Combinatorics for Computer Science

COMPUTERS AND MATH SERIES

Series Editor
MARVIN MARCUS, *University of California at Santa Barbara*

Lowell A. Carmony, Robert J. McGlinn, Ann Miller Millman, and Jerry P. Becker
Apple Pascal: A Self-Study Guide for the Apple II Plus, IIe, and IIc

Lowell A. Carmony and Robert L. Holliday
Macintosh Pascal

Marvin Marcus
Discrete Mathematics: A Computational Approach Using BASIC

S. Gill Williamson
Combinatorics for Computer Science

OTHER BOOKS OF INTEREST FROM COMPUTER SCIENCE PRESS

Shimon Even
Graph Algorithms

Ellis Horowitz and Sartaj Sahni
Fundamentals of Computer Algorithms

Donald J. Spencer
Computers in Number Theory

Combinatorics for Computer Science

S. Gill Williamson
University of California
at San Diego

Computer Science Press, Inc.
1803 Research Boulevard
Rockville, Maryland 20850

1 2 3 4 5 6   89 88 87 86 85

Library of Congress Cataloging in Publication Data

Williamson, S. Gill (Stanley Gill)
   Combinatorics for computer science.

   Includes index.
   1. Combinatorial analysis.   2. Electronic data
processing—Mathematics.   I. Title.
QA164.W55   1985   511'.6   84-17018
ISBN 0-88175-020-4

"Which shall be the Laureate's notebook?"

"'Sbodikins! I am wholly fuddled! Eight species of common notebook?"
"Sixteen, sir; sixteen, if I may," Bragg said proudly. "Ye may have

> A thin plain cardboard folio,
> A thin plain cardboard quarto,
> A thin plain leather folio,
> A thin ruled cardboard folio,
> A fat plain cardboard folio,
> A thin plain leather quarto,
> A thin ruled cardboard quarto,
> A fat plain cardboard quarto,
> A thin ruled leather folio,
> A fat ruled cardboard folio,
> A fat plain leather folio,
> A thin ruled leather quarto,
> A fat ruled cardboard quarto,
> A fat plain leather quarto,
> A fat ruled leather folio, or
> A fat ruled leather quarto."

"Stop!" cried Ebenezer, shaking his head as though in pain. "'Tis the Pit!"

—John Barth, *The Sotweed Factor*

CONTENTS

PREFACE

This book is the result of a beginning graduate-level course taught by the author at the University of California, San Diego, for the last eight years. The students have had diverse backgrounds with the majority of them being applied mathematics or computer science majors. Many topics were covered during this period that do not appear in this book. The topics presented here are those that, in our opinion (author and students), contain the most basic and useful ideas for the computer scientist and applied mathematician. More recently, selections from this book have been the basis for an upper-division undergraduate course (see SUGGESTIONS ON HOW TO USE THIS BOOK).

This book's organization reflects my preference for presenting this material in a "seminar style," with many trips to the blackboard by students. Each PART is divided into a BASIC CONCEPTS chapter followed by four TOPICS chapters. The two PARTS reflect the general division of combinatorics into "enumeration" and "graph theory," although we have taken considerable liberties with the classical approach to both of these subjects. These PARTS are independent of each other and can be done in either order.

For most students, even very clever ones, the process of learning to express their mathematical ideas both orally and in writing is a somewhat painful experience. For pure mathematicians, this learning process traditionally takes place in the first rigorous course in analysis or algebra. The desire to provide similar training for applied mathematicians and computer scientists through the presentation of material more directly related to their needs was a principal concern in the organization of this book. Combinatorial mathematics provides an ideal subject area for students to learn basic techniques of proof. At the same time, we have tried to convey, through many figures and examples, the important role of intuition in the process of developing an explanation of a mathematical concept.

Finally, some comments regarding data structures and complexity of algorithms are in order. Basic data structures are introduced early in this book, and the student is periodically encouraged to think about the complexity of various algorithms. However, it is a mistake for the student at this level to be overly concerned with "optimality" of algorithms in terms of theoretical running time estimates. Optimality and complexity results are generally asymptotic in nature. If algorithms A for a family of problems $\{P_n\}$ has worst-case complexity $O(n)$, then algorithm B = "Use whatever algorithm seems to work best on your computer for solving P_n. If no answer has been found by the end of 10,000,000,000 years, switch over to algorithm A'' also has worst-case complexity $O(n)$. In other words, to be really useful, complexity results must take into consideration programming and system-related factors that involve the actual program being constructed. On the positive side, the attempt to create theoretically optimal algorithms has led to the invention of many interesting and imaginative data structures. It is the general form of these data structures and not the optimality results per se that should be the first concern of the student. It is better for the student to experiment with these data structures, even if the algorithms produced are "suboptimal," than it is to memorize a collection of optimal algorithms. Combinatorial mathematics provides a powerful intuitive or "geometric" framework for the discussion of algorithmic concepts. The systematic exploitation of this geometry of algorithms is emphasized over the complexity of algorithms in this book.

S. Gill Williamson

ACKNOWLEDGMENTS

I am greatly indebted to my many fine graduate students who, over the years, have contributed to the contents of this book. David Perlman contributed to the material on constructive Polyá theory. Dennis White, in his dissertation and subsequent research on enumeration and symmetry, has contributed substantially to that subject. Chris Parrish's work on multivariate umbral calculus added to my understanding of that class of problems. My interest in planarity algorithms and related questions began with a series of lectures by Tony Trojanowski. Rod Canfield's lectures on sorting largely influenced the contents of that chapter. The chapter on triconnectivity, and other aspects of the material on graph theory, were inspired by the work of Phong Vo and Wayne Dick. Some important examples were contributed by Christine Alfaro. Most recently, a number of helpful ideas were contributed by my students Sue O. Hart, Paul Kaschube, and Mark Mummy. Sue Hart, in particular, read the entire manuscript and found and corrected numerous errors.

I also wish to express my thanks to my colleague and friend, Dominique Foata, for providing me with the opportunity to visit France during the academic year 1979–80 when I presented much of the material on graph theory to a helpful, critical, and highly capable audience at the Université Louis Pasteur, Strasbourg.

During the years that this material and many other topics were presented to and by graduate students, the activities of the class continued into the summer as a seminar. This seminar was inspired and organized by my colleague, Adriano Garsia, who has generously shared his many ideas and insights with me and all of my students. In addition, I have enjoyed workng with and have learned much from my colleagues Ed Bender, Jay Fillmore, and Gérard Viennot. For me personally, no acknowledgments would be complete without stating that my original interest in the field of combinatorics was inspired by the impressive combinatorial works of N. G. de Bruijn, G.-C. Rota, and M. P. Schutzenberger.

In regard to the preparation of this manuscript, I wish to thank Neola Crimmins who is not only a great technical typist, but an alert and most helpful critic as well. Also, I wish to thank my friend and long-time secretary, Elaine Morici, for an important assist at a difficult time in the preparation of the manuscript. The helpfulness and patience of the librarians at UCSD's Science and Engineering Library helped make the task of writing this book more pleasant. In particular, I wish to thank Beverlee French for her help on many occasions and, in particular, for explaining the workings of MATHFILE and INSPEC to me.

SUGGESTIONS ON HOW TO USE THIS BOOK

Here are some ways this book has been used in various classroom and programmatic situations:

1. In a small (fewer than 15 students), beginning-level graduate class, the material can be presented by the students in the style of a seminar. One may start with either PART I or PART II, each of which contains ample material for a semester course. Each PART begins with a BASIC CONCEPTS chapter which should be completed first. The STUDY GUIDES which follow these SUGGESTIONS are designed to facilitate the making of assignments for class presentation. It seems best to keep the presentations fairly short so that four or five students may make their presentations per class session. There should be a number of written assignments, at least during the first part of the course. Careful proofs should be demanded. After completing the BASIC CONCEPTS chapter, one can choose selections from the various TOPICS chapters according to the interests of the students and the instructor. Except for Chapters 7 and 8, these TOPICS chapters are essentially independent of each other. The seminar format sometimes results in slower coverage of the material than if the instructor were to give most of the presentations. If time is a factor, the instructor can present the material. The benefit to the students of presenting the material themselves generally seems well worth the price of a slightly slower pace.

2. In a small, upper-division undergraduate course, the seminar format described above can be followed. One must go slower and emphasize the BASIC CONCEPTS chapters. Generally, upper-division courses where this material has been used have been larger (40 to 50 students). In this case one can again start with PART I or PART II. The material is presented by standard classroom lectures. Written assignments are made each week. It was found helpful in such classes to periodically have the students work exercises and examples in class. The instructor can help the students get started and can give them hints. Students who finish first can then help the others, and so on. Generally, one or two programming projects have been assigned each quarter. One way to assign projects is to divide the class into small groups based on programming ability, including one good programmer in each group as "group leader." Each group is given a different assignment and demonstrates their software to the instructor

at the end of the course. A question for each group may be included on the final exam to see that all in that group have learned at least the basic ideas of the project. A typical one-quarter course from PART I might be Chapter 1, Chapter 2, and selections from Chapter 3, 4, or 5. A one-quarter course from PART II might include Chapter 6 and Chapter 7 together with a related programming project, or Chapter 6 together with selections from Chapters 7 and 9.

3. In a program which includes both a graduate and undergraduate course covering this material, the two BASIC CONCEPTS chapters (plus other selections as indicated in 2 above) may be covered in the undergraduate course. A two-quarter undergraduate course may be followed by a two-quarter graduate course. Some of the better undergraduate students may then take the graduate course. If the undergraduate course is not a prerequisite to the graduate course, one will be faced with a class where some of the students will not have studied the BASIC CONCEPTS chapters. In this case it is essential to have a rapid review of the BASIC CONCEPTS chapters. To speed things up, the instructor, perhaps together with some of the students who have taken the undergraduate course, can present the material with all students doing written exercises. One can then proceed to a selection of material from the TOPICS as in 1 above.

Study Guide for PART I: Linear Order

This study guide is intended to give the reader a quick overview of the material covered. It should be consulted periodically to help keep things in perspective. If the material is being presented "seminar style," the more passive participants will find the study guide to be a helpful outline.

BASIC CONCEPTS (1.1–1.77) is a preview of the ideas that will occur in more depth in the TOPICS that follow. We begin (1.1–1.13) with some useful descriptive tools from elementary set theory.

Although informal, our discussion of complexity of algorithms still requires some common ground in terms of data structures (1.14–1.19).

The important idea of lexicographic order is developed and its relation to backtracking and isomorph rejection is explored (1.20–1.38).

Ordered partition trees as conceptual devices for studying lists of basic combinatorial objects are introduced (1.39–1.61).

Lexicographic order, isomorph rejection, and ordered partition trees are brought together in connection with the n-queens problem (1.62–1.77).

Basic ideas about sorting, including some practical techniques and interesting data structures, are presented first (2.1–2.11).

Sorting strategies and sorting networks are discussed. Sorting networks constructed from adjacent comparators are related to the combinatorial idea of inversions of permutations. Of all sorting networks, the one that is optimal from the point of view of periodicity and geometric simplicity is the odd-even transposition sort (2.12–2.26).

Some more theoretical aspects of merging and sorting are discussed. The recursively defined methods of Ford-Johnson and Batcher are described. Two elementary but important results, the 0–1 Principle and the Generalized Matrix Principle, are derived (2.27–2.40).

Chapter 3   TOPIC II: BASIC COMBINATORIAL LISTS 76

We consider the basic sets of enumerative combinatorics. To "enumerate" can either mean to count or to list. We take the latter approach and study the familiar sets of combinatorics in terms of natural methods for linearly ordering these sets. The most frequently occurring combinatorial objects are studied first (3.1–3.27).

The ordered and unordered set partitions are the basic building blocks for many other combinatorial objects. We study their structure in some detail (3.28–3.53).

In certain questions involving linear orders on combinatorial objects, the data structures for computing the next object in the list play a central role (3.54–3.55).

**Chapter 4   TOPIC III: SYMMETRY—ORBIT ENUMERATION
                AND ORDERLY ALGORITHMS**

The computer scientist or applied mathematician who lacks the language and conceptual tools to deal with the idea of symmetry is at a great disadvantage. The most elementary concepts of group theory are a big help (4.1–4.21). After studying this material the reader can learn more about the orbit enumeration problem (4.22–4.61) or go directly to the treatment of orderly algorithms and the orbit listing problem (4.62–4.70).

Pólya's theorem is an important specialization of Burnside's lemma (4.34–4.45).

We next consider some of the numerous extensions of Pólya's theorem (4.46–4.61).

In the section BASIC CONCEPTS, we considered several approaches to the isomorph rejection problem. For certain problems with special structure, a more refined technique called the method of "orderly algorithms" is sometimes helpful (4.62–4.70).

Chapter 5   TOPIC IV: SOME CLASSICAL COMBINATORICS 165

We now give a brief survey of several important topics that are traditionally part of a course in combinatorial mathematics. The topics are: A. GENERATING FUNCTIONS, B. INCLUSION-EXCLUSION, C. MÖBIUS INVERSION, and D. NETWORK FLOWS. These topics may be read independently of each other.

We begin with the standard combinatorial facts about generating functions. A number of important tricks are included in the exercises (5A.1–5A.13).

Systematic methods for relating combinatorial models to their generating functions are of interest in combinatorial mathematics. One such approach is concerned with exponential generating functions, classes of combinatorial objects constructed from set partitions and classes of polynomials called "polynomials of binomial type." We give a brief glimpse of some of these ideas (5A.14–5A.34).

The "principle of inclusion-exclusion" is an important classical combinatorial technique. A number of different versions of this idea are used (5B.1–5B.13).

In solving a certain class of combinatorial problems it is necessary to invert finite sums over partially ordered sets. These problems are often referred to as involving "Möbius inversion" (5C.1–5C.24).

The topic of flows in networks is generally part of a course in combinatorial optimization or linear programming. Many of the ideas involved relate to the material in Part II. We present the basic ideas only (5D.1–5D.21).

Study Guide for PART II:
Graphs, Trees, and Recursion

As is PART I, this study guide is designed to facilitate the presentation of the material in a classroom seminar. All key ideas are numbered sequentially. The BASIC CONCEPTS section focuses on graph theory as a descriptive tool in the study of algorithms. The concepts introduced in this section are developed in more depth in the TOPICS.

We begin with the elementary definitions and some algorithmic insights into trees.

...

We shall use trees extensively as geometric devices for understanding algorithms. First we develop some necessary terminology and illustrate its use in connection with recursion.

We now develop and give examples of the important algorithmic concepts, depth first search in graphs and orderly algorithms.

*At this point, we give a quick preview of some ideas that we shall see again
in connection with TOPIC IV: MATROIDS.*

*In TOPICS I, II, and III we study the algorithmic aspects of embeddings of
graphs. We now develop the intuitive ideas needed for this task.*

Our first TOPIC is concerned with the algorithmic aspects of planarity. Our approach is a combination of depth first search and the use of auxiliary graphical structures called ''segment graphs.''

Chapter 7   TOPIC I: DEPTH FIRST SEARCH

**Chapter 8   TOPIC II: DEPTH FIRST SEARCH
              AND NONPLANARITY** **319**

*What if a graph cannot be embedded on the plane or sphere? An important
first start in the algorithmic study of nonplanar graphs is to learn how to locate
the minimal obstructions to planarity. This is our next task.*

Chapter 9   TOPIC III: TRICONNECTIVITY 337

In TOPICS I and II biconnectivity played a key role. Higher orders of connectivity can be defined. The most important of these is "triconnectivity" which plays a very special role in the study of planar embeddings.

The concept of a "matroid" and related ideas are becoming increasingly important in algorithmic combinatorics and optimization. The term matroid was originally intended to imply an extension of the idea of a "matrix." Most important matroids, however, can be studied in the context of matrix theory. They are called the "representable matroids." For the computer scientist or applied mathematician, the most direct and useful route to understanding matroid theory is to develop the subject first for representable matroids. We carry out this approach in this TOPIC. We begin with a review of some ideas from matrix theory and then give the basic definitions of matroids.

Next we exploit matrix canonical forms to study some of the most interesting classes of matroids. We can do this because all of these matroids are easily seen to be representable.

A number of important operations (taking duals, restriction, contraction, truncation, elongation, series, and parallel extension) can be performed on matroids. All of these operations preserve representability. Thus, we can again use matrix theory to study these operations.

Connectivity in matroids corresponds to biconnectivity in graphs and is equally important. As is the case of graphs, the notion of a "bridge" provides an important recursive tool for studying matroids. For representable matroids, these concepts all have easily understood matrix theoretic interpretations.

A central theme of this book has been the relationship between tree structures and recursion. We use these ideas to study the "delete-contract" recursion for matroids and develop an understanding of some important classes of polynomials associated with matroids.

We conclude with a brief introduction to the important topic of matroid algorithms. To be effective at designing matroid algorithms it helps to know something about matroids. This is why this aspect of the subject has been left for last. The reader who would like to explore this subject in more depth will find extensive references at the end of the chapter. Again we shall exploit matrix theory.

PART I

Linear Order

Chapter 1

Basic Concepts of Linear Order

We shall be concerned with studying basic finite sets from a point of view that facilitates computations with these sets. Permutations, subsets, graphs, tree structures, partially and totally ordered sets, etc., are interesting in their own right. They are also the fundamental building blocks for describing and constructing a variety of algorithms. Our point of view will be motivated largely by these algorithmic considerations. The construction and manipulation of linear lists is one of the most fundamental techniques in the design and analysis of algorithms. We begin by looking at the idea of a *linear order* from a somewhat "formal" point of view. In the process we develop some basic ideas to be used later on.

1.1 DEFINITION.

Let S be a set. A relation on S is a function from the Cartesian product, $S \times S$ to any set T with two elements.

For example, $T = \{0,1\}$, $T = \{-1,+1\}$, and $T = \{\text{false, true}\}$ could all be used as the range T of a relation ρ on S. If the set T is fixed and S is finite, then it is easily seen that there are 2^p, $p = |S|^2$, functions from $S \times S$ to T (if S is a finite set, $|S|$ denotes the *cardinality* or *number of elements* of S). The notion of a relation is, of course, a triviality in full generality. Two special classes of relations, however, play an important descriptive role in the study of algorithms. For the next definition, let $\rho : S \times S \to T$ be a relation. Fix $T = \{\text{false, true}\}$. We shall use the equivalent but more suggestive notation "x ρ y" for "$\rho(x,y) = \text{true}$" and "x $\not\rho$ y" for "$\rho(x,y) = \text{false}$."

1.2 DEFINITION.

A relation ρ on S is

(1) *Reflexive* if for all $x \in S$, $x \rho x$.
(2) *Symmetric* if for all $x, y \in S$, $x \rho y$ implies $y \rho x$.
(2') *Antisymmetric* if for all $x, y \in S$, $x \rho y$, and $y \rho x$ implies $x = y$.
(3) *Transitive* if for all $x, y, z \in S$, $x \rho y$ and $y \rho z$ implies $x \rho z$.

A relation ρ that satisfies 1, 2, and 3 is called an *equivalence relation*. A relation ρ that satisfies 1, 2', and 3 is called an *order relation*.

3

The general structure of equivalence relations is easy to understand because of the well-known correspondence between equivalence relations and partitions of a set.

1.3   DEFINITION.

Let S be a set. A *partition* of S is a collection $\mathscr{C}$ of subsets of S such that $\bigcup_{A \in \mathscr{C}} A = S$, and if A and B are elements of $\mathscr{C}$, then either $A = B$ or A and B are disjoint. The elements of $\mathscr{C}$ (which are subsets of S by definition) are called the *blocks* of $\mathscr{C}$. $\mathscr{C}$ is *discrete* if each block has one element. The empty set $\phi \notin \mathscr{C}$.

Thus, if N^+ is the set of positive integers, then $\mathscr{C} = \{E, O\}$, where E is the set of even numbers and O is the set of odd numbers in N^+, is a partition of N^+. The collection $\{\{1,3,7\}, \{2,4,5,6\}, \{8\}\}$ is a partition of $S = \{1, \ldots, 8\}$.

1.4   DEFINITION.

Let ρ be an equivalence relation on S. For each $s \in S$, let E_s be the set $\{x: x \in S, x \rho s\}$. The set E_s is called the *equivalence class of s with respect to ρ or the equivalence class of s*.

1.5   THEOREM.

If ρ is an equivalence relation on a set S, then the collection $\mathscr{C} = \{E_s: s \in S\}$ of all ρ equivalence classes is a partition of S. Conversely, if $\mathscr{C}$ is any partition of S, and x and y are elements of S, then define $x \rho y$ if x and y belong to the same block of $\mathscr{C}$. Then ρ is an equivalence relation on S, and $\mathscr{C}$ is the collection of equivalence classes.

THEOREM 1.5 finds its way into many undergraduate courses in mathematics (discrete math, real analysis, logic, algebra, group theory, linear algebra). The reader should attempt to reconstruct the proof and consult a reference if necessary. Although the general structure of equivalence relations is quite clear from THEOREM 1.5, particular relations might not obviously be equivalence relations at first glance. Transitivity, in particular, is sometimes a bit tricky to verify. Once the axioms are verified for ρ, then the partition into equivalence classes follows from THEOREM 1.5.

1.6   NOTATION.

The set of integers $1, \ldots, n$ will be denoted by $\underline{n}$. If A and B are sets, we write $f: A \rightarrow B$ for a function f with domain A and range B. The set of all such functions will be denoted by B^A (note that if A and B are finite with cardinality $|A| = a$ and $|B| = b$, then $|B^A| = b^a$, hence the notation). The *Image*(f) is the set $\{f(a): a \in A\}$. For each $b \in B$, $f^{-1}(b)$ is called the "inverse image of b" and is the set $\{a: a \in A, f(a) = b\}$. The collection $\mathscr{C} = \{f^{-1}(b): b \in Image(f)\}$

is a partition of A and is called the Coimage(f). If Image(f) = B, then f is a
surjection. If Coimage(f) is discrete, then f is an *injection*. If f is both an injection
and a surjection, it is a *bijection*. It is easily seen that if $|A| = |B|$ (both finite),
then f is an injection if and only if it is a surjection. The injections of A^A are
called the *permutations* of A, A finite.

As an example of the above ideas, consider $f \in \underline{6}^{\underline{6}}$ where f =
$\begin{pmatrix} 1 & 2 & 3 & 4 & 5 & 6 \\ 1 & 3 & 1 & 3 & 2 & 2 \end{pmatrix}$. The Image(f) = {1,2,3}. Coimage(f) = {{1,3}, {5,6}, {2,4}}.

This function can be written in *one-line notation* as (1 3 1 3 2 2). This notation
specifies the function if the domain is known and specified in some order. Some
permutations of $\underline{6}$ in one-line notation are (5 6 3 2 1 4) or (4 2 3 5 6 1).

We shall see many examples in the text of equivalence relations. We mention
a few examples here (it is conventional to use a symbol such as ~ rather than
ρ when working with equivalence relations).

1.7 EXAMPLES OF EQUIVALENCE RELATIONS.

(1) S = $\underline{2}^{\underline{3}}$ with f ~ g if Image(f) = Image(g). The equivalence classes are
{(1 1 1)}, {(1 1 2), (1 2 1), (2 1 1), (1 2 2), (2 1 2), (2 2 1)}, and {(2 2 2)}.
We use one line notation for all functions.

(2) S = $\underline{2}^{\underline{3}}$ with f ~ g if Coimage(f) = Coimage(g). The equivalence classes
are {(1 1 1), (2 2 2)}, {(1 1 2), (2 2 1)}, {(1 2 1), (2 1 2)}, and {(1 2 2),
(2 1 1)}.

(3) S = $\underline{2}^{\underline{3}}$ with f ~ g if Max(f) = Max(g). There are two equivalence classes.

(4) S = $\underline{2}^{\underline{3}}$ with f ~ g if f is a cyclic shift of g: (1 1 2),(2 1 1), and (1 2 1)
are cyclic shifts of each other.

(5) S = $\underline{2}^{\underline{3}}$ with f ~ g if f(1) + f(2) + f(3) = g(1) + g(2) + g(3).

For the reader who knows a little graph theory:

(6) Let G = (V,E) be a graph. Define an equivalence relation on V by x ~ y
if there is a path in G from x to y. The equivalence classes are used to define
the connected components of G.

(7) Let G = (V,E) be a graph. Define an equivalence relation on E by e ~ f
if e and f lie on the same simple (not self-intersecting) cycle of G. The
equivalence classes are used to define the biconnected components of G.
Check transitivity here. Assume e ~ e.

(8) Let S = {(a,b): a and b integers, b ≠ 0}. Define (a,b) ~ (a',b') if ab' = ba'.
This is the equivalence relation used in the formal definition of the rational
numbers.

(9) Let {a_n} and {b_n} be two infinite sequences of rational numbers. Define {a_n}
~ {b_n} if $\lim_{n \to \infty} (a_n - b_n) = 0$. Such an equivalence relation is used in the
formal development of the real number system.

The general structure of order relations is more complex than that of equivalence relations. The notation $x \leq y$ or $x \mathrel{\underline{\alpha}} y$ is often used for order relations rather than $x \rho y$. A set S together with an order relation $\underline{\alpha}$ is often called a "partially ordered set" or "poset." We write $(S, \underline{\alpha})$ to designate such a poset. We use $x \propto y$ to mean $x \underline{\alpha} y$, but $x \neq y$.

1.8 DEFINITION.

Let $(S, \underline{\alpha})$ be an ordered set. We say y *covers* x if $x \propto y$ and if, for all $z \in S$, $x \underline{\alpha} z \underline{\alpha} y$ implies $x = z$ or $y = z$. If y covers x, we write $x \mathrel{\overset{\propto}{c}} y$ and we say that y is a successor of x and x a predecessor of y.

1.9 EXAMPLES OF ORDERED SETS.

(1) $(R, \leq)$ Real numbers with usual ordering.
(2) $(N, \leq)$ Positive integers with usual ordering.
(3) Given a set A, let $S = \mathscr{P}(A)$, the set of all subsets of A. Then $(S, \subseteq)$ is a poset where "$\subset$" denotes the usual set inclusion.
(4) $(\pi(A), \underline{\alpha})$, where $\pi(A) =$ partitions of a set A, and $\pi_2 \underline{\alpha} \pi_1$ if π_2 is a refinement of π_1, e.g., if $A = \underline{8}$, $\pi_1 = \{\{1,3,5\}, \{2,4,6\}, \{7,8\}\}$ and $\pi_2 = \{\{1,3\}, \{5\}, \{2,6\}, \{4\}, \{7,8\}\}$, then $\pi_2 \underline{\alpha} \pi_1$. (Blocks of π_1 are split further to get blocks of π_2).
(5) $(N, \underline{\alpha})$, where $x \underline{\alpha} y$ if and only if $x|y$ ("x divides y").
(6) $\underline{r}^{\underline{d}}$ (set of functions from $\underline{d}$ to $\underline{r}$), with $f \underline{\alpha} g$ if and only if $f(i) \leq g(i)$ for all i.

1.10 DEFINITION.

Given a poset $P = (S, \leq)$, let $P_{cov} = (S, \mathrel{\overset{\propto}{c}})$. We create a diagram of P_{cov} by connecting a to b with a line *if and only if* a covers b. This diagram of P_{cov} is called the *Hasse diagram* of P.

1.11 HASSE DIAGRAM FOR S = 12, WITH x|y AS THE ORDER RELATION.

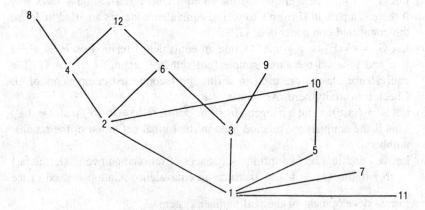

Figure 1.11

1.12 HASSE DIAGRAMS OF $(\mathscr{P}(\underline{2}), \subseteq)$, ALL SUBSETS OF $\underline{2}$ WITH INCLUSION AND $(\underline{5}, \leq)$.

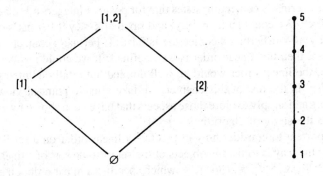

Figure 1.12

1.13 EXERCISE.

(1) Let $\mathscr{M}_n$ be the set of all $n \times n$ matrices with real entries. Define a relation $\sim$ on $\mathscr{M}_n \times \mathscr{M}_n$ by $(A,B) \sim (C,D)$ if $A + D = B + C$. Show that $\sim$ is an equivalence relation on $\mathscr{M}_n \times \mathscr{M}_n$.

(2) Let $\mathscr{M}_n$ be as in (1). Define $A \sim B$ if there is a nonsingular matrix P such that $P A P^{-1} = B$. Show that $\sim$ is an equivalence relation on $\mathscr{M}_n$. A student who has studied *linear algebra* should be able to give a good description of the equivalence classes for this equivalence relation.

(3) Let ρ_1 be a relation on S and ρ_2 a relation on T. Define a relation ρ_3 on $S \times T$ by $(s,t)\rho_3(s',t')$ if $s\rho_1 s'$ *and* $t\rho_2 t'$. Show that ρ_3 is an equivalence relation if both ρ_1 and ρ_2 are equivalence relations. Show ρ_3 is an order relation if both ρ_1 and ρ_2 are order relations.

(4) Construct the Hasse diagram of $(\mathscr{P}(\underline{4}), \subseteq)$ and $(\underline{18}, |)$. See EXAMPLES 1.9(3) and 1.9(5). See Figure 1.11 for $(\underline{12}, |)$.

(5) Let ρ be a reflexive, symmetric relation on S. Define a relation ρ' on S by $s\rho't$ if there exists some sequence $u_1, \ldots, u_p$ in S such that $s\rho u_1, u_1\rho u_2, \ldots, u_p\rho t$. Show that ρ' is an equivalence relation on S.

(6) Referring to EXAMPLES 1.9(3) and 1.9(6), consider $(\mathscr{P}(\underline{d}), \subseteq)$ and $(\{0,1\}^{\underline{d}}, \leq)$. For $A \in \mathscr{P}(\underline{d})$, let $f_A \in \{0,1\}^{\underline{d}}$ be defined by $f_A(x) = 0$ if $x \notin A$, 1 if $x \in A$. Show that the map $\varphi(A) = f_A$ is a bijection from $\mathscr{P}(\underline{d})$ to $\{0,1\}^{\underline{d}}$. Show that $A \subseteq B$ if and only if $f_A \leq f_B$. Such a map φ is called an *order preserving bijection* between the two posets. The function f_A is called the *characteristic function* of A.

There is an extensive and quite fascinating mathematical theory of partially ordered sets. From an algorithmic point of view, however, the most basic techniques involve working with various types of *linear orders*. A poset $(S, \leq)$ is *linearly ordered* if for every x and y in S either x ≤ y or y ≤ x. The Hasse diagram of a linearly ordered set is a chain (as, for example, ($\underline{5}$,≤) of Figure 1.12). The purely mathematical idea of a linear order still permits many other digressions. Fermat's conjecture states that for positive integers a,b,c and n > 2, $a^n + b^n \neq c^n$. We could let S = {x,y} and say that x < y if Fermat's conjecture is true and y < x if Fermat's conjecture is false. If Fermat's conjecture is either true or false, then this linear order is well defined. If we could resolve Fermat's conjecture, the linear order would be well defined but totally uninteresting *as a linear order*. In the rest of this chapter, we take a naive point of view towards linear orders and simply explore those aspects that have been shown by experience to relate to the study of algorithms.

It is important to consider how in practice a linear order on a set S might be specified. One way is to list the objects of the set in some sort of "linear array." Consider ¢, %, &, $, *, #, (,@,), + which specifies a linear order on a standard set of text symbols. Is $ < #? One way to decide this is to read the array from first to last (left to right here) and check which of the two symbols being compared comes first. In some cases, this might be the only way to decide which of two elements in a linearly ordered set is the smaller. Consider the linearly ordered set @, ¢, x, z, #. The number of straight line segments in these symbols is respectively 0, 1, 2, 3, and 4. Thus, associated with each symbol in the list is an intrinsic method for computing its position in the list. This idea can be important when deciding which of two elements should appear first in long lists. Even if the correspondence is not bijective (unique for each symbol), such an intrinsic association might be helpful. Consider the list @, &, +, x, v, y, z, N, #. Here, the straight line segment computation yields 0, 0, 2, 2, 2, 2, 3, 3, 4. Consider Table 1.14, as follows.

1.14 HASHING TABLE.

0:	@ &
1:	empty
2:	+ x v y
3:	z N
4:	#

In order to compare two elements in the list one might first compute the number of straight line segments in the two symbols. For + one would compute 2, and for N one would compute 3. If one can then recognize easily that 2 is less than 3, then one can conclude that + < N. If one is required to compare + and v, then one computes 2 for both symbols. In this case it is necessary to go to the line labeled 2 in TABLE 1.14. One then can look at the sublist of symbols in line 2 to decide if + < v. One can imagine large-scale applications of this sort of idea (called "hashing" by computer scientists). Many interesting questions then arise. First of all, how easy is it really to find the sublists corresponding to those of TABLE 1.14 given the integer or symbol that labels the sublist (such as 2)?

Suppose that instead of comparing two symbols in the list we want to simply find the next element following or preceding a given element in a list. Does this sort of organization of the data help? How do we measure the degree of help provided by such a scheme? One very simple model of computation (direct access model) assumes that certain special classes of symbols are "directly accessible." Roughly speaking, this means that if such a symbol labels a sublist such as TABLE 1.14, then given the symbol, we can go directly to that sublist in a small constant amount of time independent of the "size of the problem" measured in some way. For example, imagine a very large version of TABLE 1.14. Given an integer n, we would assume in this model we can go directly to the list labeled by n in the same amount of time it took us to find the sublist labeled by 2 in the smaller TABLE 1.14. This is, of course, not true in reality. Just to read the digits of a *very* large number might take 1,000 years. A *very* large table such as TABLE 1.14 might be forced to have some of its entries at the bounds of the known universe. Nevertheless, experience shows that the basic idea of the direct access model is a good way to get a feeling for the complexity of certain basic computations. It will be useful at this point to look at one method for organizing computations with linearly ordered sets called *linked lists*.

Figure 1.15 shows an array of squares or "locations" in which we can store certain classes of basic symbols. The array is rectangular only for typographical convenience. Each square has an "address" such as A4, B6, etc. Given such an address, we can go to and read the contents of the designated square. In Figure 1.15, we are instructed to start at address D3 and follow the instructions contained in the square (as in the classical treasure hunt game). Doing this and reading the symbols we read @ # $ % ¢ &. Such a "data structure" is called a *linked list*.

1.15   LINKED LIST FOR LIST @ # $ % ¢ &.

Start at D3.

	1	2	3	4	5	6
A						$ GO TO B1
B	% GO TO D6				# GO TO A6	
C			&			
D			@ GO TO B5			¢ GO TO C2
E						

Figure 1.15

The basic assumption of the "direct access model" would be that, given a symbol such as "D5" or "E2," one can go to the corresponding region of the structure shown in 1.15 in "constant time." Courses in computational complexity can go into what this means in rigorous terms. For our purposes, the obvious intuitive ideas will suffice. The basic idea is that structures such as 1.15 can be allowed to grow in size over a fairly wide range with the same constant access time for all structures. This rough idea is all that is needed to get one started in thinking about "how efficient" certain computational ideas are. Studies of "computational complexity" can be overdone and carried to a point where they bear a rather questionable relationship to actual programming problems!

1.16   STRUCTURAL DIAGRAM OF FIGURE 1.15.

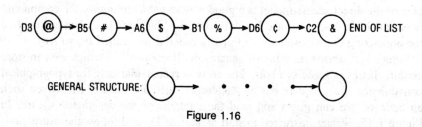

GENERAL STRUCTURE:

Figure 1.16

Associated with a "data structure" such as FIGURE 1.15 one can ask a number of basic questions. To get a more "global" or "geometric" feeling for the linked list of 1.15, one can represent the situation by a structural diagram such as shown in 1.16. The elements of the list are shown inside the circles; the "address" of each element is written just to the left of the circle. The arrows of 1.16 represent the fact that each location containing an element of the list also contains the address of the next entry in the list. The address of the next entry (represented by the arrow) is called a "pointer."

The reader should consider certain basic questions associated with the linked list data structure of 1.15. For instance, how would one carry out the instruction to "insert a new symbol * between $ and %?" Clearly, one would first locate an unused square in 1.15 (such as E6) and put the new symbol * in that square. One would then go to the square A6, which contains $, and replace the pointer "GO TO B1" with "GO TO E6." One would add to square E6 a pointer "GO TO B1." How much time is required to make these changes? First of all, we have to find an empty location or square. Do we have to scan a large number of squares to find one or can we be clever in how we keep track of empty squares so we can find one in "constant time?" Next, we have to find the square containing the symbol $. We have assumed that we can go to a square in constant time given the *address* (such as "A6") but not given the *contents* "$." We can get around this problem if the symbols of the list are address symbols.

These problems that arise in our very simple-minded model can be magnified many times in dealing with a "real world" computational situation. If we are optimists, we can agree that the above computations required to insert a new symbol can be done in constant time. If we believe this in the context of the direct access model, then we would probably believe that the time required to insert a new symbol is *independent of the length of the list*. This follows, since one symbol is added and two pointers are changed independent of the length of the list. If our data structure consisted of typing each list symbol with one space between symbols, then we would represent the list of 1.15 by @ # $ % ¢ &. Now, inserting a new symbol * between $ and % would not, even viewed by an optimist, require constant time independent of the length of the list if the new list is to be represented in the same manner.

1.17 A MORE COMPLEX DATA STRUCTURE.

LIST 1: START E5   LIST 2: START D6   LIST 3: START D3   LIST OF LISTS: START E1

STRUCTURAL DIAGRAM
FOR LIST OF LISTS: E1   (D6) ──► D5   (E5) ──► E6   (D3) ──►E1 (START)

	1	2	3	4	5	6
A	D2 LIST 1	E2 LIST 1	E5 LIST 1 (START)	C3 LIST 1	D1 LIST 3	D3 LIST 3 (START)
B	D4 LIST 2	C1 LIST 2	C4 LIST 2	D6 LIST 2 (START)	C6 LIST 3	C2 LIST 3
C	B2 LAST ENTRY START D6	B6 AHEAD C6	A4 BACK D2 LAST ENTRY START E5	B3 AHEAD C1 START D6		B5 START D3
D	A5 AHEAD C2	A1 BACK E2 AHEAD C3	A6 AHEAD D1	B1 AHEAD C4 START D6	E5 (LIST 1) AHEAD E6	B4 AHEAD D4 FIRST ENTRY
E	D6 (LIST 2) AHEAD D5	A2 BACK E5 AHEAD D2			A3 FIRST ENTRY AHEAD E2 END C3	D3 (LIST 3) START E1

Figure 1.17   (Top)

STRUCTURAL DIAGRAMS:

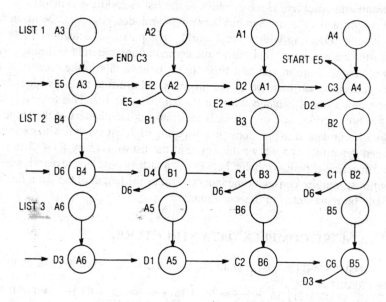

Figure 1.17   (Bottom)

A more complex data structure involving the idea of linked lists is shown in FIGURE 1.17. Three lists are stored in the 5 by 6 array shown. The symbols appearing in the lists are symbols such as "A2," "B3," etc. These symbols are also possible address symbols for squares in the array. We assume we can go to the addressed square in constant time for a wide range of such arrays. Thus, although the lists shown here are only of length 4, we can think of the analogous situation for lists of length n, n being much larger than 4. In Figure 1.17, LIST 1 is a "doubly linked" list in that each square containing a symbol of the list (except the first and last) has a pointer AHEAD to the location of the next symbol in the list and a pointer BACK to the previous symbol in the list. As the symbols stored in the list are also addresses, we have used those addresses to store (for each symbol in the list) its address *in the list*. Thus in A2 we find E2, which is the square that contains A2 in LIST 1. Also, the square containing the first entry in LIST 1 contains a pointer to the last entry in LIST 1 and vice versa. LIST 2 is a simple linked list where each square contains a pointer to the first square in the list. LIST 3 is a linked list with a pointer from the last entry to the first. FIGURE 1.17 also illustrates an important idea concerning how complex data structures may be manipulated using pointers.

In addition to the above mentioned lists, there is a list called LIST OF LISTS. The elements of this list are the three addresses to the first entries of LIST 1, LIST 2, and LIST 3. The LIST OF LISTS starts at E1 and contains the address

D6 of the first entry in LIST 2. Also in E1 we find a pointer AHEAD to the next square in LIST OF LISTS which is D5. This square contains the address E5 to the start of LIST 1 and a pointer AHEAD to E6. In E6 we find the last square in LIST OF LISTS, which contains the address D3 of the first entry of LIST 3, and a pointer back to the start of LIST OF LISTS.

The important thing to notice here is that the sequence of addresses D6, E5, and D3 defines a linear order on the lists: LIST 2, LIST 1, LIST 3. The reader should think carefully about this situation. How would a new list be added to the LIST OF LISTS? How would the order on the lists be changed? The basic advantage here is the ease with which these operations can be done in that only pointers to the lists are being moved and not the entries in the lists themselves. The reader should also think about what might happen here if the lists are allowed to get larger and more numerous. How does this model relate to one's own experience in programming? Is the direct access model really nonsense or does it give you some useful ideas? One thing to keep in mind in playing this game is that the amount of information stored in each square of an array such as that of FIGURE 1.17 *should be constant* (not depend on the number or length of lists). Also, the reader should try to develop a good notation for structural diagrams in the general case (arbitrary length list n in this example).

FIGURE 1.18 gives a suggestion for one possible notation. A good notation for structural diagrams of data structures is especially important as the data structures become more complex, as in the case of graphs.

1.18 STRUCTURAL DIAGRAMS FOR GENERAL CASE.

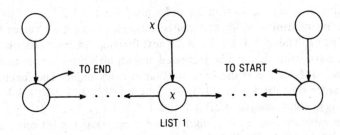

Figure 1.18

1.19 EXERCISE.

Discuss in detail how the data structure of FIGURE 1.17 would be modified in order to insert and delete elements from the various lists and change the order of the lists. Consider the general (m lists of length n) as m and n get large. Can these changes be made "in constant time?"

An important method for constructing linear orders on products of linear ordered sets involves the notion of lexicographic order. This is a familiar idea to most readers but it can involve some subtle ideas when applied to combinatorial problems.

"Lexicographic order" derives its name from the order imposed on the words in a dictionary. As before, the set $\{1,2,\ldots,n\}$ will be denoted by $\underline{n}$. The *functions* from $\underline{d}$ to $\underline{r}$ will be denoted by $\underline{r}^{\underline{d}}$. We denoted such functions by length d strings of numbers from $\underline{r}$ ("one line" notation). For example, 1 3 1 is a function in $\underline{3}^{\underline{3}}$. This function sends $1 \rightarrow 1$, $2 \rightarrow 3$, and $3 \rightarrow 1$. Of course, 1 3 1 may be regarded as a function in $\underline{r}^{\underline{3}}$ for any $r \geq 3$. The *domain* of this function is the set $\underline{3}$. The *range* is $\underline{r}$. The *image* is the set $\{1,3\}$. The *coimage* is the *partition* $\{\{1,3\}, \{2\}\}$ of $\underline{3}$ (i.e., the collection of subsets of the domain on which the function takes on its various values). Two functions $i_1 \ldots i_d$ and $j_1 \ldots j_d$ are equal if $i_k = j_k$ for all k.

1.20 DEFINITION.

Given two functions $f = i_1 \ldots i_d$ and $g = j_1 \ldots j_d$, we scan from left to right until we find the first k such that $i_k \neq j_k$. If $i_k < j_k$, we say f is *lexicographically less* than g. If $i_k > j_k$, we say f is *lexicographically greater* than g. If $i_k = j_k$ for all k, then $f = g$.

1.21 REMARK.

The order defined by DEFINITION 1.20 is linear (why?). This order on $\underline{r}^{\underline{d}}$ is called the *lexicographic order*. We shall call it *lex order* for short. If we scan instead from right to left in DEFINITION 1.20, the resulting order will be called the *colex order*.

To find the next function in lex order after 3 3 1 3 1 2 3 in $\underline{3}^{\underline{7}}$ we increase by one the right-most value that can be increased and set all values further to the right to 1. Thus 3 3 1 3 1 3 1 is the next function. In colex order we increase the left-most value that can be increased and set all values further to the left to 1. Thus 1 1 2 3 1 2 3 is the next function in colex order. The functions in $\underline{3}^{\underline{3}}$ in lex order start off 1 1 1, 1 1 2, 1 1 3, 1 2 1, 1 2 2, 1 2 3, 1 3 1, etc. The functions in colex order start off 1 1 1, 2 1 1, 3 1 1, 1 2 1, 2 2 1, 3 2 1, 1 3 1, etc. The *permutations* (or *injections* or *one-to-one maps*) in lex order are 1 2 3, 1 3 2, 2 1 3, 2 3 1, 3 1 2, 3 2 1. In colex order they are 3 2 1, 2 3 1, 3 1 2, ... More interesting are the *nondecreasing* functions. In lex order they come out 1 1 1, 1 1 2, 1 1 3, 1 2 2, 1 2 3, 1 3 3, 2 2 2, 2 2 3, 2 3 3, 3 3 3. In colex order they are 1 1 1, 1 1 2, 1 2 2, 2 2 2, 1 1 3, 1 2 3, 2 2 3, 1 3 3, 2 3 3, 3 3 3. *Notice that any subset of a linearly ordered set is automatically linearly ordered by the same order relation* (e.g., the *nondecreasing* functions as a subset of $\underline{3}^{\underline{3}}$).

1.22 EXERCISE.

(1) List all of the 27 functions in $\underline{3}^{\underline{3}}$ in lex and colex order. Find the nondecreasing functions in each list and think about the induced order on this subset. What

are the "mirror images" of these various lists (the lists obtained by writing each element in reverse order)?

(2) Write a computer program to list all permutations on $\underline{n}$ in lex order. Execute the program for n = 4, 5.

(3) List all of the *strictly increasing* functions in $\underline{5}^3$ in lex order and colex order. These correspond to the subsets of size 3 from $\underline{5}$.

The notions of lex and colex order extend easily to a product of linearly ordered sets $A_1 \times \ldots \times A_n$. For example, to list in lex and colex order the elements of $\underline{3} \times \{a,b\} \times \{\alpha,\beta\}$, we start off 1 a α, 1 a β, 1 b α, 1 b β, etc. and 1 a α, 2 a α, 3 a α, 1 b α, etc. We assume the natural order on $\underline{3}$ and a < b, $\alpha < \beta$.

One can also define lexicographic order recursively. Consider the product $\mathscr{A}_n = A_1 \times \ldots \times A_n$ of linearly ordered sets A_i. If n = 1, then lex order on $\mathscr{A}_n$ is just the order on A_1. In general, $(a_1, \ldots, a_n)$ is lexicographically less than $(a'_1, \ldots, a'_n)$ if a_1 is less than a'_1 in the order on A_1 *or* $a_1 = a'_1$ and $(a_2, \ldots, a_n)$ is lexicographically less than $(a'_2, \ldots, a'_n)$ in $A_2 \times \ldots \times A_{\dot{n}}$.

1.23 EXERCISE.

(1) Define colexicographic order recursively. Prove that the recursive definitions of lex and colex order give the same linear orders as DEFINITION 1.20 and REMARK 1.21.

(2) Let $(L_1, \underline{\simeq})$ and $(L_2, \leq)$ be linearly ordered sets. Define a relation on $L_1 \times L_2$ by $(x,y) \; \underline{\alpha} \; (x',y')$ if $x \underline{\simeq} x'$ in L_1 *and* $y \leq y'$ in L_2. By EXERCISE 1.13(3) this relation is an order relation. Consider $L_1 = \underline{2} \times \underline{2} = L_2$ with lexicographic order. Draw the Hasse diagram for the order on $L_1 \times L_2$.

The recursive definition of lex order gives a clear conceptual picture of how a card sorter works. Suppose we are given some subset $\mathscr{B}_n$ of $\mathscr{A}_n$. We want to put the elements of $\mathscr{B}_n$ into lexicographic order. To be a little more precise about the data structures involved, suppose that the elements (each a sequence of length n) of $\mathscr{B}_n$ are written on cards, one per card. Suppose we have $A_1 = \ldots = A_n = \underline{m}$ to simplify the notation. Imagine m buckets into which the cards can be placed. Given the cards of $\mathscr{B}_n$ in some order, they will be distributed into the various buckets according to some rules to be explained below. The critical idea will be that cards are put into the buckets *carefully* so that within each bucket the cards are stacked in such a way as to preserve the *same relative order* that they just had. The sorting algorithm is to first place the cards into buckets according to their right-most symbols. The cards are then removed from the buckets and stacked together (concatenated), cards from bucket 1 first, then bucket 2, etc. This process is repeated on the next symbol to the left, then the next, etc. The process is illustrated in FIGURE 1.24 for n = 2.

1.24   LEXICOGRAPHIC BUCKET SORT.

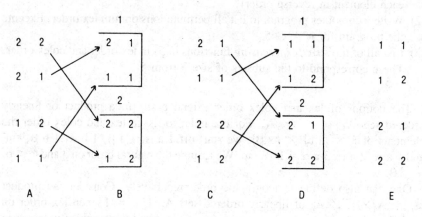

Figure 1.24

A. Reading from top to bottom, the list is in some order but not lex order.
B. The elements of the list are placed into "buckets" according to the right-most value. In each bucket the order is the same as the starting order. Thus in bucket 1 the element 2 1 is before 1 1 as in the starting order.
C. The contents of the buckets are concatenated.
D. The elements are placed in buckets according to the value of next symbol to the left. The order in C is preserved within each bucket.
E. The buckets are again concatenated and the list is now in lex order.

1.25   EXERCISE.

Give a careful proof that the lexicographic bucket sort algorithm will correctly put any sublist $\mathcal{B}_n$ of $\underline{m} \times \ldots \times \underline{m}$ into lex order.

Next we shall consider some variations on the idea of lexicographic order and related combinatorial problems.

Consider $\underline{r}^{\underline{d}}$ again. Introduce a new symbol $*$, which we add to the set $\underline{r}$. First assume $*$ precedes all elements of $\underline{r}$ so $\underline{r} \cup \{*\} = \bar{\underline{r}}$ is linearly ordered. Consider the usual lexicographic order on $\bar{\underline{r}}^{\underline{d}}$. We are interested in the subset $W_{d,r} \subseteq \bar{\underline{r}}^{\underline{d}}$ of functions of the form $i_1 i_2 \ldots i_k * * \ldots *$, $k = 1, 2, \ldots, d$, where $i_t \in \underline{r}$ for $t = 1, \ldots, k$. In these strings (or functions) $*$ acts as a "terminal symbol" in the sense that if it appears at all in a position, then all subsequent positions contain $*$. For example, look at $\underline{2}^3$. Here $\underline{2} = \{*, 1, 2\}$. In lex order $W_{3,2}$ becomes $1 * *$, $1 1 *$, $1 1 1$, $1 1 2$, $1 2 *$, $1 2 1$, $1 2 2$, $2 * *$, $2 1 *$, $2 1 1$, $2 1 2$, $2 2 *$, $2 2 1$, $2 2 2$. A common way to graphically represent $W_{3,2}$ is shown in FIGURE 1.26(a) (the terminal $*$'s are omitted). The order in which $W_{3,2}$ appears in the above lex order is shown in FIGURE 1.26(b).

1.26 TREE DIAGRAM OF PRELEX ORDER.

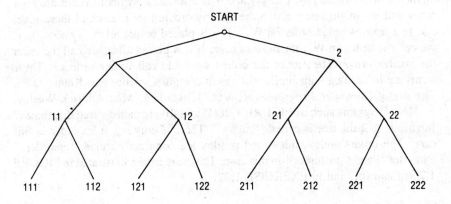

Figure 1.26a

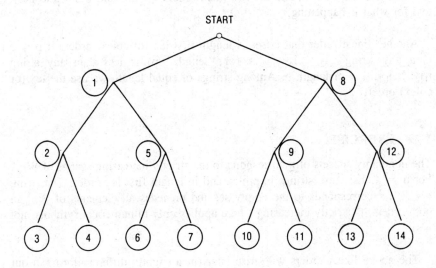

Figure 1.26b

1.27 EXERCISE.

Draw the analogous figures to 1.26(a) and 1.26(b) for the cases where ∗ is located {1,∗,2} and {1,2,∗} in the order on $\underline{2}$.

In general, let $W_{d,r}$ (words of length at most d on r symbols) denote the elements of $\bar{r}^d$ where $\bar{r} = r \cup \{*\}$ and $*$ is a terminal symbol. There are $r+1$ ways that we might insert $*$ into the linearly ordered set r. Each of these gives rise to a lexicographic order on $W_{d,r}$. If $*$ is placed before all the symbols in r, we call the order on $W_{d,r}$ the *prelex order*. If it is placed after, we call the order the *postlex order*. The rest of the orders we could call "inlex orders." These terms are in keeping with similar notions in computer science (see Knuth, D.E., *The Art of Computer Programming*, Vol. 1, Reading, MA: Addison-Wesley, p. 316). Diagrams such as FIGURE 1.26(a) and (b) are called "tree diagrams." In case r = 2 the tree is called "binary." There is only one inlex order in this case. The orders prelex, inlex, and postlex are commonly called "preorder," "inorder," and "postorder" in this case. These orders are illustrated in FIGURE 1.26(a) and (b), and in EXERCISE 1.27.

1.28 EXERCISE.

Draw enough of the analogs for FIGURE 1.26(a) and (b) for $W_{3,3}$ for prelex $* 1\ 2\ 3$, postlex $1\ 2\ 3\ *$, and the two inlex orders $1 * 2\ 3$ and $1\ 2 * 3$ to get a feel for what is happening.

Another linear order that arises is length-first lex (or colex) order. If $p < q$ then any string $i_1 i_2 \ldots i_p * * \ldots *$ (of "length" p) is less than any string $i_1 i_2 \ldots i_q * \ldots *$ of length q. Among strings of equal length we use the lex (or colex) order.

1.29 EXERCISE.

The nonempty subsets of n correspond to the strictly increasing strings of $W_{n,n}$. For n = 4, list these strings in prelex and in length first lex order. The string $* * \ldots *$ corresponds to the empty set and precedes all elements of $W_{n,n}$ in both orders. ("strictly increasing" here applies only to numerical symbols, not $*$'s).

The above linear orders will arise later (in a slightly different form) in our discussion of graphs and trees. Postlex order will be called *postorder*, prelex order will be called *preorder*, and length-first order will be called *breadth-first order*.

The various lexicographic orders on $W_{d,r}$ are inherited by any subset $S \subseteq W_{d,r}$. Also, the discussion of these orders applies if d or r is replaced by any finite linearly ordered set. The discussion of prelex (or postlex) order applies equally well to a direct product of arbitrary linearly ordered sets $A_1 \times \ldots \times A_d$ as the symbol $*$ may be addended to the beginning (or end) of all of the sets A_i. In particular, the linear order on A_i may itself be a lex, colex, prelex, etc., order.

1.30   EXAMPLE.

In FIGURE 1.31(b) we have indicated the list of all possible positions for five different "tiles" that might be placed on the 4 × 4 board shown in FIGURE 1.31(a). The numbers in FIGURE 1.31(b) indicate the squares of FIGURE 1.31(a) covered by that position of the tile (read as in a book).

1.31   LEX LISTS OF TILINGS OF A BOARD (backtracking problem).

(a)

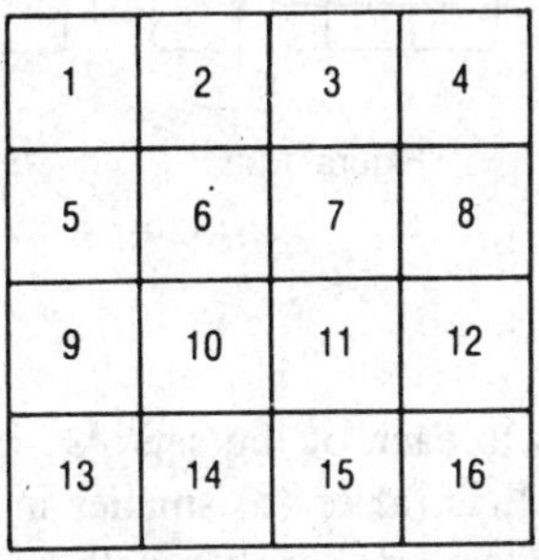

1	2	3	4
5	6	7	8
9	10	11	12
13	14	15	16

$\tilde{A}_i = \{*\} \cup A_i$,

A SEQUENCE SUCH AS $((1,2,3,6), (5,9,10,14), *,*,*)$ IS WRITTEN $((1,2,3,6),(5,9,10,14))$ AND IS SAID TO HAVE "LENGTH 2."

(b)

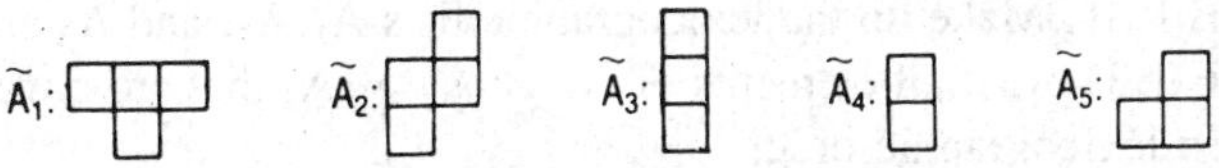

$\tilde{A}_1$:	$\tilde{A}_2$:	$\tilde{A}_3$:	$\tilde{A}_4$:	$\tilde{A}_5$:
*	*	*	*	*
(1,2,3,6)	(1,2,6,7)	(1,2,3)	(1,2)	(1,2,5)
(1,5,6,9)	(1,5,6,10)	(1,5,9)	(1,5)	(1,2,6)
(2,3,4,7)	(2,3,5,6)	(2,3,4)	(2,3)	(1,5,6)
(2,5,6,7)	(2,3,7,8)	(2,6,10)	(2,6)	(2,3,6)
(2,5,6,10)	(2,5,6,9)	(3,7,11)	(3,4)	(2,3,7)
⋮	⋮	⋮	⋮	⋮

Figure 1.31

Observe that each list A_1 is ordered lexicographically. The natural order on $A_1 \times \ldots \times A_5$ is the prelex order ($\underline{r}^d$ replaced by $\tilde{A}_1 \times \ldots \times \tilde{A}_5$). In covering the board with these "tiles," only strings with all sets disjoint—such as the length 2 string, $(1,2,3,6)$, $(5,9,10,14)$ (FIGURE 1.32(c)), or length 5 string, $(1,2,3,6)$ $(4,7,8,11)$, $(5,9,13)$, $(10,14)$, $(12,15,16)$ (FIGURE 1.32(a))—will even be considered. In prelex order, the string $(1,2,3,6)$, $(5,9,10,14)$ would be encountered before any longer string starting off with the same two terms. This is desirable because we see (FIGURE 1.32(c)) that this string leaves the square number 13 isolated. Hence no continuation of this string can lead to a solution. Thus we immediately take a *leap forward* in the prelex order on $A_1 \times \ldots \times A_5$, skipping many strings. This technique of testing and leaping forward is called (strange as it may seem) "backtracking."

1.32   SAMPLE TILING CONFIGURATIONS.

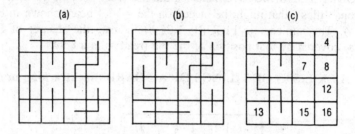

Figure 1.32

1.33   EXERCISE.

(1) Add the next five entries to each of the sets A_1, $i = 1, \ldots, 5$, in FIGURE
    1.31(b). In FIGURE 1.32, is (a) or (b) smaller in lex order? Is there any
    solution to this tiling problem smaller than both (a) and (b)?

(2) The 3×3 board below is to be covered with the tiles shown below just as
    in FIGURE 1.31. Make up the lexicographic lists A_1, A_2, and A_3 analogous
    to FIGURE 1.31. List all elements of $A_1 \times A_2 \times A_3$ that are coverings of
    the board in lexicographic order.

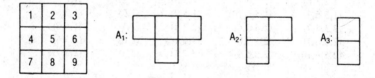

Figure 1.33   (Top)

(3) Solutions to the problem of placing five nonattacking queens on a 5×5
    chessboard are specified by sequences such as $(1,4,2,5,3)$ and $(4,1,3,5,2)$.
    The numbers represent the location of the queen in the respective columns
    of the board:

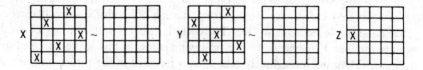

Figure 1.33   (Bottom)

(a) Two solutions are equivalent if one can be made to coincide with the other by rotating and/or reflecting the board. Are X and Y above in the same equivalence class? Explain. If a lexicographically minimal system of representatives is to be selected, what element or elements would be selected equivalent to X and Y? (See EXERCISE 1.38(2) for related ideas.)

(b) Show that there is no minimal representative that starts off (3,. . .) as in Z above.

1.34 EXERCISE.

The "Mathematical Games" section of *Scientific American* (Vol. 227, No. 3, September 1972, pp. 176–182) describes a game called SOMA cube (Parker Brothers, Inc., Salem, Massachusetts). How would you linearly order the solutions and partial solutions to this game?

1.35 EXAMPLE.

The string of symbols v v h h h v v h describes a covering of the 4×4 board of FIGURE 1.36(a) with dominoes (or "dimers"). To interpret the string, read the first symbol, a v, and place a vertical domino on the square numbered 1. The second symbol is a v so place a vertical domino on the lowest numbered uncovered square (number 2). The third symbol is an h so place a horizontal domino on the lowest uncovered square, etc. The configuration after the first four symbols of the string have been interpreted is shown in FIGURE 1.36(b) and the final configuration in FIGURE 1.36(c). Of course, not all of the $2^8 = 256$ strings of length 8 represent coverings of the square with dominoes (v v v h . . . wouldn't!) There are 36 "grammatically correct" strings that do represent coverings.

If we let A = {h,v} be a two-point ordered set with h < v, then the strings of length 8 or less (call them $W_{8,A}$) are ordered by the prelex order. In particular, the solutions (all of length 8) are ordered by the lex order on A^8. The 36 solutions are shown in FIGURE 1.37. They are not in lex order.

1.36 CODING DOMINO COVERINGS.

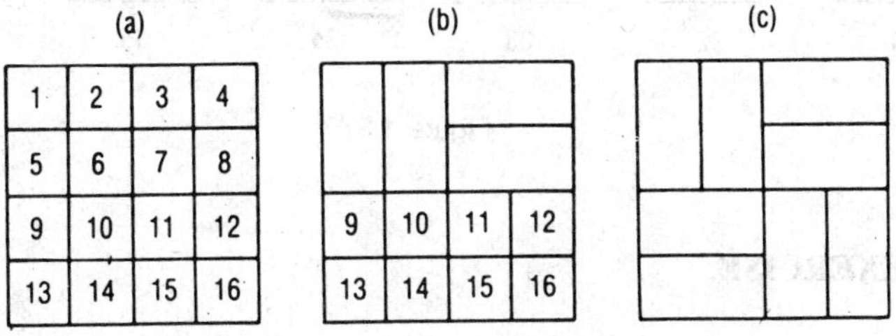

Figure 1.36

1.37   ALL DOMINO COVERINGS OF A 4 × 4 BOARD.

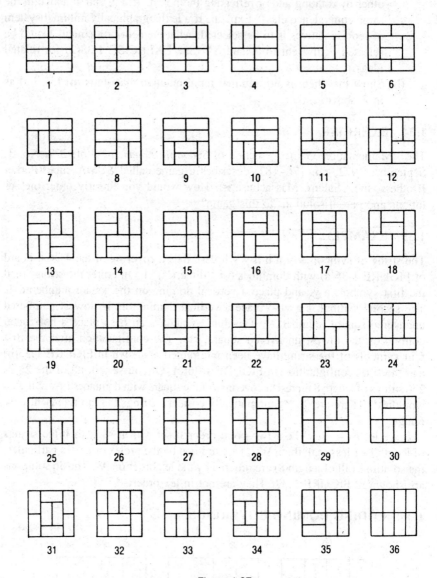

Figure 1.37

1.38   EXERCISE.

(1) Find the next to last solution of FIGURE 1.37 in lex order. Carry out a systematic procedure for putting the solutions of FIGURE 1.37 in correct lex order.

(2) Look at solution 27 of FIGURE 1.37. A rotation by 90° produces a lex smaller figure, so cross out 27. Look at solution 25. It is the smallest among all possible rotations (90°, 180°, 270°) and reflections of itself. So keep 25. Do this for all of the 36 figures. Verify that the final list of solutions that you keep by this procedure has the following properties (such lists are called "systems of representatives"):

  (a) No two solutions are "isomorphic" in the sense that a rotation and/or reflection of one produces the other.

  (b) All of the 36 solutions are "isomorphic" to some solution in your list.
    Problems of selecting sublists satisfying (a) and (b) with respect to groups of symmetries are called *isomorph rejection* problems. We will discuss them later.

(3) Think up a totally different algorithm than EXERCISE 1.38(2) to perform isomorph rejection in FIGURE 1.37. Which algorithm is easier for a standard computer? Which is easier for you?

(4) Invent your own algorithms for making a list of all possible ways to color the faces of a tetrahedron and a cube with r different colors up to (a) rotations and (b) rotations and reflections. First try r = 2, 4, 6.

(5) List all ways of coloring the vertices of a hexagon with three colors, B, G, R, up to rotations and reflections, such that adjacent vertices are never given the same color. How many such figures are there for r colors?

(6) Try to write some programs along the lines of the previous problems.

Conceptually, there is another way to regard the set $W_{d,r}$. Given a string $i_1 i_2 \ldots i_t$ we can think of it as a key or label for a *subset* of $\underline{r}^d$. The subset is the set of all $j_1 j_2 \ldots j_d$ with $j_1 \ldots j_t = i_1 \ldots i_t$. Consider $W_{3,2}$. The strings 1 and 2 are associated with the sets $B_1 = \{1\,1\,1,\ 1\,1\,2,\ 1\,2\,1,\ 1\,2\,2\}$ and $B_2 = \{2\,1\,1,\ 2\,1\,2,\ 2\,2\,1,\ 2\,2\,2\}$. The strings 1 1, 1 2 are associated with the sets $B_{11} = \{1\,1\,1,\ 1\,1\,2\}$ and $B_{12} = \{1\,2\,1,\ 1\,2\,2\}$. The strings 21 and 22 are associated with the sets $B_{21} = \{2\,1\,1,\ 2\,1\,2\}$ and $B_{22} = \{2\,2\,1,\ 2\,2\,2\}$. The string 1 1 1 is associated with the one element set $B_{111} = \{1\,1\,1\}$ consisting of itself, as are the rest of the length 3 strings. An *ordered partition* of a set S is a sequence $(Q_1, \ldots, Q_p)$, $p \geq 1$, of subsets (possibly empty) of S, pairwise disjoint, with union S. Thus (B_1, B_2) is an ordered partition of $\underline{r}^d$ and (B_{11}, B_{12}) is an ordered partition of B_1, etc. The ordered partition $(B_{11}, B_{12}, B_{21}, B_{22})$ is an ordered partition of $\underline{r}^d$ which is a *refinement* of (B_1, B_2) in the sense that each of its subsets is contained in some subset of the ordered partition (B_1, B_2). This conceptual association between strings and successive refinements by ordered partitions is quite common in mathematics. For example the binary decimal .1 0 1 refers to the set $B_1 = \{x: 1/2 \leq x < 1\}$, refined by $B_{10} = \{x: 1/2 \leq x < 3/4\}$, refined by $B_{101} = \{x: 5/8 \leq x < 3/4\}$, refined by $\{x: 5/8 \leq x < 11/16\}$, etc. The number of refinements corresponding to .10100 . . . is infinite, defining in the limit one real number. There is a conceptually natural way to associate linear orders with successive refinements by ordered partitions. We now explore this method.

FIGURE 1.39 shows a structure that we will call an *ordered partition tree* for the set S (in this case S = 6). We shall give a more formal definition of the idea of an *ordered tree* later. As for now, we shall use this idea intuitively to discuss linear orders on sets.

1.39   ORDERED PARTITION TREE.

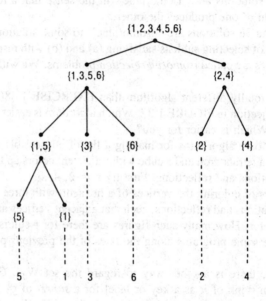

Figure 1.39

The *vertices* of the tree of FIGURE 1.39 are nonempty subsets of 6. The set 6 is the *root* of the tree (the tree is upside down). The root has two *sons*: {1, 3, 5, 6} (the first son) and {2, 4} the second son. The sons of each vertex define an ordered partition of that vertex. None of the sets in the ordered partition are empty. The vertices such as {5},{1},{3}, etc., are *terminal vertices* or *leaves* in the tree. Each terminal vertex corresponds to a subset of 6 with one element. The dotted lines project the terminal vertices onto a horizontal line. When reading the elements of 6 as they appear on the horizontal line one obtains 5, 1, 3, 6, 2, 4. This defines the linear order associated with the ordered partition tree of FIGURE 1.39.

A given order, such as 5, 1, 3, 6, 2, 4, may be defined by many different ordered partition trees. The *nodes* or *vertices* in FIGURE 1.39 are labeled by subsets of 6. Note that only the labels of the leaves need be given to recover all of the other labels. That is, each label of an internal node is exactly the set of elements in the leaves descendant to that label. There is one leaf corresponding to each element in the set associated with the root of the partition tree (6 in FIGURE 1.39). Why bother to label the internal nodes at all if they are determined by the leaves? The reason is that we may wish to define the partition tree "locally" by giving rules for constructing the tree rather than by drawing the whole tree, as in FIGURE 1.39. We now discuss some examples of this type of situation.

Consider $\underline{r}^{\underline{d}}$ as above. Let $(i_1, \ldots, i_t, \_, \ldots, \_)$ denote the set of all functions in $\underline{r}^{\underline{d}}$ whose first t values are the ones specified. In our above notation, $B_1 = (1, \_, \_)$. Note that in a tree diagram such as FIGURE 1.39 there is a unique path (sequence of edges) from the root to any given node of the tree. We call the number of edges in that path the *height* of that node. Figure 1.40 gives a local description of one possible partition tree for $\underline{r}^{\underline{d}}$.

1.40 LOCAL DESCRIPTION OF A PARTITION TREE FOR $\underline{r}^{\underline{d}}$.

(1) ROOT $= (\_, \ldots, \_) = \underline{r}^{\underline{d}}$
(2) INTERNAL NODES:

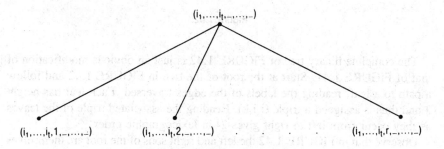

LEXICOGRAPHIC ORDER

Figure 1.40

(3) ANY NODE OF HEIGHT d IS A LEAF.

The order defined by the partition tree of FIGURE 1.40 is lexicographic order on $\underline{r}^{\underline{d}}$. The case $r = 2$ and $d = 3$ is shown in FIGURE 1.41.

1.41 PARTITION TREE FOR $\underline{2}^3$.

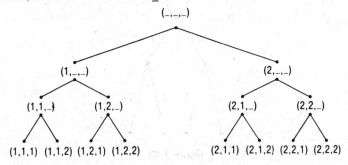

Figure 1.41

A tree is a *binary tree* if each internal node has one or two sons, a *full binary tree* if each internal node has exactly two sons, and a *complete binary* tree if it is full and all leaves are at the same level (see FIGURE 1.42 for an example).

1.42 LEXICOGRAPHIC ORDER ON $\underline{2}^3$.

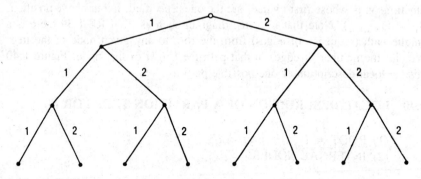

Figure 1.42

The complete binary tree of FIGURE 1.42 is just an obvious modification of that of FIGURE 1.41. Start at the root of the tree in FIGURE 1.42 and follow a path to a leaf, reading the labels of the edges traversed. Each leaf has height 3 and thus is assigned a triple (i,j,k). Reading the associated triple of the leaves as they occur from left to right gives $\underline{2}^3$ in lexicographic order.

Observe that in FIGURE 1.42 the left and right sons of the root are themselves roots of complete binary trees of height 2. These two subtrees are identical, so they may be superimposed on each other as seen in FIGURE 1.43. In this figure, paths from the root to the terminal nodes still correspond to elements of $\underline{2}^3$ in lex order. The resulting "graph" is no longer a tree.

1.43 A MODIFICATION OF FIGURE 1.42.

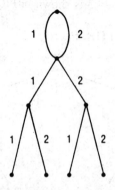

Figure 1.43

The two subtrees of FIGURE 1.43 may be superimposed in the same manner and the terminal vertices identified to get FIGURE 1.44. Paths from the top-most vertex in this figure to the bottom vertex still correspond to paths in $\underline{2}^3$. To describe the linear order (lex order) in terms of FIGURE 1.44 one must essentially give the definition of lex order (DEFINITION 1.20).

1.44 A MODIFICATION OF FIGURE 1.43.

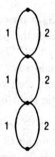

Figure 1.44

We shall now consider partition trees for some additional linear orders. Let S_n denote the set of all permutations from $\underline{n}$ to $\underline{n}$. Using notation similar to that above, let $(i_1, \ldots, i_k, \_, \ldots, \_)$ denote the set of all permutations in S_n with first k values as specified. We let $S_n = (\_, \ldots, \_)$. The partition tree of FIGURE 1.45 is associated with lex order on S_3.

1.45 LEX ORDER ON S₃.

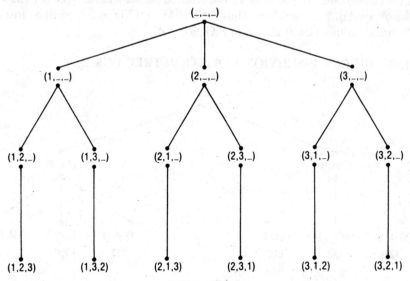

Figure 1.45

1.46   EXERCISE.

(1) Consider the general case of a partition tree for S_n as suggested by the example for S_3 in FIGURE 1.45. Give a careful local description of the general case along the lines of FIGURE 1.40.

(2) What is the analog of FIGURE 1.44 for FIGURE 1.45 and for the general case? *Hint*: Note that all subtrees at the same level are identical.

.nother basic partition tree for S_n is based on the "direct insertion" method ,ur generating permutations. Consider the permutation 426153 in S_6. Note that the 2 is to the left of the 1. We say that "2 is in position two relative to 1." If the 2 were to the right of 1 we would say "2 is in position one relative to 1." For any permutation in S_n we consider the two possible positions of the 2 relative to the 1: $\frac{-}{2} 1 \frac{-}{1}$. The position on the right is called the first position, the other position is the second position. Let $(2 \text{ in } 1)_n$ denote the subset of S_n of all permutations with 2 in position 1 and let $(2 \text{ in } 2)_n$ denote all permutations with 2 in position 2. Thus, $465213 \in (2 \text{ in } 2)_6$ and $4123 \in (2 \text{ in } 1)_4$. Similarly, if we consider a permutation in S_n, $n \geqslant 3$, then we define 3 positions of 3 relative to the symbols 1 and 2: $\frac{-}{3} x \frac{-}{2} y \frac{-}{1}$. The x and y can be either 1 or 2. Thus 4231 and 4132 are both elements of the set $(3 \text{ in } 2)_4$, 4321 and 4312 are both in $(3 \text{ in } 3)_4$, etc. In the same manner, we define sets $(k \text{ in } j)_n$, $j \in \underline{k}$. Another way to view the set $(k \text{ in } j)_n$ is as follows: Given a permutation in S_n, and an integer k, remove all symbols greater than k from the permutation. The permutation is in $(k \text{ in } j)_n$ if k is the jth symbol from the right in the reduced permutation. Consider 957862431 and k = 7. The reduced permutation is 5762431 and 7 is the 6th symbol from the right. Thus, $957862431 \in (7 \text{ in } 6)_9$. A partition tree for S_3 based on this idea is shown in FIGURE 1.47.

1.47   DIRECT INSERTION PARTITION TREE FOR S_3.

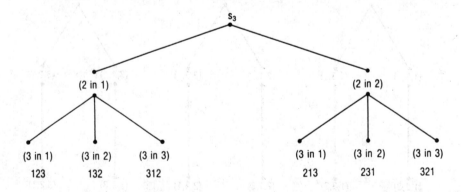

Figure 1.47

The labels in the partition tree of FIGURE 1.47 are not the actual partitions (except labels of sons of the root). In FIGURE 1.47 and in its generalization to S_n, the partition associated with a vertex v is obtained by taking the intersection of all sets labeling vertices on the path from the root to v. The intersection of all sets on a path from the root to a leaf is a set consisting of a single permutation. Thus the order of the leaves from left to right defines a linear order on S_n. For example, (2 in 1) ∩ (3 in 3) = {312} in FIGURE 1.47. The permutations associated with each leaf are shown in FIGURE 1.47.

Note that in the first three permutations of FIGURE 1.47, the "1,2" pattern remains fixed and the 3 is inserted in the three positions right to left relative to this pattern. Then, the pattern becomes "2,1" and the 3 is again inserted right to left. This basic idea extends to the case of S_n and is the reason for the name "direct insertion method." Another way of representing the tree in FIGURE 1.47 is shown in FIGURE 1.48.

1.48   CODED VERSION OF DIRECT INSERTION TREE.

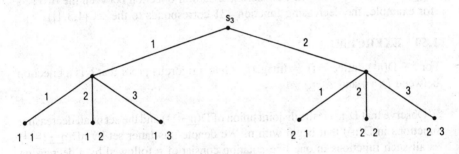

Figure 1.48

In FIGURE 1.48, the labels on the edges tell where the corresponding integer is to be inserted. In any path from the root to a leaf, the first edge tells where to insert the symbol 2, the second edge where to insert 3, etc. This tree represents the same linear order on permutations as the direct insertion tree. It is interesting to label each leaf of the tree of FIGURE 1.48 with the sequence of edge labels obtained by following the path from the root to that leaf. This has been done in FIGURE 1.48. Note that the labels on the leaves, read left to right, is just lex order on $\underline{2} \times \underline{3}$. Thus there is a natural bijection between S_n in direct insertion order and $\underline{2} \times \ldots \times \underline{n}$ in lex order. This is an example of an *order isomorphism*. Between linearly ordered sets, only one bijection preserves order.

1.49   EXERCISE.

(1) Extend FIGURES 1.47 and 1.48 to S_n by giving the local description such as in FIGURE 1.40 or EXERCISE 1.46(1).

(2) Give a careful proof of the correspondence between S_n in direct insertion order and $\underline{2} \times \ldots \times \underline{n}$ in lex order.

(3) What is the successor and predecessor of 87612543 in lex and direct insertion order on S_8? What is the first entry in the second half of the list of S_8 in lex and direct insertion order?

As one can see from the above examples, the idea of "partition tree" has many different variations. The general idea is that given a set S and a linear order on S, we wish to construct some geometric object that aids our intuition. Thus, we seek a tree or graph together with a bijection between certain classes of paths and the elements of our set S. The idea of a partition tree is a general idea that can be modified as needed in various particular situations. We have discussed permutations above. Now we consider "combinations" or subsets of fixed size k from a set of size n. Let $\mathcal{P}_k(n)$ denote the set of all subsets of size k chosen from $\underline{n}$. Let $D(\underline{n}^{\underline{k}})$ denote the set of all decreasing functions from $\underline{k}$ to $\underline{n}$. For example, $D(\underline{4}^{\underline{3}}) = \{321,421,431,432\}$ where the functions are listed in one line notation and in lexicographic order. Clearly, to list the elements of $\mathcal{P}_k(\underline{n})$ it suffices to list $D(\underline{n}^{\underline{k}})$ as there is a natural bijection between the two sets (for example, the decreasing function 431 corresponds to the set $\{4,3,1\}$).

1.50   EXERCISE.

For $f \in D(\underline{n}^{\underline{k}})$ define $F(f) = \text{Image}(f)$. Give a rigorous proof that F is a bijection between $D(\underline{n}^{\underline{k}})$ and $\mathcal{P}_k(\underline{n})$.

Observe that $D(\underline{n}^{\underline{k}})$ is the disjoint union of $D(\underline{n-1}^{\underline{k}})$ and the set of all decreasing functions in $D(\underline{n}^{\underline{k}})$ that begin with n. We denote this latter set by $nD(\underline{n-1}^{\underline{k-1}})$ as all such functions in one line notation consist of n followed by a decreasing function from $\underline{k-1}$ to $\underline{n-1}$. In the same manner, $D(\underline{n-1}^{\underline{k}})$ is a disjoint union of $D(\underline{n-2}^{\underline{k}})$ and $(n-1)D(\underline{n-2}^{\underline{k-1}})$. Repeating this process we arrive at a partition tree with local description as shown in FIGURE 1.51.

1.51   PARTITION TREE FOR DECREASING FUNCTIONS.

(1) Root $D(\underline{n}^{\underline{k}})$

(2) INTERNAL NODES

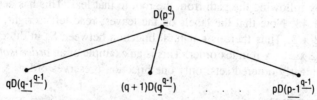

(3) ANY NODE OF HEIGHT k IS A LEAF

Figure 1.51

The basic idea of FIGURE 1.51 is very simple, the decreasing functions from $\underline{k}$ to $\underline{n}$ are decomposed first into all functions that start with k, then all functions that start with $k + 1$, etc. It is better to represent this process in a manner analogous either to FIGURE 1.42 or 1.48. This is done in FIGURE 1.52.

1.52 TREE DIAGRAM FOR $D(\underline{6}^{\underline{4}})$ IN LEX ORDER.

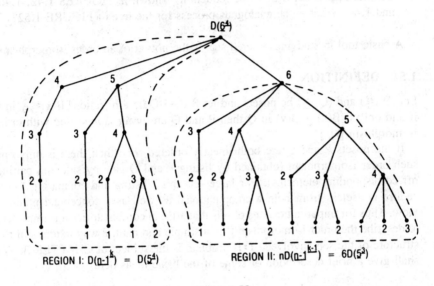

Figure 1.52

The interpretation of FIGURE 1.52 is the obvious one—start at the root and descend to a leaf, reading the labels on the vertices encountered on the way. Thus, each terminal node corresponds to a unique decreasing function (the sequence of labels from the root to the terminal node). The order defined by left to right order on terminal nodes is lex order on decreasing functions from $\underline{4}$ to $\underline{6}$. The sons of the root are labeled 4, 5, and 6 and the corresponding subtrees rooted at these vertices give all decreasing functions of length 4 starting with 4, 5, and 6, respectively (as specified in FIGURE 1.51). The basic recursion that $D(\underline{n}^{\underline{k}})$ is the disjoint union of $D(\underline{n-1}^{\underline{k}})$ and $nD(\underline{n-1}^{\underline{k-1}})$ is shown by the dotted REGION I and REGION II of FIGURE 1.52.

1.53 EXERCISE.

(1) Try to prove the standard result $|\mathscr{P}_k(\underline{n})| = \dfrac{n!}{k!(n-k)!}$ without consulting your previous notes or textbook.

(2) FIGURES 1.51 and 1.52 show geometrically that $\binom{n}{k} = \sum_{j=k-1}^{n-1} \binom{j}{k-1}$

and $\binom{n}{k} = \binom{n-1}{k-1} + \binom{n-1}{k}$. Prove these results by induction using the

formula for $\binom{n}{k}$ in problem (1) above (assume $k \geq 1$).

(3) Consider the process of "tree reduction" shown in FIGURES 1.42, 1.43, and 1.44. What is the analogous process for the tree of FIGURE 1.52?

A basic tool in studying ordered sets is the notion of an order isomorphism.

1.54   DEFINITION.

Let $(P, \leq)$ and $(Q, \propto)$ be posets and let $\beta:P \to Q$ be a bijection. If $x \leq y$ in P if and only if $\beta(x) \propto \beta(y)$ in Q then P and Q are *order isomorphic* with order isomorphism β.

If the posets P and Q are both linearly ordered sets, then there is only one such order isomorphism (obtained by listing P and Q side by side and pairing off corresponding elements). For large sets this "listing and comparing" procedure is useless from both a computational as well as a conceptual point of view. Thus for important classes of sets that arise in combinatorics it is important to describe the order isomorphism β in a simple and natural way in terms of the structure of the sets involved. This problem is the subject of CHAPTER 3. We shall give a brief description of some of the basic ideas here.

1.55   DEFINITION.

Let S be a linearly ordered set with $|S| = s$. Let $_{\lfloor}s_{\rfloor}$ denote the linearly ordered set $0, 1, \ldots, s-1$. We denote the order isomorphism between S and $_{\lfloor}s_{\rfloor}$ by RANK and its inverse by UNRANK.

Thus, if $x \in S$ then RANK(x) is the number of elements of S that occur *before* x in the linear order on S. If $k \in {}_{\lfloor}s_{\rfloor}$ then UNRANK(k) is the element of S that has exactly k elements preceding it. FIGURE 1.56 shows an edge $e = (a,b)$ in a tree structure such as those we have previously examined. The upper vertex of the edge is a and the lower vertex is b. Let $R(e) = R(a,b)$ denote the tree structure that consists of all paths of the form $a, x, \ldots$ and ending at a leaf of the tree where x is to the left of b. This tree structure is shown in FIGURE 1.56. We call $R(e)$ the *residual tree* of the edge e.

1.56 RESIDUAL TREE OF AN EDGE.

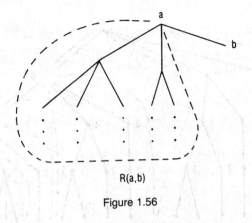

R(a,b)

Figure 1.56

In FIGURE 1.57, a tree structure is shown together with a path a_1, a_2, a_3, a_4 from the root to a leaf. The residual tree of each edge in the path is shown. If we let S denote the set of all leaves of the tree (equivalently, the set of all paths from the root to a leaf) linearly ordered from left to right, then the RANK(a_4) (equivalently, RANK(path a_1, a_2, a_3, a_4)) is just the sum of the number of leaves (or paths) in the residual tree of each edge of the path. If we let $\Delta(a_i, a_j)$ denote the number of leaves in R(a_i, a_j), then RANK(a_4) $= \Delta(a_1, a_2) + \Delta(a_2, a_3) + \Delta(a_3, a_4) = 5 + 3 + 2 = 10$. There are 10 leaves or terminal vertices before $a_4 = k$, namely, a,b,c,d,e,f,g,h,i, and j.

1.57 THE RANK OF A LEAF IN TERMS OF RESIDUAL TREES.

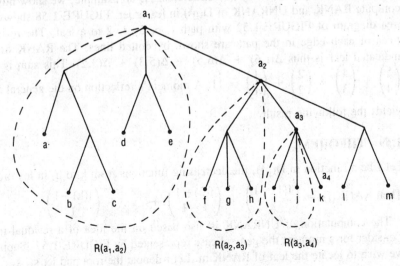

R(a_1, a_2) R(a_2, a_3) R(a_3, a_4)

Figure 1.57

1.58 RANK OF A LEAF OF D(6^4).

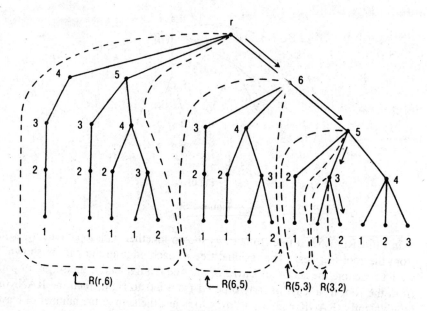

Figure 1.58

The idea illustrated in FIGURE 1.57 for computing the RANK of a leaf in a tree may be used to compute the RANK function of many important combinatorial lists. FIGURES 1.42, 1.45, 1.47, 1.48, and 1.52 are examples of basic lists that have been represented by tree structures. As an example, we show how to compute RANK and UNRANK of D($\underline{n}^{\underline{k}}$) in lex order. FIGURE 1.58 shows the tree diagram of FIGURE 1.52 with path r, 6, 5, 3, 2 to a leaf. The residual trees of each edge in the path are shown by dotted lines. The RANK of the indicated leaf is thus $\Delta(r,6) + \Delta(6,5) + \Delta(5,3) + \Delta(3,2)$. This sum is just

$$\binom{5}{4} + \binom{4}{3} + \binom{2}{2} + \binom{1}{1} = 11.$$ A moment's reflection on the general case yields the following result.

1.59 THEOREM.

Let f be a function in D($\underline{n}^{\underline{k}}$), the decreasing functions from $\underline{k}$ to $\underline{n}$, in lex order. Then RANK(f) = $\binom{f(1)-1}{k} + \binom{f(2)-1}{k-1} + \ldots + \binom{f(k)-1}{1}$.

The computation of UNRANK is also based on the idea of a residual tree. Consider for a moment the general case represented by FIGURE 1.57. Suppose we wish to locate the leaf of RANK m. Let r denote the root and let s_1, s_2, ...,

s_p be the sons of the root in order from left to right. Which edge (r,s_i) must we take to eventually arrive at the leaf x with RANK(x) = m? Clearly, if $\Delta(r,s_i)$ > m then x lies in the residual tree $R(r,s_i)$, so we had better not descend along the edge (r,s_i). Also, if $\Delta(r,s_i) < m$ *and* $\Delta(r,s_{i+1}) \leq m$ then the largest (i.e., right-most) leaf in $R(r,s_{i+1})$ has RANK strictly less than m, so in this case also we would not want to descend along (r,s_i). Thus we must choose the index i such that $i = \max \{t: \Delta(r,s_t) \leq m\}$. We then let $m' = m - \Delta(r,s_i)$ and repeat the same procedure on the subtree rooted at s_i. This is the basis for the following result.

1.60 THEOREM.

Let UNRANK be the inverse of the function RANK of THEOREM 1.59. The following algorithm computes UNRANK:

procedure UNRANK(m) (Computes f = (f(1), . . . , f(k)) in $D(\underline{n}^k)$, RANK(f) = m)

> *initialize* $m' := m$, $t := 1$, $s := k$; $(1 \leq k \leq n, 0 \leq m \leq \binom{n}{k} - 1)$

>> *while* $t \leq k$ *do*
>> *begin*

$$f(t) - 1 := \max \{y : \binom{y}{s} \leq m'\};$$

$$m' := m' - \binom{f(t)-1}{s};$$

$$t := t + 1;$$

$$s := s - 1;$$

> *end.*

1.61 EXERCISE.

(1) Prove by induction that the procedure of THEOREM 1.60 is correct.
(2) Find the element UNRANK (99) of $D(\underline{10}^5)$ in lex order. Find RANK (10,8,6,5,2) in this list.
(3) State and prove the analogous results to THEOREM 1.59 and 1.60 for the list of permutations S_n in lex order and direct insertion order.
(4) Let S be a set (finite as usual). To "select an element at random from S" is to define a procedure that selects an element from S in such a way that any element of S is equally likely to be selected. In probability terms, the procedure selects an element from S according to the *uniform distribution* on S. Write procedures that select a permutation from S_n at random and a subset of size k from $\mathcal{P}_k(n)$ at random.

(5) How would you linearly order, rank, and unrank all ways of placing k indistinguishable balls into n bins? Try some examples first.

We put aside for now the computation of basic order isomorphisms for combinatorial lists. In CHAPTER 3 a detailed discussion of this subject will be given. The reader should note that if we have a nice algorithm for computing the order isomorphism RANK for a linearly ordered set, then, by computing RANK(x) where x is the last element of S, we also know the number of elements of S, $|S| = $ RANK(x) + 1. The problem of counting the number of elements of a set S is a central problem of classical combinatorial theory (enumerative combinatorics). Thus the problem of computing RANK and UNRANK as posed above is in general more difficult than simply counting the total number of elements in the corresponding sets. In fact, many of the classical techniques for counting the number of elements of a set can be modified to produce methods for linearly ordering the elements of the set and computing RANK and UNRANK. This is particularly so for counting methods based on recursions as one can then use the partition tree concepts as previously discussed. Other methods with which the reader may be familiar (such as the principle of inclusion-exclusion) may not be readily modified to compute RANK and UNRANK. In some problems of listing combinatorial objects, the partition tree provides a useful framework but the trees do not have enough regularity to allow for a simple characterization of the residual trees. This situation is common in so-called backtracking problems ("forward leaping" problems, as noted previously). Problems involving both backtracking and isomorph rejections are especially complex and interesting in this regard.

We conclude our discussion with a famous example of this type of problem, the "8-queens problem." The great 19th century mathematician, Carl Friedrich Gauss, got the wrong answer to this problem! The classical "8-queens" problem is to discover all ways of placing 8 nonattacking queens on an 8 × 8 chessboard. A more general problem is to place n *or fewer* nonattacking queens on an n × n chessboard. An n × n board has eight basic symmetries—the identity, rotation by 90, 180, and 270 degrees and reflections about the four axes ρ_1, ρ_2, ρ_3, ρ_4, as shown in FIGURE 1.62(a) for the case n = 4.

1.62   THE SYMMETRIES OF A CHESSBOARD.

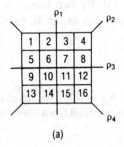

(a)

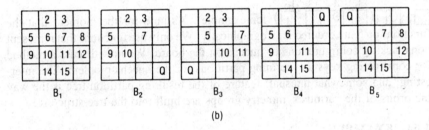

(b)

Figure 1.62

We number the squares of the board as one would read a book, from left to right and from top to bottom. Consider square 1 of FIGURE 1.62. By applying the group of symmetries G to the square, square 1 can be moved to the position occupied by square 4, 13, or 16, but to no other squares. The set $\{1, 4, 13, 16\}$ is called an *orbit* of G on the 4×4 board. This orbit could have been generated by rotations alone. An orbit that requires reflections as well as rotations is the set $\{2, 3, 5, 8, 9, 12, 14, 15\}$. There is one other orbit on the 4×4 board, $\{6, 7, 10, 11\}$. The orbits of a group of symmetries are always disjoint (they form a partition of the set of squares of the board). We linearly order the orbits according to the label of the *smallest* integer in the orbit. In FIGURE 1.62, B_1 shows the 4×4 board with the squares of the first orbit blanked out. In B_2 a queen has been placed on the S.E. (southeast) corner square. All squares attacked by this queen are also blanked out. Let Q_n denote the set of all solutions to the n or fewer queens problem and let $Q_n^=$ denote the set of all solutions to the exactly n queens problem. We regard the picture B_1 of FIGURE 1.62 as a symbolic representation of the subset of Q_4 consisting of all solutions that, when restricted to the first orbit (the corner squares), looks exactly like B_1 (i.e., the corner squares are empty). Likewise, B_2 stands for the subset of Q_4 consisting of all solutions with a queen in the S.E. corner and all other corners empty, etc.

We call the B_i "keys" or symbolic representations of certain subsets of solutions. We could equally well regard the B_i as specifying subsets of $Q\overline{\overline{4}}$. In this case, the set specified by B_1 has exactly two elements and the other B_i specify the empty set. We shall use keys such as the B_i to construct partition trees for Q_n or $Q\overline{\overline{n}}$.

1.63 EXERCISE.

Prove that there are only two solutions to the exactly 4-queens problem (they are isomorphic, as one can be obtained from the other by reflection ρ_1 of FIGURE 1.62).

The keys of FIGURE 1.62 are specified by giving an ordered subset S of the board (S = $\{1, 4, 13, 16\}$) and then a function from S to the ordered set $\square$, $\boxed{Q}$ (($\begin{smallmatrix}1\\\square\end{smallmatrix}$ $\begin{smallmatrix}4\\\boxed{Q}\end{smallmatrix}$ $\begin{smallmatrix}13\\\square\end{smallmatrix}$ $\begin{smallmatrix}16\\\square\end{smallmatrix}$) for example). Assume for the moment that the functions on S are ordered lexicographically. We only use functions that represent nonattacking configurations of queens on the board. We now discuss a method for constructing keys and refining partitions for the queens problem. The interesting, and somewhat unusual, feature of the resulting partition tree is the way the orbits of the various symmetry groups are built into the tree structure.

1.64 EXAMPLE.

Consider the 4×4 board. The first (in lexicographic order) *orbit* of the full group of eight symmetries of the board is the ordered set $\{1, 4, 13, 16\}$ (remember, we order the collection of orbits *by their smallest element*). The four keys for this orbit are shown in FIGURE 1.62. Call the associated sets of solutions B_1, . . . , B_5. For this example assume "solution" means a configuration of four or fewer queens on the board (i.e., Q_4). Suppose we select B_2. How do we refine B_2 into an ordered partition? A natural way that is recursive with respect to symmetry is to construct the next collection of keys on the first orbit with respect to the group of symmetries that leave the key B_2 unchanged. This group consists of the identity and a reflection about the line through the N.W. and S.E. corner of the board. The first orbit (with respect to this reflection group) in the region of the board that is not attacked by the queen is $\{2, 5\}$. The three keys for this orbit, B_{21}, B_{22}, B_{23}, are shown in FIGURE 1.65.

1.65 KEYS FOR REFINING ORBIT.

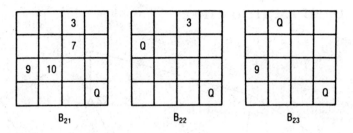

Figure 1.65

The set B_{21} again is fixed by the same group of order 2. The first orbit is $\{3, 9\}$, which gives rise to B_{211}, B_{212}, and B_{213}, shown in FIGURE 1.66.

1.66 THIRD ORDER REFINEMENT OF ORBIT.

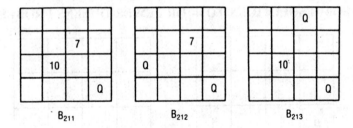

Figure 1.66

The set B_{211} again is fixed by the same group. The first (and last!) orbit is $\{7, 10\}$. This gives rise to B_{2111}, B_{2112}, B_{2113} (each consisting of one solution), as shown in FIGURE 1.67.

1.67 FOURTH ORDER REFINEMENT OF ORBIT.

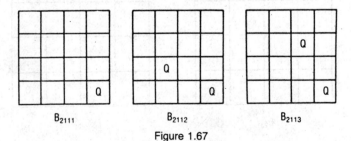

Figure 1.67

Discarding the B's and keeping their subscripting strings, the partition tree rooted at B_2 is shown by the tree diagram in FIGURE 1.68.

1.68   ORBIT PARTITION TREE.

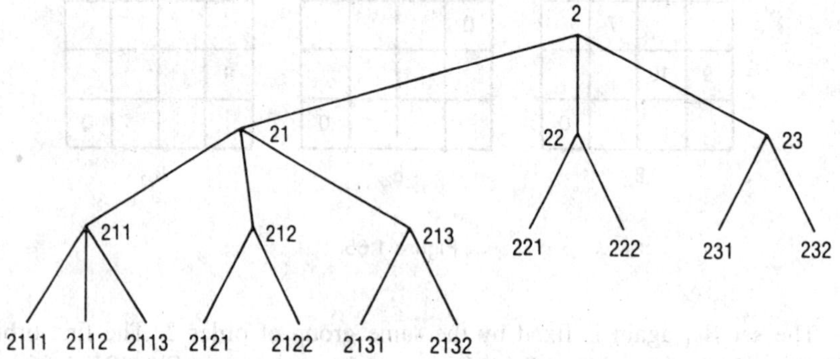

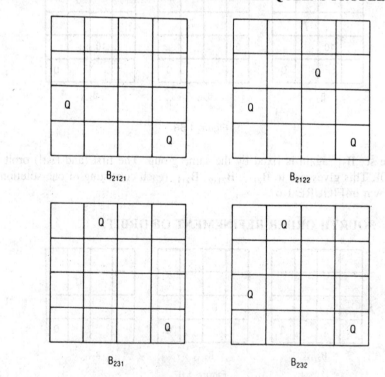

Figure 1.68

Some sample solutions are shown in FIGURE 1.69.

1.69   SOME SOLUTIONS TO 4- OR FEWER QUEENS PROBLEM.

Figure 1.69

1.70   EXERCISE.

As in FIGURE 1.69, draw the solutions corresponding to the rest of the terminal nodes in FIGURE 1.68.

1.71   EXERCISE.

A direct way (not regarding symmetry recursively) to organize the n or fewer queens problem is column by column. A configuration of queens can be regarded as functions in $(\underline{n} \cup \{*\})^{\underline{n}}$. For n = 4 the configurations of FIGURE 1.69 would be specified by 2 * * 1, 2 * 3 1, * 4 * 1, and 2 4 * 1. The numbers refer to height up the corresponding column. A * means empty column. Carry out enough of this method of generating solutions to the 4- or fewer queens problem to get a feel for what is happening. What shortcuts can you make if you use this method on the "exactly n queens" problem?

1.72   EXERCISE.

Write a computer program to find all (there are 92) solutions to the 8- queens problem, $Q_8^{\pm}$. Can you also reject isomorphs (there are 12 solutions up to symmetries)?

Two solutions to the 8-queens problem are shown in FIGURE 1.73.

1.73   TWO SOLUTIONS TO 8-QUEENS PROBLEM.

(a)   (b)

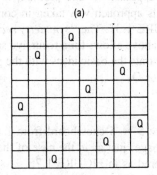
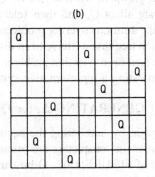

Figure 1.73

We use the symmetry-recursive ordering as in EXAMPLE 1.64. Consider 1.73(a). The first orbit under the symmetry group of order 8 of the board is {1, 8, 57, 64}. The first function $\Box$, $\Box\,\Box$, $\Box$ is on this orbit, so write down B_1. The whole group fixes this function (i.e., leaves the key B_1 unchanged). The first orbit in the complement of the orbit and the region attacked by the queen configuration on the orbit (the latter, empty in this case) is {2, 7, 9, 16,

49, 56, 58, 63}. The configuration on this orbit is again the first function, so write down B_{11}. The group fixing B_{11} is still the full group G. The first orbit in what remains is {3, 6, 17, 24, 41, 48, 59, 62}. The configuration ☐ ☐ ☐ ☐ ☐ Ⓠ Ⓠ ☐ is the 5th (nonattacking) configuration in lex order. Write down B_{115}. The group that fixes B_{115} is the identity. From now on orbits consist of single squares on the board. The first orbit in what remains is {4}. The configuration Ⓠ is the 2nd (of two possible). Write down B_{1152}. The solution of 1.73(a) is thus contained in the set of solutions B_{1152}. Continuing this process we find that 1.73(a) is the one element in the set $B_{115222222}$.

1.74 EXERCISE.

Duplicate on 1.73(b) the procedure just employed on 1.73(a) to find the key (corresponding to 1 1 5 2 2 2 2 2 2 for 1.73(a)) that identifies 1.73(b). Do you see any pattern emerging on the keys that might help in finding solutions?

In Chapter 4 we shall study a class of algorithms called *orderly algorithms*, which may be used to deal with certain classes of *isomorph rejection* problems. The isomorph rejection problem for Q_n would be to obtain a subset Δ_n of Q_n such that no two elements of Δ_n can be transformed from one to the other by rotations and reflections of the board (they are inequivalent with respect to the group of symmetries of the board) but every element of Q_n can be obtained from some element of Δ_n by a rotation or reflection of the board (Δ_n is complete relative to Q_n). The set Δ_n is called a *system of representatives* of Q_n with respect to the group of symmetries of Q_n. One approach to this problem is to first generate all of Q_n and then select Δ_n. This approach was taken in connection with the domino covering problem of FIGURE 1.37. The "*symmetry recursive*" partition tree that we have been discussing above allows for a recursive approach to the isomorph rejection problem. We illustrate the basic ideas with the problem of generating a representative system Δ_5 for Q_5.

1.75 GENERATING Δ_5 for Q_5.

We begin by numbering the squares of the 5×5 chessboard from 1 to 25 in the order that characters are printed on a page, just as in the case of the 4×4 board of FIGURE 1.62. Orbits are numbered as in FIGURE 1.76.

Take the empty square bearing the smallest number, in this case 1, and compute its orbit under the full symmetry group of the square—in this case, squares 1, 5, 21, and 25. The largest number of queens that may be placed in these four squares is one; the other possibility is zero. We begin by placing one queen on square 1. By the use of the symmetry group, we need not consider placing one queen on square 5, square 21, or square 25; this amounts to picking a representative of an orbit for the symmetry group acting on the configuration of queens on these four squares. Later we will pick another representative of an orbit under this action. We will keep track of these choices by always placing

the "largest" first. That is, if the presence or absence of a queen on a square
is interpreted as a binary digit, square 1 is the most significant bit, and square
25 is the least significant bit. A record must be kept of the orbits as they are
used. *This represents a variation on the linear order that results on Q_5 as
compared with the order on Q_4 discussed previously.*

From the recursive viewpoint, the problem is now the following: place four
or fewer nonattacking queens on the 21 squares that are exclusive of squares 1,
5, 21, and 25 so that they are not attacked by the queen in square 1. Note there
is to be a queen in square 1, and no queen in squares 5, 21, and 25. The
symmetry group of this problem is the group of order two consisting of the
identity and reflection in the diagonal through squares 1 and 25. The orbit in
the chessboard containing the least numbered unspecified square consists of
squares 2 and 6. The "largest" placement of queens on this orbit is to place no
queen on either square 2 or square 6.

The algorithm now continues in this recursive fashion. As soon as the identity
group is reached, isomorphs are rejected, and the search may proceed in any
manner. When orbits of various groups acting on the chessboard fill up all 25
squares, a solution has been reached. One then finds the largest orbit (in the
sequence of orbits of the various symmetry groups) for which the configuration
of queens on that orbit can be advanced. "Advanced" means changed to the
next orbit representative for the symmetry group of that orbit acting on the
configuration of queens in that orbit.

An initial and a terminal segment of this algorithm is executed step by step
in FIGURES 1.76 and 1.77. Orbits are numbered as they are set down; queens
are denoted by circles. For the sake of brevity, only those steps in the execution
of the algorithm that change the configuration of queens, are a backtrack, or are
terminal are recorded. Terminal steps (when the whole board is filled by labeled
orbits) are solutions.

1.76   INITIAL SEGMENT IN THE GENERATION of Δ_5.

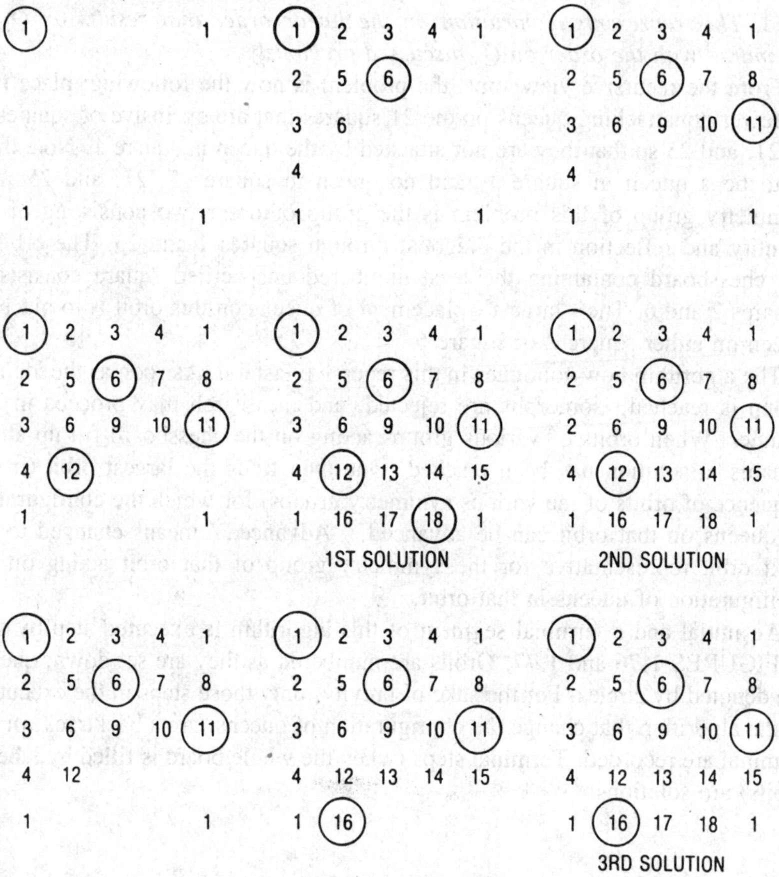

```
 (1)              1        (1)  2   3   4   1        (1)  2   3   4   1
                           2   5  (6)                2   5  (6)  7   8
                           3   6                     3   6   9  10 (11)
                           4                         4
  1               1         1               1         1               1


(1)  2   3   4   1        (1)  2   3   4   1        (1)  2   3   4   1
 2   5  (6)  7   8         2   5  (6)  7   8         2   5  (6)  7   8
 3   6   9  10 (11)        3   6   9  10 (11)        2   6   9  10 (11)
 4  (12)                   4  (12) 13  14  15        4  (12) 13  14  15
 1               1         1   16  17 (18)  1        1   16  17  18   1
                               1ST SOLUTION              2ND SOLUTION


(1)  2   3   4   1        (1)  2   3   4   1        (1)  2   3   4   1
 2   5  (6)  7   8         2   5  (6)  7   8         2   5  (6)  7   8
 3   6   9  10 (11)        3   6   9  10 (11)        3   6   9  10 (11)
 4   12                    4   12  13  14  15        4   12  13  14  15
 1               1         1  (16)                   1  (16) 17  18   1
                                                          3RD SOLUTION
```

Figure 1.76

1.77 TERMINAL SEGMENT IN THE GENERATION OF Δ_5.

```
1  (2)  3   2   1        1   2  (3)  2   1        1   2  (3)  2   1
2   4   5   6   2        2               2        2   4   5   4   2
7   8   9  10  11        3               3        3  (6)      6   3
2  12  13  14   2        2               2        2               2
1   2  15   2   1        1   2   3   2   1        1   2   3   2   1
```

55TH SOLUTION

```
1   2  (3)  2   1        1   2  (3)  2   1        1   3  (3)  2   1
2   4   5   4   2        2   4   5   4   2        2   4   5   4   2
3  (6)  7   6   3        3  (6)  7   6   3        3   6       6   3
2   8   9 (10)  2        2   8   9  10   2        2               2
1   2   3   2   1        1   2   3   2   1        1   2   3   2   1
```

56TH SOLUTION   57TH SOLUTION

```
1   2  (3)  2   1        1   2  (3)  2   1        1   2  (3)  2   1
2   4   5   4   2        2   4   5   4   2        2   4   5   4   2
2   6   7   6   3        3   6   7   6   3        3   6   7   6   3
2  (8)      8   2        2  (8)  9   8   2        2   8       8   2
1   2   3   2   1        1   2   3   2   1        1   2   3   2   1
```

58TH SOLUTION

```
1   2  (3)  2   1        1   2   3   2   1        1   2   3   2   1
2   4   5   4   2        2               2        2  (4)      4   2
2   6   7   6   3        3               3        3   3           3
2   8   9   8   2        2               2        2   4       4   2
1   2   3   2   1        1   2   3   2   1        1   2   3   2   1
```

59TH SOLUTION

Figure 1.77

(cont.)

```
1   2   3   2   1        1   2   3   2   1        1   2   3   2   1
2  (4)  5   4   2        2  (4)  5   4   2        2   4       4   2
3   5   6  (7)  3        3   5   6   7   3        3               3
2   4   7   4   2        2   4   7   4   2        2   4       4   2
1   2   3   2   1        1   2   3   2   1        1   2   3   2   1

   60TH SOLUTION            61ST SOLUTION
```

```
1   2   3   2   1        1   2   3   2   1        1   2   3   2   1
2   4  (5)  4   2        2   4  (5)  4   2        2   4   5   4   2
3   5       5   3        3   5   6   5   3        3   5       5   3
2   4   5   4   2        2   4   5   4   2        2   4   5   4   2
1   2   3   2   1        1   2   3   2   1        1   2   3   2   1

                            62ND SOLUTION
```

```
I   2   3   2   1        1   2   3   2   1
2   4   5   4   2        2   4   5   4   2
3   5  (6)  5   3        3   5   6   5   3
2   4   5   4   2        2   4   5   4   2
1   2   3   2   1        1   2   3   2   1

   63RD SOLUTION            64TH SOLUTION
```

Figure 1.77 (continued)

Chapter 2

Topic I: Sorting

As our first topic we consider the problem of "sorting." The intuitive idea of sorting is that objects in a linearly ordered set are "out of order" and must be put "in order." As an example, consider a large bag of oranges on a table together with a beam balance sufficiently accurate to distinguish between any pair of oranges. We thus have a set ORANGES together with a rule of comparison that defines a linearly ordered set.

Strictly from the point of view of defining a linearly ordered set, the job is done! What is missing in this framework is the ability to answer certain basic questions about the linear order conveniently. Which orange is the heaviest? One might have to work through the whole bag of oranges before figuring out the answer to this question. Given an orange, which orange is the next heaviest? Which orange is the next lighter orange? Suppose that the oranges are lined up left to right on the table from lightest to heaviest, each orange just touching its predecessor. Now it is quite easy to see which orange is heaviest and which is lightest. Given an orange one can also see easily its predecessor and successor in the linear order. Now, however, if a new orange is to be added to the set ORANGES, and the same linear array is to be maintained, then many oranges might have to be moved to make room for the new orange. If one is content to describe the linear order with just the bag of oranges and the beam balance, then the addition of a new orange is simple (just toss it into the bag!).

The problem of "sorting" a linearly ordered set is concerned with just these types of questions in a slightly more sophisticated sounding setting. Basically, the sorting problem is concerned with various data structures that are defined on linear ordered sets and the complexity of the computations involved in going back and forth between these various data structures. The most basic problem is that of starting with a linearly ordered set (the bag of oranges and the beam balance) and storing the elements of the set sequentially in an array, linked list, doubly linked list, tree structure, etc.

A separate but very important topic is to study how these various data structures behave with respect to insertion, deletion, locating objects, finding maxima and minima, etc. Such questions are more appropriate for a course in data structures and the complexity of algorithms than a course in combinatorics. We shall take a fairly quick look at some of the basic ideas that arise in connection with sorting problems, and leave the reader to pursue a more detailed study in some of the excellent references that exist on the subject.

For someone who might be faced with an actual sorting problem, it is important to notice at the outset how small additional pieces of information about the problem might drastically change one's approach to sorting. In the case of the bag of oranges, for example, suppose one has a digital scale, all oranges in the bag weigh between seven and nine ounces, and weighing to two significant figures is enough to differentiate between oranges. One might divide the table into squares labeled 7.00, 7.01, . . ., 8.99, and 9.00. Each orange may then be weighed and placed in the appropriate square. This is called a "bucket sort." The beam balance model is called a "comparison sort."

A variation of the bucket sort is the lexicographic bucket sort or "radix sort" of FIGURE 1.24. Some problems may require a combination of the two approaches together with some sort of hashing (as in TABLE 1.14). The sorting problem completely degenerates if one has the integers, $1, . . ., n$ placed in some order in an array $A(1), . . ., A(n)$ and wishes to put them in order. One simply sets $A(1) := 1, . . ., A(n) := n$. Other factors such as how the information is stored may become important (on tape or in high-speed memory, for example). It is important for the computer scientist or applied mathematician to take a look at the general theory of sorting at some point in his or her studies. In this manner, one can accumulate a certain bag of tricks. As in many applied areas, however, the real challenge is often how to best exploit special features of a problem that could not have been anticipated in the general development. In addition to "useful tricks," the theory of sorting contains some very pretty mathematics. We shall try to include a little of both aspects in our brief discussion.

Imagine a set of "labels" or "keys" $K_1, K_2, . . ., K_n$ that refer to locations in computer memory; each location contains data, consisting at least of an object from a linearly ordered set. Thus we are concerned with a linearly ordered set of size n whose elements are stored in locations $K_1 . . . K_n$. Theoretically, we may know absolutely nothing about the elements themselves—they could be a set of numbers computed by the machine, and we ourselves would not even know what the set is—however, we shall assume a procedure within the machine that, given two of the elements, can decide which is "larger." Perhaps it is desired to know the largest, or the smallest, or the $t^{\underline{th}}$ largest, or, in general, a printout of all n objects *in order*. This model leads to sorting techniques based on comparisons alone. Some basic ideas are now discussed.

2.1 SOME GENERAL IDEAS FOR COMPARISON SORTING.

(1) Selection—determine the smallest; print it; continue with the shortened list.
(2) Enumeration—compare each item with all the others; counting the number of smaller items determines an entry's proper position in the sorted list.
(3) Insertion—start with one element; bring in a new element and determine its position relative to the one there; . . .finally insert the $n^{\underline{th}}$ into its proper place among the $n - 1$ already ordered.

(4) Exchange—compare two items in the list, and if they are out of order, reverse them. Continue this until the list is in order.

As we noted above in connection with our "bag of oranges" model, additional information may make sorting by using only comparisons unnecessary, undesirable, or both. As a start, however, we shall just use "number of comparisons" as our measure of complexity of certain basic sorting problems. In TABLE 2.3 we evaluate the number of comparisons that we might naively expect to make in each of the above general ideas for comparison sorting.

2.2 DEFINITION.

For a real number x, $\lfloor x \rfloor$ denotes the largest and $\lceil x \rceil$ denotes the smallest integer such that $\lfloor x \rfloor \leq x \leq \lceil x \rceil$.

2.3 NUMBER OF COMPARISONS FOR THE METHODS OF TABLE 2.1.

(1) To select the smallest (or largest) of n elements requires $n - 1$ comparisons at most, and you must make that many to be absolutely certain of having the desired element. (Compare 1st and 2nd, then the smaller to 3rd, then the smaller of those to 4th, etc. Making fewer than $n - 1$ comparisons means one element was not used, and so you could not be certain.) Hence, for method (1),

$$n-1 + n-2 + \ldots + 1 = \frac{n(n-1)}{2} = \binom{n}{2}$$

comparisons will suffice.

(2) Similar in complexity to (1).

(3) One way to insert K into $K_{i_1} < K_{i_2} < \ldots < K_{i_\ell}$ is to first compare K with K_{i_1}, then, if $K > K_{i_1}$, compare K with K_{i_2}, etc., until K's place is found. Again this leads to $1 + 2 + 3 + \ldots + n - 1 = \binom{n}{2}$ comparisons total. Alternatively, compare K with the K_i closest to the middle of the existing list—if K is larger, compare it next to the middle of the second half, if K is smaller compare it next to the middle of the first half. Continue in this fashion until K's proper position is determined. This may require a total of $\lceil \log_2 2 \rceil + \lceil \log_2 3 \rceil + \ldots + \lceil \log_2 n \rceil$ comparisons. A list of length ℓ has $\ell + 1$ possible places for inserting the $(\ell + 1)^{\text{st}}$ element; each comparison in the above scheme reduces the possibilities by as close to one-half as possible. Hence, $\lceil \log_2(\ell + 1) \rceil$ comparisons suffice (prove it!) to insert the $(\ell + 1)^{\text{st}}$ element. For example, one element may be inserted into seven with no more than three comparisons; change seven to eight and strictly more than three may be necessary. This technique is known as *binary insertion*.

There will be more information on this later.

In all of the above we are counting the cost of the worst outcome. There is a great theoretical difference in the two approaches of (3); this will be covered in the *sorting networks* discussion that follows later. Depending on the data structure used for sorting the list entries, a count of comparisons alone may be a poor measure of sorting complexity. If the keys K1,. . .,Kn refer to a fixed array rather than a linked list structure, then each insertion of a list entry into a new location might require considerable data movement. This data movement may result in much more waste of time than that due just to comparisons. Even with a linked list data structure, if only adjacent interchanges are allowed in order to move list entries, there will be a severe restriction on the complexity of the sorting problem.

To get a feel for this, let S_n denote all permutations from $\underline{n}$ to $\underline{n}$. Any sorting method that moves entries one space at a time will have at least as many interchanges to sort $f \in S_n$ as $|f(1) - 1| + |f(2) - 2| + \ldots + |f(n) - n|$. This is because f(k) is the symbol in position k and it must move "distance" $|f(k) - k|$ to go to its correct position, f(k). This sum has an average of $\dfrac{n^2 - 1}{3}$ over all of S_n (see EXERCISE 2.7(7)). Thus, any sorting procedure that only allows adjacent interchanges when moving data will have an average time complexity of at least order n^2. One method that addresses this problem is called "Shell's Method."

2.4 SHELL'S METHOD.

Let $h_t, h_{t-1}, \ldots, h_1 = 1$ be a decreasing sequence of integers. Using the selection method, say, "h_s-sort" the given data $K_1, K_2, \ldots, K_n$ successively for s = t, t−1,. . .,1. A sequence is "h-sorted" when $K_i < K_{i+h}$ for all relevant i. For example, we do the following to sort 7 5 1 3 2 8 6 4 with $\vec{h}$ = (4,3,1).

2.5 AN h-SORT

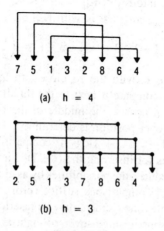

(a) h = 4

(b) h = 3

Figure 2.5

On the first pass we separately sort the subsequences (7,2), (5,8), (1,6), (3,4) as represented by FIGURE 2.5(a) (note that these are subsequences of the form $K_i, K_{i+h}, K_{i+2h} \ldots$ with h = 4) giving 2 5 1 3 7 8 6 4. On the second pass we 3-sort—separately sort the subsequences (2,3,6),(5,7,4),(1,8,-) as in FIGURE 2.5(b) giving 2 4 1 3 5 8 6 7. Finally, this is "1-sorted"—which just means it is sorted. The idea is that by the time we reach that final 1-sort, enough larger jumps have already taken place to cut down on the number of 1-moves. There is total freedom in the choice of numbers $\vec{h}$. As yet, it is unresolved how to choose $\vec{h}$ in such a way as to minimize the average running time. We saw that when $\vec{h} = (1)$, the trivial choice for $\vec{h}$, the average running time was $O(n^2)$. Using the standard notation $t(n) = O(f(n))$, to mean "t(n) is bounded by a constant times f(n) for all sufficiently large n," we state without proof the following results. (See references at end of Part I, in particular Knuth, Vol. 3.)

2.6 SOME COMPLEXITY RESULTS FOR SHELL'S METHOD.

(1) If $\vec{h} = (h,1)$, then the best choice of h is $\approx 1.72 \sqrt[3]{n}$, giving an average *total* time (including the selection-method comparisons) of $O(n^{5/3})$, already an improvement.
(2) For a fixed t, when $\vec{h} = (h_t, \ldots, 1)$, under the constraint that h_s divides h_{s+1} for $t > s \geq 1$, the running time decreases to $O(n^{1.5 + \varepsilon/2})$, $\varepsilon = 1(2^t - 1)$ for large n.
(3) $O(n^{1.5})$ when $h_s = 2^s - 1$ for $1 \leq s \leq t = \lfloor \log_2 n \rfloor$.
(4) $O(n(\log_2 n)^2)$ when h_s = all numbers of form $2^p 3^q$ that are less than n.

The following exercises illustrate some ideas related to other aspects of sorting.

2.7 EXERCISE.

(1) FIGURE 2.8(a) shows a *complete binary tree* (recall discussion of FIGURES 1.41 and 1.42). The tree in FIGURE 2.8(a) has $15 = 2^4 - 1$ vertices. The *height* of a tree is the maximum length of a path (number of edges) from the root to a leaf. Thus the height of both trees shown in FIGURE 2.8 is 3. If the vertices of the tree are read as one would read a book, level by level starting with the root, one obtains 15, 12, 14, 9, 7, 13, 11, 8, 4, 6, 5, 1, 10, 2, 3 for FIGURE 2.8(a) and 15, 12, 14, 9, 7, 13, 11, 8, 4, 6 for FIGURE 2.8(b). This is called *breadth first order on vertices* and corresponds to length first lexicographic order discussed earlier (see EXERCISE 1.29). The tree in FIGURE 2.8(b) is obtained from that in FIGURE 2.8(a) by removing a terminal sequence (5, 1, 10, 2, 3) from the breadth first sequence of vertices. Such a tree will be called a *truncated complete binary tree* or TCBT. A complete binary tree, CBT, is a TCBT in which the empty sequence is removed. Prove that the height of a TCBT with n vertices is $\lfloor \log_2(n) \rfloor$.

(2) A TCBT with vertex labels from a linearly ordered set will be called a HEAP
if the label of each internal vertex is larger than the labels of its sons. FIGURE
2.8(a) is a HEAP on the linearly ordered set 15 with the natural order.
Suppose we are given a TCBT of height h with vertex labels from a linearly
ordered set. Describe an efficient procedure for converting this TCBT into
a HEAP. Call your procedure MAKEHEAP. *Hint:* A good idea for doing
this is provided in the procedure REHEAP of the next exercise.

2.8   A TRUNCATED COMPLETE BINARY TREE.

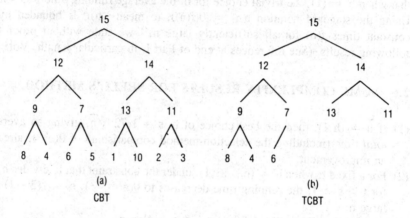

Figure 2.8

2.9   DELETE AND REHEAP.

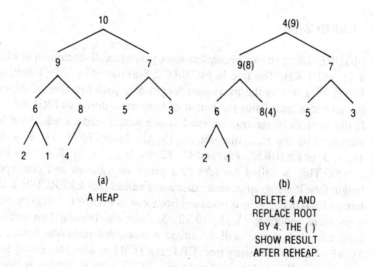

Figure 2.9

2.10 DATA STRUCTURE FOR BINARY TREE AND REVERSE BREADTH FIRST LIST.

ROOT := B3, START RBF := C6 (RBF = REVERSE BREADTH FIRST LIST OF VERTICES)

	1	2	3	4	5	6
A						
B			20 ROOT FATH ∅ BRO ∅ SON C5 RBF (END)			
C	13 FATH C5 BRO C3 SON ∅ RBF D5		10 FATH C5 BRO ∅ SON ∅ RBF C1		15 FATH B3 BRO D5' SON C1 RBF B3	4 FATH D5 BRO ∅ SON ∅ RBF C3
D					8 FATH B3 BRO ∅ SON C6 RBF C5	
E						

Figure 2.10 (Top)

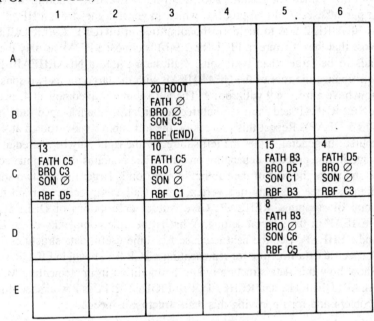

STRUCTURAL DIAGRAM   RBF LIST

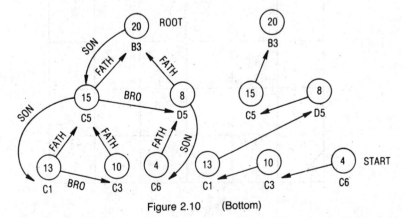

Figure 2.10 (Bottom)

2.7   EXERCISE 2.7 (continued).

(3) FIGURE 2.9(a) shows a HEAP on 10. Remove the breadth first last vertex (a 4 in this case) from the HEAP and replace the root (10 in FIGURE 2.9(a)) with this value. The result is shown in FIGURE 2.9(b), ignoring the values in parentheses. Call the process, which in general goes from a HEAP such as FIGURE 2.9(a) to the corresponding tree in FIGURE 2.9(b), DELETE. Note that the structure in FIGURE 2.9(b) is almost a HEAP as only the root fails to be larger than both sons. Call such a tree a NEARHEAP. Now, interchange the root of the NEARHEAP with the larger of its two sons. We now have a tree on 9 with root 9. The left subtree, rooted now at 4, is again a NEARHEAP and the right subtree rooted at 7, is unchanged (and hence still a HEAP). Repeat this process on the left subtree (now rooted at 4). Of course, in general, either the left subtree or the right may be altered at each stage in this process, depending on which one contains the maximal son. If at any stage the root of the subtree in question is larger than its two sons or if the subtree has only one vertex, stop. Call this process, carried to the point of stopping, REHEAP. Give careful descriptions of DELETE and REHEAP in the general setting. What is the time complexity of DELETE and REHEAP? See the next exercise for some useful data structures.

(4) A specific data structure for representing a TCBT is shown in FIGURE 2.10. Show how this data structure would be modified in implementing MAKE-HEAP, DELETE, and REHEAP. Use FIGURE 2.11 as a worksheet for this problem and for improving this data structure as needed.

2.11   WORKSHEET FOR EXERCISE 2.7(4) and FIGURE 2.10.

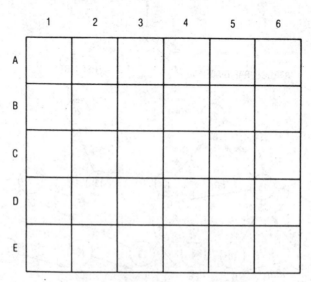

Figure 2.11

2.7   EXERCISE (continued)

(5) Consider the permutation 4 3 9 1 8 5 2 7 6,of 9 in one line notation. Select a particular value, say 5, and let LEFT(5) denote the longest initial sequence of consecutive values in the permutation that are less than 5, RIGHT(5) denote the longest consecutive terminal string of values greater than 5. In this example, LEFT(5) = 4 3 and RIGHT(5) = 7 6. Either LEFT(x) or RIGHT(x) may be empty in the general case.

   Here are two more examples with LEFT(5) and RIGHT(5) underlined: 1 3 4 8 5 6 9 2 7 and 8 9 7 6 5 4 3 2 1 (both LEFT(5) and RIGHT(5) are empty). This idea obviously extends to any sequence of values from a linearly ordered set. If x is an element of such a sequence, let L(x) denote the next element following LEFT(x) and R(x) the element just preceding RIGHT(x). For x = 5 and for the three sequences above, L(x) = 9, 8, and 8 and R(x) = 2, 2, and 1. Clearly, L(x) = R(x) if and only if x is in its correct position (where it would be in the sorted sequence) and all elements to the left of x are smaller than x, and all elements to the right of x are larger than x, in the linear order. We describe this situation by saying that x is *strongly positioned* in the sequence. Consider the following algorithm:

   procedure   STRONGPOS(x,LIST) (LIST is a sequence of elements
                                          from a linearly ordered set,
                           x ∈ LIST)
     while   L(x) ≠ R(x)   *do*   LIST: = LIST with L(x) and R(x)
                  interchanged

   Prove that STRONGPOS terminates with a list in which x is strongly positioned. (Note: Applying this algorithm to x = 5, LIST: = 4 3 9 1 8 5 2 7 6 gives the sequences 4 3 2 1 8 5 9 7 6, and 4 3 2 1 5 8 9 7 6, the latter being STRONGPOS(x,439185276). As above, underlined values represent LEFT(x) and RIGHT(x). These sequences, together with L(x) and R(x), are recomputed at each iteration, but x is not changed.)

(6) As in the previous problem, let LIST be a sequence of elements from a linearly ordered set and let x ∈ LIST. Compute STRONGPOS(x,LIST) and let LEFT(x) be the sequence of elements before x and RIGHT(x) the sequence of elements after x in this new sequence. Now choose x_1 in LEFT(x) and x_2 in RIGHT(x) and repeat the process, computing STRONG-POS(x_1,LEFT(x)) and STRONGPOS(x_2,RIGHT(x)). Continuing in this manner, the original LIST will eventually be sorted. Work several nontrivial examples and then describe carefully a sorting algorithm along these lines. If you are a good programmer, it is very interesting to write a program to sort permutations of n based on this idea. Try to compute the average number of comparisons plus interchanges required by your program to sort all permutations in S_n for n = 2,. . .,8 and plot this value as a function of n (you will probably have to do this experimentally by actually sorting all permutations of S_n for each n = 2,. . .,8).

(7) Let f be a permutation in S_n. We wish to evaluate the average value with respect to the uniform distribution on S_n of the sum $D_f = |f(1) - 1| + \ldots + |f(n) - n|$. For each j consider $|f(j) - j|$ as f(j) ranges over values $1, \ldots, n$. We obtain values for $|f(j) - j|$ of $j - 1, j - 2, \ldots, 0, 1, \ldots, n - j$ for the respective values of f(j). Let M_n be the $n \times n$ matrix whose j^{th} column is the above sequence. In other words, $M_n(i,j) = |i - j|$. Prove that the average value of D_f is $\Sigma M_n/n$ where ΣM_n denotes the sum of all the entries in M_n. Use this result to prove that the average of D_f is $(n^2 - 1)/3$ as asserted just prior to paragraph 2.4 SHELL'S METHOD.

In TABLE 2.3(3), two approaches to sorting by insertion were indicated. There is a basic difference between them. In the first approach, we may list the comparisons to be made for inserting K into $K_{i_1} < \ldots < K_{i_k}$:

First comparison—K with K_{i_1}
Next comparison—the larger of the previous with K_{i_2}
Next comparison—the larger of the previous with K_{i_3}, etc.

No such list is possible in the second approach.

To more precisely describe the difference between the two strategies, consider the "binary insertion" sorting strategy of FIGURE 2.13(a). This strategy is represented by a full binary tree with internal nodes labeled by pairs (i,j) with $i \neq j$. The function f will, in general, stand for an injection from $\underline{n}$ to a linearly ordered set L. For example, $f = (234, 0.45, 9)$ has $n = 3$ and L the real numbers (we use one-line notation). Imagine the function f starting at the root of the tree of FIGURE 2.13(a). The root has label (1,2) so the values of the function in the first and second position are compared (in this case f(1) and f(2)). If the first value is less, then, in general, a certain computation is done on f and its associated data structures, and the transformed function travels to the left subtree. If the second value is less, then the function travels to the right subtree. In our strategy the function is not changed when it goes left and its first two values are transposed when it goes right. By the time the function reaches a leaf of the tree it has been rearrranged so that its values are in increasing order (i.e., sorted). The pairs (i,j) refer to the entries in position i and j of the sequence representing the function. Thus, to compare the (1,2) entry of (f(3),f(1),f(2)), one compares f(3) and f(1). Any given function f will travel a unique path. For example, (45,11,23) applied to FIGURE 2.13(a) has $45 > 11$, so goes right (R) to become (11,45,23). Then it has $11 < 23$, so goes left (L), remaining (11,45,23), and finally has $45 > 23$, so goes right (R) to become (11,23,45), which is the sorted sequence. The path traveled is given by the sequence R,L,R.

2.12   VAGUE IDEA.

A *comparison-based sorting strategy* or, simply, *sorting strategy* is a method of sorting that can be sensibly represented by a full binary tree such as that of FIGURE 2.13(a) or (b). An injection $f: \underline{n} \rightarrow L$ is entered at the root of the tree and travels down to a leaf. At each node of the tree a comparison is made and as a result certain elementary computations are done on the function and its associated data structures (pointers are changed, linked lists changed, etc.). The transformed function and data structures travel to the next node where the next comparison and changes are made, and so on. *We assume that different injections with the same image will never end up at the same leaf.* Thus, there are *at least* n! leaves. When f arrives at the leaf it has been transformed into increasing order.

The idea that different injections with the same image all end up at different leaves is the intuitive expression of the phrase "comparison based." If two different rearrangements of the same function followed the same path and were sorted, then some other criterion than the comparisons made on the path would have had to have been "critical" in making the distinction between the two functions. This is what we rule out in order to bring the notion of *comparisons* to the forefront. We have already pointed out that this is an oversimplification of the "complexity" of a sorting method, but this is the game we are playing for the moment. We now consider a special class of sorting strategies where the transformations at each node are defined by "comparators."

2.13   A SORTING STRATEGY AND SORTING NETWORK.

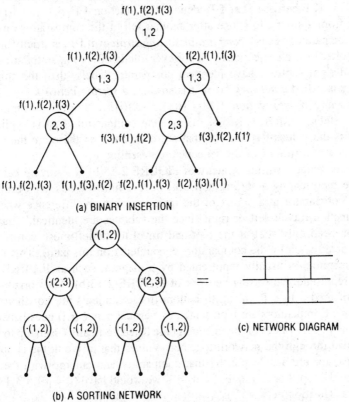

(a) BINARY INSERTION

(c) NETWORK DIAGRAM

(b) A SORTING NETWORK

Figure 2.13

For $1 \le i < j \le n$, let $\cdot(i,j)$ denote a map from functions to functions defined by $f \cdot (i,j) = f$ if $f(i) < f(j)$, otherwise, $f \cdot (i,j) = g$, where $g = (f(1), \ldots, f(j), \ldots, f(i), \ldots, f(n))$ has $g(i) = f(j)$, $g(j) = f(i)$, and $g(t) = f(t)$ for $t \ne i$ or j. The operator $\cdot(i,j)$ is called a *comparator*. If $f \cdot (i,j) = f$ we say that the comparator *acts trivially* on f, otherwise we say the comparator acts *nontrivially*. The notation $f \cdot (i_1,j_1) \cdots \cdot (i_t,j_t)$ indicates the result of applying a sequence of comparators to f, starting with $\cdot(i_1,j_1)$ and ending with $\cdot(i_t,j_t)$.

2.14 DEFINITION.

A *comparator tree* or *comparator strategy* is a full binary tree with internal nodes labeled by comparators $\cdot(i,j)$. A path from the root $\cdot(i_1,j_1)$ to a leaf is specified by $\cdot(i_1,j_1)X_1 \cdot (i_2,j_2)X_2 \cdots \cdot (i_p,j_p)X_p$ where each X_t is either an L or an R, indicating whether the path branches left or right at the node $\cdot(i_t,j_t)$. To each injection $f: \underline{n} \to L$, we associate a unique such path P_f from the root to a leaf defined by the rule $X_1 = L$ if $\cdot(i_1,j_1)$ acts trivially on f and $X_1 = R$ otherwise, and in general, $X_t = L$ if $\cdot(i_t,j_t)$ acts trivially on $f \cdot (i_1,j_1) \cdots \cdot (i_{t-1},j_{t-1})$ and $X_t = R$ otherwise. Let $f \cdot P_f$ denote the function $f \cdot (i_1,j_1) \cdots \cdot (i_p,j_p)$ that results from applying to f, one after another, all of the comparators on the path P_f. A comparator tree is a *comparator sorting strategy* if $f \cdot P_f$ is strictly increasing (i.e., sorted) for all injections f. If for every node of a comparator strategy, the left and right subtrees have identical comparator labels, then the comparator strategy is called a *network* or, if it is sorting, a *sorting network*.

A warning about notation. If $f = (f(1), \ldots, f(i), \ldots, f(j), \ldots)$ is transformed to $g = (f(1), \ldots, f(j), \ldots, f(i), \ldots)$ and the comparator $\cdot(i,t)$ is applied to g, then it is the values $f(j)$ and $f(t)$ that are compared, as these are the values in the ith and t^{th} *positions* of the sequence representing g.

The comparator sorting strategy of FIGURE 2.13(b) is a *sorting network*. In the tree representing a sorting network, once a function has been transformed by the comparator at a vertex of the tree, it makes no difference whether the new function travels left or right since the subtrees are identical. Thus, every function need only start at the root and travel to the left-most leaf of the tree (being acted upon by the comparators encountered on this path). This sequence of comparators is usually represented by a diagram such as FIGURE 2.13(c) which represents the sorting network of FIGURE 2.13(b). The horizontal lines are numbered 1 to n from top to bottom (these numbers are not shown in the diagram). Comparators are represented by vertical bars ($\cdot(i,j)$ goes between line i and line j). The values of the injection f are listed vertically (from top to bottom) and travel through the network together. Values that arrive at the endpoints of a comparator are acted upon by that comparator and emerge with the smaller value on the top. For example, for n = 4 we would have (f = (9,5,3,1), "odd-even transposition network"):

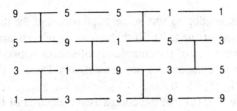

Figure 2.14

For n = 6, the sorting strategy "selection" of 2.3(1) can be realized by the networks of FIGURE 2.15(a) or (b). The insertion method, 2.3(3), is represented by the network of FIGURE 2.15(c) and should be compared with FIGURE 2.15(b). The "odd-even" transposition sort is shown in FIGURE 2.15(d). A variation of the odd-even transposition sort is shown in FIGURE 2.15(e). FIG-URE 2.15(d) generalizes to any n (EXERCISE 2.26(2)). FIGURE 2.15(e) generalizes to any even n.

2.15 EXAMPLES OF SORTING NETWORKS.

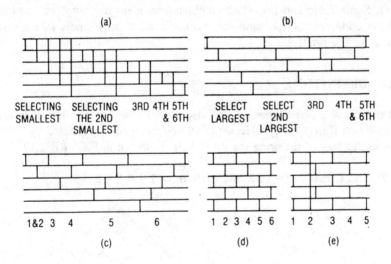

Figure 2.15

The vertical bars in the diagram of a sorting network are called "comparators." The number of vertical layers of comparators in a diagram is called the "delay time" of the diagram. If the elements being sorted were able to travel in parallel from left to right through the diagram, then the delay time represents the actual time required to sort the worst case sequence (assuming the last layer of comparators is actually needed to sort some sequence, and the travel time between layers of comparators is one unit). Both the number of comparators and the delay time are used as measures of the complexity of sorting networks. In EXAMPLE 2.15, the number of comparators are respectively 15, 15, 15, 15, 14 and the delay times are 15, 15, 15, 6, and 5.

Notice in Figure 2.15(b) that the comparisons required of the 6th comparator are independent of those required of comparators 5, 4, 3, but not of comparator 2. Thus, we can slide this comparator from vertical layer 6 to vertical layer 3 without encountering any other comparators. The 7th comparator can now slide to level 4 in the same manner. Doing this for all comparators, we obtain a *minimal diagram* for the network (minimal in the sense of delay time). The delay time of a sorting network is, by definition, the delay time of a minimal diagram for that network. FIGURES 2.15(d) and (e) are minimal. The reader should construct minimal diagrams from FIGURES 2.15(a), (b), and (c). Note that these diagrams are the same for (b) and (c).

The sorting network in EXAMPLE 2.15(d) is called the "odd-even transposition sort" and is certainly optimal over all sorting networks with respect to its beautiful geometric simplicity. It is not optimal with respect to either number of comparators or delay time as EXAMPLE 2.15(e) shows (at least for the even case). Some basic and important combinatorial ideas are involved in proving that the odd-even transposition sort works for all n, so we now take a careful look at such a proof.

2.16   DEFINITION.

Let $\sigma \in S_n$ be a permutation. A pair (i,j), $1 \le i < j \le n$ is called an *inversion* relative to σ if $\sigma(i) > \sigma(j)$. The set of all inversions of σ is denoted by INV(σ).

A useful way of picturing the set INV(σ) is shown in FIGURE 2.17.

2.17   INVERSION DIAGRAM FOR σ = 7 1 6 5 4 8 3 2.

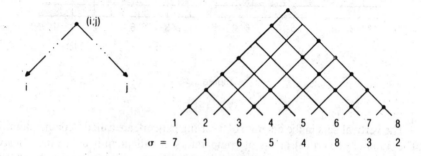

A LARGE DOT INDICATES AN INVERSION

Figure 2.17

2.18 INVERSION GRID.

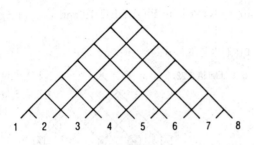

Figure 2.18

In FIGURE 2.17 the large dots correspond to the coordinates of inversions as indicated. The reader should copy the basic grid shown in FIGURE 2.18 and practice constructing inversion diagrams for several permutations. In particular, experiment with how the diagram changes when pairs of symbols are interchanged in a permutation. Of particular interest is the case when the symbols interchanged in the permutation are adjacent. If $\tau = (i,j)$ is a pair of integers, $1 \le i < j \le n$, σ a permutation, then let $\sigma \cdot \tau$ denote the permutation gotten by interchanging the ith and j^{th} symbols in σ (in one line notation) if τ is an inversion of σ, and doing nothing if τ is not an inversion. An example of a σ and $\sigma \cdot \tau$ is given in FIGURES 2.19 and 2.20 with $\tau = (4,5)$. ($\cdot \tau$ is a comparator in the sense of DEFINITION 2.14). FIGURES 2.19 and 2.20 show the case where $\tau = (i, i+1)$ is an "adjacent comparator." Let $A_\tau(\sigma) = \{(x,y) \in INV(\sigma): x = i$ or $y = i+1$ but not both$\}$ and let $B_\tau(\sigma) = \{(x,y) \in INV(\sigma): x = i+1$ or $y = i\}$. These sets are shown in FIGURE 2.19 for an example. In FIGURE 2.19, $(i, i+1)$ $= (4,5)$ is an inversion. Compare FIGURE 2.19 with FIGURE 2.20, which is the inversion diagram for $\sigma \cdot \tau$.

2.19 AN ADJACENT INVERSION

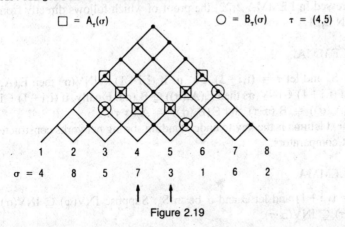

Figure 2.19

2.20 VARIATION OF FIGURE 2.19.

$A_\tau(\sigma \cdot \tau)$ and $B_\tau(\sigma \cdot \tau)$ for σ is in FIGURE 2.19 and $\tau = (4,5)$.

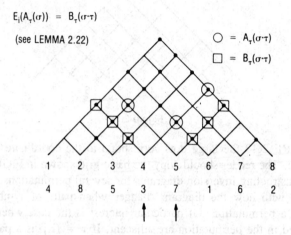

$$E_i(A_\tau(\sigma)) = B_\tau(\sigma \cdot \tau)$$

(see LEMMA 2.22)

$\bigcirc = A_\tau(\sigma \cdot \tau)$

$\square = B_\tau(\sigma \cdot \tau)$

Figure 2.20

2.21 DEFINITION.

Let E_i be the transformation defined on all pairs $(x,y) \neq (i,i+1)$ with $1 \leq x < y \leq n$ by the rule $E_i(x,y) = (x',y')$ where (x',y') is obtained from (x,y) by replacing i by $i+1$ (if either $i = x$ or y) or $i+1$ by i (if either $i+1 = x$ or y). If neither i nor $i+1$ occurs in (x,y) then $E_i(x,y) = (x,y)$.

The geometric effect of applying the "exchange i and $i+1$" transformation E_i is seen in the transition from FIGURE 2.19 to FIGURE 2.20. Note in particular how the "boxed" and "circled" points interchange roles. These geometric ideas are expressed in LEMMA 2.22, the proof of which follows directly from DEFINITION 2.21.

2.22 LEMMA.

Let $\sigma \in S_n$ and let $\tau = (i,i+1)$, $i < n$. If $(i,i+1) \in \text{INV}(\sigma)$ then $E_i(A_\tau(\sigma)) \supseteq B_\tau(\sigma)$. If $(i,i+1) \notin \text{INV}(\sigma)$ then $E_i(A_\tau(\sigma)) \subseteq B_\tau(\sigma)$. Finally, if $(i,i+1) \in \text{INV}(\sigma)$ then $E_i(A_\tau(\sigma)) = B_\tau(\sigma \cdot \tau)$ and $E_i(B_\tau(\sigma)) = A_\tau(\sigma \cdot \tau)$.

The next lemma is the key to understanding sorting networks constructed from adjacent comparators.

2.23 LEMMA.

Let $\tau = (i,i+1)$ and let φ and σ be in S_n. Suppose $\text{INV}(\varphi) \subseteq \text{INV}(\sigma)$. Then $\text{INV}(\varphi \cdot \tau) \subseteq \text{INV}(\sigma \cdot \tau)$.

Proof. If τ is an inversion of both φ and σ, or is an inversion of neither, then the result is easily seen to be true (think of FIGURES 2.19 and 2.20 together with LEMMA 2.22 as applied to both φ and σ). Since we have assumed that INV(φ) is a subset of INV(σ), the only other possibility is that $\tau \in$ INV(σ) but $\tau \notin$ INV(φ). The situation in this case is summarized in FIGURE 2.24 from which we see that $A_\tau(\varphi \cdot \tau)$ is contained in $A_\tau(\sigma \cdot \tau)$ and $B_\tau(\varphi \cdot \tau)$ is contained in $B_\tau(\sigma \cdot \tau)$ (identify each of the sets in the two chains of equalities and inclusions at the bottom of FIGURE 2.24, remembering LEMMA 2.22 and 2.23). Thus, INV(φ) is contained in INV(σ).

2.24 DIAGRAMMATIC REPRESENTATION OF PROOF OF LEMMA 2.23.

INV(φ) $\subseteq$ INV(σ) AND $\tau \in$ INV(σ) BUT $\tau \notin$ INV(φ).

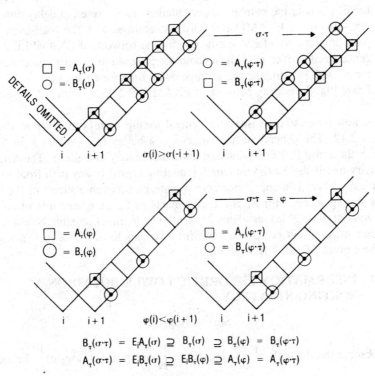

$$B_\tau(\sigma \cdot \tau) = E_i A_\tau(\sigma) \supseteq B_\tau(\sigma) \supseteq B_\tau(\varphi) = B_\tau(\varphi \cdot \tau)$$
$$A_\tau(\sigma \cdot \tau) = E_i B_\tau(\sigma) \supseteq E_i B_\tau(\varphi) \supseteq A_\tau(\varphi) = A_\tau(\varphi \cdot \tau)$$

Figure 2.24

The following is a remarkable theorem that follows from LEMMA 2.23.

2.25 THEOREM.

A network constructed from adjacent comparators sorts all permutations if it sorts the reverse permutation $\rho = n, n-1, \ldots, 1$.

Proof. An adjacent comparator is $\tau = (i, i+1)$ acting as has been recently discussed. $INV(\rho) = \{(i,j) : 1 \le i < j \le n\}$ is the set of all possible pairs. Thus, for any permutation φ, $INV(\varphi) \subseteq INV(\rho)$. Apply LEMMA 2.23 for each comparator τ in the network and use the fact that ρ is sorted.

2.26 EXERCISE.

(1) Give a careful proof of LEMMA 2.22.
(2) Prove that the odd-even transposition sort (EXAMPLE 2.15(d)) extended to the general case, n, sorts all permutations in S_n by showing that it sorts the reverse permutation $\rho = n, n-1, \ldots, 1$. *Hint:* Look at the path followed by n as the network sorts ρ. By ignoring comparators involved in interchanges with n and looking carefully at what is happening to the other symbols you will see the basis for an inductive proof.
(3) Let $d_{n,k}$ denote the number of permutations in S_n sorted in delay time k for the network of EXAMPLE 2.15(d) generalized to n the (odd-even transposition sort). Similarly, define $e_{n,k}$ for the network of EXAMPLE 2.15(e) generalized to even n. Write a computer program to compute these numbers for $n = 4, 6, 8$. Compute the average delay time for each case.
(4) Prove that the sorting network of EXAMPLE 2.15(e) sorts for any even n.

We now return to the case of the general sorting strategy as given in VAGUE IDEA 2.12. The general sorting strategy is a binary tree (in fact a *full* binary tree in the sense that every internal node has exactly two sons). The height of a binary tree is the maximum length (counting edges) in any path from the root to a leaf. There is a one-to-one correspondence between a subset of the leaves of a sorting strategy for S_n and the elements of S_n. A binary tree of height h can have at most 2^h leaves. Thus $2^h \ge n!$. The minimal possible height for any sorting strategy will be denoted by S(n). We thus have $2^{S(n)} \ge n!$. Taking logarithms gives LOWER BOUND 2.27.

2.27 INFORMATION THEORETIC LOWER BOUND ON A SORTING STRATEGY.

$$S(n) \ge \lceil \log_2(n!) \rceil.$$

Observe that $\log_2(n!) = \sum_{k=1}^{n} \log_2(k) \ge \int_1^n \log_2(x)dx = \log_2(e)\int_1^n \ln(x)dx = \log_2(e)(n\ln(n) - n + 1) = n\log_2(n) - n\log_2(e) + \log_2(e)$. Thus $S(n) \ge n(\log_2(n) - 1.5)$. But the binary insertion strategy of TABLE 2.3(3) required $\sum_{k=1}^{n} \lceil \log_2(k) \rceil = B(n)$ comparisons. Thus $S(n) \le B(n) \le n \lceil \log_2(n) \rceil \le n\log_2(n) + n$. Thus, S(n) is asymptotic to B(n) (in the usual sense that $\lim_{n \to \infty} S(n)/B(n) = 1$) and both are asymptotic to $n\log_2(n)$. This proves the following theorem.

2.28 THEOREM.

The optimal number of comparisons of a sorting strategy for S_n, denoted by $S(n)$, is asymptotic to the number of comparisons $B(n)$ for the binary insertion method (TABLE 2.3(3)). Both $S(n)$ and $B(n)$ are asymptotic to $n\log_2(n)$.

Of course, other factors than number of comparisons must be considered in actually evaluating a sorting strategy. As a result of THEOREM 2.28, however, aficionados of the subject of sorting are always pleased with reasonable sorting strategies with numbers of comparisons close to $n\log_2(n)$. It is possible to implement the sorting strategy suggested by EXERCISE 2.7(2) and (3) such that the number of comparisons in the worst case is less than a constant times $n\log_2(n)$. This strategy is called HEAPSORT. The strategy suggested in EXERCISE 2.7(6) does not have any obvious implementation with worst-case upper bound of order $n\log_2(n)$. The average number of comparisons required by this sorting strategy (called QUICKSORT) is proportional to $n\log_2(n)$, however. These are standard topics in a course in the complexity of algorithms. If we let $S_{av}(n)$ denote the optimal average number of comparisons required by a sorting strategy defined for all n (uniform distribution on S_n), then obviously $S_{av}(n) \leq S(n)$. An optimal sorting strategy is a full binary tree with exactly n! leaves. Hence, $S_{av}(n)$ is just the sum of the lengths of the paths from the root to the leaves of the tree (PALN(tree)) divided by n!. In EXERCISE 2.30 we investigate this type of sum. Using the results of EXERCISE 2.30, the following theorem is obtained.

2.29 THEOREM.

$S_{av}(n) \geq \lfloor \log_2(n!) \rfloor$ and hence $S_{av}(n)$ is asymptotic to $S(n)$ and both are asymptotic to $n\log_2(n)$.

2.30 EXERCISE.

(1) Let T be a full binary tree (FBT) with HEIGHT(T) = h and λ leaves. Show that there is a FBT T′ with λ leaves, HEIGHT(T′) = h′ $\leq$ h and *all leaves* at height h′ − 1 or h′ such that PALN(T′) $\leq$ PALN(T). (For any tree T, PALN(T) denotes the sum of the lengths of all paths from the root to a leaf.) *Hint:* Apply a series of transformations to T to get T′. Each transformation relocates a pair of leaves of maximal height and decreases PALN(T).

(2) Let T be a full binary tree with λ leaves and HEIGHT(T) = h. If all leaves occur at height h or h − 1 then show that h = $\lceil \log_2(\lambda) \rceil$ (for λ not a power of 2, h − 1 = $\lfloor \log_2(\lambda) \rfloor$). Show that PALN(T) = $\lambda(h - 1) + 2(\lambda - 2^{h-1})$. Using this result, prove THEOREM 2.29.

The study of the exact values of $S(n)$—the number of comparisons in an optimal sorting strategy—is much more difficult than the asymptotics. For n = 2, 3, and 4, $B(n)$, the number of comparisons in the binary insertion strategy, is $\lceil \log_2(n!) \rceil$ and thus is optimal and equal to the theoretical lower bound. For

$n=5$, however, $B(n) = 8$ while $\lceil \log_2(n!) \rceil = 7$. Thus, $S(5)$ is either 7 or 8. It was once conjectured that $S(n) = B(n)$ for all n, but the following strategy shows that this fails even at $n=5$.

Make two disjoint comparisons and then compare the smallest elements of the two sorted pairs. After three comparisons we know

$$b \underset{\underset{a}{\wedge}}{\cdot} > \underset{\underset{d \quad e}{\wedge}}{\cdot} c$$

e may be inserted into the chain a b c in two comparisons. After this, d may be inserted into the resulting chain, still in two comparisons. Thus, $S(6) = 7$. A generalization of the above procedure is called *merge insertion*.

Suppose we know this much information:

$$x_1 > x_2 > x_3 > x_4 > x_5 > x_6$$
$$\underset{y_4}{\wedge} \quad \underset{y_5}{\wedge} \quad \underset{y_6}{\wedge}$$

y_6 may be inserted into the x's with $\lceil \log_2 6 \rceil =$ three comparisons.
y_5 may be inserted into the resulting chain, *still* three comparisons.
y_4 may be inserted into the resulting chain, *still* three comparisons.

This sort of reasoning holds for any m and n, not just 4 and 6. Hence, the following is the case.

2.31 MERGE INSERTION (Ford-Johnson).

(1) Partition the n elements into $\lfloor n/2 \rfloor$ pairs, comparing each pair. Denote these pairs by $\{x_i, y_i\}$, $x_i < y_i$.

(2) Sort the $\lfloor n/2 \rfloor$ smaller elements recursively to obtain $x_1 > x_2 > \ldots > x_{\lfloor n/2 \rfloor}$.
This gives

$$x_1 > x_2 > \ldots > x_{\lfloor n/2 \rfloor}$$
$$\underset{y_1}{\wedge} \quad \underset{y_2}{\wedge} \qquad \underset{y_{\lfloor n/2 \rfloor}}{\wedge}$$

(an extra element z must be inserted if n is odd.)

(3) Call $y_1 > x_1 > \ldots > x_{\lfloor n/2 \rfloor}$ the main chain. Then y_2, y_3 may be inserted into the main chain, resulting in two comparisons each starting with y_3. Next, y_4, y_5 may be inserted into the resulting main chain in three comparisons each starting with y_5. Then $y_6, y_7, y_8, y_9, y_{10}, y_{11}$ may each be inserted in four comparisons starting with y_{11}, etc.

2.32 Theorem

We shall now give a more careful analysis of the MERGE INSERTION sorting strategy. This analysis shows that MERGE INSERTION is remarkably good for small values of n (with respect to comparison counting). We have the following theorem:

2.32 THEOREM.

Let $F(n)$ denote the number of comparisons in the worst case for MERGE INSERTION on S_n. Then $F(n)$ equals $S(n)$—the corresponding value for the optimal strategy—for $1 \le n \le 12$ and $n = 20,21$. For $1 \le n \le 11$ and for $n = 20,21$ we have $F(n) = \lceil \log_2(n!) \rceil$, so in this range MERGE INSERTION gives the theoretical lower bound for sorting strategies. For $n = 12$, $S(n) = F(n) > \lceil \log_2(n!) \rceil$, so the theoretical lower bound is not attainable for $n = 12$. In general, $F(n) = \sum_{k=1}^{n} \lceil \log_2(3k/4) \rceil$.

Proof. The proof is by now a fairly standard calculation in this subject but presents a somewhat bewildering display of calculations with $\log_2(x)$, $\lceil x \rceil$, and $\lfloor x \rfloor$ for the beginner. Typically, these types of results are discovered by computing examples, conjecturing a formula, and proof by induction. We give the basic steps in deriving the formula for $F(n)$. The reader should verify these formulas by trying out examples and computing the first few terms of the various series expansions. Induction proofs and general cases will then become obvious.

We need numbers $(t_2, t_3, t_4, \ldots) = (3, 5, 11, \ldots)$ so that y_j for $j = t_k$, $t_k - 1, \ldots, t_{k-1} + 1$, may each be inserted in k comparisons. At the point where we are going to insert these values we have:

$$\overbrace{y_1 > x_1 > x_2 > \ldots > x_{t_k-1}}^{\text{includes previously inserted y's}} > x_{t_k}.$$
$$\wedge$$
$$y_{t_k}$$

Note that the $t_{k-1} - 1$ previously inserted y's (i.e., $y_2, y_3, y_4, \ldots, y_{t_{k-1}}$) are included in the above values. Hence, y_{t_k} is to be binarily inserted into a list with $t_k + t_{k-1} - 1$ elements in k comparisons. Then by the reasoning explained above, all of $y_{t_k-1}, y_{t_k-2} \cdots y_{t_{k-1}+1}$ will go in k also. To binary insert with k comparisons, the list must have $< 2^k$ elements. So $t_k + t_{k-1} - 1 = 2^k - 1$; $t_k + t_{k-1} = 2^k$; $t_1 = 1$ for convenience.

$$t_k = 2^k - t_{k-1} = 2^k - (2^{k-1} - t_{k-2})$$
$$= 2^k - 2^{k-1} + t_{k-2}$$
$$= 2^k - 2^{k-1} + 2^{k-2} - t_{k-3}$$
$$\vdots$$
$$= \sum_{i=0}^{k} (-1)^i \cdot 2^{k-i} = \frac{2^{k+1} + (-1)^k}{3}$$

This then defines the algorithm. Let $F(n)$ denote the number of comparisons used. Clearly, $F(n) = \lfloor n/2 \rfloor + F(\lfloor n/2 \rfloor) + G(\lfloor n/2 \rfloor)$ where G represents the comparisons from part (3) in the algorithm. So

$$G(m) = \sum_{1 \leq j < k} j(t_j - t_{j-1}) + k(m - t_{k-1}),$$

where

$$t_{k-1} < m \leq t_k.$$

Thus, $G(m) = km - (t_0 + \ldots + t_{k-1})$, where $t_0 = 1$. Let $w_k = t_0 + \ldots + t_{k-1} = \left\lfloor \dfrac{2^{k+1}}{3} \right\rfloor$. Then an elementary but tedious consideration of cases shows that $F(n) - F(n-1) = k$ if and only if $w_k < n \leq w_{k+1}$. This leads to $F(n) - F(n-1) = \lceil \log_2(3n/4) \rceil$ which implies that

$$F(n) = \sum_{1 \leq k \leq n} \lceil \log_2(3k/4) \rceil.$$

This compares favorably with $B(n) = \sum_{1 \leq k \leq n} \lceil \log_2 k \rceil$ (binary insertion). Direct computation now gives

$$F(n) = \lceil \log_2 n! \rceil \text{ for } 1 \leq n \leq 11, \quad n = 20, 21$$

So MERGE INSERTION is optimal for those n. A computer search revealed that $30 = S(12) = F(12) > \lceil \log_2 12! \rceil$. This completes the proof of THEOREM 2.32.

The MERGE-INSERTION algorithm was discovered in 1959 by Lester Ford, Jr., and Selmer Johnson. It is still the best known sorting algorithm among all algorithms with a reasonable parametric description for all n (from the point of view of counting comparisons). It has been a difficult problem to find any n for which it can be proved that $S(n) < F(n)$. G. K. Manacher has produced a method for constructing infinitely many $n \geq 189$ for which $S(n) < F(n)$. In fact, $S(189) < F(189)$ although $S(189)$ is not known. It has been shown by F. K. Hwang and S. Lin that $F(n) = n \log_2 n - n\kappa(n) + \lambda(n)$ where $1.329 \leq \kappa(n) \leq 1.415$ and $\lambda(n) = 0(\log_2(n))$. It is easily seen that the theoretical lower bound $\lceil \log_2(n!) \rceil = n \log_2 n - 1.44n + \mu(n)$, where $\mu(n) = 0(\log_2 n)$ ($1.44 \approx \log_2(e)$). Thus, improvements on MERGE INSERTION will never be very dramatic from an asymptotic point of view. These and other references are given at the end of PART I (in particular, look at Knuth, Vol. 3).

2.33 EXERCISE.

(1) Describe and carry out MERGE INSERTION on several examples of size n = 16.
(2) Explain why MERGE INSERTION is a sorting strategy but not a sorting network.

We now consider sorting with the network constraint. Let $\hat{S}(n)$ denote the minimum number of comparators in a sorting net that sorts S_n. $\hat{S}(n)$ is an even more difficult function to study than $S(n)$. Unlike $S(n)$, the asymptotic value of $\hat{S}(n)$ is not known. It is known that there is a c such that for all n, $\hat{S}(n) \leq cn(\log_2(n))$. The values of $\hat{S}(n)$ for n = 1, . . . , 8 are 0, 1, 3, 5, 9, 12, 16, 19, respectively.

2.34 EXERCISE.

(1) Prove that $\hat{S}(3) = 3$ and $\hat{S}(4) = 5$.
(2) Prove that $\hat{S}(n+1) \leq \hat{S}(n) + n$ for all n.

S_n contains n! elements and $n! \sim \sqrt{2\pi n}\left(\dfrac{n}{e}\right)^n$ by Stirling's formula. The following theorem shows that for any sorting net it suffices to consider inputs from a much smaller set (though still quite large).

2.35 THEOREM (zero-one principle).

If a network sorts all inputs of zeroes and ones, then it sorts all permutations.

Proof. The result follows from the observation that for a monotonic function f,

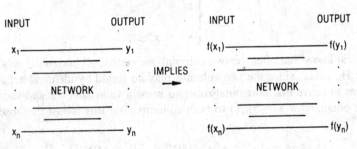

Figure 2.35

That is, however the network handles a comparison of x_i and x_j, it will handle a comparison of $f(x_i)$ and $f(x_j)$ in the same fashion. Suppose a network failed to sort $(\sigma(1), . . . , \sigma(n))$. Let k be the first out-of-place output:

$$\text{line 1 output} = 1, . . . , \text{line } k - 1 \text{ output} = k - 1$$

$$\text{line k output} \neq k. \text{ (In particular, } k < n)$$

Define f, monotonic, by

DOMAIN	1	2	$\cdots$	k	k+1	$\cdots$	n
$\downarrow f$	$\downarrow$	$\downarrow$		$\downarrow$	$\downarrow$		$\downarrow$
RANGE	0	0		0	1		1

Then $(f(\sigma(1)), \ldots, f(\sigma(n)))$ is an input of zeroes and ones which the network fails to sort.

Another basic result is the following theorem.

2.36 THEOREM (generalized matrix principle).

Let $\mathscr{C} \subseteq \{(i,j): 1 \leqslant i, j \leqslant n, i \neq j\}$ be a collection of ordered pairs of distinct integers. Suppose that for $1 \leqslant k \leqslant m$, $X^k = \{x_1^k, x_2^k, \ldots x_n^k\}$ is a set of numbers satisfying the relations of $\mathscr{C}$: $x_i^k < x_j^k$ for all $1 \leqslant k \leqslant m$ and $(i,j)\ \varepsilon\ \mathscr{C}$. For each i, $1 \leqslant i \leqslant n$, sort the set of numbers $\{x_i^1, x_i^2, \ldots, x_i^m\}$ and write the result as $\hat{x}_i^1 \leqslant \hat{x}_i^2 \leqslant \ldots \leqslant \hat{x}_i^m$. Then the new sets $\hat{X}^k = \hat{x}_1^k, \ldots, \hat{x}_n^k$ *still* satisfy the relations of $\mathscr{C}$:

$$\hat{x}_i^k < \hat{x}_j^k \text{ for all } 1 \leqslant k \leqslant m \text{ and } (i,j)\ \varepsilon\ \mathscr{C}.$$

Remark. When $\mathscr{C} = \{(i,i+1): i = 1, 2, \ldots, n-1\}$, the proposition states that if first the rows of an $m \times n$ matrix are sorted and then the columns, then the rows remain sorted.

Proof. Take any $(i,j)\ \varepsilon\ \mathscr{C}$. We start with

$$\begin{cases} x_i^1 \leqslant x_j^1 \\ x_i^2 \leqslant x_j^2 \\ \quad \vdots \\ x_i^m \leqslant x_j^m, \end{cases}$$

and must know that after the two columns are sorted, all horizontal $\leqslant$'s remain valid. However, since the two columns may be sorted by identical networks, it suffices to prove that horizontal relations remain valid after the application of a single comparator $\tau = (k,\ell)$ to both columns. But this is just the observation that

$$x_i^k \leqslant x_j^k \text{ and } x_i^\ell \leqslant x_j^\ell \Rightarrow MIN\{x_i^k, x_i^\ell\} \leqslant MIN\{x_j^k, x_j^\ell\} \text{ and}$$

$$MAX\{x_i^k, x_i^\ell\} \leqslant MAX\{x_j^k, x_j^\ell\}.$$

EXERCISE 2.34(2) gives an easily verifiable upper bound on the growth of $\hat{S}(n)$. The following theorem gives a lower bound on the growth of $\hat{S}(n)$.

2.37 THEOREM.

$$\hat{S}(n+1) \geqslant \hat{S}(n) + \lceil \log_2(n+1) \rceil$$

Proof. Starting from each input of an $(n+1)$ sorter, draw the path that ∞ would follow were it entered in the network. Here is an example $(n=4)$:

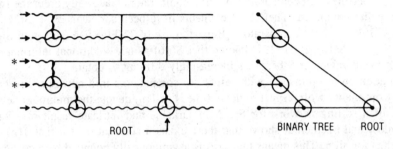

Figure 2.37a

The result may be viewed as a full binary tree (as just shown) with root corresponding to bottom line output position and external nodes corresponding to all input positions. The internal nodes are circled above. A binary tree with $n+1$ external nodes must have at least one path of length $\lceil\log_2(n+1)\rceil$ from root to external node. The external nodes marked * have this property above. This means that $\lceil\log_2(n+1)\rceil$ comparators have predictable behavior when ∞ is entered at such an input; these comparators may then be pruned to leave an n sorter. Hence, $\hat{S}(n) \leqslant \hat{S}(n+1) - \lceil\log_2(n+1)\rceil$. Here is how the above 5-sorter would be pruned to produce a 4-sorter:

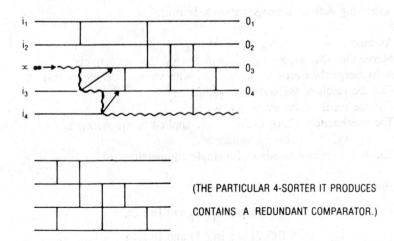

(THE PARTICULAR 4-SORTER IT PRODUCES

CONTAINS A REDUNDANT COMPARATOR.)

Figure 2.37b

Computer search has revealed that $\hat{S}(7) = 16$. Hence, $\hat{S}(8) \geqslant 19$ by THEOREM 2.37. We prove $\hat{S}(8) \leqslant 19$ by showing that 2^n elements may be sorted with $3^n - 2^n$ comparators. For $n = 1$ this is clear. Proceed by induction. Given 2^{n+1} elements, make 2^n disjoint ordered pairs; apply a 2^n sorter to these pairs, replacing each comparator by three comparators that totally order the two pairs being compared. Then 2^{n+1} elements have been sorted in $2^n + 3(3^n - 2^n) = 3^{n+1} - 2^{n+1}$ comparators. Repeated use of THEOREM 2.37 with $\hat{S}(8) = 19$ gives $\hat{S}(16) \geq 51$. It is known that $\hat{S}(16) \leq 60$. Additional information about exact values of $\hat{S}$ becomes increasingly difficult to obtain.

In addition to optimality with respect to comparators in a network, one can study optimality with respect to delay time. Let $\hat{T}(n)$ denote the minimum delay time of a sorting network for S_n. A remarkable and intricate result of Ajtai, Komlós, and Szemerédi shows that there exists a constant c such that $\hat{T}(n) \leq c\log_2(n)$ for all n. This means that $\hat{S}(n)$ is asymptotically bounded by a constant times $n\log_2(n)$ as mentioned above. At present, the exact asymptotic value of $\hat{S}(n)$ is still unknown. For $n \leq 8$, $\hat{T}(n) = 0, 1, 3, 3, 5, 5, 6, 6$.

We conclude our discussion of sorting with some interesting examples of sorting networks constructed recursively from merging networks. The reader should try to construct some nontrivial examples of networks based on the recursive techniques that we now describe.

A B(m,n)-merge network sorts $m + n$ elements, given that the first m (x's) and last n (y's) are already in order. Batcher devised the following recursive procedure for producing a B(m,n)-merge network.

2.38   THEOREM (Batcher odd-even merge).

The following defines a merge network B(m,n):

(1) Assume $x_1 < \ldots < x_m$, $y_1 < \ldots y_n$.
Merge the odds $x_1, x_3, x_5 \ldots$ with $y_1, y_3, \ldots$ recursively.
Also merge the evens $x_2, x_4, x_6 \ldots$ with $y_2, y_4, \ldots$ recursively.
Call the result of the odds $v_1, v_2, v_3 \ldots$
Call the result of the evens $w_1, w_2, w_3, \ldots$
(2) The comparators $(2,3), (4,5), \ldots$, applied to $z_1, z_2, z_3, z_4, \ldots = v_1, w_1, v_2, w_2, \ldots$, sort the sequence.
(3) The B(1,1) merge consists of a single comparator.

To construct

$$B(5,4) \text{ use } B(3,2) \text{ and } B(2,2)$$

$$B(3,2) \text{ use } B(2,1) \text{ and } B(1,1)$$

$$B(2,2) \text{ use } B(1,1) \text{ and } B(1,1)$$

$$B(2,1) \text{ use } B(1,1) \text{ and } B(1,0).$$

These can be built up as follows:

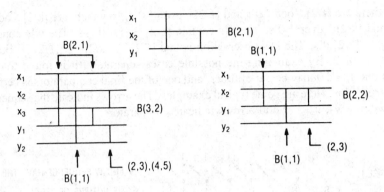

Figure 2.38a

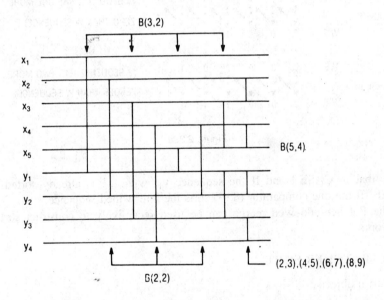

Figure 2.38b

Proof. The proof uses the ZERO-ONE PRINCIPLE, THEOREM 2.35 (we actually use an obvious variation of THEOREM 2.35). The reader should be sure to try a few examples. Let the input be $\vec{x} = $ "ℓ zeroes followed by $m-\ell$ ones" followed by $\vec{y} = $ "k zeroes followed by $n-k$ ones." Inductively the even and odd merges work:

$$v_1, v_2, \ldots = 0, \ldots 0, 1, \ldots 1$$

$$w_1, w_2, \ldots = 0, \ldots 0, 1, \ldots 1$$

In $\vec{x}$ there are $\lceil \ell/2 \rceil$ "odd" 0's and $\lfloor \ell/2 \rfloor$ "even" 0's. In $\vec{y}$ there are $\lceil k/2 \rceil$ "odd" 0's and $\lfloor k/2 \rfloor$ "even" 0's. The v's contain $\lceil \ell/2 \rceil + \lceil k/2 \rceil$ 0's. The w's contain $\lfloor \ell/2 \rfloor + \lfloor k/2 \rfloor$ 0's. The key observation is that $\lceil \ell/2 \rceil + \lceil k/2 \rceil - (\lfloor \ell/2 \rfloor + \lfloor k/2 \rfloor)$ $= 0, 1,$ or 2. By examining the possible cases separately, it is found that at most one 1 and 0 may be out of order, and one of the final comparators is certain to remedy this. Here are some typical examples. The arrows indicate the sequence $v_1, w_1, v_2, w_2, \ldots$ Solid arrows indicate comparators.

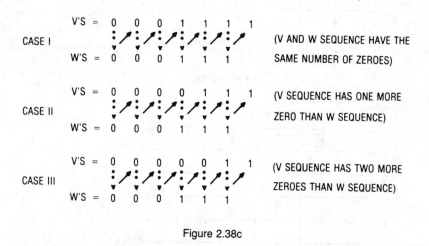

Figure 2.38c

Note that in CASE I and II the sequence $v_1, w_1, \ldots$ is already sorted. In CASE III the one comparator (8, 9) sorts the intertwined sequence.

The Batcher odd-even merge can be used recursively to construct sorting networks.

2.39 BATCHER SORT.

To sort n objects,

(1) Sort first $\lceil n/2 \rceil$, recursively.
(2) Sort second $\lfloor n/2 \rfloor$, recursively.
(3) Apply B($\lceil n/2 \rceil$, $\lfloor n/2 \rfloor$) merge.

The following exercises explore some ideas associated with these recursively defined merging and sorting networks.

2.40 EXERCISE.

(1) Construct some Batcher odd-even merge networks of larger order than B(5,4) (shown following THEOREM 2.38).
(2) Construct some examples of Batcher sorting networks.

(3) It is known that the delay time $\delta(n)$ of a Batcher sorting network satisfies

$$\delta(n) \leq \binom{1 + \lceil \log_2(n) \rceil}{2} = (\lceil \log_2 n \rceil + 1)(\lceil \log_2 n \rceil)/2 \quad \text{(see (4))}. \text{ Suppose you}$$

design a family of networks of delay time $c \log_2 n$, c a constant. The actual value of c is critical in determining when your networks are better than the Batcher sorting networks 2.38. Discuss this situation.

(4) Verify the inequality of EXERCISE (3) above. *Hint*: First consider the case where n is a power of 2.

Chapter 3

Topic II: Basic Combinatorial Lists

The goal of TOPIC II is to describe linear orders on basic sets (various classes of functions, permutations, partitions, subsets, etc.) such that the natural order isomorphisms RANK and UNRANK (see DEFINITION 1.55) can be computed easily. In doing so we shall gain an important detailed understanding of these sets, which are themselves the basic building blocks of many algorithms. The reader might wish to review the material in Chapter 1 from DEFINITION 1.55 to the paragraph just following EXERCISE 1.61.

We have used the notation $\underline{r} = \{1,2,...,r\}$. Define $\underline{r} = \{0,1,...,r-1\}$. Note that 3 is the 4th element of $\underline{5}$, or in general j is the $(j+1)^{st}$ element of $\underline{r}$. We use this notation throughout this TOPIC. When numbering the elements of a set from 0 instead of 1 we speak of the "rank k" element of the set, k = $0,...,r-1$. Thus, the rank 3 element of $\underline{5}$ is 3. The rank 3 element of $\underline{5}$ is 4 (DEFINITION 1.55).

Consider the functions mapping $\underline{4} \rightarrow \underline{3}$, denoted by $\underline{3}^{\underline{4}}$. In lexicographic order (DEFINITION 1.20), this set is 0 0 0 0, 0 0 0 1, 0 0 0 2, 0 0 1 0, 0 0 1 1, etc. We have just listed the elements of rank 0 through 4. What is the element of rank 40? What is the rank of the function 1 0 1 1? How many functions are there between 1 0 1 1 and 2 1 0 2? Consider TABLE 3.1.

3.1 LEXICOGRAPHIC LIST OF FUNCTIONS (a_3, a_2, a_1, a_0) from $\underline{4}$ to $\underline{3}$.

$$\rho = a_3{\cdot}27 + a_2{\cdot}9 + a_1{\cdot}3 + a_0$$

a_3	a_2	a_1	a_0	ρ
0	0	0	0	0
0	0	0	1	1
0	0	0	2	2
0	0	1	0	3
0	0	1	1	4
0	0	1	2	5
0	0	2	0	6
0	0	2	1	7
0	0	2	2	8
0	1	0	0	9
1	1	1	1	40
2	2	2	2	80

It is apparent from TABLE 3.1 that the formula $\rho = a_3{\cdot}27 + a_2{\cdot}9 + a_1{\cdot}3 + a_0$ gives the ranks of the elements in the list of functions $\underline{3}^{\underline{4}}$ in lex order. But $\rho = a_3\,3^3 + a_2\,3^2 + a_1\,3 + a_0$ defines the coefficients a_3, a_2, a_1, a_0 of ρ in the *base 3 number system*. In general, the element $(a_{d-1}, a_{d-2}, \ldots, a_0)$ of $\underline{r}^{\underline{d}}$ has rank $a_{d-1}r^{d-1} + a_{d-2}r^{d-2} + \ldots + a_0$ in the list $\underline{r}^{\underline{d}}$ given in lex order. That is, given an element $(a_{d-1}, a_{d-2}, \ldots, a_0)$ in the lex list of $\underline{r}^{\underline{d}}$, its rank m in the list is found by interpreting the numbers $a_{d-1}, a_{d-2}, \ldots, a_0$ as coefficients base r. Conversely, the rank q element in the list $\underline{r}^{\underline{d}}$ in lex order is gotten by finding the coefficients of q base r.

Let S and T be ordered sets (DEFINITION 1.2) and let $\eta{:}S \to T$ be a bijection such that $x \le y$ if and only if $\eta(x) \le \eta(y)$. Then η is called an ORDER ISOMORPHISM and S and T are called ORDER ISOMORPHIC (DEFINITION 1.54).

3.2 EXERCISE.

There are 32 subsets of $\underline{5}$. Can you linearly order these subsets so that you have a simple order isomorphism between your list and $\{0,1,2,\ldots,31\}$? Extend your method to the general case.

We should learn to recognize other descriptions of the set $\underline{r}^{\underline{d}}$. In FIGURE 3.3(a), (b), and (c) we see three descriptions of the same function $(5,1,0,1,4)$ in $\underline{6}^{\underline{5}}$. The notation "$(5,1,0,1,4)$" is called *one line notation*. We often write simply 5 1 0 1 4.

3.3   THREE DESCRIPTIONS OF THE SAME FUNCTION.

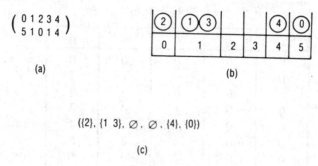

$$\begin{pmatrix} 0\ 1\ 2\ 3\ 4 \\ 5\ 1\ 0\ 1\ 4 \end{pmatrix}$$

(a)

(b)

$(\{2\},\ \{1\ 3\},\ \varnothing,\ \varnothing,\ \{4\},\ \{0\})$

(c)

Figure 3.3

FIGURE 3.3(a) shows one standard way of writing down the function 5 1 0 1 4 (in which the domain is explicitly shown). FIGURE 3.3(b) shows the distribution of five labeled balls into six labeled boxes. FIGURE 3.3(c) shows a *length 6 ordered partition* of $\underline{5}$: $(A_0, A_1, \ldots, A_5)$, $A_i \cap A_j = \phi$ if $i \neq j$, $\bigcup_i A_i = \underline{5}$.

The set A_t, $t = 0, \ldots, 5$, is the set where $f = 5\ 1\ 0\ 1\ 4$ takes on the value t $(A_t = f^{-1}(t))$. The corresponding (unordered) partition $\{\{2\}, \{1,3\}, \{4\}, \{0\}\}$ is the "coimage" of f referred to at the beginning of Chapter 1 (NOTATION 1.6). Thus, we are able to list lexicographically and rank the distributions of d labeled balls into r labeled boxes and the ordered partitions of a set $\underline{d}$. Another intuitive interpretation of the string 5 1 0 1 4 is the statistical one as an "ordered sample" of "length 5" "with repetition" from $\underline{6}$. Which functions in $\underline{r}^{\underline{d}}$ would correspond to the "unordered samples"?

3.4   EXERCISE.

List the first, middle, and last five ordered partitions of length 3 on $\underline{4}$. Interpret these as distributions of labeled balls into labeled boxes.

More generally, we are interested in ranking the lex list of functions in $R_{d-1} \times \ldots \times R_0$ where each R_t is a linearly ordered set. Assume for convenience that $R_t = \underline{r_t}$ for $t = 0, \ldots, d-1$. Consider, for example, $\underline{3} \times \underline{4} \times \underline{2}$. The list starts off 0 0 0, 0 0 1, 0 1 0, 0 1 1, 0 2 0, 0 2 1, 0 3 0, 0 3 1, 1 0 0, 1 0 1, 1 1 0, etc. Define $c_0 = 1$, $c_1 = r_0 c_0 = 2$, and $c_2 = r_1 c_1 = 8$. Consider $\rho(a_2, a_1, a_0) = a_0 c_0 + a_1 c_1 + a_2 c_2$. Computing the values of ρ on the part of the list written above gives 0, 1, 2, 3, 4, 5, 6, 7, 8, 9, 10, etc. It appears that this ρ is the ranking function for $\underline{3} \times \underline{4} \times \underline{2}$ in lex order. This observation extends to the general case as stated in THEOREM 3.5.

3.5   THEOREM.

For each $(a_{d-1}, \ldots, a_0)$ in $\underline{r_{d-1}} \times \ldots \times \underline{r_0}$, let $\rho(a_{d-1}, \ldots, a_0) = \sum_{t=0}^{d-1} a_t c_t$
where $c_t = r_{t-1} c_{t-1}$ and $c_0 = 1$. This ρ is the order isomorphism between
$\underline{r_{d-1}} \times \ldots \times \underline{r_0}$ in lex order and the linearly ordered set $\{0, 1, \ldots, m\}$ where
$m = (r_0 r_1 \ldots r_{d-1}) - 1$.

Proof.   The proof of THEOREM 3.5 is an easy consequence of the relationship
between residual trees and ranks of leaves of an unordered tree discussed in
connection with FIGURES 1.57 and 1.58. FIGURE 3.6(a) shows the idea for
modifying the tree diagram of FIGURE 1.42 to cover the situation of
THEOREM 3.5. The residual tree associated with an edge at level t is shown
in FIGURE 3.6(c). The number of leaves in the residual tree R(e) of the edge
e is clearly $a_{d-t} c_{d-t}$. Thus, $\rho(a_{d-1}, \ldots, a_0)$ is just the sum of these quantities
along the path associated with $a_{d-1}, \ldots, a_0$ in the tree analogous (in the general
case) to FIGURE 3.6(a).

3.6   RESIDUAL TREE DIAGRAM FOR THEOREM 3.5.

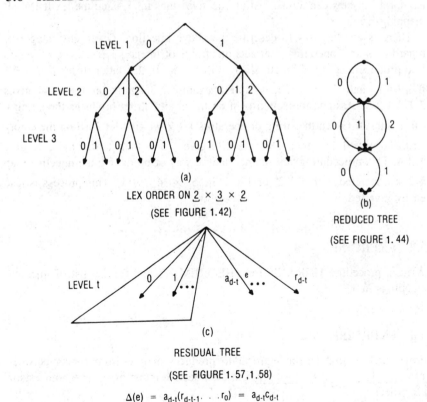

(a)

LEX ORDER ON $\underline{2} \times \underline{3} \times \underline{2}$

(SEE FIGURE 1.42)

(b)

REDUCED TREE

(SEE FIGURE 1. 44)

(c)

RESIDUAL TREE

(SEE FIGURE 1. 57, 1.58)

$\Delta(e) = a_{d-t}(r_{d-t-1} \cdots r_0) = a_{d-t} c_{d-t}$

The lex list of injective mappings (NOTATION 1.6) in $5^{\underline{3}}$ starts off 0 1 2,
0 1 3, 0 1 4, 0 2 1, 0 2 3, 0 2 4, 0 3 1, 0 3 2, 0 3 4, 0 4 1, 0 4 2, 0 4 3, 1 0 2,
1 0 3, ... To construct such a mapping $i_1 i_2 i_3$ we have five choices for i_1, then
four choices for i_2, then three choices for i_3. There are $5 \cdot 4 \cdot 3 = 60$ such mappings.
There are also 60 mappings in $5 \times 4 \times 3$. In lex order this list starts off
0 0 0, 0 0 1, 0 0 2, 0 1 0, 0 1 1, 0 1 2, 0 2 0, 0 2 1, 0 2 2, 0 3 0, 0 3 1, 0 3 2,
1 0 0, 1 0 1, ... Suppose we are given a mapping in $5 \times 4 \times 3$, say
1 1 2. Associate with 1 1 2, by reading left to right, an injective mapping as
follows: The first integer in 1 1 2 is a 1, so write down the rank 1 element (the
integer 1 in this case) of the linearly ordered set $5 = \{0,1,2,3,4\}$. Write $\boxed{1}$.
Delete this element from 5 to get 0,2,3,4. The second integer in 1 1 2 is also
a 1 so write down the rank 1 element (the integer 2) of $\{0,2,3,4\}$. Write
$\boxed{1\,2}$. Delete the 2 to obtain $\{0,3,4\}$. The last integer is a 2 so write the
rank 2 element (the integer 4) of $\{0,3,4\}$. Write $\boxed{1\,2\,4}$. In this manner we
interpret the successive digits of 1 1 2 as these ranks (among all allowable
choices) of the elements in the corresponding injection. In this case we obtain
the injective mapping 1 2 4. Given 1 2 4 the process is easily inverted (1 is the
rank 1 element of 5, 2 the rank 1 element of $5 - \{1\}$, 4 the rank 2 element
of $5 - \{1,2\}$, giving 1 1 2). The process just described gives a natural order
isomorphism between the lex list of injective maps in $5^{\underline{3}}$ and the lex list of all
mappings in $5 \times 4 \times 3$.

There is another way to describe the above bijection. Given any integer n,
regard $\hat{n}$ as an "operator" that acts on strings of integers $i_1, i_2, \ldots, i_k$ of length
k to produce a string of length $k+1$, $n\, i_1' i_2' \ldots i_k'$. In this latter string $i_t' = i_t + 1$
if $i_t \geq n$, and $i_t' = i_t$ if $i_t < n$. For example, $\hat{3}$ acting on 1 3 3 2 4 gives
3 1 4 4 2 5. Assume the action of $\hat{n}$ on the empty string produces the string n
(of length 1). Given the string of operators $\hat{1}\ \hat{1}\ \hat{2}$ we first let $\hat{2}$ act on the empty
string to give $\hat{1}\ \hat{1}\ 2$, then $\hat{1}$ act on 2 to give $\hat{1}\ 1\ 3$, then $\hat{1}$ act on 1 3 to give
1 2 4. This procedure gives another natural way of producing the injective map
1 2 4 associated with 1 1 2 (or $\hat{1}\ \hat{1}\ \hat{2}$) in $5 \times 4 \times 3$. This process is also
easily inverted.

3.7 EXERCISE.

Write a procedure UNRANK for THEOREM 3.5 and for the list of injective
mappings in $r^{\underline{d}}$.

3.8 EXERCISE.

Prove carefully that the above procedure produces an order isomorphism between
$r \times r-1 \times \ldots \times r-d+1$ and the injective mappings in $r^{\underline{d}}$ (both lists in
lex order).

3.9 EXERCISE.

Write a computer program that, given r, d, and a function in $\underline{r} \times \underline{r-1} \times \ldots \times \underline{r-d+1}$, produces the corresponding injective mapping in $\underline{r}^{\underline{d}}$. Do the same starting with an injection in $\underline{r}^{\underline{d}}$ to produce the function in $\underline{r} \times \ldots \times \underline{r-d+1}$.

We have seen in THEOREM 3.5 above how to rank the lex list of functions $\underline{r} \times \underline{r-1} \times \ldots \times \underline{r-d+1}$. According to THEOREM 3.5 the rank of a function $(a_{d-1}, \ldots, a_0)$ is given by $\rho(a_{d-1}, \ldots, a_0) = \sum_{t=0}^{d-1} a_t c_t$ where $c_0 = 1$, $c_1 = r-d+1$, $c_2 = (r-d+2)(r-d+1), \ldots, c_{d-1} = (r-1)(r-2) \ldots (r-d+1)$. If we denote by $(p)_q$ the product $p(p-1) \ldots (p-q+1)$ (a total of q factors— sometimes called the "q falling factorial of p") then $c_t = (r-d+t)_t$ (define $(p)_0 \equiv 1$). For example, consider $\underline{5} \times \underline{4} \times \underline{3}$. The rank of $(a_2, a_1, a_0) = (1, 0, 1)$ would be given by $a_2 c_2 + a_1 c_1 + a_0 c_0$ where $c_0 = 1$, $c_1 = 3$, $c_2 = 12$. Thus, the rank of 1 0 1 is 13. Conversely, we may ask for the function with rank, say, 33. Observe that $33 = 2c_2 + 3c_1 + 0c_0$. Thus, 2 3 0 is the function with rank 33 in the lex list of $\underline{5} \times \underline{4} \times \underline{3}$. Using our order isomorphism between $\underline{5} \times \underline{4} \times \underline{3}$ and the injective mappings in $\underline{5}^{\underline{3}}$ we obtain immediately that the injection 1 0 3 (corresponding to the function 1 0 1) has rank 13 and the injection with rank 33 is 2 4 0.

3.10 EXERCISE.

(1) Write a computer program that, given r and d, produces a list of the injective mappings of $\underline{r}^{\underline{d}}$.

(2) Write a program that, given an integer n, $0 \leqslant n < (r)_d$, produces the rank n injective mapping of $\underline{r}^{\underline{d}}$.

(3) Write a program that, given an injective mapping in $\underline{r}^{\underline{d}}$, produces its rank.

There is a natural recursive procedure for generating the injective mappings of $\underline{r}^{\underline{d}}$. Consider, for example, the injective mappings of $\underline{5}^{\underline{3}}$. There are $(5)_3 = 5 \cdot 4 \cdot 3 = 60$ such mappings. In lex order the rank 0 map is 0 1 2, the rank 59 map is 4 3 2. In this list, 24 of the mappings do not contain a 4. These are the injective mappings in $\underline{4}^{\underline{3}}$ (i.e., 0 1 2, 0 1 3, 0 2 1, 0 2 3, 0 3 1, 0 3 2, 1 0 2, 1 0 3, etc.). The remaining injective mappings can be constructed from the list of injective mappings in $\underline{4}^{\underline{2}}$ (i.e., 0 1, 0 2, 0 3, 1 0, 1 2, 1 3, . . .) by direct insertion of the symbol 4. For example, from 0 1 we construct 0 1 4, 0 4 1, and 4 0 1. The list then looks as follows: 0 1 4, 0 4 1, 4 0 1, 0 2 4, 0 4 2, 4 0 2, 0 3 4, 0 4 3, 4 0 3, 1 0 4, 1 4 0, 4 1 0, ... There are $3 \cdot (4)_2 = 36$

such mappings that, together with the previous $(4)_3 = 24$ mappings, make up the $(5)_3 = 60$ injective mappings of $\underline{5}^{\underline{3}}$.

3.11 EXERCISE.

Describe in general the recursive procedure just covered for constructing the injective mappings in $\underline{r}^{\underline{d}}$. Develop a method for ordering and ranking the mappings in this list based on the associated recursion $(r)_d = d(r-1)_{d-1} + (r-1)_d$.

An important special case of the injective mappings occurs when $d = r$. In this case the injective mappings are called *permutations* of r. Basic methods for listing permutations were discussed in connection with FIGURES 1.45 and 1.47. We now discuss lists of permutations in more detail.

The permutations in $\underline{r}^{\underline{r}}$ will be denoted by S_r. Thus, in lex order, S_3 is 0 1 2, 0 2 1, 1 0 2, 1 2 0, 2 0 1, 2 1 0. The permutations in lex order are ranked as in the previous section (injective mappings with $d = r$). For example, the permutation 3 0 1 4 5 2 in S_6 is associated with $(\alpha_5, \alpha_4, \ldots, \alpha_0) = (3, 0, 0, 1,$ 1, 0) in $\underline{6} \times \ldots \times \underline{1}$. Thus, it has rank $\sum_{k=0}^{r-1} \alpha_k c_k = 0 \cdot 1 + 1 \cdot 1! + 1 \cdot 2! +$ $0 \cdot 3! + 0 \cdot 4! + 3 \cdot 5! = 363$. Thus, 3 0 1 4 5 2 is the rank 363 permutation in the lex list of permutations S_6 (720 permutations with ranks 0 through 719). In general, if $(\alpha_{r-1}, \alpha_{r-2}, \ldots, \alpha_0)$ is the function in $\underline{r} \times \ldots \times \underline{1}$ corresponding to the permutation $\sigma = \sigma_{r-1}\sigma_{r-2} \ldots \sigma_0$ in S_r, then the rank of σ is $\sum_{k=0}^{r-1} \alpha_k k!$. This fact is a special case of the corresponding result for injective mappings which, in turn, follows immediately from THEOREM 3.5.

As discussed in the previous section, the above ranking of the permutations S_r is based on an order isomorphism between permuations in lex order and the functions in $\underline{r} \times \ldots \times \underline{1}$ in lex order. There is also an interesting order isomorphism between functions in $\underline{1} \times \ldots \times \underline{r}$ in lex order and the permutations generated recursively by direct insertion. This method is related to EXERCISE 3.11. S_1 consists of 0. S_2 contains 0 1 and 1 0. S_3 contains 0 1 2, 0 2 1, 2 0 1, 1 0 2, 1 2 0, 2 1 0. The new symbol 2 is inserted right to left in the successive permutations of S_2. Generated in this manner, S_4 starts off 0 1 2 3, 0 1 3 2, 0 3 1 2, 3 0 1 2, 0 2 1 3, 0 2 3 1, ... Given $(\alpha_{r-1}, \ldots, \alpha_0)$ in $\underline{1}$ $\times \ldots \times \underline{r}$, we show how to construct a corresponding permutation. We always have $\alpha_{r-1} = 0$. Write down $\square \, 0 \, \square$. The symbol α_{r-2} tells us where to put the 1. If $\alpha_{r-2} = 0$ we write $\square \, 0 \, \boxed{1}$, if $\alpha_{r-2} = 1$ we write $\boxed{1} \, 0 \, \square$. At this stage the only thing we know about the permutation we are constructing is whether or not the symbol 0 appears to the left or to the right of the 1. Now write down $\square \, * \, \square \, * \, \square$. The *'s stand for the locations of the 0 and 1. The symbol α_{r-3} in $\underline{3}$ is either a 0, 1, or 2. If 0 write $\square \, * \, \square \, * \, \boxed{2}$, if 1 write $\square$ $* \, \boxed{2} \, * \, \square$, if 2 write $\boxed{2} \, * \, \square \, * \, \square$. Thus, α_{r-2} gives the rank (read right to left) of the location of the symbol 2 relative to 0 and 1 (or, equivalently, the *position* read right to left of the symbol 2). At this stage we know the relative order of the symbols 0, 1, and 2 in the permutation we are associating with $(\alpha_{r-1}, \ldots, \alpha_0)$. Continuing this procedure gives the relative locations of all of the symbols $1, 2, \ldots, r-1$ and hence determines uniquely the permutation.

For example, consider $(\alpha_5, \ldots, \alpha_0) = (0, 1, 1, 2, 1, 4)$. We write down $\square$ 0 $\square$. Then $\alpha_4 = 1$ tells us to write $\boxed{1}$ 0 $\square$ (i.e., the 1 is in the rank-1 position reading right to left). The next $\alpha_3 = 1$ tells us the rank of the 2 or that 1 2 0 is the correct order for the symbols 0, 1, 2. The $\alpha_2 = 2$ gives 1 3 2 0, the $\alpha_1 = 1$ gives 1 3 2 4 0, and the $\alpha_0 = 4$ gives 1 5 3 2 4 0, which is the permutation associated with the function $(0, 1, 1, 2, 1, 4)$. Conversely, if we were given the permutation 1 5 3 2 4 0, we write $\alpha_{r-1} = \alpha_5 = 0$ (always!), $\alpha_4 = 1$ (the 1 is in the rank-1 position relative to the 0), $\alpha_3 = 1$ (the 2 is in the rank-1 position relative to the 0 and 1), etc. Similarly, in general, the correspondence we have described can be reversed and hence describes a bijection.

3.12 EXERCISE.

Prove that the bijection just described is the order isomorphism between $\underline{1} \times \ldots \times \underline{r}$ in lex order and the permutations S_r in the order defined by the method of direct insertion.

As a consequence of this order isomorphism we can rank the permutations S_r when generated by direct insertion. By THEOREM 3.5 the rank of $(\alpha_{r-1}, \ldots, \alpha_0)$ in $\underline{1} \times \ldots \times \underline{r}$ is $\displaystyle\sum_{t=0}^{r-1} \alpha_t c_t$, where $c_0 = 1$, $c_1 = r$, $c_2 = r(r-1), \ldots, c_k = (r)_k, \ldots, c_{r-1} = (r)_{r-1}$. Thus, the permutation 1 5 3 2 4 0 in S_6 which has $(\alpha_{r-1}, \ldots, \alpha_0) = (0, 1, 1, 2, 1, 4)$ has rank $4 \cdot 1 + 1 \cdot 6 + 2(6 \cdot 5) + 1 \cdot (6 \cdot 5 \cdot 4) + 1 \cdot (6 \cdot 5 \cdot 4 \cdot 3) = 550$.

3.13 EXERCISE.

Which permutation in the direct insertion list of S_6 has rank 599? What is the rank in this list of the permutation 1 2 5 3 0 4?

In the above order isomorphism between $\underline{1} \times \ldots \times \underline{r}$ and S_r we interpreted the coefficients of $(\alpha_{r-1}, \ldots, \alpha_0)$ as the relative ranks read right to left of each successive digit of the permutation. If we read left to right instead, the list starts off 3 2 1 0, 2 3 1 0, 2 1 3 0, 2 1 0 3, 3 1 2 0, etc. An interesting variation is obtained by making the convention "left to right" or right to left for interpreting a given digit α_{r-t} depend on the values of $\alpha_{r-1}, \ldots, \alpha_{r-t+1}$. One way of doing this leads to a basic algorithm for generating permutations. Consider TABLE 3.14.

3.14   TABLE OF FALLING FACTORIALS.

c_6	c_5	c_4	c_3	c_2	c_1	c_0	r
						1	1
					2	1	2
				6	3	1	3
			24	12	4	1	4
		120	60	20	5	1	5
	720	360	120	30	6	1	6
5040	2520	840	210	42	7	1	7

COEFFICIENTS $c_j = (r)_j$

Given any function $(\alpha_{r-1}, \ldots, \alpha_0)$ in $\underline{1} \times \underline{2} \times \ldots \times \underline{r}$ its rank in the lex order is given by $\sum_{j=0}^{r-1} \alpha_j c_j$ and may be conveniently computed for $r \leqslant 7$ from TABLE 3.14. In the method we now consider, we interpret the coefficient α_{r-j-1} as the relative rank of j, read right to left if the function $(\alpha_{r-1}, \ldots, \alpha_{r-j})$ has even rank in $\underline{1} \times \ldots \times \underline{j}$, and read left to right if $(\alpha_{r-1}, \ldots, \alpha_{r-j})$ has odd rank.

3.15   REMARK.

We observe immediately that, as c_j is even if $j \geqslant 2$, the above function is odd (even) if and only if $\alpha_{r-j+1}c_1 + \alpha_{r-j}c_0 = j(\alpha_{r-j+1}) + \alpha_{r-j}$ is odd (even).

Consider, for example, the function (0, 1, 1, 3, 3, 2, 6) in $\underline{1} \times \ldots \times \underline{7}$. We begin with $\square$ 0 $\square$. The $\alpha_5 = 1$ tells us that the 1 is in the rank-1 position read right to left (0 has rank 0 in $\underline{1}$). The function (0,1) has odd rank (rank 1) in $\underline{0} \times \underline{1}$ so the $\alpha_4 = 1$ is the rank of 2 in $\square$ 1 $\square$ 0 $\square$ read left to right. This gives $\square$ 1 $\square$ 2 $\square$ 0 $\square$. The function (0, 1, 1) has even rank so $\alpha_3 = 3$ is the rank of 3 read right to left giving $\square$ 3 $\square$ 1 $\square$ 2 $\square$ 0 $\square$. Next, (0, 1, 1, 3) has odd rank so we obtain the sequence $\square$ 3 $\square$ 1 $\square$ 2 $\square$ 4 $\square$ 0 $\square$. Next, (0, 1, 1, 3, 3) has even rank giving $\square$ 3 $\square$ 1 $\square$ 2 $\square$ 5 $\square$ 4 $\square$ 0 $\square$. Finally, (0, 1, 1, 3, 3, 2) has even rank giving 6 3 1 2 5 4 0 as the final permutation.

This process can be easily reversed. For example, start with 6 3 1 2 5 4 0. The 1 is in rank-1 position relative to 0 giving $\alpha_{r-2} = \alpha_6 = 1$ (α_{r-1} is always 0, and α_{r-2} is always interpreted right to left). This gives $(\alpha_{r-1}, \alpha_{r-2}) = (0, 1)$, which has odd rank in $\underline{1} \times \underline{2}$. Thus, the relative position of the 2 is interpreted left to right giving $\alpha_{r-3} = \alpha_4 = 1$. Next $(\alpha_6, \alpha_5, \alpha_4) = (0, 1, 1)$ has even rank, so 3 is read right to left giving $\alpha_3 = 3$, etc. We end up with (0, 1, 1, 3, 3, 2, 6).

This procedure, illustrated above for r = 7, can be extended in the obvious way to an arbitrary positive integer r, giving a bijection between $\underline{1}$ × . . . × $\underline{r}$ and S_r. If we start with lex order of $\underline{1}$ × . . . × $\underline{r}$ and define the order on S_r to be the way the successive permutations come out under the above bijection, we may trivially regard this bijection as an order isomorphism. In TABLE 3.16, the resulting order on S_4 is shown. Observe that each permutation is obtained from its predecessor by switching the relative positions of two adjacent symbols. We now prove this in general.

3.16 TABLE OF PERMUTATIONS BY ADJACENT MARKS.

	12 4 1 $\alpha_2\ \alpha_1\ \alpha_0$	S_4
0	0 0 0	0 1 2 3
1	0 0 1	0 1 3 2
2	0 0 2	0 3 1 2
3	0 0 3	3 0 1 2
4	0 1 0	3 0 2 1
5	0 1 1	0 3 2 1
6	0 1 2	0 2 3 1
7	0 1 3	0 2 1 3
8	0 2 0	2 0 1 3
9	0 2 1	2 0 3 1
10	0 2 2	2 3 0 1
11	0 2 3	3 2 0 1
12	1 0 0	3 2 1 0
13	1 0 1	2 3 1 0
14	1 0 2	2 1 3 0
15	1 0 3	2 1 0 3
16	1 1 0	1 2 0 3
17	1 1 1	1 2 3 0
18	1 1 2	1 3 2 0
19	1 1 3	3 1 2 0
20	1 2 0	3 1 0 2
21	1 2 1	1 3 0 2
22	1 2 2	1 0 3 2
23	1 2 3	1 0 2 3

Consider a typical element $(\alpha_{r-1}, . . .,\alpha_0) = (\alpha_{r-1}, . . .,\alpha_{r-j}, j, j+1, . . ., r-1)$ of $\underline{1}$ × . . . × $\underline{r}$ and let $(\alpha'_{r-1}, . . .,\alpha'_0) = (\alpha_{r-1}, . . ., \alpha'_{r-j} + 1, 0, . . ., 0)$ be the next element in lex order. Here α_{r-j} is the last coordinate (reading left to right) that is not maximal and as such is always defined if $(\alpha_{r-1}, . . .,\alpha_0)$ is not the last function in the list. As $\alpha_{r-1}, . . .,\alpha_{r-j+1}$ are the same in the two sequences, the relative postions of the symbols 0, . . .,j−2 are unchanged. As α_{r-j} is changed to $\alpha_{r-j} + 1$, the symbol j−1 is moved one place to the left or right depending on whether or not $(\alpha_{r-1}, . . ., \alpha_{r-j+1})$ is of even or odd rank. In doing this the symbol j−1 is switched with a symbol 0, 1, . . ., j−2 since

α_{r-j} is not maximal and the remaining coefficients $\alpha_{r-j-1} = j,\ldots,\alpha_0 = r-1$ are maximal. This is the single interchange referred to above. Any other symbol $t \geq j$ is not moved relative to the symbols $0, 1,\ldots,t-1$. To prove this we show that $(\alpha_{r-1},\ldots,\alpha_{r-t})$ is odd (even) if and only if $(\alpha'_{r-1},\ldots,\alpha'_{r-t})$ is even (odd). If we show this, then t being in its maximal position relative to $0,\ldots,t-1$ in the permutation corresponding to $(\alpha_{r-1},\ldots,\alpha_0)$ implies t is already in its minimal position $(\alpha'_{r-t} = 0)$ in the permutation corresponding to $(\alpha'_{r-1},\ldots,\alpha'_0)$. To verify this we need to show (using here REMARK 3.15) that A is odd (even) if and only if B is even (odd) for the following three cases:

(1) $t = j$ $A = \alpha_{r-j+1}j + \alpha_{r-j}$

                 $B = \alpha_{r-j+1}j + (\alpha_{r-j}+1)$

(2) $t = j + 1$ $A = \alpha_{r-j}(j+1) + j$

                 $B = (\alpha_{r-j}+1)(j+1)$

(3) $t > j + 1$ $A = (t-2)t + (t-1)$

                 $B = 0$

All cases are easily verified.

There are numerous other ways to construct order isomorphisms between $\underline{1} \times \underline{2} \times \ldots \times \underline{r}$ or $\underline{r} \times \underline{r-1} \times \ldots \times \underline{1}$ and S_r. With a little practice the reader can invent her or his own algorithms based on the same ideas. The method discussed in connection with TABLE 3.16 is called the method of "adjacent marks."

3.17 EXERCISE.

Write a computer program to generate the permutations by the method of adjacent marks.

We now consider similar ideas to the above for increasing and nondecreasing functions. In lex order the list of (strictly) increasing functions in $\underline{5}^{\underline{3}}$ is 0 1 2, 0 1 3, 0 1 4, 0 2 3, 0 2 4, 0 3 4, 1 2 3, 1 2 4, 1 3 4, 2 3 4. The list of nondecreasing functions starts off 0 0 0, 0 0 1, 0 0 2, 0 0 3, 0 0 4, 0 1 1, 0 1 2, 0 1 3, 0 1 4, 0 2 2, ... There are 10 increasing functions and 35 nondecreasing functions. The increasing functions in $\underline{r}^{\underline{d}}$ can be regarded as the list of all subsets of size d chosen from $\underline{r}$. In this manner, 0 1 2 is the subset $\{0,1,2\} \subset \underline{5}$. This correspondence was, for decreasing functions, the subject of EXERCISE 1.50. In EXERCISE 3.2 a ranking function for the list of all subsets of $\underline{5}$ was requested. The subsets of $\underline{5}$ correspond in an obvious way to functions in $\underline{2}^{\underline{5}}$ (regarded as "characteristic functions" of the corresponding sets, EXERCISE 1.13(6)). The functions in $\underline{2}^{\underline{5}}$ in lex order may be ranked using the base 2 number representation as previously discussed. This method, of course, extends to $\underline{2}^{\underline{r}}$, the subsets of $\underline{r}$. To rank the subsets of size d from $\underline{r}$, a different approach is required. Consider TABLE 3.18.

3.18 INCREASING FUNCTIONS IN COLEX ORDER.

$$\rho = \binom{\alpha_0}{1} + \binom{\alpha_1}{2} + \binom{\alpha_2}{3}.$$

ρ	α_0	α_1	α_2	β_0	β_1	β_2	ρ'
0	0	1	2	2	3	4	9
1	0	1	3	1	3	4	8
2	0	2	3	1	2	4	7
3	1	2	3	1	2	3	6
4	0	1	4	0	3	4	5
5	0	2	4	0	2	4	4
6	1	2	4	0	2	3	3
7	0	3	4	0	1	4	2
8	1	3	4	0	1	3	1
9	2	3	4	0	1	2	0

The increasing functions $(\alpha_0,\alpha_1,\alpha_2)$ of $\underline{5}^{[3]}$ are listed in colex order in TABLE 3.18.

The ranking function ρ (the order isomorphism for this list in colex order to $0,\ldots,9)$ is given by the formula $\rho = \binom{\alpha_0}{1} + \binom{\alpha_1}{2} + \binom{\alpha_2}{3}$. Thus, the rank

of $(0,3,4)$ is $\binom{0}{1} + \binom{3}{2} + \binom{4}{3} = 0 + 3 + 4 = 7$. Given $(\alpha_0,\alpha_1,\alpha_2)$ we

construct $(\beta_0,\beta_1,\beta_2)$ by the rule $\beta_0 = 4 - \alpha_2$, $\beta_1 = 4 - \alpha_1$, $\beta_2 = 4 - \alpha_0$. Observe that the functions $(\beta_0,\beta_1,\beta_2)$ of TABLE 3.18 are in reverse lex order. To compute the rank ρ' of $(\beta_0,\beta_1,\beta_2)$ in lex order we compute the rank ρ of the corresponding $(\alpha_0,\alpha_1,\alpha_2)$ and observe that $\rho + \rho' = 9$. For example, $(\beta_0,\beta_1,\beta_2)$

$= (0,2,3)$ corresponds to $(1,2,4)$ with $\rho = \binom{1}{1} + \binom{2}{2} + \binom{4}{3} = 6$ and ρ'

is thus 3. This procedure works in general for ranking the increasing functions in $\underline{r}^{[d]}$ (or the subsets of size d of $\underline{r}$) in lex order.

3.19 EXERCISE.

Convince yourself and be prepared to convince others that the transformation $(\alpha_0,\ldots,\alpha_{d-1}) \rightarrow (\beta_0,\ldots,\beta_{d-1})$ where $\beta_i = r - 1 - \alpha_{d-1-i}$, $i = 0,\ldots,d-1$, is an order isomorphism between the list of increasing functions in $\underline{r}^{[d]}$ in colex order and the same list in reverse lex order.

3.20 THEOREM.

The mapping ρ defined by $\rho(\alpha_0,\ldots,\alpha_{d-1}) = \binom{\alpha_0}{1} + \ldots + \binom{\alpha_{d-1}}{d}$ is the order isomorphism between the list of increasing functions in $\lfloor r \rfloor^{\lfloor d \rfloor}$ in colex order

and $\{0,1,2,\ldots, \binom{r}{d} - 1\}$.

Proof. Consider any increasing function $(\alpha_0,\ldots,\alpha_{d-1})$ in $\lfloor r \rfloor^{\lfloor d \rfloor}$. We must have $d - 1 \leqslant \alpha_{d-1} \leqslant r - 1$. Suppose $\alpha_{d-1} = j$ in this range. For α_{d-1} fixed at this value the remaining coordinates $(\alpha_0,\ldots,\alpha_{d-2})$ range over all increasing functions in $\lfloor j \rfloor^{\lfloor d-1 \rfloor}$. Suppose the theorem is true for d replaced by $d-1$. By the definition of colex order, the increasing functions of the form $(\alpha_0,\ldots,\alpha_{d-2},j)$ (as $(\alpha_0,\ldots,\alpha_{d-2})$ ranges over the increasing functions of $\lfloor j \rfloor^{\lfloor d-1 \rfloor}$ in colex order) are consecutive elements of $\lfloor r \rfloor^{\lfloor d \rfloor}$ in colex order. We would then have ρ mapping

these elements into $0 + \binom{j}{d}, 1 + \binom{j}{d}, \ldots, \binom{j+1}{d} - 1$. We use here *Pascal's*

identity $\binom{j}{d-1} + \binom{j}{d} = \binom{j+1}{d}$. Letting j take on the various possible values

of α_{d-1} from $d-1$ to $r-1$ and piecing together the respective intervals gives the result for $\lfloor r \rfloor^{\lfloor d \rfloor}$. The case $d = 1$ is trivially true so the theorem follows by induction.

3.21 EXERCISE.

Restate the proof of THEOREM 3.20 in terms of residual trees as was done in the case of THEOREM 3.5. What is the relationship between THEOREM 3.20 and THEOREM 1.59?

3.22 COROLLARY.

Consider the list of increasing functions in $\lfloor r \rfloor^{\lfloor d \rfloor}$ in lex order and let $(\beta_0,\ldots,\beta_{d-1})$ be such a function. The mapping ρ' defined by

$$\rho'(\beta_0,\ldots,\beta_{d-1}) = \binom{r}{d} - 1 - \binom{\alpha_0}{1} - \ldots - \binom{\alpha_{d-1}}{d}$$

where $\alpha_i = r - 1 - \beta_{d-1-i}$, $i = 0,\ldots,d-1$, is an order isomorphism between

this list and $\{0,1,\ldots, \binom{r}{d} - 1\}$.

Proof. This is exactly the procedure followed in connection with TABLE 3.18.

Given an integer m, it is quite easy to compute $\rho^{-1}(m) = (\alpha_0,\ldots,\alpha_{d-1})$. First let α_{d-1} be the largest integer such that $\binom{\alpha_{d-1}}{d} \leqslant m$. If equality holds,

$(0,\ldots,0,\alpha_{d-1})\;=\;\rho^{-1}(m)$. Otherwise replace m by $m\,-\,\begin{pmatrix}\alpha_{d-1}\\d\end{pmatrix}$ and d by

$d-1$ and repeat. When $d\,=\,1$, $\begin{pmatrix}\alpha_0\\1\end{pmatrix}\,=\,m$ is always possible so the procedure

terminates. As $m\,<\,\begin{pmatrix}r\\d\end{pmatrix}$ we must have $\begin{pmatrix}\alpha_{d-1}\\d\end{pmatrix}\,<\,\begin{pmatrix}r\\d\end{pmatrix}$ or $\alpha_{d-1}\,<\,r$. In the

general step, we have chosen α_j to be the largest integer such that $\begin{pmatrix}\alpha_j\\j+1\end{pmatrix}\,\leqslant$

m and α_{j-1} to be the largest integer such that $\begin{pmatrix}\alpha_{j-1}\\j\end{pmatrix}\,\leqslant\,m\,-\,\begin{pmatrix}\alpha_j\\j+1\end{pmatrix}$. If α_{j-1}

$\geqslant\,\alpha_j$ then we have

$$\begin{pmatrix}\alpha_j+1\\j+1\end{pmatrix}\,=\,\begin{pmatrix}\alpha_j\\j\end{pmatrix}\,+\,\begin{pmatrix}\alpha_j\\j+1\end{pmatrix}\,\leqslant\,\begin{pmatrix}\alpha_{j-1}\\j\end{pmatrix}\,+\,\begin{pmatrix}\alpha_j\\j+1\end{pmatrix}\,\leqslant\,m$$

which contradicts the maximality of α_j. Thus, $\alpha_{j-1}\,<\,\alpha_j$ and the sequence $(\alpha_0,\ldots,\alpha_{d-1})$ produced by the above procedure is the desired increasing function

in $\underline{r}^{\underline{d}}$ satisfying $\rho(\alpha_0,\ldots,\alpha_{d-1})\,=\,\begin{pmatrix}\alpha_0\\1\end{pmatrix}\,+\,\ldots\,+\,\begin{pmatrix}\alpha_{d-1}\\d\end{pmatrix}\,=\,m$.

3.23 EXERCISE.

(1) Consider the subsets of size 5 from $\underline{30}_{\underline{\,}}$. What is the rank of (3,5,9,11,15) in colex lists of these subsets? What is the $10{,}000^{th}$ subset in the lex and colex lists? (TABLE 3.24 gives a partial list of binomial coefficients).

(2) Construct the tree diagram for increasing functions in lex and colex order (see FIGURE 1.52).

(3) Describe the computation of UNRANK(m) $=\rho^{-1}(m)$ as a procedure (such as THEOREM 1.60) for THEOREM 3.20.

We now consider the nondecreasing functions. The nondecreasing functions in $\underline{5}^{\underline{3}}$ in lex order start off 0 0 0, 0 0 1, 0 0 2, 0 0 3, 0 0 4, 0 1 1, 0 1 2, 0 1 3, 0 1 4, 0 2 2, 0 2 3, 0 2 4, 0 3 3, 0 3 4, 0 4 4, 1 1 1, ... It is instructive to leave spaces between the consecutive symbols in a nondecreasing function $(\alpha_0,\ldots,\alpha_{d-1})$ in $\underline{r}^{\underline{d}}$. Leave $\alpha_i\,-\,\alpha_{i-1}$ spaces in front of α_i. Thus, write 0 2 2 as $\boxed{0\ \ \ \ 2\,2\ \ \ }$, 0 2 4 as $\boxed{0\ \ \ \ 2\ \ \ \ 4}$, 1 3 3 as $\boxed{\ \ 1\ \ \ \ 3\,3\ \ \ }$, and 1 3 4 as $\boxed{\ \ 1\ \ \ \ 3\ \ \ 4}$. By convention we leave α_0 spaces in front of α_0 and $(r-1)\,-\,\alpha_{d-1}$ spaces after α_{d-1}. There are d symbols α_i and $\alpha_0\,+\,(\alpha_1\,-\,\alpha_0)\,+\,\ldots\,+\,((r-1)\,-\,\alpha_{d-1})\,=\,r-1$ spaces for a total of $d\,+\,r\,-\,1$ boxes in the array $\boxed{\ \ \ \ \ \ }\cdots\boxed{\ \ \ \ }$ in which we write the nondecreasing functions of $\underline{r}^{\underline{d}}$. In the above case of $\underline{5}^{\underline{3}}$ we use $3\,+\,5\,-\,1\,=\,7$ boxes. Observe now that with this method of writing the nondecreasing functions all we need to know is which boxes have symbols in them or which boxes are blank to reconstruct the function. For example, $\boxed{\ \ |*|\ \ |*|*|\ \ }$ indicates where the α_i appear by a *. There are $\alpha_0 = 1$ initial spaces, so $\alpha_1 = \alpha_0 + 2 = 3$. Similarly $\alpha_2 = 3$ so $\boxed{\ \ |1|\ \ |3|3|\ \ }$ must be the function. Now rank the boxes of the array 0 to $r + d - 2$ reading left to right:

$$0\ \ 1\ \ 2\ \ 3\ \ 4\ \ 5\ \ 6$$
$$\boxed{\ \ |\ \ |\ \ |\ \ |\ \ |\ \ |\ \ }.$$

We can represent the nondecreasing function 1 3 3 $\boxed{\ \ |*|\ \ |\ \ |*|*|\ \ }$ by either the set $\{1,4,5\}$ indicating where the *'s appear in the array, or the set $\{0,2,3,6\}$ indicating where the blanks appear. In TABLE 3.25 we list some of the nondecreasing functions in $\underline{5}^{\underline{3}}$ together with these two alternative descriptions.

3.24   TABLE OF BINOMIAL COEFFICIENTS $\binom{n}{k}$, n = 0,. . .,20,

k = 0,. . .,5.

1	0	0	0	0	0
1	1	0	0	0	0
1	2	1	0	0	0
1	3	3	1	0	0
1	4	6	4	1	0
1	5	10	10	5	1
1	6	15	20	15	6
1	7	21	35	35	21
1	8	28	56	70	56
1	9	36	84	126	126
1	10	45	120	210	252
1	11	55	165	330	462
1	12	66	220	495	792
1	13	78	286	715	1287
1	14	91	364	1001	2002
1	15	105	455	1365	3003
1	16	120	560	1820	4368
1	17	136	680	2380	6188
1	18	153	816	3060	8568
1	19	171	969	3876	11628
1	20	190	1140	4845	15504

3.25 CODING NONDECREASING FUNCTIONS.

Rank	Functions	*'s A	(Right-Left) B	Blanks C	(Right-Left) D
0	0 0 0	0 1 2	(4 5 6)	3 4 5 6	(0 1 2 3)
1	0 0 1	0 1 3	(3 5 6)	2 4 5 6	(0 1 2 4)
2	0 0 2	0 1 4	(2 5 6)	2 3 5 6	(0 1 3 4)
3	0 0 3	0 1 5	(1 5 6)	2 3 4 6	(0 2 3 4)
4	0 0 4	0 1 6	(0 5 6)	2 3 4 5	(1 2 3 4)
5	0 1 1	0 2 3	(3 4 6)	1 4 5 6	(0 1 2 3)
6	0 1 2	0 2 4	(2 4 6)	1 3 5 6	(0 1 3 5)
7	0 1 3	0 2 5	(1 4 6)	1 3 4 6	(0 2 3 5)
8	0 1 4	0 2 6	(0 4 6)	1 3 4 5	(1 2 3 5)
9	0 2 2	0 3 4	(2 3 6)	1 2 5 6	(0 1 4 5)
10	0 2 3	0 3 5	(1 3 6)	1 2 4 6	(0 2 4 5)
11	0 2 4	0 3 6	(0 3 6)	1 2 4 5	(1 2 4 5)
12	0 3 3	0 4 5	(1 2 6)	1 2 3 6	(0 3 4 5)
13	0 3 4	0 4 6	(0 2 6)	1 2 3 5	(1 3 4 5)
14	0 4 4	0 5 6	(0 1 6)	1 2 3 4	(2 3 4 5)
15	1 1 1	1 2 3	(3 4 5)	0 4 5 6	(0 1 2 6)
⋮	⋮	⋮	⋮	⋮	⋮

A is lex order, B is reverse colex order, C is reverse lex order, and D is colex order.

We have made the convention that we read the ranks of the *'s or blanks from left to right. We could equally well have read from right to left:
6 5 4 3 2 1 0
☐☐☐☐☐☐☐. The lists in TABLE 3.25 indicate that if the nondecreasing functions of $_r \lfloor^{d} \rfloor$ are listed in lex order then the sets of *'s are produced in lex order read left to right and reverse colex order read right to left. Similarly, the sets of blanks are produced in reverse lex order read left to right and colex order read right to left. Proofs of these facts in the general case should be routine by now. We have seen in the first part of the section how to rank the subsets of fixed cardinality of a set. This ranking is of course the key to ranking the nondecreasing functions. The rank of the last subset of size d from $\lfloor r+d-1 \rfloor$ is

of course $\binom{r+d-1}{d} - 1$, so there are clearly $\binom{r+d-1}{d} = \binom{r+d-1}{r-1}$

nondecreasing functions in $_r\lfloor^{d}\rfloor$.

As we saw in the first part of this section, we could easily rank the subsets of fixed size when listed in colex order. Thus, the most immediate ranking of the nondecreasing functions is in terms of the blanks read right to left. For example, the function 0 3 3 is associated with the set 0 3 4 5 which has rank

$$\rho(0,3,4,5) = \binom{0}{1} + \binom{3}{2} + \binom{4}{3} + \binom{5}{4} = 0 + 3 + 4 + 5 = 12.$$ If

instead we were given the *'s read left to right for 0 3 3, which is 0 4 5, we would first form $(6-5,\ 6-4,\ 6-0) = (1,2,6)$, which has rank $\binom{1}{1} + \binom{2}{2}$

$+ \binom{6}{3} = 1 + 1 + 20 = 22$ in the list of subsets of size 3 from $\underline{7}$, in colex

order, or rank $\binom{7}{3} - 1 - 22 = 34 - 22 = 12$ in reverse colex order, again

giving the rank of 0 3 3 in our basic list.

The general procedure is exactly the same. Start with a nondecreasing function $(\alpha_0, \ldots, \alpha_{d-1})$ in $\underline{r}^{\underline{d}}$. As above, write this function in a linear array:

$$
\begin{array}{c}
\overset{0\ \ 1\ \ 2}{\boxed{\ \ }\boxed{*}\boxed{*}\boxed{\ \ }\boxed{*}} \cdots \overset{m}{\boxed{\ \ }\boxed{*}\boxed{\ \ }}, \quad m = (r+d-1) - 1.
\end{array}
$$

This latter step, of course, is more conceptual than necessary! Locate the ranks of the $*$'s or blanks regarded as a subset of size d or size $r-1$, respectively, of $\underline{d+r-1}$. Depending on how this subset is described (right-left or left-right) apply the appropriate version of THEOREM 3.20 or COROLLARY 3.22 as suggested by TABLE 3.25.

In actually doing this, we of course omit the "linear array." Given $(\alpha_0, \ldots, \alpha_{d-1})$ we can, for example, write down immediately the location of the $*$'s read left to right:

$$\{\alpha_0,\ \alpha_0 + (\alpha_1 - \alpha_0) + 1,\ \alpha_0 + (\alpha_1 - \alpha_0) + 1 + (\alpha_2 - \alpha_1) + 1, \ldots\}.$$

For 0 3 3 in $\underline{5}^{\underline{3}}$ we get $\{0,4,5\}$. For $(5,10,10,30,30)$ in $\underline{50}^{\underline{5}}$ we get $\{5,11,12,33,34\}$. In the latter case the set associated with the blanks has cardinality 49 so we work with the $*$'s! In particular we work with the analog of column B in TABLE 3.25. First go from $\{5,11,12,33,34\}$ to $\{19,20,41,42,48\}$ by subtracting each integer from $(r+d-1) - 1 = (50+5-1) - 1 = 53$. This gives the $*$'s read right to left. The rank of $\{19,20,41,42,48\}$ in the colex

order (see TABLE 3.24) is $\binom{19}{1} + \binom{20}{2} + \binom{41}{3} + \binom{42}{4} + \binom{48}{5} = 19$

$+\ 190 + 10,660 + 111,930 + 1,712,304 = 1,835,103$. Column B is in

reverse colex order so we subtract this figure from $\binom{54}{5} - 1 = 3,162,509$ to

obtain 1,327,406, which is the rank of the nondecreasing function $(5,10,10,30,30)$ in the lex list of nondecreasing functions in $\underline{50}^{\underline{5}}$.

3.26 EXERCISE.

Ponder quietly to yourself the various possible ways suggested by TABLE 3.25 for computing the rank of a function in the lex list of nondecreasing functions in $\underline{r}^{\underline{d}}$. Be sure to give actual examples and to consider such things as the relative sizes of d and r. What happens if instead we work with the colex list of non-decreasing functions in $\underline{r}^{\underline{d}}$?

There is a one-to-one correspondence between nondecreasing functions in $\underline{r}^{\underline{d}}$ and "distributions of d indistinguishable balls into r labeled boxes." To describe the latter set we (a) define how to construct a "distribution of d indistinguishable balls into r labeled boxes," and (b) define when two such constructions are equal. The recipe for (a) is to take d balls $(0,0,. . .,0)$ and distribute them in some manner among r labeled boxes:

$$\boxed{}\,\boxed{0}\,\boxed{00}\,\boxed{}\,\boxed{} \quad \text{or} \quad \boxed{0}\,\boxed{}\,\boxed{}\,\boxed{}\,\boxed{00}$$
$$\;\;0\;\;\,1\;\;\,2\;\;\,3\;\;\,4 \qquad\qquad\;\; 0\;\;\,1\;\;\,2\;\;\,3\;\;\,4$$

We could have first lined up the three balls before putting them in the boxes, tagging each ball with a temporary label giving the box number in which it is to be placed. The above distributions would have been specified by ① ③ ③ and ⓪ ④ ④, or simply by 1 3 3 and 0 4 4. In this manner we clearly have a bijection between nondecreasing functions in $\underline{r}^{\underline{d}}$ and distributions of d indistinguishable balls into r labeled boxes. We can list and rank the former set and hence also the latter. The rank of the last nondecreasing function is of course $\binom{r+d-1}{d} - 1$ and hence there are $\binom{r+d-1}{d}$ distributions of the above type

(a well known classical result).

3.27   EXERCISE.

What is the rank 1,000,000 distribution of five indistinguishable balls into 50 labeled boxes?

In FIGURE 3.3 and EXERCISE 3.4 we discussed the bijection between ordered partitions of a set $\underline{d}$ and functions in $\underline{r}^{\underline{d}}$. The correspondence was given by $f^{-1}(t) = A_t$ where $(A_0,. . .,A_{r-1})$ was the ordered partition of length r. For example, if r = 4, d = 6, and $(A_0,. . .,A_{r-1}) = (\{1\ 4\}, \phi, \{2\ 3\ 5\}, \{0\})$, then $f^{-1}(0) = \{1\ 4\}$, $f^{-1}(1) = \phi$, $f^{-1}(2) = \{2\ 3\ 5\}$, and $f^{-1}(3) = 0$. Thus, f = $\begin{pmatrix} 0\ 1\ 2\ 3\ 4\ 5 \\ 3\ 0\ 2\ 2\ 0\ 2 \end{pmatrix}$ or f = (3, 0, 2, 2, 0, 2) in $\underline{4}^{\underline{6}}$. The ranking of the ordered partitions of length r of $\underline{d}$ in the order corresponding to lex order on $\underline{r}^{\underline{d}}$ is thus immediate from this discussion. If we consider instead only those ordered partitions where $|A_0| = a_0,. . .,|A_{r-1}| = a_{r-1}$ for a fixed multinomial index $(a_0,. . .,a_{r-1})$, then a different ranking and order must be considered.

Suppose that $(a_0,a_1,a_2,a_3) = (2, 2, 1, 1)$, r = 4, d = 6. We may choose any set $A_0 \subseteq \underline{6}$ with $|A_0| = 2$. List the subsets of $\underline{6}$ of cardinality 2 in colex order. There are $\binom{6}{2} = 15$ sets in this list. For each such A_0 set there are $\binom{4}{2} = 6$

subsets of $\underline{d}$ $-$ A_0 that may be chosen for A_1 (again use colex order on these

sets). There are $\begin{pmatrix} 2 \\ 1 \end{pmatrix}$ $=$ 2 subsets of $\underline{d}$ $-$ A_0 $-$ A_1 to choose for A_2 and

$\begin{pmatrix} 1 \\ 1 \end{pmatrix}$ $=$ 1 subset for A_3. In this manner we have a natural bijection between the

functions in $\underline{15}$ $\times$ $\underline{6}$ $\times$ $\underline{2}$ $\times$ $\underline{1}$ and ordered partitions of $\underline{6}$ of length 4
corresponding to the multinomial index (2,2,1,1). List the functions of $\underline{15}$ $\times$
$\underline{6}$ $\times$ $\underline{2}$ $\times$ $\underline{1}$ in lex order and let the order on the partitions be the corresponding
order defined by this bijection. In TABLE 3.28, the initial part of this list is
shown. We write the entries of each block, such as {2,5}, in increasing order
and emphasize this fact by writing (2,5) instead of {2,5}.

3.28 ORDERED PARTITIONS WITH FIXED MULTINOMIAL INDEX.

ρ	$\underline{15}$ $\times$ $\underline{6}$ $\times$ $\underline{2}$ $\times$ $\underline{1}$	(2,2,1,1)—Partitions of $\underline{6}$
0	0 0 0 0	((0,1), (2,3), (4), (5))
1	0 0 1 0	((0,1), (2,3), (5), (4))
2	0 1 0 0	((0,1), (2,4), (3), (5))
3	0 1 1 0	((0,1), (2,4), (5), (3))
4	0 2 0 0	((0,1), (3,4), (2), (5))
5	0 2 1 0	((0,1), (3,4), (5), (2))
6	0 3 0 0	((0,1), (2,5), (3), (4))
7	0 3 1 0	((0,1), (2,5), (4), (3))
8	0 4 0 0	((0,1), (3,5), (2), (4))
9	0 4 1 0	((0,1), (3,5), (4), (2))
10	0 5 0 0	((0,1), (4,5), (2), (3))
11	0 5 1 0	((0,1), (4,5), (3), (2))
12	1 0 0 0	((0,2), (1,3), (4), (5))
13	1 0 1 0	((0,2), (1,3), (5), (4))
14	1 1 0 0	((0,2), (1,4), (3), (5))
15	1 1 1 0	((0,2), (1,4), (5), (3))
	⋮	⋮

Suppose we wish to locate the rank 89 partition of the list of TABLE 3.28.
The functions of $\underline{15}$ $\times$ $\underline{6}$ $\times$ $\underline{2}$ $\times$ $\underline{1}$ in lex order are ranked by THEOREM
3.5. The coefficients are $c_0 = 1$, $c_2 = 1$, $c_3 = 2$, $c_4 = 12$. Thus, $89 = 7 \cdot 12$
$+ 2 \cdot 2 + 1 \cdot 1 + 0 \cdot 1$ or (7,2,1,0) is the rank 89 function in the lex list. To find
the corresponding partition we find the rank-7 subset (colex order) of size 2
from $\underline{d}$. In general we use THEOREM 3.20 to do this. In this case, $\begin{pmatrix} \alpha_0 \\ 1 \end{pmatrix}$ $+$

$\begin{pmatrix} \alpha_1 \\ 2 \end{pmatrix}$ $= 7$ or $(\alpha_0, \alpha_1) = (1,4)$. Next we find the rank-2 subset in the colex list

of subsets of size 2 from the set {0,2,3,5}. This is the set corresponding to (α_0, α_1)

$= (1,2)$ consisting of $(2,3)$—the rank-1 and rank-2 element of $\{0,2,3,5\}$. Continuing in this manner we find the ordered partition $((1,4), (2,3), (5), (0))$ which is the rank 89 partition of TABLE 3.28.

3.29   EXERCISE.

What is the rank 100 partition of TABLE 3.28? What is the rank of the partition $((3,5,9), (0,1,2,8), (4,6), (7))$ in the list of $(3,4,2,1)$—partitions of $\underline{10}$? How would you choose a partition at random from this list?

We remark that in general the procedure for ranking and listing ordered partitions corresponding to a multinomial index $(a_0,...,a_{r-1})$ is directly analogous to the above example. The functions in

$$\underbrace{\binom{d}{a_0}} \times \underbrace{\binom{d-a_0}{a_1}} \times \ldots \times \underbrace{\binom{d-a_0-\ldots-a_{r-2}}{a_{r-1}}}$$

are listed in lex order and ranked as specified by THEOREM 3.5. Given a function $(\alpha_0,\alpha_1,...,\alpha_{r-1})$ in this list construct $(A_0,...,A_{r-1})$ by finding (in colex order) the rank α_0 subset A_0 of size a_0 of $\underline{d}$, the rank α_1 subset A_1 of size a_1 of $\underline{d} - A_0$, etc. Note that the last ordered partition of this list has rank one less than the product

$$\binom{d}{a_0}\binom{d-a_0}{a_1}\cdots\binom{d-a_0-\ldots-a_{r-2}}{a_{r-1}}$$

which equals $\dfrac{d!}{a_0!a_1!\ldots a_{r-1}!}$. This number is called a MULTINOMIAL COEFFICIENT:

$$\binom{d}{a_0\ldots a_{r-1}} = \frac{d!}{a_0!a_1!\ldots a_{r-1}!}.$$

This is the size of the list of ordered partitions of $\underline{d}$ corresponding to $(a_0,a_1,...,a_{r-1})$.

We now consider "unordered set partitions," henceforth called simply "partitions." If $\{A_0,...,A_p\}$ is a partition of $\underline{d}$ we require that $A_t \neq \phi$ for all t and we call these sets the "blocks" of the partition. As usual we can write each such subset or block as a strictly increasing sequence of integers from $\underline{d}$: $d = 8$, $A_t = (1, 2, 5) \equiv \{1, 2, 5\} \subseteq \underline{8}$. In the discussion that follows, we adopt a convention for ordering the blocks of a partition.

3.30   ORDER CONVENTION FOR BLOCKS A$_0$,A$_1$,...,A$_p$ OF A PARTITION.

(1) 0 is in A_0.
(2) the smallest integer not in $A_0 \cup \ldots \cup A_{t-1}$ is in A_t, for $t = 1,...,p$.

Of course, adopting the convention that the blocks of a partition are written in this order does not make the partition an "ordered partition" in the sense used previously because equality of partitions does not depend on the order. We still have $\{(0,1,4,6), (2,3), (5), (7)\} = \{(7), (0,1,4,6), (5), (2,3)\}$ for example.

Given a partition $\{A_0, \ldots, A_p\}$ (blocks in ORDER 3.30) we construct a function f by the rule $f^{-1}(0) = A_0$, $f^{-1}(1) = A_1, \ldots, f^{-1}(p) = A_p$. We may regard f as in $\underline{r}^{\underline{d}}$ as long as $r > p$. For example, to $\{(0,1,4,6), (2,3), (5), (7)\}$ we associate

$$f = \begin{pmatrix} 0\ 1\ 2\ 3\ 4\ 5\ 6\ 7 \\ 0\ 0\ 1\ 1\ 0\ 2\ 0\ 3 \end{pmatrix},\ \text{or simply}\ f = (0, 0, 1, 1, 0, 2, 0, 3).\ \text{The coimage}$$

of f is the partition $\{f^{-1}(t): t = 0, \ldots, p\} = \{(0,1,4,6), (2,3), (5), (7)\}$—the partition we started with. Note that this list of blocks $f^{-1}(0)$, $f^{-1}(1), \ldots, f^{-1}(p)$ is in order. We can easily characterize those functions in $\underline{r}^{\underline{d}}$ that correspond to partitions whose blocks are in order as above. Let RG (for "restricted growth") denote the set of functions $f = (\alpha_{d-1}, \ldots, \alpha_0)$ in $\underline{r}^{\underline{d}}$ defined by

     (1) $\alpha_{d-1} = 0$ and
     (2) $\alpha_t \leq \max (\alpha_{d-1}, \ldots, \alpha_{t+1}) + 1$ for $t = 0, \ldots, d-2$.

For example, $(0,0,1,1,0,2,0,3)$ is such a function but $(0,0,1,1,0,3,0,3)$ is not.

3.31 EXERCISE.

Show that f is in RG if and only if the nonzero blocks of the coimage of f are in ORDER 3.30 when written $f^{-1}(0), \ldots, f^{-1}(p)$.

From EXERCISE 3.31 and the above remarks, we see that making a list of the functions in RG is equivalent to making a list of the partitions of $\underline{d}$ into r or fewer blocks (the case $r > d$ need not be considered for these purposes). The RG functions in $\underline{d}^{\underline{d}}$ ($d = 2,3,4$) with corresponding partitions are shown in TABLE 3.32.

3.32 RESTRICTED GROWTH FUNCTIONS IN LEX ORDER.

	d = 2		d = 3		d = 4
0 0	(0,1)	0 0 0	(0 1 2)	0 0 0 0	(0 1 2 3)
0 1	(0)(1)	0 0 1	(0 1)(2)	0 0 0 1	(0 1 2)(3)
		0 1 0	(0 2)(1)	0 0 1 0	(0 1 3)(2)
		0 1 1	(0)(1 2)	0 0 1 1	(0 1)(2 3)
		0 1 2	(0)(1)(2)	0 0 1 2	(0 1)(2)(3)
				0 1 0 0	(0 2 3)(1)
				0 1 0 1	(0 2)(1 3)
				0 1 0 2	(0 2)(1)(3)
				0 1 1 0	(0 3)(1 2)
				0 1 1 1	(0)(1 2 3)
				0 1 1 2	(0)(1 2)(3)
				0 1 2 0	(0 3)(1)(2)
				0 1 2 1	(0)(1 3)(2)
				0 1 2 2	(0)(1)(2 3)
				0 1 2 3	(0)(1)(2)(3)

Referring to TABLE 3.32, note that for d = 4, the rank 2, 3, and 4 functions (0 0 1 0, 0 0 1 1, and 0 0 1 2) all arise from the function 0 0 1 for d = 3. In terms of partitions, 0 0 1 is (0 1)(2). The corresponding partitions for d = 4 are (0 1 3)(2), (0 1)(2 3), and (0 1)(2)(3), formed by inserting the new symbol 3 into each block of (0 1)(2) successively and finally tagging on the singleton block (3). This is the general pattern. The transition from d = 4 to d = 5 may be seen from TABLE 3.32 and TABLE 3.33. If $S(d,k)$ denotes the number of partitions of d into k parts (or the number of RG functions with image 0,. . .,k−1), then the above pattern implies that $S(d,k) = k\,S(d-1,k) + S(d-1,k-1)$. This classical recursion may be used in general to rank partitions as listed in TABLES 3.32 and 3.33. If this recursion is to be used, however, it is better to linearly order the partitions such that partitions with the same number of blocks occur consecutively in the list. The reader is asked to explore the consequences of this recursion for listing and ranking partitions in EXERCISE 3.50, seen later in this chapter. We now consider a more direct method of ranking the lex list of RG functions and hence the partitions.

Consider in TABLE 3.33 the functions that start off 0 1 1 ∗ ∗. The ∗ ∗ part we call the "tail of length n = 2." The maximum of 0, 1, 1 is m = 1. There are $T(2,1) = 10$ ways to complete the ∗ ∗ and they are completely determined by the rule for generating RG and by the fact that n = 2 and m = 1. *In general, let $T(n,m)$ denote the number of ways to complete a tail of length n with a previous maximum of m.* If we put any j, $0 \le j \le m$, in the first ∗ of the tail, then the maximum for the remaining ∗'s is still m so we have $T(n-1,m)$ ways of completing the ∗'s. If j = m + 1 is the first ∗, then there are $T(n-1,m+1)$ ways of completing. We thus have (define $T(0,m) = 1$):

$$T(n,m) = (m+1)\,T(n-1,m) + T(n-1,m+1).$$

A table computed from this recursion is shown in TABLE 3.34. Note that $T(d-1,0)$ is the total number of partitions of $\underline{d}$.

3.33 PARTITIONS ASSOCIATED WITH RESTRICTED GROWTH FUNCTIONS.

ρ	f in $5^{\underline{5}}$	Coimage of f	ρ	f in $5^{\underline{5}}$	Coimage of f
0	0 0 0 0 0	(0,1,2,3,4)	26	0 1 1 0 1	(0 3)(1,2,4)
1	0 0 0 0 1	(0,1,2,3)(4)	27	0 1 1 0 2	(0,7)(1,2)(4)
2	0 0 0 1 0	(0,1,2,4)(3)	28	0 1 1 1 0	(0,4)(1,2,3)
3	0 0 0 1 1	(0,1,2)(3,4)	29	0 1 1 1 1	(0)(1,2,3,4)
4	0 0 0 1 2	(0,1,2)(3)(4)	30	0 1 1 1 2	(0)(1,2,3)(4)
5	0 0 1 0 0	(0,1,3,4)(2)	31	0 1 1 2 0	(0,4)(1,2)(3)
6	0 0 1 0 1	(0,1,3)(2,4)	32	0 1 1 2 1	(0)(1,2,4)(3)
7	0 0 1 0 2	(0,1,3)(2)(4)	33	0 1 1 2 2	(0)(1,2)(3,4)
8	0 0 1 1 0	(0,1,4)(2,3)	34	0 1 1 2 3	(0)(1,2)(3)(4)
9	0 0 1 1 1	(0,1)(2,3,4)	35	0 1 2 0 0	(0,3,4)(1)(2)
10	0 0 1 1 2	(0,1)(2,3)(4)	36	0 1 2 0 1	(0,3)(1,4)(2)
11	0 0 1 2 0	(0,1,4)(2)(3)	37	0 1 2 0 2	(0,3)(1)(2,4)
12	0 0 1 2 1	(0,1)(2,4)(3)	38	0 1 2 0 3	(0,3)(1)(2)(4)
13	0 0 1 2 2	(0,1)(2)(3,4)	39	0 1 2 1 0	(0,4)(1,3)(2)
14	0 0 1 2 3	(0,1)(2)(3)(4)	40	0 1 2 1 1	(0)(1,3,4)(2)
15	0 1 0 0 0	(0,2,3,4)(1)	41	0 1 2 1 2	(0)(1,3)(2,4)
16	0 1 0 0 1	(0,2,3)(1,4)	42	0 1 2 1 3	(0)(1,3)(2)(4)
17	0 1 0 0 2	(0,2,3)(1)(4)	43	0 1 2 2 0	(0,4)(1)(2,3)
18	0 1 0 1 0	(0,2,4)(1,3)	44	0 1 2 2 1	(0)(1,4)(2,3)
19	0 1 0 1 1	(0,2)(1,3,4)	45	0 1 2 2 2	(0)(1)(2,3,4)
20	0 1 0 1 2	(0,2)(1,3)(4)	46	0 1 2 2 3	(0)(1)(2,3)(4)
21	0 1 0 2 0	(0,2,4)(1)(3)	47	0 1 2 3 0	(0,4)(1)(2)(3)
22	0 1 0 2 1	(0,2)(1,4)(3)	48	0 1 2 3 1	(0)(1,4)(2)(3)
23	0 1 0 2 2	(0,2)(1)(3,4)	49	0 1 2 3 2	(0)(1)(2,4)(3)
24	0 1 0 2 3	(0,2)(1)(3)(4)	50	0 1 2 3 3	(0)(1)(2)(3,4)
25	0 1 1 0 0	(0,3,4)(1,2)	51	0 1 2 3 4	(0)(1)(2)(3)(4)

Using TABLE 3.34 we can easily compute the rank of any partition of $\underline{d}$ for $d \le 8$. For example, consider $(0)(1,3)(2)(4)$ corresponding to f = 0 1 2 1 3. First write $\underline{0}$ 1 2 1 3. Let m be the maximum over the first underlined string and let n be the length of the second underlined string. In this case m = 0, n = 3, and $T(3,0) = \boxed{15}$. Multiply the number not underlined times $T(3,0)$ and record 15 . Now increase the length of the first string by one and decrease by one the second string $\underline{0\ 1}$ 2 $\underline{1\ 3}$ and repeat. Now m = 1, n = 2, $T(2,1) = 10$, so record $2 \cdot T(2,1) = \boxed{20}$. Next do $\underline{0\ 1\ 2}$ 1 $\underline{3}$ to get $1 \cdot T(1,2) = \boxed{4}$. Finally do $\underline{0\ 1\ 2\ 1}$ 3 to get $3 \cdot T(0,2) = \boxed{3}$. Add the boxed numbers to get 42, which is the rank of $(0)(1,3)(2)(4)$.

3.34   TABLE OF TAIL COEFFICIENTS.

n \ m	0	1	2	3	4	5	6	7
0	1	1	1	1	1	1	1	1
1	2	3	4	5	6	7	8	
2	5	10	17	26	37	50		
3	15	37	77	141	235			
4	52	151	372	799				
5	203	674	1915					
6	877	3263						
7	4140							

The corresponding calculation for the partition (0,4,6) (1,2) (3,5) (7) with
f = 0 1 1 2 0 2 0 3 is

$$\underline{0\ 1}\ 1\ 2\ 0\ 2\ 0\ 3 \qquad n = 6,\ m = 0,\ \boxed{877}$$

$$0\ 1\ \underline{1}\ 2\ 0\ 2\ 0\ 3 \qquad n = 5,\ m = 1,\ \boxed{674}$$

$$0\ 1\ 1\ \underline{2}\ 0\ 2\ 0\ 3 \qquad n = 4,\ m = 1,\ \boxed{302}$$

$$0\ 1\ 1\ 2\ \underline{0}\ 2\ 0\ 3 \qquad n = 3,\ m = 2,\ \boxed{0}$$

$$0\ 1\ 1\ 2\ 0\ \underline{2}\ 0\ 3 \qquad n = 2,\ m = 2,\ \boxed{34}$$

$$0\ 1\ 1\ 2\ 0\ 2\ \underline{0}\ 3 \qquad n = 1,\ m = 2,\ \boxed{0}$$

$$0\ 1\ 1\ 2\ 0\ 2\ 0\ \underline{3} \qquad n = 0,\ m = 2,\ \boxed{3}$$

Thus, this partition has rank 1890 in the lex list of partitions of 8.

In these examples we have considered the RG functions in d^{d}. The result of EXERCISE 3.31 is valid for r^{d} for any positive integer r. In general, the RG functions in r^{d} correspond to partitions of d into r or fewer blocks. We may, of course, define analogous coefficients $T^{(r)}(n,m)$ for these functions as well. Start with $T^{(r)}(0,m) = 1$ if $m \leq r - 1$ and $T^{(r)}(0,m) = 0$ if $m \geq r$. The basic recursion $T^{(r)}(n,m) = (m + 1)\, T^{(r)}(n-1,m) + T^{(r)}(n-1,m+1)$ is still valid. These coefficients for r = 3 and 4, $d \leq 8$, are given in TABLE 3.35(a) and (b), respectively.

What is the rank of (0,3,4)(1,2) in the lex list of partitions of 5 into three or fewer parts? The calculations are as just given. Note first that (0,3,4)(1,2) corresponds to the RG function 0 1 1 0 0. Using TABLE 3.35(a), we have

$$\underline{0\ 1\ \underline{1\ 0}\ 0}\quad 1 \cdot T(3,0) = \boxed{14}$$

$$\underline{0\ 1\ 1\ \underline{0}\ 0}\quad 1 \cdot \dot{T}(2,1) = \boxed{9}$$

$$\underline{0\ 1\ 1\ 0\ \underline{0}}\quad 0 \cdot T(1,1) = \boxed{0}$$

$$\underline{0\ 1\ 1\ 0\ 0}\quad 0 \cdot T(0,1) = \boxed{0}.$$

Thus, the rank of $(0,3,4)(1,2)$ in the list of partitions of $\underline{5}$ into three or fewer blocks is 23. Note that this partition has rank 25 in TABLE 3.33. There are two partitions into four blocks, namely $(0,1)(2)(3)(4)$ and $(0,2)(1)(3)(4)$, which occur prior to this one, giving this one rank 23 in the restricted list.

Suppose in the lex list of RG functions in $\underline{3}^{\underline{5}}$ we list only functions where max $(\alpha_4, \alpha_3, \alpha_2, \alpha_1, \alpha_0) = 2$. Such functions are easily generated by the rules: max $(\alpha_4, \alpha_3, \alpha_2) < 1$ implies $\alpha_1 = 1$ and max $(\alpha_4, \alpha_3, \alpha_2, \alpha_1) < 2$ implies $\alpha_0 = 2$. Thus we start off $0\ 0\ 0\ 1\ 2, 0\ 0\ 1\ 0\ 2, 0\ 0\ 1\ 1\ 2, 0\ 0\ 1\ 2\ 0, 0\ 0\ 1\ 2\ 1, 0\ 0\ 1\ 2\ 2,$ $0\ 1\ 0\ 0\ 2$, etc. The corresponding partitions are $(0,1,2)(3)(4)$, $(0,1,3)(2)(4)$, $(0,1)(2,3)(4)$, $(0,1,4)(2)(3)$, $(0,1)(2,4)(3)$, $(0,1)(2)(3,4)$, $(0,2,3)(1)(4)$, ... This is the list of partitions of $\underline{5}$ into exactly three blocks. The reader should scan TABLE 3.33 and rank these partitions $0, . . . ,24$. To rank these partitions in the lex order of TABLE 3.33 we define $E^{(r)}(n,m) = T^{(r)}(n,m) - T^{(r-1)}(n,m)$, where $T^{(r)}(n,m)$ is the tail coefficient for the partitions of $\underline{d}$ into r or fewer blocks. Start with $E^{(r)}(0,m) = 0$ if $m \neq r-1$, else $E^{(r)}(0,m) = 1$. Then apply the recursion

$$E^{(r)}(n,m) = (m+1)\ E^{(r)}(n-1,m) + E^{(r)}(n-1,m+1) .$$

Alternatively, if one has already computed tables of $T^{(r)}$ and $T^{(r-1)}$, one may simply take differences of corresponding entries. The coefficients $E^{(r)}(n,m)$ for $r = 3$, and 4 and $d \leq 8$ are given in TABLE 3.37(a) and (b).

For example, consider the partition $(0,3)(1,4)(2)$ with corresponding function $(0,1,2,0,1)$. We shall compute its rank in the lex list of partitions of $\underline{5}$ into exactly three blocks. Use TABLE 3.37(a):

$$\underline{0\ 1\ \underline{2}\ 0\ 1}\quad 1 \cdot E^{(3)}(3,0) = \boxed{6}$$

$$\underline{0\ 1\ 2\ 0\ 1}\quad 2 \cdot E^{(3)}(2,1) = \boxed{10}$$

$$\underline{0\ 1\ 2\ 0\ 1}\quad 0 \cdot E^{(3)}(1,2) = \boxed{0}$$

$$\underline{0\ 1\ 2\ 0\ 1}\quad 1 \cdot E^{(3)}(0,2) = \boxed{1}$$

Thus, the rank of $(0,3)(1,4)(2)$ is 17.

3.35   TABLE OF RESTRICTED TAIL COEFFICIENTS.

n \ m	0	1	2	3	4	5	6	7
0	1	1	1	0	0	0	0	0
1	2	3	3	0	0	0	0	
2	5	9	9	0	0	0		
3	14	27	27	0	0			
4	41	81	81	0				
5	122	243	243					
6	365	729						
7	1094							

(a) $T^{(3)}(n,m)$—at most three blocks.

n \ m	0	1	2	3	4	5	6	7
0	1	1	1	1	0	0	0	0
1	2	3	4	4	0	0	0	
2	5	10	16	16	0	0		
3	15	36	64	64	0			
4	51	136	256	256				
5	187	528	1024					
6	715	2080						
7	2795							

(b) $T^{(4)}(n,m)$—at most four blocks.

Note: The number of partitions of $\llcorner d \lrcorner$ into r or fewer blocks is $T^{(r)}(d-1,0)$.

3.36 EXERCISE.

(1) Consider (a) all partitions of ⌊8⌋, (b) the partitions of ⌊8⌋ into four or fewer blocks, (c) the partitions of ⌊8⌋ into exactly four blocks, all lists in lex order on partitions. In each case compute the rank of (0,4,5)(1,3,7)(2)(6) and compute the partition that has rank 1000. Write a program to generate the lists.

(2) Two computers working simultaneously are to list the lists (a), (b), and (c) of EXERCISE (1). One computer is twice as fast as the other. The slow computer is to start at the beginning of each list. In each case, at which partition should the fast computer start so that they finish together as nearly as possible? (In each case the two computers work on the same list and never generate the same partition).

3.37 TABLE OF TAIL COEFFICIENTS $E^{(r)}(n,m)$.

n \ m	0	1	2	3	4	5	6	7
0	0	0	1	0	0	0	0	0
1	0	1	3	0	0	0	0	
2	1	5	9	0	0	0		
3	6	19	27	0	0			
4	25	65	81	0				
5	90	211	243					
6	301	665						
7	966							

(a) $E^{(3)}(n,m)$—exactly three blocks.

n \ m	0	1	2	3	4	5	6	7
0	0	0	0	1	0	0	0	0
1	0	0	1	4	0	0	0	
2	0	1	7	16	0	0		
3	1	9	37	64	0			
4	10	55	175	256				
5	65	285	781					
6	350	1351						
7	1701							

(b) $E^{(4)}(n,m)$—exactly four blocks.

Note: The number of partitions of $\llcorner d \lrcorner$ into r blocks is $E^{(r)}(d-1,0) = S(d,r)$.

3.38   EXERCISE.

(1) Write a program that, given a partition and an integer j, produces the rank of that partition and, upon request, the next j partitions in the list.

(2) Write a program that, given d and p, produces the rank p partition of $\llcorner d \lrcorner$. (See THEOREM 3.41 and its following discussion for a general description).

We now describe these techniques in the general case and give proofs.

3.39   DEFINITION.

A function $f = (\alpha_{n-1}, \ldots, \alpha_0)$ will be called a function of m-restricted growth if $0 \le \alpha_{n-1} \le m+1$ and for each $t = 0, \ldots, n-2$, $\alpha_t \le \max(m, \alpha_{t+1}, \ldots, \alpha_{n-1}) + 1$. Denote the set of such functions in $\llcorner r \lrcorner^n$ by $RG(m)$. We write simply RG for $RG(-1)$. Let $T^{(r)}(n,m)$ denote the cardinality of $RG(m) \subseteq \llcorner r \lrcorner^n$. Define $T^{(r)}(n,m) = 0$ if $m \ge r$.

Adopt the convention $T^{(r)}(0,m) = 1$ if $m \le r-1$, and $T^{(r)}(0,m) = 0$ if $m > r-1$. With these conventions the $T^{(r)}(n,m)$ satisfy the basic recursion that follows.

3.40   RECURSION.

$$T^{(r)}(n,m) = (m+1) T^{(r)}(n-1,m) + T^{(r)}(n-1,m+1).$$

We have observed that there is a natural bijection between functions in $RG \subseteq \llcorner r \lrcorner^d$ and partitions of d into at most r blocks, with these blocks ordered in postlex order (with each such f we associate the partition $\{f^{-1}(0) \ f^{-1}(1), \ldots\}$). We order RG in lex order and call the induced order on partitions the "lex order" on partitions. Every RG function $f = (\alpha_{d-1}, \alpha_{d-2}, \ldots, \alpha_0)$ has $\alpha_{d-1} = 0$. Thus, $|RG(-1)| = T^{(r)}(d,-1) = T^{(r)}(d-1,0) = |RG(0)|$ $(n = d-1)$.

3.41 THEOREM.

Let $f = (\alpha_{d-1},\ldots,\alpha_0)$ be in the lex list of RG functions in $\underline{r}^{\underline{d}}$. For each t, $t = 0,1,\ldots,d-2$, let $m_t = \max\{\alpha_j: j > t\}$. Then the function ρ defined by

$$\rho(f) = \sum_{t=0}^{d-2} \alpha_t\, T^{(r)}(t,m_t)$$

gives the rank of f and hence of the partition associated with f on the lex list of all partitions of d into r or fewer blocks.

Proof. The proof of THEOREM 3.41 and many other similar results (such as COROLLARY 3.45 and EXERCISES 3.44, 3.50, 3.52, 3.53) can be described in terms of residual trees analogous to the proof of THEOREM 3.5 and the associated FIGURE 3.6. Consider FIGURE 3.42. FIGURE 3.42(a) shows the complete tree of RECURSION 3.40 for the case r = 4, n = 4, and m = -1. If the edge labeled 3—the bottom rightmost edge—is removed from this tree, we have the tree associated with r = 3, n = 4, and m = -1. In the first case, there are 15 leaves to the tree, corresponding to the fact that $T^{(4)}(4,-1) = T^{(4)}(3,0) = 15$ (as can be read from TABLE 3.35(b)). In the second case, there are 14 leaves, corresponding to the fact that $T^{(3)}(3,0) = 14$ (TABLE 3.35(a)). Each leaf of the tree of FIGURE 3.42(a) corresponds to an RG function as may be determined by reading the sequence of edge labels on the edges connecting the root to that leaf. The path $(\alpha_3,\alpha_2,\alpha_1,\alpha_0) = (0,1,0,0)$ is indicated on FIGURE 3.42(a). The vertices of the tree of FIGURE 3.42(a) are labeled with the parameter m and represent, in each case, the maximum edge label on the path from the root to that vertex. Associated with each level of the tree is a value of n that represents the number of edges on any path from a vertex at that level to a leaf. The general rule for constructing a tree such as that of FIGURE 3.42(a) is shown in FIGURE 3.42(b). This rule is obtained directly from RECURSION 3.40. In FIGURE 3.42(b), each subtree at level n = t that has root labeled m_t has $T^{(r)}(t,m_t)$ leaves. There are α_t such subtrees to the left of the edge labeled α_t, and hence the number of leaves of the residual subtree of that edge is $\alpha_t T^{(r)}(t,m_t)$. Thus, just as in the case of THEOREM 3.5, THEOREM 3.41 follows from the relationship between residual trees and ranks of leaves of ordered trees discussed in connection with FIGURES 1.57 and 1.58.

The reduced tree of FIGURE 3.6(b) is, in the case of THEOREM 3.41, represented by the graph of FIGURE 3.43. The set of all directed paths starting at S in FIGURE 3.43 and ending at either A, B, or C corresponds to all functions in RG(-1) for r = 3 and n = 6. The set of functions RG(1) corresponds to all directed paths from R to either B, C, or D if r = 4 and n = 3. The reader is asked to explore some of the properties of such directed graphs associated with recursions in EXERCISES 3.44, 3.50, 3.52, and 3.53.

The RG functions in $\underline{r}^{\underline{d}}$ which are onto (or alternatively, surjective) correspond to partitions of d into exactly r parts. These functions are easily generated by the rule that if the symbol j $(1 \leq j \leq r-1)$ has not occurred in $(\alpha_{d-1}, \ldots, \alpha_0)$ to the left of α_{r-j-1} then set $\alpha_{r-j-1} = j$.

3.42   RESIDUAL TREE DIAGRAM FOR THEOREM 3.41.

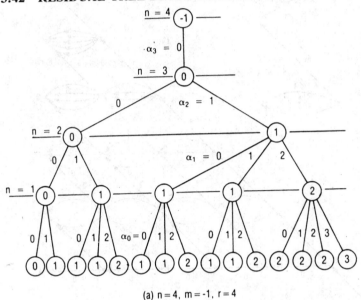

(a) n = 4, m = -1, r = 4

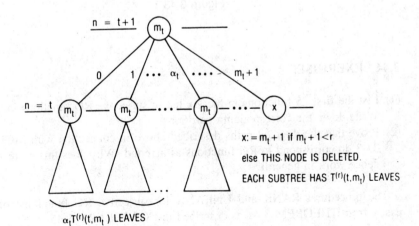

x := m_t + 1 if m_t + 1 < r

else THIS NODE IS DELETED.

EACH SUBTREE HAS $T^{(r)}(t, m_t)$ LEAVES

$\alpha_t T^{(r)}(t, m_t)$ LEAVES

(b) GENERAL CASE

Figure 3.42

3.43 REDUCED TREE DIAGRAM OF FIGURE 3.42.

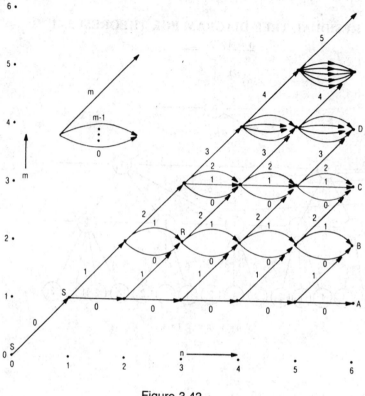

Figure 3.43

3.44 EXERCISE.

(1) List the first 25 functions in the lex list of surjective RG functions in $\underline{3}^{\underline{5}}$. Write down the corresponding partitions.

(2) Prove that the directed paths described above in connection with FIGURE 3.43 do correspond to RG functions as asserted. Why does this correspondence work in general?

The procedures RANK and UNRANK for surjective RG functions follow easily from THEOREM 3.41 as described in COROLLARY 3.45.

3.45 COROLLARY.

The rank of a function $f = (\alpha_{d-1}, \ldots, \alpha_0)$ in the lex list of surjective RG functions in $\underline{r}^{\underline{d}}$ is given by

$$\rho(f) = \sum_{t=0}^{d-2} \alpha_t E^{(r)}(t, m_t)$$

where $E^{(r)}(n,m) = T^{(r)}(n,m) - T^{(r-1)}(n,m)$. This is the ranking function for the lex list of partitions of d into exactly r parts.

Proof. Recall that $T^{(r)}(n,m)$ is the cardinality of $RG(m) \subseteq \underline{r}^{\underline{n}}$, as defined in DEFINITION 3.39. Thus, $T^{(r)}(n,m) - T^{(r-1)}(n,m)$ represents the number of ways of completing an RG function $(\alpha_{d-1},\ldots,\alpha_{n+1},\alpha_n,*,\ldots,*)$ to a surjective mapping on $RG \subseteq \underline{r}^{\underline{d}}$ when $\max(\alpha_{d-1},\ldots,\alpha_n) = m$. Note that if $m = r-1$ the $*$'s can be completed with any function in $\underline{r}^{\underline{n}}$. This is why, for example, column three of TABLE 3.37(b) is a list of powers of 4. With these observations, if we now replace "RG functions" by "surjective RG functions" and "$T^{(r)}$" by "$E^{(r)}$" in THEOREM 3.41, we obtain COROLLARY 3.45.

By either a direct combinatorial argument or by taking the difference $T^{(r)}(n,m) - T^{(r-1)}(n,m)$ in terms of the right-hand side of RECURSION 3.40 and applying the definition of $E^{(r)}(n,m)$, we obtain the following.

3.46 RECURSION.

$$E^{(r)}(n,m) = (m+1) E^{(r)}(n-1,m) + E^{(r)}(n-1,m+1).$$

Note that initially we have $E^{(r)}(0,m) = 1$ if $m = r-1$, 0 otherwise.

In EXERCISE 3.38(2) you were asked to invert (i.e., UNRANK) the order isomorphism of THEOREM 3.41. The basic question is, given p, find the rank p function $f = (\alpha_{d-1}, \alpha_{d-2}, \ldots, \alpha_0)$ in $RG \subseteq \underline{r}^{\underline{d}}$. Of course $\alpha_{d-1} = 0$. The term $\alpha_{d-2} T^{(r)}(d-2,0)$ will appear in computing the rank of f, so choose α_{d-2} to be the largest integer $0 \le \alpha_{d-2} \le 1$ such that $\alpha_{d-2} T^{(r)}(d-2,0) \le p$. If equality holds $(\alpha_{d-1}, \alpha_{d-2}, 0, \ldots, 0) = f$. If not $p \leftarrow p - \alpha_{d-2} T^{(r)}(d-2,0)$, $m \leftarrow \max(\alpha_{d-1}, \alpha_{d-2})$, and α_{d-3} is chosen similarly: $0 \le \alpha_{d-3} \le m+1$, and $\alpha_{d-3} T^{(r)}(d-3,m) \le p$. The general inductive step is easily described. At each state one produces a sequence $(\alpha_{d-1}, \ldots, \alpha_t)$ which is the initial segment of an RG function and which is lexicographically maximal among all such sequences with $\sum_{j=t}^{d-2} \alpha_j T^{(r)}(j, m_j) \le p$. Thus, when $t = 0$, we must have $(\alpha_{d-1}, \ldots, \alpha_0)$ in RG and $\sum_{j=0}^{d-2} \alpha_j T^{(r)}(j, m_j) = p$ if $p \le (|RG| - 1)$. The same technique applies to COROLLARY 3.45. The reader should compare these results to THEOREM 1.60 and to the discussion just preceding THEOREM 1.60 of the general UNRANK procedure in terms of residual trees.

For example, to find the rank 500 partition of 8 into exactly 4 parts we work with FIGURE 3.37(b).

(1) $\alpha_7 = 0$.

(2) $0 \le \alpha_6 \le 1$, $\alpha_6 E^{(4)}(6,0) = \alpha_6 350 \le 500$ gives maximal $\alpha_6 = 1$, $m = \max(0,1) = 1$, $p = 500 - 350 = 150$.

(3) $0 \le \alpha_5 \le 2$, $\alpha_5\, E^{(4)}(5,1) = \alpha_5\, 285 \le 150$ maximal $\alpha_5 = 0$, m $= 1$, p $=$
150 $- 0 = 150$.
(4) $0 \le \alpha_4 \le 2$, $\alpha_4\, E^{(4)}(4,1) = \alpha_4\, 55 \le 150$ maximal $\alpha_4 = 2$, m $= 2$, p $= 40$.
(5) $0 \le \alpha_3 \le 3$, $\alpha_3\, E^{(4)}(3,2) = \alpha_3\, 37 \le 40$ maximal $\alpha_3 = 1$, m $= 2$, p $= 3$.
(6) $0 \le \alpha_2 \le 3$, $\alpha_2\, E^{(4)}(2,2) = \alpha_2\, 7 \le 3$ maximal $\alpha_2 = 0$, m $= 2$, p $= 3$.
(7) $0 \le \alpha_1 \le 3$, $\alpha_1\, E^{(4)}(1,2) = \alpha_1 \le 3$ maximal $\alpha_1 = 3$.

Thus, (0,1,0,2,1,0,3,0) or the partition (0,2,5,7)(1,4)(3)(6) has rank 500 in the lex list of all partitions of 8 into exactly 4 blocks.

3.47 EXERCISE.

Explain and prove the general UNRANK algorithm for inverting the order iso-morphism ρ of THEOREM 3.41 and COROLLARY 3.45. Be sure to describe the general inductive step carefully and relate these descriptions to a general UNRANK procedure in terms of residual trees.

We have considered lex order on partitions, what about colex order? How do the RG functions look in colex order? The RG functions in $3^{\underline{3}}$ in colex order read 0 0 0, 0 1 0, 0 0 1, 0 1 1, 0 1 2. Compare this with TABLE 3.32. The transition from 0 1 1 to 0 1 2 is interesting. Scan 0 1 1 from left to right erasing all entries that are maximal: $\boxed{0\,1\,1} \to \boxed{1}$. The last entry is not maximal as it can be increased to 2 and the initial squares can still be filled in to give an RG function: Thus, write $\boxed{2}$. Now scanning left to right, fill each square with the smallest integer that still is compatible with the definition of an RG function: $\boxed{0\,1\,2}$. The reader should develop some of the analogs of the above results for colex order.

Of course many other linear orders are possible for the partitions. Consider the unrestricted partitions of d. Linearly order them as follows:

d = 1: (0).
d = 2: (0,1); (0)(1).
d = 3: (0,1,2); (0,1)(2), (0,2)(1), (0)(1,2); (0)(1)(2).
d = 4: (0,1,2,3); (0,1,2)(3), (0,1,3)(2), (0,1)(2,3), (0,2,3)(1), (0,2)(1,3),
(0,3)(1,2), (0)(1,2,3); (0,1)(2)(3), (0,2)(1)(3), (0,1,2)(3), (0,3)(1)(2),
(0)(1,3)(2), (0)(1)(2,3); (0)(1)(2)(3).

The order for d is obtained from the order for d − 1. Partitions with k blocks are all consecutive. The partitions of d with k blocks are obtained by first addending the block (d) to each of the partitions of d − 1 into k − 1 blocks in the order in which they appear in that list, then inserting d into each block ((. . .d)(. . .). . .(. . .), (. . .)(. . .d) (. . .). . .(. . .), etc.) of the partitions of d − 1 into k blocks. Clearly, the number S(d,k) of partitions of d into k blocks satisfies the recursion.

3.48 RECURSION.

$$S(d,k) = S(d-1,k-1) + k\, S(d-1,k).$$

A table of this recursion is given in TABLE 3.49. These numbers are often called the STIRLING NUMBERS OF THE SECOND KIND.

3.49 S(d,k)—THE NUMBER OF PARTITIONS OF d INTO k PARTS

n/k	1	2	3	4	5	6	7	8	9	10
1	1									
2	1	1								
3	1	3	1							
4	1	7	6	1						
5	1	15	25	10	1					
6	1	31	90	65	15	1				
7	1	63	301	350	140	21	1			
8	1	127	966	1701	1050	266	28	1		
9	1	255	3025	7770	6951	2646	462	36	1	
10	1	511	9330	34105	42525	22827	5880	750	45	1

3.50 EXERCISE.

Derive a ranking function for the recursively defined linear order suggested above using RECURSION 3.48. Describe the figures analogous to FIGURES 3.42 and 3.43 for this case.

We have classified partitions according to restrictions on the number of blocks. One can also consider the sizes of the blocks. A nondecreasing sequence 1 1 1 2 2 3 3 . . . of positive integers that adds up to d is called an *integral partition* of d. For example, 1 1 1 2 2 2 3 3 is an integral partition of 15. We might also use the notation $1^3\, 2^3\, 3^2$ to specify such a string of integers. How do we list and rank in lex order the set partitions corresponding to a given "type" such as $1^3\, 2^3\, 3^2$? By this we mean those partitions that have exactly three blocks of size 1, three blocks of size 2, and two blocks of size 3. For example, where would (1)(5)(3)(2,4)(6,7)(10,14)(0,8,9)(11,12,13) occur in the lex list of partitions of 15 of type $1^3\, 2^3\, 3^2$? Using lex order on RG functions this question is hard to answer. If we modify lex order, however, this question can be answered in a reasonably straightforward manner. Consider, for example, (1)(8)(2,7)(5,6)(0,3,4) of type $1^2\, 2^2\, 3$. In general we have a partition $\{A_1,. . .,A_p\}$ of type $1^{k_1} 2^{k_2}. . .d^{k_d}$. Consider the multinomial index $(b_1,. . .,b_d)$ when $b_t = tk_t$. In the example, it is (2,4,3,0,0,0,0,0,0,0). Let M denote the list of all ordered partitions of d corresponding to this multinomial index as in our previous discussion of this problem. From $\{A_1,. . .,A_p\}$ construct $(B_1,. . .,B_d)$ where $B_t = \cup \{A_j: |A_j| = t\}$. In the example we construct ((1,8), (2,5,6,7),(0,3,4),\phi,\phi,\phi,\phi,\phi,\phi). Clearly $(B_1,. . .,B_d)$ is of type $(b_1,. . .,b_d)$.

Our first task is to find the rank of $(B_1, \ldots, B_d)$ in the list of ordered partitions of $\underline{d}$ corresponding to $(b_1, \ldots, b_d)$. We do this as previously discussed by considering the functions in Cartesian product space

$$\underbrace{\binom{d}{b_1}} \times \underbrace{\binom{d-b_1}{b_2}} \times \cdots \times \underbrace{\binom{d-b_1-\cdots-b_{d-1}}{b_d}}$$

in lex order. In the example, this space is

$$\underbrace{\binom{9}{2}} \times \underbrace{\binom{7}{4}} \times \underbrace{\binom{3}{3}} \times \underbrace{1} \times \underbrace{1} \times \underbrace{1} \times \underbrace{1} \times \underbrace{1} \times \underbrace{1}.$$

The ordered partition $((1,8), (2,5,6,7), (0,3,4), \phi, \ldots, \phi)$ corresponds to $(29,32,0,0,\ldots,0)$ in this space. $((1,8)$ has rank 29 in the colex order on subsets of size 2 from $\underline{9}$, $(2,5,6,7)$ has rank 32 in colex order on subsets of size 4 from $0,2,3,4,5,6,7,$etc.). The coefficients $c_0 = \ldots = c_7 = 1$, $c_8 = 35$ so our ordered partition has rank $29 \cdot 35 + 32 \cdot 1 + 0 \cdot 1 = 1047$.

Now, fix $\{B_1, \ldots, B_d\}$. Let L_t denote the list of all unordered partitions of the block B_t into k_t blocks of size t. We shall linearly order L_t in a moment! As for now, let $N = L_1 \times \ldots \times L_d$. In our example, L_1 consists of all partitions of $(1,8)$ into two blocks of size 1, L_2 all partitions of $(2,5,6,7)$ into two blocks of size 2, etc. If the L_t are ordered, then N is ordered lexicographically. Thus, $M \times N$ is ordered lexicographically. Clearly there is a bijective correspondence between elements of $M \times N$ and unordered partitions of type $1^{k_1} \ldots d^{k_d}$ (this is just what we have been describing). Thus, it remains only to order each L_t. But an element of L_t has k_t blocks each of size t. They are not ordered so we might as well list the block with the smallest element of B_t first. We are free in general to choose $t-1$ other elements from the n_t-1 remaining elements $(n_t = tk_t)$. This can be done in $\binom{n_t-1}{t-1}$ ways. We may assume that the next block contains the smallest element not yet chosen. Again we choose $t-1$ elements from the remaining n_t-t-1 elements. In this manner we construct a bijection between L_t and

$$\underbrace{\binom{n_t-1}{t-1}} \times \underbrace{\binom{n_t-t-1}{t-1}} \times \underbrace{\binom{n_t-2t-1}{t-1}} \times \cdots \times \underbrace{1}.$$

This latter set we list in lex order. In our example $L_1 \approx \underline{1} \times \underline{1}$, $L_2 \approx \underline{3} \times \underline{1}$, $L_3 \approx \underline{1}$. The partition $(1)(8)$ of $(1,8)$ has rank 0 in L_1, the partition $(2,7)(5,6)$ has rank 2 in L_2, and $(0,3,4)$ has rank 0 in L_3. Thus, translated into ranks, we have the element $(0,2,0)$ in $N = L_1 \times L_2 \times L_3$, which happens to have rank 2 in this list. Thus, in terms of ranks we have the element $(1047,2)$, which has rank $3 \cdot 1047 + 2 = 3143$. Thus, $(1)(8)(2,7)(5,6)(0,3,4)$ is the rank 3143 partition in the above described linear order on partitions of $\underline{9}$ of type $1^2 \, 2^2 \, 3$.

3.51 EXERCISE.

(1) Find the rank of $(1)(5)(3)(2,4)(6,7)(10,14)(0,8,9)(11,12,13)$ in the list of unordered set partitions of 15 of type $1^3 \, 2^3 \, 3^2$.

(2) How would you list, RANK, and UNRANK the integral partitions of n? Construct the analogs of FIGURES 3.42 and 3.43 for your method.

As another exercise we suggest that the reader look back over the basic sets that we have listed and ranked and consider how one might select elements at random (*uniform distribution* on the list) from these lists. Observe that the algorithms for computing the inverse of the ranking function together with a random number table always provides a method for doing this. In many instances, less complicated algorithms than those required to rank the lists will allow for random selection from the lists.

3.52 EXERCISE.

Write a program that, given d and r, selects a partition of d into at most r parts at random from the list of all such partitions.

A standard result about permutations is that each permutation can be written as a product of "disjoint cycles" and this representation is unique up to order of the cycles. We refer the reader to any algebra book. If a permutation has no cycles of length 1 in its disjoint cycle decomposition (corresponding to no "fixed points"), then it is called a *derangement*.

3.53 EXERCISE.

Let $D(n,k)$ denote the derangements of $n = \{0,\ldots,n-1\}$ with k cycles. The standard recursion is $d(n,k) = (n-1)(d(n-1,k) + d(n-2,k-1))$ where $d(n,k) = |D(n,k)|$. The combinatorial interpretation of this recursion is to consider the cycle containing the number $n-1$. If this is a 2-cycle, then there are $n-1$ choices for the other element in the same cycle. The remaining cycles are identified with $D(n-2,k-1)$. If it is not a 2-cycle, then by removing $n-1$ we identify a derangement in $D(n-1,k)$. Using this recursion, describe algorithms for listing, ranking, and unranking derangements. Construct the analogs of FIGURES 3.42 and 3.43.

As a final exercise, we explore some interesting ideas associated with linear orders such as that of TABLE 3.16 and EXERCISE 3.17 (generating permutations by adjacent transpositions of symbols). The basic idea of such a linear order is that adjacent strings of symbols in the list are "very close" to being the same. In addition to the strings being "close to each other" we also want to be able to easily identify (using clever data structures) which symbols are to be changed in moving from one element in our list to the next.

Consider this example. Let $\{r_t : t = 1,2,\ldots\}$ be a sequence of positive integers. Let $\underline{r_t} = \{0,1,2,\ldots,r_t-1\}$, and let $F_n = \underline{r_n} \times \ldots \times \underline{r_1}$. Consider the set of strings of the form $\alpha_1 \ldots \alpha_{3n+2} = a_n \ldots a_1 \, d_n \ldots d_1 \, \ell_n \ldots \ell_0 \rho$ where $a_n \ldots a_1$ is the desired element of F_n and the remaining symbols are defined by ALGORITHM 3.54.

3.54 LOOP FREE ALGORITHM (combinatorial Gray Code).

"Loop free" listing of $\underline{r_n} \times \ldots \times \underline{r_1}$.

Initially we start with $\ell_0 \leftarrow 1$, $p \leftarrow 1$ and with $a_t \leftarrow 0$, $d_t \leftarrow +1$, $\ell_t \leftarrow t+1$
   for $t = 1,\ldots,n$.
procedure LIST $(\underline{r_n} \times \ldots \times \underline{r_1})$
while $p \leq n$ *do*
begin

     write $a_n \, a_{n-1} \ldots a_1$
     $\ell_0 \leftarrow 1;$
     $a_p \leftarrow a_p + d_p;$
     if $a_p = 0$ or $a_p = r_p - 1$ *then* $d_p \leftarrow -d_p$, $\ell_{p-1} \leftarrow \ell_p$, $\ell_p \leftarrow p+1;$
     $p \leftarrow \ell_{0j}$
end
write $a_n a_{n-1} \ldots a_1$

EXAMPLE LIST $(\underline{2} \times \underline{2} \times \underline{3})$ *Changed entries circled:*

a_3	a_2	a_1	d_3	d_2	d_1	ℓ_3	ℓ_2	ℓ_1	ℓ_0	p
0	0	0	+1	+1	+1	4	3	2	1	1
0	0	①	+1	+1	+1	4	3	2	1	1
0	0	②	+1	+1	⊝	4	3	2	②	②
0	①	2	+1	⊝	−1	4	3	3	1	1
0	1	①	+1	−1	−1	4	3	3	1	1
0	1	⓪	+1	−1	⊕	4	3	②	③	③
①	1	0	⊝	−1	+1	4	④	2	①	①
1	1	①	−1	−1	+1	4	4	2	1	1
1	1	②	−1	−1	⊝	4	4	2	②	②
1	⓪	2	−1	⊕	−1	4	③	④	①	①
1	0	①	−1	+1	−1	4	3	4	1	1
1	0	⓪	−1	+1	⊕	4	3	②	④	④	$p = 4$ so *stop*.

There are at most six changes independent of n between list elements. The reader should prove this assertion in general for ALGORITHM 3.54.

3.55   EXERCISE.

Develop a "loop free" listing algorithm for permutations based on the method of "adjacent marks" (see TABLE 3.16 and EXERCISE 3.17). The goal is to be able to keep track of the elements to be switched in each permutation in a way that is "independent of n" in the sense of ALGORITHM 3.54. Describe RANK and UNRANK for your list.

Chapter 4

Topic III: Symmetry—Orbit Enumeration and Orderly Algorithms

In this TOPIC we concern ourselves with the basic problem of selecting a "system of representatives" from the equivalence classes of an equivalence relation on a set S. By THEOREM 1.5, this corresponds to selecting a system of representatives from the blocks of a partition of S. By a system of representatives we mean a subset of S consisting of exactly one element from each equivalence class or block. The reader should review the material in the first chapter from DEFINITION 1.1 to EXAMPLE 1.7.

As usual, interesting results come from exploiting special features of particular classes of equivalence relations rather than from totally general considerations. We consider an important class of equivalence classes called "orbits of group actions." The problem of selecting systems of representatives for these equivalence classes is sometimes referred to as the "isomorph rejection problem." A number of important ideas associated with isomorph rejection problems have already been discussed in EXERCISE 1.38 and in connection with the n-queens problem, in FIGURE 1.62 through FIGURE 1.77.

We first explore some classical combinatorial ideas generally referred to as "Pólya enumeration theory."

It is shown in this chapter that, in spite of some beautiful insights provided by this approach, there are important problems to which these methods don't extend. Pólya enumeration theory is not generally a good tool for actually listing the system of representatives, providing instead methods for counting the number of elements in a system of representatives. To clarify this distinction, we present Pólya enumeration theory from the point of view that shows exactly what it is that is being said about the objects themselves.

Also, Pólya enumeration theory is not stable under slight restrictions on the problem under consideration. From a purely algorithmic point of view, a more useful technique for actually constructing systems of representatives is the method of "orderly algorithms" (if this is your primary interest you should go directly to the paragraph following EXERCISE 4.61). By combining these various methods with the recursive methods discussed in connection with the n-queens problem, the reader will have a number of useful techniques for solving isomorph rejection problems.

We recall some elementary ideas from group theory. If A is a set, then a *binary operation* on A is a map β from A × A to A. We denote the element of A obtained by applying β to (x,y) by juxtaposition of x and y. Thus, β(x,y) = xy. The binary operation is *associative* if (xy)z = x(yz) for all x, y, and z in A. If A is a set with an associative binary operation, then A is called a *group* if it satisfies the following two conditions:

(1) There is a fixed element e in A (called the *identity*) such that ex = xe = x for all x in A.
(2) For every x in A there is an element y (called the inverse, x^{-1}, of x) such that xy = yx = e.

If A and B are groups and ν a mapping from A to B that satisfies the equation $\nu(xy) = \nu(x)\nu(y)$ for all x and y in A, then ν is called a *homomorphism* from A to B. If S is a set, then we denote by PER(S) the set of all permutations of S (see NOTATION 1.6). For S = $\underline{r}$ = {1,2,. . .,r} or S = $\underline{r}$ = {0,1,. . .,r−1} we have used the notation S_r for the permutations of S. If f and g are permutations of S (i.e., elements of PER(S)), then fg is the permutation obtained by composing f and g (thus fg(x) = f(g(x)) for all x in S). The set of all permutations PER(S) is easily seen to be a group with this binary operation (prove it!).

4.1 DEFINITION.

Let A be a group and let S be a set. A homomorphism ν from A to PER(S), the group of permutations of S, will be called "an action of A on S." We write "A: S with ν" for "A acts on S with homomorphism ν." When there is no need to explicitly mention ν we write simply "A: S."

The study of group actions is basically the study of permutation groups. The reason for introducing the idea of a homomorphism of an abstract group is to clarify the intuitive idea of a single group having a number of different ways of acting as a permutation group, as indicated by EXAMPLE 4.2. In what follows we shall adopt our usual convention that sets are finite.

The group A associated with EXAMPLE 4.2 is the "group of symmetries" of the square. This group consists of all rotations and reflections in the plane of the square that leave the set of points representing the square invariant. Obviously, this group can be thought of as the identity, e, rotation counterclockwise by τ = 90°, by τ^2 = 180°, and by τ^3 = 270°, and the four reflections ρ_r, ρ_s, ρ_t, ρ_u, about the axes indicated in FIGURE 4.2.

4.2   EXAMPLE OF A GROUP ACTION: DIHEDRAL GROUP.

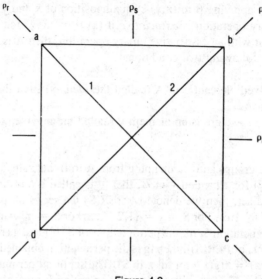

Figure 4.2

A is the group of symmetries of the square: $e, \tau, \tau^2, \tau^3, \rho_r, \rho_s, \rho_t, \rho_u$.
Action of A on vertices $\{a,b,c,d\}$ defined by homomorphism ν:

$$\nu(\tau) = \begin{pmatrix} a\ b\ c\ d \\ d\ a\ b\ c \end{pmatrix}, \ \nu(\tau^2) = \begin{pmatrix} a\ b\ c\ d \\ c\ d\ a\ b \end{pmatrix},$$

$$\nu(\tau^3) = \begin{pmatrix} a\ b\ c\ d \\ b\ c\ d\ a \end{pmatrix}, \ \nu(\tau^4) = \begin{pmatrix} a\ b\ c\ d \\ a\ b\ c\ d \end{pmatrix} = \nu(e)$$

$$\nu(\rho_r) = \begin{pmatrix} a\ b\ c\ d \\ a\ d\ c\ b \end{pmatrix}, \ \nu(\rho_s) = \begin{pmatrix} a\ b\ c\ d \\ b\ a\ d\ c \end{pmatrix},$$

$$\nu(\rho_t) = \begin{pmatrix} a\ b\ c\ d \\ c\ b\ a\ d \end{pmatrix}, \ \nu(\rho_u) = \begin{pmatrix} a\ b\ c\ d \\ d\ c\ b\ a \end{pmatrix}.$$

Action of A on diagonals 1 and 2 defined by homomorphism μ:

$$\mu(\tau) = \mu(\tau^3) = \begin{pmatrix} 1\ 2 \\ 2\ 1 \end{pmatrix}, \ \mu(\tau^2) = \mu(e) = \begin{pmatrix} 1\ 2 \\ 1\ 2 \end{pmatrix},$$

$$\mu(\rho_r) = \mu(\rho_t) = \begin{pmatrix} 1\ 2 \\ 1\ 2 \end{pmatrix}, \ \mu(\rho_s) = \mu(\rho_u) = \begin{pmatrix} 1\ 2 \\ 2\ 1 \end{pmatrix}$$

Imagine now that the square of FIGURE 4.2 is rotated counterclockwise by $\tau = 90°$. The vertex labeled a moves to where d used to be, b moves to where a used to be, etc. We record this transformation of vertices by $\nu(\tau) =$

$\begin{pmatrix} a\ b\ c\ d \\ d\ a\ b\ c \end{pmatrix}$. Similarly, $\nu(\rho_r) = \begin{pmatrix} a\ b\ c\ d \\ a\ d\ c\ b \end{pmatrix}$. From the defnition of the elements

τ and ρ_r of A, it is evident that the result of applying first ρ_r and then τ, which we indicate by the product $\tau\rho_r$, is the same as the reflection ρ_u. To see this, one can think of how the group elements transform the edges of the square, the interior triangular regions, or the vertices. One can also, without thinking at all of the geometry, simply compose the two permutations $\nu(\tau)$ and $\nu(\rho_r)$ to obtain $\begin{pmatrix} a\ b\ c\ d \\ d\ c\ b\ a \end{pmatrix}$ and note that the latter permutation is $\nu(\rho_u)$. The composition, by our rules, of $\nu(\tau)$ and $\nu(\rho_r)$ is computed with the argument on the right. For example, $\nu(\tau)\nu(\rho_r)(b)$ is computed first by computing $\nu(\rho_r)(b) = d$ and then $\nu(\tau)(d) = c$.

4.3 EXERCISE.

(1) Let A be the group of symmetries of the square (FIGURE 4.2). Show that for any reflection ρ, $\tau\rho = \rho\tau^{-1}$. Show that for any fixed choice of ρ, each element of the group A can be written uniquely in the form $\tau^i\rho^j$ where $0 \leqslant i \leqslant 3$, and $0 \leqslant j \leqslant 1$.

(2) Prove that ν and μ of FIGURE 4.2 are homomorphisms. (*Hint*: The previous exercise is a help here.) In fact, ν is also a bijection. A bijective homomorphism is called an *isomorphism*.

(3) Isn't the fact that ν and μ are isomorphisms intuitively obvious? There is one detail worth considering, however. Suppose we had interpreted $\nu(\tau) = \begin{pmatrix} a\ b\ c\ d \\ d\ a\ b\ c \end{pmatrix}$ geometrically as: "a is replaced by d," "b is replaced by a," "c is replaced by b," "d is replaced by c." At first glance it again is "obvious" that ν is an isomorphism. Is it true that ν is an isomorphism with this geometric interpretation? *Hint*. Check that $\nu(\alpha\beta) = \nu(\beta)\nu(\alpha)$ so ν is an *antiisomorphism*.

4.4 NOTATION.

In most instances it is not necessary to make explicit reference to the homomorphism ν in connection with group actions. In this case, instead of writing $\nu(a)(x)$ for the image of x under $\nu(a)$, we simply write ax. If a and b are elements of A, then the fact that ν is a homomorphism is expressed by the identity (ab)x $= a(bx)$ for all x in S (we assume A: S).

4.5 DEFINITION.

Let A be a group and S a set with A: S. We define an equivalence relation $\sim$ on S by s $\sim$ t if there is an a $\in$ A such that as $=$ t. The equivalence classes of this equivalence relation are called the *orbits* of A acting on S.

4.6   EXERCISE.

Prove that the relation ~ defined in DEFINITION 4.5 is actually an equivalence relation in the sense of DEFINITION 1.2.

4.7   DEFINITION.

Let A: S and let s be an element of S. The set of all elements a of A for which as = s is a subgroup A_s of A, called the *stability subgroup of* A *at* s or the *stabilizer subgroup of* A *at* s.

   The orbits of a group A acting on squares with vertices labeled with two symbols are shown in FIGURE 4.8. If s is the first element shown in Orbit 4, then $A_s = \{e, \rho_u\}$ where ρ_u is as shown in FIGURE 4.2. Note that $|A| = 8$ and $|A_s| = 2$ and there are $|A|/|A_s| = 4$ elements in Orbit 4. This is a general result, stated in LEMMA 4.9.

4.8   ORBITS OF A DIHEDRAL GROUP ACTION.

Let S = the set of all functions $\{1,2,3,4\} \to \{g,r\}$, or equivalently, the set of all 2-colorings of the four vertices of a square. If A is the group of rotations and reflections of a square, then A: S has six different orbits.

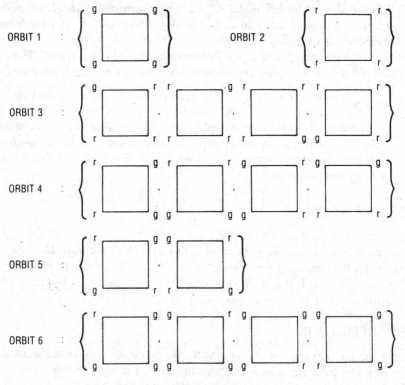

Figure 4.8

The reader should recall from elementary group theory that if A is a group and B is a subgroup of A, then A/B is the set $\{aB: a \in A\}$ of cosets of B in A.

4.9 LEMMA.

Let A: S and for each $s \in S$ let $O_s = \{as: a \in A\}$ be the orbit, of s. Let $A/A_s = \{aA_s: a \in A\}$ be the set of cosets of A_s in A. Then the map f: $O_s \to A/A_s$ defined by $f(as) = aA_s$ is a bijection. Hence, $|O_s| = |A|/|A_s|$.

Proof. Observe that for a and b in A and s in S, we have $as = bs$ if and only if $b^{-1}as = s$ if and only if $b^{-1}a \in A_s$ if and only if $aA_s = bA_s$. Reading this chain of implications from left to right shows that f is a function, and reading from right to left shows that f is an injection. It is obvious that f is a surjection, hence f is a bijection.

It is immediate from LEMMA 4.9 that if $s \sim t$ (i.e., s and t lie in the same orbit) then $|A_s| = |A_t|$. Again, from elementary group theory, recall that if A is a group with subgroups B and C, then B and C are said to be *conjugate subgroups* of A if there is an element $a \in A$ such that $aBa^{-1} = C$. LEMMA 4.10 asserts that elements in the same orbit of A: S have conjugate stabilizer subgroups.

4.10 LEMMA.

Let A: S and suppose that for s and t in S there is an a in A such that $as = t$. Then $aA_sa^{-1} = A_t$.

Proof. Note that $bt = t$ if and only if $b(as) = as$ if and only if $a^{-1}bas = s$ if and only if $a^{-1}ba$ is in A_s. Thus, $A_s = a^{-1}A_t a$.

If A is a group, then we can use the idea of conjugation to define an action A: A. For a in A and x in A define $\nu(a)x = axa^{-1}$. Then it is easily seen that ν is a homomorphism from A to PER(A). We say that "A acts on itself by conjugation." The orbits of this action are called the *conjugacy classes* of A. If x is in A, then the stabilizer subgroup of x in A under conjugation, $\{a: axa^{-1} = x\}$, is denoted by C_x and is called the *centralizer* of x in A. If K is the conjugacy class containing x then, by LEMMA 4.9, $|K| = |A|/|C_x|$.

We now discuss a class of results that are related to "Burnside's Lemma" in group theory. Let A: S be a group action. We order the group elements A and also order the elements of the set S. A matrix M whose entries M(a,s) are indexed by the pairs $A \times S$ will be called an *action matrix* for A: S. An action matrix for the case where A is the group of rotations and reflections of the triangle and S is the set of triangles with vertices labeled either r or g is shown in FIGURE 4.11. In FIGURE 4.11, $M(a,s) = 1$ if $as = s$ and $M(a,s) = 0$ if $as \neq s$. In general, an action matrix M(a,s) that satisfies $M(a,s) = 0$ if $as \neq s$ will be called *stable*. Thus, the action matrix of FIGURE 4.11 is stable. If it is the case that whenever a and b are conjugate elements of A then the row sums $\sum_{s \in S} M(a,s)$ and $\sum_{s \in S} M(b,s)$

are equal, then M will be called *class consistent*. Similarly, if s and t in the same orbit of A: S implies that the column sums $\sum\limits_{a \in A} M(a,s)$ and $\sum\limits_{a \in A} M(a,t)$ are equal, then M will be called *orbit consistent*. Assume addition and subtraction of entries of M are defined (see the examples that follow).

Note that the action matrix of FIGURE 4.11 is both orbit and class consistent. In fact, $\sum\limits_{a \in A} M(a,s) = |A_s|$, the size of the stabilizer subgroup of A at s. Thus, orbit consistency follows from LEMMA 4.10. The row sum $\sum\limits_{s \in S} M(a,s) = |S_a|$ where $S_a = \{s: s \in S, as = s\}$. The reader should verify that if a,b, and c are elements of A with $c^{-1}bc = a$ (i.e., a and b are conjugate elements of A), then $cS_a = S_b$. This fact implies immediately that the matrix M of FIGURE 4.11 is class consistent.

We have, in fact, two actions of the group A. The group A acts on S and also acts on itself by conjugation. Thus, A acts on A × S by the rule, a(x,s) = (axa^{-1},as) where $x \in A$ and $s \in S$. We call this action the *product action of A on A × S*.

4.11 ACTION MATRIX FOR ROTATIONS AND REFLECTIONS OF A TRIANGLE.

		0₁		0₂		0₃			0₄
K₁ {	e	1	1	1	1	1	1	1	1
K₂ {	τ	1	0	0	0	0	0	0	1
	τ²	1	0	0	0	0	0	0	1
K₃ {	ρ₁	1	1	0	0	1	0	0	1
	ρ₂	1	0	1	0	0	1	0	1
	ρ₃	1	0	0	1	0	0	1	1

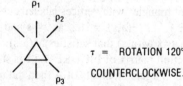

τ = ROTATION 120° COUNTERCLOCKWISE.

Figure 4.11

4.12   DEFINITION.

Let A: S. A stable action matrix M will be called a *Burnside* matrix if $M(x,s)$ $= M(axa^{-1},as)$ for all a and x in A and s in S. In other words, an action matrix M that is stable ($M(x,s) = 0$ if $xs \neq s$) and is constant on orbits of the product action of A on $A \times S$ is a Burnside matrix.

4.13   EXERCISE.

(1) Prove that the "product action" of A on $A \times S$ as defined above is a group action in the sense of DEFINITION 4.1.
(2) Prove that any action matrix M (stable or not) that satisfies the equation $M(x,s) = M(axa^{-1},as)$ for all $a,x \in A$ and $s \in S$ is orbit and class consistent as defined in the discussion following LEMMA 4.10.

4.14   DEFINITION.

Let A: S be a group action. For $a \in A$, $S_a = \{s: s \in S, as = s\}$ is the subset of S stabilized by a. For $s \in S$, $A_s = \{a: a \in A, as = s\}$ is the stabilizer subgroup of A at s. $C_x = \{a: a \in A, axa^{-1} = x\}$ is the centralizer of x in A. Let $\Delta(S)$ be a system of representatives for the orbits of A: S. Let $\Delta(A)$ be a system of representatives for the conjugacy classes of A (the orbits of A: A by conjugation).

4.15   LEMMA (generalized Burnside's lemma).

Let A: S be a group action with action matrix M. If M is a Burnside matrix, then the following are equal:

(1) $\displaystyle\sum_{s \in S} \sum_{a \in A_s} M(a,s)$

(2) $\displaystyle\sum_{a \in A} \sum_{s \in S_a} M(a,s)$

(3) $\displaystyle\sum_{s \in \Delta(S)} \frac{|A|}{|A_s|} \sum_{a \in A_s} M(a,s)$

(4) $\displaystyle\sum_{a \in \Delta(A)} \frac{|A|}{|C_a|} \sum_{s \in S_a} M(a,s)$.

Proof.   Using the fact that $M(a,s) = 0$ if $as \neq s$ (i.e., M is stable), it is obvious that (1) equals (2) because both equal the sum of all of the entries in M. By EXERCISE 4.13(2), (1) equals (3) since $|A|/|A_s|$ is the number of elements in the orbit of s. Similarly, (2) equals (4) since $|A|/|C_a|$ is the number of elements in the conjugacy class of a.

LEMMA 4.15 is an important and very basic tool in many different types of orbit enumeration problems. The action matrix M is more a conceptual tool than a practical one. Conceptually, M is used to give one insights into how to apply LEMMA 4.15. The entries of M can be numbers, variables, polynomials, formal power series, and even the entries of A and S themselves (the symbols of A and S can be regarded as variables in polynomials and formal power series). We shall now give a number of examples of the application of LEMMA 4.15. In the case where $M(a,s) = W(s)$ does not depend on $a \in A_s$ LEMMA 4.15 takes on a particularly simple form which we state in COROLLARY 4.16.

4.16 COROLLARY.

If $M(a,s) = W(s)$ does not depend on the group element a, we have:

(1) $\displaystyle \sum_{s \in \Delta(S)} W(s) = \frac{1}{|A|} \sum_{a \in A} \left(\sum_{s \in S_a} W(s) \right)$

(weighted Burnside's lemma)

(2) $\displaystyle |\Delta(S)| = \frac{1}{|A|} \sum_{a \in A} |S_a|$

(classical Burnside's lemma)

Proof.   Identity (1) follows by setting 4.15 (3) equal to 4.15 (2) and dividing by $|A|$. Identity (2) follows from (1) by setting $W(s) = 1$ for all s.

4.17 ACTION MATRIX FOR EXAMPLE 4.18 (see FIGURE 4.20 for symmetries of triangle)

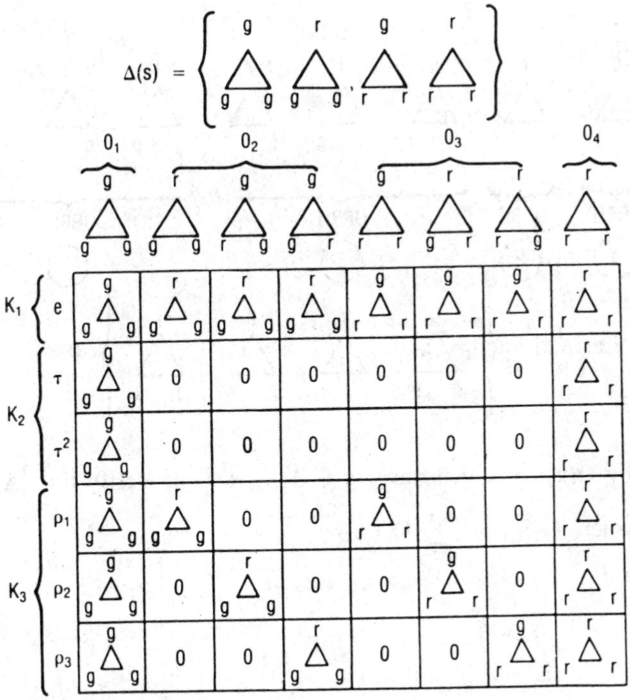

Figure 4.17

As our first example, we consider the "weighted Burnside's lemma" of COROLLARY 4.16(1). The action matrix for this example is shown in FIGURE 4.17. The group is the group of symmetries of a triangle shown in Figure 4.20. We take $W(s') = s$ where s is the unique element of $\Delta(S)$ equivalent to s'. The set of representatives $\Delta(s)$ is shown in FIGURE 4.17. It may seem odd to the reader to take sums of labeled triangles as is done in EXAMPLE 4.18. The easiest way to adjust to this idea is to think of the labeled triangles (i.e., the elements of S in general) as symbols representing variables in a polynomial (a linear polynomial in this case). The reader would not be shocked to see a polynomial in variables x, y, and z or other letters of the alphabet. If our ancestors had chosen to represent the letters of the alphabet with labeled triangles instead of the present symbols then polynomials such as those in EXAMPLE 4.18 would have seemed perfectly all right! The reader should look at EXAMPLE 4.18 in detail but should also interpret the result directly in terms of the action matrix of FIGURE 4.17. Basically, the result says that each element of $\Delta(S)$ occurs exactly $|A| = 6$ times in the action matrix and expresses this fact in terms of row sums.

4.18 EXAMPLE OF BURNSIDE'S LEMMA AS MANIPULATION OF SET ELEMENTS.

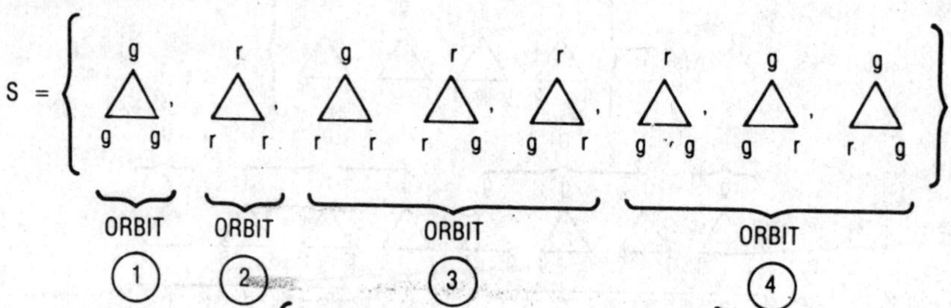

$$S = \left\{ \triangle^{g}_{g\ g},\ \triangle^{r}_{r\ r},\ \triangle^{g}_{r\ r},\ \triangle^{r}_{r\ g},\ \triangle^{r}_{g\ r},\ \triangle^{r}_{g\ g},\ \triangle^{g}_{g\ r},\ \triangle^{g}_{r\ g} \right\}$$

ORBIT (1)   ORBIT (2)   ORBIT (3)   ORBIT (4)

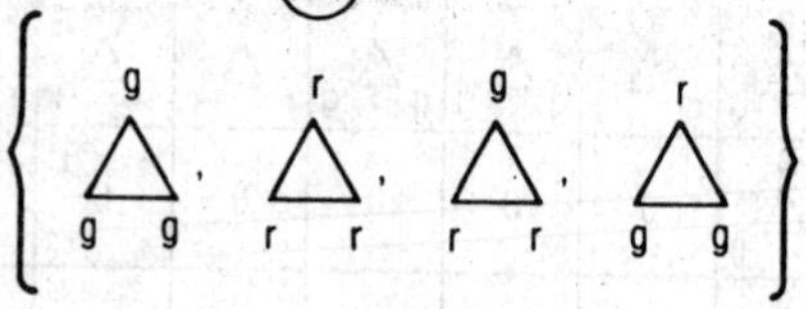

$$\text{Let } \Delta(S) = \left\{ \triangle^{g}_{g\ g},\ \triangle^{r}_{r\ r},\ \triangle^{g}_{r\ r},\ \triangle^{r}_{g\ g} \right\}$$

Define O by $O(x) = s$, whenever $s \in \Delta(S), x \sim s$. Verify that $|A| \sum\limits_{s \in \Delta} s = \sum\limits_{a \in A} O(S_a)$ where $O(S_a) = \sum\limits_{x \in S_a} O(x)$.

$$S_e = S$$

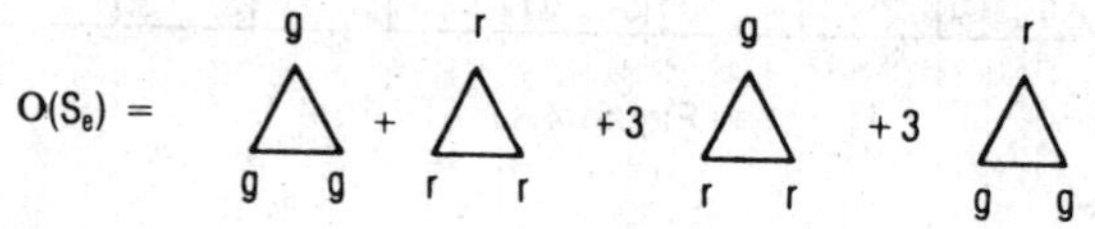

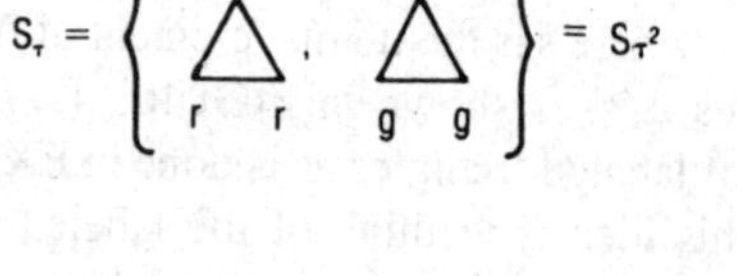

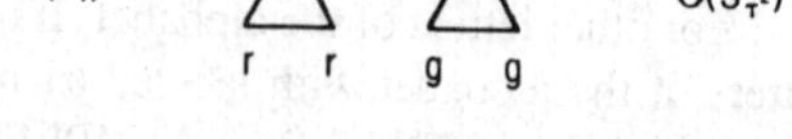

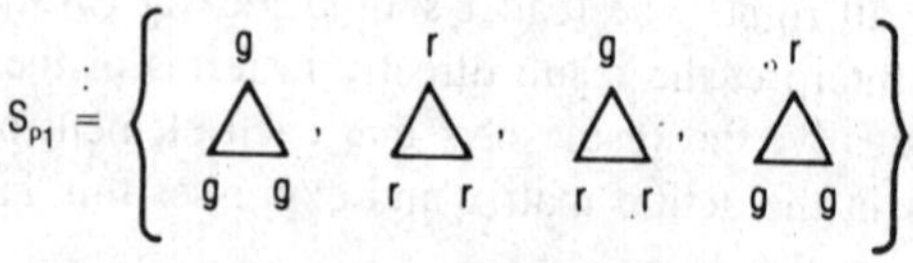

$$O(S_e) = \triangle^{g}_{g\ g} + \triangle^{r}_{r\ r} + 3\ \triangle^{g}_{r\ r} + 3\ \triangle^{r}_{g\ g}$$

$$S_r = \left\{ \triangle^{r}_{r\ r},\ \triangle^{g}_{g\ g} \right\} = S_{r^2}$$

$$O(S_r) = \triangle^{r}_{r\ r} + \triangle^{g}_{g\ g} = O(S_{r^2})$$

$$S_{p_1} = \left\{ \triangle^{g}_{g\ g},\ \triangle^{r}_{r\ r},\ \triangle^{g}_{r\ r},\ \triangle^{r}_{g\ g} \right\}$$

Figure 4.18

(cont.)

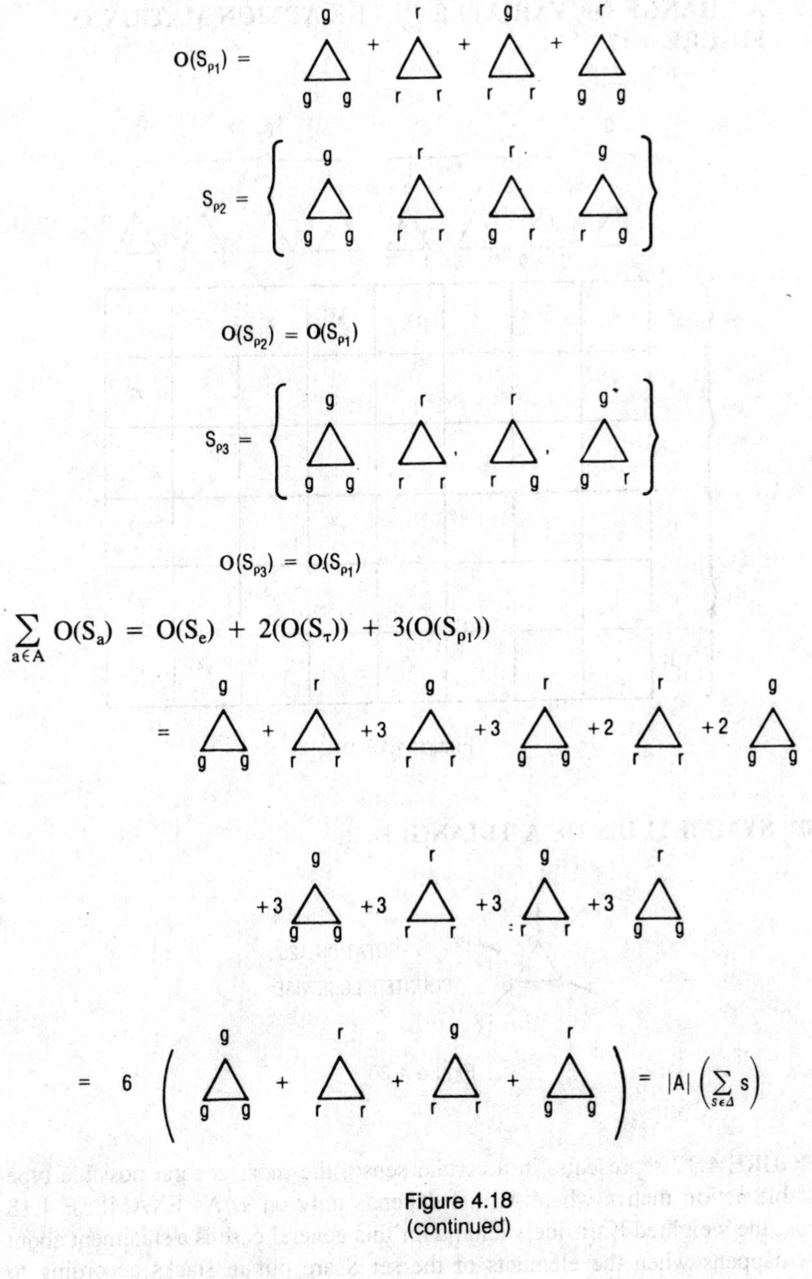

$$O(S_{\rho_1}) = \triangle + \triangle + \triangle + \triangle$$

$$S_{\rho_2} = \left\{ \triangle \quad \triangle \quad \triangle \quad \triangle \right\}$$

$$O(S_{\rho_2}) = O(S_{\rho_1})$$

$$S_{\rho_3} = \left\{ \triangle \quad \triangle, \quad \triangle, \quad \triangle \right\}$$

$$O(S_{\rho_3}) = O(S_{\rho_1})$$

$$\sum_{a \in A} O(S_a) = O(S_e) + 2(O(S_\tau)) + 3(O(S_{\rho_1}))$$

$$= \triangle + \triangle + 3 \triangle + 3 \triangle + 2 \triangle + 2 \triangle$$

$$+ 3 \triangle + 3 \triangle + 3 \triangle + 3 \triangle$$

$$= 6 \left(\triangle + \triangle + \triangle + \triangle \right) = |A| \left(\sum_{s \in \Delta} s \right)$$

Figure 4.18
(continued)

4.19   A CHANGE OF VARIABLE IN THE ACTION MATRIX OF FIGURE 4.17.

		O_1	O_2			O_3			O_4
		g	r	g	g	g	r	r	r
		g g	g g	r g	g r	r r	r g	r g	r r
K_1 {	e	1	x	x	x	x^2	x^2	x^2	x^3
K_2 {	τ	1							x^3
	τ^2	1							x^3
K_3 {	ρ_1	1	x			x^2			x^3
	ρ_2	1		x			x^2		x^3
	ρ_3	1			x			x^2	x^3

Figure 4.19

4.20   SYMMETRIES OF A TRIANGLE.

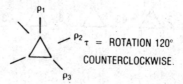

τ = ROTATION 120° COUNTERCLOCKWISE.

Figure 4.20

FIGURE 4.17 represents, in a certain sense, the most general possible type of stable action matrix where M(a,s) depends only on s. As EXAMPLE 4.18 shows, the weighted Burnside's lemma for this general case is a statement about what happens when the elements of the set S are put in stacks according to stabilizer elements. Other weaker statements can be obtained by replacing the objects themselves by various algebraic quantities. Thinking of the objects as variables, this amounts to making a change of variable in the resulting polynomials. In FIGURE 4.19, each object s is replaced by the expression $x^{r(s)}$ where

$r(s)$ is the number of times the symbol r occurs in the object s. In this case, the identity 4.16(1) becomes the expression $1 + x + x^2 + x^3 = (1/6)$ $(6 + 2x + 2x + 2x + 2x^2 + 2x^2 + 2x^2 + 6x^3)$. In more complex examples, the expression for the right-hand side of identity 4.16(1) is easier to compute than the left-hand side of 4.16(1). In this case, both sides are trivial. The expression $1 + x + x^2 + x^3$ tells us that there is one element of $\Delta(S)$ with no r's, one with one r, one with two r's, and one with three r's. For more complex examples this type of information is not obvious.

4.21   EXAMPLE OF THE CLASSICAL BURNSIDE'S LEMMA.

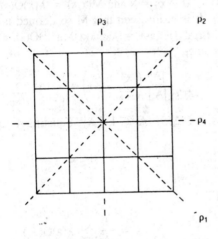

Figure 4.21

Given a square array of 16 squares, how many different ways are there to put 8 x's into these 16 squares, up to rotations and reflections? Let τ be counter-clockwise rotation by $90°$ and let ρ_1, ρ_2, ρ_3, and ρ_4 be the reflections about the axes indicated in the above figure. Let $A = \{e, \tau, \tau^2, \tau^3, \rho_1, \rho_2, \rho_3, \rho_4\}$. Using 4.16(2) we see that

$$|\Delta(S)| = 1/|A| \sum_{a \in A} |S_a|$$

$$= 1/8 \, (|S_e| + |S_\tau| + |S_{\tau^2}| + |S_{\tau^3}| + |S_{\rho_1}|$$

$$+ |S_{\rho_2}| + |S_{\rho_3}| + |S_{\rho_4}|)$$

$$= 1/8 \left(\binom{16}{8} + \binom{4}{2} + \binom{8}{4} + \binom{4}{2} \right.$$

$$\left. + 2 \left(\binom{6}{4} + \binom{4}{2}\binom{6}{3} + \binom{6}{2} \right) + 2 \binom{8}{4} \right) = 1{,}674.$$

For our next example we consider an action matrix M in which $M(a,s)$ depends on both a and s. Let A be any group. Suppose $\lambda: A \to \mathbb{C}$ is a complex valued group homomorphism; i.e., $\lambda(aa') = \lambda(a)\lambda(a')$ for all a, a' $\in$ A. If A' is a subgroup of A, then what possible values can $\sum_{a' \in A'} \lambda(a')$ have? Choose any x $\in$ A'. Then $\lambda(x) \sum_{a' \in A'} \lambda(a') = \sum_{a' \in A'} \lambda(xa') = \sum_{a \in A'} \lambda(a)$. If we let $\beta = \sum_{a' \in A'} \lambda(a')$, this says that if x $\in$ A', $\lambda(x)\beta = \beta$. This implies that either $\beta = 0$, or $\lambda(x) = 1$ for all x $\in$ A' (i.e., $\beta = |A'|$). Hence $\lambda(A') = \sum_{a' \in A'} \lambda(a') = |A'|$ or 0. The former case occurs only if A' $\subseteq$ ker $\lambda = \{a: a \in A, \lambda(a) = 1\}$. Assume A: S. We define $M(x,s) = 0$ if $xs \neq s$ and $M(x,s) = \lambda(x)O(s)$ if $xs = s$ ($O(s)$ as 'in EXAMPLE 4.18). It is easily seen that M so defined is a Burnside matrix as $M(axa^{-1},as) = \lambda(axa^{-1})O(as) = \lambda(a)\lambda(x)\lambda(a^{-1})O(s) = \lambda(x)O(s) = M(x,s)$. Thus, 4.15(3) becomes

$$\sum_{s \in \Delta(S)} \frac{|A|}{|A_s|} \left(\sum_{a \in A_s} \lambda(a) \right) s = |A| \sum_{s \in \hat{\Delta}(S)} s$$

where $\hat{\Delta}(S) = \{s: s \in \Delta(S), A_s \subseteq \ker \lambda\}$. Equating 4.15(2) and 4.15(3) gives IDENTITY 4.22.

4.22   IDENTITY.

$$\sum_{s \in \hat{\Delta}(S)} s = \frac{1}{|A|} \sum_{a \in A} \lambda(a)O(S_a).$$

IDENTITY 4.22 forms the basis for EXAMPLE 4.23 and EXAMPLE 4.24.

4.23   BURNSIDE'S LEMMA WITH A GROUP CHARACTER.

Let S = all functions from $\{1,2,3,4\} \to \{g,r\}$. Let A = $\{e,\tau,\tau^2,\tau^3\}$ where τ is a 90° rotation counterclockwise. S has six orbits under A. Let

$$\Delta = \left\{ \begin{smallmatrix} g & & g \\ & \square & \\ g & & g \end{smallmatrix}, \begin{smallmatrix} g & & g \\ & \square & \\ g & & r \end{smallmatrix}, \begin{smallmatrix} g & & g \\ & \square & \\ r & & r \end{smallmatrix}, \begin{smallmatrix} g & & r \\ & \square & \\ r & & r \end{smallmatrix}, \begin{smallmatrix} r & & r \\ & \square & \\ r & & r \end{smallmatrix}, \begin{smallmatrix} r & & g \\ & \square & \\ r & & g \end{smallmatrix} \right\}.$$

Let $\lambda = \begin{pmatrix} e & \tau & \tau^2 & \tau^3 \\ 1 & i & -1 & -i \end{pmatrix}$. We verify that $1/|A| \sum_{a \in A} \lambda(a)O(S_a) = \sum_{s \in \hat{\Delta}(S)} O(s)$, where $O(x) = s$ if $s \in \Delta$ and $x \sim s$. $\hat{\Delta}(S) = \{s: s \in \Delta, A_s \subseteq \ker \lambda\} =$

$$\left\{ \begin{smallmatrix} g & & g \\ & \square & \\ g & & g \end{smallmatrix}, \begin{smallmatrix} g & & g \\ & \square & \\ r & & r \end{smallmatrix}, \begin{smallmatrix} r & & g \\ & \square & \\ r & & r \end{smallmatrix} \right\}.$$

Compute $\lambda(a)O(S_a)$ for each $a \in A$:

$$\lambda(e)O(S_e) = 1\ O(S)$$

$$= \begin{smallmatrix}g&&g\\&\square&\\g&&g\end{smallmatrix} + 4\begin{smallmatrix}g&&g\\&\square&\\g&&r\end{smallmatrix} + 4\begin{smallmatrix}g&&g\\&\square&\\r&&r\end{smallmatrix} + 4\begin{smallmatrix}g&&r\\&\square&\\r&&r\end{smallmatrix}$$

$$+ 2\begin{smallmatrix}g&&r\\&\square&\\r&&g\end{smallmatrix} + \begin{smallmatrix}r&&r\\&\square&\\r&&r\end{smallmatrix}$$

$$\lambda(\tau)O(S_\tau) = i\begin{smallmatrix}g&&g\\&\square&\\g&&g\end{smallmatrix} + i\begin{smallmatrix}r&&r\\&\square&\\r&&r\end{smallmatrix}$$

$$\lambda(\tau^2)O(S_{\tau^2}) = -1\begin{smallmatrix}g&&g\\&\square&\\g&&g\end{smallmatrix} - 2\begin{smallmatrix}g&&r\\&\square&\\r&&g\end{smallmatrix} - 1\begin{smallmatrix}r&&r\\&\square&\\r&&r\end{smallmatrix}$$

$$\lambda(\tau^3)O(S_{\tau^3}) = -i\begin{smallmatrix}g&&g\\&\square&\\g&&g\end{smallmatrix} - i\begin{smallmatrix}r&&r\\&\square&\\r&&r\end{smallmatrix}$$

$$1/|A| \sum_{a \in A} \lambda(a)O(S_a) = 1/4\left(4\begin{smallmatrix}g&&g\\&\square&\\g&&r\end{smallmatrix} + 4\begin{smallmatrix}g&&g\\&\square&\\r&&r\end{smallmatrix} + 4\begin{smallmatrix}g&&r\\&\square&\\r&&r\end{smallmatrix}\right)$$

$$= \begin{smallmatrix}g&&g\\&\square&\\g&&r\end{smallmatrix} + \begin{smallmatrix}g&&g\\&\square&\\r&&r\end{smallmatrix} + \begin{smallmatrix}g&&r\\&\square&\\r&&r\end{smallmatrix} = \sum_{s \in \hat{\Delta}(S)} O(s).$$

4.24 SECOND EXAMPLE OF BURNSIDE'S LEMMA AND A GROUP CHARACTER.

Let S, A, and Δ be as in EXAMPLE 4.23, but let $\lambda = \begin{pmatrix} e & \tau & \tau^2 & \tau^3 \\ +1 & -1 & +1 & -1 \end{pmatrix}$.

We show that $1/|A| \sum_{a \in A} \lambda(a)O(S_a) = \sum_{s \in \hat{\Delta}(S)} O(s)$, where $\hat{\Delta}(S) = \{s: s \in \Delta,\ A_s$ $\subseteq \ker \lambda\} = \{s: s \in \Delta,\ A_s \subseteq \{e, \tau^2\}\}$

$$= \left\{\begin{smallmatrix}g&&g\\&\square&\\g&&r\end{smallmatrix}, \begin{smallmatrix}g&&g\\&\square&\\r&&r\end{smallmatrix}, \begin{smallmatrix}g&&r\\&\square&\\r&&r\end{smallmatrix}, \begin{smallmatrix}g&&r\\&\square&\\r&&g\end{smallmatrix}\right\}$$

$$\lambda(e)O(S_e) = \begin{smallmatrix}g&&g\\&\square&\\g&&g\end{smallmatrix} + 4\begin{smallmatrix}g&&g\\&\square&\\g&&r\end{smallmatrix} + 4\begin{smallmatrix}g&&g\\&\square&\\r&&r\end{smallmatrix} + 4\begin{smallmatrix}g&&g\\&\square&\\r&&r\end{smallmatrix}$$

$$+ 2\begin{smallmatrix}g&&r\\&\square&\\r&&g\end{smallmatrix} + \begin{smallmatrix}r&&r\\&\square&\\r&&r\end{smallmatrix}$$

$$\lambda(\tau)O(S_\tau) = -\begin{smallmatrix}g&&g\\&\square&\\g&&g\end{smallmatrix} - \begin{smallmatrix}r&&r\\&\square&\\r&&r\end{smallmatrix} = \lambda(\tau^3)O(S_{\tau^3})$$

$$\lambda(\tau^2)O(S_{\tau^2}) = \begin{smallmatrix}g&&g\\&\square&\\g&&g\end{smallmatrix} + 2\begin{smallmatrix}g&&r\\&\square&\\r&&g\end{smallmatrix} + \begin{smallmatrix}r&&r\\&\square&\\r&&r\end{smallmatrix}. \text{ So}$$

4.25 IDENTITY.

$$1/|A| \sum_{a \in A} \lambda(a)O(S_a) = 1/4 \left(4 \; {}^g_g\square^{\dot g}_r + 4 \; {}^g_r\square^g_r + 4 \; {}^g_r\square^r_r + 4 \; {}^g_r\square^r_g \right)$$

$$= {}^g_g\square^g_r + {}^g_r\square^g_r + {}^g_r\square^r_r + {}^g_r\square^r_g$$

$$= \sum_{s \in \hat\Delta(S)} O(s).$$

4.26 EXERCISE.

(1) Use the ideas associated with LEMMA 4.15 and COROLLARY 4.16 to discuss EXERCISE 1.38(4) and (5).
(2) Use the ideas associated with LEMMA 4.15 and COROLLARY 4.16 to discuss the domino covering problem of FIGURE 1.37, EXERCISE 1.38(2) and (3). Try to analyze some larger boards than the 4 × 4 board.
(3) Use the ideas associated with LEMMA 4.15 and COROLLARY 4.16 to analyze the problem of covering a 2 × n board with dominoes.

We conclude our discussion of Burnside's lemma and its variations by proving White's lemma on orbit representatives with conjugate stability subgroups.

4.27 NOTATION.

We define $X(statement) = 1$ if *statement* is true and $X(statement) = 0$ if *statement* is false.

Consider $\sum_{s \in S} W(s)X(H \subseteq A_s)$ where $W(s)$ is as in COROLLARY 4.16. This sum represents all values of W for elements of s whose stability subgroup contains a fixed group H as a subgroup. For many examples, this sum is not too difficult to calculate and, so it seems, is also not very interesting! A much more interesting and difficult sum to compute is $\sum_{s \in \Delta(S)} W(s)X(A_s \sim K)$ where K is a fixed subgroup of A. This sum represents all elements s in $\Delta(S)$ (DEFINITION 4.14) whose stability subgroups A_s are conjugate to a fixed subgroup K (the notation $A_s \sim K$ means "A_s is conjugate to K"). There is a remarkable relationship between these two sums that represents an important combinatorial technique (one that we shall see more of in Chapter 5). Using the fact that W is constant on orbits of A: S, we see that $\sum_{s \in S} W(s)X(H \subseteq A_s) = \sum_{s \in \Delta(S)} W(s) \left(\sum_{s' \sim s} X(H \subseteq A_{s'}) \right)$. Note that $\sum_{s' \sim s} f(s') = \frac{1}{|A_s|} \sum_{a \in A} f(as)$ for any function f so that above sum becomes

$$\sum_{s\in\Delta(S)} \frac{W(s)}{|A_s|} \left(\sum_{a\in A} \chi(H \subseteq A_{as}) \right) \quad \text{which, from LEMMA 4.10, equals}$$

$$\sum_{s\in\Delta(S)} \frac{W(s)}{|A_s|} \left(\sum_{a\in A} \chi(a^{-1}Ha \subseteq A_s) \right).$$ If we let $\mathscr{A}$ be the set of all subgroups of A, then A acts on $\mathscr{A}$ by conjugation ($K \in \mathscr{A}$ is sent to aKa^{-1}). Let $\mathscr{H}$ be a list of orbit representatives for this action (a complete list of nonconjugate subgroups). Using the fact that $\sum_{a\in A} \chi(a^{-1}Ha \subseteq A_s) = \sum_{a\in A} \chi(aHa^{-1} \subseteq A_s)$. We can now rewrite the above expression as $\displaystyle\sum_{K\in\mathscr{H}} \sum_{s\in\Delta} \frac{W(s)}{|A_s|} \chi(A_s \sim K) \sum_{a\in A} \chi(aHa^{-1} \subseteq A_s)$

$$= \sum_{K\in\mathscr{H}} \left(\frac{1}{|K|} \sum_{a\in A} \chi(aHa^{-1} \subseteq K) \right) \sum_{s\in\Delta(S)} W(s)\chi(A_s \sim K).$$ To get this expression we have simply reorganized the sum over $s \in \Delta \equiv \Delta(s)$ according to the element $K \in \mathscr{H}$ to which A_s is conjugate. We use the fact that $\sum_{a\in A} \chi(aHa^{-1} \subseteq A_s)$

$$= \sum_{a\in A} \chi(aHa^{-1} \subseteq K)$$ if A_s is conjugate to K. These observations lead one to DEFINITION 4.28 and THEOREM 4.29.

4.28 DEFINITION.

Let H and K be subgroups of A. We define $M_K(H)$, called the *mark of* K *at* H, to be the sum

$$\frac{1}{|K|} \sum_{a\in A} \chi(aHa^{-1} \subseteq K).$$

We have thus proved LEMMA 4.29.

4.29 LEMMA (White's lemma).

Let W be constant on orbits of A: S. Then

$$\sum_{K\in\mathscr{H}} M_K(H) \sum_{s\in\Delta(S)} W(s)\chi(A_s \sim K) = \sum_{s\in S} W(s)\chi(H \subseteq A_s).$$

It is conceptually useful to interpret White's lemma in matrix terms. Order the complete list of nonconjugate subgroups $K_1, K_2, \ldots, K_p$ such that $|K_1| \geqslant |K_2| \geqslant \ldots \geqslant |K_p|$. Define a $p \times p$ matrix $\mathscr{M}$ whose entry in the position i,j is $M_{K_j}(K_i)$. Obviously, $\mathscr{M}$ is lower triangular with nonzero diagonal entries.

4.30 DEFINITION.

The nonsingular lower triangular matrix $\mathscr{M} = (M_{K_j}(K_i))$, where $|K_1| \geqslant |K_2| \geqslant \ldots \geqslant |K_p|$ is a complete list of nonconjugate subgroups of A, is called the *matrix of marks* of A.

Let X denote the $p \times 1$ column vector with j^{th} entry $\sum\limits_{s \in \Delta(S)} W(s)X(A_s \sim K_j)$ and let Y denote the $p \times 1$ column vector with i^{th} entry $\sum\limits_{s \in S} W(s)X(K_i \subseteq A_s)$. Then IDENTITY 4.31 gives the matrix version of White's lemma.

4.31   IDENTITY (Matrix version of White's lemma).

$$\mathcal{M}X = Y \text{ and } X = \mathcal{M}^{-1}Y.$$

Given $\mathcal{M}$, the matrix $\mathcal{M}^{-1}$ is easily computed since $\mathcal{M}$ is lower triangular. The matrix $\mathcal{M}$ itself is not generally easy to compute. It is possible to compute $\mathcal{M}$ for certain important crystallographic groups. For some interesting applications of White's lemma, see the articles by McLarnan and McLarnan and Moore cited in the references at the end of PART I.

4.32   EXERCISE.

(1) Let A be a group with subgroups K and H. Show that the mark of K at H, $M_K(H)$, is given by the formula $\dfrac{|A| \, [H \subseteq K]}{|K| \, [H]}$ where $[H \subseteq K]$ denotes the number of subgroups of A conjugate to H and contained in K and $[H] = [H \subseteq A]$.

(2) Calculate the matrix of marks for the symmetry groups of the triangle and square.

(3) TABLE 4.33 gives the list of nonconjugate subgroups for the rotations and reflections of the hexagon. The matrix of marks for this group is also given in TABLE 4.33. Compute the vector X of IDENTITY 4.31 for the case where S is the set of all hexagons labeled with two symbols g and r. Do the same when S is the set of labeled hexagons of EXERCISE 1.38(5).

4.33   MATRIX OF MARKS FOR THE SYMMETRY GROUP OF THE HEXAGON.

$K_1 = G$;

$K_2 = $ cyclic group of order 6;

$K_3 = $ dihedral group of order 6 generated by 120° rotation and reflection through line through opposite vertices;

$K_4 = $ dihedral group of order 6 generated by 120° rotation and reflection through line through opposite midpoints;

$K_5 = $ dihedral group of order 4 generated by 180° rotation and a reflection;

$K_6 = $ cyclic group of order 3;

$K_7 = $ cyclic group of order 2 generated by 180° rotation;

$K_8 = $ cyclic group of order 2 generated by reflection through line through opposite vertices;

K_9 = cyclic group of order 2 generated by reflection through line through opposite midpoints;

K_{10} = identity.

$$
\mathcal{M} = \begin{bmatrix}
1 \\
1\ 2 \\
1\ 0\ 2 & & & & 0 \\
1\ 0\ 0\ 2 \\
1\ 0\ 0\ 0\ 1 \\
1\ 2\ 2\ 2\ 0\ 4 \\
1\ 2\ 0\ 0\ 3\ 0\ 6 \\
1\ 0\ 2\ 0\ 1\ 0\ 0\ 2 \\
1\ 0\ 0\ 2\ 1\ 0\ 0\ 0\ 2 \\
1\ 2\ 2\ 2\ 3\ 4\ 6\ 6\ 6\ 12
\end{bmatrix}
$$

We now consider some interesting results, such as the classical Pólya's enumeration theorem, which are specializations of the generalized Burnside's lemmas (LEMMA 4.15 and COROLLARY 4.16). These results gain computational advantage by restricting the group action A: S and the action matrix M or "weight function" W of LEMMA 4.15 or COROLLARY 4.16. The set S will be a set of functions, R^D, and the group A will act on these functions by permuting the elements of D. The cycle structure of permutations of D will play a critical role here, so we first review some ideas already familiar to the reader in order to collect together the necessary terminology.

Let D and R be sets. A function f from D to R is a rule that assigns to each element of D an element of R. Each element of D must be assigned something in R. The set D is called the *domain* of the function and the set B is called the *range*. The set $\{f(x): x \in D\}$ is called the *image* of f.

4.34   EXAMPLE OF FUNCTIONS f: D → R.

Here, the *domain* of the function is D, the *range* is R, the *image* is {a,c,d}. The arrows indicate the element of R that is being assigned to a particular element of D.

This function is *surjective* or *onto* because its image is equal to its range. To be precise, if $y \in R$, then there exists $x \in D$ such that $f(x) = y$.

Figure 4.34, cont.

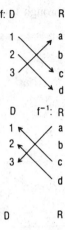

This function is *injective* or one-to-one because each element of D is assigned to a different element of R. In other words, if x,y $\in$ D and x $\neq$ y, then f(x) $\neq$ f(y).

Every injective function has an "inverse" function denoted by f^{-1}. The domain of the inverse is the image of f. Clearly, f^{-1} is also injective. The function shown here is the inverse of the preceding example.

A function that is both injective and surjective is called bijective. The image of a bijective function is its range. In this case, f^{-1} is also a bijection. If f is a bijection, then D and R must have the same size (if they are finite). For finite sets, there exists a bijection f: D $\rightarrow$ R if and only if D and R have the same size (or "cardinality").

If f is a bijection and D equals R, then f is called a permutation of D. The set of all permutations of D is designated PER(D). When D = $\underline{n}$ or $\underline{n}$, we have used $S_n \equiv$ PER(D).

Figure 4.34

There are many ways of describing functions. Any such description must specify the domain, the range, and, for each element of the domain, the rule for computing the corresponding element of the range.

Here are some different ways of writing the function given by the first diagram in EXAMPLE 4.34: (1,a), (2,c), (3,a), (4,d) or $\begin{pmatrix} 1234 \\ acad \end{pmatrix}$ or "assign a to 1 and 3, c to 2, and d to 4." If D is infinite (all integers, the real numbers, etc.), then a tabulation of all values of the function is impossible. Instead, tables for some values are given if the function has a smooth graph (like sin and cos) or a rule for computing the corresponding value is given (like f(x) = x^2).

Of particular interest are ways of writing permutations of finite sets. The permutation of EXAMPLE 4.34 (the last diagram) can be written in three standard ways: $\begin{pmatrix} 1234 \\ 4213 \end{pmatrix}$ or 4213 or (143)(2). The first way is called "two-line notation,"

the second way is called "one-line notation," and the third way is called "cycle notation." One-line notation is the same as two-line notation except that the domain values are just imagined to be there. The cycle notation is really different. The cycle f = (143) is read "1 goes to 4 (i.e., f(1) = 4), 4 goes to 3, 3 goes to 1." The cycle (2) is read "2 goes to 2." If the domain of the permutation is known, then cycles like (2) are omitted from the cycle notation. Thus, (143)(2) equals (143) *plus* the information that the domain is {1,2,3,4}.

If f and g are permutations then the "product" of f and g, written fg, is the *composition* of f and g as functions: fg(x) = f(g(x)). Suppose, for example, that f = (143) and g = (1562) are permutations of A = {1,2,3,4,5,6}. To "compose" f and g (i.e., to compute fg) we must compute for each integer x ∈ A *first* g(x) and *then* f(g(x)). Take x = 5. Then g(5) = 6 and f(6) = 6. Thus, fg(5) = 6. For x = 2, g(2) = 1 and f(1) = 4. By going through the elements of the set A (in any order) one computes fg in two line notation fg = $\begin{pmatrix} 123456 \\ 541362 \end{pmatrix}$. In cycle notation fg = (156243). The reader should practice composing functions in both two-line notation and in cycle notation.

4.35 EXERCISE.

(1) Write down three pairs of permutations and compose them. Work both in two-line notation and in cycle notation.
(2) Write down five permutations of 1,2,3,4,5,6,7,8 in two-line notation and convert each one to cycle notation.

Every cycle can be written as a product of cycles of length two in many different ways. For example (1432) = (23)(14)(24) = (12)(13)(14) = (14)(42)(43) = (12)(13)(14)(43)(42)(14)(23)(14)(24). The reader should verify these expressions. Note that the number of cycles in the first three cases is three and in the last case is nine. A cycle of length two is called a *transposition*. It is a general result that whenever a cycle is written in different ways as a product of transpositions, then the number of transpositions in the different products have the same "parity." That is, both numbers are odd or both are even.

Two cycles are said to be disjoint if they have no entries in common. A permutation written such as (25174)(346) where the cycles are pair-wise disjoint is said to be written in "disjoint cycle" notation. By permuting the symbols cyclically in any cycle, that cycle is not changed *as a permutation*: (2517) = (5172) = (1725) = (7251). Also, in disjoint cycle notation the cycles themselves may be written down in any order ((2517)(346) or (346)(2517) for example). The *disjoint cycle notation* is unique up to these transformations. If any permutation is written in two different ways as a product of transpositions then the result mentioned above for single cycles is still true (the parity of the number of transpositions in each case is the same).

4.36 DEFINITION (Pólya action).

Suppose A acts on D, A: D, D finite. Let $S = R^D$, where both D and R are finite sets (i.e., $S =$ all functions from D to R). Then we can define an action of A on R^D by

$$(af)(x) = f(a^{-1}x), \text{ for all } a \in A, f \in R^D, x \in D$$

Note that for a and b in A, $(ab)f(x) = f((ab)^{-1}x) = f(b^{-1}a^{-1}x) = a(bf(x))$ and hence $(ab)f = a(bf)$ so the rule of DEFINITION 4.36 does define an action of A on S. This action is called the *Pólya action* of A on S.

4.37 EXAMPLE OF PÓLYA ACTIONS.

(1) Let $D = \{1,2,3,4\}$, $R = \{g\ r\ t\}$, $A = S_4$. Consider $\tau = (1\ 2\ 3\ 4) \in A$. If

$$f = \begin{pmatrix} 1\ 2\ 3\ 4 \\ g\ r\ g\ r \end{pmatrix}, \tau f = \begin{pmatrix} 1\ 2\ 3\ 4 \\ r\ g\ r\ g \end{pmatrix}. \text{ If } f = \begin{pmatrix} 1\ 2\ 3\ 4 \\ g\ r\ t\ r \end{pmatrix}, \tau f = \begin{pmatrix} 1\ 2\ 3\ 4 \\ r\ g\ r\ t \end{pmatrix},$$

etc.

(2) $S = \{g,r\}^{\{1,2,3,4\}}$, $A = \{e,\tau,\tau^2,\tau^3\}$, where $\tau = (1\ 2\ 3\ 4)$. Note $\tau^2 = (1\ 3)(2\ 4)$, and S_{τ^2}, the functions unchanged by τ^2, are given by

$$S_{\tau^2} = \begin{pmatrix} 1\ 3\ 2\ 4 \\ g\ g\ r\ r \end{pmatrix}, \begin{pmatrix} 1\ 3\ 2\ 4 \\ r\ r\ g\ g \end{pmatrix}, \begin{pmatrix} 1\ 3\ 2\ 4 \\ g\ g\ g\ g \end{pmatrix}, \begin{pmatrix} 1\ 3\ 2\ 4 \\ r\ r\ r\ r \end{pmatrix}$$

$$\cong \begin{pmatrix} (1\ 3)\ (2\ 4) \\ g \qquad r \end{pmatrix}, \begin{pmatrix} (1\ 3)\ (2\ 4) \\ r \qquad g \end{pmatrix}, \begin{pmatrix} (1\ 3)\ (2\ 4) \\ g \qquad g \end{pmatrix}, \begin{pmatrix} (1\ 3)\ (2\ 4) \\ r \qquad r \end{pmatrix}.$$

In fact, for all $a \in A$, $S_a = \{f: af = f\} \cong R^{cyc(a)}$ where cyc(a) is the set of all disjoint cycles of a (including cycles of length one).

The last observation of EXAMPLE 4.37(2) is extremely important to our present discussion: there is a natural correspondence between the functions unchanged by the action of a fixed permutation $a \in A$ and the set of *all* functions from cyc(a) to R, denoted by $R^{cyc(a)}$. This correspondence is shown in EXAMPLE 4.37(2) and extends in an obvious way to the general case.

In our discussion of the generalized Burnside lemma previously mentioned, we adopted the point of view that the objects of the sets themselves could be viewed as "variables" in polynomials. To adopt that point of view here would be to treat the functions $f \in R^D$ as variables. This is fine, and was done in EXAMPLE 4.18 where D was the vertices of the triangle and $R = \{g,r\}$. A natural variation of this idea in our present discussion is to think of the elements of D and R as variables. This can be done no matter what the elements of D and R are. In the following examples, we shall want to be free to choose D and R to suit the problem at hand. If however, $D = \{1,2,3\}$ and we think of the objects of D as "variables" rather than integers, then one might confuse the polynomial $2^2 + 2 + 3$ with an arithmetic statement about integers. If, on the other hand, we set $D = \{x_1, x_2, x_3\}$, then the same polynomial becomes $x_2^2 + x_2 + x_3$ and there is no confusion. When we wish to avoid such confusions, we shall choose $D = \{x_1, x_2, \ldots, x_d\}$ and $R = \{y_1, y_2, \ldots, y_r\}$ as sets of variables. Otherwise, we shall choose D and R for conceptual or notational convenience:

4.38 DEFINITION.

Let $D = \{x_1, x_2, \ldots, x_d\}$ and $R = \{y_1, y_2, \ldots, y_r\}$. Given $f \in R^D$, define

$$O(f) = \prod_{j=1}^{r} y_j^{|f^{-1}(y_j)|} = \prod_{i=1}^{d} f(x_i).$$

We call the reader's attention to the difference between $O(f)$ of DEFINITION 4.38 and $O(x)$ of EXAMPLE 4.18. The latter is an "Orbit selection" function and hence has different values on different orbits. $O(f)$ may equal $O(h)$ even though f and h are in different orbits of $A: R^D$ (see EXAMPLE 4.39(2)).

4.39 EXAMPLES OF DEFINITION 4.38.

(1) If $f = \begin{pmatrix} x_1 & x_2 & x_3 & x_4 \\ y_1 & y_2 & y_1 & y_2 \end{pmatrix}$, $O(f) = \prod_{i=1}^{4} f(x_i) = y_1 y_2 y_1 y_2 = y_1^2 y_2^2.$

(2) Note $O(S_a) = \sum_{f \in S_a} O(f) = \sum_{f \in S_a} \prod_{i=1}^{d} f(x_i)$. But since $S_a \cong R^{\mathrm{cyc}(a)}$ the sum

$\sum_{f \in S_a} \prod_{i=1}^{d} f(x_i)$ is equal to $\sum_{g \in R^{\mathrm{cyc}(a)}} \prod_{c \in \mathrm{cyc}(a)} (g(c))^{|c|}$ where $g(c)$ is the value of f at any element c of $\mathrm{cyc}(a)$ and $|c|$ is the length (number of elements) of the cycle c. For instance, if $f = \begin{pmatrix} 1 & 2 & 3 & 4 \\ a & b & a & b \end{pmatrix}$; $O(f) = \prod_{i=1}^{4} f(i) = a^2 b^2$; $f \in S_{\tau^2}$ where $\tau^2 = (1\ 3)(2\ 4)$. But $f \cong g = \begin{pmatrix} (1\ 3)(2\ 4) \\ a \qquad b \end{pmatrix} \in R^{\mathrm{cyc}(\tau^2)}$, and

$\prod_{c \in \mathrm{cyc}(\tau^2)} (g(c))^{|c|} = a^{|(1\ 3)|} b^{|(2\ 4)|} = a^2 b^2 = O(f)$. Note that if $A = \{e, \tau, \tau^2, \tau^3\}$ is the cyclic group of order 4, then $h = \begin{pmatrix} 1 & 2 & 3 & 4 \\ a & b & b & a \end{pmatrix}$ also has $O(h) = a^2 b^2$, but f and h are in different orbits of $A: R^D$. Observe that with $R = \{y_1, y_2, \ldots, y_r\}$, $\sum_{g \in R^{\mathrm{cyc}(a)}} \prod_{c \in \mathrm{cyc}(a)} (g(c))^{|c|} = \prod_{c \in \mathrm{cyc}(a)} \sum_{j=1}^{r} y_j^{|c|}$ by interchanging product and sum. Therefore

$$O(S_a) = \sum_{f \in S_a} O(f) = \sum_{f \in S_a} \prod_{i=1}^{d} f(x_i)$$

$$= \sum_{g \in R^{cyc(a)}} \prod_{c \in cyc(a)} (g(c))^{|c|} = \prod_{c \in cyc(a)} \sum_{j=1}^{r} y_j^{|c|}.$$

Thus we have proved the basic PÓLYA ACTION IDENTITY 4.40.

4.40 PÓLYA ACTION IDENTITY AND AN EXAMPLE.

$$\sum_{f \in S_a} \prod_{i=1}^{d} f(x_i) = \prod_{c \in cyc(a)} \sum_{j=1}^{r} y_j^{|c|}$$

where $S_a = \{f: af = f\}$.

Let $R = \{y_1, y_2\}$, $a = (1\ 2)(3\ 4\ 5)$. Then

$$R^{cyc(a)} = \left(\binom{(1\ 2)(3\ 4\ 5)}{y_1 \quad y_1} \right), \left(\binom{(1\ 2)(3\ 4\ 5)}{y_1 \quad y_2} \right), \left(\binom{(1\ 2)(3\ 4\ 5)}{y_2 \quad y_1} \right), \left(\binom{(1\ 2)(3\ 4\ 5)}{y_2 \quad y_2} \right).$$

So

$$\sum_{g \in R^{cyc(a)}} \prod_{c \in cyc(a)} (g(c))^{|c|} = y_1^2 y_1^3 + y_1^2 y_2^3 + y_2^2 y_1^3 + y_2^2 y_2^3.$$

But

$$\prod_{c \in cyc(a)} \sum_{j=1}^{r} y_j^{|c|} = \left(\sum_{j=1}^{2} y_j^{|(3\ 4\ 5)|} \right) \left(\sum_{j=1}^{2} y_j^{|(1,2)|} \right)$$

$$= (y_1^3 + y_2^3)(y_1^2 + y_2^2)$$

$$= y_1^2 y_1^3 + y_1^2 y_2^3 + y_2^2 y_1^3 + y_2^2 y_2^3$$

$$= \sum_{g \in R^{cyc(a)}} \prod_{c \in cyc(a)} (g(c))^{|c|}.$$

Using COROLLARY 4.16 and IDENTITY 4.40, we can now easily prove Pólya's enumeration theorem.

4.41 THEOREM (Pólya's theorem).

Let $D = \{x_1, x_2, \ldots, x_d\}$ and let $R = \{y_1, y_2, \ldots, y_r\}$. Let the group A act on D and hence on $S = R^D$ by the Pólya action (DEFINITION 4.40). Then

$$\sum_{f \in \Delta} \left(\prod_{i=1}^{d} f(x_i) \right) = 1/|A| \sum_{a \in A} \prod_{c \in cyc(a)} \sum_{j=1}^{r} y_j^{|c|}$$

Proof. Using IDENTITY 4.40, this result is a special case of the weighted Burnside lemma COROLLARY 4.16(1). In COROLLARY 4.16(1), set $s = f$,

$W(s) = \prod_{i=1}^{d} f(x_i)$. Then $\sum_{s \in S_a} W(s) = \sum_{f \in S_a} \prod_{i=1}^{d} f(x_i) = \prod_{c \in cyc(a)} \left(\sum_{j=1}^{r} y_j^{|c|} \right)$ by IDEN-

TITY 4.40.

Another standard formulation of THEOREM 4.41 is in terms of the polynomial $P_A(z_1,. . .,z_d)$ associated with the action A: D called the *cycle index polynomial.*

4.42   DEFINITION.

For each permutation a $\in$ A, let $\nu(a,i)$ denote the number of cycles in a of length i (as a permutation of D). The vector $(\nu(a,1),. . .,\nu(a,d))$ is called the *type* of a. The polynomial

$$P_A(z_1,. . .,z_d) = \frac{1}{|A|} \sum_{a \in A} z_1^{\nu(a,1)} z_2^{\nu(a,2)} \cdots z_d^{\nu(a,d)}$$

is called the *cycle index polynomial of* A *acting on* D.

Using DEFINITION 4.42, we have the obvious rephrasing of Pólya's theorem as IDENTITY 4.43.

4.43   CYCLE INDEX VERSION OF PÓLYA'S THEOREM.

$$\sum_{f \in \Delta} \prod_{i=1}^{d} f(x_i) = P_A\left(\sum_{j=1}^{r} y_j, \sum_{j=1}^{r} y_j^2,. . .,\sum_{j=1}^{r} y_j^d \right).$$

The main feature of Pólya's theorem as distinct from the general Burnside lemma (from which Pólya's theorem is obtained) is that it allows information about the range R to be included as a variable or "parameter" in the formulas in a particularly nice way. We now consider some examples.

The symmetries of the cube under rotations only (no reflections) is shown in FIGURE 4.44. Imagine the faces of the cube labeled 1 through 6. Looking at the cube as in FIGURE 4.44(b), we label the front face 1, the top face 2, the back face 3, the bottom face 4, the right-side face 5, and the left-side face 6. The permutation (1 2 3 4)(5)(6) is interpreted as "1 is sent to where 2 used to be, 2 is sent to where 3 used to be, etc.," just as in the case of the symmetries of the square in FIGURE 4.2. FIGURE 4.44 shows how the cycle index polynomial is computed. The number of distinct cubes with r colors is gotten by setting $y_j = 1, j = 1,. . .,r$, in IDENTITY 4.43. The reader is asked to explore some additional ideas related to Pólya's theorem in EXERCISE 4.45.

4.44   ROTATION GROUP OF CUBE ACTING ON FACES.

$$4$$
$$3$$
$$6\ 2\ 5$$
$$1 \leftarrow \text{Front face}$$

(a) identity = e   type = (6, 0, 0, 0, 0, 0)
                                    (see DEF. 4.42)   Figure 4.44 (cont.)

(b) 6 90° rotations of type $= (2, 0, 0, 1, 0, 0)$
e.g., $(1\ 2\ 3\ 4)(5)(6)$

(c) 3 180° rotations of type $(2, 2, 0, 0, 0, 0)$
e.g., $(13)(24)(5)(6)$

(d) 6 180° rotations of type $(0, 3, 0, 0, 0, 0)$
e.g., $(16)(53)(24)$

(e) 8 120° rotations of type $(0, 0, 2, 0, 0, 0)$
e.g., $(1\ 6\ 4)(2\ 3\ 5)$

Figure 4.44
(continued)

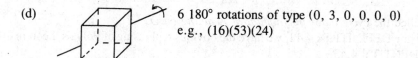

$$P_A(z_1, z_2, z_3, z_4, z_5, z_6) = \frac{1}{24}(z_1^6 + 6z_1^2 z_4 + 3z_1^2 z_2^2 + 6z_2^3 + 8z_3^2)$$

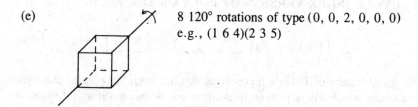

NUMBER OF DISTINCT CUBES
WITH r COLORS (FACES) $= \frac{1}{24}(r^6 + 12r^3 + 3r^4 + 8r^2).$

4.45 EXERCISE.

(1) The group of rotations of the cube, considered in FIGURE 4.44, also acts on the edges and the vertices of the cube in an analogous fashion. What are the cycle index polynomials for these actions?

(2) The full group of symmetries of the cube includes both rotations and reflections and has 48 elements. What is the cycle index polynomial of this group?

(3) The rotational group of symmetries of the regular polygon with d vertices is the cyclic group Z_d generated by the cycle $(1, 2, 3, \ldots, d)$ (if we think of this group acting on vertices). Show that the cycle index polynomial of this action is given by $P_{Z_d}(z_1, \ldots, z_d) = \frac{1}{d} \sum_{i|d} \varphi(i) z_i^{d/i}$ where the sum is over all

divisors of d and $\varphi(i)$ is the number of integers less than or equal to i and relatively prime to i (Euler's φ-function).

(4) The group of symmetries of the regular polygon with d vertices allowing reflections has 2d elements and is called the *dihedral group* D_{2d}. We have considered certain aspects of this group in the previous material (d = 4 in FIGURE 4.2, d = 3 in FIGURE 4.11, d = 6 in EXERCISE 4.32(3)). Prove that the cycle index polynomial $P_{D_{2d}}(z_1, \ldots, z_d) = \frac{1}{2}(P_{Z_d}(z_1, \ldots, z_d) + \frac{1}{2}(z_2^{d/2} + z_1^2 z_2^{(d-2)/2}))$ if d is even and $P_{D_{2d}}(z_1, \ldots, z_d) = \frac{1}{2}(P_{Z_d}(z_1, \ldots, z_d) + z_1 z_2^{(d-1)/2})$ if d is odd.

(5) Using IDENTITY 4.22, extend Pólya's theorem to include group characters. Illustrate your theorem with the rotational group of symmetries of the polygon with d vertices (i.e., the cyclic group Z_d). Recall EXAMPLES 4.23 and 4.24. Prove White's theorem, the Pólya theorem analog of Lemma 4.29.

As our final example of a cycle index polynomial, we consider the cycle index polynomial of the symmetric group on $\underline{d} = \{1, \ldots, d\}$. The result is of theoretical rather than practical importance as the index of summation is over a set whose size grows exponentially with d. We denote by S_d the group of all permutations (symmetric group) of $\underline{d}$. For $a \in S_d$ we define the vector $(\nu(a,1), \nu(a,2), \ldots, \nu(a,d))$ to be the *type* of a (the $\nu(a,i)$ are as in DEFINITION 4.42). For example, if a = (1 2 3)(4 5)(6 7)(8)(9), then type (a) = (2, 2, 1, 0, \ldots, 0). So

$$P_{S_d} = 1/d! \sum_{\substack{(\alpha_1, \ldots, \alpha_d) \\ \alpha_1 + 2\alpha_2 + \ldots + d\alpha_d = d}} |\{a : \text{type } (a) = (\alpha_1, \ldots, \alpha_d)\}| z_1^{\alpha_1} \ldots z_d^{\alpha_2}.$$

Now let us try to determine, given type $(\alpha_1, \alpha_2, \ldots, \alpha_d)$, how many permutations have this type?

If a has type $(\alpha_1, \ldots, \alpha_d)$, then the "form" of the cycle decomposition of a is

$$a = \underbrace{(\square)(\square) \ldots (\square)}_{\alpha_1 \text{ 1-cycles}} \underbrace{(\square\square)(\square\square) \ldots (\square\square)}_{\alpha_2 \text{ 2-cycles}}$$

$$\ldots \underbrace{(\square \ldots \square) \ldots (\square \ldots \square)}_{\alpha_k \text{ k-cycles}}$$

$$\ldots \underbrace{(\square \ldots \square) \ldots (\square \ldots \square)}_{\alpha_d \text{ d-cycles } (\alpha_d = 0 \text{ or } 1)}$$

There are d! different ways of putting integers in the above boxes. Each placement may be regarded as a permutation of type $(\alpha_1, \ldots, \alpha_d)$. But not all of these will give a *different* permutation, for instance $(5)(4)(3\ 2\ 1) = (4)(5)(2\ 1\ 3)$, etc. It turns out that by dividing by the number of such duplications we obtain

$$\left|\{a: \text{type } (a) = (\alpha_1, \alpha_2, \ldots, \alpha_d)\}\right| = \frac{d!}{\alpha_1! \alpha_2! \ldots \alpha_d! \, 1^{\alpha_1} 2^{\alpha_2} \ldots d^{\alpha_d}}.$$

Thus, we obtain IDENTITY 4.46.

4.46 CYCLE INDEX POLYNOMIAL OF SYMMETRIC GROUP.

$$P_{S_d}(z_1, \ldots, z_d) = \frac{1}{d!} \sum_{\substack{(\alpha_1, \ldots, \alpha_d) \\ \alpha_1 + 2\alpha_2 + \ldots + d\alpha_d = d}} \frac{d!}{\displaystyle\prod_{i=1}^{d} \alpha_i! \, i^{\alpha_i}} z_1^{\alpha_1} \ldots z_d^{\alpha_d}.$$

4.47 EXERCISE.

(1) Let $P_{S_d}(z_1, \ldots, z_d)$ be the cycle index polynomial of the symmetric group S_d. Prove that

$$P_{S_d}(z_1, \ldots, z_d) = \frac{1}{d} \sum_{k=1}^{d} z_k P_{S_{d-k}}(z_1, \ldots, z_{d-k}).$$

For small d this provides a useful recursion for calculating P_{S_d}. Try it for d = 1,2,3,4.

(2) Prove that $P_{S_d}(z_1, \ldots, z_d)$ is the coefficient of u^d in the development of

$$\exp\left(uz_1 + \frac{u^2 z_2}{2} + \frac{u^3 z_3}{3} + \ldots\right)$$

as a power series in u.

(3) Consider Pólya's theorem (IDENTITY 4.43) applied to the group of rotational symmetries of the cube (FIGURE 4.44). Suppose $R = \{y_1, y_2, y_3\}$ has three elements ("colors"). Let $y_1 = u$, $y_2 = y_3 = 1$. What is the interpretation of the left-hand side of IDENTITY 4.43? Such a "change of variables" for the values of R is called an "assignment of Pólya weights." Try to think up some imaginative assignments of Pólya weights for the various Pólya actions we have constructed thus far (cube groups, cyclic groups, dihedral groups, symmetric groups).

There are two basic techniques for extending the scope of Pólya's theorem. One may attempt to systematically enlarge the class of group actions A: D for which reasonable formulas are known for the cycle index polynomial, or one may enlarge the class of group actions analogous to the Pólya action for which a similar result may be obtai d. We shall conclude our discussion of Pólya's theorem with some examples of each approach.

Let A and B be groups and P and Q sets such that A: P and B: Q. The set of all functions from P to B, B^P, is also a group where, for φ and ψ in B^P, i in P, $\varphi\psi(i) = \varphi(i)\psi(i)$. This is called the "pointwise product of φ and ψ" for obvious reasons. Each pair (a,φ), $a \in A$ and $\varphi \in B^P$, may be regarded as a permutation of the set of all pairs $PxQ = \{(i,j): i \in P, j \in Q\}$ by defining $(a,\varphi)(i,j) = (ai, \varphi(i)j)$. With this definition we see that composition of permutations of this form goes as follows: $(a_1,\varphi_1)(a_2,\varphi_2)(i,j) = (a_1,\varphi_1)(a_2i,\varphi_2(i)j)$ $= (a_1a_2i,\varphi_1(a_2i)\varphi_2(i)j)$. Thus, the permutations of this type are closed under composition (i.e., multiplication of permutations) according to the rule $(a_1,\varphi_1)(a_2,\varphi_2)$ $= (a_1a_2,(\varphi_1a_2)\varphi_2)$. The identity permutation is of this form: (e,ε) where e is the identity in A and ε is the function that maps each element of P to the identity of B. If (a,φ) is a permutation, then (a^{-1},ψ) is its inverse where ψ is the inverse of φa^{-1} in B^P. Thus, the set of all permutations of the form (a,φ) with $a \in A$ and $\varphi \in B^P$ forms a subgroup of the group of all permutations PER(PxQ). This permutation group will be called the *wreath product* of A: P and B: Q and will be denoted by A[B]. The reader familiar with a little group theory will note that the wreath product is an action of a semidirect product of A and B^P. The group B^P is a normal subgroup of this product. We regard A and B as subgroups of A[B] by the obvious identifications.

4.48   WREATH PRODUCT OF S_3 AND S_2 ACTING ON $\underline{3} \times \underline{2}$.

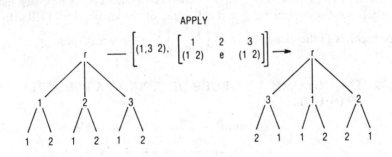

Figure 4.48

An example of the product of elements in a wreath product is given in FIGURE 4.48. There, we consider the wreath product of S_3 and S_2 acting on $\underline{3} \times \underline{2}$. The set $\underline{3} \times \underline{2}$ is represented by the standard ordered tree diagram (see FIGURES 1.42 and 3.6). In FIGURE 4.48, we compose two elements of $S_3[S_2]$. The composition is $(a,\varphi)(b,\psi)$ where $a = (1\ 3)$, $b = (1\ 3\ 2)$, $\varphi = \begin{pmatrix} 1 & 2 & 3 \\ e & e & (1\ 2) \end{pmatrix}$ and $\psi = \begin{pmatrix} 1 & 2 & 3 \\ (1\ 2) & e & (1\ 2) \end{pmatrix}$. The reader should check carefully the computation of FIGURE 4.48 against the definitions of the previous paragraph. In general, a wreath product A[B] acting on $P \times Q$ has $|A||B|^{|P|}$ elements. Thus, $S_3[S_2]$ has 48 elements and acts on a set, $\underline{3} \times \underline{2}$, which has six elements. The reader who has worked EXERCISE 4.45(2) will be struck by the similarities of this group with the full symmetry group of the cube (48 elements) acting on the faces of the cube (six elements). In fact, the wreath product $S_3[S_2]$ is exactly the group of symmetries of the cube acting on the faces of the cube (up to certain natural identifications). More generally, $S_d[S_2]$ is the full symmetry group of the d-dimensional cube acting on faces. The basic idea is shown in FIGURE 4.49. The set P is identified with the three oriented axes as shown by the labels 1, 2, and 3. The endpoints of each axis are identified with the labels 1 and 2 corresponding to the set Q. One can easily verify how the group $S_3[S_2]$ relates to the symmetries of the cube. For example, reflection through the plane passing through the left-most and right-most vertical edges of the diagram of FIGURE 4.49 corresponds to the element $\left((2\ 3), \begin{pmatrix} 1 & 2 & 3 \\ e & e & e \end{pmatrix} \right)$ of the wreath product.

4.49 FULL SYMMETRY GROUP OF CUBE AS A WREATH PRODUCT.

$A = S_3[S_2]$ with $P = \underline{3}$ and $Q = \underline{2}$ has order 48

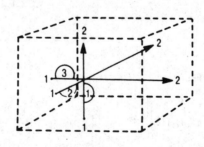

Figure 4.49

In FIGURE 4.50 we see a square whose vertices are labeled with labeled triangles. The vertices of the triangles are labeled with symbols g,r. Imagine that the square can be rotated 0°, 90°, 180°, or 270° and at the same time the triangles can be rotated independently of the square and of each other by 0°,

120°, or 240°. This is intuitively what is meant by the action of the wreath product $C_4[C_3]$ on the structures such as that of FIGURE 4.50. If we think of the vertices of the square as $\{1,2,3,4\} = \underline{4}$ and the vertices of the triangle as $\{1,2,3\} = \underline{3}$, then the twelve vertices of FIGURE 4.50 can be identified with $\underline{4} \times \underline{3}$. The transformations of FIGURE 4.50 just described represents the Pólya action of $C_4[C_3]$ on $\{g,r\}^{\underline{4} \times \underline{3}}$.

Again referring to FIGURE 4.50, the set $\Delta_t(3)$ is a system of orbit representatives for the Pólya action of C_3 on $\{g^t,r^t\}^{\underline{3}}$, t a positive integer. By Pólya's theorem (IDENTITY 4.43) we have

$$\sum_{f \in \Delta_t(3)} \prod_{i=1}^{3} f(i) = g^{3t} + g^{2t}r^t + g^t r^{2t} + r^{3t} \equiv \eta_t$$

$$= P_{C_3}(g^t + r^t, g^{2t} + r^{2t}, g^{3t} + r^{3t}) .$$

We may also consider the Pólya action of C_4 on $(\Delta_1(3))^{\underline{4}}$. That is, we imagine the vertices of the square of FIGURE 4.50 being labeled in all possible ways with elements of $\Delta_1(3)$. The structure shown in FIGURE 4.50 is one such labeling. It is intuitively obvious that an orbit representative system for $C_4[C_3]$ acting on $(\Delta_1(3))^{\underline{4}}$ is also an orbit representative system for $C_4[C_3]$ acting on $\{g,r\}^{\underline{4} \times \underline{3}}$. If in each case we take the Pólya weights (see EXERCISE 4.47(3)) to be the product of all labels g or r that occur in the structure we consequently obtain the wreath product identity for $C_4[C_3]$ (IDENTITY 4.51).

4.50 ACTION OF WREATH PRODUCT C₄[C₃].

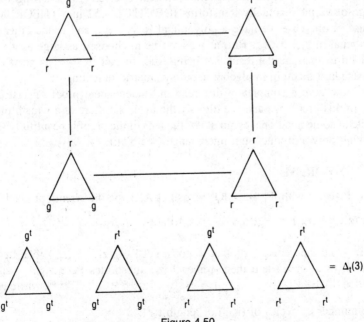

Figure 4.50

4.51 WREATH PRODUCT IDENTITY FOR $C_4[C_3]$.

$$P_{C_4[C_3]}(g + r,. . .,g^t + r^t,. . .,g^{12} + r^{12}) = P_{C_4}(\eta_1,\eta_2,\eta_3,\eta_4)$$

where

$$\eta_t = g^{3t} + g^{2t}r^t + g^t r^{2t} + r^{3t} = P_{C_3}(g^t + r^t, g^{2t} + r^{2t}, g^{3t} + r^{3t}).$$

This is the sense in which a cycle index polynomial of a wreath product is a composition of cycle index polynomials. Instead of just having $R = \{g,r\}$ we might have $R = \{y_1,. . .,y_r\}$ and we might have the general case of $A[B]$ acting on $P \times Q$ ($|P| = p$, $|Q| = |q|$). Then IDENTITY 4.51 becomes IDENTITY 4.52.

4.52 WREATH PRODUCT IDENTITY FOR THE GENERAL CASE.

$$P_{A[B]}\left(\sum_{j=1}^{r} y_j,. . .,\sum_{j=1}^{r} y_j^{pq}\right) = P_A(\eta_1,\eta_2,. . .,\eta_p)$$

where

$$\eta_t = P_B\left(\sum_{j=1}^{r} y_j^t, \sum_{j=1}^{r} y_j^{2t},. . .,\sum_{j=1}^{r} y_j^{qt}\right).$$

By making the change of variable $z_k = \sum_{j=1}^{r} y_j^k$ for $k = 1,. . .,pq$ we obtain THEOREM 4.53. There is a slight technical difficulty in asserting that this change of variable actually transforms IDENTITY 4.52 into THEOREM 4.53 because in one case we have a polynomial in $y_1,..,y_r$, and in the other case a polynomial in $z_1,. . .,z_{pq}$. But, as we are free to choose r as large as we please it is hard to imagine the result not being true. In fact, $r = pq$ is good enough by a standard theorem in algebra about symmetric functions.

We now give a completely different and independent proof of THEOREM 4.53. In this proof, we analyze directly the cycle structure of a wreath product. In spite of some notational complexity, the idea of the proof is beautifully simple, involving only a product-sum interchange (see STEP 4).

4.53 THEOREM.

Let $A: P$, $B: Q$ with $|P| = p$, $|Q| = q$. Let $A[B]$ be the wreath product. Then

$$P_{A[B]}(z_1,. . .,z_{pq}) = P_A(P_B(z_1,. . .,z_q),P_B(z_2,. . .,z_{2q}),. . .,P_B(z_p,. . .,z_{pq})) .$$

Proof. The theorem asserts that to construct $P_{A[B]}(z_1,. . .,z_{pq})$, one first constructs $P_A(z_1,. . .,z_p)$ and then, for each z_t, substitutes $P_B(z_t,z_{t2},. . .,z_{tq})$. By definition, $|A[B]| \, P_{A[B]}(z_1,. . .,z_{pq}) = \sum_{(a,\varphi)\in A[B]} z_1^{\nu(a,\varphi,1)} \cdots z_{pq}^{\nu(a,\varphi,pq)}$ where $\nu(a,\varphi,t)$ is the number of cycles of (a,φ) of length t.

STEP 1. Fix $(a,\varphi) \in A[B]$ and $(i,j) \in P \times Q$. Suppose that i is in a cycle of a of length 3 (as A acts on P). The cycle of (a,φ) containing (i,j) can be written

$$((i,j),(ai,\varphi(i)j),(a^2i,\varphi(ai)\varphi(i)j),(i,\varphi(a^2i)\varphi(ai)\varphi(i)j). \ldots) \, .$$

Let $b = \varphi(a^2i)\varphi(ai)\varphi(i) \in B$ and suppose that j is in a cycle of length h of b (as B acts on Q). Thus, the cycle of j is $(j,bj,\ldots,b^{h-1}j)$. Then the cycle of (a,φ) containing (i,j) can be written $((i,j),\ldots,(i,bj),\ldots,(i,b^{h-1}j),\ldots)$ and has length $3h$. If i is contained in a cycle of length g of a then we set $b = \varphi(a^{g-1}i)\ldots\varphi(i)$ and, if j is in a cycle of b of length h we find that (i,j) is in a cycle of (a,φ) of length gh.

STEP 2. As a result of STEP 1, for each cycle $c = (i,ai,\ldots,a^{g-1}i)$ of $a \in A$, there is a permutation $b_c = \varphi(a^{g-1}i)\ldots\varphi(i)$. If $\mathrm{cyc}(a)$ denotes the cycles of a, the correspondence $c \to b_c$ is a function from $\mathrm{cyc}(a)$ to B. Let $|c|$ denote the length of c. Each permutation (a,φ) contributes the term

$$\prod_{c \in \mathrm{cyc}(a)} \prod_{c' \in \mathrm{cyc}(b_c)} z_{|c| \, |c'|} \quad \text{to} \quad P_{A[B]}$$

STEP 3. We now count the number of different functions φ such that (a,φ) produces the same correspondence $c \to b_c$ and hence the same terms of STEP 2. Let $b_c = \varphi(a^{g-1}i)\ldots\varphi(ai)\varphi(i)$. The value of φ may be specified arbitrarily on the values $a^{g-1}i,\ldots,ai$. We may then choose $\varphi(i)$ so that the product is b_c. Thus, we have $|B|^{|c|-1}$ such choices for each cycle c and hence each map $c \to b_c$ contributes

$$\prod_{c \in \mathrm{cyc}(a)} |B|^{|c|-1} \prod_{c \in \mathrm{cyc}(a)} \prod_{c' \in \mathrm{cyc}(b_c)} z_{|c| \, |c'|} \quad \text{to} \quad P_{A[B]}$$

STEP 4. This is the key step and involves a product-sum interchange. From STEP 3 we now see that each fixed $a \in A$ contributes (to $P_{A[B]}$)

$$\prod_{c \in \mathrm{cyc}(a)} |B|^{|c|-1} \sum_{c \to b_c} \prod_{c} \prod_{c'} z_{|c| \, |c'|}$$

where the sum is over all maps $c \to b_c$ from $\mathrm{cyc}(a)$ to B. By the standard rule for interchanging sums and products this becomes

$$\prod_{c \in \mathrm{cyc}(a)} |B|^{|c|-1} \prod_{c \in \mathrm{cyc}(a)} \sum_{b \in B} \prod_{c' \in \mathrm{cyc}(b)} z_{|c| \, |c'|} \, .$$

STEP 5. (Last step!) This step is nothing more than a change of notation. As usual, let $\nu(a,k)$ denote the number of cycles of $a \in A$ of length k. Note that

$$\prod_{c \in \mathrm{cyc}(a)} |B|^{|c|-1} = |B|^{|P|} \prod_{c \in \mathrm{cyc}(a)} \frac{1}{|B|} \, . \text{Thus, the last expression of STEP 4 becomes}$$

$$|B|^{|P|} \prod_{k=1}^{p} \left(\frac{1}{|B|} \sum_{b \in B} z_{k1}^{\nu(b,1)} \ldots z_{kq}^{\nu(b,q)} \right)^{\nu(a,k)}$$

Summing over all a $\in$ A we thus obtain the sum over all $(a,\varphi) \in A[B]$ of terms $z_1^{\nu(a,\varphi,1)} \ldots z_{pq}^{\nu(a,\varphi,pq)}$ as $|A| \, |B|^{|P|} \, P_A(P_B(z_1, \ldots, z_q), \ldots, P_B(z_p, \ldots, z_{pq}))$. Dividing by $|A| \, |B|^{|P|} = |A[B]|$ gives the result.

4.54 EXERCISE.

(1) Let $\mathcal{P}(n)$ denote the set of all polynomials $p(x_1, \ldots, x_n)$ in n variables. The symmetric group S_n acts on $\mathcal{P}(n)$ by the rule, $\sigma \in S_n$, $\sigma p(x_1, \ldots, x_n) = p(x_{\sigma^{-1}1}, \ldots, x_{\sigma^{-1}n})$. Let $(S_n)_p$ denote the stability subgroup at p (i.e., all σ such that $\sigma p = p$). For $p(x_1, \ldots, x_9) = x_1 x_2 x_3 + x_4 x_5 x_6 + x_7 x_8 x_9$, what is $(S_9)_p$? What is the size of the orbit containing p as S_9 acts on $\mathcal{P}(9)$?

(2) We consider structures such as those shown in FIGURE 4.50. Instead of just two labels $\{g,r\}$, consider labels $\{y_1, y_2, \ldots, y_r\}$ (now "r" is a parameter counting the number of labels, not a label). Give explicit polynomials in r that count the number of labeled structures up to the action of $C_4[C_3]$, $D_8[C_3]$, $C_4[D_6]$, and $D_8[D_6]$. Recall that D_8 is the dihedral group of all rotations and reflections of the square and D_6 is the group of all rotations and reflections of the triangle. Graph these polynomials and compare their behavior for large values of r.

(3) Let A and B be groups, A: P and B: Q. The *direct product* A $\times$ B of A and B is the group of ordered pairs (a,b) with a $\in$ A and b $\in$ B where multiplication is defined by the rule $(a,b)(a',b') = (aa',bb')$. A $\times$ B acts on P $\times$ Q in the obvious way: $(a,b)(i,j) = (ai,bj)$. Express the cycle index polynomial of A $\times$ B: P $\times$ Q in terms of the cycle index polynomials of A: P and B: Q.

(4) Give procedures for listing, ranking, and unranking $S_m[S_n]$.

(5) Construct a bijection between the orbits of the Pólya action of A[B] on $R^{P \times Q}$ and the Pólya action of A on $(\Delta(Q))^P$ where $\Delta(Q)$ is the list of orbits of the Pólya action of B on R^Q. Give careful proofs.

(6) Describe explicitly an orbit representative system for the Pólya action of $S_m[S_n]$ on $R^{\underline{m} \times \underline{n}}$ where $R = y_1, y_2, \ldots, y_r$ is a linearly ordered set. How would you linearly order, rank, and unrank this list? Hint: The nondecreasing functions are a list of orbit representatives for $S_n: R^{\underline{n}}$. Recalling EXERCISE 3.26 one can then use (5) above. Give explicit formulas for the number of orbits of the action of $S_m[S_2]$ on the faces of the m-cube with r possible labels. Note that Pólya's theorem is not needed for this exercise.

We now consider how one can develop analogous theorems to Pólya's theorem for other group actions. There is by now an extensive literature on the subject of Pólya theory or "pattern enumeration." We shall only give a brief description of some of the most basic ideas and refer the reader to the references at the end of the chapter for further study. Much of what we now describe is based on the extensive work of N. G. deBruijn on pattern enumeration.

4.55 DEFINITION.

Let A be a group such that A acts on a set P and a set Q. The *Cartesian action* of A on P × Q is defined by a(i,j) = (ai,aj) where a ∈ A, i ∈ P, j ∈ Q.

The Cartesian action has many variations. First of all, if G and H are groups such that G: P and H: Q, then we can set A = G × H to be the direct product of G and H. Then for (g,h) in A, define (g,h)i = gi for all i ∈ P. Thus, A acts on P. Similarly, A acts on Q. In this case the Cartesian action of A on P × Q satisfies (g,h)(i,j) = ((g,h)i,(g,h)j) = (gi,hj). Thus, the direct product action of EXERCISE 4.54(3) is a special case of the Cartesian action. Given any function f ∈ Q^P we define the graph of f to be the set GRAPH(f) = {(i,j): i ∈ P, j ∈ Q such that f(i) = j}, GRAPH(f) is a subset of P × Q. If A acts on P × Q by the Cartesian action (or any action for that matter) then A acts on the set of all subsets of P × Q. In particular, for a ∈ A, aGRAPH(f) = {(ai,aj): f(i) = j} = {(s,t): f(a^{-1}s) = a^{-1}t} = GRAPH(afa^{-1}). In other words, A acts on the set of functions Q^P by acting on their graphs. Thus, the action f→afa^{-1} on Q^P is a special case of the Cartesian action. If A = G × H is the direct product action, and (g,h) is in A, then we have (g,h)f = hfg^{-1}. Finally, if A acts as the identity on Q, then f→fa^{-1} is the Pólya action. We also should note that the Cartesian action on functions sends injective functions to injective functions and also sends surjective functions to surjective functions.

We return now to the notation used in connection with Pólya's theorem. Let D = {x_1,. . .,x_d} and let R = {y_1,. . .,y_r}. Let R^D denote the set of all functions from D to R.

4.56 DEFINITION.

Let A be a group, A: R and A: D. Let v be the homomorphism from A to PER(R^D) defined by v(a)(f) = afa^{-1}. Then v defines an action of A on R^D that we call the *Cartesian action on functions*.

4.57 INTUITIVE IDEA OF LEMMA 4.58.

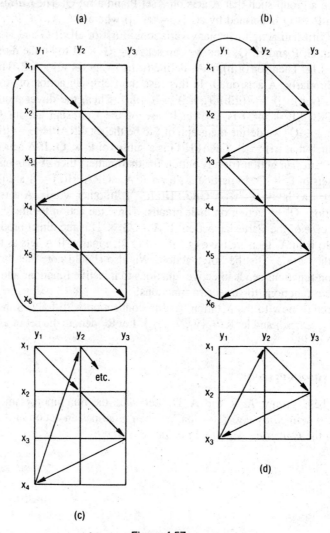

Figure 4.57

As just stated, the Cartesian action on functions has both the injective and surjective functions as invariant subsets of R^D. Just as in the case with Pólya's theorem, we shall apply the general Burnside's lemma (COROLLARY 4.16) to obtain an analog of THEOREM 4.41. As with these earlier results, the central problem is to describe the set S_a of all functions f such that $afa^{-1} = f$ for a fixed $a \in A$. Let $cyc_D(a)$ denote the set of cycles of the cycle decomposition of a acting on D and similarly define $cyc_R(a)$. We describe the intuitive idea involved in characterizing S_a in terms of the Cartesian action of A on GRAPH(f). Thus, we want to have aGRAPH(f) = GRAPH (f). This means that if $(x_i,y_j) \in$

GRAPH(f) then $(ax_i, ay_j) \in$ GRAPH(f). FIGURE 4.57 shows the sort of things
that can happen.

Suppose we have an element $a \in A$ and suppose that $c = (x_1, \ldots, x_6) \in$
$cyc_D(a)$. Suppose also that $c' = (y_1, y_2, y_3) \in cyc_R(a)$. FIGURE 4.57(a) shows
the cycle of $a \in A$ acting on $D \times R$ containing (x_1, y_1). This cycle, indicated
by the arrows in FIGURE 4.57(a), is $((x_1, y_1), (ax_1, ay_1), \ldots, (a^5 x_1, a^5 y_1))$. It is
evident that if $f \in S_a$ and hence aGRAPH(f) = GRAPH(f), then the condition
$(x_1, y_1) \in$ GRAPH(f) forces all other points $(ax_1, ay_1) \ldots$ in this cycle to be in
GRAPH(f). In the same manner, if $(x_1, y_2) \in$ GRAPH(f) then all other points
shown in FIGURE 4.57(b) must be in GRAPH(f). There is one other possibility,
namely $(x_1, y_3) \in$ GRAPH(f). For both FIGURES 4.57(a) and (b) it is quite
possible to have functions whose graphs are as shown. Thus, if $f \in S_a$ and $f(x_1)$
$\in \{y_1, y_2, y_3\}$, then there are only $|c'| = 3$ possibilities for f restricted to c.

Now consider FIGURE 4.57(c). Here $c = (x_1, \ldots, x_4)$ and $c' = (y_1, y_2, y_3)$.
Again, suppose that $f \in S_a$ and $(x_1, y_1) \in$ GRAPH(f). For the same reasons, we
must have all elements of the cycle $((x_1, y_1), (ax_1, ay_1), \ldots)$ in GRAPH(f). But,
from FIGURE 4.57(c) it is clear that this means that both (x_1, y_1) and (x_1, y_2)
must be in GRAPH(f). This is impossible since f is a function. Comparing the
situation in FIGURES 4.57(a) and (b) with that in FIGURE 4.57(c), we see that
for $c \in cyc_D(a)$ and $c' \in cyc_R(a)$ and $x \in c$, it is possible to have $f(x) \in c'$,
$f \in S_a$, *only if* the length of c' divides the length of c (we write $|c'| \big| |c|$). In the
case where $|c'| \big| |c|$, there are exactly $|c'|$ values we can assign to $f(x)$. Once $f(x)$
is specified, then the value of f at all other points of c is determined. These
observations obviously extend to the general case and clearly specify how one
might construct all elements of S_a.

If we denote by R_*^D the injective maps from D to R, then, as we have observed
above R_*^D is invariant under the Cartesian action of A. If f is an injective function
and $f \in S_a$, then f must be of the type described in the previous paragraph. The
fact that f is injective, however, rules out situations such as that shown in
FIGURES 4.57(a) and (b) as these cannot be the graphs of an injective function.

It is easily seen that in addition to having $|c'| \big| |c|$, we must in fact have $|c'| =$
$|c|$ for injective maps. But there is still another difference between the general
case and injective map! If c and c' are as above and $x \in c$, $f(x) \in c'$ then f is
an injection from c to c' (assume $f \in R_*^D$). In this case we say that f *associates*
c' to c. If $|c| = k$ then there are, in general, other cycles of $a \in A$: D of length
k. Let $\nu_D(a,k)$ denote the number of cycles of $a \in A$ of length k (as a permutation
of D). Similarly, define $\nu_R(a,k)$. Clearly, no fixed c' can be associated by f to
more then one cycle c if f is injective. In other words, associated with each
injection, $f \in R_*^D$, and each integer k, there is an injection θ from the k-cycles
of a in D to the k-cycles of a in R. The map θ is defined by $\theta(c) = c'$ if f
associates c' to c. Let Im(θ) be the image of θ. Let $cyc_D(a,k)$ be the set of cycles
of $a \in A$: D of length k and similarly define $cyc_R(a,k)$. The set of all injective
maps θ from $cyc_D(a,k)$ to $cyc_R(a,k)$ will be denoted by $\mathscr{I}_k(a)$. LEMMA 4.58
summarizes the ideas of the previous two paragraphs and FIGURE 4.57 and is

the extension of the Pólya action IDENTITY 4.40 to the Cartesian action of A on R^D and R^D_* (DEFINITION 4.56). Recall X of NOTATION 4.27.

4.58 LEMMA.

Let A act on R^D by the Cartesian action $f \rightarrow afa^{-1}$. Let $D = \{x_1, \ldots, x_d\}$ and $R = \{y_1, \ldots, y_r\}$. Let $S_a = \{f: f \in R^D, afa^{-1} = f\}$ and let $S_a^* = \{f: f \in R_*^D, afa^{-1} = f\}$. In the notation of the previous two paragraphs we have:

$$(1) \quad \sum_{f \in S_a} \prod_{i=1}^{d} f(x_i) = \prod_{k=1}^{d} \left(\sum_{c' \in cyc_R(a)} |c'| \cdot \left(\prod_{i \in c'} y_i \right)^{k/|c'|} X(|c'| \| k) \right)^{\nu_D(a,k)}$$

$$(2) \quad \sum_{f \in S_a^*} \prod_{i=1}^{d} f(x_i) = \prod_{k=1}^{d} k^{\nu_D(a,k)} \sum_{\theta \in \mathcal{F}_k(a)} \prod_{c' \in Im(\theta)} \prod_{j \in c'} y_j .$$

Proof. The proof is the discussion of the previous two paragraphs extended in the obvious way to the general case. The factor $k^{\nu_D(a,k)}$ in (2) comes from the fact that if c' is associated to c and $x \in c$, then there are exactly k different choices for $f(x)$ to construct an invariant f. Once this choice is made, the value of f on all of c is determined. This choice among k values must be made for $\nu_D(a,k)$ different c' and hence the factor.

To find interesting applications of LEMMA 4.58 in the generality stated requires as much ingenuity as proving the theorem in the first place. The problem is that the expressions depend on the actual cycles c' and not just on the type of permutation a acting on R. A more tractable result is obtained if we set $y_j = 1$ for all j.

4.59 LEMMA.

If we set $y_j = 1$ for $j = 1, \ldots, r$ then LEMMA 4.58(1) and (2) become

$$(1) \quad |S_a| = \prod_{k=1}^{d} \left(\sum_{j|k} j \nu_R(a,j) \right)^{\nu_D(a,k)}$$

$$(2) \quad |S_a^*| = \prod_{k=1}^{d} k^{\nu_D(a,k)} (\nu_R(a,k))_{\nu_D(a,k)} .$$

Proof. Recall that $j|k$ means "j divides k." The sum in LEMMA 4.58(1) is over all c' such that $|c'|$ divides k. For each fixed j such that $j|k$, there are $\nu_R(a,j)$ such terms. This explains 4.59(1). With $y_j = 1$ for all j, LEMMA 4.58(2) involves only the $|\mathcal{F}_k|$. In general, the number of injective mappings from a set of q elements to a set of p elements is $p(p-1)(p-2)\ldots(p-q+1)$. This number is called the "falling factorial" and is denoted by $(p)_q$. By definition, $(p)_q = 0$ if $q > p$. Thus, $|\mathscr{S}_k| = (\nu_R(a,k))_{\nu_D(a,k)}$ appears in 4.59(2).

LEMMA 4.59 together with Burnside's lemma (COROLLARY 4.16(2)) gives THEOREM 4.60, a result of deBruijn.

4.60 THEOREM (deBruijn).

Let A act on R^D by the Cartesian action $f \rightarrow afa^{-1}$. Let Δ be a system of representatives for the orbits of A acting on R^D and let Δ_* be a system of representatives for A acting on the injective functions R_*^D. Then

$$(1) \quad |\Delta| = \frac{1}{|A|} \sum_{a \in A} \prod_{k=1}^{d} \left(\sum_{j|k} j\nu_R(a,j) \right)^{\nu_D(a,k)}$$

$$(2) \quad |\Delta_*| = \frac{1}{|A|} \sum_{a \in A} \prod_{k=1}^{d} k^{\nu_D(a,k)} (\nu_R(a,k))_{\nu_D(a,k)} .$$

In EXERCISE 4.61, we explore these results further. The references at the end of the chapter should be consulted in connection with these exercises (in particular, see the chapter by de Bruijn in the book *Applied Combinatorial Mathematics*). Also in EXERCISE 4.61 we indicate some other directions one might go in exploring the topic of orbit enumeration. There are many interesting applications of this material that make ideal topics for classroom presentations by students!

4.61 EXERCISE.

(1) Show how the identity of LEMMA 4.58(1) specializes to the Pólya action IDENTITY 4.40.
(2) Consider the case where $A = G \times H$ is the direct product of two groups G and H, G: D, H: R. Thus, for $a = (g,h)$, $f \in R^D$ is transformed into hfg^{-1}. Show that THEOREM 4.60(2) can be written

$$|\Delta_*| = P_G\left(\frac{\partial}{\partial z_1}, \ldots, \frac{\partial}{\partial z_d}\right) P_H(1+z_1, 1+2z_2, \ldots, 1+rz_r)$$

evaluated at $z_1 = \ldots = z_r = 0$.
Hint: Note that if $|\Delta_*| \neq 0$ then we must have $r \geq d$. For any integers p, q, and s, where $q \leq s$, we have

$$\left[\frac{\partial}{\partial z}\right]^q (1+pz)^s \big|_{z=0} = p^q s(s-1)(s-2) \ldots (s-q+1) = p^q(s)_q.$$

This latter expression occurs in THEOREM 4.60(2) with $k = p$, $q = \nu_D(a,k)$ and $s = \nu_R(a,k)$.

(3) Show that in the case where $|D| = |R|$ the identity of (2) becomes $|\Delta_*| =$

$$P_G\left(\frac{\partial}{\partial z_1}, \ldots, \frac{\partial}{\partial z_d}\right) P_H(z_1, 2z_2, \ldots, dz_d) \text{ evaluated at } z_1 = \ldots = z_d = 0.$$

Hint: Note that $\left(\dfrac{\partial}{\partial z_1}\right)^{q_1} \cdots \left(\dfrac{\partial}{\partial z_d}\right)^{q_d} z_1^{s_1} (2z_2)^{s_2} \cdots (dz_d)^{s_d}$ is equal to

$\left(\dfrac{\partial}{\partial z_1}\right)^{q_1} \cdots \left(\dfrac{\partial}{\partial z_d}\right)^{q_d} (1+z_1)^{s_1} (1+2z_2)^{s_2} \cdots (1+dz_d)^{s_d}$ if $q_i = s_i$ for all

i. Otherwise, using $|D| = |R|$, show $q_i > s_i$ for some i and both expressions are zero.

(4) Illustrate the result of EXERCISE (3) with some examples.

(5) Consider $A = G \times H$ as in EXERCISE (2) above. Show that THEOREM 4.60(1) can be written

$$|\Delta| = P_G\left(\frac{\partial}{\partial z_1}, \ldots, \frac{\partial}{\partial z_d}\right) P_H(g_1, \ldots, g_r)\big|_{z_1 = z_2 = z_3 = \ldots = 0}$$

where $g_t = \exp\left(j \sum_t z_{t \cdot j}\right)$. The notation $z_{t \cdot j}$ means z with subscript equal to the product of t and j. Thus, $z_{2 \cdot 3} = z_6$.

(6) Consider the following two problems:
   (a) The faces and the vertices of a cube are to be labeled (simultaneously) with symbols from a set R. How many ways are there to do this up to rotations of the cube?
   (b) The faces of a cube are to be labeled with symbols from a set R_1 and the vertices of a cube are to be labeled with symbols from a set R_2 ($R_1 \cap R_2 = \phi$). How many ways are there to do this up to the rotations of the cube?

   Discuss the solutions to these problems. Does either problem require an extension of Pólya's theorem? If so, formulate this extension in the general case.

(7) Let T and D be sets and A a group that acts on T and D. Let A act on R^D by the Pólya action. Thus, A acts on $T \times R^D$ by the Cartesian action $(a(t,f) = (at, fa^{-1}))$. Let $U_A(z_1, \ldots, z_d) = \sum_{t \in \Delta(T)} P_{A_t}(z_1, \ldots, z_d)$ where A_t is the stability subgroup of A at t (relative to A: T) and $\Delta(T)$ is a system of orbit representatives for A: T. Show that $U_A(r, \ldots, r)$ is the number of orbits of A acting on $T \times R^D$ where $r = |R|$. What are some combinatorial interpretations of this result? *Hint.* The collection of sets $\{\{t\} \times R^D : t \in T\}$ is a partition of $T \times R^D$. Note that the blocks of this partition are invariant under the action of the group A in the sense that $a \in A$, $a(\{t\} \times R^D) = \{at\} \times R^D$, and the latter set is still a block of the partition. This type of generalization has been developed by deBruijn (see references list at end of Part I). In fact, the idea of invariant partitions extends to any group action and was the basis

of our isomorph rejection algorithms earlier in Chapter 1 (for example, the n-queens problem of FIGURE 1.62 through FIGURE 1.77).

(8) If G acts on D and H acts on R then we have noted that the action of $G \times H$ on $D \times R$ defines an action on the sets $\{\text{GRAPH}(f): f \in R^D\}$. In this action, f is sent to hfg^{-1} by the element (g,h) of $G \times H$. But, the wreath product $G[H]$ also acts on $D \times R$ by the rule $(g,\varphi)(i,j) = (gi,\varphi(i)j)$. Thus, $G[H]$ also acts on the set $\{\text{GRAPH}(f): f \in R_D\}$. Under this action, f is sent by (g,φ) to a function whose value at $x \in D$ is $\varphi(g^{-1}x)f(g^{-1}x)$. Compare these two actions on R^D by giving some examples for small order cases ($C_3[C_2]$, $C_4[C_3]$, or $S_3[S_2]$). Various applications of this action as well as a formula for this cycle index polynomial are given in the Palmer and the Robinson references cited at the end of Part I.

(9) Consider the following figure:

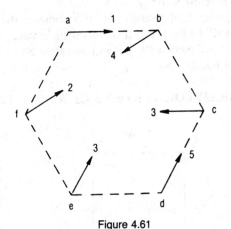

Figure 4.61

This figure shows the correspondence between functions in R^D and hexagons with unit vectors attached to each vertex. ($D = \{a,b,c,d,e,f\}$, $R = \underline{5}$). If one stands at a vertex of the hexagon and looks toward the center, then the other vertices are referred to as "1,2,3,4,5," left to right. Thus, at vertex a the arrow points to the first vertex left to right (which is b), at vertex b the arrow points to the fourth vertex (which is f), etc. This figure corresponds to the function $f = \begin{pmatrix} a\ b\ c\ d\ e\ f \\ 1\ 4\ 3\ 5\ 3\ 2 \end{pmatrix}$. How many such "vector labeled" hexagons are there up to rotations of the hexagon? How many up to rotations and reflections?

We conclude this TOPIC with a discussion of the constructive isomorph rejection problem. That is, we wish to actually construct a system of representatives for the orbits of any group action A: S. The reader who has not read the development of the various orbit enumeration techniques presented thus far in this TOPIC should read the material through LEMMA 4.10 and also read EXAMPLE 4.34, EXERCISE 4.35, DEFINITION 4.36, and DEFINITIONS 4.55 and 4.56. We have already presented the most basic techniques for solving isomorph rejection problems in EXERCISE 1.38 and in connection with the discussion of the solution to the n-queens problem (FIGURES 1.62–1.77). We now discuss a more specialized but very useful technique called the method of "orderly algorithms." A graph theoretic applications of this method are presented independently in Part II (items 6.67, 6.76–6.79 of study guide). They are in BASIC CONCEPTS Chapter 6. Our approach to orderly algorithms will emphasize a particular but very important case, the generation of set partitions of a fixed type. We first consider a class of problems where such set partitions arise naturally. If you wish, you may look quickly at the material from here through EXERCISE 4.64 and then return to this material for careful study in connection with EXERCISE 4.70(3).

We consider the group A of rotations and reflections of the square as shown in FIGURE 4.2. Let R^D be the set of functions with domain $D = \{a,b,c,d\}$ and range $R = \{L,M,R\}$. A function $f \in R^D$ will be called an "LMR-diagram" as shown in FIGURE 4.62.

4.62 LMR-DIAGRAM FOR VERTICES OF A SQUARE.

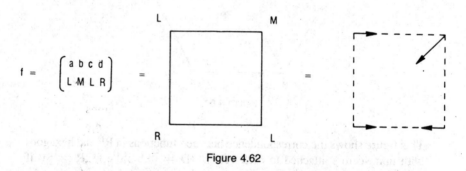

Figure 4.62

The function f of FIGURE 4.62 corresponds to the labeling of the vertices of a square with unit vectors. If $f(a) = L$, then as one stands at vertex a and faces the center of the square, a unit vector is drawn pointing to the left. If $f(a) = M$ the vector is drawn towards the middle, and if $f(a) = R$, the vector is drawn towards the right as shown in FIGURE 4.62. This idea was explored in a slightly more complex situation in EXERCISE 4.61(9). Associated with each such function is its coimage (NOTATION 1.6). The coimage(f) is the set partition of D defined by $\{f^{-1}(x): x \in \text{image}(f)\}$. For the function f of FIGURE 4.62, we have image(f) = $\{L,M,R\}$ and hence coimage(f) = $\{f^{-1}(L),f^{-1}(M),f^{-1}(R)\}$ = $\{\{a,c\},\{b\},\{d\}\}$. A rotation τ acts on an L,M,R diagram by rotating the structure 90° counterclockwise $(f \rightarrow \tau f \tau^{-1})$ and does not change the L, M, or R labels (only their positions). A reflection ρ acts by the rule $f \rightarrow \rho f \rho^{-1} = \rho f \rho$ and changes L to R and R to L. Thus, the reflection $\rho_r = (b,d)$ applied to the function f of FIGURE 4.62 produces the function $g = \begin{pmatrix} a & b & c & d \\ R & L & R & M \end{pmatrix}$. The action of A on

R^D is the Cartesian action on functions of DEFINITION 4.56.

If a group A acts on a set D, then A acts on the set $\Pi(D)$ of all partitions of D in an obvious way. If $\mathscr{C} = \{B_1, B_2, \ldots, B_p\}$ is a partition of D with blocks B_s, and if $a \in A$ then $a\mathscr{C} = \{aB_1, aB_2, \ldots, aB_p\}$ where aB_s is the set obtained by applying a to each element of B_s. Let $\nu(\mathscr{C}, j)$ denote the number of blocks B_t of $\mathscr{C}$ with $|B_t| = j$. The vector $(\nu(\mathscr{C},1), \nu(\mathscr{C},2), \ldots, \nu(\mathscr{C},d))$ is called the *type* of the partition $\mathscr{C}$. This is sometimes an awkward notation (suppose $d = 20$, $\nu(\mathscr{C},10)$ = 2, then the type is $(0,0,0,0,0,0,0,0,0,2,0,0,0,0,0,0,0,0,0,0))$. Another notation is $1^{\nu(\mathscr{C},1)} 2^{\nu(\mathscr{C},2)} \ldots d^{\nu(\mathscr{C},d)}$ where an expression of the form k^0 is always omitted. Thus, 10^2 would denote a partition of 20 with two blocks of size 10, $1^3 2^4 5^2$ would denote a partition of 21 with three blocks of size 1, four blocks of size 2, and two blocks of size 5.

If we wish to construct a system of orbit representatives for the Cartesian action of a group A acting on a set of functions R^D, then we may first construct a system $\Delta(\Pi)$ of representatives for A acting on the partitions of D (i.e., $\Pi(D)$). If $\mathscr{C} \in \Delta(\Pi)$ then let $A_{\mathscr{C}}$ denote the stability subgroup of A at $\mathscr{C}$ (all $a \in A$ such that $a\mathscr{C} = \mathscr{C}$). We may then construct a system of orbit representatives for $A_{\mathscr{C}}$ acting on the set of all functions $f \in R^D$ such that coimage(f) = $\mathscr{C}$. The resulting set will be a system of representatives for $A: R^D$. This process is illustrated in FIGURE 4.63. The general idea is developed in EXERCISE 4.64(3) and relates to the example of this paragraph by taking $S = R^D$ and $\mathscr{I} = \Pi(D)$. For $i \in \Pi(D)$, F_i of EXERCISE 4.64(3) is all functions in $R^D = S$ with coimage equal to i. For $a \in A$, $F_i \in \mathscr{F}$, a $F_i = F_{ai}$ where ai is defined as in the previous paragraph (take $i = \mathscr{C}$ there).

In FIGURE 4.63, a system of representatives $\Delta(\Pi)$ for the dihedral group D_8 acting on the partitions of the set $\{a,b,c,d\}$ is shown. The symbols a, b, c, and d refer to the vertices of the square of FIGURE 4.2. The set $\Delta(\Pi)$ is obtained by a simple inspection in this case but will be obtained below by a specific algorithm for the general case. For each $\mathscr{C}$ in $\Delta(\Pi)$ we compute the stability subgroup $A_{\mathscr{C}}$. For $\{\{a\}\{b\}\{c\}\{d\}\} = \mathscr{C}$ there are no LMR diagrams with $\mathscr{C}$ as coimage. For $\{\{a\ b\}\{c\}\{d\}\} = \mathscr{C}$, $A_{\mathscr{C}} = \{e, \rho_s\}$. For $\{\{a\ c\}\{b\}\{d\}\} = \mathscr{C}$, $A_{\mathscr{C}} = \{e, \rho_r, \rho_t, \tau^2\}$. For $\{\{a\ c\}\{b\ d\}\}$, the stability subgroup is all of D_8. For $\{\{a\ b\ c\}\{d\}\}$, the stability subgroup is $\{e, \rho_t\}$ and for $\{a\ b\ c\ d\}$ the stability subgroup is again D_8. For each $\mathscr{C}$ we list a system of representatives for the set of LMR diagrams with coimage equal to $\mathscr{C}$ under the action of $A_{\mathscr{C}}$. This set is obviously complete for $A: R^D$. In general, this method defines a recursive algorithm for isomorph rejection in the case of the Cartesian action of A on R^D. For each $\mathscr{C}$, the problem is reduced to an isomorph rejection problem for the Cartesian action of A on

$R_*^{\mathscr{C}}$, the injective functions from $\mathscr{C}$ to R. In general, each of these subproblems may be treated recursively in the same manner.

4.63　ORBIT REPRESENTATIVE SYSTEMS FOR LMR DIAGRAMS.

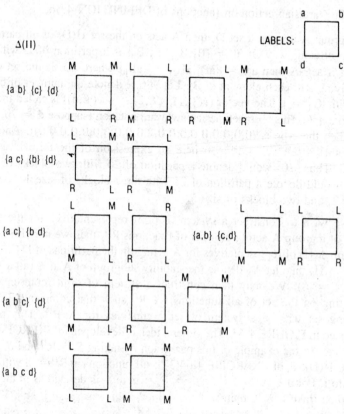

Figure 4.63

4.64　EXERCISE.

(1) Let A be a group that acts on D and hence on R^D by the Pólya action (DEFINITION 4.36). Let D = {a,b,c,d}, R = {$y_1, y_2, \ldots, y_r$}, A = D_8 as in FIGURE 4.63. Using $\Delta(\Pi)$ of FIGURE 4.63, describe for each $\mathscr{C} \in \Delta(\Pi)$ the system of orbit representatives for $A_{\mathscr{C}}$ acting on the functions $f \in R^D$ with coimage(f) = $\mathscr{C}$. For each $\mathscr{C}$, express the number of such orbit representatives as a function of r and, by summing over all $\mathscr{C}$ in $\Delta(\Pi)$, express the total number of orbit representatives for A acting on R^D as a function of r. Compare this result with the formula obtained by applying PÓLYA'S THEOREM 4.43 to the same problem.

(2) Work EXERCISE 4.64(1) above where $D = \{a,b,c,d,e,f\}$ are the vertices of a hexagon and A is the dihedral group (all rotations and reflections). Suppose that "side conditions" are placed on the structures being listed such as (a) if any symbol y_i of R appears at a vertex of the hexagon it must also appear at at least one other vertex, and (b) no two adjacent vertices of the hexagon are labeled with the same symbol of R. Describe the orbit representatives that satisfy conditions (a) and (b). Can PÓLYA'S THEOREM 4.43 or BURNSIDE'S LEMMA 4.15, COROLLARY 4.16 be applied to this situation? Explain.

(3) Let S be a set, and let A be a group that acts on S. Let $\mathscr{F} = \{F_i : i \in \mathscr{I}\}$ be a partition of S (the set $\mathscr{I}$ is an "index set"). If for all $i \in \mathscr{I}$ and all $a \in A$, $aF_i = F_j$ for some $j \in \mathscr{I}$, then $\mathscr{F}$ is called an A-*invariant partition* or simply an *invariant partition*. In this case, we say that A acts on the partition $\mathscr{F}$. Let $\Delta(\mathscr{F})$ be a system of orbit representatives for A: $\mathscr{F}$ and let $\Delta(F)$ be a system of orbit representatives for A_F acting on F where F is a block of $\mathscr{F}$ and A_F is the stability subgroup of A at F (all $a \in A$, $aF = F$). Let $\Delta(S)$ be the union over all F in $\Delta(\mathscr{F})$ of $\Delta(F)$. Prove that $\Delta(S)$ is a system of orbit representatives for A acting on S. What are $\mathscr{I}$, $\Delta(\mathscr{F})$, and $\Delta(F)$ for the example of FIGURE 4.63?

(4) Let G and H be groups and $G \times H$ their direct product. Let $G \times H$ act on R^D by the Cartesian action $((g,h)f = hfg^{-1})$. If $H = PER(R)$ is the symmetric group on R, find a natural bijection between the orbits of $G \times H$ acting on R^D and the orbits of G acting on $\Pi(D)$, the set of all partitions of D.

4.65   STRUCTURE OF ORDERLY ALGORITHM 4.66:
The orderly map B.

BASIC CONDITION: $B(\Delta_\mu) \subseteq \Delta_\theta$

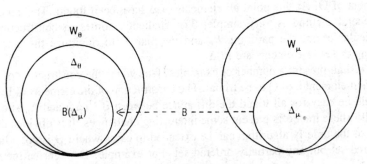

Figure 4.65

As EXERCISE 4.64 indicates, certain basic combinatorial isomorph rejection problems are central to a number of related problems. The generation of set partitions by type under a group action is such a problem. Independent of any group theoretic considerations, the problem we are dealing with is, given W and a subset Δ, find Δ. We assume that, given an element of W, we can test it to see if it is an element of Δ. Suppose that $\{W_\theta : \theta \in \Theta\}$ is a partition of W where Θ is a linearly ordered set. For each block W_μ, let $\Delta_\mu = W_\mu \cap \Delta$. An *orderly map* B for this partition is a function defined on blocks W_μ, $\mu \neq$ first element of Θ, which maps W_μ to W_θ where θ is the predecessor of μ in the linear order on Θ. In addition, B must satisfy the condition $B(\Delta_\mu) \subseteq \Delta_\theta$. The situation is illustrated in FIGURE 4.65. A number of useful algorithms have the general structure of ALGORITHM 4.66.

4.66 ORDERLY ALGORITHM WITH ORDERLY MAP B.

procedure FIND Δ.
    $\theta := $ first element of Θ;
    $U := \Delta_\theta$
    while . $\theta \neq$ last element of Θ *do*
        begin
                $\mu := $ successor of θ in Θ;
                compute $B^{-1}(\Delta_\theta)$;
                find $B^{-1}(\Delta_\theta) \cap \Delta$;
                $\Delta_\mu := B^{-1}(\Delta_\theta) \cap \Delta$;
                $U := U \cup \Delta_\mu$;
                $\theta := \mu$;
        end
    $\Delta := U$; .

The intuitive idea of ALGORITHM 4.66 is that one starts with the first element θ of Θ and constructs, in a manner unspecified, Δ_θ. One then computes $B^{-1}(\Delta_\theta)$. The condition $B(\Delta_\mu) \subseteq \Delta_\theta$, μ the successor of θ, assures us that all elements of Δ_μ are contained in $B^{-1}(\Delta_\theta)$. One then searches the elements of $B^{-1}(\Delta_\theta)$ for all elements of Δ to obtain Δ_μ. This process is repeated until θ becomes the last element of Θ. At this point all elements of Δ have been found. This process as a general method is very simple. The challenge comes in constructing, for particular cases, the partition W_θ and the map B to minimize the amount of testing to see if elements are in Δ.

We shall present a number of examples. One wants the construction of Δ_θ for the first element θ of Θ to be trivial. The construction of the elements of $B^{-1}(\Delta_\theta)$ should be easy for all θ and the difference between $B^{-1}(\Delta_\theta)$ and Δ_μ should be small. These tradeoffs present some interesting challenges. It is obvious that the idea of the orderly algorithm can be extended to cases where Θ is not a linearly ordered set but any partially ordered set. For example, Θ might be the vertex set of a rooted tree. The algorithm would start with Δ_θ given, θ the root of the tree. The map B in this case would map W_μ for all μ, $\mu \neq$ root, to W_θ, where θ is the farther of μ. For the orderly algorithm one first computes $B^{-1}(\Delta_\theta)$ where θ is the root and searches for the sets Δ_μ for each son μ of θ. The process is then repeated on each subtree of the root. We shall illustrate this approach with an example rather than formally describe the method in this generality (see FIGURE 4.69 and related discussion).

4.67 ORDERLY ALGORITHM FOR RANGE ACTIONS.

Let $W = \bigcup\limits_{d=1}^{p} \underline{r}^{\underline{d}}$. Let H be a group acting on $\underline{r}$. Then H acts on W by the rule $f \rightarrow hf$, for $f \in W$, $h \in H$. Let $W_d = \underline{r}^{\underline{d}}$ and $\Theta = \underline{p}$. Using one line notation, let $f = (f_1, \ldots, f_d)$ and define $B(f) = (f_1, \ldots, f_{d-1})$. Let Δ_d be a lexicographically minimal system of orbit representatives for H acting on $\underline{r}^{\underline{d}}$. Then it is easily seen that $B(\Delta_d) \subseteq \Delta_{d-1}$ (EXERCISE 4.68(1)). Hence, B is an orderly map in the sense of FIGURE 4.65. In order to be more specific, take $r = 4$ and $H = D_8$, the dihedral group. H may be thought of as the permutations of the vertices of the square

Figure 4.67

resulting from all rotations and reflections of the square (as in the case of FIGURE 4.2 with {a,b,c,d} replaced by {1,2,3,4}). In this case, $\Delta_1 = \{1\}$. $B^{-1}(\Delta_1) = \{(1,1),(1,2),(1,3),(1,4)\}$. We must check to see if each of these elements of $\underline{4}^{\underline{2}}$ is minimal in its orbit under the action of H. Consider (1,4) for example. For $h \in H$, $h(1,4) = (h1,h4)$. Clearly, if (h1,h4) is less than (1,4) in lex order, then $h1 = 1$. This means that h is the identity or the reflection about the line joining vertex 1 to vertex 3 in the above figure. For this reflection, $h4 = 2$, so (1,4) is not lex minimal in its orbit and is thus not an element of Δ_2. The elements (1,1), (1,2), and (1,3) are all in Δ_2 as they are easily seen to be lex minimal. For simplicity, we write $\Delta_2 = \{11,12,13\}$. Then $B^{-1}(\Delta_2) = \{111,112,113,\underline{114},121,122,123,124,131,132,133,\underline{134}\}$ where the elements not in Δ_3 are indicated.

4.68 EXERCISE.

(1) Prove that the map B of EXAMPLE 4.67 is an orderly map (satisfies $B(\Delta_d) \subseteq \Delta_{d-1}$).

(2) Extend EXAMPLE 4.67 to the general case where $H = D_{2r}$ is the dihedral group acting on the set $\underline{r}$. This may be thought of as the permutations of the vertices of a regular polygon with r vertices resulting from all rotations and reflections. Describe Δ_d for all d.

(3) Let $W = \underline{r}^d$ and let $W_k = \left\{ f: \sum_{i=1}^{d} f(i) = k \right\}$. Let $\Theta = (dr, dr-1, \ldots, d)$. Write $f = (f_1, f_2, \ldots, f_t, r, \ldots, r)$ where $f_t < r$, $t \leq d$. Define the orderly map B by the rule $B(f) = (f_1, \ldots, f_t + 1, r, \ldots, r)$. Let Δ be a lexicographically minimal system of orbit representatives for the Pólya action of G on $\underline{r}^d$ (DEFINITION 4.36). Prove that $B(\Delta_k) \subseteq \Delta_{k+1}$ and hence that B is an orderly map. (Note that k is "larger" than k+1 in the order on Θ.) Give some examples of the resulting algorithm.

We now give an example of an orderly algorithm where the index set for the blocks of the partition of W has the structure of an ordered rooted tree. We consider the important case of the generation of set partitions by type discussed above. Consider FIGURE 4.69. FIGURE 4.69(a) is a binary tree whose vertices are integral partitions of 6. We use the mixed notation $(\tau_1, \ldots, \tau_j, 1^k)$ to indicate the integral partition $(\tau_1, \tau_2, \ldots, \tau_j, 1, \ldots, 1)$ of d where the entries are in nonincreasing order and there are k ones. The general rule for constructing the tree is given in FIGURE 4.69(b). If the rule for constructing a son of a vertex is not applicable, then that vertex is labeled by ∅. The terminal nodes of the tree are either the symbol ∅ or an integral partition without 1's. The reader is asked, in EXERCISE 4.70(1), to show that this method, in fact, generates all partitions of d. We call the tree of FIGURE 4.69 the *type tree of order* d (order 6 is shown in FIGURE 4.69(a)).

4.69 THE TYPE TREE.

(a)

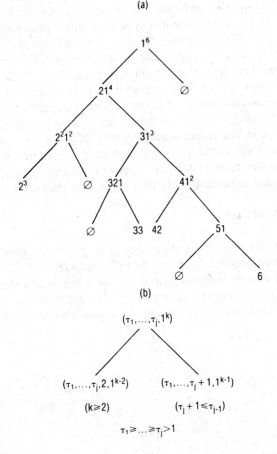

(b)

$$\tau_1 \geq \ldots \geq \tau_j > 1$$

Figure 4.69

Let Θ denote the vertices of the type tree. Let W be all set partitions of $\underline{d}$ and let W_θ, $\theta \in \Theta$ be all partitions of type θ. If G is a group that acts on $\underline{d}$, then G acts on W as explained in connection with FIGURES 4.62 and 4.63. We say that a partition $\mathscr{C} = \{B_1, \ldots B_p\}$ of $\underline{d}$ is *in order* if $i < j$ implies that $|B_i| > |B_j|$ or, if $|B_i| = |B_j|$, then the minimum element of B_i is less than the minimum element of B_j. If $\mathscr{C}$ has its blocks in order, and each block is written in increasing order, then the sequence of integers obtained by concatenating these blocks will be called the *standard form* of $\mathscr{C}$. For example, the partition $\mathscr{C} = \{\{3,5,8\},\{1,4\},\{2,6\},\{7\}\}$ is in order and the blocks are in increasing order. The standard form of this partition is $3,5,8,1,4,2,6,7$.

It is obvious that given the type and the standard form of a partition, one can construct the partition. The reader should practice applying some permutations to partitions in standard form. For instance, suppose that $\sigma = (1,3,5,7)(2,4,6,8)$

is a permutation of $\underline{8}$ in cycle notation. Let $\mathcal{C}$ be as above, then $\sigma\mathcal{C}$ is 2,5,7,3,6,4,8,1 in standard form. We order the sets W_θ lexicographically in standard form. For each $\theta \in \Theta$ let Δ_θ be a minimal system of orbit representatives with respect to this lex order. We now define, for each θ, not the root of the type tree, the map $B: W_\theta \to W_\mu$ where μ is the father of θ in the type tree. Let $\mathcal{C} = \{B_1, . . ., B_p\}$ be in order. Let j be the largest index such that $|B_j| > 1$. Define $B(\mathcal{C})$ to be the partition obtained from $\mathcal{C}$ by removing the largest element from B_j and creating from that element a new block of size 1. We ask the reader to show in EXERCISE 4.70(2) that $B(\Delta_\theta) \subseteq \Delta_\mu$, and hence that B is an orderly map. We call B the *type tree map*. The reader is asked in EXERCISE 4.70(3) to describe and give examples of the resulting orderly algorithm. For further reading, consult the paper "Construction of Minimal Representative Systems" by White and Williamson cited in the references for Chapter 4 at the end of Part I.

4.70 EXERCISE.

(1) Prove that every integral partition of d appears just once as a vertex of the type tree of order d, defined by FIGURE 4.69.
(2) Prove that the type tree map B defined above is an orderly map.
(3) Describe the orderly algorithm based on the type tree map B of (2). Give some examples of applications to the problems of EXERCISE 4.64.

Chapter 5

Topic IV: Some Classical Combinatorics

The purpose of this TOPIC is to give a brief presentation of several classical subjects in the field of combinatorics. The subjects are:

- A. Generating functions
- B. Inclusion-exclusion
- C. Möbius inversion
- D. Network flows

The last subject has an extensive literature and involves many interesting algorithmic and data structure related ideas. A thorough discussion of network flows is beyond the scope of this book. We present only the basic ideas. The other subjects represent interesting and important ideas in combinatorics but are of less direct interest to the study of algorithms than the material we have been considering thus far. Generating functions are often useful in obtaining asymptotic complexity results in the theory of algorithms. Inclusion-exclusion and Möbius inversion are interesting classical techniques in enumerative combinatorics where "enumeration" means counting and not listing. These four topics are presented independently of each other. In each case we present only the basic ideas involved. The reader interested in pursuing these subjects further will find appropriate references at the end of Part I. We shall use certain aspects of these topics to motivate some of the material in Part II, and will at certain points refer the reader to the relevant sections within Part II.

5A. GENERATING FUNCTIONS

5A.1 DEFINITION.

The *ordinary generating function* of a sequence $a_0, a_1, \ldots$ is the "formal power series" $a(x) = \sum_{n=0}^{\infty} a_n x^n$.

It is convenient initially to think of the a_i as real or complex numbers but in general they may be polynomials or other functions of x, or may themselves be formal power series. In some instances it is important to consider the question of convergence of the generating function a(x). We shall give some elementary examples of the uses of ordinary generating functions. The references at the end of the chapter contain many additional examples.

5A.2 PRODUCTS OF ORDINARY GENERATING FUNCTIONS.

Let $a(x) = \sum_{n=0}^{\infty} a_n x^n$ and $b(x) = \sum_{n=0}^{\infty} b_n x^n$. Then $c(x) = a(x)b(x) = \sum_{n=0}^{\infty} c_n x^n$

where $c_n = \sum_{k=0}^{n} a_k b_{n-k}$. The sequence $(c_0, c_1, \ldots)$ is said to be the *convolution* of the sequences $(a_0, a_1, \ldots)$ and $(b_0, b_1, \ldots)$.

For example, suppose we wish to find the coefficient of x^{37} in

$$f(x) = \frac{1 - 3x^2 + 4x^7 + 12x^{21} - 5x^{45}}{1 - x}.$$

We note that $\dfrac{1}{1-x} = \sum_{n=0}^{\infty} x^n = b(x)$ is the generating function of $(b_0, b_1, \ldots)$

$= (1, 1, \ldots)$. If we set $a(x) = \sum_{n=0}^{\infty} a_n x^n = 1 - 3x^2 + 4x^7 + 12x^{21} - 5x^{45}$

then the coefficient of x^{37} in $a(x)b(x)$ is $\sum_{k=0}^{37} a_k b_{37-k} = \sum_{k=0}^{37} a_k = 1 - 3 + 4$

$+ 12 = 14$.

As a variation on the interpretation of products of generating functions consider

$(1+x)^m = \sum_{k=0}^{m} \binom{m}{k} x^k$, the generating function of the sequence $\left(\binom{m}{0}, \right.$

$\binom{m}{1}, \ldots, \binom{m}{m}, 0, 0, \ldots \Big)$. Thus $(1+x)^m (1+x^{-1})^m$ has $\sum_{k=0}^{m} \binom{m}{k}^2$ as

constant term. But $(1+x)^m (1+x^{-1})^m = x^{-m}(1+x)^{2m} = x^{-m} \sum_{k=0}^{2m} \binom{2m}{k} x^k$

which has constant term $\binom{2m}{m}$. Thus we have proved that $\sum_{k=0}^{m} \binom{m}{k}^2 =$

$\binom{2m}{m}$.

5A.3 EXERCISE.

(1) Find the following indicated coefficients:
   (a) The coefficient of x^{20} in $(x^4 + x^5 + x^6 + x^7 + x^8)^3$.
   (b) The coefficient of x^{12} in $\dfrac{x + 3}{x^2 - 3x + 2}$.
   (c) The coefficient of x^{12} in $(1 + x^4)^{-3}$.
   (d) The coefficient of x^k in $\dfrac{t^n x^m}{(1 + tx)^{n+1}}$.
   (e) The coefficient of x^k in $(1 - x)^{-n}$.

(2) Prove that $\displaystyle\prod_{i=1}^{\infty} (1 + x^i) = \prod_{i=1}^{\infty} (1 - x^{2i-1})^{-1}$ and find the first few coefficients
   in the power series expansion. (*Hint*: Write out the first five or six factors
   in each product and the idea of the proof will become obvious).

As the above examples indicate, it is often important to find "closed form"
expressions for generating functions. An important general method is represented
in EXAMPLE 5A.4.

5A.4 EXAMPLE: TWO-TERM LINEAR RECURRENCES.

Consider infinite sequences $(a_0, a_1, \ldots)$ which satisfy the "linear two-term recurrence relation" $a_{k+2} = pa_k + qa_{k+1}$ where p and q are constants (all numbers
are complex numbers which, of course, includes real numbers). Such a sequence,
or its corresponding ordinary generating function $a(x)$, is determined completely
by the first two terms, a_0 and a_1. Thus $a(x)$ may be specified by giving a pair
of complex numbers (a_0, a_1). If $a(x)$ is determined by (a_0, a_1), and $b(x)$ is determined by (b_0, b_1), then $a(x) + b(x)$ is determined by $(a_0 + b_0, a_1 + b_1)$, and
$ra(x)$, where r is a complex number, is determined by (ra_0, ra_1). Thus, as a vector
space, the space of all formal power series that satisfy the given two-term
recursion is isomorphic to $\mathbb{C}^2$, the two-dimensional vector space of all complex
numbers. The standard "unit vectors" for $\mathbb{C}^2$ are $\underline{i} = (1,0)$ and $\underline{j} = (0,1)$ with
corresponding sequences $(1,0,p,qp,\ldots)$ and $(0,1,q,p+q^2,\ldots)$ and correspond-
ing power series $i(x) = 1 + px^2 + qpx^3 + \ldots$ and $j(x) = x + qx^2 +
(p+q^2)x^3 + \ldots$. Any power series whose coefficients satisfy the given two-
term recursion can be written as a linear combination of $\underline{i}(x)$ and $\underline{j}(x)$, but generally
this is not much help as $\underline{i}(x)$ and $\underline{j}(x)$ are awkward expressions. Note, however,
that if r is a root of the equation $x^2 = qx + p$ then the sequence $(1,r,r^2,r^3,\ldots)$
satisfies the two-term recursion. The corresponding generating function is $u(x)$
$= 1 + rx + r^2x^2 + \ldots = (1-rx)^{-1}$. If $s \neq r$ is another root, then its
generating function $v(x) = (1 - sx)^{-1}$ is linearly independent from the generating
function corresponding to the root r, and hence any generating function that
satisfies the given recursion can be written as a linear combination of these two
simple generating functions.

Consider, for example, the sequence $(1; 0, -2, -6, -14, \ldots)$ or the generating function $a(x) = 1 - 2x^2 - 6x^3 - 14x^4 \ldots$ which correspond to $q = 3$ and $p = -2$. The equation $x^2 = 3x - 2$ has two roots, $r = 1$ and $s = 2$. Thus the two basis generating functions $u(x) = (1 - x)^{-1}$ and $v(x) = (1 - 2x)^{-1}$ may be used to express this generating function. As $(1,0) = 2(1,1) + (-1)(1,2)$ we have $a(x) = 2(1 - x)^{-1} + (-1)(1 - 2x)^{-1}$. It is immediate from this expression that the nth coefficient of $a(x)$, a_n, is given by the formula $a_n = 2 - 2^n$. An expression such as this is sometimes called a "closed form" expression for a_n.

5A.5 EXERCISE.

(1) A Fibbonacci sequence is a sequence $(a_0, a_1, a_2, \ldots)$ that satisfies the linear two-term recurrence $a_{k+2} = a_k + a_{k+1}$ (i.e., $p = q = 1$ in EXAMPLE 5A.4). Find the basis series $u(x)$ and $v(x)$ for these sequences (as in EXAMPLE 5A.4). Find a closed form expression for the nth term of the Fibonacci sequence $(0,1,1,2,3,5,8, \ldots)$.

(2) Given that the sequence $(0,1,3,13,51, \ldots)$ satisfies a linear two-term recurrence, find the recurrence relation and the basis series $u(x)$ and $v(x)$. Find a closed form expression for the nth term.

(3) How should the results of EXAMPLE 5A.4 be modified if $r = s$? (*Hint*: If
$$u(x) = \frac{1}{1 - rx}, \text{ take } v(x) = \frac{d}{dr}\left(\frac{1}{1 - rx}\right).)$$

(4) Suppose that the sequence $(a_0, a_1, a_2, \ldots)$ satisfies a recurrence relation of the form $a_{k+2} = c + pa_k + qa_{k+1}$ where c is a fixed complex number. How should EXAMPLE 5A.4 be modified?

(5) Suppose that the sequence $(a_0, a_1, a_2, \ldots)$ satisfies a linear three-term recurrence $a_{k+3} = pa_k + qa_{k+1} + ta_{k+2}$. How should the results of EXAMPLE 5A.4 and EXERCISE 5A.5 (3) above be modified? Give some examples of the various possibilities. The theory of the linear m-term recurrence follows in the obvious way but becomes increasingly intractable in practice.

5A.6 EXAMPLE: GENERATING FUNCTIONS FOR COMPOSITIONS.

In TABLE 3.25 and in the associated discussion we considered nondecreasing functions. Consider, for example, the nondecreasing functions from $\underline{4}$ to $\underline{3}$. In one line notation, $(1,1,1,1)$, $(1,1,1,2)$, $(1,2,2,2)$, $(1,1,2,2)$, and $(1,1,2,3)$ are such functions. Another way to "code" or represent these functions is to specify instead triples (x_1, x_2, x_3) where x_1 is the number of 1's, x_2 is the number of 2's, and x_3 is the number of 3's in the corresponding nondecreasing function. The above functions would be represented by $(4,0,0)$, $(3,1,0)$, $(1,3,0)$, $(2,2,0)$, and $(2,1,1)$, respectively. The sum of the entries in these triples must, of course, add up to 4. A composition of n into p parts is a sequence $(x_1, x_2, \ldots, x_p)$ of non-negative integers whose sum is n. As we have just seen, there is a natural bijection between the compositions of n into p parts and the nondecreasing functions of $\underline{n}$ to $\underline{p}$. In connection with TABLE 3.25, we showed that there are $\binom{n+p-1}{n}$ such nondecreasing functions. In terms of generating functions, let

$a(x) = a_0 + a_1 x + \ldots$ be the generating function of the sequence $(a_0, a_1, \ldots)$ where a_n is the number of compositions of n into p parts. If $b(x) = 1 + x + x^2 + \ldots$ is the generating function of the sequence $(b_0, b_1, b_2, \ldots)$ where $b_i = 1$ for all i, then b(x) can be thought of as the generating function for the number of compositions of n into one part. Clearly, $c(x) = a(x)b(x)$ is the generating function of the compositions of n into $p+1$ parts. Thus, inductively, we see that $a(x) = (b(x))^p = (1-x)^{-p}$ is the generating function for the number of compositions of n into p parts. By the binomial theorem, $(b(x))^p = \sum_{n=0}^{\infty} \binom{-p}{n} (-x)^n$. But,

$$\binom{-p}{n} = \frac{-p(-p-1)(-p-2)\ldots(-p-n+1)}{n!} = (-1)^n \binom{n+p-1}{n}$$

and hence we derive again the formula for the number of nondecreasing functions or, equivalently, the number of compositions of n into p parts. By modifying this argument slightly, we can put various restrictions on the compositions. If no part is zero in the composition of n into p parts, then the generating function becomes $(c(x))^p = (x + x^2 + \ldots)^p$ or $\left(\dfrac{x}{1-x}\right)^p$. The generating function f(x)

$= \sum_{p=0}^{\infty} (c(x))^p$ is the generating function of the number of compositions of n without zero parts. Clearly,

$$f(x) = \frac{1}{1 - c(x)} = \frac{1-x}{1-2x} = 1 + \sum_{n=1}^{\infty} 2^{n-1} x^n.$$

One can easily derive this result directly by associating compositions of n with functions $\underline{2^{n-1}}$. The generating function for the number of compositions of n into 10 parts where the first part can be at most 5 and the last part can never be zero is $(1 + x + \ldots + x^5)(1-x)^{-8}(x/(1-x))$. As the references at the end of the chapter testify, an endless variety of cute word problems can be made up based on the idea of compositions with restricted parts.

5A.7 EXERCISE.

(1) Relate the following two problems to the discussion of EXAMPLE 5A.6:

(a) How many ways are there to get a sum of 36 when 12 dice are rolled?

(b) Suppose there are four large boxes. The first box is filled with green balls, the second is filled with blue balls, the third is filled with red balls, and the fourth is filled with yellow balls. How many ways are there to select 24 balls from these boxes if at least one ball must be selected from each box?

(2) Give an expression for the generating function for the number of compositions of n into p parts if the kth part is divisible by k, k = 1, . . . , p.

5A.8 EXAMPLE: GENERATING FUNCTIONS FOR INTEGRAL PARTITIONS.

Consider a sequence $1 \leqslant \lambda_1 \leqslant \lambda_2 \leqslant \lambda_3 \leqslant \lambda_4 \leqslant 4$ whose sum $\lambda_1 + \lambda_2 + \lambda_3 + \lambda_4 = 9$. For example, (1,2,2,4) and (2,2,2,3) are two such sequences. Such sequences are "integral partitions of 9 into four parts with maximum part size 4". We have considered integral partitions in the paragraph just following EXERCISE 3.50, in EXERCISE 3.51(2), and in FIGURE 4.69 and EXERCISE 4.70. The sequence (1,4,4) is also an integral partition of 9 with maximum part size 4 but it has only three parts. An integral partition such as these may be described by the notation $1^{j_1} 2^{j_2} 3^{j_3} 4^{j_4}$ which is read "j_1 1's, j_2 2's, j_3 3's, j_4 4's." We must have $j_1 + 2j_2 + 3j_3 + 4j_4 = 9$. The number of parts is $j_1 + j_2 + j_3 + j_4$. With this notation (1,2,2,4) would be written $1^1 2^2 4^1$ and (2,2,2,3) would be written $2^3 3^1$. Note that we omit terms such as 3^0 for convenience of notation. We could also describe such integral partitions by expressions of the form $(x)^{j_1} (x^2)^{j_2} (x^3)^{j_3} (x^4)^{j_4} = x^9$. From this latter description, it is easy to see that the number of integral partitions of 9 with maximum part size 4 is the coefficient of x^9 in the expansion of the product $(1 + x + x^2 + . . .)$ $(1 + (x^2) + (x^2)^2 + . . .) (1 + (x^3) + (x^3)^2 + . . .) (1 + (x^4) + (x^4)^2 + . . .)$. The reader should note that each integral partition of 9 with maximum part size 4 corresponds to a composition $(j_1, 2j_2, 3j_3, 4j_4)$ of 9 into four parts where the kth part is divisible by k (see EXERCISE 5A.7(2)). In any case, the generating function for the number of integral partitions of n with maximum part size 4 can obviously be written as the product $(1 - x)^{-1}(1 - x^2)^{-1}(1 - x^3)^{-1}(1 - x^4)^{-1}$. More generally, we have that the generating function for the number of integral partitions of n with maximum part size p is $\prod_{i=1}^{p} (1 - x^i)^{-1}$ and the generating function for the number of integral partitions of n (no restriction on part size) is $\prod_{i=1}^{\infty} (1 - x^i)^{-1}$.

Many variations on these ideas are possible.

5A.9 EXERCISE.

(1) Let c_n denote the number of ways to represent n cents in terms of pennies, nickels, dimes, and quarters. Find an expression for the generating function $c(x) = \sum_{n=1}^{\infty} c_n x^n$ and evaluate c_{100}.

(2) Explain why the generating function for the number of integral partitions with no repeated parts is given by $\prod_{i=1}^{\infty} (1+x^i)$ and the generating function for the number of integral partitions with each part odd is given by $\prod_{i=1}^{\infty} (1-x^{2i-1})^{-1}$. Note by EXERCISE 5A.3(2) we have the remarkable fact that these two classes of integral partitions are "equinumerous" as their generating functions are equal (see Remmel, 1982, in Part I References).

(3) Let (a_n) denote the sequence $(a_0, a_1, \ldots)$ with generating function $a(x)$. Note that $(d/dx)a(x)$ is the generating function for the sequence $((n+1)a_{n+1})$ and $x(d/dx)a(x)$ is the generating function for the sequence (na_n). We have already noticed that $(1-x)^{-1}a(x)$ is the generating function for the sequence $(a_0 + a_1 + \ldots + a_n)$. By combining these types of operations, generating functions of more complicated sequences can be constructed. Thus, $b(x) = (1-x)^{-1}x(d/dx)a(x)$ is the generating function of the sequence $(a_1 + 2a_2 + \ldots + na_n)$. For example, if we take $a(x) = (1-x)^{-1}$ then $b(x) = x/(1-x)^3$ must have as its coefficient of x^n the sum $1 + 2 + \ldots + n$. But, using EXERCISE 5A.3(1(e)), we see that the coefficient of x^n in $(1-x)^{-3}$ is $\binom{-3}{n} (-1)^n$ and hence the coefficient of x^n in $b(x)$ is $\binom{n+1}{2}$. This proves the standard result (easily proved geometrically or by induction) that $1 + 2 + \ldots + n = \binom{n+1}{2}$. Using these techniques, derive some more complicated identities of your own. One obvious one to try is $1^2 + 2^2 + \ldots + n^2 = \binom{n+1}{3} + \binom{n+2}{3}$.

(4) A product of three matrices $A_1 A_2 A_3$ can be taken in two ways: $(A_1 A_2)A_3$ and $A_1(A_2 A_3)$. In the first case, A_1 and A_2 are multiplied first, and in the second case A_2 and A_3 are multiplied first. For four matrices, there are five ways to form the product: $(A_1 A_2)(A_3 A_4)$, $((A_1 A_2)A_3)A_4$, $(A_1(A_2 A_3))A_4$, $A_1((A_2 A_3)A_4)$, and $A_1(A_2(A_3 A_4))$ (all yield the same answer).

(a) Let p_n denote the number of ways to take the product of n matrices. Show that $p_n = p_1 p_{n-1} + p_2 p_{n-2} + \ldots + p_{n-1}p_1$ when $n > 1$.

(b) Let $p(x) = p_1 x + p_2 x^2 + \ldots + p_n x^n + \ldots$ be the generating function for the p_n. Show that $p(x) - x = (p(x))^2$.

(c) Using the quadratic formula, solve the equation of part (b) for $p(x)$ to obtain $p(x) = (1 - (1-4x)^{1/2})/2$.

(d) Using the binomial theorem $(1+z)^a = \sum_{n=0}^{\infty} \binom{a}{n} z^n$ with $a = 1/2$ and $z = -4x$, show that $p_n = \frac{1}{n}\binom{2n-2}{n-1}$. The p_n are called "Catalan" numbers.

For certain computations the ordinary generating function becomes awkward, and it is best to introduce slight variations on this idea.

5A.10 DEFINITION.

The exponential generating function of a sequence $(a_0, a_1, \ldots)$ is the formal power series $\sum_{n=0}^{\infty} a_n x^n / n!$.

5A.11 PRODUCTS OF EXPONENTIAL GENERATING FUNCTIONS.

Let $a(x) = \sum_{n=0}^{\infty} a_n x^n / n!$ and $b(x) = \sum_{n=0}^{\infty} b_n x^n / n!$ and $c(x) = a(x)b(x)$

$$= \sum_{n=0}^{\infty} c_n x^n / n!.$$

Then $c_n = \sum_{k=0}^{n} \binom{n}{k} a_k b_{n-k}$.

Note that the exponential generating function of the sequence $(1, 1, \ldots)$ is e^x. We shall give some examples of the use of exponential generating functions. Many additional examples can be found in the references.

5A.12 EXAMPLE: EXPONENTIAL GENERATING FUNCTIONS AND DERANGEMENTS.

We use the standard notation S_n for the set of all permutations of $\underline{n}$. For $Q \subseteq \underline{n}$, let $D(Q) = \{f : f \in S_n \text{ and } f(i) = i \text{ if and only if } i \in \underline{n} - Q\}$. In other words, f is in $D(Q)$ if the set of elements of $\underline{n}$ that are fixed by f is $\underline{n} - Q$. The set $D(Q)$ will be called the set of Q-*derangements* of $\underline{n}$. The set of permutations $D(\underline{n})$ is called the set of *derangements* of $\underline{n}$. Let $d_n = |D(\underline{n})|$ denote the number of derangements of $\underline{n}$ ($d_0 = 1$). Clearly, if $|Q| = q$ then $|D(Q)| = d_q$. Obviously, S_n is the disjoint union of the $D(Q)$ as Q ranges over all subsets of $\underline{n}$. Thus we have $n! = \sum_{k=0}^{n} \binom{n}{k} d_k$. Let $d(x) = \sum_{n=0}^{\infty} d_n x^n / n!$ be the exponential generating function of the sequence (d_n). Using the rule for PRODUCTS OF EXPONENTIAL GENERATING FUNCTIONS 5A.11, we must have $\sum_{n=0}^{\infty} n! x^n / n! = d(x)e^x$

or $d(x) = e^{-x}(1-x)^{-1} = \sum_{n=0}^{\infty} c_n x^n / n!$ where $c_n = n! \sum_{k=0}^{n} (-1)^k / k!$. For large n, c_n is thus approximately $n!/e$ (e is about 2.7). This is the basis for the assertion that, if an irate hatcheck person scrambles the hatcheck receipts, the probability that no one gets their own hat back is e^{-1}. We shall derive this result from another point of view in the section on INCLUSION-EXCLUSION (EXAMPLE 5B.3).

5A.13   EXERCISE.

(1) Use generating functions to derive the recurrence relation $d_n = nd_{n-1} + (-1)^n$. *Hint*: $d(x)(1-x) = e^{-x}$.

(2) Use generating functions to derive the recurrence relation $d_{n+1} = n(d_n + d_{n-1})$. Explain why this recurrence relation is true using only the definition of derangements. (See EXERCISE 3.53.) Show $x\, d(x) + x\, d'(x) = d'(x)$.

(3) Consider $e^x(1-x)^{-p} = \sum\limits_{n=1}^{\infty} c_n x^n/n!$. It turns out that c_n is the number of ways to choose k balls (k = 0, 1,. . .,n) from n balls, labeled 1,. . .,n, and distribute them into p boxes where the order of the balls in the boxes matters. Thus $\lfloor 1,2 \mid 3 \rfloor$ is a different distribution of three balls into two boxes than $\lfloor 2,1 \mid 3 \rfloor$. Explain why the c_n have this interpretation.

We conclude our discussion of the exponential generating function with a discussion of "polynomials of binomial type." There are a number of approaches to the problem of giving a combinatorial model for generating functions. The reader will find some suggested articles in the references at the end of Part I.

We now give an elementary version of such a model. Imagine that, given a set S of integers, we are able to print the integers in g_s different colors where s = |S| (all integers in the set are printed the *same color*, but we have g_s different colors to choose from). We might denote by S_{red} the set S with all integers printed red, S_{blue} all integers printed blue, etc. Our basic assumption is that the number of colors that the set can be printed in depends only on the size of the set. Consider an ordered partition $(A_1, A_2, . . ., A_p)$ of $\underline{n}$ with multinomial index $(a_1, a_2, . . ., a_p)$. Such partitions were discussed in connection with FIGURE 3.3, EXERCISE 3.4, in the paragraph following EXERCISE 3.27, and in connection with FIGURE 3.28 and EXERCISE 3.29. We only need to recall here that the A_i form a pair-wise disjoint collection of subsets of $\underline{n}$ whose union is $\underline{n}$. For each i, $a_i = |A_i|$. We assume that the $a_i > 0$. For each set A_i, the integers of A_i can be printed in g_{a_i} different choices of colors (for each choice, all elements of A_i are printed in the same color as above). This means that there are $g_{a_1} g_{a_2} \cdots g_{a_p}$ different ways to print the given ordered partition. There are $n!/a_1! a_2! . . . a_p!$ ways to select an ordered partition on $\underline{n}$ with multinomial index $(a_1, a_2, . . ., a_p)$. This number is called the *multinomial coefficient*. (See EXERCISE 5A.34(1).)

5A.14   NOTATION FOR THE MULTINOMIAL COEFFICIENT

$$\frac{n!}{a_1! a_2! . . . a_p!} = \binom{n}{a_1 a_2 . . . a_p}.$$

Each set A_i in an ordered partition is called a *block* of the partition. The ordered partition $(A_1, A_2, . . ., A_p)$ has p blocks (the blocks are nonempty in this

discussion). The total number of color printed ordered partitions with p blocks
is given by IDENTITY 5A.15.

5A.15 IDENTITY: THE NUMBER $c_n^*(g,p)$ OF COLOR PRINTED ORDERED PARTITIONS OF $\underline{n}$ with p BLOCKS.

$$c_n^*(g,p) = \sum_{a_1 + \ldots + a_p = n} g_{a_1} g_{a_2} \cdots g_{a_p} \binom{n}{a_1 \, a_2 \, \ldots \, a_p}.$$

The sum is over all compositions $(a_1, a_2, \ldots, a_p)$ of n, where $a_i > 0$ for all i.

We now observe that each of the p! different rearrangements of a color printed
ordered partition with p blocks is distinct. Thus, if we divide $c^*(g,p)$ by p! then
we obtain $c(g,p)$, the total number of color printed set (unordered) partitions of
$\underline{n}$ into p blocks. This modification of IDENTITY 5A.15 is given by
IDENTITY 5A.16.

5A.16 IDENTITY: THE NUMBER, $c_n(g,p)$, OF COLOR PRINTED SET PARTITIONS OF $\underline{n}$ WITH p BLOCKS.

$$c_n(g,p) = \frac{1}{p!} \sum_{a_1 + \ldots + a_p = n} g_{a_1} g_{a_2} \cdots g_{a_p} \binom{n}{a_1 \, a_2 \, \ldots \, a_p}.$$

The sum is over all compositions $(a_1, a_2, \ldots, a_p)$ of n, where $a_i > 0$ for all i.

In EXAMPLE 5A.17 we discuss the relationship between exponential generating functions and color printed partitions. This model relates to a number of
basic combinatorial problems.

5A.17 EXAMPLE: COLOR PRINTED PARTITIONS AND EXPONENTIAL GENERATING FUNCTIONS.

Consider $e^{xg(u)}$ where $g(u) = g_1 u + g_2 u^2/2! + g_3 u^3/3! + \ldots$ is the exponential
generating function of the sequence $(g_1, g_2, \ldots)$. Using the power series expansion for the exponential function, we write $e^{xg(u)} = 1 + (xg(u)) + (xg(u))^2/2!
+ \ldots$. This expression can be rewritten in the form $1 + p_1(x)u + p_2(x)u^2/
2! + \ldots$. This latter expression may be regarded as the exponential generating
function of a sequence of polynomials $\{p_n(x)\}$. In order to avoid convergence
problems, we have assumed that the constant term of $g(u)$ is zero. We wish to
express the coefficients of the polynomials $p_n(x)$ in terms of the g_i. Consider a
typical term $(xg(u))^p/p!$. The coefficient of x^p in $p_n(x)$ will be

$$\frac{n!}{p!} \sum_{a_1 + \ldots + a_p = n} \frac{g_{a_1}}{a_1!} \frac{g_{a_2}}{a_2!} \cdots \frac{g_{a_p}}{a_p!}$$

where the sum is over all compositions $(a_1, a_2, \ldots, a_p)$ of n where $a_i > 0$ for all i. This sum is obviously $c_n(g,p)$ of IDENTITY 5A.16. Thus we have derived IDENTITY 5A.18.

5A.18   IDENTITY: COEFFICIENTS OF $p_n(x)$ ARE THE $c_n(g,p)$ OF IDENTITY 5A.16.

$$e^{xg(u)} = 1 + p_1(x)u + \ldots + p_n(x)u^n/n! + \ldots$$

$$\text{where } p_n(x) = \sum_{p=1}^{n} c_n(g,p)x^p.$$

We assume that $g(u) = g_1u + g_2u^2/2! + \ldots$. *Henceforth we shall also assume that $g_1 \neq 0$.*

There are many interesting combinatorial interpretations of IDENTITY 5A.18. We have already discussed color printed partitions. For these we assume that for the integers in a set $S \subseteq \underline{n}$ with $|S| = s$, we have exactly g_s choices for the color of the print (all integers are printed the same color once a choice is made). We showed that a partition of $\underline{n}$ into p blocks can be printed in $c_n(g,p)$ different ways, given by IDENTITY 5A.16. The model of "color printed partitions" may seem too restrictive to be of much interest. However, if we let our imaginations soar a bit, we may interpret the idea of coloring a set more generally as imposing some structure on the set. For example, given a set $S \subseteq \underline{n}$ with $|S| = s$, there are s! ways to linearly order the elements of S. We might think of such rearrangement as a "color." In this case $g_s = s!$. A "color printed partition with p blocks" thus corresponds to a partitioning of a set of n elements into p blocks and the selection of a linear order on each block.

As another example, if $|S| = s$ there are $(s-1)!$ ways to arrange the elements of S in cyclic order. In this case, $g_s = (s-1)!$ and a color printed partition of $\underline{n}$ with p blocks corresponds to a partitioning of $\underline{n}$ into p blocks and the selection of a cyclic order on the elements of each block. The reader familiar with the disjoint cycle notation for permutations (EXAMPLE 4.34, EXERCISE 4.35) will recognize that, in this case, $c_n(g,p)$ is the number of permutations on $\underline{n}$ with exactly p cycles. Looking ahead to CHAPTER 6, we may let g_s denote the number of connected graphs with s vertices (CHAPTER 6, DEFINITION 6.11). In this case, $c_n(g,p)$ is the number of graphs with n vertices and p components. Or, let g_s be the number of trees with s vertices (CHAPTER 6, DEFINITION 6.12.). In this case $c_n(g,p)$ is the number of forests with n vertices and p components. There are many other possibilities. One that we have not yet mentioned is the trivial case where $g_s = 1$ for all s. In this case, $c_n(g,p)$ corresponds to the number of partitions of n with p blocks (Stirling numbers of the second kind, TABLE 3.49).

5A.19   EXAMPLE: SET PARTITIONS.

As mentioned above, if $g_s = 1$ for all s, then $c_n(g,p)$ is the number of partitions of $\underline{n}$ with p blocks. In this case, $g(u) = u + u^2/2! + \ldots = e^u - 1$ and $e^{xg(u)}$ is $e^{x(e^u-1)}$. If we set $x = 1$ we obtain e^{e^u-1} as the generating function for the number of set partitions of a set of n elements (the coefficient of $u^n/n!$).

5A.20   EXAMPLE: LAH NUMBERS.

If $g_s = s!$ then $c_n(g,p)$ is the number of partitions of n with p nonempty ordered blocks. We might think of constructing such a partition by first specifying a permutation of n. For example, let $n = 6$ and consider 6 3 5 2 4 1. Next we choose $p - 1$ of the $n - 1$ spaces between symbols in this permutation, and insert vertical bars in these spaces to define the p ordered blocks. In our example, if $p = 3$ we might choose 6 3 5 | 2 4 | 1, giving the ordered blocks (6,3,5), (2,4), (1). This process can be carried out in $n! \begin{pmatrix} n-1 \\ p-1 \end{pmatrix}$ ways. In this way we would construct all *ordered* partitions of n into p nonempty ordered blocks. To get *unordered* partitions into p ordered blocks we divide by p! giving $\dfrac{n!}{p!} \begin{pmatrix} n-1 \\ p-1 \end{pmatrix}$, the so called "Lah numbers." But, $g(u) = u + u^2 + u^3 = \ldots = u/(1-u)$. From IDENTITY 5A.18 we thus have $e^{xu/(1-u)} = 1 + p_1(x)u + p_2(x)u^2/2! + \ldots$ where $p_n(x) = \sum_{p=1}^{n} \dfrac{n!}{p!} \begin{pmatrix} n-1 \\ p-1 \end{pmatrix} x^p$.

5A.21   EXAMPLE: STIRLING NUMBERS OF THE FIRST KIND.

A permutation on $\underline{n}$ with only one cycle (including cycles of length one) is called a "full cycle" on $\underline{n}$. For example, (1,4,5,3,2,6) is a full cycle on $\underline{6}$. A full cycle on $\underline{6}$ can always start with (1, . . .) and the remaining entries can be any of the 5! permutations of 2, . . .,6. All full cycles on $\underline{6}$ can be constructed in this way. Thus by defining $g_s = (s-1)!$ we are counting full cycles on a set of size s. For this choice of g_s, the $c_n(g,p)$ count the number of permutations of $\underline{n}$ with p cycles. These numbers are called the "Stirling numbers of the first kind" (strictly speaking, the absolute values of these numbers). For this choice of g_s, $g(u) = u + u^2/2 + u^3/3 + \ldots = -\ln(1-u)$. Again, by IDENTITY 5A.18, $e^{-x\ln(1-u)} = 1 + p_1(x)u + p_2(x)u^2/2! + \ldots$ is the exponential generating function for these polynomials. It can be shown that $p_n(x) = (x)^n$, the "upper factorial" polynomial, where $(x)^n = x(x+1) \ldots (x+n-1)$.

5A.22   EXAMPLE: GRAPHICAL STRUCTURES.

Many types of graphical structures are constructed from "connected" structures of the same type. A graph has its connected components (DEFINITION 6.11 of CHAPTER 6). A forest is a graph whose components are trees

(DEFINITION 6.12 of CHAPTER 6). A rooted forest is a graph whose components are rooted trees (DEFINITION 6.23 of CHAPTER 6). In all of these cases, if g_s is the number of connected structures with vertex set of size s then $c_n(g,p)$ is the number of structures with vertex set of size n and p components. An interesting example is the case of rooted forests. We shall see in CHAPTER 6 that $g_s = s^{s-1}$ (LEMMA 6.20, EXERCISE 6.22(1)). We shall see in the following material that, for this case, $p_n(x) = x(x+n)^{n-1}$ (EXAMPLES 5A.32, 5A.33).

We conclude our discussion of the exponential generating function with a brief presentation of some linear algebraic properties of sequences of polynomials. Note that the sequence of polynomials $\{x^n/n!\}$ is a basis for the vector space of all polynomials. The differentiation operator D is a linear transformation on this vector space, and "shifts" this basis in the sense that $D(x^n/n!) = x^{n-1}/(n-1)!$ for all $n \geq 1$.

5A.23 DEFINITION.

A sequence of polynomials $\{p_n(x)\}$ where the degree of p_n is n for all n will be called a *basis sequence*. If $p_0 = 1$ and $p_n(0) = 0$ for all $n > 0$ then the basis sequence will be called a *normalized basis sequence*. A linear transformation S on polynomials for which there exists a basis sequence $\{p_n\}$ such that $S(p_n/n!) = p_{n-1}/(n-1)!$ for all $n \geq 1$ and $Sp_0 = 0$ will be called a *basis shift* operator with *shift basis* $\{p_n/n!\}$. (*Note*: To say that the degree of a polynomial is zero implies that the polynomial is a nonzero constant.)

Obviously, a *basis sequence* is a basis for the vector space of all polynomials. If $\mathcal{P}_n$ denotes the vector space of all polynomials of degree less than or equal to n then S is a linear transformation from $\mathcal{P}_n$ to $\mathcal{P}_{n-1}$ of rank $n-1$ and nullity 1. This observation is the basic fact needed to prove LEMMA 5A.24.

5A.24 LEMMA.

Let S be a basis shift operator. Suppose that both $\{p_n/n!\}$ and $\{q_n/n!\}$ are shift bases for S. Then, there exists a sequence of numbers $(a_0, a_1, \ldots, a_n, \ldots)$ such that $a_0 \neq 0$ and for all n, $q_n/n! = \sum_{k=0}^{n} a_{n-k} \, p_k/k!$. Conversely, if such a sequence relates the two sequences $\{p_n/n!\}$ and $\{q_n/n!\}$, then if either sequence is a shift basis for S, the other is also.

Proof. The converse is left to the reader. Suppose that $\{p_n/n!\}$ and $\{q_n/n!\}$ are shift bases for S. We use induction. As p_0 and q_0 are both of degree 0 (i.e., nonzero constants) we have $q_0 = a_0 p_0$. Assume that there is a sequence $(a_0, a_1, \ldots, a_n)$ such that for all $m \leq n$, $q_m/m! = \sum_{k=0}^{m} a_{m-k} p_k/k!$. Let $f =$

$q_{n+1}/(n+1)! - \sum_{k=1}^{n+1} a_{n+1-k}p_k/k!$. Then by our hypotheses, $S(f) = 0$. Since

the basis shift operator S has nullity 1, and p_0 is in the null space of S, we have $f = a_{n+1}p_0$ for some number a_{n+1} (this is how a_{n+1} is determined). Thus

$$q_{n+1}/(n+1)! = \sum_{k=0}^{n+1} a_{n+1-k}p_k/k!.$$

COROLLARY 5A.25 follows from LEMMA 5A.24. (EXERCISE 5A.34(2)).

5A.25 COROLLARY.

Let S be a basis shift operator. Then there is one and only one normalized basis sequence $\{p_n\}$ such that $\{p_n/n!\}$ is a shift basis for S.

COROLLARY 5A.26 is a rephrasing of LEMMA 5A.24.

5A.26 COROLLARY.

Let S be a basis shift operator with shift basis $\{p_n/n!\}$. A basis sequence $\{q_n/n!\}$ is also a shift basis for S if and only if there is a formal power series $f(S) = a_0 + a_1S + a_2S^2 + \ldots$ with $a_0 \neq 0$ such that $f(S)p_n = q_n$ for all n.

5A.27 DEFINITION.

The sequence $\{p_n\}$ of polynomials defined by IDENTITY 5A.18 (with the assumption $g_1 \neq 0$) defines a normalized basis sequence which we call the *normalized basis sequence of* g(u).

LEMMA 5A.28 is an important technical lemma that relates LEMMA 5A.24 and DEFINITION 5A.27. If $g(u) = g_1u + g_2u^2 + \ldots$ is a formal power series with $g_1 \neq 0$ then there always exists a formal power series $h(u) = h_1u + h_2u^2 + \ldots$ with $h_1 \neq 0$ such that $g(h(u)) = u$. Assume all coefficients are real or complex numbers. The power series h(u) is called the *compositional inverse* of g(u) and is denoted by $g^{-1}(u)$ (see EXERCISE 5A.34(3)). If D denotes differentiation with respect to x, and if f(u) is a formal power series with real or complex coefficients, then f(D) is defined as an operator on polynomials. Similarly, D or f(D) acts on formal power series with polynomial coefficients by transforming each coefficient. If $\sum_{m=0}^{\infty} c_n(x)u^n$ is such a formal power series and

g(u) is as above, we can define a transformation $A_g \sum_{m=0}^{\infty} c_n(x)u^n = \sum_{m=0}^{\infty} c_n(x)(g(u))^n$.

Thus D, f(D), and A_g all act as transformations on power series with polynomial coefficients.

5A.28 LEMMA.

Let $\{p_n\}$ be the normalized basis sequence (DEFINITION 5A.27) of the formal power series $g(u) = g_1u + g_2u^2 + \ldots$ and let $S = g^{-1}(D)$ where D is differentiation with respect to x. Then S is a basis shift operator with shift basis $\{p_n/n!\}$.

Proof. As above, let A_g denote the operator which replaces u with $g(u)$ in a formal power series. Clearly, as transformations on power series with polynomial coefficients, $DA_g = A_gD$ and hence $f(D)A_g = A_gf(D)$ for any formal power series f. Note that $g^{-1}(D)e^{xg(u)} = g^{-1}(D)A_ge^{xu} = A_gg^{-1}(D)e^{xu} = A_gg^{-1}(u)e^{xu} = ue^{xg(u)}$. Interpreting the equality between the first and last of these expressions in terms of coefficients of powers of u gives the result.

Of course, not all normalized basis sequences can be associated with a formal power series $g(u)$ in the sense of DEFINITION 5A.27. LEMMA 5A.29 is sometimes useful in identifying those that do have this property.

5A.29 LEMMA.

Let $\{p_n\}$ be a normalized basis sequence and let $h(u) = h_1u + h_2u^2 + \ldots$, where $h_1 \neq 0$, be a formal power series. If $\{p_n/n!\}$ is a shift basis for $h(D)$ then p_n is the normalized basis sequence of $g(u) = h^{-1}(u)$.

Proof. Let $\{q_n\}$ be the normalized basis sequence associated with $g(u)$. By LEMMA 5A.28, $\{q_n/n!\}$ is a shift basis for $g^{-1}(D) = h(D)$. By COROLLARY 5A.25, $p_n = q_n$ for all n.

We shall give several examples of the use of LEMMA 5A.29, but first we define an important class of operators on polynomials that are power series in the differentiation operator.

5A.30 DEFINITION.

For any number a, E^a is the linear operator on polynomials defined by $E^ap(x) = p(x+a)$. E^a is called "translation by a," or "(argument) shift by a." We use the former terminology to avoid confusion with the basis shift operators.

Remark. By Taylor's theorem, $p(x+a) = \sum_{k=0}^{\infty} \frac{a^k}{k!} D^kp(x)$ and thus $E^a = \sum_{k=0}^{\infty} \frac{a^k}{k!} D^k = e^{aD}$ is a formal power series in the differentiation operator D.

5A.31   EXAMPLE: APPLICATIONS TO ABEL AND FACTORIAL POLYNOMIALS.

The polynomials $(x)_n = x(x-1)\ldots(x-n+1)$ and $(x)^n = x(x+1)\ldots(x+n-1)$ are called the lower and upper factorial polynomials respectively. The reader may easily verify that $E-1 = e^D - 1$ is a basis shift operator with shift basis $(x)_n/n!$. Similarly, $1 - E^{-1} = 1 - e^{-D}$ is a basis shift operator with shift basis $(x)^n/n!$. Thus $(x)_n$ is the normalized basis sequence of $g(u) = h^{-1}(u)$ where $h(u) = e^u - 1$. In this case we have $g(u) = \ln(1+u)$. Similarly, $(x)^n$ is the normalized basis sequence for $g(u) = -\ln(1-u)$. A more interesting example is the sequence of polynomials $x(x+an)^{n-1}$, called the *Abel polynomials*. A basis shift operator for these polynomials is $DE^{-a} = De^{-aD}$ (EXERCISE 5A.34(4)). Thus, the sequence of Abel polynomials is a normalized basis sequence for $g(u) = h^{-1}(u)$ where $h(u) = ue^{-au}$. No simple closed form expression for $g(u)$ is known. The coefficient of x in $x(x+an)^{n-1}$ is $(an)^{n-1}$ thus by IDENTITY 5A.18 and 5A.16, $g(u) = \sum_{n=1}^{\infty} (an)^{n-1} \dfrac{u^n}{n!}$.

5A.32   EXAMPLE: ABEL POLYNOMIALS AND ENUMERATION OF TREES.

Suppose that $\{p_n(x)\}$ is the normalized basis sequence for the power series $g(u)$. From IDENTITIES 5A.18 and 5A.16, we see that the sequence of polynomials $\{p_n(x)\}$ is determined completely by the coefficients of x alone, since these values determine the power series $g(u)$. Suppose that $p_n(x) = \sum_{p=1}^{n} c_n(g,p)x^p$ where $c_n(g,p)$ is the number of rooted forests on n vertices with p components. We have noted in EXAMPLE 5A.22 that the sequence $\{p_n\}$ is a normalized basis sequence for $g(u) = g_1 u + g_2 u^2/2! + \ldots$ where g_n is the number of rooted trees on a set of n vertices. We did not need to know that $g_n = n^{n-1}$ to conclude this fact. A little thought reveals that these polynomials must satisfy the identity $g_n = np_{n-1}(1)$. To see this, one notes that to construct a rooted tree on n vertices one can select the root (this accounts for the factor n) and then construct a rooted forest on $n-1$ vertices (this accounts for the factor $p_{n-1}(1)$). The forest is just the collection of principal subtrees of the root (CHAPTER 6, DEFINITION 6.28). Direct substitution reveals that the Abel polynomials $x(x+n)^{n-1}$ also satisfy this relation and hence both have the same power series $g(u)$. Thus $e^{xg(u)}$ generates both sequences and, hence, the polynomials are equal. This is an independent and rather curious verification of the fact that n^{n-1} counts the number of rooted trees on n vertices!

If p_n is the normalized basis sequence of $g(u)$ then the functional equation $e^{(x+y)g(u)} = e^{xg(u)}e^{yg(u)}$ implies that $p_n(x+y) = \sum_{k=0}^{n} \binom{n}{k} p_k(x)p_{n-k}(y)$ holds.

Thus the normalized basis sequence of a power series $g(u)$ is a sequence of polynomials of *binomial type* in the sense of DEFINITION 5A.33.

5A.33   DEFINITION.

A basis sequence $\{p_n\}$ (DEFINITION 5A.23) that satisfies $\sum\limits_{k=0}^{n} \binom{n}{k} p_k(x)p_{n-k}(y)$

$= p_n(x+y)$ for all n is called a *sequence of polynomials of binomial type.*

As we previously noted, a normalized basis sequence of a power series $g(u)$ $= g_1u + g_2u^2/2! + \ldots$ (as usual, $g_1 \neq 0$) is always a sequence of polynomials of binomial type. The converse is also true (EXERCISE 5A.34(5)). For this reason, the theory of exponential generating functions of the form $e^{xg(u)}$ is sometimes referred to as the "theory of polynomials of binomial type."

5A.34   EXERCISE.

(1) Prove that the number of ordered partitions $(A_1, A_2, \ldots, A_p)$ of a set of n elements is given by the multinomial coefficient of NOTATION 5A.14 where $a_i = |A_i|$ (the a_i may be zero, in which case $0! = 1$).

(2) Using LEMMA 5A.24, prove COROLLARY 5A.25.

(3) Let $\mathcal{G}$ denote the set of all power series of the form $a(u) = a_1u + a_2u^2 + a_3u^3 + \ldots$ where $a_1 \neq 0$. Show that $\mathcal{G}$ is a group under composition of power series. (The identity in $\mathcal{G}$ is the trivial power series u.)

(4) Show that $E-1$, $1-E^{-1}$, and DE^{-a} are the basis shift operators for the shift bases $(x)_n/n!$, $(x)^n/n!$, and $x(x+an)^{n-1}/n!$ respectively.

(5) Prove that every sequence $\{p_n\}$ of polynomials of binomial type (DEFINITION 5A.33) is the normalized basis sequence of a power series $g(u)$ as defined in DEFINITION 5A.27. *Hint*: First show that $\{p_n\}$ must in fact be *normalized* in the sense of DEFINITION 5A.23. Define $g(u) = g_1u + g_2\dfrac{u^2}{2!} + \ldots$ by defining g_n to be the coefficient of x in $p_n(x)$.

(6) Each element $g \in \mathcal{G}$ (the group of (3) above) defines a linear transformation U_g on polynomials. The defining relation is $U_gx^n = p_n(x)$ where $e^{xg(u)} = 1 + p_1(x)u + p_2(x)u^2/2! + \ldots$. If $g \circ h$ denotes the composition of g and h (i.e., the group operation of $\mathcal{G}$) show that $U_{g \circ h} = U_gU_h$ and thus that the correspondence $g \rightarrow U_g$ is a "representation" of the group $\mathcal{G}$. The operators U_g, $g \in \mathcal{G}$, are called *umbral operators.*

(7) The Dirichlet generating function of a sequence $a_1, a_2, \ldots$ is the formal sum $\sum\limits_{n=1}^{\infty} a_n n^{-x}$. State the rule for taking products of Dirichlet generating functions analogous to PRODUCT RULES 5A.2 and 5A.11. The Dirichlet generating function for the sequence $1, 1, \ldots$ is $\zeta(x) = \sum\limits_{n=1}^{\infty} n^{-x}$ and is called the "Riemann zeta function." A famous unsolved mathematical conjecture called the "Riemann Hypothesis" is concerned with the zeroes of the analytic continuation of $\zeta(x)$, $x > 1$.

5B. THE PRINCIPLE OF INCLUSION-EXCLUSION.

Consider the product $(1 - x_1)(1 - x_2). . .(1 - x_n)$ where $x_1, . . ., x_n$ are variables.
Expanding this product, we get $\sum\limits_{Q \subseteq \underline{n}} (-1)^{|Q|} \prod\limits_{q \in Q} x_q$. The sum is over all subsets
Q of $\underline{n}$. Intuitively, each term in this product arises by choosing a subset Q of
the index set $1, . . ., n$ and choosing the factor $-x_q$ for each $q \in Q$ and choosing
the factor 1 for each $q \notin Q$. All possible terms are obtained by varying Q over
all possible subsets of $\underline{n}$. Given any set S, we may consider real valued functions
$f_1, f_2, . . ., f_n$ instead of the variables $x_1, x_2, . . ., x_n$. Sums and products of functions
are interpreted point-wise: $(f_i + f_j)(t) = f_i(t) + f_j(t)$ and $(f_i f_j)(t) = f_i(t) f_j(t)$. With
this interpretation, the above expansion is obviously still true and is called the
"principle of inclusion-exclusion," as stated in THEOREM 5B.1.

5B.1 THEOREM (PRINCIPLE OF INCLUSION-EXCLUSION).

Let $f_1, f_2, . . ., f_n$ be real valued functions. Then, if u is the identically 1 function,
$u(t) = 1$ for all t,

$$\prod_{i=1}^{n} (u - f_i) = \sum_{Q \subseteq \underline{n}} (-1)^{|Q|} \prod_{q \in Q} f_q.$$

The most elementary combinatorial applications of THEOREM 5B.1 occur
when the functions f_i are chosen to be characteristic functions f_{P_i} of subsets
$P_1, . . ., P_n$ of a set P (see EXERCISE 1.13(6)). In this case $u - f_{P_i}$ is the characteristic function of the set $P - P_i$ (the domain of all functions is P). Thus, the
product on the left-hand side of the identity of THEOREM 5B.1 is the characteristic function of the set of all elements of P that do not belong to any of
the P_i, $i = 1, . . ., n$. It is an interesting fact that in some cases the right-hand
side of THEOREM 5B.1 is easier to compute than the left-hand side. Note that
if f_A is a characteristic function of a subset $A \subseteq P$, then $\sum\limits_{t \in P} f_A(t) = |A|$. Thus,
by evaluating both sides of the identity of THEOREM 5B.1 at t and summing
over all t, we obtain, in the case $f_i = f_{P_i}$, COROLLARY 5B.2.

5B.2 COROLLARY (ENUMERATIVE INCLUSION-EXCLUSION).

$$\left| \bigcap_{i=1}^{n} (P - P_i) \right| = \sum_{Q \subseteq \underline{n}} (-1)^{|Q|} \left| \bigcap_{q \in Q} P_q \right|.$$

A standard example of the application of COROLLARY 5B.2 is to the problem
of derangements (also considered in EXAMPLE 5A.12).

5B.3 EXAMPLE: DERANGEMENTS AND INCLUSION-EXCLUSION.

We let P denote the set S_n of all permutations of $\underline{n}$. Let $D(\underline{n})$ be the derangements as defined in EXAMPLE 5A.12. Let P_i be the set of all permutations σ in S_n such that $\sigma(i) = i$. P_i is defined for $i = 1,\ldots,n$. Clearly, $\left| \bigcap_{q \in Q} P_q \right| = (n - |Q|)!$. This example is typical in that this quantity does not depend on the set Q but only on $|Q|$. Since $\bigcap_{i=1}^{n} (P - P_i) = D(\underline{n})$, we have from COROLLARY 5B.2 the identity $|D(\underline{n})| = \sum_{Q \subseteq \underline{n}} (-1)^{|Q|} (n - |Q|)! = \sum_{k=0}^{n} (-1)^k \binom{n}{k} (n-k)! = n! \sum_{k=0}^{n} (-1)^k/k!$. Again, we note that this is approximately $n!e^{-1}$. This approach should be compared carefully with that of EXAMPLE 5A.12.

For some applications it is convenient to have a slight generalization of THEOREM 5B.1.

5B.4 COROLLARY.

Let $f_1,\ldots,f_n$ be as in THEOREM 5B.1. Let $T \subseteq \underline{n}$ and let $T^c = \underline{n} - T$. Then

$$\prod_{i \in T} f_i \prod_{i \in T^c} (u - f_i) = \sum_{R \supseteq T} (-1)^{|R| - |T|} \prod_{i \in R} f_i.$$

Proof. The left side equals (using THEOREM 5B.1)

$$\prod_{i \in T} f_i \sum_{Q \subseteq T^c} (-1)^{|Q|} \prod_{q \in Q} f_q.$$

If we set $R = T \cup Q$, this expression becomes $\sum_{R \supseteq T} (-1)^{|R| - |T|} \prod_{i \in R} f_i$, which is the right side of the identity.

As above, we may let $f_i = f_{P_i}$ in COROLLARY 5B.4. In this case, the left-hand side of COROLLARY 5B.4 becomes the cardinality of the set (which we call "IN(T)") of all elements of P that belong to P_i if and only if $i \in T$. This leads to DEFINITION 5B.5.

5B.5 DEFINITION.

Let P_i, $i = 1,\ldots,n$, be subsets of P. Let $T \subseteq \underline{n}$ be a subset of $\underline{n}$. Define IN(T) $= \{p: p \in P, p \in P_i \text{ if and only if } i \in T\}$ and define $IN(k) = \bigcup_{|T| = k} IN(T)$ where the union is over all subsets T of $\underline{n}$ with $|T| = k$. IN(k) is the set of all elements of P that belong to exactly k of the sets P_i.

5B.6   COROLLARY.

Let P_i, $i = 1,\ldots,n$, be subsets of P and let $T \subseteq \underline{n}$. Let IN(T) and IN(k) be as in DEFINITION 5B.5. Then the following identities are valid

(1) $|\text{IN}(T)| = \displaystyle\sum_{R \supseteq T} (-1)^{|R|-|T|} |\bigcap_{i \in R} P_i|.$

(2) $|\text{IN}(k)| = \displaystyle\sum_{r=k}^{n} \binom{r}{k} (-1)^{r-k} \sum_{|R|=r} |\bigcap_{i \in R} P_i|$ where the sum is over all subsets $R \subseteq \underline{n}$ with $|R| = r.$

Proof.   Identity (1) follows from COROLLARY 5B.4 just as COROLLARY 5B.2 follows from THEOREM 5B.1. Identity (2) requires a change of order of summation as follows:

$$|\text{IN}(k)| = \sum_{|T|=k} \sum_{R \supseteq T} (-1)^{|R|-|T|} |\bigcap_{i \in R} P_i|$$

$$= \sum_{|R| \geqslant k} \binom{|R|}{k} (-1)^{|R|-k} |\bigcap_{i \in R} P_i|$$

$$= \sum_{r=k}^{n} \binom{r}{k} (-1)^{r-k} \sum_{|R|=r} |\bigcap_{i \in R} P_i|$$

which is the right-hand side of identity (2).

5B.7   EXAMPLE OF COROLLARY 5B.6 APPLIED TO DERANGEMENTS.

As in EXAMPLE 5B.3, let $P = S_n$ and let $P_i = \{\sigma: \sigma(i) = i\}$. The set IN(k) is the set of all permutations that fix exactly k elements of $\underline{n}$. We recall from EXAMPLE 5B.3 that $|\bigcap_{i \in R} P_i| = (n-|R|)!$ and hence from COROLLARY 5B.6 we have

$$\text{IN}(K) = \sum_{r=k}^{n} (-1)^{r-k} \binom{r}{k} \sum_{|R|=r} (n-|R|)!$$

$$= \sum_{r=k}^{n} (-1)^{r-k} \binom{r}{k} \binom{n}{r} (n-r)!$$

$$= \frac{n!}{k!} \sum_{r=k}^{n} \frac{(-1)^{r-k}}{(r-k)!}$$

$$= \frac{n!}{k!} \sum_{j=0}^{n-k} \frac{(-1)^j}{j!} \cong \frac{n!}{k!} e^{-1} \quad (n-k \text{ large enough}).$$

5B.8 EXAMPLE OF COROLLARY 5B.6 APPLIED TO DIVISIBILITY CONDITIONS.

Let $P = \underline{m}$ and let $\{a_1,\ldots,a_n\}$ be a set of pairwise relatively prime positive integers (two integers are *relatively prime* if their greatest common divisor is 1). Let $P_i = \{t: t \in \underline{m}$ and a_i divides $t\}$. We also write $a_i|t$ for "a_i divides t." For any subset $Q \subseteq \underline{n}$, $\bigcap_{i \in Q} P_i = \{t: t \in \underline{m}$ and $\prod_{i \in Q} a_i|t\} = \{\prod_{i \in Q} a_i, 2\prod_{i \in Q} a_i,\ldots,k\prod_{i \in Q} a_i\}$ where $k = \lfloor x \rfloor$ (see DEFINITION 2.2) with $x = \dfrac{m}{\prod_{i \in Q} a_i}$. For this example IN(k) is the set of all integers of $\underline{m}$ divisible by exactly k of the integers in the set $\{a_1,\ldots,a_n\}$. Applying COROLLARY 5B.6(2), we see that

$$|IN(k)| = \sum_{r=k}^{n} \binom{r}{k} (-1)^{r-k} \sum_{|R|=r} \left\lfloor \frac{m}{\prod_{i \in R} a_i} \right\rfloor.$$

R is a subset of $\underline{n}$. If each of the integers a_i is a divisor of m then $\dfrac{m}{\prod_{i \in R} a_i}$ is an integer for all R. In this case, $|IN(0)| = m \prod_{t=1}^{n} \left(1 - \dfrac{1}{a_t}\right)$. The number $|IN(0)|$ is sometimes denoted by $\varphi(m)$ and is called the *Euler φ-function*.

5B.9 EXERCISE.

(a) How many ways are there of placing eight nonattacking rooks on an 8×8 chessboard with exactly one rook on the white diagonal? *Hint*: Rook placements correspond in a natural way to permutations (elements of S_8). A rook on the white diagonal corresponds to a fixed point of such a permutation.

(2) How many integers between one and 1000 are divisible by exactly k of the integers 3,5, and 7 for $k = 0,1,2$, and 3?

We now develop a more intricate example of the principle of inclusion-exclusion. The problem we consider is called the "problème des ménages." Suppose n couples are to be seated at a circular table. The n husbands take alternate seats. At this point, how many ways are there to seat the n wives such that no wife sits next to her own husband? A seating may be described by a permutation $\varphi \in S_n$ by specifying that wife $\varphi(i)$ is to be seated to the left of gentleman i. We must have $\varphi(i-1) \neq i$ and $\varphi(i) \neq i$ for all i (arithmetic mod n). We thus may consider sets $P_{2i-1} = \{\varphi: \varphi(i-1) = i\}$ and $P_{2i} = \{\varphi: \varphi(i) = i\}$, $i = 1,\ldots,n$. Our problem is to determine the number $|S_n - \bigcup_{j=1}^{2n} P_j|$. The solution is described in EXERCISE 5B.10.

5B.10 EXERCISE.

(See the previous paragraph for statement of problem.)

(1) Show that for $Q \subset \underline{2n}$, $\left|\bigcap_{i \in Q} P_i\right| = 0$ if Q contains two consecutive integers
mod 2n and $\left|\bigcap_{i \in Q} P_i\right| = (n - |Q|)!$ if Q does not contain two consecutive
integers mod 2n (assume n > 1).

(2) Show that for $k \leq n$ the number of ways of selecting a set Q with $|Q| = k$
from $\underline{2n}$ such that no two elements of Q are consecutive mod 2n is

$$N^*(2n,k) = \frac{2n}{2n-k}\binom{2n-k}{k}.$$

Hint: Let N(m,k) denote the number of sequences of zeroes and ones with
length m, k ones, and no two ones consecutive. Show that N(m,k) =
$\binom{m-k+1}{k}$. For m = 4, k = 2, 1 0 0 1 is such a sequence. Let $N^*(m,k)$
denote the number of such sequences where "consecutive" now applies to
the position 1 and m (consecutive mod m). Thus 1 0 0 1 would not be
included in this count. Show $N^*(m,k) = N(m-1,k) + N(m-3,k-1) =$
$\frac{m}{m-k}\binom{m-k}{k}$. The correspondence between these sequences and the set
Q is obtained by considering the characteristic function f_Q.

(3) Show that the number of solutions to the "problème des ménages" is given
by $\displaystyle\sum_{k=0}^{n} (-1)^k (n-k)! \frac{2n}{2n-k}\binom{2n-k}{k}$, n > 1.

Certain applications of the principle of inclusion-exclusion require a slight
generalization of COROLLARIES 5B.2 and 5B.6. Both of these results were
obtained from THEOREM 5B.1 by choosing the functions $f_1, \ldots, f_n$ to be characteristic functions $f_{P_1}, \ldots, f_{P_n}$. We then used the fact that, for any subset $A \subseteq P$,
$\sum_{t \in P} f_A(t) = |A|$ to pass from THEOREM 5B.1 to COROLLARIES 5B.2 and
5B.6. If w: P → X is any function from P to an algebraic structure X where
addition and subtraction are defined (an abelian group, ring, etc.) we can define
$w(A) = \sum_{t \in A} w(t) = \sum_{t \in P} w(t)f_A(t)$. In the case where w(t) = 1 for all t ∈ P we
get $w(A) = |A|$. We call w a "weight function." COROLLARIES 5B.11 and
5B.12 are obvious extensions of COROLLARIES 5B.2 and 5B.6 to the case of
weight functions.

5B.11   COROLLARY (WEIGHTED INCLUSION-EXCLUSION).

Using the notation of COROLLARY 5B.2 we have

$$w\left(\bigcap_{i=1}^{n} (P - P_i)\right) = \sum_{Q \subseteq \underline{n}} (-1)^{|Q|} w\left(\bigcap_{q \in Q} P_q\right).$$

5B.12   COROLLARY.

Using the notation of COROLLARY 5B.6 we have

(1) $w(IN(T)) = \sum_{R \supseteq T} (-1)^{|R| - |T|} w(\bigcap_{i \in R} P_i).$

(2) $w(IN(k)) = \sum_{r=k}^{n} \binom{r}{k} (-1)^{r-k} \sum_{|R|=r} w(\bigcap_{i \in R} P_i).$

We now give an example of the use of the weighted principle of inclusion-exclusion.

5B.13   EXAMPLE OF WEIGHTED INCLUSION-EXCLUSION AND PERMANENTS.

In this example, we let $P = \underline{n}^{\underline{m}}$ be the set of all functions from $\underline{m}$ to $\underline{n}$ where we assume that $m \le n$. Let P_i, $i = 1, \ldots, n$, be defined by $P_i = \{f : i \notin \text{image}(f)\}$. For $k = n - m$ the set $IN(k)$ is the set of injective mappings from $\underline{m}$ to $\underline{n}$ (note that any $f \in IN(k)$ has $|\text{image}(f)| = n - k = m$ and hence must be an injection). Let $A = (a_{ij})$ be an $m \times n$ matrix. For each f in P we define the weight of f by

$$w(f) = \prod_{t=1}^{n} a_{t,f(t)}.$$ We define the permanent of A, $\text{per}(A)$, to be $w(IN(k))$ where

$k = n - m$. In other words, $\text{per}(A) = \sum_{f \in IN(k)} \prod_{t=1}^{n} a_{t,f(t)}$ where the sum is over

all injections from $\underline{m}$ to $\underline{n}$. If $m = n$ the permanent is the same as the determinant

except that the determinant uses the weight function $w(f) = \text{sgn}(f) \prod_{t=1}^{n} a_{t,f(t)}$

where the sgn(f) is $+1$ for even permutations and -1 for odd permutations. The properties of the permanent are such that it is generally much more difficult to compute than the determinant. In some cases, COROLLARY 5B.12(2) provides the best means for computing the permanent as we now explain. We have

immediately, from COROLLARY 5B.12(2), that $\text{per}(A) = \sum_{r=k}^{n} \binom{r}{k} (-1)^{r-k} W_A(r)$

where $W_A(r) = \sum_{|R|=r} w(\bigcap_{i \in R} P_i)$ with w defined as above. But, the set $\bigcap_{i \in R} P_i$ is

just the set of all functions f with image(f) contained in $\underline{n} - R$. In other words, the set of *all* functions from $\underline{m}$ to $\underline{n} - R$, $(\underline{n} - R)^{\underline{m}}$. Thus, it is easy to see that

$w(\cap\limits_{i \in R} P_i) = \prod\limits_{t=1}^{m} \sum\limits_{j \in R} a_{tj}$. This formula can be used in certain instances to compute $W_A(r)$. As an example, consider the 3×4 matrix

$$A = \begin{pmatrix} 1 & -1 & -1 & 1 \\ 1 & 1 & 1 & -1 \\ 1 & -1 & 1 & -1 \end{pmatrix}.$$

There are four subsets $R \subseteq \underline{4}$ of size 1: $\{1\},\{2\},\{3\},\{4\}$. For $r = 1$, we have (using the above formula) $W_A(1) = (-1)(+1)(-1) + (+1)(+1)(+1) + (+1)(+1)(-1) + (-1)(+3)(+1) = -2$. Similarly, we find that $W_A(2) = 0$, $W_A(3) = 2$ and hence that per(A) $= W_A(1) - \begin{pmatrix} 2 \\ 1 \end{pmatrix} W_A(2) + \begin{pmatrix} 3 \\ 1 \end{pmatrix} W_A(3)$

$= -2 + 6 = 4$. This method should be compared with the direct method of computing per(A) (using the definition).

5C. MÖBIUS INVERSION.

We now present a more general classical technique than the method of inclusion-exclusion. The expository article of Bender and Goldman (1975) referred to at the end of this chapter contains many examples of this technique. We give a brief presentation of the most important concepts, and refer the reader to this article and the other references listed in the section on MÖBIUS INVERSION for further study. The reader should also review the material at the beginning of Chapter 1 through EXERCISE 1.13.

We refer to an ordered set $P = (S, \leq)$ as a "poset." We refer to elements $x, y, \ldots$ of the set S of the poset P as "elements of the poset P" and write $x \in P$, $y \in P, \ldots$.

5C.1 DEFINITION.

Let P be a poset, $x, y \in P$, $x \leq y$. Define the interval [x,y] to be the set $\{z: x \leq z \leq y\}$.

5C.2 EXAMPLE OF AN INTERVAL IN A POSET.

Consider the poset of all subsets of A, $\mathcal{P}(A)$, where $A = \underline{4}$ (EXAMPLE 1.9(3)). The interval $[\{1,2\}, \{1,2,3,4\}] = \{\{1,2\}, \{1,2,3\}, \{1,2,4\}, \{1,2,3,4\}\}$. An interval [x,y] in a poset $P = (S, \leq)$ is itself a poset $([x,y], \leq)$ with the same order relation as P restricted to $[x,y] \times [x,y]$. We refer to this poset as the "subposet [x,y]." The Hasse diagram for the subposet of this example is shown in FIGURE 5C.3.

5C.3   HASSE DIAGRAM OF AN INTERVAL.

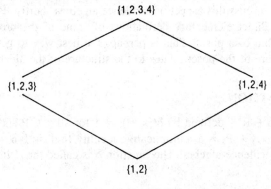

Figure 5C.3

A poset P is "locally finite" if every interval has finitely many elements.

5C.4   DEFINITION.

A poset P is *locally finite* if $|[x,y]|$ is finite for all $x, y \in P$.

Henceforth, "poset" will mean "locally finite poset."

Let D be any set and let R be the real numbers. Then the set of all functions from D to R, which we denote by R^D, is a vector space over R under the usual operations of function addition and scalar multiplication. A vector space together with a rule for multiplying vectors is called an *algebra*. Formally, the rule of multiplication must satisfy certain axioms, but these axioms will be trivially true for the examples we shall be considering. The reader already knows a number of such algebras (the vector space R^D under pointwise multiplication was considered in connection with the INCLUSION-EXCLUSION section of this chapter, the vector space of polynomials under polynomial multiplication, the vector space of $n \times n$ matrices under matrix multiplication). We now take the set D to be the set i(P) of all intervals of a (locally finite) poset P. The vector space $R^{i(P)}$ will be called the "incidence vector space" of the poset P. We now define a multiplication on $R^{i(P)}$.

5C.5   DEFINITION.

Let P be a poset, and let f and g be elements of $R^{i(P)}$. The *convolution* of f and g, denoted by f∗g is defined by

$$f*g([x,y]) = \sum_{x \leq z \leq y} f([x,z])g([z,y]) .$$

The vector space $R^{i(P)}$ with the convolution rule of multiplication is called the *incidence algebra* of the poset P.

Incidence algebras of finite posets are all isomorphic to subalgebras of $n \times n$ matrices where $n = |P|$. In fact the matrices may always be taken to be upper triangular. We discuss this aspect of incidence algebras shortly. First, however, we shall give direct elementary derivations of some of the properties of the incidence algebra of a poset. This is perhaps the best way to get a feeling for how the structure of the poset relates to the structure of the algebra.

5C.6 DEFINITION.

The function $\delta \in R^{i(P)}$ defined by $\delta([x,x]) = 1$ for all $x \in P$ and $\delta([x,y]) = 0$ for all $x \neq y$, $x,y \in P$, is a multiplicative identity ($\delta*f = f*\delta = f$ for all $f \in R^{i(P)}$) for the incidence algebra. The function δ is called the *delta function*.

5C.7 LEMMA.

The incidence algebra is associative: $f*(g*h) = (f*g) * h$.

Proof.   Verify that $(f*g)*h = f*(g*h)$. We have

$$((f*g)*h)[x,y] = \sum_{x \leq z \leq y} (f*g)[x,z]h[z,y] = \sum_{x \leq z \leq y} \sum_{x \leq w \leq z} f[x,w]g[w,z]h[z,y].$$

We interchange the order of summation to obtain

$$\sum_{x \leq w \leq y} \sum_{w \leq z \leq y} f[x,w]g[w,z]h[z,y] = \sum_{x \leq w \leq y} f[x,w](\sum_{w \leq z \leq y} g[w,z]h[z,y])$$

$$= \sum_{x \leq w \leq y} f[x,w](g*h)[w,y] = f*(g*h)[x,y].$$

An element f in $R^{i(P)}$ is a "unit" or "invertible element" if there exists an element g such that $f*g = g*f = \delta$. LEMMA 5C.8 characterizes these elements.

5C.8 LEMMA.

An element $f \in R^{i(P)}$ is invertible if and only if $f([x,x]) \neq 0$ for all $x \in P$.

Proof.   Assume f is invertible. For two functions f and g in $R^{i(P)}$ we have $f*g[x,x] = f[x,x]g[x,x]$. Thus if $f*g = \delta$, then $f[x,x] \neq 0$.

Assume $f[x,x] \neq 0$. We define g inductively on the cardinality of the interval. If $x \in P$ define $g[x,x] = \dfrac{1}{f[x,x]}$. Assume we have defined g on all intervals $[x,y]$, $|[x,y]| \leq n$. Let $|[x,y]| = n+1$. For $f*g[x,y] = \delta[x,y] = 0$ we must have

$$f[x,x]g[x,y] + \sum_{x < z \leq y} f[x,z]g[z,y] = 0 .$$

Thus we define (note that $\|[x,z]\|$ and $\|[z,y]\|$ are $\le$ n)

$$g[x,y] = \frac{-1}{f[x,x]} \sum_{x < z \le y} f[x,z]g[z,y] .$$

With g[x,y] so defined we have constructed a right inverse for f (i.e., f*g = δ). Thus *any element* f *with* f[x,x] $\ne$ 0 *has a right inverse* g, f*g = δ. But then (g*f)*g = g*(f*g) = g. Since f[x,x]g[x,x] = δ[x,x] = 1, g[x,x] $\ne$ 0 so let h be the right inverse of g. Thus g*f = (g*f)*(g*h) = ((g*f)*g)*h = g*h or g*f = δ. Thus g is also a left inverse of f and hence g is the inverse of f.

LEMMA 5C.8 provides a constructive method for defining the inverse of any invertible f, although in most instances a more concise representation of the inverse is required. This method is essentially "Gaussian elimination" of matrix theory.

Combinatorially, the most important functions in the incidence algebra are the zeta function and its inverse, the Möbius function. These functions are defined in DEFINITION 5C.9.

5C.9 DEFINITION.

The function $\zeta \in R^{i(P)}$ which is identically 1 for all intervals [x,y] $\in$ i(P) is called the zeta function. The inverse μ of the zeta function is called the Möbius function of P.

As $\zeta([x,y])$ = 1 for all [x,y] in i(P), ζ is clearly invertible by LEMMA 5C.8. We shall be interested in obtaining simple formulas for the value of $\mu([x,y])$ in terms of x and y for interesting posets P. For example, we shall see that for the poset $\mathcal{P}(A)$ of all subsets of a set A, $\mu([x,y]) = (-1)^{|y-x|}$ where $|y-x|$ is the number of elements in the subset y but not in the subset x. Before going into this topic in detail, we make some simple observations about the Möbius function μ. Note that if x $\in$ P, then $\mu[x,x] = \dfrac{1}{\zeta[x,x]}$ = 1. If $\|[x,y]\|$ = 2 then $\mu*\zeta[x,y]$ = 0 = δ[x,y] implies that $\mu[x,x]$ + $\mu[x,y]$ = 0 so $\mu[x,y]$ = -1. If $\|[x,y]\|$ = 3 then again, if x < z < y, then $\mu[x,x]$ + $\mu[x,z]$ + $\mu[x,y]$ = 0 so $\mu[x,y]$ = 0. If $\|[x,y]\|$ = 4 there are two possibilities shown in FIGURE 5C.10. In FIGURE 5C.10(a) $\mu[x,y]$ = 0 but in FIGURE 5C.10(b) $\mu[x,x]$ + $\mu[x,z_1]$ + $\mu[x,z_2]$ = 1 + (-1) + (-1) = -1 so $\mu[x,y]$ = $+1$.

Thus, one sees that as the situation grows more complex the nature of μ depends very much on the structure of the poset and more sophisticated techniques will be required to characterize μ. One should note that if P is linearly ordered (x,y $\in$ P implies that x $\le$ y or y $\le$ x) then the function f defined by f[x,x] = 1 for all x, f[x,y] = -1 if $\|[x,y]\|$ = 2, and f[x,y] = 0 if $\|[x,y]\|$ > 2 inverts ζ and hence (by uniqueness of inverses) must be equal to μ.

5C.10   TWO INTERVALS OF CARDINALITY FOUR.

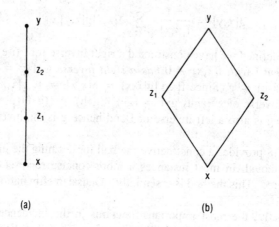

(a)   (b)

Figure 5C.10

We have already mentioned that, as an algebra, the incidence algebra of a finite poset is isomorphic to a subalgebra of $n \times n$ upper triangular matrices. We now indicate why this is so. Consider the 6×6 matrix of FIGURE 5C.11. The rows and columns of this matrix are indexed by the elements of the poset $\mathcal{P}(\underline{3})$ of all subsets of $\underline{3}$. In order to write down such a matrix, the elements of the poset must be linearly ordered. We have chosen the linear order on $\mathcal{P}(\underline{3})$ such that, if the subset x is contained in the subset y, then x comes before y in the linear order. This can be done in general, and is not difficult to show for the case of finite posets (EXERCISE 5C.12(1)). When such a linear order is specified, the matrix Z, called the incidence matrix, corresponding to that of FIGURE 5C.11 is always upper triangular. Note that the matrix Z of FIGURE 5C.11 has a 1 in position (x,y) if and only if $x \subseteq y$.

Thus the incidence matrix is just one possible way of representing the zeta function of the poset. Let $\mathcal{A}(P)$ denote the set of all matrices M with $M(x,y) = 0$ whenever $Z(x,y) = 0$. Note that the convolution product of DEFINITION 5C.5 when applied to these matrices as members of $R^{i(P)}$ (which they are, because M is the function $[x,y] \rightarrow M(x,y)$) is just the standard rule for multiplying matrices. The product of two matrices in $\mathcal{A}(P)$ is again a matrix in $\mathcal{A}(P)$. It is easily seen that the matrix algebra $\mathcal{A}(P)$ is isomorphic to the incidence algebra $R^{i(P)}$. We skip the algebraic formalities, as the result should have strong intuitive appeal at this point. With the matrix algebra model in mind, some of our previous results become obvious to the reader familiar with a little matrix theory. For example, LEMMA 5C.7 is just the statement that matrix multiplication is associative. LEMMA 5C.8 states the obvious fact that an upper triangular matrix is invertible if and only if all of its diagonal entries are nonzero. It turns out to be useful to have both the matrix point of view and the more local point of view in mind when studying the incidence algebras of posets. The standard linear algebraic ideas are not enough to answer the questions that arise in the study of incidence algebras. The special structures of the various posets of combinatorics must be exploited. We shall now study some specific examples where we try to give concise formulas for the entries of the inverse of Z. Using Cramer's rule or Gaussian elimination or other standard linear algebraic results is not enough to provide these results.

5C.11 AN INCIDENCE MATRIX.

$Z =$

	φ	1	2	3	12	13	23	123
φ	1	1	1	1	1	1	1	1
1	0	1	0	0	1	1	0	1
2	0	0	1	0	1	0	1	1
3	0	0	0	1	0	1	1	1
12	0	0	0	0	1	0	0	1
13	0	0	0	0	0	1	0	1
23	0	0	0	0	0	0	1	1
123	0	0	0	0	0	0	0	1

Figure 5C.11

5C.12 EXERCISE.

(1) Let S be a finite set with order relation $\leq$. Give an algorithm that lists the elements of S sequentially: $x_1, x_2, \ldots, x_s$, such that $x_q < x_p$ implies x_p is to the right of x_q in the list (q < p as integers). Call such a listing *order compatible* for the given order relation $\leq$. The column headings (read left to right) for the matrix Z of FIGURE 5C.11 specify an order compatible listing of the elements of the poset $\mathcal{P}(3)$. An order compatible listing of S, when used to define the incidence matrix Z of the poset $P = (S, \leq)$, forces Z to the upper triangular, as in FIGURE 5C.11.
(2) Find the inverse of the matrix Z of FIGURE 5C.11 using any one of the standard methods of elementary linear algebra.

We now show how one computes the Möbius function of a product of posets from those of its factors. This result is the most important elementary tool for computing formulas for Möbius functions of posets. Let $\{P_i : i \in I\}$ be a family of posets indexed by the possibly infinite set I. Suppose $P_i = (S_i, \leq_i)$. Consider the Cartesian product $\underset{i \in I}{\times} S_i = S$. If $f \in S$ then $f(i)$ denotes the "component" of f in S_i. For f and g in S, we define $f \leq g$ if $f(i) \leq_i g(i)$ for all $i \in I$. $P = (S, \leq)$ is easily seen to be a poset (EXERCISE 1.13(3)). We write $P = \underset{i \in I}{\times} P_i$ and call P the *product* of the posets P_i, $i \in I$. If the index set I is infinite then P may not be locally finite even if all of the P_i are locally finite (almost any example shows this). For this reason, we fix some element $f_0 \in S$ and let $S_0 = \{f: |\{i: f(i) \neq f_0(i)\}| < \infty\}$. S_0 is the set of all elements of S that are equal to f_0 except for finitely many components. Define $P_0 = (S_0, \leq)$. The poset P_0 is clearly locally finite if all of the P_i are locally finite. For example, let $P_i = \{0, 1, 2, \ldots\} = N$ be the non-negative integers ordered in the usual manner. Let $I = \{1, 2, 3, \ldots\}$ be the positive integers. Then $P = \underset{i \in I}{\times} P_i = N^I$ corresponds to all functions from I to N. If f_0 is chosen to be the identically zero function, the P_0 consists of all functions that are zero except at finitely many values of I. The general result we need is stated in THEOREM 5C.13.

5C.13 THEOREM.

Let $f \leq g$ be in P_0 (defined in the previous paragraph) and let μ denote the Möbius function of P_0. Then $\mu([f,g]) = \underset{i \in I}{\prod} \mu_i([f(i), g(i)])$ where μ_i is the Möbius function of P_i.

Proof.   Let $[f,g] \in i(P_0)$ be an interval of P_0. Define $\tau[f,g] = \underset{i \in I}{\prod} \mu_i[f(i), g(i)]$. This product is finite. Consider $\tau * \zeta[f,g] = \underset{f \leq h \leq g}{\sum} \tau[f,h] = \underset{f \leq h \leq g}{\sum} \underset{i \in I}{\prod} \mu_i[f(i), h(i)]$. Let $\mu_i[f(i), j] = a_{ij}$ and let $f(i) = b_i$ and $g(i) = c_i$. Then $\tau * \zeta[f,g] = \underset{h}{\sum} \underset{i \in I}{\prod} a_{ih(i)}$ where the sum is over all h in $\underset{i \in I}{\times} [b_i, c_i]$. By the standard "sum-product interchange" rule, $\tau * \zeta[f,g] = \underset{i \in I}{\prod} (\underset{b_i \leq j \leq c_i}{\sum} a_{ij})$. Thus $\tau * \zeta[f,g] = \underset{i \in I}{\prod} (\underset{f(i) \leq j \leq g(i)}{\sum} \mu_i[f(i), j])$ $= \underset{i \in I}{\prod} \mu_i * \zeta_i[f(i), g(i)] = \underset{i \in I}{\prod} \delta_i[f(i), g(i)] = \delta[f,g]$ where ζ_i and δ_i are the zeta and delta functions of P_i and δ is the delta function of P_0. Thus τ is the inverse of ζ and hence, by uniqueness of the inverse, $\tau = \mu$.

We now consider three important examples of the use of THEOREM 5C.13.

5C.14   THE MÖBIUS FUNCTION OF THE POSET OF SUBSETS.

Consider the set of all subsets $\mathcal{P}(D)$ of a finite set D with set inclusion as the order relation. The poset $\mathcal{P}(D)$ is obviously order isomorphic (DEFINITION 1.54) to the set of functions $\{0,1\}^D$ where each $Z \in \mathcal{P}(D)$ is associated with its characteristic function f_Z. We apply THEOREM 5C.13 with $P_i = \{0,1\}$ (with $0 < 1$) for all $i \in D = I$. P_i is linearly ordered so its Möbius function is given by (see the paragraph following DEFINITION 5C.9) $\mu_i[x,x] = 1$, $\mu_i[x,y] = -1$ if $x < y$. Since D is finite, we take $P = P_0 = \{0,1\}^D$. The identity of THEOREM 5C.13 becomes $\mu[A,B] = \mu[f_A,f_B] = \prod_{i \in A} \mu_i[f_A(i),f_B(i)] = (-1)^{|B-A|}$.

Thus $\mu[A,B] = (-1)^{|B-A|}$ is the Möbius function of the poset of subsets.

5C.15 THE MÖBIUS FUNCTION OF THE INTEGERS UNDER DIVISIBILITY.

Let $I = \{p_1, p_2, p_3, \ldots\}$ be the prime numbers in their natural order as integers. Let N be the non-negative integers, and consider the poset $P = N^I$. Using the function $f_0(p_i) = 0$ for all $p_i \in I$, define P_0 as above in connection with THEOREM 5C.13. The poset P_0 is easily seen to be order isomorphic to the integers under divisibility (using the unique factorization of integers as powers of primes). Thus each $f \in P_0$ corresponds to the integer $n_f = \prod_{i=1}^{\infty} p_i^{f(p_i)}$ where this product has finitely many terms not equal to 1. Using THEOREM 5C.13, we have that $\mu[f,g] = \prod_{i \in I} \mu_i[f(p_i),g(p_i)]$. Since N is linearly ordered, its Möbius function is as described in the paragraph following DEFINITION 5C.9. Hence, $\mu[f,g] = 0$ if $g(p_i) - f(p_i) \geq 2$ for any prime p_i. Otherwise, $\mu[f,g] = (-1)^t$ where t is the number of primes p_i for which $g(p_i) - f(p_i) = 1$. Another way to describe this Möbius function is to form the quotient n_g/n_f of the integers n_g and n_f associated with g and f. If this number is divisible by the square of a prime, then $\mu[f,g]$ is 0. If this number is "square free" then $\mu[f,g] = (-1)^t$ where t is the number of primes (all to the power 1) in its prime factorization. This is the classical description of the Möbius function of number theory.

Our final application of THEOREM 5C.13 will be to the poset of partitions of a set. Before doing this we discuss briefly the most important combinatorial use of the Möbius function, namely, the inversion of finite series. Suppose that g and f are in the incidence algebra of a finite poset P. Suppose also that $g = f*\zeta$ where ζ is the zeta function of the incidence algebra. Expressed as a summation, this identity becomes $g[x,y] = \sum_{x \leq z \leq y} f[x,z]$. The identity $g = f*\zeta$ implies that $f = g*\mu$ where μ is the Möbius function of the poset. In terms of sums this becomes $f[x,y] = \sum_{x \leq z \leq y} g[x,z]\mu[z,y]$. A similar rule holds if $g = \zeta*f$. We thus have LEMMA 5C.16.

5C.16 LEMMA.

Let f and g be functions from the intervals i(P) of a poset P to R. The following rules for inverting finite sums apply:

(1) If $g[x,y] = \sum\limits_{x \le z \le y} f[x,z]$ then $f[x,y] = \sum\limits_{x \le z \le y} g[x,z]\mu[z,y]$.

(2) If $g[x,y] = \sum\limits_{x \le z \le y} f[z,y]$ then $f[x,y] = \sum\limits_{x \le z \le y} \mu[x,z]g[z,y]$.

5C.17   EXAMPLE OF INVERSION OF FINITE SUMS.

Let P be the positive integers with the usual linear order. Suppose that we are given a function g in the incidence algebra of P, $g[x,y] = xy^2$. We define a function f on $\{[x,y]: x \le y\}$ by the finite series $xy^2 = \sum\limits_{x \le z \le y} f[x,z]$. Clearly $f[x,x] = g[x,x] = x^3$. Using LEMMA 5C.16(1) we see that for $x < y$, $f[x,y]$ $= \sum\limits_{x \le z \le y} xz^2 \mu[z,y] = x(y-1)^2\mu[y-1,y] + xy^2 \mu[y,y] = -x(y-1)^2 + xy^2$ $= x(2y-1)$. Thus, given the explicit formula $g[x,y] = xy^2$ for g together with the implicit definition of f as a finite sum, we obtain, using the Möbius function of the poset, an explicit formula for f. This is a typical application of "Möbius inversion" of a finite sum. The Möbius function in this example is trivial, but we shall now consider some more complex examples.

There is a variation on LEMMA 5C.16 that is sometimes confusing to the beginner in this subject. The functions f and g of LEMMA 5C.16 are given directly as functions from the intervals i(P) of the poset P to R. In many applications of LEMMA 5C.16 the functions f and g are functions from P to R instead. Thus, we are given a finite series of the form $g(y) = \sum\limits_{x \le z \le y} f(z)$ or $g(x) =$ $\sum\limits_{x \le z \le y} f(z)$ where x is regarded as fixed in the former equation (giving g as a function of the variable y) and y is regarded as fixed in the latter. A given function f: P → R may be regarded as a function in the incidence algebra in two natural ways. We may define $\underline{f}[x,y] = f(x)$ for all intervals x,y or we may define $\bar{f}[x,y] = f(y)$. We call $\underline{f}$ the *lower representation* of f and $\bar{f}$ the *upper representation* of f. We then see that the identity $g(y) = \sum\limits_{x \le z \le y} f(z)$ is equivalent to the identity $\bar{g} = \bar{f}*\zeta$ and the identity $g(x) = \sum\limits_{x \le z \le y} f(z)$ is equivalent to the identity $\underline{g} = \zeta*\underline{f}$. With these correspondences, LEMMA 5C.18 follows from LEMMA 5C.16.

5C.18   LEMMA.

Let f and g be functions from a poset P to R. The following rules for inverting finite sums apply:

(1) If $g(y) = \sum\limits_{x \le z \le y} f(z)$ then $f(y) = \sum\limits_{x \le z \le y} g(z)\mu[z,y]$.

(2) If $g(x) = \sum\limits_{x \le z \le y} f(z)$ then $f(x) = \sum\limits_{x \le z \le y} \mu[x,z]g(z)$.

We shall now give some examples of the use of LEMMA 5C.18.

5C.19 EXERCISE.

(1) Prove LEMMA 5C.18.
(2) In LEMMA 5C.16 and LEMMA 5C.18, R denotes the real numbers. For what other algebraic structures are these lemmas valid? For example, if R were to denote all polynomials in a variable x, would these lemmas still be valid? *Hint*: This is an occasion where the "matrix point of view" might be helpful, at least conceptually.

5C.20 THE MÖBIUS FUNCTION OF THE POSET OF PARTITIONS OF A SET.

Consider the poset $\Pi(D)$ of partitions of a finite set D, $|D| = d$, where $\pi_1 \leq \pi_2$ means "π_1 refines π_2" (see DEFINITION 1.3 and EXAMPLE 1.9(4)). The "elements" of a partition are subsets of D and are called the "blocks" of the partition. We use the usual notation $|\pi|$ to denote the number of blocks of the partition π. Let S be a set with $|S| = s$. For any function $f \in S^D$ recall that the coimage(f) is the partition of D whose blocks are the sets $f^{-1}(t)$ for $t \in$ image(f) (see NOTATION 1.6). Given $\pi \in \Pi(D)$, one may easily verify that $|\{f: \text{coim-age}(f) = \pi\}| = (s)_{|\pi|}$. Here, $(s)_k = s(s-1)(s-2)\ldots(s-k+1)$ is the *falling factorial*. Let θ denote the discrete partition $\{\{t\}: t \in D\}$ and let τ denote the one block partition. By classifying the functions of S^D by the cardinality of their coimage, we obtain the identity $s^d = s^{|\theta|} = \sum_{\theta \leq \pi \leq \tau} (s)_{|\pi|}$. Using the inversion formula of LEMMA 5C.18(2) we obtain $(s)_d = (s)_{|\theta|} = \sum_{\theta \leq \pi \leq \tau} \mu(\theta,\pi)s^{|\pi|}$. This identity is valid for all values of s, so we may view it as a polynomial identity and think of s as a variable. When we compare the coefficients of s on both sides of the identity, we obtain $\mu[\theta,\tau] = (-1)^{d-1}(d-1)!$. Thus, we have computed the value of μ on the total interval $[\theta,\tau]$.

Suppose now that we are given partitions $\eta \leq \rho$ in $\Pi(D)$. Let $B_1,B_2,\ldots,B_q$ denote the blocks of the partition ρ. Since η is a refinement of ρ, each block B_i is further partitioned by η. We call this partition of B_i induced by η, η_i. Since η_i is a set (of blocks) we may consider $\Pi(\eta_i)$. Note that the interval $[\eta_i,\{B_i\}]$ in the poset $\Pi(B_i)$ is order isomorphic to the total interval in the poset $\Pi(\eta_i)$. Hence, the interval $[\eta,\rho]$ in the poset $\Pi(D)$ is isomorphic to the product $\underset{i}{\times} \Pi(\eta_i)$. Thus, by THEOREM 5C.13, we obtain the formula $\mu[\eta,\rho] = (-1)^{|\eta|-|\rho|}(|\eta_1|-1)!$ $(|\eta_2|-1!)\ldots(|\eta_q|-1)!$ where $\eta_1,\ldots,\eta_q$ are the restrictions of η to the blocks of ρ. This completely specifies the Möbius function of the poset of partitions of a set.

5C.21 MÖBIUS INVERSION AND THE PRINCIPLE OF INCLUSION-EXCLUSION.

In a certain sense, the principle of inclusion-exclusion can be regarded as a special case of Möbius inversion. Consider COROLLARY 5B.4. Let $\mathcal{N}_=(T) = \prod_{i \in T} f_i \prod_{i \in T^c} (u - f_i)$ and let $\mathcal{N}_\supseteq(T) = \prod_{i \in T} f_i$. We observe that

$$\sum_{T \subseteq R \subseteq \underline{n}} \mathcal{N}_=(R) = \sum_{T \subseteq R \subseteq \underline{n}} \prod_{i \in R} f_i \prod_{i \in \underline{n} - R} (u - f_i)$$

$$= \prod_{i \in T} f_i \sum_{Q \subseteq \underline{n} - T} \prod_{i \in Q} f_i \prod_{i \in (\underline{n} - T) - Q} (u - f_i)$$

$$= \prod_{i \in T} f_i \prod_{i \in \underline{n} - T} (f_i + (u - f_i)) = \prod_{i \in T} f_i = \mathcal{N}_\supseteq(T) .$$

Thus we have $\mathcal{N}_\supseteq(T) = \sum\limits_{T \subseteq R \subseteq \underline{n}} \mathcal{N}_=(R)$ which is a form of LEMMA 5C.18(2)

where the poset is $\mathscr{P}(\underline{n})$ (EXAMPLE 5C.14). We are actually using a slight extension of LEMMA 5C.18 suggested in EXERCISE 5C.19(2). Thus we see that

$$\mathcal{N}_=(T) = \sum_{T \subseteq R \subseteq \underline{n}} \mu(T,R) \mathcal{N}_\supseteq(R)$$

when $\mu(T,R) = (-1)^{|R| - |T|}$. This gives COROLLARY 5B.4 from which all other results on inclusion-exclusion follow. Of course, the proof of COROLLARY 5B.4 is a trivial algebraic manipulation, so using Möbius inversion to prove the result is a case of "using a sledgehammer to kill a fly." We point out that we use P and P_i as sets in connection with the discussion of inclusion-exclusion and as posets in connection with Möbius inversion. In both cases this is standard notation. In the former case, P_i stands for the subset of P with "property" i (in the case of derangements, P_i is the subset of $P = S_n$ with the property that i is a fixed point). In COROLLARY 5B.2, for example, the underlying poset is $(\mathscr{P}(\underline{n}), \subseteq)$. The P_i are just subsets of a set P and are not to be confused with the posets of the Möbius inversion discussion.

5C.22   MÖBIUS INVERSION AND DIVISIBILITY OF INTEGERS: EULER'S φ-FUNCTION.

We refer to EXAMPLE 5C.15. For a positive integer n, we let $\varphi(n)$ denote the number of positive integers x that are less than or equal to n and are relatively prime to n (g.c.d.$(x,n) = 1$, where g.c.d. stands for "greatest common divisor"). The function φ is called the Euler φ-function. Let $S_d = \{i \le n: \text{g.c.d.}(i,n) = d\}$. It is evident that $\underline{n} = \bigcup\limits_{d|n} S_d$ and the sets S_d are disjoint. Thus $n = \sum\limits_{d|n} |S_d|$. Note that $|S_d| = \varphi(n/d)$ and hence $n = \sum\limits_{d|n} \varphi(n/d) = \sum\limits_{d|n} \varphi(d)$. This identity is of the form of LEMMA 5C.18(1) so we obtain the identity $\varphi(n) = \sum\limits_{d|n} d\,\mu(d,n)$.

Now, let $\{p_i: i \in T\}$ be the set of primes that are divisors of n. From EXAMPLE 5C.15 we see that $\mu(d,n) = 0$ unless $d = n/\prod\limits_{i \in Q} p_i$ where $Q \subseteq T$, in which case $\mu(d,n) = (-1)^{|Q|}$. Thus, $\varphi(n) = \sum\limits_{Q \subseteq T} (-1)^{|Q|} n/\prod\limits_{i \in Q} p_i = n \prod\limits_{p|n} (1 - 1/p)$ where the product is over all prime divisors of n. This result should be compared with EXAMPLE 5B.8.

5C.23 MÖBIUS INVERSION AND THE POSET OF PARTITIONS: CONNECTED GRAPHS.

For this example, the reader should look at the material in CHAPTER 6 up to DEFINITION 6.11. Let $G = (V,E)$ be a graph (no loops). From the definition, it is immediate that there are $2^{\binom{n}{2}}$ such graphs if $|V| = n$. Associated with each graph G is a partition π of V determined by the connected components of G (each block of π is a connected component's vertex set). We call π the *component partition of* G. We say that a partition π is of type $(b_1,b_2,\ldots,b_n)$ if there are b_t blocks of cardinality t in π, $t = 1,\ldots,n$. We have seen this idea in connection with ranking ordered partitions with fixed multinomial index (see TABLE 3.28 and the related discussion). The idea of type was also discussed in connection with permutations (in the derivation of IDENTITY 4.46) and for partitions (in connection with FIGURE 4.63). One can show that the number of partitions π with type $(b_1,b_2,\ldots,b_n)$ is $n!/\prod_{t=1}^{n} (t!)^{b_t} b_t!$ (EXERCISE 5C.24(1)). As in EX-AMPLE 5C.20, we let θ be the discrete partition (minimal element of $\Pi(V)$) and τ the one-block partition (maximal element of $\Pi(V)$). For a given partition π, let $N_=(\pi)$ denote the number of graphs $G = (V,E)$ with component partition π and let $N_\le(\pi)$ denote all graphs whose component partition is a refinement of π. We thus have

$$2^{\binom{n}{2}} = N_\le(\tau) = \sum_{\theta \le \pi \le \tau} N_=(\pi) .$$

This identity is in the form of LEMMA 5C.18(1). Applying LEMMA 5C.18(1) we obtain

$$N_=(\tau) = \sum_{\theta \le \pi \le \tau} N_\le(\pi)\mu(\pi,\tau)$$

where μ is the Möbius function of the poset $\Pi(V)$ (EXAMPLE 5C.20). Thus $\mu(\pi,\tau) = (-1)^{\Sigma b_i - 1} (\Sigma b_i - 1)!$. It is easily seen that $N_\le(\pi) = \prod_i 2^{\binom{i}{2} b_i}$. $N_=(\tau)$ is the number c_n of connected graphs $G = (V,E)$ with $|V| = n$. Thus we obtain

$$c_n = \sum_b (-1)^{\Sigma b_i - 1} \left(\sum b_i - 1\right)! \prod_i 2^{\binom{i}{2} b_i} \frac{n!}{\prod_i (i!)^{b_i} b_i!}$$

where the sum is over all possible types $(b_1,...,b_n)$ or all n-tuples of non-negative integers $(b_1,...,b_n)$ such that $\sum_i ib_i = n$. Simplifying, we obtain that the number c_n of connected graphs $G = (V,E)$ with $|V| = n$ is:

$$c_n = -n! \sum_b \left(\sum b_i - 1\right)! \prod_i \left[\frac{-2^{\binom{i}{2}}}{i!}\right]^{b_i} \frac{1}{b_i!}$$

where the product is over $b_i > 0$ and the sum is over all $(b_1,...,b_n)$ such that $\sum_i ib_i = n$. Unfortunately, the number of terms in this sum grows exponentially with n so the formula is only useful for small values of n.

5C.24 EXERCISE.

(1) Try to give a reasonably convincing argument that the number of partitions π with type $(b_1,b_2,...,b_n)$ is $n!/\prod_{t=1}^{n} (t!)^{b_t} b_t!$. *Hint:* The argument is similar to that used in deriving IDENTITY 4.46.

(2) Additional applications of Möbius inversion (Waring's formula, convex polytopes, finite vector space, etc.) are given in the references at the end of Part I. Organize and present some of this material to the class.

5D. NETWORK FLOWS.

For this section, the reader should study the material in CHAPTER 6 through DEFINITION 6.11. FIGURE 5D.1(a) shows a directed graph $G = (V,E)$ with $V = \{s,p,q,r,t\}$. Each edge is labeled with a value c, called the "capacity of the edge" and a value f, called the "flow of the edge." The vertex s is called the "source" of G and the vertex t is called the "sink" of G. Imagine that each edge represents a tube through which water is flowing in the direction indicated. The capacity c of each edge or "tube" represents the maximum amount of water that can flow through the tube in the indicated direction (in m^3/sec, say). Suppose that at all vertices except s and t the amount of water flowing into that vertex must equal the amount of water flowing out of that vertex. Generally, one thinks of water being put into the system at s and flowing out at t, but the roles of s and t are symmetrical. The flow f represents the actual amount of water flowing through the "network."

5D.1   FLOW THROUGH A NETWORK.

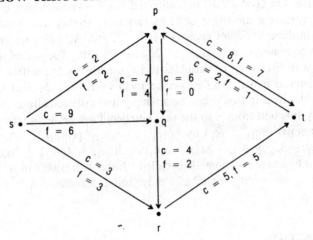

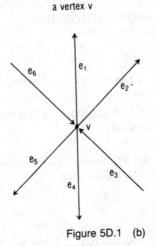

Figure 5D.1   (a)

The undirected path (s,q,p,t) with edge sequence ((s,q),(q,p),(t,p)) is augmentable. Edges (s,q) and (q,p) are forward directed, edge (t,p) backward directed. The edge sequence ((s,q),(q,p),(p,t)) also may be associated with this path.

Figure 5D.1   (b)

$OUTOF(v) = e_1 + e_2 + e_4 + e_5$

$INTO(v) = e_3 + e_6$

$STAR(v) = e_1 + e_2 + e_4 + e_5 - e_3 - e_6$

LINEAR EXTENSION for h: $E \rightarrow R$, $h(STAR(v)) = h(e_1) + h(e_2) + h(e_4) + h(e_5) - h(e_3) - h(e_6)$

Before proceeding further with networks, we discuss briefly an important conceptual idea. Let $G = (V,E)$ be a directed graph. We think of the symbols $e_1, e_2, \ldots$ representing the edges of G as variables. In this way we can form polynomials in these variables such as $4e_1 + e_3^2$, etc. Actually, we shall only need linear polynomials such as $e_1 - 2e_2 + 3e_3$, etc. The set of all linear polynomials with E as a set of variables and real numbers as coefficients has a fancy mathematical name: *the free vector space of* E *over the real numbers*. Name aside, the idea is trivial but notationally and conceptually useful. If h: $E \to R$ is any function from E to the real numbers then we define the value of h on a polynomial $p(e_1, \ldots, e_n)$ by $hp(e_1, \ldots, e_n) = p(h(e_1), \ldots, h(e_n))$. For example, $h(e_1 - 3e_2 + 4e_3 - 2e_4) = h(e_1) - 3h(e_2) + 4h(e_3) - 2h(e_4)$. This extension of h to *linear* polynomials is called "linear extension" of h. In DEFINITION 5D.2, we specify some basic polynomials associated with a directed graph.

5D.2   DEFINITION.

Let $G = (V,E)$ be a directed graph without loops (i.e., no edges of the form (x,x)). For each v in V, let INTO(v) be the polynomial formed by summing all edges incident on v and directed towards v, let OUTOF(v) be the sum of all edges incident on v and directed away from v, and let $STAR(v) = OUTOF(v) - INTO(v)$. An example is shown in FIGURE 5D.1(b).

Referring again to FIGURE 5D.1, we give the formal definitions needed in connection with networks in DEFINITION 5D.3.

5D.3   DEFINITION.

A network is a 4-tuple (G,s,t,c) where G is a directed graph, s and t are distinct vertices of G called the *source* and the *sink* respectively, and c: $E \to R^+$ is a function from the edges E of G to the positive real numbers. The function c is called the *capacity* of the network.

In DEFINITION 5D.4, we define the "flow" of a network in terms of the polynomials defined in DEFINITION 5D.2.

5D.4   DEFINITION.

Let (G,s,t,c) be a network. A function f: $E \to R_0^+$ that maps E to the non-negative real numbers and satisfies $f(STAR(v)) = 0$ for all v not equal to s or t and $f(e) \le c(e)$ for all $e \in E$ will be called a *flow on the network*.

The intuitive idea of a flow has been presented above in connection with water flowing in tubes (FIGURE 5D.1). The condition $f(STAR(v)) = 0$ says that "the water flowing into v equals the water flowing out of v."

For each edge e $\in$ E, let IN(e) denote the initial vertex of e and let TM(e) denote the terminal vertex of e. (See NOTATION 6.41 of CHAPTER 6 for more discussion.)

5D.5   DEFINITION.

Let (G,s,t,c) be a network. A partition $\{P,\bar{P}\}$ of V into two blocks (DEFINITION 1.3) with s $\in$ P and t $\in$ $\bar{P}$ will be called a *cut partition*. Let OUTCUT(P,$\bar{P}$) be the polynomial formed by summing all edges e with IN(e) $\in$ P and TM(e) $\in$ $\bar{P}$ (i.e., all edges that go from P to $\bar{P}$) and let INCUT(P,$\bar{P}$) be the sum over all edges going from $\bar{P}$ to P. Define CUT(P,$\bar{P}$) = OUTCUT(P,$\bar{P}$) + INCUT(P,$\bar{P}$). We define the number c(OUTCUT(P,$\bar{P}$)) to be the *capacity of the cut partition* $\{P,\bar{P}\}$, or the *capacity of the cut*.

In terms of the "water in tubes" analogy, the capacity of $\{P,\bar{P}\}$ represents the maximum amount of water that could possibly be flowing from P to $\bar{P}$.

5D.6   LEMMA.

Let (G,s,t,c) be a network and let $\{P,\bar{P}\}$ be a partition of V with s $\in$ P and t $\in$ $\bar{P}$ as in DEFINITION 5D.5. Using the notation of DEFINITIONS 5D.2 and 5D.5, the following identities hold:

(1) $\sum_{v \in P}$ STAR(v) = OUTCUT(P,$\bar{P}$) $-$ INCUT(P,$\bar{P}$).

(2) $\sum_{v \in \bar{P}}$ STAR(v) = INCUT(P,$\bar{P}$) $-$ OUTCUT(P,$\bar{P}$).

(3) $\sum_{v \in P}$ STAR(v) = $- \sum_{v \in \bar{P}}$ STAR(v).

(4) For any flow f, f(STAR(s)) = $-$f(STAR(t)) = f(OUTCUT(P,$\bar{P}$)) $-$ f(INCUT(P,$\bar{P}$)). This number is called the *value of the flow*.

(5) For any flow f, f(STAR(s)) $\leq$ c(OUTCUT(P,$\bar{P}$)) (the value of the flow is less than or equal to the capacity of the cut).

Proof.   We first prove (1). Let e = (v,w) be an edge with both v and w in P. Then, e occurs in the polynomial STAR(v) and $-$e occurs in the polynomial STAR(w). The edge e does not occur in STAR(x) if x is not equal to v or w. Thus all edges with both vertices in P cancel in forming the sum that is the left-hand side of identity (1). This leaves only the right-hand side of identity (1). Identity (2) is derived in the same manner. Identity (3) follows trivially from (1) and (2). To prove (4), note that, from (1), $\sum_{v \in P}$ f(STAR(v)) = f(OUTCUT(P,$\bar{P}$))

$- f(\text{INCUT}(P,\bar{P}))$ for any function f, whether or not f is a flow. If f is flow, however, we have $f(\text{STAR}(v)) = 0$ if $v \neq s$ or t. As $s \in P$ but $t \notin P$, identity (4) follows. To prove (5), note that the stronger identity $f(\text{STAR}(s)) \leq f(\text{OUTCUT}(P,\bar{P}))$ is obvious from (4). From the definition of a flow, $f(\text{OUTCUT}(P,\bar{P})) \leq c(\text{OUTCUT}(P,\bar{P}))$.

Note that the inequality of LEMMA 5D.6(5) is valid for any flow and any partition $\{P,\bar{P}\}$ such that $s \in P$ and $t \in \bar{P}$. In particular, the maximum value over all flows f of $f(\text{STAR}(s))$ is less than or equal to the minimum over all such $\{P,\bar{P}\}$ of $c(\text{OUTCUT}(P,\bar{P}))$. In fact, we shall see by THEOREM 5D.8 that these numbers are always equal.

5D.7. DEFINITION.

Let (G,s,t,c) be a network. The maximum value over all flows f on the network of $f(\text{STAR}(s))$ will be denoted by MAXFLOW. The minimum over all partitions $\{P,\bar{P}\}$ of $c(\text{OUTCUT}(P,\bar{P}))$ will be denoted by MINCUT.

As we have remarked, the fact that MAXFLOW $\leq$ MINCUT follows easily from LEMMA 5D.6(5).

5D.8 THEOREM.

For any network (G,s,t,c), MAXFLOW = MINCUT.

Proof. Let f be any flow. Let $\bar{G}$ be the undirected version of the graph G. Consider a path $s = x_1, x_2, \ldots, x_j = v$ in $\bar{G}$ from s to a vertex v. A directed edge of G of the form (x_i, x_{i+1}), $1 \leq i < j$, will be called *forward directed* relative to this path and an edge of G of the form (x_{i+1}, x_i) *backward directed*. If it is possible to choose a sequence of such edges $(e_1, e_2, \ldots, e_{j-1})$ of G such that for each forward directed $e_i = (x_i, x_{i+1})$, $f(e_i) < c(e_i)$ and for each backward directed $e_t = (x_{t+1}, x_t)$, $f(e_t) > 0$ then the path $x_1, \ldots, x_j$ will be called *augmentable* relative to the flow f. The sequence $(e_1, e_2, \ldots, e_{j-1})$ will be called an *edge sequence* of the path, and may not be unique (see FIGURE 5D.1(a)).

Let P_f denote the set of all vertices v of G for which there exists an augmentable path from s to v. We assume $s \in P_f$. Suppose that $t \in P_f$ and let $s = x_1, x_2, \ldots, x_k = t$ be an augmentable path joining s to t with edge sequence $(e_1, e_2, \ldots, e_{k-1})$. Let M be the set of all numbers of the form $c(e) - f(e)$ for "forward-directed" edges $e = (x_i, x_{i+1})$ and of the form $f(e)$ for "backward-directed" edges $e = (x_{i+1}, x_i)$. Let $m > 0$ be the minimum value of M. Define a new flow f' on G by $f'(e) = f(e) + m$ on each forward-directed edge of the augmentable path, $f'(e) = f(e) - m$ on each backward-directed edge of the augmentable path, and $f'(e) = f(e)$ for all other edges of G. It is easily seen that f' is a flow and that $f'(\text{STAR}(s)) > f(\text{STAR}(s))$ (i.e., the value of f' is greater than the value of f so f *cannot be a flow of maximal value*). By elementary topological considerations (trivial in the case of "integral flows" where f and c take on only non-negative integral values) there exists *a flow* F *of maximal value.* By what we have just shown, t $\notin$ P_F so $\{P_F, \overline{P}_F\}$ is a cut partition (DEFINITION 5D.5). By the definition of P_F, any edge e in OUTCUT($P_F, \overline{P}_F$) must have F(e) = c(e) and any edge in INCUT($P_F, \overline{P}_F$) must have F(e) = 0. Thus, by LEMMA 5D.6(4), F(STAR(s)) = c(OUTCUT($P_F, \overline{P}_F$)). This completes the proof as we remarked above, MAX-FLOW $\leq$ MINCUT is a trivial consequence of LEMMA 5D.6.

There are many applications of THEOREM 5D.8. We shall mention some of the more interesting combinatorial consequences. The literature on this subject is extensive and quite accessible. The classical reference, and still one of the best, is the book *Flows in Networks* by Ford and Fulkerson (Princeton University Press, 1962).

An important technical result is stated in THEOREM 5D.9.

5D.9   THEOREM (Integrity theorem).

For any network (G,s,t,c) where c is integral valued there exists a maximal flow f that is integral valued.

Proof.   An inspection of the proof of THEOREM 5D.8 reveals that the augmentation process can always be done in such a way as to transform an integral valued flow into another integral valued flow of larger value.

One obvious and important extension of THEOREM 5D.8 is to networks of the form (G,s,t,c,d) where (G,s,t,c) is a network as above but d: $V \rightarrow R^+$ is a function from the vertices V of G to the positive real numbers (a vertex capacity function). We must have f(INTO(v)) $\leq$ d(v) and f(OUTOF(v)) $\leq$ d(v) for all v. A simple trick of replacing each vertex v $\in$ V by a directed edge reduces such networks to the case where only an edge capacity is considered. This idea is shown in FIGURE 5D.10. In the second network of FIGURE 5D.10, the source is s and the sink is t'.

5D.10   VERTEX CAPACITIES REDUCED TO EDGE CAPACITIES.

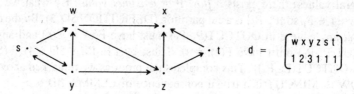

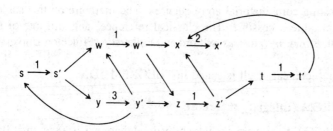

Figure 5D.10

VERTEX CAPACITY FUNCTION d ASSIGNS CAPACITIES TO NEW EDGES

Another trivial extension of THEOREM 5D.8 arises when the source s is replaced by a set S of sources and the sink t is replaced by a set T of sinks. Thus one has a network of the form (G,S,T,c). Such networks can be reduced to the case of a single source and sink as indicated in FIGURE 5D.11 where a single source s and sink t are added to the network. An edge of infinite (the same as "finite but very large" in this case) capacity is added to the network joining s to each element of S and each element of T to t.

5D.11   MANY SOURCES AND MANY SINKS.

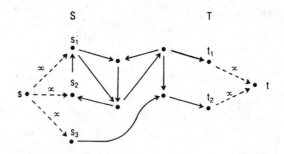

Figure 5D.11

An important graph theoretic version of THEOREM 5D.8 is called "Menger's Theorem" (THEOREM 5D.12). Let $G' = (V',E')$ be an undirected graph and let S' and T' be two disjoint subsets of V'. Let $a_1, a_2, \ldots, a_n$ be the vertex sequence of a path in G' (see CHAPTER 6, DEFINITION 6.9). The vertex a_1 is called the "initial vertex" of the path and the vertex a_n is called the "terminal vertex." The other vertices are called "internal vertices" of the path. Two paths in G' will be called *vertex disjoint* if they have no vertices in common and *internally vertex disjoint* if they have no internal vertices in common. Let S' and T' be two nonempty disjoint subsets of V'. A subset D' of V' will be called an S', T' *blocking set* (or disconnecting set, or separator) if every path with initial vertex in S' and terminal vertex in T' (i.e., a path from S' to T') has a vertex in D' (passes through D'). In what follows, "a path from S' to T'" means a path with initial vertex in S', terminal vertex in T' and all other vertices in $V' - S' - T'$.

5D.12   THEOREM (Menger).

Let $G' = (V', E')$ be an undirected graph and let S' and T' be nonempty disjoint subsets of V'. The maximum number of pairwise vertex disjoint paths from S' to T' is equal to the minimum size of an S', T' blocking set D'.

Proof.   (See EXERCISE 5D.21(1).)

A frequently occurring special case of THEOREM 5D.12 happens when $S' \cup T' = V'$ and all edges of G' have one vertex in S' and the other in T'. In this case, the graph is called *bipartite* with vertex partition $\{S', T'\}$. An example of a bipartite graph is shown in FIGURE 5D.14. In this case the only paths starting in S' and ending in T' are single edges. Any S', T' blocking set D' must be a subset of $S' \cup T'$ as this set is all of V'. In this case, the set D' is sometimes referred to as a "vertex cover" of the bipartite graph because the union of all edges of G' incident on D' is all of E' ("covers" E'). A picturesque rephrasing of Menger's theorem in the bipartite case is sometimes called the "rook-plank" theorem (EXERCISE 5D.21(2)).

5D.13   COROLLARY.

Let G' be a bipartite graph with vertex partition $\{S', T'\}$. The maximum size of a pairwise disjoint collection of edges is equal to the minimum size of a vertex cover.

If G' is a bipartite graph with vertex partition $\{S', T'\}$ then each edge $e = \{x, y\}$, $x \in S'$, $y \in T'$, may be thought of as "matching some element of S' to an element of T'." Correspondingly, a collection of disjoint edges may be thought of as matching a subset of S' to a subset of T' (i.e., defining a bijection between these subsets). Thus we call any collection of disjoint edges of G' a *matching*. Suppose $|S'| \leq |T'|$. A subset of edges of G' that is pairwise disjoint (i.e., is a matching) and whose union contains S' is called a *complete matching* of S'.

Conditions for the existence of complete matchings are sometimes of interest. One standard example is the case where S' is a set of girls and T' is a set of boys. A bipartite graph is constructed by defining {x,y} to be an edge if girl x knows boy y. A dating service might be interested in a complete matching that would pair each girl with one boy that she already knows. FIGURE 5D.14 shows a bipartite graph with a complete matching.

5D.14 A BIPARTITE GRAPH WITH A COMPLETE MATCHING.

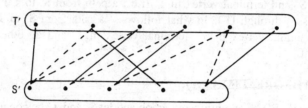

SOLID EDGES GIVE A COMPLETE MATCHING

Figure 5D.14

Let G' be a graph and let x be a vertex of G'. A vertex y for which there is an edge of the form {x,y} is said to be *adjacent* to x. Let A_x denote the set of all vertices adjacent to x. THEOREM 5D.15 gives the standard conditions for the existence of a complete matching in a bipartite graph.

5D.15 THEOREM (Matching theorem).

Let G' be a bipartite graph with vertex partition {S',T'}. There exists a complete matching of S' if and only if for every subset $Q \subseteq S'$, $|\underset{x \in Q}{\cup} A_x| \geq |Q|$.

Proof. The "only if" part is trivial. Suppose the inequality of the hypothesis holds. Consider a minimal vertex cover $D' = A' \cup B'$ where $A' \subseteq S'$ and $B' \subseteq T'$. The situation is shown in FIGURE 5D.16. Note that by the definition of D' there can be no edge from $S' - A'$ to $T' - B'$. Thus $B' \supseteq \underset{x \in S' - A'}{\cup} A_x$ and, by our hypothesis, $|B'| \geq |\underset{x \in S' - A'}{\cup} A_x| \geq |S'| - |A'|$. Thus $|D'| = |A'| + |B'| \geq |S'|$. Of course $|D'| = |S'|$ as S' is itself a vertex cover. The result now follows immediately from COROLLARY 5D.13.

5D.16   MINIMAL VERTEX COVER FOR MATCHING THEOREM.

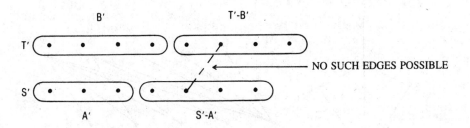

D′ = A′ ∪ B′ IS THE MINIMAL VERTEX COVER

Figure 5D.16

As our final example, we consider Dilworth's theorem for ordered sets (DEF-INITION 1.8). An ordered set $P = (X,\underline{\alpha})$ is also called a "poset" and we say "x is an element of P" when $x \in X$. A subset $Q \subseteq X$ which has the property that $x,y \in Q$ implies that $x \underline{\alpha} y$ or $y \underline{\alpha} x$ is called a *linearly ordered subset* of P or a *chain*. A partition of P in which each block is a chain is called a "*chain cover*" of P. A subset $T \subseteq Q$ with the property that if $x,y \in T$ then $x \underline{\alpha} y$ implies that $x = y$ is called a *transversal* for P. Note that any single element $x \in P$ defines a *singleton chain* $\{x\}$. The cardinality of a chain cover $\mathscr{C}$ is the number of blocks in $\mathscr{C}$. We say that "s and t are *comparable* in P" if either $s \underline{\alpha} t$ or $t \underline{\alpha} s$. A transversal T is a subset of X such that every pair of distinct elements is *not comparable*. The *length* of a chain Q is $|Q| - 1$.

5D.17   THEOREM (Dilworth).

The minimum cardinality of a chain cover of a poset P equals the maximum cardinality of a transversal of P.

Proof.   We use COROLLARY 5D.13. For convenience of notation, let $P = (\underline{n},\underline{\alpha})$ and let $P' = (\underline{n}',\underline{\alpha})$ be an order isomorphic copy of P where $\underline{n}' = \{1',2',\ldots,n'\}$. Construct a bipartite graph G′ with vertex partition $S' = \underline{n}$ and $T' = \underline{n}'$ by defining a pair $\{i,j'\}$ to be an edge if $i \alpha j$ in the poset P. An example is shown in FIGURE 5D.18. The poset there is specified by its Hasse diagram (DEFINITION 1.10).

5D.18   BIPARTITE GRAPH OF A POSET.

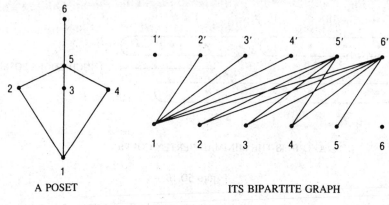

A POSET   ITS BIPARTITE GRAPH

Figure 5D.18

We now define a bijection β between disjoint edge sets of G' and chain covers of P. Suppose we are given a disjoint edge set, DES, in G'. Every edge in DES corresponds to a 2-vertex chain in P, e.g., $\{1,3'\} \leftrightarrow \vert_1^3$. If any two of the chains thus formed from DES are not disjoint, then they must be of the form $\vert_a^b$ and $\vert_b^d$ (by disjointness of their corresponding edges in G'). We can link these chains to form $\vert_a^d$. By forming all such linkages we construct a set of disjoint chains in P. Let $\beta(DES) = \{$disjoint chains in P as constructed above$\} \cup \{$all points left in P, considered as singleton chains$\}$. Clearly, $\beta(DES)$ is a chain cover of P. Note that β is an injection: if DES and DES' are two different disjoint edge sets of G', $\beta(DES)$ and $\beta(DES')$ are two distinct chain covers for P. To see that β is a bijection, consider a chain cover CHC of P. Break every (nonsingleton) chain of length n in P into n (nondisjoint) 2-chains. (n $\geq$ 1), e.g.

$$\begin{matrix} e \\ d \\ b \\ a \end{matrix} \longrightarrow \vert_a^b \quad \vert_b^d \quad \vert_d^e$$

Associate with each 2-chain an edge in G':

$$\vert_a^b \longleftrightarrow (a,b').$$

Note that by the way we formed the 2-chains, their corresponding edges in G' will be disjoint. Let $\gamma(CHC)$ be the disjoint edge set formed in this manner. Clearly, for any disjoint edge set DES,

$$\gamma(\beta(\text{DES})) = \text{DES}$$

and for any chain cover CHC in P,

$$\beta(\gamma(\text{CHC})) = \text{CHC} .$$

So $\gamma = \beta^{-1}$. β as defined above is a bijection.

Now, consider any disjoint edge set DES in G′ and look at the chain cover β(DES) in P. Circle the top element in each of the chains in β(DES), and circle all singleton-chain points. (See FIGURE 5D.19.) Clearly the number of circled points is equal to |β(DES)|. Notice that to each chain of length k (k ≥ 1) in β(DES), there correspond k edges in DES. Also, each chain of length k has k uncircled points. So the number of uncircled points is equal to |DES|. But the number of circled points plus the number of uncircled points equals |P|. Hence |DES| + |β(DES)| = |P|.

5D.19   RELATING |β(DES)| TO |DES|.

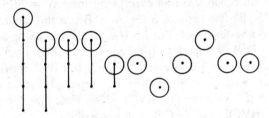

Figure 5D.19

The above ideas relate disjoint edge sets and chain covers. We now must relate vertex covers and transversals. Consider any vertex cover VC of G′. Let A = VC ∩ S′ and let B′ = VC ∩ T′. Let B be the copy of B′ in S′ and let A′ be the copy of A in T′. These sets are shown in FIGURE 5D.20.

5D.20   RELATING TRANSVERSALS TO VERTEX COVERS.

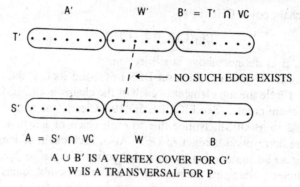

Figure 5D.20

Notice that we cannot have an edge going from $W = S' - A - B$ to $W' = T' - A' - B'$ (the copy of $S' - A - B$), as this would violate the fact that $A \cup B'$ is a vertex cover. But this is equivalent to saying that no two points in $S' - A - B$ are comparable (i.e., $S' - A - B$ is a transversal). Hence, given any vertex cover VC, we can define A and B as above, and let $\tau(VC)$ equal the transversal $W = S' - A - B$. Conversely, given a transversal W, we can construct a VC such that $\tau(VC) = W$. Note that, for any vertex cover VC, $|VC| + |\tau(VC)| \geq |P|$ ($A \cap B \neq \phi$ is possible).

Given the two basic identities $|DES| + |\beta(DES)| = |P|$ and $|VC| + |\tau(VC)| \geq |P|$. Dilworth's theorem follows easily, for maximizing the size of a disjoint edge set, $|DES|$, corresponds to minimizing the size of a chain cover, $|\beta(DES)|$. By COROLLARY 5D.13, the maximum $|DES|$ is equal to the minimum $|VC|$, and thus, by the two basic identities above, the maximum possible $|\tau(VC)|$ is greater than or equal to the minimum possible $|\beta(DES)|$. The reverse inequality is trivial (each chain contains at most one transversal element).

5D.21   EXERCISE.

(1) Prove Menger's theorem (THEOREM 5D.12). *Hint:* Construct a network with S' as the set of sources and T' as the set of sinks by replacing each edge of G' by a pair of opposite directed edges. Put unit capacity on all vertices and infinite capacity on all edges. Use the integrity theorem (THEOREM 5D.9).

(2) Consider an $n \times n$ chessboard diagram with rows labeled r1,r2,. . .,rn and columns labeled c1,c2,. . .,cn. Draw N rooks on the chessboard. Let NAT denote the size of the largest subset of these rooks such that no two rooks attack each other. Suppose that one has available a box of $n \times 1$ planks (very thin but not transparent) that can be used to cover a row or column of the board. Let PLK denote the smallest number of planks that can be laid on

the board (each plank covering a row or a column) such that all rooks are covered. The statement that NAT = PLK is just COROLLARY 5D.13 in disguise. Can you explain why?

(3) Given a network (G,s,t,c) how would you actually find a maximum flow and a minimum cut partition? A careful look at the proof of THEOREM 5D.8 gives one basic idea in the form of the "augmentable path." Try to devise your own algorithm for finding a maximum flow in a network, and illustrate it with some examples. Try to avoid looking up the standard algorithms given in the references until you have at least made a serious attempt yourself!

(4) State and prove a version of Menger's theorem for directed graphs. *Hint:* Menger's theorem in its various forms can be found in the references if you have difficulty with this problem or become interested in learning more about this class of results.

REFERENCES

PART I: LINEAR ORDER

There are by now a large number of excellent books on combinatorics. Since individual tastes vary widely as to which topic is the most interesting or which book is the most well written, the reader should spend some time in the library browsing through the books on combinatorics and graph theory. We make no attempt to give a comprehensive list of references. The suggestions we give are only to get the reader started in the process of exploring the literature.

To get an overall feeling for the subject, we recommend:

Beckenbach, E.F. (Editor), *Applied Combinatorial Mathematics*, Wiley, New York, 1964.

For a general background in discrete mathematics there is again a wide-ranging selection of books to be found in the library. Here are a few suggestions:

Birkhoff, G., and Bartee, T.C., *Modern Applied Algebra*, McGraw-Hill, New York, 1970.
Fraleigh, J.B., *A First Course in Abstract Algebra*, Addison-Wesley, Reading, Mass., 1982.
Liu, C.L., *Elements of Discrete Mathematics*, McGraw-Hill, New York, 1977.
Marcus, M., *A Survey of Finite Mathematics*, Houghton Mifflin, Boston, 1969.
Perlis, S., *Theory of Matrices*, Addison-Wesley, Reading, Mass., 1952.

Chapter 1 BASIC CONCEPTS OF LINEAR ORDER

Here are some books that together give a fairly comprehensive coverage of the basic ideas of combinatorial mathematics:

Aigner, M., *Combinatorial Theory*, Wiley, New York, 1980.
Berge, C., *Principle of Combinatorics*, Academic Press, New York, 1971.
Cohen, D.I.A., *Basic Techniques of Combinatorial Theory*, Wiley, New York, 1978.
Comtét, L., *Advanced Combinatorics*, D. Reidel, Dordrecht, Boston, 1974.
Goulden, I.P., and Jackson, D.M., *Combinatorial Enumeration*, Wiley, New York, 1983.
Hall, M., *Combinatorial Theory*, Blaisdell, Waltham, Mass., 1967.
Liu, C.L., *Introduction to Combinatorial Mathematics*, McGraw-Hill, New York, 1968.

Lovász, L., *Combinatorial Problems and Exercises*, North Holland, Amsterdam, New York, 1979.

Riordan, J., *An Introduction to Combinatorial Analysis*, Wiley, New York, 1958.

Ryser, H.J., *Combinatorial Mathematics*, Mathematical Association of America, Wiley, New York, 1963.

Tucker, A., *Appiled Combinatorics*, Wiley, New York, 1980.

Our selection of topics in combinatorics is motivated by algorithmic ideas. Here are some references that relate to this approach to the subject:

Aho, A.V., Hopcroft, J.B., and Ullman, J.D., *The Design and Analysis of Computer Algorithms*, Addison-Wesley, Reading, Mass., 1974.

Baase, S., *Computer Algorithms*, Addison-Wesley, Reading, Mass., 1978.

Even, Shimon, *Algorithmic Combinatorics*, Macmillan, New York, 1973.

Greene, D.H., Knuth, D.E., *Mathematics for the Analysis of Algorithms*, Birkhauser, Boston, Basel, Stuttgart, 1981.

Knuth, D.E., *The Art of Computer Programming*, vol. 1,2,3, Addison-Wesley, Reading, Mass., 1973.

Nijenhuis, A., and Wilf, H.S., *Combinatorial Algorithms*, Academic Press, New York, 1975.

Page, E.S., and Wilson, L.B., *An Introduction to Computational Combinatorics*, Cambridge University Press, Cambridge, 1979.

Reingold, E.M., Nievergelt, J., and Deo, N., *Combinatorial Algorithms: Theory and Practice*, Prentice-Hall, Englewood Cliffs, N.J., 1977.

Wells, M.B., *Elements of Combinatorial Computing*, Pergamon Press, New York, 1971.

Wirth, N., *Algorithms + Data Structure = Programs*, Prentice-Hall, Englewood Cliffs, N.J., 1976.

The problem of listing the configurations of eight nonattacking queens on a chessboard has an interesting history. F. Schuh in his book, *Master Book of Mathematical Recreations* (Dover), attributes the problem to Nauck, 1850. The famous mathematician, Gauss, worked on the problem and got the wrong answer! The problem is sufficiently complex that boredom becomes a significant factor when working it by hand. It thus becomes an advantage to have a systematic method that both rejects isomorphs and linearly orders the partial solutions so one is very likely to detect mistakes. A list of solutions is given in Schuh's book. Some related references are as follows:

Fillmore, J., and Williamson, S.G., *On backtracking: a combinatorial description of algorithm*, SIAM J. Comp. *3* (March 1974), 41–55.

Ginsburg, J., *Gauss's arithmetization of the problem of 8 queens*, Scripta Math. *5* (1938), 63–66.

Golumb, S.W., and Baumert, L., *Backtrack programming*, J. Assoc. Comp. Mach. *12* (1965), 516–524.

Schuh, F., *Master Book of Mathematical Recreations*, Dover, New York, 1968.

We now give specific references for the various TOPICS.

Chapter 2 TOPIC I: SORTING

The most comprehensive work on sorting is the third volume of Knuth's series, *The Art of Computer Programming*. This book has an extensive bibliography and discusses the historical development of the subject.

Knuth, D.E., *The Art of Computer Programming*, vol. 3. Addison-Wesley, Reading, Mass., 1973.

In selecting material for our very brief presentation of sorting, we had to make some tough decisions about what seemed most important. Before taking on a serious study of Knuth's vol. 3, the reader might like to look at the choices made by some other authors in this regard. In particular, the books mentioned above by Aho, Hopcroft, and Ullman; by Baase; by Reingold, Nievergelt, and Deo; and by Wirth all have material on sorting. For references to the original works of Ford, Johnson, and Batcher, as well as numerous other papers, we refer the reader to Knuth, vol. 3. Four papers that relate to our discussion that are not in Knuth, vol. 3 are as follows:

Ajtai, M., Komlós, J., and Szemerédi, E., *An O(nlog(n)) sorting network*, Proc. 15th Annual ACM Symposium on the Theory of Computing (SIGACT), (1983). Boston, Mass.

Hwang, F.K., Lin, S. *An analysis of Ford and Johnson's sorting algorithm*, Proc. Third Annual Princeton Conf. on Inform. Sci. and Syst., (1969), 292–296.

Incerpi, J., Sedgewick, R., *Improved upper bounds on Shellsort*, IEEE 24th Annual Symposium on the Foundations of Computer Science, (1983), 48–55. Nov. 7–9, 1983, Tucson, Arizona.

Manacher, G.K., *The Ford-Johnson algorithm is not optimal*, JACM 26 (July 1979), 441–456.

Chapter 3 TOPIC II: BASIC COMBINATORIAL LISTS

Again, we do not attempt to give detailed references to the research work in this field. The author's interest in this approach to enumerative combinatorics was inspired by the article, "The Machine Tools of Combinatorics," by D. H. Lehmer, found in the book edited by Beckenbach mentioned in the beginning of this reference list. The book by Nijenhuis and Wilf contains many useful algorithms in a form readily transferable to working programs. The books mentioned previously by Page and Wilson and by Reingold, Nievergelt, and Deo also contain many related ideas as well as references to the literature. An approach to ranking and unranking similar to that which we have presented in this TOPIC was described by the author in "On Ordering, Ranking, and Random Generation of Basic Combinatorial Sets," *Editor* Foata, D., Springer-Verlag Lecture Notes in Mathematics 579, 1977, *Combinatoire et Représentation du Groupe Symétrique*, 311–339. A unified setting for sequencing, ranking, and selection algorithms is described by Wilf in Advances in Mathematics, *24* (1977), 281–291 and in the following book:

Alspach, B., Hell, P., and Miller, D.J., *Algorithmic Aspects of Combinatorics*, North Holland, Amsterdam, 1978.

Some results on an important aspect of this TOPIC that we have not covered (ranking and unranking trees) may be found in the following titles:

Hu, T.C., and Ruskey, F., *Generating binary trees lexicographically*, SIAM J. Comp. *6* (1977), 745–758.
Ruskey, F., *Generating t-ary trees lexicographically*, SIAM J. Comp. *7* (1978), 424–439.
Ruskey, F., *Listing and counting subtrees of a tree*, SIAM J. Comp. *10* (1981), 141–150.
Trojanowski, A.E., *Ranking and listing algorithms for k-ary trees*, SIAM J. Comp. *7* (1978), 492–509.

Combining isomorph rejection and ranking algorithms can rapidly lead to difficult problems. A case where nice results can be obtained is suggested in EXERCISE 4.54(6). A related article is the following:

Fillmore, J.P., and Williamson, S.G., *On ranking functions: The symmetries and colorations of the n-cube*, SIAM J. Comp. *5* (1975), 297–304.

For some more theoretical applications of restricted growth functions, see the following article:

Milne, S., *Restricted growth functions and incidence relations of the lattice of partitions of an n-set*, Advances in Math. *26* (1977), 290–305.
Milne, S., *Restricted growth functions, rank row matchings of partition lattices, and q-Stirling numbers*, Advances in Math. *43*(2) (1982), 173–196.

The idea of a "loop free" algorithm or "combinatorial Gray code" given in ALGORITHM 3.54 can be extended to more complex combinatorial structures. Shimon Even (in the book *Algorithmic Combinatorics* mentioned previously, Sections 1.3 and 2.4) describes loop free algorithms for permutations and combinations due to Ehrlich. A general method for constructing such algorithms is described in the following article:

Joichi, J.T., White, D.E., and Williamson, S.G., *Combinatorial Gray codes*, SIAM J. Comp. *9* (1980), 130–141.

Chapter 4 TOPIC III: SYMMETRY—ORBIT ENUMERATION AND ORDERLY ALGORITHMS

Most algebra texts contain an introduction to the subject of permutation groups and groups acting on sets. For example, Chapter 7 of *Modern Applied Algebra*, by Birkhoff and Bartee (previously mentioned) contains a good introduction. An excellent introduction to Pólya theory is contained in the following book, *Applied Combinatorial Mathematics*:

deBruijn, N.G., "Pólya's Theory of Counting," *Applied Combinatorial Mathematics*, Beckenbach, E.F. (Editor), Wiley, New York, 1964.

Other related articles follow:

deBruijn, N.G., *Enumerative combinatorial problems concerning structures*, Nieuw. Arch. Wisk. *11* (1963), 142–161.
deBruijn, N.G., and Klarner, D.A., *Enumeration of generalized graphs*, Indag. Math. *31*(1) (1969), 1–9.
deBruijn, N.G., *A survey of generalizations of Pólya's enumeration theorem*, Nieuw. Arch. Wisk. *19* (1971), 89–112.

The proof of White's lemma is based on the following paper:

White, D.E., *Counting patterns with a given automorphism group*, Proc. AMS *47* (1975), 41–44.

For some related references take a look at the following articles:

Sheehan, J., *The number of graphs with a given automorphism group*, Can. J. Math. *20* (1968), 1068–1076.
Stockmeyer, P.K., "Enumeration of graphs with prescribed automorphism group," Ph.D. Thesis, Univ. of Michigan, Ann Arbor, Mich., 1971.
White, D.E., *Classifying patterns by automorphism group: An operator theoretic approach*, Discrete Math. *13* (1975), 277–295.

For an introduction to the applications of Burnside's lemma to chemistry, see:

McLarnan, T.J., and Moore, P.B., "Graph-Theoretic Enumeration of Structure Types: A Review," in *Structure and Bonding in Crystals* II, O'Keeffe, M., Navrotsky, A. (Editors), Academic Press, New York, 1981.
McLarnan, T.J., *Mathematical tools for counting polytypes*, Zeitshrift für Kristallographie *155* (1981), 227–245. (See also, pp. 247–268 and pp. 269–291.)

The first systematic treatment of the subject of enumerating orbits of group actions was by Redfield and was reported in:

Redfield, J.H., *The theory of group-reduced distributions*, American J. Math. *49* (1927), 433–455.

Little notice was taken of Redfield's paper until after the following famous paper by Pólya:

Pólya, G., *Kombinatorische Ansahlbesstimmungen für Gruppen, Graphen, und Chemishe Verbindungen*, Acta Math. *68* (1937), 145–254.

Several of the combinatorial mathematics books in the list of texts in this reference list contain treatments of Pólya's theorem. Numerous examples are given in the books by Tucker, Liu, and Cohen.

One area where Pólya's theorem has been applied extensively is in graph theory. For more information refer to the following text:

Harary, F., and Palmer, E.M., *Graphical Enumeration*, Academic Press, New York, 1973.

For an interesting application of wreath products, we refer the reader to the following article:

Hanlon, P., *A cycle index sum inversion theorem*, J. Comb. Theory *30* (1981), 248–269.

The action of the wreath product described in EXERCISE 4.61(8) is discussed, together with some applications, in:

Palmer, E.M., and Robinson, R.W., *Enumeration under two representations of the wreath product*, Acta Math. *131* (1973), 123–143.

Orbit enumeration problems play a basic role in multilinear algebra. The reader interested in extensions of Burnside's lemma and Pólya's theorem along these lines might look at the following:

Merris, R., *Generalized matrix functions and pattern inventory*, Linear and Multilinear Algebra v. 12, 1983, 315–327.

White, D.E., *Multilinear techniques in Pólya enumeration theory*, Linear and Multilinear Algebra 7 (1979), 299–315.

Williamson, S.G., *Isomorph rejection and a theorem of deBruijn*, SIAM J.Comp. *2*(1973), 44–59.

The basic idea of an "orderly algorithm" seems to have occurred to a number of people working on applied problems in chemistry, engineering, and computer science. The first careful statement of the general method seems to be due to Read in the interesting paper

Read, R.C., *Every One a Winner or How to Avoid Isomorphism Search When Cataloguing Combinatorial Configurations*, Annals of Discrete Math. *2* (1978), 107–120.

An alternative description of orderly algorithms with additional combinatorial applications may be found in

White, D.E., and Williamson, S.G., *Construction of Minimal Representative Systems*, Linear and Multilinear Algebra. *9* (1981), 167–180.

Chapter 5   TOPIC IV: SOME CLASSICAL COMBINATORICS

A. GENERATING FUNCTIONS

A discussion of generating functions is found in most combinatorics texts. The books by Cohen, Liu, and Tucker referred to previously contain many examples of standard generating function techniques. Additional facts are to be found in the books of Hall; Comtét; Goulden and Jackson; and Riordan. The subject of combinatorial models for generating functions and the relationship between generating functions and the theory of special functions is an extensive topic in combinatorics. We list some papers that one might look at to get a feeling for this subject as follows:

Bender, E.A., and Goldman, J.R., *Enumerative uses of generating functions*, Indiana Univ. Math. J. *20*(8) (1971), 753–765.
Doubilet, P., Rota, G.-C., and Stanley, R., *On the foundations of combinatorial theory (IV): The idea of a generating function*, Proceedings of the Sixth Berkeley Symposium on Mathematical Statistics and Probability, vol. 2 (Probability), Berkeley, Calif., 1971.
Cartier, P., and Foata, D., *Problèmes combinatories de commutation et réarrangements*, Lecture Notes in Mathematics #85, Springer-Verlag, Berlin-Heidelberg-New York, 1969.
Fillmore, J.P., and Williamson, S.G., *A linear algebra setting for the Rota-Mullin theory of polynomials of binomial type*, Linear and Multilinear Algebra *1* (1973), 119–138.
Foata, D., *La série génératrice exponentielle dans les problèmes d'énumeration*, Le Presses de l'Université de Montréal, 1974.
Garsia, A., *An exposé of the Rota-Mullin theory of polynomials of binomial type*, Linear and Multilinear Algebra *1* (1973), 47–65.
Garsia, A., and Joni, S.A., *Composition sequences*, Comm. in Algebra *8* (1980), 1195–1266.
Remmel, J., *Bijective proofs of some classical partition identities*, J. Combinatorial Theory A *33*(3) (1982), 273–286.

The following paper originated the modern form of the "theory of polynomials of binomial type":

Rota, G.-C., and Mullin, R., "On the foundations of combinatorial theory III: Theory of binomial enumeration," in *Graph Theory and Its Applications*, B. Harris (Editor), pp. 167–213, Academic Press, New York, 1970.

An extensive amount of material plus numerous references can be found in the following "direct descendants" of the above paper:

Rota, G.-C., Kahaner, D., and Odlyzko, A., "On the foundations of combinatorial theory VIII: Finite operator calculus," J. Math. Analysis and Applications 42 (1973), 684–760.

Roman, S.M., and Rota, G.-C., "The umbral calculus," Advances in Math. 27 (1978), 95–188.

B. THE PRINCIPLE OF INCLUSION-EXCLUSION

As we have shown in our development of this topic, the various forms of the principle of inclusion-exclusion have trivial algebraic proofs. The trick is in learning to apply the results in various situations. The best way to learn to do this is to study a number of examples such as those found in the books by Cohen, Comtét, Liu, Ryser, and Tucker referred to previously. In addition, the reader might be interested in the way the same ideas are proved and applied in probability theory. Many probability texts discuss the principle of inclusion-exclusion under the topic of "combinations of events." For example:

Feller, W., An Introduction to Probability Theory and Its Applications, Wiley, New York, 1959. (See Chapter 4.)

Parzen, E., Modern Probability Theory and Its Applications, Wiley, New York, 1960. (See Chapter 2, Section 6.)

C. MÖBIUS INVERSION

The classical paper on Möbius inversion in combinatorics is listed as follows:

Rota, G.-C., On the foundations of combinatorial theory I: Theory of Möbius functions, Z. Wahrscheinlichkeitstheorie, Band 2, heft 4, S. 340–368 (1964).

Two other articles that constitute a good introduction to the subject are:

Bender, E.A., and Goldman, J.R., On the application of Möbius inversion in combinatorial analysis, Am. Math. Monthly 82 (1975), 789–803.

Greene, C., On the Möbius algebra of a partially ordered set, Advances in Math. 10 (1973), 177–187.

A careful development of Möbius inversion is also given in the book by Aigner, Combinatorial Theory, listed previously.

For a discussion of the connection between group actions and Möbius inversion, take a look at the following:

Rota, G.-C., and Smith, D.A., Enumeration under group action, Annali Scuola Normale Superiore-Piza Classe di Scienze, Serie IV, V, IV, #4 (1977), 637–646.

D. NETWORK FLOWS

The classical reference on the subject of network flows is the book:

Ford, L.R., and Fulkerson, D.R., Flows in Networks, Princeton University Press, 1962.

The following books contain algorithmically oriented introductions to the topic of network flows (plus numerous additional references):

Even, S., *Graph Algorithms*, Computer Science Press, Rockville, Md., 1979.
Hu, T.C., *Combinatorial Algorithms*, Addison-Wesley, Reading, Mass., 1982.
Lawler, E.L., *Combinatorial Optimization: Networks and Matroids*, Holt, Rinehart & Winston, New York, 1976.

For additional reading, consult the following article:

Burr, S.A. (Editor), *The mathematics of networks*, Proc. Symposia in Applied Math. *26* (1981).

PART II

Graphs, Trees, and Recursion

Chapter 6

Basic Concepts of Graphs, Trees, and Recursion

In this chapter, we study a selection of topics from a vast area of combinatorial theory called "graph theory." One definition of a graph is that a graph G is a pair of sets (V,E) where V is arbitrary and E is a subset of the set of all subsets of E of size 2. Never mind for the moment if this definition seems unclear. Note, however, that E may be taken as the empty set ϕ. Thus, all pairs (V,ϕ), where V is any set whatsoever, are graphs by this standard definition. These sets are in obvious correspondence with all sets V $\Leftrightarrow$ (V,ϕ). Thus, to embark blindly on the task of trying to learn all there is to know about graphs in general (without some application or outside motivation in mind) is to learn all there is to know about arbitrary sets (i.e., all of mathematics).

This example is a bit silly, but there is still an element of truth to it that will become apparent to anyone spending an afternoon in the library browsing through the literature of graph theory. The conceptual motivations for selecting a particular topic in graph theory are very important, especially to the beginner. The topics we shall consider in this chapter are selected because of their relationship to the study of algorithms. Even with this point of view in mind, we can only make a small selection from a very wide range of possibilities.

FIGURE 6.1 shows a labeled geometric configuration of lines (arcs, edges) and points (vertices) that represents the intuitive idea behind one standard definition of a graph.

6.1. THE INTUITIVE IDEA OF A GRAPH.

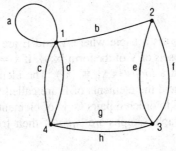

Figure 6.1

To describe the labeled geometric structure of FIGURE 6.1 in set theoretic terms, we can specify the *vertex* set $V = \underline{4} = \{1,2,3,4\}$, the *edge* set $\{a,b,c,d,e,f,g,h\}$ = E, and an *incidence* function φ from E to V. In FIGURE 6.1, the function φ is given by

$$\varphi = \begin{pmatrix} a & b & c & d & e & f & g & h \\ \{1\} & \{1,2\} & \{1,4\} & \{1,4\} & \{2,3\} & \{2,3\} & \{3,4\} & \{3,4\} \end{pmatrix}.$$

Given the triple (V,E,φ) we could draw a figure such as FIGURE 6.1. For $V = \underline{4}$ we would put four vertices on the plane (all distinct). Then, for each edge $a,b,\ldots$ of E we would draw a smooth arc joining the two vertices of $\varphi(a)$, $\varphi(b),\ldots$. The drawing need not look like FIGURE 6.1. FIGURE 6.2 shows some alternative drawings or "embeddings" of the graph (V,E,φ).

6.2 ALTERNATIVE REPRESENTATIONS OF FIGURE 6.1.

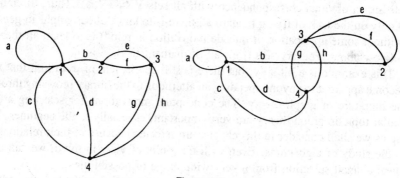

Figure 6.2

We shall take the point of view that a graph *is* a triple such as (V,E,φ). The geometrically (as point sets) different representations of FIGURES 6.1 and 6.2 all represent the same graph.

6.3 DEFINITION.

A graph $G = (V,E,\varphi)$ is a triple where V and E are arbitrary sets and φ is a function from E to subsets of V of the form $\{x,y\}$. If $x = y$ then the corresponding element of E is called a *loop* ($\{x,x\} \equiv \{x\}$). The elements of V are called the vertices of G, V(G), and the elements of E are called the edges, E(G), of G. If the function φ maps E to ordered pairs (x,y) of elements from V, then the graph is called a *directed* graph. Graphs are *equal* if their triples are equal.

6.4 PICTORIAL REPRESENTATION OF A DIRECTED GRAPH.

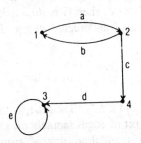

AN EDGE e IS REPRESENTED BY AN ARROW FROM x TO y IF φ(e) = (x,y).

Figure 6.4

In many applications of graph theory a slightly simpler definition of a graph than that of DEFINITION 6.3 is used. The set E is arbitrary, so suppose E is itself a set of pairs of the form {x,y}, x and y in V. Suppose also that the function φ is the identity φ({x,y}) = {x,y}. The resulting triple is then a graph by DEFINITION 6.3. However, the function φ is redundant, so in this case the graph may be specified by a pair, G = (V,E) where E is a collection of pairs of the form {x,y}, x and y in V. FIGURE 6.5(a) shows a pictorial representation of the graph G = (4, {1,2}, {2,3}, {2,4}, {2}). For graphs of the form (V,E), only one edge joins any pair of vertices in its pictorial representation. There are many other variations on the definition of a graph. One could define a *multigraph* to be a pair (V,E) where E is a *multiset* (set with repeated elements) of elements of the form {x,y}, x and y in V. FIGURE 6.5(b) represents a graph of this type with {1,2} repeated three times. One could consider instead pairs of the form (V,E) where the elements of E are arbitrary subsets of V. Such structures are called *hypergraphs*. Are either of these latter examples covered by DEFINITION 6.3?

6.5 GRAPH OF THE FORM (V,E) AND A MULTIGRAPH.

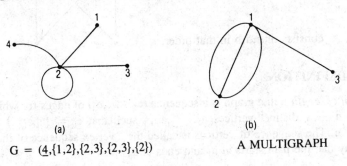

(a)

G = (4,{1,2},{2,3},{2,3},{2})

(b)

A MULTIGRAPH

Figure 6.5

For the most part, we shall use graphs of the form $G = (V,E)$ and only occasionally the more general graphs specified by DEFINITION 6.3. If $G = (V,E)$ and E is a subset of $V \times V$, then G is *directed*.

We now introduce the idea of an ordered graph. This idea is basic to the material that follows.

6.6 DEFINITION.

Let $G = (V,E,\varphi)$ be a graph and $x \in V$. The set I_x is the set of all edges e such that $x \in \varphi(e)$. I_x is called the set of edges *incident on* x. If for all $x \in V$ a linear order is defined on I_x then G is called an *ordered graph*.

If the graph G is of the form (V,E), and y is such that $\{x,y\}$ is an edge of G, then y is said to be *adjacent* to x. Assume G has no *loops* (pairs of the form $\{x,x\}$). Let A_x denote the set of all vertices adjacent to x. The integer $|A_x|$ is called the *degree* of x (see DEFINITION 6.14). To define a linear order on I_x it now suffices to define a linear order on A_x. Thus we have the following definition for loopless graphs of the form (V,E).

6.7 REMARK.

Let $G = (V,E)$ be a graph without loops. If for all $x \in V$ the set A_x is linearly ordered, then G is an *ordered graph*. *Unless otherwise stated, graphs will henceforth be of the form* (V,E), *without loops*. We assume V is *finite*.

6.8 EXAMPLE.

One common method for specifying an ordered graph is with an "adjacency table." For each vertex one lists the vertex followed by an ordered list of its adjacent vertices $(x:A_x)$.

    a: c,d,b
    b: a,c,d
    c: a,b
    d: b,a

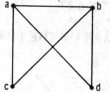

Thus, A_a consists of c,d,b in that order.

6.9 DEFINITION.

A *path of length* n in a graph is a sequence $(e_1,\ldots,e_n)$ of edges for which there exists $n + 1$ distinct vertices $a_1,\ldots,a_{n+1}$ such that $e_i = \{a_i,a_{i+1}\}$ for $i = 1,\ldots,n$. The sequence of vertices is called the "vertex sequence of the path." We say that the path starts at a_1 and ends at a_{n+1}.

6.10   DEFINITION.

A *cycle of length* n in a graph $G = (V,E)$ is a subset $\{e_1,\ldots,e_n\}$ of E such that $(e_1,\ldots,e_{n-1})$ is a path, and if the vertex sequence of this path is $a_1,\ldots,a_n$, then $e_n = \{a_1,a_n\}$. We assume $n \geqslant 3$.

The following diagrams represent a path and a cycle (both of which may be regarded as subgraphs of G, DEFINITION 6.43).

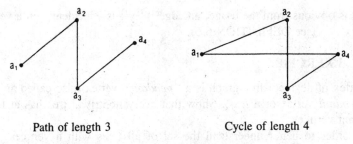

Path of length 3   Cycle of length 4

Figure 6.10

If we start with any graph and define $u \sim v$ if there is a path starting at u and ending at v, then, adopting the convention that $u \sim u$ for all u, it is easily seen that $\sim$ is an equivalence relation (reflective, symmetric, and transitive) on vertices V of G. Thus V decomposes into equivalence classes A,B, . . . under this equivalence relation. Each class A,B,. . . defines a graph by associating with that class all edges of G with both endpoints in that class (i.e., edges contained in that class as sets). The resulting graphs $G_A,G_B,\ldots$ are called the "connected components" of G. DEFINITIONS 6.9, 6.10, and 6.11 have obvious analogs for the general graph of DEFINITION 6.3.

6.11   DEFINITION.

A graph is *connected* if it has only one connected component.

6.12   DEFINITION.

A graph which is connected and acyclic is called a *tree*. Let TR(V) denote the set of all trees with vertex set V.

Here "acyclic" means "without cycles." We consider any graph with just one vertex, $|V| = 1$, a tree (the trivial tree). All graphs with two or three vertices are trees except for the cycle of length 3. In general, there are n^{n-2} trees on a vertex set V of cardinality $n \geqslant 2$. We give one of the many proofs of this fact below.

6.13   EXERCISE.

With V = $\underline{n}$ = {1,2,. . .,n}, list all trees with n $\leqq$ 4 vertices.

6.14   DEFINITION.

The degree of a vertex x in a general loopless graph is the number of edges incident on x (or $|A_x|$, the number of vertices adjacent to x if G = (V,E) and G is loopless).

As is obvious from the usage, an edge {x',y'} is "incident" on a vertex x if x $\in$ {x',y'} (see DEFINITION 6.6).

6.15   EXERCISE.

A vertex of degree 1 in a graph is a "*pendant*" vertex (also called an *external* or *terminal* vertex or a *leaf*). Show that every nontrivial tree has at least two pendant vertices.

In order to better understand the set of all trees with n vertices, we now consider a classical bijection between the set of all such trees and the set of functions $V^{\underline{n-2}}$ = {f: f: $\underline{n-2}$ → V}. First we give a canonical ordering of the edges of a tree. Each edge in this sequence will be a *directed edge* (i.e., an ordered pair (x,y)). Let T = (V,E), $|V|$ ≥ 2, be a tree. Let PEND(T) denote the set of pendant vertices of T. For sake of notational convenience, we assume that V is a set of nonnegative integers. Thus "x > y" means x is a larger integer than y.

6.16   *procedure* ESEQ(T).

("ESEQ" stands for *Edge Sequence*)
if $|V|$ = 2 *then* ESEQ(T): = (x,y) where V={x,y}, x > y *else*
begin
    m: = MAXPEND(T);   the integer m is taken to be the maximum of the set
                    PEND(T))
    m': = the vertex adjacent to m;
    T': = (V − {m},E − {{m,m'}});
    ESEQ(T): = (m,m')ESEQ(T');
end

As an example, consider the tree T = ($\underline{4}$, {{1,3},{3,2},{3,4}}) with diagram:

Executing the algorithm 16 for this example yields the following values:

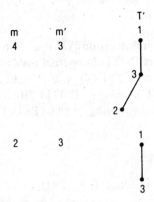

m	m'
4	3
2	3

Thus ESEQ(T): $= (4,3)(2,3)(3,1)$. *Note that these edges are directed.*

It is obvious that given the edge sequence ESEQ(T) of a tree T, one can reconstruct the tree (simply ignore ordering and direction on the edges and one obtains immediately the pair (V,E)). It is less obvious but not difficult to see that, given only the second term of each pair in the edge sequence, one can also reconstruct the whole edge sequence if V is known.

6.17   DEFINITION.

Let T be a tree and let ESEQ(T) $= (a_1,b_1)(a_2,b_2) \cdots (a_{n-1},b_{n-1})$ be the edge sequence of T ($|V| = n$). The sequence $b_1,b_2,\ldots,b_{n-2}$ is called the *Prüffer sequence* of T.

It is useful to write a procedure for generating the Prüffer sequence directly

6.18   *procedure* **PRU(T).**

if $|V| = 2$ *then* PRU(T) is the empty sequence *else*
begin
    m: = MAXPEND(T);
    m': = vertex adjacent to m;
    T': = $(V - \{m\}, E - \{\{m,m'\}\})$;
    PRU(T): = m'PRU(T');
end

We now prove some basic facts about the map PRU, including the fact that PRU is a bijection between the set TR(V) of all trees with vertex set V ($|V| = n$) and the set V^{n-2} of all functions from $\{1,\ldots,n-2\}$ to V (or, equivalently, "all sequences of length $n-2$ with entries from V").

6.19 LEMMA

If $PRU(T) = b_1,...,b_{n-2}$ then the set $\{b_1,...,b_{n-2}\}$ is the set of all internal nodes (i.e., not pendant) of T.

Proof. The proof is by induction on $|V| = n$. If $n = 2$ then $PRU(T)$ is the empty sequence and the set $INT(T)$ of internal nodes is empty. Assume that the lemma is true for all $p < n$. If $PRU(T) = b_1,...,b_{n-2}$, then it is evident from *Procedure* 6.18 that $INT(T') \cup \{b_1\} = INT(T)$. But by the induction hypothesis it follows that $INT(T') = \{b_2,...,b_{n-2}\}$ since $PRU(T') = b_2,...,b_{n-2}$. The lemma follows.

6.20 LEMMA.

The mapping PRU is an injection (i.e., $PRU(T) = PRU(S)$ implies $T = S$, where equality of trees means they are equal as graphs).

Proof. The proof is by induction on $|V| = n$. The result is easily verified for $n = 2,3$. Assume the lemma is true if $p < n$. Let T and S be in $TR(V)$ (DEFINITION 12) where $|V| = n$. Assume that $PRU(T) = PRU(S)$ and show that this implies that $T = S$. Following *Procedure* $PRU(T)$, 6.18, we see immediately that $MAXPEND(T) = MAXPENDT(S) = m$ and $m' = b_1$ where $PRU(T) = PRU(S) = b_1,...,b_{n-2}$. Let T' and S' represent T and S after removing the vertex m and the edge $\{m,m'\}$ from both trees. Notice that by 6.18 we have $PRU(S') = PRU(T') = b_2,...,b_{n-2}$ and hence by induction $S' = T'$. Thus $S = T$.

We now give a procedure (INVPRU or "inverse Prüffer") that, given a sequence $b_1,...,b_{n-2}$ in $V^{\underline{n-2}}$, constructs a tree T such that $PRU(T) = b_1,...,b_{n-2}$. The set V is given, $|V| = n \geqslant 2$.

6.21 *procedure* INVPRU.

$(b_1,...,b_{n-2},V)\{$Constructs $ESEQ(T)$ hence T$\}$
if the sequence $b_1,...,b_{n-2}$ is empty $(n = |V| = 2)$
then $INVPRU(\phi,V) = (x,y)$ where $V = \{x,y\}$, $x > y$,
else
begin
  $m := MAX(V - \{b_1,...,b_{n-2}\})$;
  $V' := V - \{m\}$;
  $INVPRU(b_1,...,b_{n-2},V) := (m,b_1)INVPRU(b_2,...,b_{n-2},V')$;
end

6.22 EXERCISE.

(1) Give several examples of INVPRU for $n = 8$. Give a *careful* proof that INVPRU is correct in general.

(2) Using PRU and INVPRU, give procedures for ordering trees lexicographically (CHAPTER 1, DEFINITION 1.20) in some natural fashion. (*Hint:* Consider V^{n-2}.) Describe a method for constructing a tree from TR(V) at random (such that each tree in TR(V) is equally likely to be the output of your procedure, see CHAPTER 1, EXERCISE 1.61(3) and preceding discussion).

Note that LEMMA 6.20 *and* EXERCISE 6.22(1) *prove that* PRU *is a bijection between* TR(V) *and* V^{n-2} *and hence that* $|TR(V)| = n^{n-2}$.

The notion of a tree is very useful as a descriptive tool in algorithmics. For this purpose, we shall want to add a bit more structure to the idea of a "tree."

6.23 DEFINITION.

Let $T = (V,E)$ be a tree and $v \in V$. The pair (T,v) is called a *rooted tree*. The vertex v is called the *root*. The notation RTR means rooted tree.

There are exactly $n = |V|$ possible choices for the root v and hence there are n^{n-1} possible rooted trees on a vertex set of size n. For simplicity of notation we shall often say "let T be a rooted tree" with the root v being implied or otherwise specified. The diagram of a rooted tree is usually just like that of a tree except that one vertex is circled, darkened, checked, or otherwise indicated.

6.24 DEFINITION.

Let T be an ordered tree and v a vertex of T. The pair (T,v) is called an ordered rooted tree (sometimes written ORTR).

The notion of an "ordered tree" referred to in DEFINITION 6.24 is just that of an "ordered graph" of DEFINITION 6.7 (a tree is a graph).

In any tree there is only one path joining any given pair of vertices (why?). Thus, in a rooted tree, for any vertex or edge, there is only one path starting at that vertex or edge and ending at the roots. We call the number of edges in such a path the *distance* of the given edge or vertex from the root. For the example associated with *Procedure* 6.16, the distance of vertex 4 from 1 is 2 and the distance of the edge {3,4} from 1 is also 2. If x and y are vertices of a rooted tree, then "{x,y} an edge of the tree" implies that the distance of x and the distance of y from the root are different. We use this fact in the following definition.

6.25 DEFINITION.

Let (T,v) be a rooted tree. Let {x,y} be an edge and assume without loss of generality that the distance from the root to x, D(x), is less than D(y). We call the directed edge (x,y) the *natural directed edge* associated with the undirected edge $\{x,y\}$. When each edge is given its natural direction we obtain the *natural directed tree* associated with (T,v). For each such edge (x,y), y is called a *son* of x (see also NOTATION 6.41).

In other words, the natural directed version of a rooted tree is obtained by directing each edge away from the root. See FIGURE 6.27(a).

In general, if G is a directed graph, the undirected version of G is obtained by replacing each directed edge (x,y) by the undirected edge $\{x,y\}$. We denote the resulting undirected graph by UND(G).

6.26 DEFINITION.

Let $(e_1,. . .,e_n)$ be a sequence of edges in a directed graph G. If the same sequence of edges, without orientation, represents a path in UND(G) then we call the sequence $(e_1,. . .,e_n)$ a chain in G. If the vertex sequence of this path in UND(G) is $a_1,. . .,a_{n+1}$ and for each $i = 1,. . .,n$, $e_i = (a_i,a_{i+1})$ then $(e_1,. . .,e_n)$ is a *directed path* or simply *path* in G. In FIGURE 6.27 $((a,b),(a,c))$ is a chain, $((a,b)(b,e))$ a path.

In other words, *in the diagram of a directed path, all arrows point in the direction of the terminal vertex of the path.*

6.27 AN ORDERED ROOTED TREE ORTR AND DEPTH FIRST SEQUENCES.

(The order on sons, DEFINITION 6.25, is left to right.)

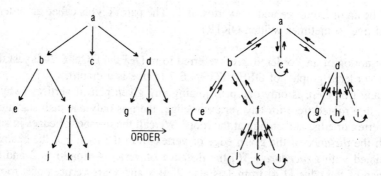

(a) An ORTR with root a (natural directed version shown for each edge).

(b) Diagram of depth first sequences. DFV(T) is abebfjfkflfbacadgdhdida.

Figure 6.27

Let (T,v) be a rooted tree where $T = (V,E)$. Let A_v be the set of vertices adjacent to the root v. Direct T according to DEFINITION 6.25.

6.28 DEFINITION.

For x in A_v, define $T_x = (V_x, E_x)$ where V_x is the set of all vertices y for which there is a directed path from x to y (we include x in V_x) and E_x is the set of all edges e such that e = {a,b} is contained in V_x. The graphs of the form T_x for x in A_v are called the *principal subtrees* of the root v. The root of T_x is x.

The reader should verify that for x and y in A_v with $x \neq y$ the sets E_x and E_y are disjoint, V_x and V_y are disjoint, and T_x is in fact a tree. If T is an ordered tree, and hence A_v is ordered, then the set of principal subtrees is also ordered by the natural order induced from A_v. In diagrams, we draw the principal subtrees below the root in order left to right.

We now consider some additional ideas involving ordered rooted trees that provide very useful descriptive tools in combinatorics and algorithmics. Consider the diagram (b) of FIGURE 6.27. By following the arrows as indicated and traversing the edges of the tree, we encounter the vertices in the following order: abebfjfkflfbacadgdhdida. We call this sequence the *depth first sequence* of vertices of T, DFV(T). Each vertex of T appears in DFV(T) as many times as its degree in T except for the root which appears once more than its degree.

6.29 EXERCISE.

For any graph, let DEG(v) denote the degree of the vertex v. Show that the sum over all v of DEG(v) is twice the number of edges of G. Thus the length of DFV(T) is twice the number of edges of T plus one $(2|E| + 1)$. Prove that in any tree T = (V,E), $|E| = |V| - 1$ and thus the length of DFV(T) is also $2|V| - 1$.

If we again follow the arrows of the second diagram of FIGURE 6.27(b) and record an edge each time it is traversed, we obtain DFE(T), the depth first sequence of edges: {a,b} {b,e} {b,e} {b,f} {f,j} {f,j} {f,k} {f,k} {f,l} {f,l} {b,f} {a,b} {a,c} {a,c} {a,d} {d,g} {d,g} {d,h} {d,h} {d,i} {d,i} {a,d}. The sequence consists of edges of the undirected ordered rooted tree. Clearly, the length of the depth first sequence of edges, DFE(T), is 2 |E|.

Both DFV(T) and DFE(T) have natural recursive descriptions. Let T be an ordered rooted tree with principal subtrees $T_1, T_2, \ldots, T_p$ in order. Let v be the root of T and v_i the root of T_i for each i.

6.30 DEFINITION.

Let T = (V,E) be an ordered rooted tree with root v. If $|V| = 1$ then DFV(T) = v and DFE(T) is empty. Otherwise, let $T_1, \ldots, T_p$ be the principal subtrees of v in order with roots $v_1, \ldots, v_p$. Then we define

$$DFV(T) = vDFV(T_1)vDFV(T_2)v. . .vDFV(T_p)v$$

and

$$DFE(T) = \{v,v_1\}DFE(T_1)\{v,v_1\}. . .\{v,v_p\}DGE(T_p)\{v,v_p\}.$$

Using the sequences DFV and DFE we can define two important linear orders on the vertices and edges of an ordered rooted tree.

6.31 DEFINITION.

The sequence of first occurrences of elements of V or E in the sequences DFV(T) or DFE(T), respectively, are all called the *preorder sequences* of vertices or edges. We write PREV(T) or PREE(T) for these sequences. Likewise, we define the *postorder sequences* of vertices or edges to be the corresponding last occurrences. We write POSV(T) or POSE(T) for these sequences.

For example, consider the tree T of FIGURE 6.27. The sequence PREV(T) is abefjklcdghi. The sequence PREE(T) is {a,b} {b,e} {b,f} {f,j} {f,k} {f,l} {a,c} {a,d} {d,g} {d,h} {d,i}. The sequence POSV(T) is ejklfbcghida. Notice that these sequences actually define linear orders on the vertices or edges of T since each vertex or edge occurs only once in the sequence. If T′ is T with the reverse order, then PREV(T′) is POSV(T) read backwards. To practice writing down the vertices of a tree in preorder and postorder, the reader should follow the arrows in the second diagram of FIGURE 6.27. Writing down a vertex the last time it is encountered (i.e., when arriving at that vertex from its rightmost son) produces postorder on vertices.

Recall that we have used the notation A_x to indicate the vertices adjacent to a vertex x in a graph. Similarly, we have used I_x to indicate the set of edges incident on x (DEFINITION 6.6).

We have already observed that between any two vertices in a tree there is one and only one path. We use that idea in the following.

6.32 DEFINITION.

Let T be a rooted tree with root v. For each edge e of T we define the stack of e, STACK(e), to be the path starting at v and ending with e. Similarly, for each vertex x ≠ v, define STACK(x). Define STACKS(T) to be the set {STACK(e): e an edge of T}.

We now define a natural version of lexicographic order ("length first lex order" CHAPTER 1, EXERCISE 1.29) on the set STACKS(T). Let T be ordered, and for each vertex x let I_x be the incident edges as above.

6.33 DEFINITION.

(BREADTH FIRST ORDER) Let $e = (e_1,. . .,e_p)$ and $e' = (e'_1,. . .,e'_q)$ be two paths in STACKS(T) where T is an ordered rooted tree. Define $e <e'$ if either

p < q or p = q and the smallest t such that $e_t \neq e_t'$ satisfies $e_t < e_t'$. *Note:* e_t and e_t' are, because of the definition of t, both incident on a common vertex x. Thus they are ordered by the ordering on I_x (or equivalently A_x) given by the ordering on the tree T. This is the meaning of "$e_t < e_t'$."

The STACK of DEFINITION 6.32 corresponds to the stack of local data maintained by any implementation of a recursive program. The mapping STACK from E to STACKS(T) is clearly a bijection. Thus the breadth first order on STACKS(T) defines a linear order on E called breadth first order on edges, BRE(T). Similarly, we define breadth first order on vertices, BRV(T). In the latter case we add the root v to the order and adopt the convention that it is the first element. If the tree T is drawn as in FIGURE 6.27, then breadth-first order on vertices is obtained by listing the root, then all vertices of distance one from the root left to right, then all of distance two left to right, etc. In this example breadth first order is just alphabetic order: abcdefghijkl.

6.34 EXERCISE.

Given just the preorder and postorder sequences of vertices of a tree, can one reconstruct the tree? Given breadth first order and preorder or breadth first order and postorder can one reconstruct the tree?

We now discuss informally the relationship between ordered rooted trees and recursively described algorithms. As an example, consider the classical Towers of Hanoi puzzle. As in FIGURE 6.35, we start with three positions A,B, and C. The stack of n discs of different size is placed initially at position A. The discs range in size from smallest to largest going from top to bottom. The problem is to transfer the discs from position A to position C according to the following rules:

(1) The discs are to be transferred one at a time and only the top disc of a stack can be moved.
(2) The disc that moved can be placed at a position with no discs or at the top of a stack at another position provided that the top disc of the stack is larger than the disc that was moved.

The sequence of moves is completed when all of the discs are transferred to position C.

The basic recursive description of the solution of the Towers of Hanoi puzzle is indicated in FIGURE 6.36.

6.35 TOWERS OF HANOI.

Let H(A,B,C,n) be the sequence of moves needed to transfer n discs from position A to position C using B for temporary placement.

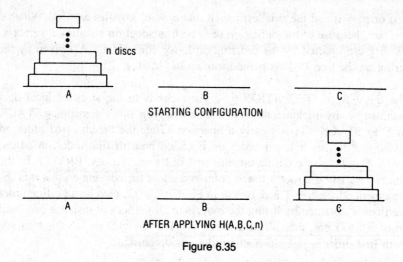

STARTING CONFIGURATION

AFTER APPLYING H(A,B,C,n)

Figure 6.35

6.36   THE BASIC RECURSION FOR THE TOWERS OF HANOI PUZZLE.

H(X,Y,Z,k) With starting configuration as in FIGURE 35 (A: = X, B: = Y, C: = Z, n: = k). *Apply* H(X,Z,Y,k − 1):

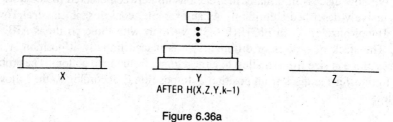

AFTER H(X,Z,Y,k−1)

Figure 6.36a

Now transfer the disc on X to Z (write "X to Z")

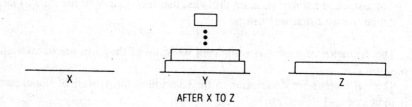

AFTER X TO Z

Apply H(Y,X,Z,k − 1):

Figure 6.36b

AFTER H(Y,X,Z,k-1)

Figure 6.36c

The steps of FIGURE 6.36 may be described in pidgin Algol as follows.

6.37 *procedure* H(X,Y,Z,k).

if k = 1 *then* write "X to Z" *else*
begin
   H(X,Z,Y,k − 1);
   write "X to Z";
   H(Y,X,Z,k − 1);
end

A program written for a computer that compiled algol and that is basically like *procedure* 6.37 would actually list the moves to solve the puzzle for various assignments of X,Y,Z, and k. We wish to have some working intuitive conventions for doing the same thing as the algol compiler.

We shall regard recursions such as described in 6.36 or 6.37 as essentially rules for constructing ordered rooted trees. In this case the rule tells us what the tree looks like "locally." The diagram of this "local" description is given by 6.38.

6.38 LOCAL DESCRIPTION OF THE TOWERS OF HANOI TREE.

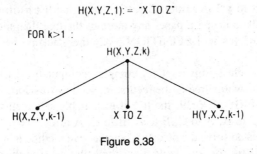

H(X,Y,Z,1): = "X TO Z"

FOR k>1 :

H(X,Y,Z,k)

H(X,Z,Y,k-1)   X TO Z   H(Y,X,Z,k-1)

Figure 6.38

To generate a particular tree using the rules of FIGURE 6.38, one starts with the root, say H(A,B,C,n), and constructs the tree using the rule of FIGURE 6.38

repeatedly. Usually the tree's vertices are constructed in preorder. H(A,B,C,3) is shown in FIGURE 6.39.

6.39   H(A,B,C,3).

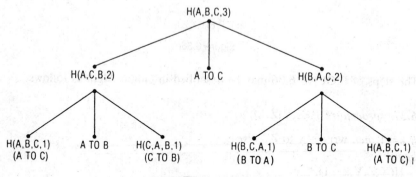

Figure 6.39

Note that we are using the symbols of the form H(X,Y,Z,k) in two ways. They are being used to stand for sequences of moves in the puzzle and as vertices for the tree of FIGURE 6.38 and FIGURE 6.39. The sequence of moves that solves the Towers of Hanoi problem H(A,B,C,3) is obtained by listing the "x to y" type statements in the tree of FIGURE 6.39 as they are encountered in a depth first listing of the vertices. (This is the order obtained by projecting the pendant vertices, or "leaves," of the tree of FIGURE 6.39 onto a horizontal line and reading from left to right. These statements of the form "x to y" form a subsequence of the preorder sequence of the tree. The reader should practice generating the tree of FIGURE 6.39 by pencil and paper using only the rules of FIGURE 6.38. Observe that if the tree is generated in depth first order (the order in which the vertices are written down is preorder in vertices) and each statement of the form "x to y" is written down in a separate list as it is generated, then one never needs to keep on paper any more of the tree than the stack of the last vertex generated (as in DEFINITION 6.32, the stack is the path back to the root).

This observation is important for complex computations when one does not wish to store the whole tree of the recursion, such as was done in FIGURE 6.39. In the case of FIGURE 6.39, the list of executable statements in preorder is A to C, A to B, C to B, A to C, B to A, B to C, A to C. The reader should check that these moves do solve the puzzle. The recursive method that we just discussed is often very useful for describing algorithms and proving theorems about combinatorics and algorithms. Often, however, the generation of the tree such as FIGURE 6.39 from the recursive description is not the most "efficient" method for generating the required output. This is certainly the case with the Towers of Hanoi problem. The geometric insight gained by thinking about the structure of the "recursion tree" of various recursions can often provide valuable clues for designing more efficient "nonrecursive" methods (see EXERCISE 6.40(3)).

The following exercises contain many beautiful and entertaining surprises!

6.40 EXERCISE.

(1) Using FIGURE 6.38, generate the moves of H(A,B,C,4) by constructing the vertices of the tree like the one shown in FIGURE 6.39. For each vertex, keep only its stack. The vertices should be generated in depth first order (i.e., in preorder as if making a list of the depth first sequence of vertices). How many moves are there in H(A,B,C,n)?

(2) For n = 20, what would be the 500,000th move? If someone abandons a Towers of Hanoi problem somewhere before completion and you find only the configuration of discs left behind, how do you find the next move?

(3) Notice that in H(A,B,C,n) the smallest disc is moved every other move. The alternate moves are forced by the rule that a disc cannot be placed on top of a smaller one. Determine the pattern of moves of the smallest disc (it depends on whether n is odd or even) and use this to give a nonrecursive rule for constructing the sequence of moves H(A,B,C,n). Give a rigorous proof that your rule works (for the proof you will probably want to go back to the recursion!).

(4) Suppose that instead of having only three places A, B, and C to stack discs, there are four places A, B, C, and D. Study H(A,B,C,D,n).

(5) Let $\Pi(n,k)$ denote the set of all partitions of the set $\underline{n}$ into k blocks (see CHAPTER I, DEFINITION 1.3). If $\alpha \in \Pi(n,k)$ is a partition, then α is, by definition, an unordered collection of subsets of $\underline{n}$. For the sake of discussion, order the blocks of any partition such as α by the smallest element in each block. Thus, $\alpha = (\{1,7,8\}, \{2,3,6\}, \{4,5\})$ is an element of $\Pi(8,3)$ ordered according to the above convention. Note that in this example, α may be thought of as having been obtained from $\beta \in \Pi(7,3)$, $\beta = (\{1,7\}, \{2,3,6\}, \{4,5\})$, by adding 8 to the first block of β. We write $\alpha = (8 \to 1)\beta$. For $\gamma = (\{1,7\}, \{2,3,6\}, \{4,5\}, \{8\})$ we write $\gamma = (8 \to \infty)\beta$. The following diagram summarizes this situation:

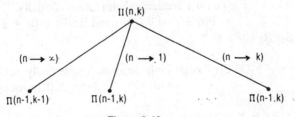

Figure 6.40

The diagram states that $\Pi(n,k)$ can be constructed by first applying the operation $(n \to \infty)$ to all partitions in $\Pi(n-1,k-1)$, then applying $(n \to 1)$

to all partitions in $\Pi(n-1,k)$, then $(n \rightarrow 2)$ to all partitions in $\Pi(n-1,k)$, etc. Note that this diagram is analogous to FIGURE 6.38 for $H(A,B,C,n)$. Thus this diagram is the local description of a tree. For particular n and k, study this tree. Use these ideas to develop a method for listing the partitions $\Pi(n,k)$. The numbers $S(n,k) = |\Pi(n,k)|$ are called the *Stirling numbers of the second kind*. Note that the above diagram implies that $S(n,k) = S(n-1,k-1) + kS(n-1,k)$. Use this recursion to make a table of the $S(n,k)$. (The reader may wish to review FIGURES 1.42, 1.48, and 1.52 of CHAPTER 1 for related ideas.)

(6) The Towers of Hanoi problem involved two recursive calls. Here is an interesting example that involves three recursive calls. This example and Problem (7) are a bit more complex than those we have been considering. Problem (7) involves a little group theory. Consider k 1's and $n - k$ 0's in an array F with $F(1) = \ldots = F(k) = 1$. We wish to make a series of single interchanges of 0's and 1's in the array F such that all k subsets of $\underline{n} = 1,2,\ldots,n$ are at some point represented in F and such that the final configuration is $F(n - k + 1) = \ldots = F(n) = 1$. If $n = k$ we do nothing. For $k = 1$ the sequence is $1000\ldots00, 0100\ldots00, 0010\ldots00, \ldots,$ $0000\ldots10,0000\ldots01$. Recursively we may specify the procedure by first moving, using the procedure, the k ones from their initial position to $F(n - k) = \ldots = F(n - 1) = 1$ thus generating all subsets of size k with $F(n) = 0$. We then set $F(n - 1) = 0$ and $F(n) = 1$. Now run the procedure in reverse moving the $k - 1$ 1's to $F(1) = \ldots = F(k - 1) = 1$ generating all k subsets of $\underline{n}$ with $F(n - 1) = 0$, $F(n) = 1$. Next set $F(k - 1) = 0$ and $F(n - 1) = 1$. Finally apply the procedure to the $k - 2$ 1's specified by $F(1) = \ldots = F(k - 2) = 1$ ending with $F(n - k + 1) = \ldots = F(n - 2) = 1$ and generating all k-subsets of $\underline{n}$ with $F(n - 1) = F(n) = 1$. The final configuration is the desired one and all subsets of size k have been generated.

We now give a formal definition of the procedure. Let $F(1),\ldots,F(n)$ be an array with $F(i) = 0$ or 1. Let $\alpha,\beta \in \underline{n}$. Suppose t (representing the number of 1's) is an integer, $0 \leqslant t \leqslant |\alpha - \beta| + 1$ and let $\delta = +1$ or -1. The procedure MOVE(t,δ,α,β) is defined if $\delta = +1$ and $\alpha \leqslant \beta$ or $\delta = -1$ and $\alpha \geqslant \beta$. MOVE(t,δ,α,β) generates sequentially in locations $F(\alpha)$, $F(\alpha+\delta),\ldots,F(\beta)$ all 0,1 sequences with t ones. Initially, if $t \geqslant 1$, $F(\alpha) = F(\alpha+\delta) = \ldots = F(\alpha+(t-1)\delta) = 1$ and finally $F(\beta) = F(\beta-\delta) = \ldots = F(\beta-(t-1)\delta) = 1$.

procedure MOVE(t,δ,α,β) {will generate sequentially in locations $F(\alpha)$,
$\qquad\qquad\qquad\qquad\qquad F(\alpha+\delta),\ldots,F(\beta)$ all 0,1 sequences with t 1's}
begin

$\qquad$ *if* $t = 0$ or $t-1 = |\alpha-\beta|$ *do* return;
$\qquad$ *if* $t = 1$ shift the 1 one step at a time from $F(\alpha)$ to $F(\beta)$;
$\qquad$ *else* {at this point $2 \leqslant t \leqslant |\alpha - \beta|$

> *begin*
>> MOVE $(t,\delta,\alpha,\beta-\delta)$; {ends with $F(\beta-t\delta) = \ldots = F(\beta-\delta)$
>>> $= 1$}
>>
>> $F(\beta-\delta):=0$ and $F(\beta):=1$; {switch a 0,1 pair}
>> MOVE $(t-1,-\delta,\beta-2\delta,\alpha)$; {ends with $F(\alpha) = \ldots$
>>> $= F(\alpha+(t-2)\delta) = 1.$
>>> $F(\beta-\delta) = 0$ and $F(\beta) =$
>>> 1 throughout}
>>
>> $F(\alpha+(t-2)\delta):=0$ and $F(\beta-\delta):=1$; {switch a 0,1 pair}
>> MOVE $(t-2,\delta,\alpha,\beta-2\delta)$; {ends with
>>> $F(\beta) = \ldots = F(\beta-(t-1)\delta) = 1$}.
>
> *end*

Execute MOVE $(3,1,1,6)$ and some other examples to get a feeling for the procedure. Given a 0,1 sequence, be able to find the next sequence in MOVE $(t,1,1,n)$. If you have studied PART I, try and find good algorithms for computing RANK and UNRANK for the list of sequences in MOVE $(t,1,1,n)$.

(7) As usual, let S_n denote all permutations of $\underline{n}$. Let C_n denote the cyclic group generated by the permutation $\tau = (12\ldots n)$. C_n acts on S_n by the rule $\tau*\sigma(i) = \sigma(\tau^{-1}(i))$. The standard "direct insertion" method (see CHAPTER 1, FIGURE 1.47) for recursively generating S_n proceeds by selecting in order (recursively) an element from S_{n-1}, $\sigma = \sigma_1,\sigma_2,\ldots,\alpha_{n-1}$, and inserting n in the various possible positions:

$$\sigma_1\sigma_2\ldots\sigma_{n-1}n, \ \sigma_1\sigma_2\ldots n\sigma_{n-1},\ldots,\sigma_1n\sigma_2\ldots\sigma_{n-1}, \ n\sigma_1\sigma_2\ldots\sigma_{n-1}.$$

Given any order on S_{n-1} we could use this procedure, denoted by $S_{n-1}(n)$ say, to form S_n. One possibility is to decompose S_{n-1} into orbits under the action of C_{n-1}: $S_{n-1} = O_1 \cup O_2 \cup \ldots \cup O_p$, $p = (n-2)!$ Order the orbits in some manner and the elements in the orbits in some manner and form $S_{n-1}(n) = O_1(n) \cup \ldots \cup O_p(n)$. It is well known that a system of orbit representatives for C_{n-1} acting on S_{n-1} is simply $\{\varphi: \varphi \in S_{n-1}, \varphi(n-1) = n-1\}$. Thus the orbits are identified with S_{n-2}. With a little care one can then proceed recursively. Consider $\sigma_1\sigma_2\ldots\sigma_{n-1}n$. After the series of insertions of n we obtain $n\sigma_1\sigma_2\ldots\sigma_{n-1}$. Switching the first and last symbols gives $\sigma_{n-1}\sigma_1\ldots\sigma_{n-2}n$ which is just $\tau*(\sigma_1\ldots\sigma_{n-1})n$ where $\tau = (12\ldots(n-1))$ is the generator of C_{n-1}. Thus $n-1$ series of n insertions followed by a switch of the first and last elements produces $O_t(n)$ where O_t is the orbit of C_{n-1} containing $\sigma_1\ldots\sigma_{n-1}$ (and returns us to the starting permutation $\sigma_1\sigma_2\ldots\sigma_{n-1}n$). Thus starting with 12345 say, we would go 12345, ..., 51234, 41235, ... 54123, 34125, ..., 53412, 23415, ..., 52341. Thus far we have formed $O_1(5)$ where O_1 is the orbit of C_4 acting on S_4 which contains 1234. The next switch brings us back to 12345 at which point we apply the procedure recursively to 123 to get the representative 1324 of the next orbit of C_4 acting on S_4. It should be obvious from the above remarks about the action of C_n on S_n that the algorithm works in general.

We give a rough pidgin algol description of the above procedure. Suppose an array $A(1)$. . .$A(n)$ contains a permutation of $\underline{m}$ in positions $A(1)$. . .$A(m)$. We define a procedure NEXTPERM(A,m) which updates the array $A(1),$. . .,$A(n)$. We suppose that a procedure $I(A,m)$ returns the location of m (if $A \leftarrow 12534$ then $I(A,5) = 3$ for example) and a procedure $T(A,m-1)$ deletes m and returns the relative position of $m-1$ mod $(m-1)$ (if $A\leftarrow$ 12534 then $T(A,4) = 0$, if $A \leftarrow 54123$ then $T(A,4) = 1$, if $A \leftarrow 34125$ then $T(A,4) = 2$, if $A \leftarrow 53142$ then $T(A,4) = 3$). Show that the following procedure may be used to generate S_n:

Procedure NEXTPERM(A,m) {To generate S_n start with $A(i) = i$, $i =$ 1,. . .,n, and set m: = n. Apply NEXTPERM(A,n) over and over again until LAST occurs}

begin
   if m = 1 *write* LAST;
   if m = 2 *then if* A(1) = 1 *then*
   begin
      SWITCH(A(1), A(2));
      write A(1),. . .,A(n)
   end
   else write LAST;
   if I(A,m) > 1 *then*
      begin
         SWITCH (A(I(A,m)),A(I(A,m) $-$ 1))
         write A(1),. . .,A(n)
      end
   else
   if T(A,m$-$1) $\neq$ m $-$ 2 *then* { in A = (5,2,3,4,1,. . .) with m = 5
                                 T(A,4) = m $-$ 2 = 3}
      begin
         SWITCH (A(1),A(m))
         write A(1),. . .,A(n)
      end
   else
      begin
         SWITCH (A(1), A(m));
         NEXTPERM (A,m$-$2)
      end
end

Generate the first 40 elements of NEXTPERM (A,5). By examples, show how to generate the predecessor and successor of selected permutations for n = 6,8. Show how to compute RANK and UNRANK for NEXTPERM.

Note. 1234, 1243, 1423, 4123, 3124, 3142, 3412, 4312, 2314, 2341, 2431, 4231, 2134, 2143, 2413, 4213, 3214, 3241, 3421, 4321, 1324, 1342, 1432, 4132, LAST is the result of applying NEXTPERM(A,4) 24 times starting with A = (1,2,3,4).

(8) Sometimes two or more recursive procedures are defined together as the following basic example illustrates. As usual, let $\{0,1\}^{\underline{n}}$ denote all functions from $\underline{n}$ to $\{0,1\}$ or, equivalently, all sequences of length n formed from the symbols 0 and 1 (i.e., using one-line notation for functions). We use $\overrightarrow{\text{GRAY}}(n)$ to denote a certain linear order on these sequences and $\overleftarrow{\text{GRAY}}(n)$ to denote this same linear order written backwards. To start with, $\overrightarrow{\text{GRAY}}(1)$ = 0,1 so $\overleftarrow{\text{GRAY}}(1)$ = 1,0. The notation $1\overrightarrow{\text{GRAY}}(n-1)$ means "adjoin 1 to the front of each string in $\overrightarrow{\text{GRAY}}(n-1)$." Thus, $1\overrightarrow{\text{GRAY}}(1)$ = 10,11. Similarly, define $0\overrightarrow{\text{GRAY}}(n-1)$, $1\overleftarrow{\text{GRAY}}(n-1)$, and $0\overleftarrow{\text{GRAY}}(n-1)$. We define $\overrightarrow{\text{GRAY}}(n)$ = $0\overrightarrow{\text{GRAY}}(n-1)$, $1\overleftarrow{\text{GRAY}}(n-1)$ and $\overleftarrow{\text{GRAY}}(n)$ = $1\overrightarrow{\text{GRAY}}(n-1)$, $0\overleftarrow{\text{GRAY}}(n-1)$. (By introducing a parameter indicating direction, these two procedures can obviously be written as one; this can be done in general for this type of recursive description.) Some examples: $\overrightarrow{\text{GRAY}}(2)$ = $0\overrightarrow{\text{GRAY}}(1)$, $1\overleftarrow{\text{GRAY}}(1)$ = 00,01,11,10. $\overrightarrow{\text{GRAY}}(3)$ = $0\overrightarrow{\text{GRAY}}(2)$, $1\overleftarrow{\text{GRAY}}(2)$ = 000,001,011,010,110,111,101,100. Prove that the sequences in the list GRAY(n) differ from their successor in exactly one coordinate. Analyze the list $\overrightarrow{\text{GRAY}}(n)$ in the same manner that the above recursions have been analyzed. (Given m, what is the mth entry in the list? Given a sequence, what is its predecessor and successor? etc.) The sequence $\overrightarrow{\text{GRAY}}(n)$ is called the "binary Gray code."

end EXERCISE

Before continuing our discussion of trees as they relate to the study of more general graphs (as spanning trees), it will be worthwhile to introduce sc additional notation.

6.41   NOTATION FOR TREES.

Let T be a rooted tree with root v. Regard T as a directed tree in the natural manner (each edge directed away from the root as in DEFINITION 6.25). If (x,y) is a directed edge, we say that x is the *father* of y and y is the *son* of x. If x and y are vertices connected by a directed path from x to y, then y *is a descendant of* x and x *is an ancestor of* y. In this case we say that x and y are *lineal descendants* or a *lineal descendant* pair. If e = {x,y} is an edge with corresponding directed edge (x,y) then we call x the initial vertex of e (we write x = IN(e)) and y the terminal vertex (TM(e)) of e.

6.42 NOTATION FOR VECTORS.

Let L = (a,b,. . .,e,f) be a vector or equivalently, a list, sequence, or linearly ordered set ab. . .ef. We use the following notations: ← L stands for the statement L: = (b,. . .,e,f); x ← L stands for the two statements x: = a and ← L; x → L stands for L: = (x,a,b,. . .,e,f). Similarly, we define L →, L → x, and L ← x.

6.43 DEFINITION.

Let G = (V,E) be a graph. A graph G′ = (V′,E′) satisfying the conditions V′ ⊆ V and E′ ⊆ E will be called a *subgraph* of G (written G′ ⊆ G).

We now give another description of how a recursive algorithm can be described using ordered rooted trees. If the Towers of Hanoi problem is solved by constructing the tree specified by the local description FIGURE 6.38 and if the tree is constructed in depth first order (i.e., the vertices or edges are constructed as they would occur in the depth first sequence of edges or vertices of the tree) then a sequence of trees $T_1, T_2, . . ., T_p$ is constructed. Each $T_i \subset T_{i+1}$ and T_p is the final tree (as shown in FIGURE 6.39 for n = 3, for example). We have noticed in EXERCISE 6.40(1) that in order to generate T_{i+1} from T_i we need only know the stack of the preorder last edge of T_i. To obtain T_{i+1} (in Towers of Hanoi) we start with the last edge in the stack (in this case, the preorder last edge of T_i) and go backwards through the stack to find the first edge (x,y) with x of degree 1 or 2 in T_i. The edge (x,y′), y′ the next son of x after y, is then added to T_i.

This idea of constructing a sequence of trees gives a useful geometric method for describing a wide class of algorithms. We give a general description of this process. Let T_i be a tree and let S be the stack of the preorder last element of T_i (T_i is ordered and rooted). We assume that S is the vertex sequence of the stack. Thus, the sequence S = (1,3,5,4) would represent the sequence of (directed) edges ((1,3),(3,5),(5,4)) in the tree of FIGURE 6.44 where 4 is the preorder last element.

6.44   STACK OF PREORDER LAST ELEMENT.

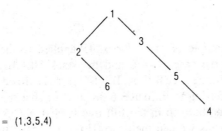

$$S = (1,3,5,4)$$

Figure 6.44

We use the notation x < y to indicate that x is closer to the root than y in S. We shall construct a sequence of trees T$_1$,. . .,T$_p$ inductively by adding one . edge at a time. Consider a tree T$_i$ (all are ordered rooted trees with the same root v). Let S be the stack of the preorder last element w. Suppose we have a function or "rule" for deciding whether or not any x ∈ S has a son in T$_p$ that is not in the tree T$_i$. We call this function SON and write SON(x,T$_i$) = φ if x does not have a son in T$_p$ − T$_i$. If x does have a son in T$_p$ − T$_i$ we assume that SON(x,T$_i$) is the first such son. Repeated applications of SON to the elements of S, starting with the last element of S and going in reverse order will either produce this latter case or find that SON(x,T$_i$) = φ for all x in S. This is the idea behind *procedure* 6.45.

In the Towers of Hanoi problem, the rule SON is specified by the local diagram of the tree given by FIGURE 6.38. The *procedure* 6.45 gives a straightforward description of how the trees of the Towers of Hanoi problem were constructed but in a slightly more general setting. Initially, we take T$_1$ = ({v},φ) and S = (v). By repeated applications of the following procedure, we construct a sequence of trees T$_1$,. . .,T$_p$. In each case, S is initially the stack of the preorder last element of T$_i$. Recall NOTATION 6.42.

6.45   *procedure* NEXT(T$_i$).

while SON(LAST(S),T$_i$) = φ *do* S→; {find vertex of S that has a son}
if S = φ exit *else*
begin
  (x,y): = (LAST(S),SON(LAST(S),T$_i$));
  NEXT(T$_i$): = T$_i$ with {x,y} added; {NEXT(T$_i$) is the tree T$_{i+1}$}
  S ← y;
end

In each tree T$_i$, the root is v and the order is determined by the order in which the edges incident to a given vertex are added. The procedure NEXT represents the basic idea involved in converting a recursive implementation of an algorithm into a nonrecursive implementation by use of a stack.

6.46 EXAMPLE.

We consider an example of *procedure* 6.45 applied to the Towers of Hanoi problem. Consider the case n = 6 and the stack H(A,B,C,6), H(B,A,C,5), H(B,C,A,4), H(C,B,A,3), H(B,C,A,2), H(C,B,A,1). Reading this stack from right to left and referring to FIGURE 6.38, we see that the largest element in the stack to have another son in the full tree is H(B,A,C,5) and the first such son is "B to C." Thus we add the edge (H,(B,A,C,5), "B to C") to the tree T_i (i.e., the existing tree, of which we actually know only the stack at the moment) and obtain the new stack: H(A,B,C,6), H(B,A,C,5), "B to C." Notice that in this example, the function SON depends on the stack of T_i and the local description of the tree T_p (the final tree). This is often the case. We need only the recursive description and the stack.

We now consider another example of an algorithm that involves the generation of a sequence of trees by successive augmentations of the stacks of the trees. It is necessary to first introduce the important notion of a spanning tree of a graph.

6.47 DEFINITION.

If G = (V,E) is a connected graph and G' = (V',E') is a subgraph with V' = V, then G' is called a *spanning subgraph*. If, in addition, G' is a tree, then G' is called a *spanning tree for* G. A graph whose components are trees is called a *forest*. For any graph G, a subgraph G' whose **components** are spanning trees for the **components** of G is called a *spanning forest* for G. If G' is a spanning forest of G, then the edges of E − E' are called the *chords* of G' in G. A pair (G', v), v ∈ V and G' a spanning tree, is called a *rooted* spanning tree. The vertex v is called *the root* of (G', v).

6.48 EXERCISE.

Give a careful proof that any connected graph G must have at least one spanning tree. *Hint:* Show that if G' = (V',E') is a subgraph of G, and G' is a tree (we call G' a *subtree* in this case), then V' not equal to V implies that a larger subtree of G can be constructed from G' by adding one more edge.

6.49 DEFINITION.

Let G = (V,E) be a graph and let (G', v) be a rooted spanning tree for G. If for every edge {x,y} of G, the vertices x and y are a lineal descendant pair with respect to the rooted tree G' then we say that G' is a *lineal spanning tree* of G (recall Notation 6.41).

If the edge {x,y} of DEFINITION 6.49 is an edge of G', then it is obvious that x and y are a lineal descendant pair. Thus the condition must be checked only on the edges of G that are not in G′. Consider EXAMPLE 6.50.

6.50 EXAMPLE.

Two rooted (at *a*) spanning trees of G, natural directions shown.

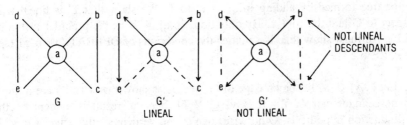

Figure 6.50

In EXAMPLE 50, the edges {b,c} and {d,e} both have vertices that do not form a lineal descendant pair with respect to the second spanning tree.

We shall now show that given any connected graph G and any vertex v of G, there is a lineal spanning tree of G rooted at v. To do so, it is convenient to extend the notion of "lineal" to subtrees of G that are not necessarily spanning. Let V(G) and E(G) denote the vertices and edges of G.

6.51 DEFINITION.

Let G be a graph and T a subtree of G rooted at v. We say that T is a lineal subtree of G if T is *ordered* and satisfies the following:

(1) If e = {x,y} is an edge of G (e ∈ E(G)) with both endpoints vertices of T (e ⊆ V(T)) then these endpoints x and y are a lineal descendant pair with respect to T.
(2) If e ∈ E(G) has exactly one vertex in common with T, then that vertex is in STACK(e′) where e′ is the preorder last edge of T (DEFINITION 6.32). Here we regard the stack as the vertex sequence of the corresponding path.

6.52 THEOREM.

Let G be any connected graph, and let v be a vertex of G. There exists a lineaɪ spanning tree for G rooted at v.

Proof. The proof is by induction. If G has only one vertex the result is trivial. If G has more than one vertex, then, by connectivity, there is an edge of the form {v,v′}. This edge of G defines a lineal subtree T with two vertices. In general, let T be a lineal subtree of G with |V(T)| = k and assume k < n =

$|V(G)|$. We shall construct a lineal subtree T' of G with $\kappa + 1$ vertices. There is some vertex $w \in V(G)$ with $w \notin V(T)$. By connectivity, there is a path $w_1, w_2, \ldots, w_t$ ($w = w_1$) arriving at the set $V(T)$ for the first time at w_t. Thus, the edge $\{w_{t-1}, w_t\}$ has exactly one vertex (namely w_t) in common with $V(T)$ and, by the induction hypothesis, this vertex must be a vertex of STACK(e) where e is the preorder last edge of T. Let p be the preorder largest (i.e., furthest from the root r) vertex of STACK(e) for which there is a vertex $q \notin V(T)$ with $\{p, q\} \in E(G)$. Let T' be the tree formed by adding $\{p, q\} = e'$ to T. We show that T' is lineal with respect to G and the root v. By defnition, $\{p, q\} = e'$ is the preorder last edge of T'. We must show that T' satisfies the conditions of DEFINITION 6.51 (see FIGURE 6.53).

(1) Let $\{x, y\} \subseteq V(T')$ be an edge of G. We must show that x and y are a lineal descendant pair of T'. If $\{x, y\} \subseteq V(T)$ then the result is evident by the induction hypothesis. Otherwise, one of the vertices of this edge, say y, is equal to q. Again, by the induction hypothesis, we must have $x \in$ STACK(e). By the maximality of p, $x \in$ STACK(p). Thus x and $y = q$ are a lineal descendant pair.

(2) Suppose that $e \in E(G)$ has exactly one vertex x in common with V(T'). If $x = q$, then x is a vertex of STACK(e'). If $x \neq q$ then, by the induction hypothesis, x is a vertex of STACK(e). But again using the maximality of p, x is a vertex of STACK(p) and hence in STACK(e').

This completes the proof of the theorem since by induction, there is a lineal subtree of G with n vertices rooted at v. This subtree must be a lineal spanning tree rooted at v.

6.53   THE INDUCTION STEP OF THEOREM 6.52.

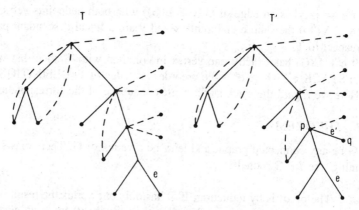

Solid lines are TREE edges, dotted lines edges of G.

Figure 6.53

We shall, in what follows, give many applications of the notion of a lineal spanning tree. An alternative way of viewing lineal spanning trees is suggested in EXERCISE 6.54.

6.54 EXERCISE.

Let G = (V,E) be a connected graph, v ∈ V. Assume $|V| \geq 2$. Choose w adjacent to v. Let W denote all x ∈ V for which there exists a path (not self-intersecting) from x to v with w as a vertex. Let U = V − W. By inductively constructing a lineal spanning tree for G restricted to W (root w) and G restricted to U (root v), prove THEOREM 6.52. *Hint:* See FIGURE 6.55.

6.55 IDEA FOR ALTERNATIVE PROOF OF THEOREM 6.52.

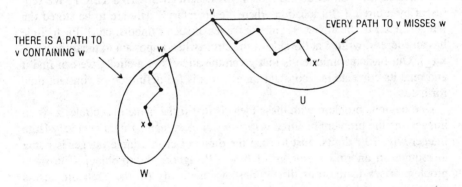

Figure 6.55

An algorithm for constructing a lineal spanning tree follows immediately from THEOREM 6.52 and follows exactly *procedure* 6.45. We need only describe the function SON for this particular case. The tree T_p will be the lineal spanning tree. Given v, the tree $T_1 = (\{v\}, \phi)$. The function $SON(x,T_i)$ is ϕ if all of the vertices adjacent to x in G are in T_i (i.e., $A_x - V(T_i)$ is empty where A_x is the set of vertices adjacent to x in G). If $A_x - V(T_i)$ is not empty, $SON(x,T_i)$ may be chosen to be any element of that set. As the choice of this element is left open one might say that the algorithm in this form is "undeterministic." Once a tree is constructed by this process, however, an order is defined on A_x each vertex x of G (the order in which the vertices of A_x are examined to see whether or not they are vertices of the current tree). This ordering of the A_x makes G into an ordered graph. If, with respect to this order, we define $SON(x,T_i)$ to be the first element of $A_x - V(T_i)$ in each case, then we construct the same final tree. Henceforth, in constructing a lineal spanning tree for G we shall assume at the outset that the connected graph G is an ordered graph (without loops). In this case, $SON(x,T) = \phi$ if $A_x - V(T)$ is empty and otherwise equals the first element of $A_x - V(T)$ with respect to the order on A_x. Using the *procedure* 6.45 NEXT(T), we have

6.56 *procedure* (construct a lineal spanning tree).

Initially T = $(\{v\},\phi)$;
while $|V(T)| < |V(G)| = $ n *do* T: = NEXT(T);

Procedure 6.56 is in fact a very efficient and easy algorithm to implement. In order to give a discussion of the "complexity" of this procedure it is necessary to have a simple model of computing. We next give such a model, intended only as a rough intuitive guide. The reader should review the discussion of basic data structures at the start of CHAPTER 1 (in particular, TABLE 1.14, FIGURE 1.15, 1.16, and 1.17, and related discussion). The discussion to follow is related to the "direct access model" as described in CHAPTER 1. We represent by a circle ◯ a location where "elementary" data are to be stored (an integer, letter of the alphabet, pairs or triples of such symbols, etc.). Each circle has an address, written at the side of the circle when important to the discussion: x ◯. Our basic assumption is that given the address of a circle, we can find it and read its contents in "constant time" (this is the definition of constant time for us!).

One obvious problem with these ideas is that if the name of a circle, x, is an integer and the problem required *very many* circles, then x might be a very large integer with 10^{10} digits. Just to scan the digits of such a large integer is going to require an enormous amount of time. We ignore this problem. The same problem arises in rigorous discussions of complexity (in the "random access model" of computation) and is ignored there also. We also do not make any attempt to define the class of possible symbols for naming circles or the possible contents of circles. We rely instead on "common sense" to dictate these choices. Our mathematical interests here do not lie in the direction of complexity analysis of algorithms. We wish only to gain some sensitivity to such problems in order to relate them to the combinatorics. We shall describe an algorithm and indicate how the computations are to be made. We then attribute costs to certain basic steps in the computation and call the total cost the measure of complexity of the algorithm. We hope to at least be reasonable enough to "get the ball rolling" in so far as complexity questions are concerned. We start with some examples.

If f is a function from a set D to a set R (assume D finite) then f can be represented in tabular form: x ⓕ⟨x⟩ . Given x, we assume that we can find $f(x)$ in constant time. In particular, arrays such as a matrix (a_{ij}) can be represented in this form: (ij) ⓐ$_{ij}$. Thus, given i and j, we can read the ij^{th} entry of the matrix in constant time. One basic type of information that we shall store in our circles is a "pointer" to another circle: x ⓨ where y is the address of another circle, y◯. The symbol y is the *pointer* in location x. This situation is also represented by the diagram x ◯ → y ◯ or simply by ◯ → ◯ when the actual names x and y are not important to the discussion. Again, we suppose that the elements of D,R and the symbols that represent points (or addresses of circles) are, in some vague sense, "elementary." If we wished to list the three symbols # $ ¢ in that order we might do so by using pointers as follows: start at x, x⟨#y⟩, y⟨$z⟩ z⟨¢⟩. In location x we read # and go to y were we read $ and go to z, etc. We must, of course, have some conventions for telling pointers from data inside a circle, but this is clear from the notation in this example. Once the pointers are given, the order or location of the corresponding circles in the text obviously has no importance as we have assumed that, given the name, a circle can be located in constant time. Thus the same list could be given by the following: start at x, y⟨$z⟩, z⟨¢⟩ x⟨#y⟩ . Such a method for listing a sequence of symbols is called a "linked list" (see FIGURE 1.15, CHAPTER 1). It is an example of what we shall refer to informally as a "data structure." The linked list structure can be indicated by the following notation: ○ → ○ → . . . → ○ (see FIGURE 1.16, CHAPTER 1).

The amount of work involved in an algorithm will depend very much on the data structure used. If one specifies an ordering of a sequence of symbols by listing them one after the other in the text (for example, #$¢) then to insert a new symbol, say &, between two others, say # and $, requires shifting all symbols to the right of the new symbol added by one space (for example #$¢ becomes #&$¢). Thus the amount of work involved in inserting a new symbol depends on the length of the list. In the case of the linked list the amount of work will not depend on the length of the list. (See the discussion associated with FIGURE 1.15, CHAPTER 1). For example, to insert & between # and $ we modify the above linked list to obtain the following: start at x, y⟨$z⟩, z⟨¢⟩ x⟨#w⟩ w⟨&y⟩ . (In general, we do not redraw the old circles but simply add the new circle and change the relevant pointers. If the old circles were redrawn then the changes would clearly not be independent of the length of the list! This should be thought of in terms of FIGURE 1.15 of CHAPTER 1.) The pointer in circle x was changed from y to w and a new circle named w was added with the symbol & and a pointer y. These changes do not depend on the length of the list.

One problem here that may or may not be minor is that of locating the name of the circle containing the symbol after which the new symbol is to be inserted. If we are asked to "insert & just after the symbol contained in x" then this is no problem by our assumptions. If, on the other hand, we are asked to "insert & just after $" then we must first find the name of the circle containing $. One possibility is to keep a *function* or *array* $\begin{pmatrix} \# & \$ & ¢ \\ x & y & z \end{pmatrix}$ that gives the location of each symbol. This means that x, y, and z become contents of circles, and #, $, and ¢ (or perhaps numerical codes associated with these symbols if that is preferred for some reason) become addresses or names of circles. Now when asked to "insert & just after $" one obtains the location of $ from the array and modifies the linked list accordingly. One then must modify the array to give the location of &. These modifications still require constant time, independent of the length of the list in our model.

We now use the above ideas to discuss the complexity of the problem of finding a lineal spanning tree of a graph. Consider the graph of FIGURE 6.57.

6.57   A GRAPH G.

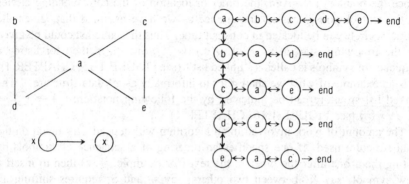

Figure 6.57

The "adjacency table" of FIGURE 6.57 has vertices as contents of circles with pointers as shown. A list with pointers both to the next element of the list and the previous element of the list is called a "doubly linked list." Thus, the list of vertices (the vertical list of FIGURE 6.57) is a doubly linked list. Associated with each vertex x there is a pointer $x\bigcirc \rightarrow \circledx$ to the location of x. The lists of adjacent elements are also doubly linked. We will not need all of these pointers for the lineal spanning tree problem. In fact, the doubly-linked list structure of the list of vertices will not be used at all for the lineal spanning tree problem. As this data structure is useful for other problems, it is a good general convention for the list of vertices. As remarked, we assume that given a vertex name x, we can go in constant time to the location where x is stored in the list of vertices. How this can be accomplished within the framework of our model was explained in the previous paragraph and in FIGURE 1.18 of CHAPTER 1. We shall construct a lineal spanning tree for G of FIGURE 6.57 rooted at *a*. G is an ordered graph as given by the adjacency table of FIGURE 6.57. We start with T = ({a},φ) and construct a sequence of trees using NEXT(T), *procedure* 6.45, until a lineal spanning tree is obtained (using *procedure* 6.56). The lineal subtree (DEFINITION 6.52) obtained at each stage of the algorithm will be denoted by T. For each such tree, we shall have a function VERT: V(T) → {0,1} defined by VERT(x) = 1 if x is a vertex of T and 0 otherwise. Initially S denotes the stack of the preorder last element of T. *We regard* T *as directed in the natural fashion* (away from the root, DEFINITION 6.25).

We now carry out the construction of a spanning tree step by step, showing at each stage the basic data structures: G, T, S, and VERT.

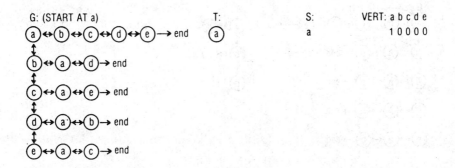

Start at *a* and check the first vertex b adjacent to *a* (follow pointer to right). VERT(b) is 0 so b must be added to T and the stack S and deleted from G. Then VERT(b): = 1. We then go to b (vertical list).

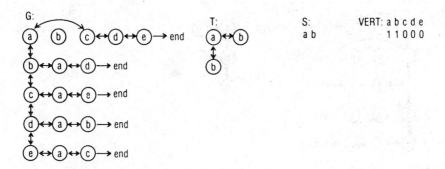

Start at b and check the first vertex in its adjacency list, *a*. VERT(a) = 1 so *a* has already been added to the tree. Change the pointers to d:

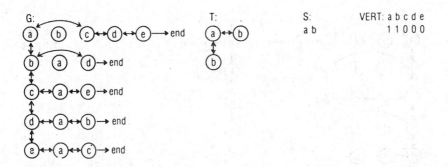

The pointer from b now points to d. VERT(d) = 0 so d has not been added to the tree T. Change the pointer from b in G to indicate that all vertices in its adjacency list have been considered, add d to T, add d to S, and set VERT(d) = 1.

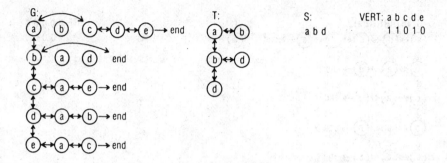

The first pointer at d points to *a*. VERT(a) = 1. Change the pointer to b. VERT(b) = 1. Change the pointer to "end" and remove d from S. Now b is the last element of S:

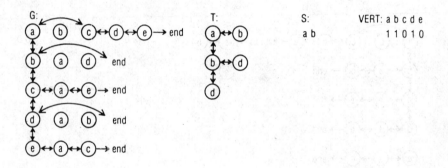

Start at b. The pointer points to "end" so remove b from S to get S = *a*. Go to *a* in G and follow pointer to c. VERT(c) = 0 so add c to S, change pointer to d, add c to S and T, change VERT(c) to 1 and go to c.

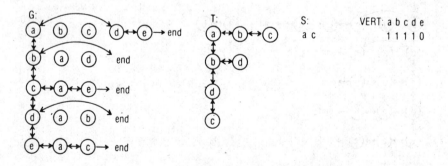

Start at c. VERT (a) = 1. Change pointers to e. VERT(e) = 0 so add e to S, VERT, T:

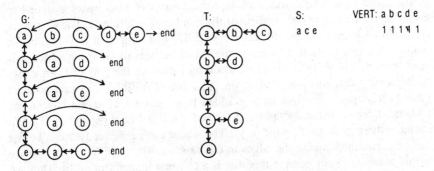

Start at e. The first pointer is to *a*, but VERT(a) = 1. Change the pointer to c. VERT(c) = 1. Change pointer to end and remove e from S. Last element of S is now c so go to c. The pointer at c points to end so remove c from S and go to last element of S which is now *a*. The pointer at *a* points to d but VERT(d) = 1 so change pointer to e. VERT(e) = 1 so change pointer to end and remove *a* from S. S is now empty so stop. The terminal configuration is shown in FIGURE 6.58.

6.58 TERMINAL DATA STRUCTURE AND LINEAL SPANNING TREE.

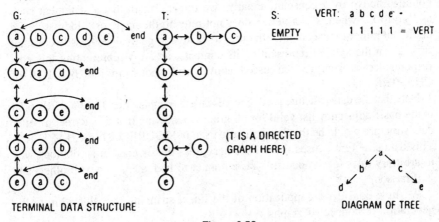

Figure 6.58

We assert that the time required to construct the spanning tree of a connected graph using the above data structures is proportional to the number of edges in the graph. As the algorithm is carried out, certain basic operations are performed (going to a specified address, reading the last element of S, changing a pointer, etc.). We observe that these basic operations can be partitioned among the edges of the graph in a natural way such that the number of basic tasks assigned to each edge is a constant independent of the number of edges in G. The first thing we do in each case is read the last entry of S. For example, if S = a b c, we read c. We then go to this vertex in the list of vertices of G. If the vertex x is read from S, and y is the vertex obtained by following the pointer from x into its adjacency list, then, depending on the value of VERT(y), certain pointers must be changed—S might have y added to it, and VERT might have to be updated. Clearly, these operations, for fixed x and y do not depend on |E|. We attribute these costs to the edge {x,y}. The reader can easily verify that all costs can be partitioned among the edges in this fashion. The maximum cost that we would attribute to any edge in this way is a constant indpendent of |E|. Thus we say that the complexity of this algorithm is bounded above by a constant times the number of edges. Clearly, all edges of a connected graph must, in general, be examined to determine a lineal spanning tree in this fashion. Thus we say that the complexity of this algorithm is linear in the number of edges of G (i.e., proportional to a constant times the number of edges). In fact, of course, we have an inequality $c_1|E| \leq \text{COST} \leq c_2|E|$ for constants c_1, c_2. In the adjacency structure for G (see FIGURE 6.57) the first column represents the linked list of vertices for G. Notice that we go to a vertex in this list as many times as that vertex appears as the last element of S in the course of the algorithm. This is equal to the degree of that vertex in the lineal spanning tree and in general is not a constant independent of |E|. We assert only that *for each x in the vertex list and each y adjacent to x*, the cost of processing that y is (as explained above) bounded above by a constant. Finally, we remark again that a statement such as "go to x" where x is a vertex does not refer to the name or "address" of a circle but rather to its contents. In order to be able to go to an address in constant time given the symbol representing its contents, an array representing this correspondence is kept (as discussed above, and shown in FIGURE 1.18 of CHAPTER 1).

Note that the data structure used to represent the spanning tree T in FIGURE 6.58 is the basic adjacency list valid for all graphs. Knowing that T is a tree, a better data structure would be the data structure used in FIGURE 1.87 of CHAPTER I. This data structure is used there for binary trees but extends in an obvious way to arbitrary trees (each node still has a pointer to its father, its next brother, and its first son).

We now consider an application of the lineal spanning tree algorithm to the generation of connected graphs.

6.59 DEFINITION.

Let G be a connected graph and T a spanning tree of G. An edge of G that is not an edge of T is called a *chord*. If T is a lineal spanning tree rooted at v then a chord is called a *backedge* and the *natural direction* of a backedge {x,y} is (y,x) where y is a descendant of x in T.

For example, the graph of FIGURE 6.57 has the lineal spanning tree shown in FIGURE 6.58. There are two directed chords, (d,a) and (e,a). Both are backedges since T is lineal.

We refer now to *procedure* 6.56 and the discussion (just preceding *procedure* 6.56) of the function SON(x,T). Suppose that the vertex set V of G is a set of nonnegative integers. Order each adjacency list by decreasing order on integers. Thus SON(x,T) always picks the largest vertex (as an integer) from among the vertices adjacent to x in G but not already added to T. Let T denote the lineal spanning tree that results from *procedure* 6.56 with this choice of SON. Suppose that (y,x) is a directed backedge of G with respect to T. There is a unique path x,t,. . .,y in T from x to y and the length of this path must be at least 2. We claim that t > y as integers. Consider the point in *procedure* 6.56 when t was the preorder last element in the tree T (a subtree of the final spanning tree). Note that at this point y was not a vertex of the current tree. Let T′ denote the tree just prior to adding t. Evidently, SON(x,T′) = t and not y. But, both t and y are adjacent to x in G and both are not vertices of T′. By the maximality property of SON we must then conclude that t > y.

6.60 DEFINITION.

Let T = (V,E) be a rooted tree with V linearly ordered. Let *a* be a vertex of T. A pair of vertices of T, (a,b), with b a descendant of *a* and b < *a* is called an inversion of T. We let I(T) denote the set of all inversions of T.

6.61 THE SET OF INVERSIONS.

I(T) = {(5,3),(6,4)}, V = {0,1,. . .,6}:

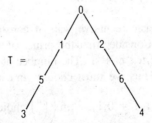

In light of DEFINITION 6.60 and the discussion just preceding, we have THEOREM 6.62. We denote by MAXSON the version of SON previously discussed that always selects the maximum available son.

6.62 THEOREM.

Let G be a connected graph and let T be a lineal spanning tree constructed using MAXSON. If (y,x) is a directed backedge of G relative to T, and x,t,. . .,y is the path from x to y in T, then (t,y) is an inversion.

Let CON(V) denote the set of connected graphs on a set of non-negative integers V and let TR(V,v) denote the set of trees on V rooted at v where v is the minimum of V. Using the procedure MAXSON we have shown how, given a connected graph G, to construct a lineal spanning tree rooted at v. Call this tree T. Define a subset S of the inversions I(T) by (t,y) $\in$ S if (y,x) is a backedge of G relative to T where x,t,. . .,y is as in 6.62. Denote the mapping INV by the rule INV(G) = (T,S).

6.63 EXERCISE.

Show that the mapping INV is a bijection between the set CON(V) and the set $\{(T,S): T \in TR(V,v)$ and $S \subseteq I(T)\}$.

We now associate with each integer n a polynomial that we call the *inversion enumerator*. Let V = $\{0,1,. . .,n\}$ and consider the sum $\sum t^{|I(T)|}$ where the sum is over all T in TR(V,0). This sum can be written in the form $p_n(t) = \sum_{s=0}^{\binom{n}{2}} a_s^{(n)} t^s$. This polynomial is the *inversion enumerator polynomial*. It is evident that $a_s^{(n)} = |\{T: |I(T)| = s\}|$. The first four such polynomials are $p_1(t) = 1$, $p_2(t) = t + 2$, $p_3(t) = t^3 + 3t^2 + 6t + 6$, $p_4(t) = t^6 + 4t^5 + 10t^4 + 20t^3 + 30t^2 + 36t + 24$. In the following exercise we develop some of the remarkable properties of these polynomials. (Note: $p_0(t) = 1$.)

6.64 EXERCISE.

(1) Show that the polynomials $p_n(t)$ satisfy the recursion

$$p_{n+1}(t) = \sum_{i=0}^{n} \binom{n}{i} p_i(t)p_{n-i}(t)(1 + t + t^2 + \ldots + t^i).$$

Hint: This reflects a basic recursive way of constructing TR(V,0) where V = $\{0,1,. . .,n+1\}$. Consider first the principal subtree of the root, say T_1, that contains the vertex n + 1. The number of vertices of this subtree can be 1,2,. . .,n+1. Thus we must choose, in each case, i other vertices besides the vertex n + 1, i = 0,1,. . .,n $\left(\binom{n}{i} \text{ choices}\right)$. For a fixed choice we must then choose a root. Finally, for a fixed choice we must consider the tree T $-$ T_1 gotten by deleting T_1 from T.

(2) Show that $p_n(0)$ = n! by constructing a bijection between all trees T $\in$ TR(V,0) with I(T) empty (no inversions) and all permutations of $\{1,. . .,n\}$ = $\underline{n}$. It is evident that $p_n(1) = (n+1)^{n-1}$ which is the number of trees on V. Do we need to know in advance that $(m+1)^{m-1}$ counts the number of trees, or does this follow from problem (1) above? Also, from the definition of p_n it is immediate that $p_n(2)$ is the number of connected graphs. Show

that the number of such directed graphs on V is given by $2^n p_n(3)$. A permutation f of $\underline{n}$ is alternating if $f(1) < f(2)$, $f(2) > f(3)$, $f(3) < f(4)$, etc. For example, if $n = 3$, there are two alternating permutations 1 3 2 and 2 3 1. For $n = 4$ there are five alternating permutations 1 3 2 4, 1 4 2 3, 2 4 1 3, 2 3 1 4, 3 4 1 2. In general, let E_n (the so called Euler number), denote the number of alternating permutations of $\underline{n}$. It is a remarkable fact that $p_n(-1) = E_n$ (try and prove it or see the references).

(3) The recursion of EXERCISE (1) contains a method for actually constructing trees classified by number of inversions. Using this idea, or any other you might think of, discuss the problem of generating all trees in TR(V,0) with a fixed number, say k, of inversions.

THEOREM 6.62 and EXERCISE 6.63 provide an interesting algorithm for constructing all connected graphs on $V = \{0,\ldots,n\}$. One first constructs all trees on V, rooted at 0. For each such tree T one then constructs all subsets S of I(T). For each such set S, one includes exactly those backedges corresponding to elements of S. The tree T can be constructed by any method (for example using INVPRU, *procedure* 6.21). We illustrate the idea by constructing all connected graphs on $\{0,1,2,3\}$.

6.65 CONNECTED GRAPHS WITH FOUR VERTICES.

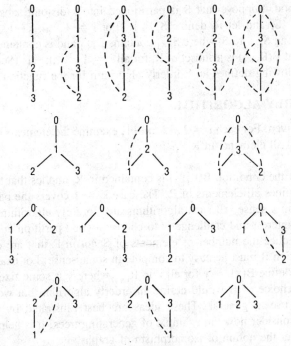

Figure 6.65

The dotted lines refer to edges that may be included or excluded. By including and excluding these edges in all possible ways, all connected graphs with vertex set V = {0,1,2,3} are obtained.

6.66   STRUCTURE OF AN ORDERLY ALGORITHM.
$B(R_{i+1}) \subseteq R_i$ IF AND ONLY IF $R_{i+1} \subseteq B^{-1}(R_i)$.

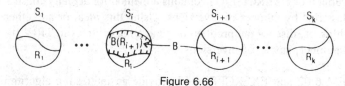

Figure 6.66

In FIGURE 6.65 it was necessary to construct all trees on a given vertex set. One method, as suggested there, is to use the map INVPRU (*procedure 6.21*). As an interesting aside, we consider another quite different method that is very general and has a wide range of applications. This method was discussed in CHAPTER 4 (see FIGURE 4.65). Let S be a set and R a subset of S. Suppose that the elements of S are to be examined one by one and a test is to be performed to see whether or not an element is in R. In practice, there are often ways to avoid examining all of the elements of S. The method we now give formalizes one such method. Suppose that S is partitioned into k disjoint subsets (called blocks) $S_1,\ldots,S_k$ and let R_i denote $S_i \cap R$. For i = 1,...,k − 1, let B be a function mapping S'_{i+1} to S_i where S'_{i+1} contains R_{i+1} and is contained in S_{i+1}. We assume that $B(R_{i+1})$ is a subset of R_i for all i = 1,...,k − 1. (See FIGURE 6.66.) The following defines an "orderly algorithm for the function B."

6.67   ORDERLY ALGORITHM.

Start with R_1 given. For each i = 1,...,k − 1, examine the elements of $B^{-1}(R_i)$ and test to find all elements in R_{i+1}.

Observe that the condition $B(R_{i+1})$ is contained in R_i implies that the orderly algorithm examines all elements of R. The case k = 1 covers the basic search procedure, so in a sense, all such algorithms are "orderly algorithms" for the trivial B. The interest and challenge is to choose a good partition and function B to greatly reduce the number of elements of S *not in* R that are examined. Also, the function B must be easy to compute in some sense. For example, one could trivially define B(x) = y for all x in R_{i+1} where y is some fixed element in R_i. Such a choice of B would define an orderly algorithm but would be of little practical use in general. These ideas are best illustrated by giving an example. We consider now the example of generating trees. It is helpful at this point to consider the notion of isomorphism of graphs.

For any set S, let $\mathscr{P}_2(S)$ denote the set of all subsets of size 2 of S. Let V and V' be sets and let f denote a bijection between V and V'. Then f induces a bijection $\underline{f}$ between $\mathscr{P}_2(V)$ and $\mathscr{P}_2(V')$ by the rule $\underline{f}\{x,y\} = \{f(x),f(y)\}$. For any graph G, define $\underline{f}(G) = (f(V),\underline{f}(E))$ where $G = (V,E)$ and f is a bijection between V and V'. Thus $\underline{f}(G)$ is a graph with vertex set $V' = f(V)$.

6.68 DEFINITION.

Two graphs $G = (V,E)$ and $G' = (V',E')$ are *isomorphic* if there is a bijection f between V and V' such that $G' = \underline{f}(G)$.

6.69 EXERCISE.

Let BIJ(A,B) denote the set of bijections from A to B. Define a map F from BIJ(V,V') to BIJ($\mathscr{P}_2(V),\mathscr{P}_2(V')$) by $F(f) = \underline{f}$. Prove carefully that $\underline{f}$ is in fact a bijection on $\mathscr{P}_2(V)$ to $\mathscr{P}_2(V')$ and show that F is an injection if $|V| > 2$.

If A is a set then we use the notation PER(A) to denote the set of all permutations of A. PER(A) is a group under compositions of permutations in the usual manner (the "symmetric group on A") (PER($\underline{n}$) = S_n). If K is any subgroup of PER(A), then we may define an equivalence relation on A by $x_{\bar{K}} y$ if there exists a permutation k in K such that $k(x) = y$. This relation is easily seen to be reflexive, symmetric, and transitive. The equivalence classes of this relation are called the *orbits* of K in ·A. The reader interested in thinking more about these ideas should read the beginning of CHAPTER 4, TOPIC III (DEFINITION 4.1 to LEMMA 4.9).

Let $\mathscr{P}(A)$ denote the set of all subsets of A (the "power set of A"). If f is an element of PER(A) then f also permutes the elements of $\mathscr{P}(A)$ in a natural way: for S in P(A), define $f(S) = \{f(x): x \text{ in } S\}$. We call this permutation group on $\mathscr{P}(A)$ the *subset action* of PER(A). Consider the situation of EXERCISE 6.69 with $V = V'$. In this case, F is an injection between PER(V) and PER($\mathscr{P}_2(V)$). It is easily seen that for f and g in PER(V), $F(fg) = F(f)F(g)$, and thus F is an *isomorphism* of PER(V) to a subgroup of PER($\mathscr{P}_2(V)$). We call this subgroup the *edge action* of PER(V) and denote it by EPER(V). Clearly, EPER(V) is the subset action of PER(V) restricted to $\mathscr{P}_2$, the subsets of size 2. We may consider also the subset action of EPER(V). Thus each element $\underline{f}$ of EPER(V) acts on subsets E of $\mathscr{P}_2(V)$. Each such subset E defines a graph $G = (V,E)$ of GRAPHS(V), the set of all graphs on V, and hence the subset action of EPER(V) defines a permutation group on GRAPHS(V). Thus we have four basic permutation groups: PER(V), EPER(V), the subset action of EPER(V), and the action of EPER(V) on GRAPHS(V). All four are isomorphic as groups to PER(V). As an example, consider $V = \{1,2,3\}$. Let $E = \{\{1,2\},\{1,3\}\}$. The group PER(V) has six elements. One such element is $\begin{pmatrix} 1 & 2 & 3 \\ 2 & 3 & 1 \end{pmatrix} = f$. Thus $\underline{f}(E) = \{\{2,3\},\{2,1\}\}$. Another element is $\begin{pmatrix} 1 & 2 & 3 \\ 1 & 3 & 2 \end{pmatrix} = g$. We have $\underline{g}(E) = \{\{1,3\},\{1,2\}\} = E$. The action of $\underline{f}$

and g on the corresponding graphs is shown in FIGURE 6.70 (the notation f and g of DEFINITION 6.68 is dropped here).

6.70   PERMUTATIONS OF V ACTING ON G = (V,E).

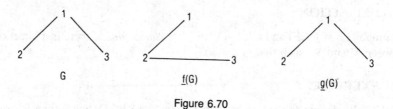

Figure 6.70

Observe that the permutation g applied to the graph G in FIGURE 6.70 does not change G. Thus G is a fixed point of g. Such a g is called an *automorphism* of G or a *stabilizer* of G. The set of all elements of PER(V) that are automorphisms of a given graph G are easily seen to form a group called the *automorphism group* of G or the *stability subgroup* of G. Let AUT(G) denote this subgroup of PER(V). Clearly, two graphs of GRAPHS(V) are isomorphic *if and only if they are in the same orbit of* EPER(V) *acting on* GRAPHS(V). Thus the number of distinct isomorphism classes of graphs is the number of orbits of this action. Given G, the number of graphs isomorphic to G (the number of elements in its orbit) is, by an elementary result from group theory, (LEMMA 4.9, Chapter 4), the ratio $n!/|AUT(G)|$. Thus, there are three graphs isomorphic to G of FIGURE 6.70. Conceptually, one may generate all graphs in the orbit of a given graph G by drawing the diagram of G, erasing all vertex labels leaving only dots, labeling the dots with all possible permutations of the original vertex labels, and then throwing out all duplicate copies of graphs. This process is illustrated for the graphs of FIGURE 6.70 in FIGURE 6.71. The pattern of dots (called the "unlabeled graph" in some books) is shown in FIGURE 6.71(b). FIGURE 6.71(a,c,d,e,f,g) give the six possible ways of labeling FIGURE 6.71(b). Note that (a) is the same as (c), (d) is the same as (e), and (f) is the same as (g) *as graphs*. Thus, there are exactly three graphs in the isomorphism class associated with the dot diagram (b), namely, (a), (d), and (f) as indicated in FIGURE 6.71.

6.71   KEEP a,d,f.
AN ORBIT CLASS OF THE GRAPH OF FIGURE 6.70.

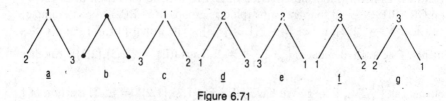

Figure 6.71

The diagram for a graph G such as shown in Figure 6.71(b) is a convenient symbolic way of representing the orbit or isomorphism class of G. We shall call such a diagram an *orbit diagram* for G. Such diagrams, as mentioned above, are often called "unlabeled graphs." We prefer not to use that terminology here, since "labeled graphs" will, for us, be graphs plus something extra (called labels). When these labels are removed we again have graphs as we have defined them, not orbit classes as above.

Orbit classes for ordered graphs may be defined in exactly the same manner. Consider, for example, the graph G of EXAMPLE 6.8 with vertex set {a,b,c,d} = V. Let $\begin{pmatrix} a & b & c & d \\ b & c & d & a \end{pmatrix}$ be in PER(V). This permutation is applied both to the edge set and to the adjacency table of G to obtain the resulting ordered graph as shown in FIGURE 6.72.

6.72   THE PERMUTATION $f = \begin{pmatrix} a & b & c & d \\ b & c & d & a \end{pmatrix}$ APPLIED TO THE EXAMPLE 6.8.

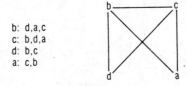

b: d,a,c
c: b,d,a
d: b,c
a: c,b

Figure 6.72

The orbit class of the ordered graph of FIGURE 6.72 can be specified by a diagram such as FIGURE 6.73. Order is indicated on incident edges by numerical labels.

6.73   THE ORBIT CLASS OF THE ORDERED GRAPH FIGURE 6.72.

Note: The numbers closest to a given vertex specify the order of the edges incident on that vertex.

Figure 6.73

Orbit classes of rooted trees have diagrams such as that of FIGURE 6.74.

6.74 THE ORBIT CLASS OF A ROOTED TREE (ROOT CIRCLED).

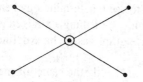

This type of structure is sometimes called a "rooted planar tree."

Figure 6.74

In the case of ordered rooted trees we draw the diagram in the standard manner with the root at the top and order specified by left to right orientation of edges as in FIGURE 6.75. In this manner the numerical labels used for ordered graphs in the general case are not required (see FIGURE 6.73) and the root is not circled.

6.75 THE ORBIT CLASS OF AN ORDERED ROOTED TREE.

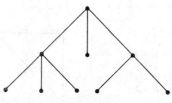

Figure 6.75

We now return to the discussion of "orderly algorithms." Referring to the ORDERLY ALGORITHM 6.67 and the discussion just preceding it, we take S to be the set of orbit diagrams of ordered rooted trees. The subset R will be a set of "canonical" diagrams. R will correspond in a natural way to the set of orbit diagrams of rooted trees (not ordered). The following definition is now necessary.

6.76 DEFINITION.

Let $\underline{T}$ be the orbit diagram of an *ordered* rooted tree T. The CODE($\underline{T}$) is the sequence obtained from the depth first sequence of edges of T, DFE(T) (see FIGURE 6.27 and DEFINITION 6.30) by replacing each first occurrence of an edge by 0 and each second occurrence by 1.

For example, the code of FIGURE 6.75 is 0010101101001011. This sequence is easily obtained geometrically by traversing FIGURE 6.75 in the same manner as indicated by the arrows of FIGURE 6.27(b). Each straight down arrow is replaced by a 0 and each straight up arrow is replaced by 1. When there is no danger of confusion, we shall write simply "tree" rather than "diagram of orbit class of a tree."

6.77   DEFINITION.

Canonical diagrams for ordered rooted trees: The orbit diagram $\underline{T}$ of an ordered rooted tree is canonical if it has one vertex or if

(1) Each principal subtree is canonical.
(2) The principal subtrees are arranged in nonincreasing order by size (number of vertices) from left to right.
(3) If two principal subtrees have the same size then the code (DEFINITION 6.76) of the one on the left is lexicographically less than or equal to the code of the one on the right.

There is a natural bijection between the *canonical* orbit diagrams of *ordered* rooted trees and orbit diagrams of rooted (not ordered) trees. The idea here is that when order does not matter for orbit diagrams of rooted trees we might as well always draw these diagrams such that they are canonical in the sense of DEFINITION 6.77. This drawing is unique and gives the desired bijection.

We now give an orderly algorithm for generating the canonical orbit diagrams R in the set of all orbit diagrams S of ordered rooted trees.

6.78   CANONICAL DIAGRAMS IN THE SENSE OF DEFINITION 6.77.
(a) IS CANONICAL   (b) IS NOT.

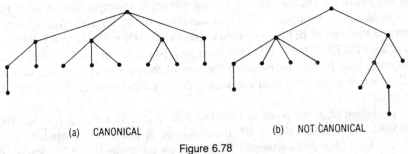

(a)   CANONICAL   (b)   NOT CANONICAL

Figure 6.78

We refer now to the ORDERLY ALGORITHM 6.67 and the preceding discussion. We classify the elements of S according to the number of edges i. The set S_i will be all orbit diagrams with i edges. S_1 contains only one element and it is canonical $(R_1 = S_1)$. We now must define the mapping B (of the ORDERLY ALGORITHM 6.67) from S'_{i+1} to S_i such that $B(R_{i+1}) \subseteq R_i$. As in most examples of orderly algorithms, we shall take $S'_i = S_i$. If $\underline{T}$ is in S_i, then $B(\underline{T})$ is the orbit diagram obtained by removing the preorder last edge from $\underline{T}$ (see DEFINITION 6.31). An example is shown in FIGURE 6.79. The pendant vertex is also removed.

6.79   THE BASIC MAPPING B FOR THE ORDERLY ALGORITHM.

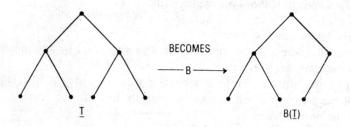

Figure 6.79

6.80   LEMMA.

If $\underline{T}$ is in R_{i+1} then $B(\underline{T})$ is in R_i.

Proof.   The proof is a trivial induction on the number of edges in $\underline{T}$. If there are just two edges the result is obvious. Otherwise, consider a $\underline{T}$ with p edges. Suppose the lemma is true for all $\underline{T}$ with fewer than p edges. Let $\underline{T}'$ denote the rightmost principal subtree of the root of $\underline{T}$. If $\underline{T}'$ has one edge then it is the preorder last edge of $\underline{T}$. In this case, it is immediate from the definition of R_i that $B(\underline{T})$ is in R_i. Otherwise, $B(\underline{T}')$ is the rightmost principal subtree of $B(\underline{T})$. By the induction hypothesis, $B(\underline{T}')$ is canonical (in R_j for some j). All other principal subtrees of $B(\underline{T})$ are canonical (DEFINITION 6.77(1)). As $\underline{T}$ satisfies (2) of DEFINITION 6.77, it is immediate that $B(\underline{T})$ does also. Condition (3) is also immediate if one observes that the size of the rightmost principal subtree of $B(\underline{T})$ is now *strictly* less than that of any other principal subtree. This completes the proof.

It is evident from the proof of LEMMA 6.80 that in fact $B(R_{i+1}) = R_i$. The ORDERLY ALGORITHM 6.67 requires that $B^{-1}(R_i)$ be computed, i = 1,2,. . .,k $-$ 1. For that we use the following rule for computing B^{-1}, described in 6.81.

6.81   RULE FOR COMPUTING B^{-1}.

Let $\underline{T}$ be in R_i. To compute $B^{-1}(\underline{T})$, construct one tree for each vertex of the stack of the preorder last vertex of $\underline{T}$ by adding an edge to that vertex.

An example of computing B^{-1} is given in FIGURE 6.82.

6.82   COMPUTING B^{-1}.
IN THIS EXAMPLE $\underline{T}$ IS NOT CANONICAL.

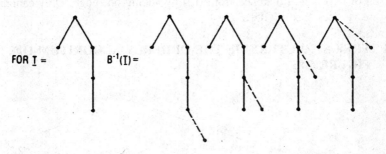

Figure 6.82

We now use the orderly algorithm to construct the first few R_i

6.83   CONSTRUCTION OF THE FIRST 4 R_i.
NC = NOT CANONICAL.

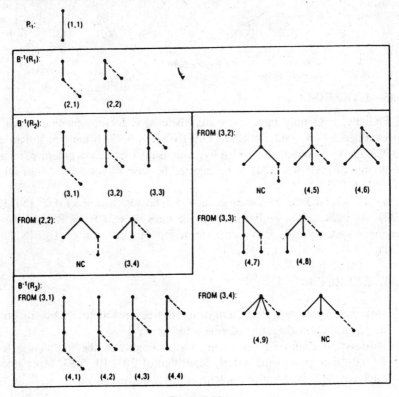

Figure 6.83

There is a natural tree structure on the trees (i,j) that are constructed by the orderly algorithm as in FIGURE 6.83. In this tree the root is (1,1). A tree (i′,j′) is a son of (i,j) if it is obtained from (i,j) by adding one edge. Only canonical trees are vertices. See FIGURE 6.84.

6.84   TREE STRUCTURE OF THE ORDERLY ALGORITHM OF FIGURE 6.83.

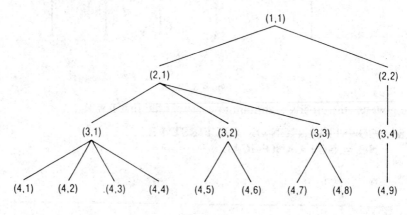

Figure 6.84

6.85   EXERCISE.

In FIGURE 6.83 only three trees are labeled NC for not canonical. All are rejected because of condition (2) of DEFINITION 6.77. If the tree structure of FIGURE 6.84 is continued through R_6, what is the first tree in preorder (relative to the tree of FIGURE 6.84) to be rejected because of condition (3) of DEFINITION 6.77?

In FIGURE 6.83 the trees were generated in breadth first order (DEFINITION 6.33). As indicated in FIGURE 6.84, the trees up to a fixed R_p can also be generated systematically in preorder (from depth first sequences, DEFINITION 6.31).

6.86   EXERCISE.

(1) How would you generate orbit diagrams of trees (not rooted)? Orbit diagrams of graphs? Orbit diagrams of connected graphs?

(2) Discuss the complexity of testing for canonicity in the sets of the form $B^{-1}(R_i)$ that arise in the orderly algorithm of FIGURE 6.83. More importantly, write a program to implement this orderly algorithm.

In FIGURE 6.65 all connected graphs with fixed vertex set are generated from all trees on that same vertex set with fixed root. These trees were generated there using the inverse Prüffer algorithm (INVPRU, procedure 6.21). These same trees can now be generated from the very different point of view of the orderly algorithm.

6.87 THE TREES OF FIGURE 6.65 OBTAINED FROM FIGURE 6.83. ALL ORBIT MEMBERS ARE ROOTED AT 0.

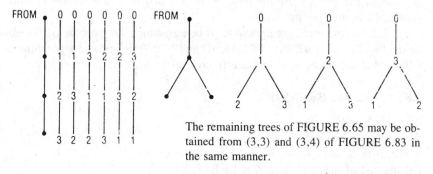

The remaining trees of FIGURE 6.65 may be obtained from (3,3) and (3,4) of FIGURE 6.83 in the same manner.

Figure 6.87

6.88 EXERCISE.

Complete the computation of the trees of FIGURE 6.87.

We have been applying the notion of a lineal spanning tree to the study of connected graphs. A graph that is connected in the sense that we have been discussing is sometimes called "1-connected." There are, as one might suspect from the terminology, notions of "2-connected," "3-connected," etc. Lineal spanning trees play an important role in the study of these higher orders of connectivity. Of particular importance are the notions of "2-connected" or "biconnected" graphs and "3-connected" or "triconnected" graphs. We shall study these cases in detail using lineal spanning trees. Before doing so, however, we consider briefly some other important ideas related to spanning trees.

6.89 DEFINITION.

Let $G = (V,E)$ be a graph and let $H = (V',E')$ be a subgraph. If $V' = V$ then H is called a *spanning subgraph* of G.

We have already introduced the idea of a *spanning forest* in DEFINITION 6.47.

6.90 DEFINITION.

Let $G = (V,E)$ be a graph. We define the *rank* of G, $r(G)$, to be the number of edges in a spanning forest of G. Let $e(G)$, $v(G)$, and $p(G)$ denote the number of edges, vertices, and components of G, respectively. We define the *nullity* of G, $n(G)$, to be $e(G) - r(G)$.

The terms "rank" and "nullity" come from the linear algebraic approach to graph theory in which the numbers $r(G)$ and $n(G)$ turn out to be the rank and nullity of a certain naturally defined linear transformation. If G is a graph and H a subgraph, then we use the notation $H + e$ and $H - e$ to denote H with e added and deleted, respectively.

Let G be a connected graph, and let H be a spanning subgraph of G. We now define two basic algorithms, BREAK(H) and JOIN(H). In these algorithms we require that the edges of G be linearly ordered: $e_1, e_2, \ldots, e_n$.

6.91   *procedure* BREAK(H).

initialize $K := H$;
for $i := n$ *step* -1 *until* 1 *do*
    if e_i is in K and $r(K) = r(K - e_i)$ *then* $K := K - e_i$;
{At the end of the procedure K is BREAK(H).}

6.92   *procedure* JOIN(H).

initialize $K := H$;
for $i := 1$ *step* 1 *until* n *do*
    if e_i is in G but not in K and $n(K) = n(K + e_i)$ *then* $K := K + e_i$;
{At the end of the procedure K is JOIN(H).}

In EXERCISE 6.94(2), the reader is asked to show that, for e_i in K, $r(K) = r(K - e_i)$ if and only if e_i belongs to some cycle in K. Similarly, for e_i in G but not in K, $n(K) = n(K + e_i)$ if and only if the endpoints of e_i lie in different components of K. With these characterizations in mind we give an example of the execution of BREAK and JOIN in EXAMPLE 6.93.

6.93   EXAMPLE OF BREAK AND JOIN.

Graph G with edges 1,2,. . .,13;
subgraph H shown by solid lines

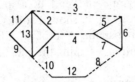

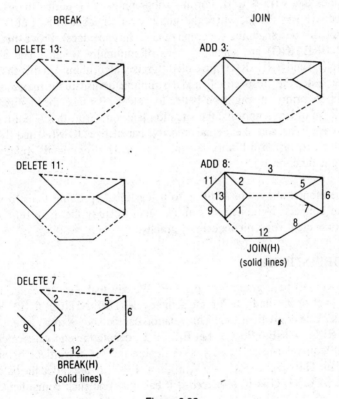

Figure 6.93

6.94   EXERCISE.

(1) Let $G = (V,E)$ be a graph. Prove that the number of edges in a spanning forest F of G is independent of the choice of F. This justifies the definition of $r(G)$, the rank of G, given in DEFINITION 6.90. Show that in fact $r(G) = v(G) - p(G)$.

(2) Let K be a spanning subgraph of G. If e is an edge of K, show that r(K) = r(K − e) if and only if e lies on some cycle of K. If e is in G but not in K, show that n(K) = n(K + e) if and only if the endpoints of e lie in different components of K. (In other words, K + e has one less component than K.)

(3) Let G be a connected graph and let T be a spanning tree for G. If e is an edge of G but not an edge of T, show that there exists an edge f of T such that (T − f) + e is a spanning tree of G. Characterize all such f. *Hint:* Consider the unique path in T joining the endpoints of e. Choose f from this path.

(4) Let G = (V,E) be a connected graph with E linearly ordered: $e_1, e_2, \ldots, e_n$. Let w: E → R be a mapping from E to the real numbers R such that i < j implies that w(i) ≤ w(j). For any subgraph K of G, define the *weight* of K to be w(K) = Σ w(e) where the sum is over all edges of K. Let D = (V,ϕ) be the discrete spanning subgraph of G (D has no edges). Prove that JOIN(D) and BREAK(G) are spanning trees of minimum weight. The algorithms JOIN(D) and BREAK(G) are called "greedy algorithms" in this case because at each step they respectively add the minimal or discard the maximal relevant edge. A priori, it might be better to not always take the minimal weight edge (in order to improve the situation later on). But, this is not required in this case. What sort of extremal property characterizes JOIN(H) and BREAK(H) in the case of an arbitrary spanning graph H ("extremal" relative to the weight function w)?

As mentioned above, in addition to using lineal spanning trees to study the notion of connected graphs, we can use them to study the more refined notion of "2-connected" or "biconnected" graphs.

6.95   DEFINITION.

Let G = (V,E) be a graph with e,f $\in$ E. We say that e is "cycle equivalent" to f if e = f or if e and f lie on the same cycle (DEFINITION 6.10). We write $e_{\hat{c}}f$ if e is cycle equivalent to f. This relation can be shown to be an equivalence relation (EXERCISE 6.96(1)). Let $E_1, \ldots, E_p$ denote the equivalence classes of the cycle equivalence relation. Let V_i denote the set of vertices belonging to edges of E_i. The subgraphs $G_i = (V_i, E_i)$, i = 1,\ldots,p, are called the *biconnected components* of G. G is *biconnected* if it has only one such component.

6.96   EXERCISE.

(1) Show that "cycle equivalence" is an equivalence relation (DEFINITION 1.2, CHAPTER 1). *Hint:* Transitivity needs some thought.

(2) Let $G_i = (V_i, E_i)$ and $G_j = (V_j, E_j)$ be two distinct bicomponents of G. Prove that $V_i \cap V_j$ has at most one element. If x $\in$ $V_i \cap V_j$ then x is called an *articulation point* of G.

(3) Let G be a connected graph and let x, y, and z be three distinct vertices of G. Show that if every path from x to y must pass through z then z is an articulation point of G.

(4) Prove that a graph G is biconnected if and only if between every pair of distinct vertices there are two vertex disjoint paths (assume G has at least two edges).

The reader should note the general "global appearance" of the bicomponents of a connected graph G. FIGURE 6.97 shows a *possible* pattern of bicomponents in (a), an *impossible* (why?) pattern in (b). Note the "tree like" structure in FIGURE 6.97(a).

6.97   GENERAL PATTERN FOR BICOMPONENTS. LARGE DOTS ARE ARTICULATION POINTS.

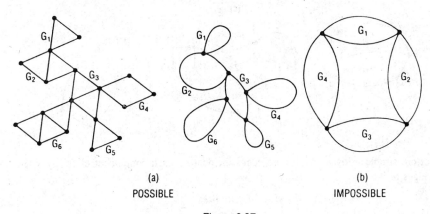

(a)
POSSIBLE

(b)
IMPOSSIBLE

Figure 6.97

In the second figure of (a) and in (b) the actual structure of the graph in the regions G_i is omitted.

6.98   THE BRIDGES OF A CYCLE IN A BICONNECTED GRAPH G.

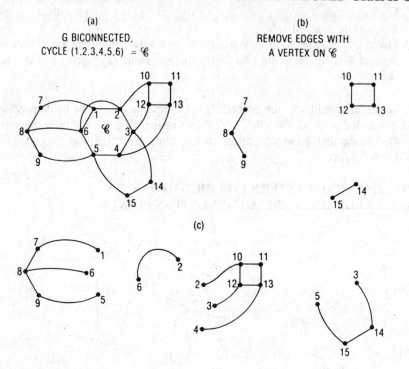

(a)

G BICONNECTED,
CYCLE (1,2,3,4,5,6) = 𝒞

(b)

REMOVE EDGES WITH
A VERTEX ON 𝒞

(c)

Restore simple bridges and restore edges incident on each component of (b) to obtain bridges of 𝒞.

Figure 6.98

6.99   A MORE FUNDAMENTAL VIEW OF BRIDGES OF A CYCLE.

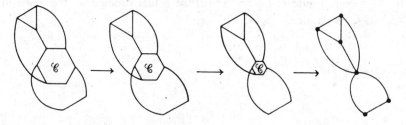

Start with a cycle 𝒞 in a biconnected graph G. Let the cycle 𝒞 shrink to a point. The edges of the biconnected components of the remaining graph are exactly the edges of the bridges in the original graph G.

Figure 6.99

We now develop the fundamental recursion for biconnected graphs. To do this, we need the notion of a *bridge* with respect to a cycle in a biconnected graph. This idea is illustrated in FIGURES 6.98 and 6.99 and EXERCISE 6.109.

6.100 DEFINITION.

Let H be a subgraph of a biconnected graph G. We define subgraphs of G called *bridges of* G *relative to* H. An edge of G that is not an edge of H is a bridge if both its vertices lie in H. Such a bridge is called a *simple bridge*. To define the other bridges, remove all vertices of H from G. Remove also all edges with a vertex in H (this includes all simple bridges and all edges of H). Let K be a component of the graph that is left. K together with all edges of G incident on K is a *bridge of* G *relative to* H. We are primarily interested in the case where H is a cycle $\mathscr{C}$ of G. (See FIGURE 6.98.)

The geometric idea behind the notion of a bridge relative to a cycle $\mathscr{C}$ is easy to visualize. Another way of presenting the same idea is shown in FIGURE 6.99. This approach to the notion of a bridge extends to structures called "matroids" and is thus a more fundamental way to look at bridges. We shall consider matroids in Chapter 10.

6.101 DEFINITION.

Let $\mathscr{C}$ be a cycle in a graph G and let B be a bridge relative to this cycle. Let $\mathscr{C}$ + B be the graph formed by taking the union of the edges in $\mathscr{C}$ and B. $\mathscr{C}$ + B is called a $\mathscr{C}$-bicomponent of the cycle.

The reader is asked to show in EXERCISE 6.109(2) that a $\mathscr{C}$-bicomponent is a biconnected graph if G is biconnected.

6.102 DEFINITION.

Let $\mathscr{C}$ + B be a $\mathscr{C}$-bicomponent. If e is an edge of $\mathscr{C}$ then $\mathscr{C}' = \mathscr{C} - e$ is called a *broken cycle* ($\mathscr{C}'$ is simply a path). The bicomponent of $\mathscr{C}'$ + B that contains B is called the *carrier* of B relative to the *broken cycle* $\mathscr{C}'$.

The reader is asked to show in EXERCISE 6.109(3) that B is in fact contained in a single bicomponent of $\mathscr{C}'$ + B. The carriers of the four bridges of the cycle $\mathscr{C}$ of FIGURE 6.98 are shown in FIGURE 6.103. In general, if $\mathscr{C}' = (v_1, v_2, \ldots, v_k)$ where e = $\{v_1, v_k\}$, let v_i be the first vertex and v_j be the last vertex of $\mathscr{C}'$ that are vertices of B. Then the carrier of B in $\mathscr{C}'$ + B is simply B together with the edges and vertices of the path $(v_i, \ldots, v_j)$.

6.103   THE CARRIERS OF THE BRIDGES OF FIGURE 6.98.
$\mathscr{C}' = (2,3,4,5,6,1)$

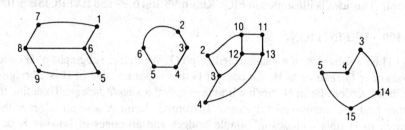

Figure 6.103

We are now prepared to describe the fundamental recursion for biconnected graphs. We do this by defining the *bicomponent tree* of a biconnected graph (DEFINITION 6.104).

6.104   DEFINITION.

A *bicomponent tree* of a biconnected graph is defined by the following rules:

(1) The root is the graph G together with a broken cycle $\mathscr{C}'$.
(2) Each internal vertex is a biconnected graph H together with a broken cycle $\mathscr{C}'$ in H.
(3) The sons of a vertex H are an ordered list of carriers (in H) of the bridges of H relative to $\mathscr{C}'$.
(4) A terminal vertex (leaf) of the bicomponent tree is an H that is itself a cycle. The broken cycle $\mathscr{C}'$ is omitted for a leaf.

A bicomponent tree of the graph of FIGURE 6.98 is shown in FIGURE 6.105. A bicomponent tree is an ordered rooted tree. There are, of course, many bicomponent trees associated with a graph G, depending on how the broken cycles are chosen and how the carriers are ordered. Two bicomponent trees for the complete graph K_5 are given in FIGURE 6.106. The complete graph K_n is a graph on n vertices in which every pair of vertices is an edge.

6.105   A BICOMPONENT TREE OF THE GRAPH OF FIGURE 6.98.

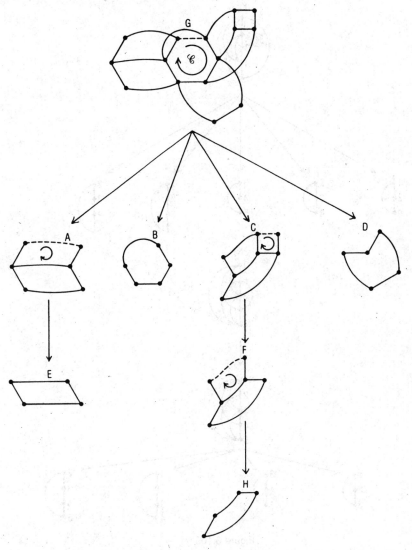

For vertex labels refer to FIGURES 6.98 and 6.103.

Figure 6.105

6.106   TWO BICOMPONENT TREES FOR K_5.

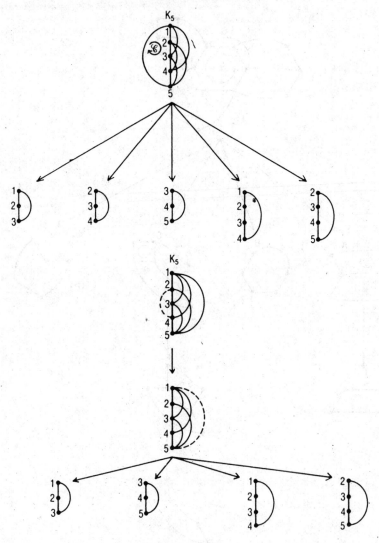

Figure 6.106

It is obvious from FIGURES 6.105 and 6.106 that there is much redundant information in the vertex labels of the bicomponent trees. Thus we introduce the idea of a *tree of cycles* or *cycle tree* of a biconnected graph.

6.107   DEFINITION.

Let $\mathcal{T}$ be the bicomponent tree of a biconnected graph G. Each internal vertex of $\mathcal{T}$ consists of a subgraph of G together with a broken cycle $\mathcal{C}'$ (obtained from a cycle $\mathscr{C}$ by removing an edge). If each such vertex is replaced by the cycle $\mathscr{C}$ (of the broken cycle $\mathscr{C}'$), then the resulting tree is called a *cycle tree* or *tree of cycles* of the graph G.

FIGURE 6.108 shows the tree of cycles corresponding to the bicomponent tree of FIGURE 6.105.

6.108 THE TREE OF CYCLES CORRESPONDING TO FIGURE 6.105.

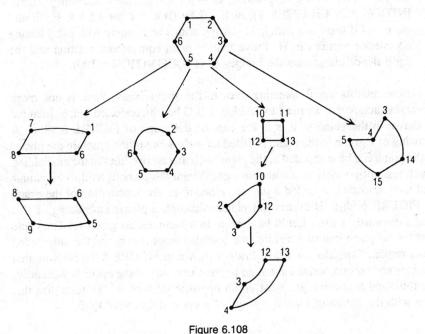

Figure 6.108

6.109 EXERCISE.

(1) Construct several nontrivial examples to illustrate the idea of *bridges, carriers, bicomponent tree,* and *cycle tree.*

(2) Let G be a biconnected graph and let $\mathscr{C}$ be a cycle in G. Prove that a bicomponent," $\mathscr{C} + B$ (see DEFINITION 6.101), is in fact a biconnected graph.

(3) Let $\mathscr{C} = (v_1, v_2, \ldots, v_k, v_1)$ be a cycle of a biconnected graph G. Let B be a bridge relative to $\mathscr{C}$. Let $\mathscr{C}' = (v_1, \ldots, v_k)$ and let v_i be the first and v_j be the last vertex of $\mathscr{C}'$ in B. Prove that $i = j$ never occurs (*Hint:* Use the fact that G is biconnected). Prove that the carrier of B relative to $\mathscr{C}'$ is B together with all vertices in the path $(v_i, \ldots, v_j)$. Call the path $(v_i, \ldots, v_j)$ the SPAN(B) relative to $\mathscr{C}'$.

(4) Let $\mathcal{T}$ be a bicomponent tree and $\mathcal{T}'$ be the corresponding cycle tree. Carefully describe data structures for representing $\mathcal{T}$ and $\mathcal{T}'$. Give an algorithm that constructs $\mathcal{T}$ from $\mathcal{T}'$ and discuss its complexity.

(5) Describe an algorithm that when given a biconnected graph G produces a bicomponent tree $\mathcal{T}$ and a cycle tree $\mathcal{T}'$. Discuss data structures and complexity.

(6) What happens if you try to construct the bicomponent tree for a graph G that is connected but not biconnected? Can you use this approach to give an algorithm for finding the biconnected components of a graph?

(7) Let H = (W,F) be a subgraph of G = (V,E). Define a relation $\sim$ (DEFINITION 1.2, CHAPTER 1) on E − F by (i) e $\sim$ e for all e $\in$ E − F and (ii) e $\sim$ f if there is a path in G starting with e and ending with f and having no interior vertices in H. Prove that $\sim$ is an equivalence relation and the equivalence classes are the bridges of H (DEFINITION 6.100).

Before relating lineal spanning trees to the above ideas, there is one more general structure that we need to develop. Let G be a biconnected graph. Imagine G drawn in the plane as it is in the case of the graph of FIGURE 6.98(a). A drawing of a graph in the plane is called an *embedding* of the graph in the plane. If the graph can be embedded in the plane such that no two lines in the embedding touch (except possibly at a common vertex) then the graph is said to be *planar* and the embedding is called a *planar embedding*. The embedding of the graph of FIGURE 6.98(a) is clearly not planar although a planar embedding of this graph obviously exists. Let $\mathcal{C}$ be a cycle in a biconnected graph G. The cycle divides the plane into two regions, the bounded inner region and the unbounded outer region. Consider the list of bridges shown in FIGURE 6.98(c). Note that the first and second bridge cannot go on the same side of the cycle $\mathcal{C}$. Similarly, the third and fourth bridges must go on opposite sides of $\mathcal{C}$. We formalize this idea with the notion of a *bridge graph* of a cycle, DEFINITION 6.110.

6.110 DEFINITION.

Let G be a biconnected graph and let $\mathcal{C}$ be a cycle in G. Let BRGR($\mathcal{C}$) = $(\mathcal{U},\mathcal{E})$ denote a graph which we call the *bridge graph* of $\mathcal{C}$ in G. The vertex set $\mathcal{U}$ is the set of bridges of the cycle $\mathcal{C}$. A pair of bridges {X,Y} is in $\mathcal{E}$ if X and Y cannot be embedded on the same side of $\mathcal{C}$ in any planar embedding of X $\cup$ Y $\cup$ $\mathcal{C}$.

As an example, consider the cycle $\mathcal{C}$ of FIGURE 6.98(a) and its list of bridges shown in FIGURE 6.98(c). Call the bridges in this list, left to right, A, B, C, and D. The bridge graph BRGR($\mathcal{C}$) = ({A,B,C,D}, {{A,B}, {C,D}}).

Again, let $\mathcal{C}$ be a cycle in a biconnected graph G and assume that all $\mathcal{C}$-bicomponents are planar (i.e., all subgraphs of the form $\mathcal{C}$ $\cup$ X, X a bridge of $\mathcal{C}$, are planar). Then G itself is planar if it is possible to place the various bridges of $\mathscr{C}$ inside the outside of $\mathscr{C}$ in such a way that no lines cross in the embedding. Such a placement of bridges can be thought of as a labeling of the vertices of the bridge graph with the two labels I (for inside $\mathscr{C}$) and O (for outside $\mathscr{C}$). A moment's thought (draw a few pictures) suggests the following lemma.

6.111 LEMMA.

Let $\mathscr{C}$ be a cycle in a biconnected graph G and assume that each $\mathscr{C}$-bicomponent is planar. Then G is planar if the vertices of BRGR($\mathscr{C}$) can be labeled with the two symbols I and O such that the vertices of every edge of BRGR($\mathscr{C}$) have different labels.

The idea behind LEMMA 6.111 is that vertices of an edge of BRGR($\mathscr{C}$) must go on opposite sides of $\mathscr{C}$ in any embedding and thus must have opposite labels. LEMMA 6.111 requires the intuitively obvious result that a closed simple curve in the plane has an inside region and an outside region. This result is known as the "Jordan Curve Theorem" in topology. In general, a graph G is called "2-colorable" or "bipartite" if its vertices can be labeled with two symbols (such as I and O) such that the two vertices of every edge are labeled differently. In EXERCISE 6.118(1) the reader is asked to show that a graph is bipartite if and only if it contains no cycle of odd length (odd number of edges).

The ideas in LEMMA 6.111 and the previous paragraph provide the basis for a number of algorithms to test whether or not a graph is planar. The obvious idea is to start with a biconnected graph G and a cycle $\mathscr{C}$ in G. If the graph being tested is not biconnected to begin with, then find its biconnected components and work with them, as a graph is planar if and only if each of its biconnected components is planar. Recursively, determine whether or not each of the $\mathscr{C}$-bicomponents is planar. If any $\mathscr{C}$-bicomponent is not planar then the graph G is not planar (why?). If all of the $\mathscr{C}$-bicomponents are planar then the graph G is planar if and only if BRGR($\mathscr{C}$) is bipartite. There is a slight hitch here, however! If $\mathscr{C}$ has only one bridge then the $\mathscr{C}$-bicomponent is G itself. One might instead work with the carrier of the one bridge. The carrier might be planar but G nonplanar, however. These complications are illustrated in FIGURE 6.112. These problems turn out to be minor ones. The reader is asked to consider them in EXERCISE 6.118(3).

6.112   A NONPLANAR GRAPH WITH ONE $\mathscr{C}$-BICOMPONENT AND PLANAR CARRIER.

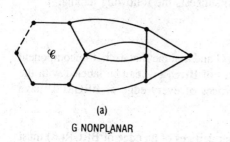

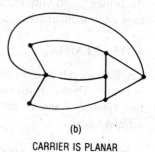

(a)   (b)

G NONPLANAR   CARRIER IS PLANAR

Figure 6.112

We shall now give a prototypic planarity algorithm based on the bicomponent tree of a biconnected graph G. This algorithm is intended as a rough guide to planarity testing (and is hence called the "sloppy planarity" algorithm). A more careful discussion will be given later on. Let $\mathscr{T}$ be a bicomponent tree of a biconnected graph G (see FIGURE 6.105, for example). Recall that each vertex X of $\mathscr{T}$ is a subgraph of G together with a broken cycle $\mathscr{C}'_X$. Recalling the notation for vectors, 6.42, let $(X,Y) \leftarrow L$, where L is a list of edges of $\mathscr{T}$, denote the operations of deleting the first edge of L and calling it (X,Y). The edge (X,Y) is directed away from the root (X is closer to the root of $\mathscr{T}$ than Y). Initially, we let L be the postorder list of edges of $\mathscr{T}$ (DEFINITION 6.31), designated by POSE$(\mathscr{T})$. For each vertex X of $\mathscr{T}$ we shall construct an embedding, EMBED(X). Initially, EMBED(X) is just the cycle $\mathscr{C}_X$.

6.113   *procedure* SLOPPY PLANARITY TEST.

begin
initialize L: = POSE$(\mathscr{T})$ ($\mathscr{T}$ a bicomponent tree of G)
        BRGR$(\mathscr{C}_X)$: = (ϕ,ϕ) for all vertices X of $\mathscr{T}$; (see DEFINITION 6.110)
        EMBED(X): = $\mathscr{C}_X$ embedded in the plane;
while L $\neq \phi$ *do*
   begin
      $(X,Y) \leftarrow L$;
      if $\mathscr{C}_X \cup Y$ is planar *then* add Y to BRGR$(\mathscr{C}_X)$ *else* STOP, G IS NON-PLANAR;
      if BRGR$(\mathscr{C}_X)$ is bipartite *then* add Y to EMBED(X) *else* STOP, G IS NONPLANAR;
   end
G IS PLANAR AND EMBED(G) IS AN EMBEDDING OF G
end

The SLOPPY PLANARITY TEST, *procedure* 6.113, is intended as an intuitive guide for "pencil and paper" execution only. The exact manner that Y is added to the bridge graph, BRGR($\mathscr{C}_x$), is not specified, the test to see if BRGR($\mathscr{C}_X$) is bipartite is not specified, and how Y is added to the embedding, EMBED(X), is not specified. We now give an example of the "execution" of the SLOPPY PLANARITY TEST in the example of FIGURE 6.105. We refer to the labels G,A,B,. . . of the vertices of the bicomponent tree of FIGURE 6.105.

6.114 SLOPPY PLANARITY TEST APPLIED TO FIGURE 6.105.

L: = (A,E),(G,A),(G,B),(F,H),(C,F),(G,C),(G,D).

(A,E) ← L: $\mathscr{C}_A \cup$ E is planar, so add E to BRGR($\mathscr{C}_A$) to get BRGR($\mathscr{C}_A$): = ({E},ϕ).
  BRGR($\mathscr{C}_A$) is bipartite so add E to EMBED(A) to get

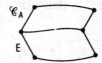

(G,A) ← L: $\mathscr{C}_G \cup$ A is planar, so add A to BRGR($\mathscr{C}_G$) to get BRGR($\mathscr{C}_G$): = ({A},ϕ).
  BRGR($\mathscr{C}_G$) is bipartite so add A to EMBED(G) to get

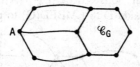

(G,B) ← L: $\mathscr{C}_G \cup$ B is planar, so add B to BRGR($\mathscr{C}_G$) to get ({A,B},{{A,B}}).
  BRGR($\mathscr{C}_G$) is bipartite so add B to EMBED(G) to get

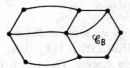

(F,H) ← L: $\mathscr{C}_F \cup$ H is planar, so add H to BRGR($\mathscr{C}_F$) to get ({H},ϕ).
  BRGR($\mathscr{C}_F$) is bipartite so add H to EMBED(F) to get

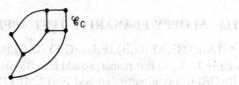

(C,F) ← L: $\mathscr{C}_C \cup$ F is planar, so add F to BRGR($\mathscr{C}_C$) to get ({F},ϕ).
    BRGR($\mathscr{C}_C$) is bipartite so add F to EMBED(C) to get

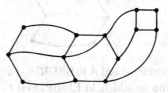

(G,C) ← L: $\mathscr{C}_G \cup$ C is planar, so add C to BRGR($\mathscr{C}_G$) to get ({A,B,C},{{A,B}}).
    BRGR(G) is bipartite so add C to EMBED(G) to get

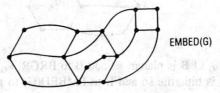

(G,D) ← L: $\mathscr{C}_G \cup$ D is planar, so BRGR($\mathscr{C}_G$):= ({A,B,C,D}, {{A,B}, {C,D}}).
    BRGR($\mathscr{C}_G$) is bipartite so add D to EMBED(G) to get

EMBED(G)

L = ϕ so STOP, G IS PLANAR

The reader is asked to explore some additional properties of the SLOPPY
PLANARITY TEST in EXERCISE 6.118. There is one very simple test of
planarity that works for some graphs. This test is stated in THEOREM 6.115
and proved in EXERCISE 6.118(4).

6.115 THEOREM.

If G = (V,E) is a connected planar graph with at least three edges then $|E| \leq$
$3|V| - 6$. If in addition G is bipartite then $|E| \leq 2|V| - 4$.

As an example, consider K_5, the complete graph on five vertices, and $K_{3,3}$, the complete bipartite graph on six vertices partitioned into two groups of 3. These graphs are shown in FIGURE 6.116.

6.116 K₅ and K₃,₃.

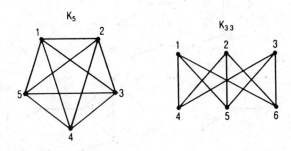

Figure 6.116

For K_5 the inequality $|E| \leq 3|V| - 6$ becomes $10 \leq 9$ and for $K_{3,3}$ the inequality $|E| \leq 2|V| - 4$ becomes $9 \leq 8$. Thus neither graph is planar.

Theorem 6.115 follows from a famous result of Euler that for any *connected* planar embedding of a graph $|V| - |E| + |R| = 2$ where $|R|$ is the number of "regions" in the embedding. It is very easy to see why this result is true. Consider the embedding of FIGURE 6.117. The regions are labeled r_1, r_2, r_3, and r_∞. The latter region is called the "unbounded region" (it would be just another bounded region if the embedding were on a sphere instead of the plane). The edge p of this embedding is called "pendant" because it has a vertex of degree 1. The edge e is not pendant and neither is the edge f. The edge f is called an "isthmus" as its removal disconnects the graph. If an edge such as e is removed (i.e., an edge that is not pendant and not an isthmus), then an embedding such as that shown in FIGURE 6.117(b) results. Call this a TYPE I deletion. Notice that a TYPE I deletion reduces $|E|$ by 1 and $|R|$ by 1. Thus a TYPE I deletion does not change the sum $|V| - |E| + |R|$. Also, the graph remains connected. A TYPE II deletion consists of removing a pendant edge and its vertex of degree 1 (see FIGURE 6.117(c)). A TYPE II deletion decreases $|V|$ by 1 and $|E|$ by 1 so again the sum is not changed. The reader can easily see by trying some examples that a series of TYPE I and TYPE II deletions will always reduce a connected planar embedding to the graph with one vertex and no edges. This graph (when embedded in the plane as a dot!) has one region, the unbounded region, and hence $|V| - |E| + |R| = 2$ for this embedding and thus for the original embedding also.

6.117   TYPE I AND TYPE II DELETIONS.

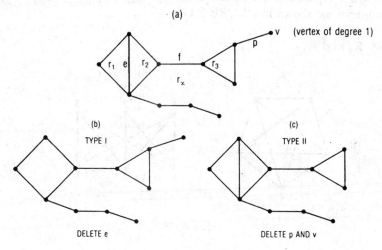

Figure 6.117

6.118   EXERCISE.

(1) A graph $G = (V,E)$ is *bipartite* if V can be partitioned into two sets $\{V_1, V_2\}$
    such that $e \in E$ implies that one vertex of e is in V_1 and the other is in V_2.
    G is *2-colorable* if the elements of V can be labeled with two symbols such
    that the two vertices of any edge have different symbols. Prove that G is
    bipartite if and only if G is 2-colorable. Prove that G is bipartite if and only
    if G has no cycles of odd length.

(2) Use the SLOPPY PLANARITY TEST, *procedure* 6.113, to show that K_5
    and $K_{3,3}$ (FIGURE 6.116) ARE NOT PLANAR.

(3) The SLOPPY PLANARITY TEST is a recursive procedure which, for each
    edge (X,Y) in the bicomponent tree, looks at the $\mathscr{C}_X$-bicomponent $\mathscr{C}_X \cup Y$.
    This is not a true recursion (reduction to simpler cases) if $\mathscr{C}_X$ has Y as its
    only bridge (see FIGURE 6.112). In this case, $X = \mathscr{C}_X \cup Y$. How can this
    problem be avoided to make the SLOPPY PLANARITY TEST a little less
    sloppy? (*Hint:* When can the cycle be changed to one that has at least two
    bridges?)

(4) Use the Euler relation, $|V| - |E| + |R| = 2$, to prove THEOREM 6.115.
    (*Hint:* Imagine a list ER of all pairs (e,r) where e is an edge "on the
    boundary" of region r. This means that all points of the edge are in contact
    with the region or "the closure of the region" in topological terms. Any
    edge can be paired with at most two regions. A pendant edge is paired with
    only one region. Under our assumptions a fixed region r must be paired with
    at least three edges or at least four if the graph is bipartite. Thus, in the

general case, we must have $3|R| \leq |ER| \leq 2|E|$ or $4|R| \leq |ER| \leq 2|E|$ in the bipartite case.)

It is a remarkable fact that by using lineal spanning trees and carefully chosen data structures the SLOPPY PLANARITY TEST can be converted into a planarity test that is (using the direct access model) linear in the number of vertices of the graph. This means that there is an algorithm and a constant c such that given any graph $G = (V,E)$, the algorithm decides in time less than or equal to $c|V|$ whether or not the graph is planar. The planar embedding, if it exists, can also be specified. Moreover, the algorithm is not a purely theoretical result of asymptotics and complexity arguments. The constant c is reasonable and the resulting algorithm appealing in practical terms. We shall, in CHAPTER 7, TOPIC I, develop in detail, using numerous examples, the basic ideas of this algorithm. One can make statements about the importance of planarity testing in applied problems (design of printed circuits, etc.) but this is risky ground. As the saying goes, "There is more than one way to skin a cat!." A better reason for us to look carefully at the linear time planarity algorithm is that it was a difficult problem to solve in the first place. Moreover, it deals with a problem of intrinsic mathematical interest that had been considered from different points of view by a number of good mathematicians. Thus it represents an excellent case study of a hard problem solved from the algorithmic point of view. The reader content with the SLOPPY PLANARITY TEST can skip to the discussions of triconnectedness or matroids, TOPICS III or IV, Chapter 9 or 10.

Chapter 7

Topic I: Depth First Search and Planarity

We begin with a quick review of certain basic ideas presented in Chapter 6. As in DEFINITION 6.6, let I_z denote the set of all edges of $G = (V,E)$ incident on $z \in V$. A graph G will be called *ordered* (DEFINITION 6.6) if for each $z \in V$ a linear order is specified on I_z. Technically, an ordered graph G is a triple $(V,E,\{(I_z, \leq_z): z \in V\})$ where the last component is a family of linear orders. We avoid this cumbersome notation. As in DEFINITION 6.28, let A_z denote the vertices adjacent to z. An ordering on A_z produces an ordering on I_z. A connected acyclic graph $T = (V,E)$ is a *tree* (DEFINITION 6.12). If in addition to T we specify a particular vertex $x \in V$ then the triple (V,E,x) is a *rooted tree* with *root* x (DEFINITION 6.23). If we delete x from V and delete all incident edges I_x from E, then the remaining graph (if not empty) will decompose into one or more connected components, themselves trees, which we call the *principal subtrees of the root* x (DEFINITION 6.28). If $T' = (V',E')$ is such a subtree then there is a unique $x' \in V'$ such that $\{x,x'\} \in I_x$. We make the convention that this x' is the *root of* T'. Any rooted tree $T = (V,E,x)$ has associated with it a natural *directed* rooted tree: to each edge $\{x,x'\}$ in I_x we assign the directed edge (x,x'), (i.e., directed "away from" the root). Recursively, we direct the edges of the subtrees of the root x to obtain a directed rooted tree which we also denote by $T = (V,E,x)$ (see DEFINITION 6.25). Using this convention we may regard any rooted tree as a directed graph, and we do so whenever it is convenient. When we speak of a *directed rooted tree* we mean directed in the above sense unless otherwise specified. The most basic structure for describing algorithms is the *ordered (directed) rooted tree*, ORTR (FIGURE 6.27, DEFINITION 6.28, and paragraph following DEFINITION 6.28). An ORTR is shown in FIGURE 7.1. The ordering on A_z is first the father of z, and then the sons, left to right (see NOTATION FOR TREES, 6.41).

Given an ordered (directed) rooted tree $T = (V,E,x)$ let $T_1 = (V_1,E_1,x_1),\ldots,T_k = (V_k,E_k,x_k)$ be the rooted subtrees of x in order. We define a sequence of edges DFE(T) ("depth first" sequence of edges) and a sequence of vertices DFV(T) ("depth first" sequence of vertices) as follows (see DEFINITION 6.30 also):

(1) If $V = \{x\}$ then DFV(T) = x and if $E = \{(x,y)\}$ then DFE(T) = (x,y),(x,y).

(2) *Otherwise*:
   DFE(T) = $(x,x_1),DFE(T_1),(x,x_1),\ldots,(x,x_k),DFE(T_k),(x,x_k)$
   DFV(T) = $x,DFV(T_1),x \ldots x,DFV(T_k),x.$

These lists, for the directed ordered rooted tree of FIGURE 7.1(a) are given in FIGURE 7.1. The intuitive interpretation of these lists comes from FIGURE 7.1(b) as follows: Follow the arrows around the tree as shown. To construct DFE(T) list each edge as it is traversed (forward or backward). To construct DFV(T) start with the root, *a*, and list each vertex when it is encountered (thus "*a*" is listed four times in FIGURE 7.1).

The reader should recall the definitions of a *spanning forest* and *spanning tree* given in DEFINITION 6.47.

7.1 MORE DEPTH-FIRST SEQUENCES.

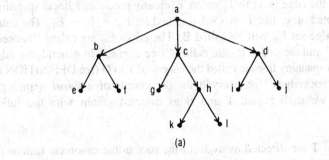

(a)

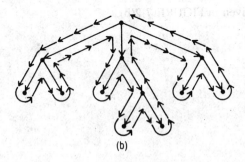

(b)

Figure 7.1

DFE(T) = (a,b),(b,e),(b,e),(b,f),(b,f),(a,b),(a,c),(c,g),(c,g),(c,h),(h,k)
            (h,k),(h,l),(h,l),(c,h),(a,c),(a,d),(d,i),(d,i),(d,j),(d,j),(a,d)
DFV(T) = a,b,e,b,f,b,a,c,g,c,h,k,h,l,h,c,a,d,i,d,j,d,a

Given any rooted tree $T = (V',E',x')$, we say that two vertices $w_1, w_2 \in V'$ are lineal with respect to T if $w_1 = w_2$ or they lie on the same directed path of T. If the path leads from w_1 to w_2 (or $w_1 = w_2$) we say that w_1 is an *ancestor* of w_2, and w_2 is a *descendant* of w_1. A rooted spanning tree $T = (V,E_T,x)$ is a *lineal* spanning tree for $G = (V,E)$ if $\{s,t\} \in E - E_T$ implies that s and t are lineal in T (DEFINITION 6.49, EXAMPLE 6.50). Given any connected graph $G = (V,E)$ and any $x \in V$, then there always exists a lineal spanning tree $T = (V,E_T,x)$ for G. This result was proved in THEOREM 6.52 and an algorithm given in *procedure* 6.56. An alternative proof was suggested in EXERCISE 6.54 and EXAMPLE 6.55.

It is worthwhile to understand both points of view, so we now discuss briefly the latter. Let $\{x,y\} \in I_x$. Referring to FIGURE 7.2, let $\bar{V}_y$ denote the set of all $s \in V$ for which no simple path from s to x includes y. Let $V_y = V - \bar{V}_y$. We assume $x \in \bar{V}_y$. Let G_y denote the restriction of G to V_y (all $\{s,t\}$ of G with $\{s,t\} \subseteq V_y$) and $\bar{G}_y$ the restriction of G to $\bar{V}_y$. From the definition of $\bar{V}_y$, the only possible edges of G not in either G_y or $\bar{G}_y$ are edges of the form $\{x,z\}$ for $z \in V_y$. Recursively we may construct lineal spanning trees T_y for G_y and $\bar{T}_y$ for $\bar{G}_y$. Adding the edge $\{x,y\}$ to T_y union $\bar{T}_y$ clearly produces a lineal spanning tree T for G rooted at x. Let $T = (V,E_T,x)$ and let $E_B = E - E_T$. The subgraph of G with edge set E_B will be called B. The edges E_B are called "backedges" or "fronds" and the edges E_T are called "tree edges." In general, the edges of $E - E_T$, T a spanning tree are called the *chords* of T in G (see DEFINITION 6.47). The term "backedges" is reserved for the chords of a *lineal* spanning tree. Henceforth we shall regard T and B as directed graphs with the following conventions:

(1) Edges of T are directed away from the root in the canonical fashion.
(2) If $(s,t) \in E_B$ then s is a descendant of t in T.

An example is given in FIGURE 7.2(b).

7.2   BASIC RECURSION FOR LINEAL SPANNING TREES.

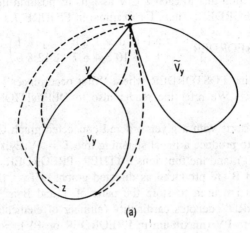

(a)

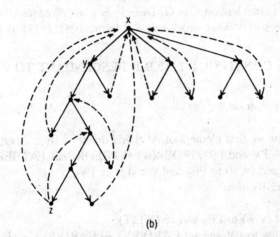

(b)

Solid arrows are edges of E_T, dashed arrows are edges of E_B.

Figure 7.2

This recursive description of the lineal spanning tree T and directed graph of backedges B (FIGURE 7.2) suggests a simple recursive algorithm for constructing T and B. First some preliminary remarks. Given an ordered directed rooted tree $T = (V,E_T,x)$ we define two functions FATHER and PREORDER on V. If $t \neq x$ then FATHER(t) is the unique $s \in V$ such that $(s,t) \in E_T$. The *preorder* linear order on V is the order specified by the sequence of first occurrences of the elements of V in the list DFV(T). For example, in the sequence DFV(T) of FIGURE 7.1 we extract just those entries z that represent a first occurrence of z to get a b e f c g h k l d i j, which is the preorder linear order of V for this example. The function that to each $z \in V$ assigns its position in preorder on V will be called PREORDER. Thus, for example in FIGURE 7.1

$$\text{PREORDER} = \begin{pmatrix} a\ b\ c\ \ d\ \ e\ f\ g\ h\ i\ \ j\ \ k\ \ l \\ 1\ 2\ 5\ 10\ 3\ 4\ 6\ 7\ 11\ 12\ 8\ 9 \end{pmatrix}.$$

Similarly, we define POSTORDER where "first occurrences" is replaced by "last occurrences." We refer the reader also to DEFINITION 6.30 and the related discussion.

Procedure 7.3 starts with a given ordered connected graph $G = (V,E)$ and $x \in V$. We wish to produce a lineal spanning tree $T = (V,E_T,x)$, DFE(T), the graph $B = (V_B,E_B)$, and the functions FATHER, PREORDER, and POSTORDER. Both T and B are produced as directed graphs. $PT = (PV,PE_T,x)$ and $PB = (PV_B,PE_B)$ are used to store the parts of T and B as they are being constructed. "CARD" denotes cardinality (number of elements) and v is the last vertex added to PV (maximum in PREORDER on PV). For each $v \in V$, A(v) initially is the list of vertices of G adjacent to v. A(v) is ordered by the order on edges I_v incident on v in G. DFE(T) is a list of edges (the depth-first sequence of edges of T when *procedure* 7.3 terminates). POST is an integer.

7.3 *procedure* CONSTRUCT T AND B DESCENDANT TO v.

begin
    while A(v) $\neq$ ϕ *do*
      begin
             w $\leftarrow$ first element of A(v) and delete w from A(v);
         if w $\in$ PV and PREORDER(w) $<$ PREORDER(FATHER(v)) *then*
             add (v,w) to PE_B and v and w to PV_B;
         if w $\notin$ PV *then*
         begin
         add (v,w) to PE_T and to DFE(T);
         add w to PV and set CARD(PV) $\leftarrow$ CARD(PV) + 1;
         FATHER(w) $\leftarrow$ v;
         PREORDER(w) $\leftarrow$ CARD(PV);
         CONSTRUCT T AND B DESCENDANT TO w;
         end
    end
    POST $\leftarrow$ POST + 1 and POSTORDER(v) $\leftarrow$ POST;
    if v $\neq$ x *then* add (FATHER(v),v) to DFE(T);
end

To construct T and B we set $PT = (\{x\},\phi,x)$, $PB = (\phi,\phi)$, PREORDER(x) = 1, POST $\leftarrow$ 0, CARD = 1, DFE(T) = ϕ and execute CONSTRUCT T AND B DESCENDANT TO x. At the end T = PT, B = PB.

7.4 COMMENTS.

(1) One can show that the above algorithm can be implemented in linear time in $|E|$ for connected graphs, $|E| + |V|$ in general. See EXERCISE 7.7(2).

(2) The statement "*if* w $\in$ PV and PREORDER(w) < PREORDER (FATHER(v)) *then*. . ." tests that (v,w) is a backedge not yet added to PB. The condition, if true, assures us that w is an ancestor of v other than the father of v.

(3) If G = (V,E) is planar, then it is a consequence of Euler's theorem on planar graphs that $|E| \leqslant 3|V| - 6$ (THEOREM 6.115, EXERCISE 6.118(4)). Suppose G is nonplanar and we apply the above procedure to each component G′ of G, keeping a count of all edges in PB′ $\cup$ PT′ at each stage of the computation for that component. If this count ever gets to 3 CARD(PV′) − 5 then we have a connected nonplanar subgraph of that component. If not, we keep the component just inspected and go to the next component. In this way we can determine a nonplanar subgraph $\bar{G} = (\bar{V},\bar{E})$ of G with $|\bar{E}| \leqslant 3 |V| - 5$. This observation is sometimes useful in dealing with nonplanar graphs, for it reduces the general case to that where the number of edges is bounded by a fixed linear function of the number of vertices. This reduction can be carried out in linear time in $|\bar{V}|$ provided one assumes that the graph G is already given and represented by a suitable data structure (such as that of FIGURE 6.57). Of course, if the graph G has to be rewritten or scanned completely prior to the computation then all edges of E must be dealt with and linearity is destroyed in the general case. Even in this case, however, the reduction might be useful in reducing the constants involved in the computation.

In DEFINITION 6.95, we defined the notion of "cycle equivalence" of edges of a graph. That is to say, we defined a relation $\sim$ on E by $e_1 \sim e_2$ if $e_1 = e_2$ or if there is an elementary (not self-intersecting) cycle of G containing both e_1 and e_2. Clearly $\sim$ is reflexive and symmetric. Less clear, but easily shown, is transitivity: $e_1 \sim e_2$ and $e_2 \sim e_3$ implies $e_1 \sim e_3$ (EXERCISE 6.96(1)). Thus, $\sim$ is an equivalence relation. The subgraphs of G determined by the equivalence classes are called the *biconnected components* ("bicomponents") of G, (DEFINITION 6.95). If $G_1 = (V_1,E_1)$ and $G_2 = (V_2,E_2)$ are two biconnected components of G then either $V_1 \cap V_2 = \phi$ or $|V_1 \cap V_2| = 1$. If x $\in V_1 \cap V_2$ then x is called an *articulation point* of G (EXERCISE 6.96(2,3)).

We indicate how one finds the biconnected components of a graph efficiently. Given an ordered connected graph G = (V,E) and x $\in$ V, construct the ordered directed graphs $T = (V,E_T,x)$ and $B = (V_B,E_B)$ as above.

7.5 DEFINITION.

For any e = (a,b) in E_T define LOW1(e) (the "first lowpoint" of e) to be the minimum of

(1) PREORDER(b)
    and
(2) The minimum value of PREORDER(t) over all $(s,t) \in E_B$ with s a descendant
    of b (including $s = b$) in T.

If we exclude from (2) above all vertices t such that PREORDER(t) = LOW1(e)
and again minimize over (1) and (2) we obtain LOW2(e) (the "second lowpoint"
of e). Note that PREORDER(b) $\geqslant$ LOW2(e) > LOW1(e) unless LOW1(e) =
PREORDER(b).

The LOW1 function may be computed recursively by examining E_T in postorder. Given $f = (p,q)$ in E_T, the edges $f_1, \ldots, f_s$ incident on q (directed away
from q) are less than f in postorder. We assume inductively that LOW1 has been
computed for all $f' < f = (p,q)$ in postorder. Let $m_1 = \text{MIN}\{\text{LOW1}(f_i); i =
1, \ldots, s\}$ and $m_2 = \text{MIN}\{\text{PREORDER}(z): (q,z) \in E_B\}$ (set $m_1 = \infty$ or $m_2 =
\infty$ if the corresponding set is empty). Then LOW1(f) =
$\text{MIN}\{m_1, m_2, \text{PREORDER}(q)\}$. It is easily seen that LOW1 can be computed in
linear time in $|E|$. Similarly LOW2 can be computed in linear time in $|E|$. If b
is not assumed connected, these computations are linear in $|V| + |E|$. *For* $e =
(a,b) \in E_B$ *we adopt the convention that* LOW1(e) = PREORDER(b) *and*
LOW2(e) = PREORDER(a).

Let $e = (a,b)$ be an edge of E_T. We say that an edge $e' = (a',b')$ is *descendant
to* e *in* T if $e' = e$ or a' is a descendant of b (as defined above for vertices).

7.6 COMPUTING BICOMPONENTS.

To compute the biconnected components ("bicomponents") of a connected graph
$G = (V,E)$, scan E_T in postorder until the first edge $f = (p,q)$ is found with
LOW1(f) $\geqslant$ PREORDER(p) (if p is the root of T this inequality must hold).
The set of tree edges of the first bicomponent is the set of all f' in E_T descendant
to f (a consecutive sequence of edges prior to f in postorder). The set of backedges
of the first bicomponent consists of all edges of E_B incident on vertices p'
descendant to q. Delete this list of edges from $E_T \cup E_B$ and continue through
E_T in postorder until the next edge $f = (p,q)$ is found such that LOW1(f) $\geqslant$
PREORDER(p), etc.

7.7 EXERCISE.

(1) In *procedure* 6.56 we gave an algorithm for computing a lineal spanning
    tree of a graph G based on the ideas of the proof of THEOREM 6.52. The
    algorithm described in *procedure* 7.3 is based on the recursive description
    (EXERCISE 6.54, FIGURE 6.55, FIGURE 7.2). Modify *procedure* 6.56
    to compute the same structures as *procedure* 7.3.
(2) Discuss the complexity of *procedure* 7.3 or your alternative version based
    on *procedure* 6.56. Describe data structures.

(3) Write a more formal description of the algorithm for computing the bicomponents of a graph outlined in 7.6, above (pidgin ALGOL or, better yet, a working program). Prove that *procedure* 7.6 actually works. (*Hint*: Suppose that e = (a,b) ≠ f is an edge descendant to f = (p,q), where f is as described in *procedure* 7.6. By construction, of·f, LOW1(e) < PREORDER(a). Thus, if a′ is the FATHER(a) then (a′,a) lies on a cycle with (a,b). Referring to the edge (a′,a) as the *father* of the edge (a,b), we have shown that each such edge e descendant to f is cycle equivalent to its father and thus, by transitivity, equivalent to f. The condition LOW1(f) ⩾ PREORDER(p) clearly implies that p is an articulation point of G and thus we see that the set of edges removed is indeed a bicomponent of G. The fact that the set of tree edges removed defines a consecutive sequence in postorder, POSE(T), gives the basis for an inductive proof.)

Thus far we have, given a connected, ordered graph G = (V,E), discussed the decomposition of G into an ordered, rooted, directed spanning tree T = (V,E_T,x) and a directed graph or backedges B = (V_B,E_B). The order on T and B is that inherited from G. *We assume henceforth that G is biconnected.* We have discussed the functions PREORDER, LOW1, and LOW2. We now consider another ordering of T and B that greatly facilitates subsequent computations. Using the notation X(*statement*) = 0 if *statement* = false and 1 if *statement* = true, we associate with each f = (p,q) ∈ E_T ∪ E_B the triple (PREORDER(p), LOW1(F), X(LOW2(f) < PREORDER(p))). Recall that for f = (p,q) in E_B, LOW1(F) = PREORDER(q) and LOW2(f) = PREORDER(p). We can, in time linear in |E| (see CHAPTER 1, FIGURE 1.24, LEXICOGRAPHIC BUCKET SORT) sort these triples in lexicographic order. First in this list will be all edges incident on the vertex v = x (the root of T) then all those edges f incident on the vertex v with PREORDER(v) = 2, etc. For a fixed vertex p, the incident edges f of T ∪ B will be sorted first according to LOW1(f). Next, given LOW1(f) = LOW1(f′) for two edges f = (p,q), f′ = (p,q′) incident to p, f will come before f′ if LOW2(f) ⩾ PREORDER(p) but LOW2(f′) < PREORDER(p). Note that, due to biconnectedness, if p ≠ x then LOW1(f) < PREORDER(p). Thus, considering all edges of T ∪ B incident to a fixed vertex p and having the same LOW1 value, all edges f = (p,q) with LOW2(f) ⩾ PREORDER(p) come first in the sorted list of edges. Within this class of edges (incident to p, same LOW1 value and LOW2 ⩾ p) and within the complement of this class (incident to p, same LOW1 value, LOW2 > p) the order is arbitrary depending on exactly how the bucket sort was carried out.

Using the above linear order on edges, we convert the ordered, directed, rooted graph T ∪ B into another such graph T̄ ∪ B̄ with only the order changed. We call this graph, together with T and B, a *properly ordered decomposition* of G. Thus to specify such a decomposition we need T = (V,E_T,x), an ordered, directed, rooted, lineal, spanning tree; B = (V_B,E_B) the associated ordered directed graph. The orders on T and B are inherited from the order on G and the order on $\bar{T} \cup \bar{B}$ is as just described above. The functions PREORDER and POSTORDER still refer to T, not the new ordered tree $\bar{T}$.

7.8 CONVENTION.

By using the function PREORDER, we can replace each vertex $v \in V$ by the integer PREORDER(v). *Henceforth we assume that* $v = $ PREORDER(v) (relative to T).

We now discuss an example. Consider the graph embedding of FIGURE 7.9. The vertices have been given the PREORDER labeling relative to the ordered spanning tree T. T and B are not shown explicitly in FIGURE 7.9 but can be reconstructed immediately from the PREORDER numbers and the given embedding. The graph $\bar{T} \cup \bar{B}$ is shown in FIGURE 7.10. The edges E_B are dashed arrows, the edges E_T are solid arrows. The order on edges (of $\bar{T} \cup \bar{B}$) incident on a vertex p is obtained by reading counterclockwise starting at 12 o'clock. The order on edges incident to p is the order in which they are encountered locally at p when read in this manner. We shall only be concerned with the order on edges e with TAIL(e) = p (the edges directed away from p). TABLE 7.11 shows the adjacency table for the ordered directed graph $\bar{T} \cup \bar{B}$.

7.9   A GRAPH EMBEDDING WITH PREORDER LABELS.

Figure 7.9

7.10 A PROPERLY ORDERED DECOMPOSITION T̂ ∪ B̄ OF THE GRAPH OF FIGURE 7.9.

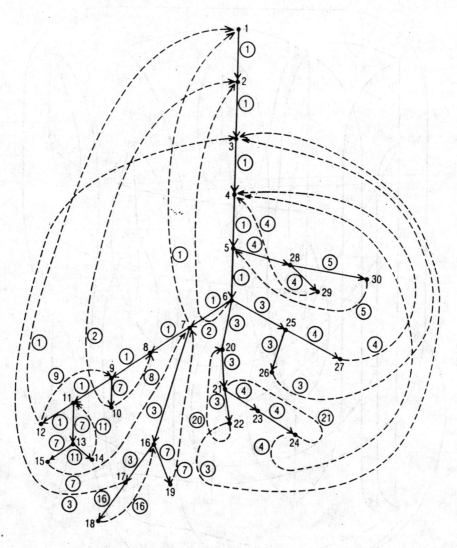

Circled edge labels are LOW1 values

Figure 7.10

7.11 ADJACENCY TABLE FOR Ť ∪ B̄ OF FIGURE 7.10.

Table 2.1

1	2	16	17,19
2	3	17	3,18
3	4	18	16
4	5	19	7
5	6,28	20	21
6	7,2,20,25	21	22,23
7	1,8,16	22	3,20
8	9	23	24
9	11,10	24	4,21
10	2,8	25	26,27
11	12,13	26	3
12	1,9	27	4
13	15,14	28	29,30
14	11	29	4
15	7	30	5

7.12 REMARKS.

(1) The order of directed edges incident on the vertex 6 in FIGURE 7.10 is $(6,7),(6,2),(6,20),(6,25)$. Notice that LOW2(6,20) = 4 and LOW2(6,25) = 4. Thus χ(LOW2(6,20) < PREORDER(6) = 6) = 1 and χ(LOW2(6,25) < 6) = 1. By our previous remarks, the order of these two edges could have been reversed in the ordering on Ť.

(2) At vertex 9 the order on edges of Ť ∪ B̄ is $(9,11),(9,10)$. Both edges are in Ť. According to the definition of PREORDER, the order of these edges is reversed in T. Thus the orders on T and Ť are not the same.

Given a properly ordered decomposition T, B, Ť ∪ B̄ of an ordered graph G, we define a new tree PATR(G,T) called the *tree of paths* of G relative to T. This tree will be needed later to give a global description of the basic recursive structure that we shall use to construct the embeddings of a planar graph. Each path will in fact define a cycle in G. Thus the "tree of paths" defines a "tree of cycles" which is, in fact, a very special case of the tree of cycles of DEFINITION 6.107 and FIGURE 6.108. The special nature of the tree of paths is critical in the construction of an efficient planarity algorithm. To each edge $e = (a,b)$ in G we assign a path, PATH(e). If $e \in E_B$ then PATH(e) ← (e). If $e \notin E_B$ then PATH(e) will be a sequence of edges PATH(e) = $(e_1,e_2,. . .,e_k)$ defined by *procedure* 131 (if $e = (a,b)$, define a = TAIL(e), b = HEAD(e)).

7.13   *procedure* PATH(e). [e = (TAIL(e), HEAD(e))]

begin

      if e $\in$ E_B *then*

           PATH(e) $\leftarrow$ (e)

      else

           begin

                    f $\leftarrow$ first edge of $\bar{T} \cup \bar{B}$ incident on and directed from

                    HEAD(e); PATH(e) $\leftarrow$ (e,PATH(f)) [e added as first edge

                    to PATH(f)];

           end

    end

Thus to obtain PATH(e), e $\in$ T, one follows the sequence of first available edges (with respect to the ordering of $\bar{T} \cup \bar{B}$) until one encounters an edge in $\bar{B}$. If PATH(e) = $(e_1,\ldots,e_k)$, with $e_i = (a_i,b_i)$, then notice that $b_k = $ LOW1(e) (as a consequence of the ordering on $\bar{T} \cup \bar{B}$) and LOW1(e) $<$ a_1 if $a_1 \neq$ x (by biconnectedness of G). The reader should recall that we have assumed that for all v $\in$ V, v = PREORDER(v). If we addend to each PATH(e) the unique sequence of tree edges from b_k to a_1 we obtain a cycle that we call CYCLE(e). CYCLE(e) may be computed easily from the function FATHER discussed previously, once PATH(e) is known. The map PATH(e) $\to$ CYCLE(e) will convert the tree of paths (defined below) to a tree of cycles in the sense of DEFINITION 6.107.

7.14   DEFINITION.

We now define the directed ordered rooted "path tree," PATR(G,T). The vertices of PATR(G,T) will be a *subset* of the set {PATH(e): e $\in$ E(G)}. PATR(G,T) will be an ordered rooted tree. Since T is lineal and G is biconnected, there is only one edge d of T incident on the root x of T. The root of PATR(G,T) is PATH(d). In general, if PATH(e) is a vertex of PATR(G,T) then let PATH(e) = $(e_1,e_2,\ldots,e_k)$ where $e_i = (a_i,b_i)$. For each i = 1,$\ldots$,k, let $\bar{E}_{a_i}$ denote the ordered (in $\bar{T} \cup \bar{B}$) list of edges incident to a_i and let $\bar{E}[e_i] = \bar{E}_{a_i} - \{e_i\}$ be this list with e_i (the first entry) removed. Let $\mathscr{E}(e)$ denote the list of edges obtained by concatenating $\bar{E}[e_i]$, i $\geq$ 2, in reverse order: $\bar{E}[e_k], \bar{E}[e_{k-1}],\ldots,\bar{E}[e_2]$. In particular, if PATH(e) = (e) then $\mathscr{E}(e)$ is empty. The ordered list of edges incident on PATH(e) in PATR(G,T) is {(PATH(e),PATH(f)): f $\in$ $\mathscr{E}(e)$} where the order is that included by the order on $\mathscr{E}(e)$. In this manner we recursively construct PATR(G,T). (It is easily verified that the directed graph constructed by this process is a tree.)

FIGURE 7.15 gives PATR(G,T) for the example of FIGURE 7.10. If PATH(e) = $(e_1,\ldots,e_k)$ with $e_i = (a_i,b_i)$, then the sequence $a_1,\ldots,a_kb_k$ specifies PATH(e).

In each vertex of FIGURE 7.15, this sequence is written in reverse order to facilitate the planar representation of the tree. (For visual clarity, we have shown edges between vertices connecting the starting value a_1 of each son to the occurrence of a_1 in the string representing its father. This is intended as an aid to reading the tree and is not a part of the definition of PATR(G,T).) Note that each backedge occurs in exactly one path so the number of vertices of PATR(G,T) is $|E_B| = |E| - |V| + 1$ (the *nullity* of G, n(G), DEFINITION 6.90).

7.15 PATR(G,T) FOR FIGURE 7.10.

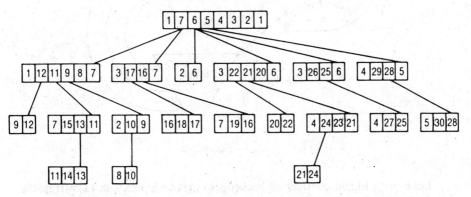

Note: PATH(e) = $(a_1,b_1) (a_2,b_2) \ldots (a_k,b_k)$ with $b_1 = a_2$, $b_2 = a_3, \ldots$, is given by the sequence $\boxed{b_k|a_k|a_{k-1}|\ldots|a_1}$.

Figure 7.15

Consider PATR(G,T) (DEFINITION 7.14, FIGURE 7.15). G = (V,E) is as above with PREORDER(v) = v for all v ∈ V. Observe that the set {PATH(e): PATH(e) a vertex of PATR(G,T)} defines a (set) partition of the set of edges E of G (the "blocks" of the partition are the sets of edges of the various paths, PATH(e)). The union of all subgraphs of $\tilde{T} \cup \tilde{B}$ of the form PATH(f) for PATH(f) a descendant of PATH(e) (including PATH(e)) in PATR(G,T) is a subgraph of $\tilde{T} \cup \tilde{B}$ which we call the *segment* of e in $\tilde{T} \cup \tilde{B}$. We denote this subgraph by SEG(e). The edges of SEG(e) contained in E_B will be called the *backedges* of SEG(e) and those contained in E_T will be called the *tree edges*. SEG(e) consists of all edges of T descendant to e = (a,b) and all backedges incident on vertices of T descendant to b. SEG(e) is ordered as a subgraph of $\tilde{T} \cup \tilde{B}$. When we speak of planar embeddings of SEG(e) we do not require that they reflect the ordering of $\tilde{T} \cup \tilde{B}$. From the definition of PATR(G,T) it is apparent that if (s,t) is a backedge of SEG(e), and PATH(e') is the father of PATH(e) in PATR(G,T), then t ≥ LOW1(e) ≥ LOW1(e'). Thus t is either a vertex of SEG(e) not on CYCLE(e') or a vertex of CYCLE(e') intersected with CYCLE(e). See

FIGURE 7.16. Note that SEG(e) is a bridge of CYCLE(e′) in the sense of DEFINITION 6.100 and FIGURES 6.98 and 6.99.

7.16 THE BRIDGE SEG(e) FOR CYCLE(e′).

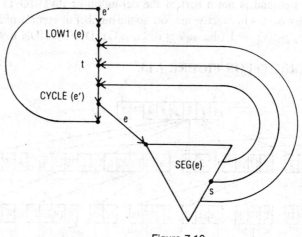

Figure 7.16

Let e $=$ (a,b) and consider all backedges (s,t) of SEG(e) with LOW1(e) < t < a. Call such backedges of SEG(e) *proper*. Observe from FIGURE 7.16 that if G is planar then the graph CYCLE(e) $\cup$ SEG(e) must be planar, and in any embedding all proper backedges must lie *inside* CYCLE(e) (as CYCLE(e′) $\cup$ CYCLE(e) $\cup$ SEG(e) is planar). We call a planar embedding of CYCLE(e) $\cup$ SEG(e) *consistent* if all proper backedges of SEG(e) lie inside CYCLE(e). FIGURE 7.17 shows an example where CYCLE(e) $\cup$ SEG(e) is planar but has no consistent embedding. If e $=$ (x,b) is the (unique by biconnectedness) edge of $\tilde{T}$ incident on the root x of $\tilde{T}$ then SEG(e) has no proper backedges (LOW1(e) $=$ x). Thus in this case $\tilde{T} \cup \tilde{B} =$ SEG(e) has a consistent embedding if and only if G is planar. Thus we have the following basic observation: G *is planar if and only if for every vertex* PATH(e) *of* PATR(G,T) *the graph* CYCLE(e) $\cup$ SEG(e) *has a consistent embedding*. The reader will note that CYCLE(e′) $\cup$ CYCLE(e) $\cup$ SEG(e) is a $\mathscr{C}$-bicomponent of the cycle $\mathscr{C} =$ CYCLE(e′) in the sense of DEFINITION 6.101. CYCLE(e) $\cup$ SEG(e) is the carrier of the bridge SEG(e) as defined in DEFINITION 6.102. If each vertex PATH(e) in PATR(G,T) is replaced by CYCLE(e), we have a cycle tree in the sense of DEFINITION 6.107.

7.17   PLANAR BUT NOT CONSISTENT.

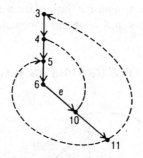

CYCLE(e) = (6,10,11,3,4,5,6)
Proper backedges: (10,4), (11,5)
e = (6,10)   LOW1(e) = 3.

Figure 7.17

We introduce some additional basic terminology. Given PATH(e), a vertex of PATR(G,T), let SEGLST(e) (called the *list of segments of* e) denote the set {SEG(f): PATH(f) a son of PATH(e) in PATR(G,T)}. Regard SEGLST(e) as linearly ordered by the order on PATR(G,T). Referring to FIGURE 7.15, let PATH(e) = PATH((7,8)) = $\boxed{1|12|11|9|8|7}$. Then SEGLST((7,8)) is (SEG((12,9)), SEG((11,13)), SEG((9,10))). These graphs may be read off directly from FIGURE 7.15. Let X, Y be segments in SEGLST(e). We say that X and Y are *directly linked* if, in any planar embedding of X ∪ Y ∪ CYCLE(e), X and Y must be on opposite sides of CYCLE(e). We define an undirected graph SEGGR(e) with vertex set SEGLST(e) and edge set {{X,Y}: X directly linked to Y}. SEGGR(e) is called the *segment graph* of e. In general, the number of edges of the segment graph may be quadratic in $|V|$. FIGURE 7.19 shows an example where the segment graph is the complete bipartite graph $K_{3,3}$. An obvious extension gives $K_{n,n}$ as a segment graph for $|V| = 2n + 3$. The reader should note that the SEGGR(e) is a *subgraph* of the more general bridge graph of CYCLE(e) as defined in DEFINITION 6.110.

It is clear that if G is planar then every SEGGR(e) associated with PATR(G,T) must be bipartite or bichromatic. We "color" each vertex of SEGGR(e) with I if the segment defined by that vertex is inside CYCLE(e) in a given planar embedding or with O if it is outside.

Due to the above remarks about consistent embeddings, the converse is not quite true. Let us define a segment X in SEGLST(e), e = (a,b), to be *internal* if it has at least one backedge (s,t) with LOW1(e) < t < a. Let $\mathscr{I}$ denote the set of internal segments in SEGLST(e).

7.18 DEFINITION.

We say that SEGGR(e) is *𝒮-bichromatic* if there exists a 2-coloring of the vertices of SEGGR(e) where all vertices in *𝒮* have the same color. Such a coloring will be called an *𝒮-bicoloring*.

7.19 COMPLETE BIPARTITE GRAPHS AS SEGMENT GRAPHS.

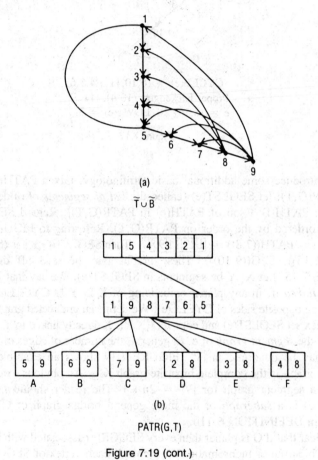

(a)

$\tilde{T} \cup \tilde{B}$

(b)

PATR(G,T)

Figure 7.19 (cont.)

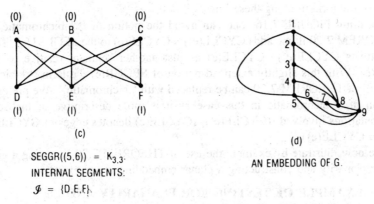

SEGGR((5,6)) = $K_{3,3}$.
INTERNAL SEGMENTS:

$\mathcal{I} = \{D,E,F\}$.

AN EMBEDDING OF G.

Figure 7.19 (continued)

These observations are summarized in THEOREM 7.20.

7.20 THEOREM.

G is planar if and only if every SEGGR(e) associated with PATR(G,T) is $\mathcal{I}$-bichromatic where $\mathcal{I}$ is the set of internal segments of SEGLST(e).

For example, consider FIGURE 7.19. If e = (5,6) and $\bar{T} \cup \bar{B}$ is as shown in FIGURE 7.19(a), then there are six segments in SEGLST(e). Each segment is a simple backedge as indicated in FIGURE 7.19(b). We label these segments A through F. D, E, and F are the internal segments so $\mathcal{I} = \{D,E,F\}$. We make the convention that when we color a segment graph, SEGGR(e), we use the two "colors" I and O. Elements of $\mathcal{I}$ will always be colored with I. FIGURE 7.19(c) shows an $\mathcal{I}$-coloring of SEGGR(e) for this example, so SEGGR(e) is $\mathcal{I}$-bichromatic. SEGGR(1,2) consists of one vertex, SEG(5,6), and no edges. $\mathcal{I} = \phi$ for this case. Thus all segment graphs are $\mathcal{I}$-bichromatic. An embedding of G (defined by $\bar{T} \cup \bar{B}$) is shown in FIGURE 7.19(d).

To specify a planar embedding for $\bar{T} \cup \bar{B}$ (order in $\bar{T} \cup \bar{B}$ ignored in the embedding) it suffices to construct SEGGR(e) for each vertex of PATR(G,T) and $\mathcal{I}$-bicolor it (let us say with I and O, vertices in $\mathcal{I}$ colored I). Assuming recursively, that for all vertices (i.e., all SEG(e) $\in$ SEGLST(e)) of SEGGR(e) we have specified a consistent embedding, then the $\mathcal{I}$-bicolored SEGGR(e) specifies how to orient these embeddings relative to CYCLE(e) to construct a consistent embedding of SEG(e) relative to CYCLE(e). If at any stage in constructing the graphs SEGGR(e) we find one that is not $\mathcal{I}$-bichromatic then G is nonplanar. As remarked above, we cannot in general compute the SEGGR(e) in linear time in $|V|$. Nevertheless, this process provides a quite effective means for constructing planar embeddings of moderately complex graphs by "pencil and paper'' computation. One can show that a *spanning forest* for SEGGR(e) can be computed in linear time in vertices of G and this leads to a linear time planarity algorithm along these lines.

Recalling FIGURE 7.16, one can avoid the notion of "$\mathcal{I}$-bichromatic" in THEOREM 7.20 if one adds CYCLE(e')\CYCLE(e) to the SEGLST(e). Thus, one treats CYCLE(e')\CYCLE(e) as just another segment relative to CYCLE(e). With this slightly extended notion of SEGGR(e) the term "$\mathcal{I}$-bichromatic" of THEOREM 7.20 can be replaced with "bichromatic." We prefer the notion of $\mathcal{I}$-bichromatic in this case as it is more descriptive of the actual computations involved. (CYCLE(e')\CYCLE(e) denotes edges of CYCLE(e') not in CYCLE(e)).

We now illustrate by example the use of THEOREM 7.20 in testing a graph G for planarity and constructing a planar embedding if one exists.

7.21 EXAMPLE OF TESTING FOR PLANARITY AND CONSTRUCTING AN EMBEDDING.

Consider $\tilde{T} \cup \tilde{B}$ of FIGURE 7.10 and PATR(G,T) shown in FIGURE 7.15. Inspect the vertices of PATR(G,T) in the depth-first sequence (i.e., generate DFV(PATR(G,T))). FIGURE 7.22 shows PATR(G,T) with the vertices replaced by their PREORDER numbers. We use these numbers to refer to the vertices of PATR(G,T).

7.22 PREORDER NUMBERS FOR PATR(G,T) OF FIGURE 7.15.

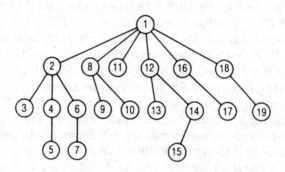

Figure 7.22

The vertices of FIGURE 7.22 listed in POSTORDER are 3, 5, 4, 7, 6, 2, 9, 10, 8, 11, 13, 15, 14, 12, 17, 16, 19, 18, 1. For each such integer k, let SEG(k), CYCLE(k), PATH(k), SEGGR(k), etc., denote the segment, cycle, path, segment graph, etc., associated with the vertex PATH(e) of PATR(G,T) having preorder number k. We attempt to construct an $\mathcal{I}$-coloration of SEGGR(k) and a consistent embedding of SEG(k) for the values of k as they occur in POSTORDER:

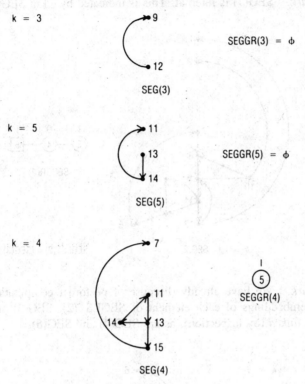

Remark.   "⑤" refers to "SEG(5)" in SEGGR(4). The manner of embedding SEG(5) relative to CYCLE(4) is left to trial and error at this stage, $\mathcal{I} = \phi$ here.

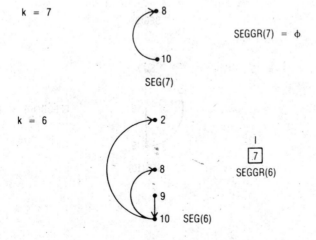

Remark.   SEG(7) is internal. This is indicated by □ in SEGGR(6).

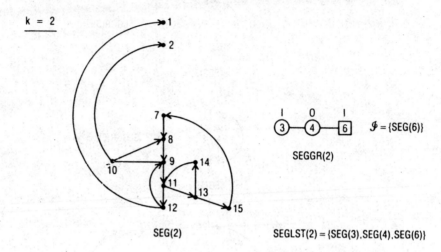

SEG(2)   SEGLST(2) = {SEG(3),SEG(4),SEG(6)}

Remark.   We have already (because of postorder computation) given consistent embeddings of each element of SEGLST(2). SEG(3) and SEG(4) are *directly linked* (by inspection), as are SEG(4) and SEG(6).

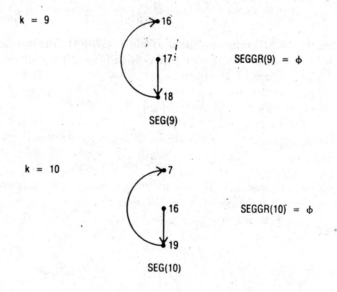

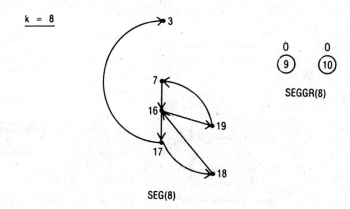

SEGGR(8)

SEG(8)

Remark.   The two vertices can be colored I or O independently, so there are three other possible $\mathcal{I}$-colorations of SEGGR(8) ($\mathcal{I} = \phi$).

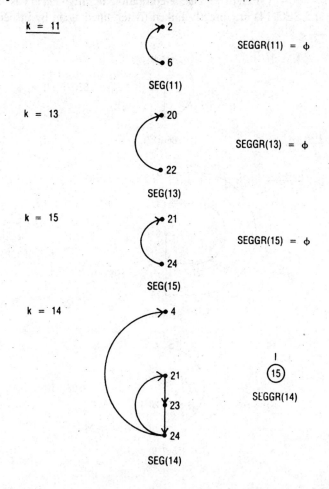

SEGGR(11) = ϕ

SEG(11)

SEGGR(13) = ϕ

SEG(13)

SEGGR(15) = ϕ

SEG(15)

SEGGR(14)

SEG(14)

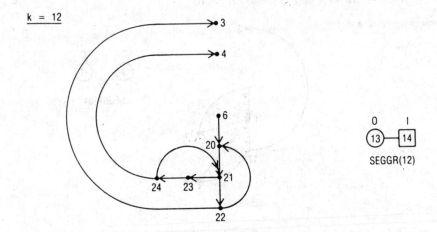

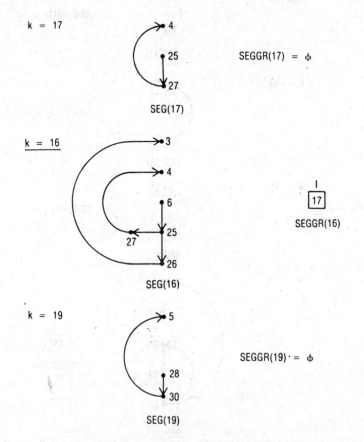

Remark. $\mathcal{S} = \{SEG(14)\}$. The $\mathcal{S}$-coloration of SEGGR(12) is unique as SEG(13) and SEG(14) are directly linked (determined again by inspection).

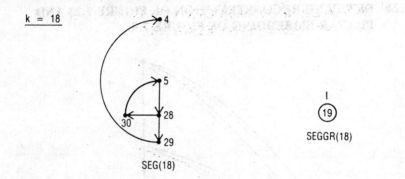

k = 18

SEG(18)

SEGGR(18)

k = 1   *Remark.*   Sons of 1 in PATR(G,T): 2, 8, 11, 12, 16, 18 are underlinked above. Only the *proper* backedges of these segments (see FIGURE 7.17) and those backedges (s,t) with t = LOW1(e) affect the construction of SEGGR(1) and the subsequent embedding. This is shown in FIGURE 7.23.

7.23   SEGGR(1) AND ITS EMBEDDING.

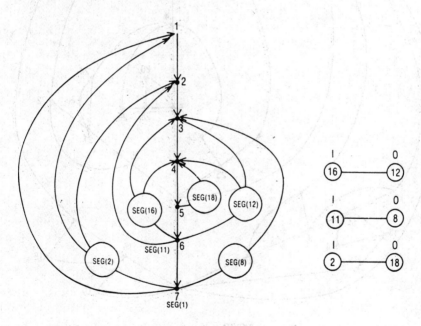

Figure 7.23

By filling in the detailed structure of the segments of the embedding shown in FIGURE 7.23 we obtain, in FIGURE 7.24, a planar embedding of the graph of FIGURE 7.9.

7.24 DETAILED RECONSTRUCTION OF FIGURE 7.23 AND PLANAR EMBEDDING OF FIGURE 7.9.

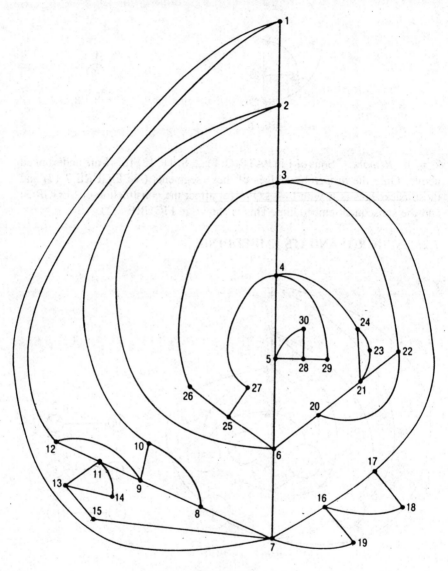

Figure 7.24

The reader should observe that the bicolorations of the segment graphs specify a labeling (with I,O) of PATR(G,T) as shown in FIGURE 7.25.

7.25 I,O LABELING OF PATR(G,T) OF FIGURES 7.15 AND 7.22.

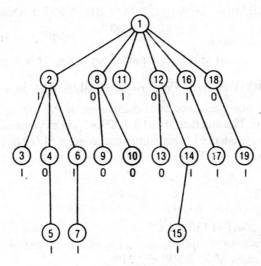

Figure 7.25

By traversing this labeled tree and, using the labels I = Inside, O = Outside, to embed the vertices of PATR(G) (as paths in G) in the plane as they are encountered in PREORDER (refer to FIGURE 7.15) we again obtain FIGURE 7.24. Thus FIGURE 7.25 may be regarded as a specification of an embedding.

We now consider two basic lemmas that aid in carrying out the type of computation illustrated by EXAMPLE 7.21. With the aid of these lemmas, the reader will find it not too difficult to set up the data structures required to test for planarity in linear time in the number of vertices. Recall that it is only necessary to consider the case where $|E| \leq 3|V| - 6$ (THEOREM 6.115). As defined above, if $SEG(f_1)$ and $SEG(f_2)$ are in SEGLST(e) then we say $SEG(f_1)$ and $SEG(f_2)$ are *directly linked* if $SEG(f_1)$ and $SEG(f_2)$ must be embedded on opposite sides of CYCLE(e) in any planar embedding of $CYCLE(e) \cup SEG(f_1) \cup SEG(f_2)$. We write $SEG(f_1)$ dl $SEG(f_2)$. Recall also that if e = (a,b) is a directed edge then TAIL(e) = a, HEAD(e) = b.

7.26 LEMMA.

Let $SEG(f_1) < SEG(f_2)$ be two segments in SEGLST(e). Then $SEG(f_1)$ is directly linked to $SEG(f_2)$ if and only if there is a backedge (s,t) of $SEG(f_1)$ with $LOW1(f_2) < t < TAIL(f_2)$.

LEMMA 7.26 is easily proved by considering cases. We note only the case where $TAIL(f_1) = TAIL(f_2)$ and $LOW1(f_1) = LOW1(f_2)$. In this case $LOW1(f_1)$

$< t < TAIL(f_1)$ so (s,t) is a *proper* backedge of $SEG(f_1)$ (as defined in connection with FIGURES 7.16 and 7.17). Recalling the definition of the order on SEGLST(e) as derived from the order on PATR(G,T) and the sorting of the triple

$$(PREORDER(p), LOW1(f), X(LOW2(f) < PREORDER(p))$$

$$\text{where } f = (p,q),$$

we see that $SEG(f_2)$ must also have a proper backedge. That is,

$$X(LOW2(f_2) < PREORDER(TAIL(f_2))) = 1.$$

This is the only place where the third component of the triple plays a role in what we have done. The fact that $SEG(f_1)$ dl $SEG(f_2)$ in this case is an immediate consequence of the existence of this proper backedge of $SEG(f_2)$. LEMMA 7.26 is a result of Hopcroft and Tarjan (see the references at the end of PART II).

7.27   EXERCISE.

(1) Complete the proof of LEMMA 7.26.
(2) What data structures would you use to implement the test of LEMMA 7.26 in the computation of EXAMPLE 7.21?

Lemma 7.26 provides the basis for efficiently constructing segment graphs or spanning forests for segment graphs insofar as deciding when a pair of segments forms an edge of the segment graph (i.e., when they are directly linked). The segments of SEGLST(e) are added one after another to SEGGR(e), checking at each stage to see if SEGGR(e) is still bipartite. This latter test is aided by the following ideas.

Consider FIGURE 7.29. $CYCLE(e) = (1,2,...,20,1)$ for the edge $e = (1,2)$ is shown. The segments of SEGLST(e) are labeled A,B,...,J in the order on SEGLST(e). The edges internal to these segments are not shown, but all backedges that go from a segment to CYCLE(e) are shown. Consider a particular segment, say H, and let SEGLST(e,H) denote all segments less than or equal to H in the ordering on SEGLST(e). Thus, SEGLST(e,H) = A,B,...,H in that order. This set of segments defines a subgraph of SEGGR(e) which we call SEGGR(e,H). The edges of this subgraph are defined by the "directly linked" relation just as in SEGGR(e). The components $\mathcal{H}_1$, $\mathcal{H}_2$, and $\mathcal{H}_3$ are shown in FIGURE 7.29. For any such component, let HEAD($\mathcal{H}$) denote the ordered sequence of vertices of CYCLE(e) of the form HEAD(f) where f is a backedge from some segment in $\mathcal{H}$ to CYCLE(e). For example, HEAD($\mathcal{H}_1$) = (1,2,3,17). In the same manner, let HEAD($\mathcal{H}$,H) denote those elements of HEAD($\mathcal{H}$) that are strictly less than the largest vertex of H on CYCLE(e) (we call this vertex TAIL(H)). In the example, TAIL(H) = 10 and HEAD($\mathcal{H}_1$,H) = (1,2,3). We say that a component $\mathcal{H}$ of SEGGR(e,H) is *relevant* if HEAD($\mathcal{H}$,H) is nonempty, otherwise $\mathcal{H}$ is called *irrelevant*. In the example, $\mathcal{H}_1$ and $\mathcal{H}_3$ are relevant to H but $\mathcal{H}_2$ is irrelevant. The basic observation that we need concerns the sets HEAD($\mathcal{H}$,H) for relevant components. In the example, HEAD($\mathcal{H}_1$,H) = (1,2,3) and HEAD($\mathcal{H}_3$,H) = (3,4,5,7,8). Note that the maximum value (last value) of the first sequence is less than or equal to the minimum value of the second sequence (in this example we have equality). In other words, the ordered sequences HEAD($\mathcal{H}$,H), as $\mathcal{H}$ ranges over all relevant components, don't overlap except possibly at their endpoints. This idea is stated in LEMMA 7.28. The order on vertices of CYCLE(e) is the natural order for integers as we are using the preorder numbers to label vertices. We order the components $\mathcal{H}_1,\mathcal{H}_2,\ldots,\mathcal{H}_p$ by their minimal segments (thus, $\mathcal{H}_1 < \mathcal{H}_2 < \mathcal{H}_3$ because A < D < F in SEGLST(e) in FIGURE 7.29). If the maximum of HEAD($\mathcal{H}_i$,H) is less than or equal to the minimum of HEAD($\mathcal{H}_{i+1}$,H) for i = 1,2,$\ldots$,p $-$ 1 we say that the sequence HEAD($\mathcal{H}_1$,H),$\ldots$,HEAD($\mathcal{H}_p$,H) is a *max-min chain* in CYCLE(e).

7.28 LEMMA.

Let H be any segment of SEGLST(e) and let $\mathcal{H}_1,\ldots,\mathcal{H}_p$ be the relevant components of SEGGR(e,H) ordered by their minimal segments. Then the sequence HEAD($\mathcal{H}_1$,H),$\ldots$,HEAD($\mathcal{H}_p$,H) is a max-min chain in CYCLE(e).

The proof of LEMMA 7.28 is left as an exercise for the reader, (EXERCISE 7.31(1)). The reader should note that LEMMA 7.28 does not involve any assumptions of planarity. The notion of a planar embedding enters only through the idea of ''directly linked'' in connection with defining the components $\mathcal{H}_i$. Referring again to FIGURE 7.29, note that SEGGR(e,H) is $\mathcal{I}$-bipartite ($\mathcal{I}$ is

7.29 MAX-MIN CHAIN.

$(\text{HEAD}(\mathcal{K}_1,H), \text{HEAD}(\mathcal{K}_3,H)) = ((1,2,3),(3,4,5,7,8))$.

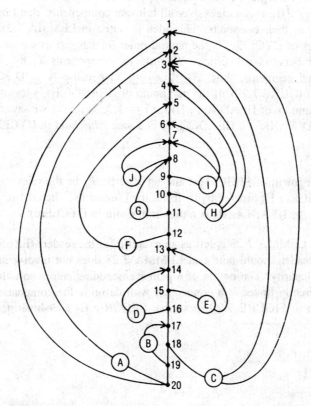

SEGLST((1,2),H) = (A,B,...,H)
SEGGR((1,2),H):

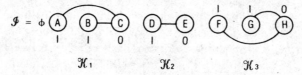

Figure 7.29

empty in this case) and that the embedding shown of SEGLST(e,H) together with CYCLE(e) is planar. This embedding gives the I,O labeling of the vertices of SEGGR(e,H) shown in FIGURE 7.29. Given this situation, we can split each sequence HEAD($\mathcal{H}$,H) into two subsequences, INHEAD($\mathcal{H}$,H) and OUT-HEAD($\mathcal{H}$,H). The sequence INHEAD($\mathcal{H}$,H) consists of all entries of HEAD($\mathcal{H}$,H) that are equal to HEAD(f) for some backedge f belonging to a segment of $\mathcal{H}$ that is labeled I (i.e., is embedded inside CYCLE(e)). OUTHEAD($\mathcal{H}$,H) is similarly defined. In FIGURE 7.29, INHEAD($\mathcal{H}_3$,H) = (5,8) and OUT-HEAD($\mathcal{H}_3$,H) = (3,4,7). For segment H, we define SPAN(H) to be the sequence of vertices of CYCLE(e) from LOW1(H) to TAIL(H) (see EXERCISE 6.109(3)). Thus, in FIGURE 7.29, SPAN(H) = (3,4,5,6,7,8,9,10) and SPAN(I) = (6,7,8,9). The *open* or *interior* span of H is SPAN(H) with its first and last entries removed. We denote this sequence by OSPAN(H). This sequence may be empty. In FIGURE 7.29, OSPAN(H) = (4,5,6,7,8,9), OSPAN(I) = (7,8). The critical observation here (FIGURE 7.29 again) is that both INHEAD($\mathcal{H}_3$,H) and OUT-HEAD($\mathcal{H}_3$,H) have entries in OSPAN(I). This means that when I is added to SEGGR(e,H) to form SEGGR(e,I) the new graph will not be $\mathcal{G}$-bipartite. In other words, SEGLST(e,H) together with CYCLE(e) is planar but SEGLST(e,I) together with CYCLE(e) is not planar. We state this observation as LEMMA 7.30. The reader should recall the relationship between CYCLE(e), CYCLE (e') and SEG(e) of FIGURE 7.16 and the notion of an internal segment defined in connection with DEFINITION 7.18.

7.30 LEMMA.

Suppose that H and I are consecutive elements of SEGLST(e) and that SEGLST(e,H) together with CYCLE(e) is planar. Suppose that an $\mathcal{G}$-bicoloration of SEGGR(e,H) has been specified (or a planar embedding of SEGLST(e,H) together with CY-CLE(e) has been specified). If there is a component $\mathcal{H}$ of SEGGR(e,H) such that both INHEAD($\mathcal{H}$,H) and OUTHEAD($\mathcal{H}$,H) have points in common with OSPAN(I), then SEGGR(e,I) is not $\mathcal{G}$-bichromatic (SEGLST(e,I) together with CYCLE(e) and hence the original graph G is not planar). If there is a component $\mathcal{H}$ of SEGGR(e,H) with a vertex A that is an internal segment and if I is an internal segment, then INHEAD ($\mathcal{H}$,H) $\cap$ OSPAN(I) $\neq$ 0 implies that SEGGR(e,I) is not $\mathcal{G}$-bichromatic (SEGLST(e,I) $\cup$ CYCLE(e) $\cup$ CYCLE(e') and hence G is not planar).

The proof of LEMMA 7.30 is essentially a restatement of LEMMA 7.26. A few sketches of cases will convince the reader of its validity.

The reader who has thought carefully about the basic data structures presented in this chapter and in PART I is now in a good position to develop any one of a number of variations of a linear time planarity algorithm.

7.31   EXERCISE.

(1) Prove LEMMA 7.28. (*Hint:* One way is by induction on the linearly ordered set SEGLST(e). Suppose X and Y are consecutive in SEGLST(e) and that the lemma is true for X. Add Y to SEGGR(e,X) to get SEGGR(e,Y) and see what happens to the max-min chain.)

(2) Using the ideas of LEMMAS 7.26, 7.28, and 7.30 try to describe the data structures for a linear time planarity algorithm. Try and convince at least two friends that your algorithm works in linear time. (*Hint:* A major hurdle will be the soporific effect on the friends. Brew a pot of strong coffee!)

(3) Extend the previous exercise to compute a spanning forest SEGFO(e,H) for each SEGGR(e,H). Specify data structures and discuss complexity. In the discussion of complexity, distinguish between the planar and nonplanar cases.

The reader interested in pursuing the topic of planarity algorithms further should begin with the seminal work of Hopcraft and Tarjan cited in the references (*Efficient Planarity Testing*, J. Assoc. Comp. March 21 (1974), 549–568).

Chapter 8

Topic II: Depth First Search and Nonplanarity

A closely related application of lineal spanning trees that we shall now consider is the problem of finding "Kuratowski subgraphs" of a nonplanar graph. Recall the graphs of FIGURE 6.116 ($K_{3,3}$ and K_5). FIGURE 8.1 shows graphs that are essentially the same as these graphs except that additional vertices of degree 2 occur along what used to be the edges of $K_{3,3}$ and K_5. Graphs that are isomorphic to graphs with the general structure of those shown in FIGURE 8.1 are called *Kuratowski graphs*. (There are infinitely many such isomorphism classes. In each class finitely many vertices of degree 2 are added, but there is no bound on this number over the whole set of classes.) THEOREM 8.2 is a famous result of Kuratowski.

8.1 KURATOWSKI GRAPHS.

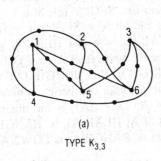

(a)

TYPE $K_{3,3}$

(b)

TYPE K_5

Figure 8.1

8.2 THEOREM.

A graph G is nonplanar if and only if it contains a subgraph that is a Kuratowski graph.

Using the idea of COMMENT 7.4(3), one can restrict one's attention to t' case where $|E| \leq 3|V| - 5$. We shall show that for this class of graphs, a

Kuratowski subgraph, if it exists, can be found in linear time in $|V|$ (or equivalently, in $|E|$). We assume that the reader has at least given some thought to EXERCISE 7.31(3). Additional references relating to the construction of segment forests can be found at the end of this chapter.

We begin by reviewing the basic structures associated with the construction of segment forests. Start with a biconnected graph G such as the one shown in FIGURE 7.9. An ordered directed lineal spanning tree T together with the directed backedge graph B is constructed. The vertex set V of G is identified with the preorder numbers of T. The order of the edges is redefined using first and second lowpoint values to obtain the ordered decomposition such as that shown in FIGURE 7.10. From the ordered decomposition, the ordered, directed path tree, PATR(G,T), is constructed as in FIGURE 7.15. Each vertex of PATR(G,T) is a path, PATH(f), associated with an edge f of T or B. Associated with each PATH(f) is a unique directed cycle, CYCLE(f). Thus, PATR(G,T) can also be regarded as a tree of cycles, CYTR(G,T). The graph obtained by taking the union of PATH(f) with all of its descendants in PATR(G,T) is called SEG(f). The graph SEG(f) is a bridge of CYCLE(e) in the standard sense (DEFINITION 6.100) where e is the edge defining the father PATH(e) of PATH(f) in PATR(G,T).

8.3 BASIC NOTATION.

(1) Let PATH(e) be a vertex of the ordered tree PATR(G,T) and let PATH(f_1),. . .,PATH(f_p) be its sons in order. The ordered set SEG(f_1),. . .,SEG(f_p) is called the *segment list*, SEGLST(e), of e.

(2) Let PATH(f) be a vertex of PATR(G,T) and let A = SEG(f), f = (a,b), be the corresponding segment. Then TAIL(f) = a and HEAD(f) = b. Define TAIL(A) = a. Let RANGE(A) be the vertices of A on CYCLE(e) (PATH(e) the father of PATH(f) in PATR(G,T)). Note that TAIL(A) is the largest element of RANGE(A) (recall the preorder numbering convention for vertices of G). The *first lowpoint* of A, LOW1(A), is the minimum element of RANGE(A). Let the *head set of* A, HEAD(A), be RANGE(A) − TAIL(A). The second smallest element of RANGE(A) is LOW2(A), if LOW2(A) < b.

(3) Let A = SEG(f) and e be as in (2). The directed path in CYCLE(e) from LOW1(A) to TAIL(A) is called the *span of* A, denoted by SPAN(A). The SPAN(A) with the first and last edges removed is called the *open span of* A, OSPAN(A). If the RANGE(A) = $v_1 < v_2 < \ldots < v_r$, then the directed paths in CYCLE(e) from v_i to v_{i+1} for i = 1,. . .,r − 1, are called the *proper gaps* of A. The directed path in CYCLE(e) from v_r to v_1 is called the *improper gap* or *cospan* of A.

(4) If A and B are segments in (elements of) SEGLST(e) and if A and B must be on opposite sides of CYCLE(e) in any planar embedding of CYCLE(e) ∪ A ∪ B then A and B are said to be *directly linked*. In this case we write

A dl B, otherwise we write A ndl B. For X in SEGLST(e), let SEGLST(e,X) denote the set of segments in SEGLST(e) that are less than or equal to X in the linear order on SEGLST(e). The graph SEGGR(e,X) has as vertices the set SEGLST(e,X) and as edges all pairs of segments A,B in SEGLST(e,X) with A dl B. If X is the last element of SEGLST(e) then SEGGR(e,X) is denoted by SEGGR(e). SEGFO(e,X) will denote a spanning forest for SEGGR(e,X).

(5) If $\mathcal{H}$ is a connected component of SEGGR(e,X), and A and B are vertices of $\mathcal{H}$ (i.e,, A and B are segments), then we say that A and B are linked, A l B. A might be linked to B but not directly linked (A l B but A ndl B). Let SPAN($\mathcal{H}$) = $\bigcup_{X}$ SPAN(X) where X is a vertex of $\mathcal{H}$. Let HEAD($\mathcal{H}$) = $\bigcup_{X}$ HEAD(X) where X is a vertex of $\mathcal{H}$. If CYCLE(e) $\cup$ SEGLST(e,X) is planar and a planar embedding has been specified, then every edge in the embedding (not in CYCLE(e)) must lie either inside or outside of CYCLE(e). Those elements of HEAD($\mathcal{H}$) that are endpoints of edges embedded inside CYCLE(e) will be denoted by INHEAD($\mathcal{H}$), and those elements that are endpoints of edges embedded outside of CYCLE(e) will be denoted by OUTHEAD($\mathcal{H}$) (see LEMMA 7.30).

We now give some examples of the BASIC NOTATION 8.3. In all of these examples we refer to FIGURE 7.29.

8.4 EXAMPLES OF BASIC NOTATION FROM FIGURE 7.29.

(1) For e = (1,2), CYCLE(e) = (1,2,. . .,20,1), SEGLST(e) = A,B,. . .,J, as shown in FIGURE 7.29 (detailed structure of segments not shown).
(2) For the segment C: TAIL(C) = 18; RANGE(C) = (1,3,18); HEAD(C) = (1,3); LOW1(C) = 1; LOW2(C) = 3.
(3) Again referring to the segment C, SPAN(C) = (1,2,. . .,18); OSPAN(C) = (2,. . .,17); the proper gaps of C are (1,2,3), (3,4,. . .,18); the cospan of C is (18,19,20,1).
(4) D dl E; B ndl D; SEGLST(e,H) = (A,B,. . .,H), ({A,. . .,H}, {{A,C}, {B,C}, {D,E}, {F,H}, {G,H}}) is SEGGR(e,H). SEGGR(e,H) = SEGFO(e,H) in this example.
(5) Components of SEGGR(e,H) are $\mathcal{H}_1$ = ({A,B,C}, {{A,C}, {B,C}}), $\mathcal{H}_2$ = ({D,E}, {{D,E}}), and $\mathcal{H}_3$ = ({F,G,H}, {{F,H}, {G,H}}). The segments A and B are both vertices of $\mathcal{H}_1$ and A l B but A ndl B. HEAD($\mathcal{H}_1$) = (1,2,3,17), INHEAD($\mathcal{H}_1$) = (2,17), OUTHEAD($\mathcal{H}_1$) = (1,3).

In EXERCISE 7.31(3) we construct a segment forest, SEGFO(e), for each PATH(e) in PATR(G,T). This construction is most naturally done in postorder on vertices of PATR(G,T). At each vertex PATH(e), we proceed in order through SEGLST(e), constructing SEGFO(e,X) for each X. For a nonplanar graph G, we arrive at a situation where CYCLE(e) $\cup$ CYCLE(e′) together with the segments of SEGLST(e,X) is a planar graph, but the addition of the next element, call it F, in SEGLST(e) destroys planarity. We thus have two vertices A and B of the same component of SEGFO(e) with A dl F and B dl F and A and B on opposite sides of CYCLE(e) in any planar embedding. The reader should recall LEMMA 7.30 in this regard. If the situation is as stated in the last sentence of LEMMA 7.30 (X = H, F = I) then it will be necessary to take F = CYCLE(e′). We leave these details to the reader. Let $(B,Y_1,\ldots,Y_p,A)$ denote the unique path in SEGFO(e,X) joining A to B. As A and B are on opposite sides of CYCLE(e), p must be even. CYCLE(e) $\cup$ B $\cup$ Y_1 $\cup$ Y_2 $\cup$ ... $\cup$ Y_p $\cup$ A is planar but this same subgraph with F added is not planar. As a result of EXERCISE 7.31(3), all of these structures can be obtained in linear time in vertices of the original graph G. If some Y_t is directly linked to F, we find the first such t. If t is even, set Y_t = B otherwise set Y_t = A. By interchanging the roles of A and B if necessary we again have a path $(B,Y_1,\ldots,Y_q,A)$ with B greater than A in the SEGLST(e) order, q even but less than p, and B and A directly linked to F (the Y_i have been relabeled). Continuing in this manner we arrive in linear time at two BASIC CASES 8.5.

8.5 BASIC CASES.

(1) F dl B dl A dl F
(2) F dl B dl Y_1 dl Y_2 dl ... dl Y_p dl A dl F, p > 0, p even, Y_i ndl F for 1 $\leq$ i $\leq$ p.

From the point of view of showing the existence of a linear time algorithm for finding a Kuratowski subgraph BASIC CASE 8.5(1) is trivial. As is shown in FIGURE 7.10, each segment Z consists of a tree rooted at TAIL(Z) together with a set of directed backedges. In BASIC CASE 8.5(1), only the tree structure of the segments F, B, and A and the backedges with vertices on CYCLE(e) are important in determining the basic nonplanar structure.

8.6 DEFINITION.

Let Z be a segment in SEGLST(e). Let P_1 and P_2 be directed paths in Z from the TAIL(Z) to LOW1(Z) and LOW2(Z) (if the latter is in HEAD(Z)). We call P_1 $\cup$ P_2 the *reduced segment* of Z, written REDSEG(Z). For A, B, and F as in BASIC CASE 8.5(1) we form the graph REDSEG(A) $\cup$ REDSEG(B) $\cup$ REDSEG(F) $\cup$ CYCLE(e). To this graph we add a path in A from TAIL(A) to a vertex of OSPAN(B), a path in A from TAIL(A) a vertex of OSPAN(F), and a path in B from TAIL(B) to a vertex of OSPAN(F). The resulting graph is called a KERNEL(A,B,F) (see FIGURE 8.8). This construction is not unique so KERNEL(A,B,F) may be thought of as a set of graphs.

8.7   DEFINITION.

Let H = (V,E) be any graph. We construct a new graph H' = (V',E') from H
as follows: V' is the set of vertices of V that are not of degree 2. E' corresponds
to the set of all paths P in H that have only their endpoints in V'. Thus P has
only vertices of degree 2 in H as internal vertices. The "edge" P is incident on
its endpoints. H' is called the *complete homeomorphic reduction of* H. If A, B,
and F are as in BASIC CASE 8.5(1), the complete homeomorphic reduction of
KERNEL(A,B,F) will be denoted by HOMKERNEL(A,B,F). In the diagram
representing a graph H all vertices of degree 2 are "ignored" to obtain the
diagram of the complete homeomorphic reduction. For an example, see FIGURE
8.8(c) relative to FIGURE 8.8(b).

8.8   KERNEL(A,B,F) AND HOMKERNEL(A,B,F).

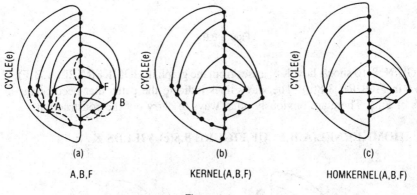

| (a) | (b) | (c) |
| A,B,F | KERNEL(A,B,F) | HOMKERNEL(A,B,F) |

Figure 8.8

In FIGURE 8.8(c) the graph HOMKERNEL(A,B,F) has 18 vertices and 27
edges. It is not difficult to devise data structures that allow one to construct a
graph in HOMKERNEL(A,B,F) in linear time. In general, the total number of
vertices and edges that occur in a graph in HOMKERNEL(A,B,F) is bounded
(at most 18 vertices and 27 edges) independent of G. It is therefore obvious that
a Kuratowski subgraph of a graph in HOMKERNEL(A,B,F), and hence of a
graph in KERNEL(A,B,F), can be found in constant time. Thus, a Kuratowski
subgraph of G can be found in linear time whenever G reduces to the case F dl
A dl B dl F. One can in fact do much better in terms of an actual algorithm
(EXERCISE 8.26(3)). A lexicographic list (up to isomorphism) of all possible
graphs in HOMKERNEL(A,B,F), each with it corresponding Kuratowski subgraph,
can be made. This list is finite and allows for a quick "table look up" of the
Kuratowski subgraphs in BASIC CASE 8.5(1). FIGURE 8.9 shows the one case
where a graph in HOMKERNEL(A,B,F) yields K_5.

8.9 HOMKERNEL(A,B,F) YIELDS K_5.

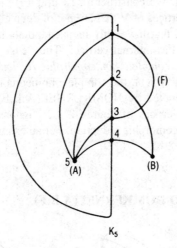

K_5

Figure 8.9

FIGURE 8.10 shows how $K_{3,3}$ arises from the graph in HOMKERNEL(A,B,F) shown in FIGURE 8.8(c). The wavy lines indicate the paths that become the edges of $K_{3,3}$. There are obviously other ways to carry out the construction.

8.10 HOMKERNEL(A,B,F) OF FIGURE 8.8(c) YIELDS $K_{3,3}$.

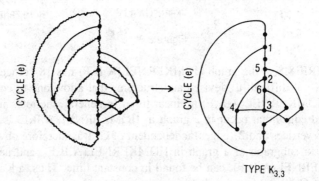

Figure 8.10

Thus far, HOMKERNEL(A,B,F) is only defined for BASIC CASE 8.5(1). The situation that results when BASIC CASE 8.5(2) occurs is more complex. We wish to construct a class of graphs HOMKERNEL(A,B,F) for these cases in an analogous fashion to the situation when F dl A dl B dl F. Again, given

G, we want to be able to find HOMKERNEL(A,B,F) in linear time and we want the class of graphs (up to isomorphism) that can arise in HOMKERNEL(A,B,F) to be finite. We shall first show how HOMKERNEL(A,B,F) is to be constructed and afterwards indicate the basic data structures needed to carry out the construction in linear time. Note: "HOMKERNEL(A,B,F)" refers to different constructions in case 8.5(1) and case 8.5(2).

To summarize, we are now assuming that F dl B dl Y_1 dl ... dl Y_p dl A dl F, p even; Y_t ndl F for t = 1,. . .,p; B ndl A; and CYCLE(e) $\cup$ B $\cup$ Y_1 $\cup$ ... $\cup$ Y_p $\cup$ A is planar. Referring to FIGURE 8.11, we prove LEMMA 8.12.

8.11 GEOMETRIC INTERPRETATIONS OF LEMMA 8.12.

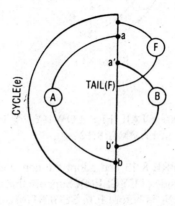

Figure 8.11

8.12 LEMMA.

Let a = max(HEAD(A) $\cap$ OSPAN(F)), b = the successor of a in RANGE(A), a' = LOW1(B), b' = TAIL(B). Then $a \leq a' \leq b' \leq b$.

Proof. If TAIL(B) = TAIL(F) then the fact that B is before F in SEGLST(e) would mean that LOW1(B) $\leq$ LOW1(F). Thus A dl F would force A dl B, a contradiction. Thus TAIL(B) > TAIL(F). But A before B in SEGLST(e) implies TAIL(A) $\geq$ TAIL(B). Thus we also have TAIL(A) > TAIL(F). This implies, using the maximality of a and the fact that A ndl B, that b > TAIL(F). Again using B ndl A gives the result.

It follows from the next lemma, LEMMA 8.14, that in fact b' < b in LEMMA 8.12. The proof of LEMMA 8.14 refers to FIGURE 8.13.

8.13   GEOMETRIC INTERPRETATION OF LEMMA 8.14.

$$X_1 = Y_j \text{ OF LEMMA 163}$$
$$x_1 = \text{LOW1}(X_1)$$
$$y_1 = \text{TAIL}(X_1)$$

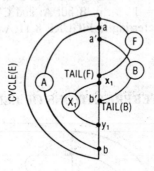

Figure 8.13

8.14   LEMMA.

At least one Y_j, j odd, satisfies $\text{TAIL}(F) \le \text{LOW1}(Y_j) < \text{TAIL}(B) < \text{TAIL}(Y_j)$ $\le$ b where b is as defined in LEMMA 8.12.

Proof.   We refer to FIGURE 8.13 and adopt the convention that A has been embedded inside and B outside of CYCLE(e). Suppose that for $k \le p$, $\text{TAIL}(Y_k)$ $\le \text{TAIL}(B)$. The fact that Y_k is before F in SEGLST(e) implies that $\text{TAIL}(Y_k)$ $\ge \text{TAIL}(F)$. If k is odd then Y_k is embedded inside of CYCLE(e) and planarity together with Y_k ndl F implies that $\text{TAIL}(F) \le \text{LOW1}(Y_k) < \text{TAIL}(Y_k) \le$ $\text{TAIL}(B)$. Each even k has Y_k dl Y_{k-1}. Thus again using planarity and the fact that Y_k ndl F gives $\text{TAIL}(F) \le \text{LOW1}(Y_k) < \text{TAIL}(Y_k) \le \text{TAIL}(B)$. Therefore, for $k \le p$, $\text{RANGE}(Y_k)$ all lie in a proper gap of A (i.e., between a and b). No such Y_k could be directly linked to A. But Y_p dl A so there must be a first j such that $\text{TAIL}(Y_j) > \text{TAIL}(B)$. But Y_j dl Y_{j-1} together with planarity implies that Y_j must be embedded inside CYCLE(e) and hence j is odd. Y_j ndl F and Y_j dl Y_{j-1} implies that $\text{TAIL}(F) \le \text{LOW1}(Y_j) < \text{TAIL}(B)$, and planarity implies that $\text{TAIL}(B) < \text{TAIL}(Y_j) \le$ b. This completes the proof.

It is, of course, possible to choose the Y_j specified by LEMMA 8.14 to be the minimal such segment in SEGLST(e) order. This choice can be made in linear time. We denote by X_1 the minimal such choice (see FIGURE 8.13).

8.15   DEFINITION.

We denote by [r,s] the sequence of vertices from r to s (r < s) on CYCLE(e). We use the notation [r,s), (r,s], (r,s) to denote this sequence with the right, left, and both right and left endpoints deleted. If I is one of these intervals (a directed path on CYCLE(e)) we say that a segment X *intrudes* on I if I $\cap$ RANGE(X) is nonempty. If X intrudes on I = (r,s), [r,s), etc. and LOW1(X) $\notin$ I, then X will be called a *retreat segment* relative to I. If X is a retreat segment relative to I and embedded outside CYCLE(e) in the planar embedding of CYCLE(e) $\cup$ B $\cup$ Y_1 $\cup$ ... $\cup$ Y_p $\cup$ A then X will be called an *external* retreat segment, otherwise an *internal* retreat segment.

8.16 LEMMA.

Suppose we have a subset $X_1, X_2, \ldots, X_{t-1}$ chosen from the set $Y_1, Y_2, \ldots, Y_p$ embedded as shown in FIGURE 8.17 (t even shown there). Suppose the following:

(1) None of the intervals $[y_0, y_1), [y_2, y_3), \ldots, [y_{2n-2}, y_{2n-1})$ with $2n < t$ have an external retreat segment, Z with $LOW1(Z) \leq LOW1(F)$.
(2) For each X_i, $x_i = LOW1(X_i)$ and $y_i = TAIL(X_i)$, $x_1 < y_0 \leq x_2 < y_1 \leq x_3 < \ldots < y_{t-1} \leq b$.
(3) For $i = 1, \ldots, t-1$, X_i is the minimal segment in SEGLST(e) order (among the $Y_1, \ldots, Y_p$) that intrudes on the interval $[y_{i-2}, y_{i-1})$, where $y_{-1} = TAIL(F)$, $y_0 = TAIL(B)$.

Then either t is even and there exists an external retreat segment Z relative to $[y_{t-2}, y_{t-1})$ with $LOW1(Z) \leq LOW1(F)$, or there exists a segment X_t (from the $Y_1, \ldots, Y_p$) such that $x_t = LOW1(X_t)$ is in the interval $[y_{t-2}, y_{t-1})$ and $y_t = TAIL(X_t)$ is greater than y_{t-1}.

Proof. Assume that $TAIL(Y_k) \leq y_{t-1} = TAIL(X_{t-1})$ for all $k = 1, \ldots, p$. Note that $TAIL(Y_k) \geq TAIL(F)$ by maximality of F. For any Y_k embedded inside of CYCLE(e), planarity requires that $RANGE(Y_k) \subseteq [a, y_{t-1}]$. Thus, for such a Y_k, $TAIL(Y_k) = TAIL(F)$ would imply that Y_k is greater than F in the linear order on SEGLST(e). This contradicts the maximality of F. Thus, for Y_k inside, $TAIL(F) < TAIL(Y_k) \leq y_{t-1}$. If, on the other hand, Y_k is embedded outside of CYCLE(e) and $TAIL(Y_k) = TAIL(F)$ then by planarity again we must have $RANGE(Y_k) \subseteq [x_0, TAIL(F)]$ and $Y_k > F$. Thus, for all k, $TAIL(F) < TAIL(Y_k) \leq y_{t-1}$.

From the remarks of the previous paragraph, note that for any Y_k embedded outside, if $LOW1(Y_k) > LOW1(F)$ then by planarity $LOW1(Y_k) \geq TAIL(F) > a$. We now observe that if, conversely, $LOW1(Y_k) \leq LOW1(F)$ then Y_k must be an external retreat segment for $[y_{t-2}, y_{t-1})$. This follows from the fact that Y_k dl Y_{k-1} and as we noted above, $RANGE(Y_{k-1}) \subseteq [a, y_{t-1}]$ since Y_{k-1} is embedded inside. Planarity then requires that Y_k be an external retreat segment for at least one of the intervals $[y_0, y_1), [y_2, y_3), \ldots, [y_{t-2}, y_{t-1})$. By assumption (1) of this Lemma, the only possibility is $[y_{t-2}, y_{t-1})$.

The proof now proceeds in a manner analogous to Lemma 8.14. Assume again that $TAIL(Y_k) \leq y_{t-1}$ for $k = 1,\ldots,p$. If $[y_{t-2}, y_{t-1})$ has no external retreat segment, then, by the previous paragraphs, $RANGE(Y_k) \subseteq [a, y_{t-1}]$ for all $k = 1,\ldots,p$. But this is impossible since Y_p dl A. Thus let q be the first integer such that $TAIL(Y_q) > y_{t-1}$. Note that Y_q dl Y_{q-1} and $RANGE(Y_{q-1}) \subseteq [a, y_{t-1}]$. Since Y_q ndl F, we see that $TAIL(F) \leq LOW1(Y_q) < y_{t-1}$. Using planarity and the fact that $X_1,\ldots,X_{t-1}$ are minimal forces $LOW1(Y_q)$ to satisfy the inequality $y_{t-2} \leq LOW1(Y_q) < y_{t-1}$. Y_q may then be taken to be the X_t specified by this Lemma.

LEMMA 8.16 suggests an obvious algorithm for constructing a sequence of segments X_i that, depending on whether or not a retreat segment is encountered, will terminate in one of two cases. These two cases are shown in FIGURE 8.18 (with $t = 6$ and $X_6 = Z'$). In FIGURE 8.18 either Z or Z' will occur, so either $a_1 = LOW1(Z)$ or $TAIL(Z')$. In either case, $b_1 = LOW1(F)$, $b_2 = LOW1(B)$, $b_3 = LOW1(X_1)$, etc. The point b_8 will be $LOW1(Z')$ but may not be $TAIL(Z)$. The point a_2 is the point that has been discovered as the head of a backedge from the segment A that directly links A to F. The point a_2 will not in general be $LOW1(A)$. Likewise, the point b_9 of FIGURE 8.18 (the point b_{t+3} in general) need not be $TAIL(A)$. Otherwise, $a_3 = TAIL(F)$, $a_4 = TAIL(B)$, $a_5 = TAIL(X_1)$, etc.

8.17 GEOMETRIC INTERPRETATION OF LEMMA 8.16.

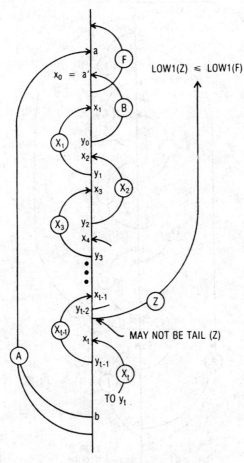

Figure 8.17

8.18   INDUCTIVE TERMINATION OF FIGURE 8.17.   (t = 6)

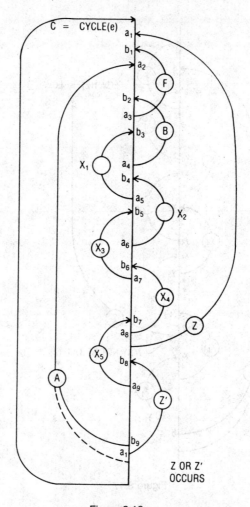

Figure 8.18

We now associate a collection of undirected paths with the structure shown in FIGURE 8.18. These paths will be defined in terms of directed paths in $T \cup B$ as we now describe.

Note that in FIGURE 8.18 we may select a directed path between each pair a_i and b_{i-2} for $i = 3, \ldots, 9$. This path is a directed path joining these vertices in $T \cup B$ and has no edges from CYCLE(e). We retain the undirected paths associated with these paths. The path joining a_2 to b_9 (b_{t+3} in general) will be taken to be the undirected version of a directed path in A from b_9 to a_2 in case b_9 (b_{t+3} in general) is TAIL(A). Otherwise let a_2' and b_9' be the vertices in A adjacent to a_2 and b_9, respectively. Let x be the preorder largest common ancestor of a_2' and b_9' in T (x is in A). The unique directed path from x to a_2' and then to a_2 together with the path from x to b_9 and then to b_9 defines the desired undirected path from a_2 to b_9. For the points a_1 and b_8 we take the undirected version of a directed path from a_1 to b_8 in the case that Z' occurs. In case Z occurs, we take the undirected version of a directed path from b_8 to a_1 if b_8 = TAIL(Z). Otherwise we use a path constructed from the preorder largest common ancestor as above in the case of a_2 and b_9. FIGURE 8.19 shows these undirected paths relative to CYCLE(e) (shown as the circle in FIGURE 8.19). The vertices of degree 2 are not shown. It is easy to see that one can construct this graph in linear time from the standard data structure for directed graphs. FIGURE 8.20 shows a further reduction of FIGURE 8.19. In the general case, b_8 becomes b_{t+2}, a_9 becomes a_{t+3}, and b_9 becomes b_{t+3}. Again ignoring vertices of degree 2, we obtain the graph of FIGURE 8.21. The smallest possible value of $t+3$ is 5 as indicated in FIGURE 8.21. In general, this graph has 10 vertices, a_1, b_1, a_2, b_2, a_3, b_3, a_4, b_{t+2}, a_{t+3}, b_{t+3}. However, for any or all of these pairs (a_i, b_i) we may have $a_i = b_i$ ($a_4 \neq b_{t+2}$ if t > 2).

8.19   FUNDAMENTAL SUBGRAPH OF FIGURE 8.18.   (t = 6)

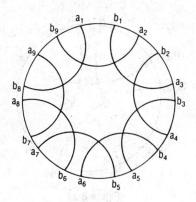

Figure 8.19

8.20   SUBGRAPH OF FIGURE 8.19.   (t = 6)

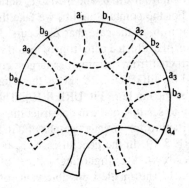

Figure 8.20

8.21   COMPLETE HOMEOMORPHIC REDUCTION OF FIGURE 8.20. (t = 6)

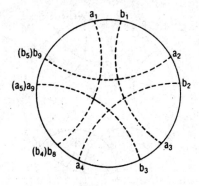

Figure 8.21

The class of graphs isomorphic to that of FIGURE 8.21, with certain vertices possibly identified as remarked above, is by definition the desired class HOMKERNEL(A,B,F) for BASIC CASE 8.5(2).

8.22   LEMMA.

If the conditions of BASIC CASE 8.5(2) hold, then G contains a subgraph whose complete homeomorphic reduction is of the type shown in FIGURE 8.21. In general, if the vertices of this graph are denoted by a_1, b_1, a_2, b_2, a_3, b_3, a_4, b_{t+2}, a_{t+3}, b_{t+3} corresponding to the associated structure specified by FIGURE 8.18, then possibly any combination of the equalities $a_1 = b_1$, $a_2 = b_2$, $a_3 = b_3$, $a_{t+3} = b_{t+3}$ holds. If $t > 2$ then a_4 never equals b_{t+2} but if $t = 2$ then possibly

$a_4 = b_4$ occurs. Thus, if $t > 2$ then G always contains a Kuratowski subgraph of type $K_{3,3}$ as shown in FIGURE 8.23. If $t = 2$ then G contains a Kuratowski subgraph of type $K_{3,3}$, unless all possible equalities $a_1 = b_1, \ldots, a_5 = b_5$ occur in which case G contains a subgraph of type K_5 (and possible also one of type $K_{3,3}$, which we have not detected).

Proof. All results directly follow from the above discussion. If $t > 2$ or $t = 2$ and at least one equality fails to occur, the subgraph with complete homeomorphic reduction $K_{3,3}$ is obtained analogous to that of FIGURE 8.23. Otherwise, the subgraph with complete homeomorphic reduction K_5 is as shown in FIGURE 8.24.

8.23 HOMKERNEL(A,B,F) CONTAINS $K_{3,3}$.

(Requires at least one inequality, in this case $a_4 \neq b_{t+2}$)

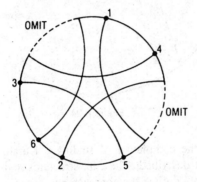

Figure 8.23

8.24   HOMKERNEL(A,B,F) CONTAINS K_5.

(Requires t = 2 and all equalities hold)

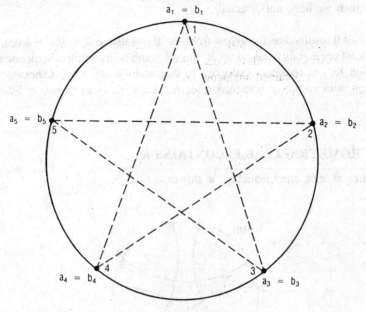

Figure 8.24

We now discuss the complexity of finding a Kuratowski subgraph by the method we have just described. The data structures and methods are all fairly standard, so we simply outline the approach and describe those areas that seem to cause some difficulty. There are three basic steps to the algorithm that must be done in linear time in vertices of the original graph G.

8.25   THREE BASIC STEPS TO FINDING A KURATOWSKI SUBGRAPH IN LINEAR TIME.

(1) The path $(B, Y_1, . . ., Y_p, A)$ joining B to A in SEGFO(e,X) with p even and A and B directly linked to F must be constructed in linear time.
(2) BASIC CASES 8.5(1) or 8.5(2) must be constructed in linear time.
(3) A graph in HOMKERNEL(A,B,F) must be constructed in linear time.

The construction of the path of 8.25(1) in linear time is the topic of EXERCISE 7.31(3) and the related references at the end of PART II. Let FLIST denote the subsequence of SEGLST(e,X) defined by the segments that occur in the path of 8.25(1) together with F. FLIST may be constructed in linear time by a "radix" or "lexicographic" bucket sort just as SEGLST(e,X) is constructed. Each segment Z in the list FLIST has the structure of a directed spanning tree together with a directed graph of backedges. The tree is represented in the standard way as a "binary" tree with each vertex having a pointer to its father, next brother, and first son. For each backedge f, there is a pointer from HEAD(f) to TAIL(f). The root of the spanning tree associated with Z is TAIL(Z). Associated with Z we also have pointers to LOW1(Z), LOW2(Z), and TAIL(Z). We also have a pointer to the linked list HEAD(Z). For each vertex x in CYCLE(e) we have a pointer to the sublist of FLIST consisting of all segments Z with x an element of HEAD(Z). We call this list F_xLIST. It is constructed by going through the list FLIST and for each segment Z going through HEAD(Z) adding Z to the list associated with each vertex of HEAD(Z). This construction is obviously linear in edges and hence also linear in vertices of G (using the reduction to the case $|E| \leq 3|V| - 5$). Also, with each element Z of F_xLIST we keep a pointer to the location of x in the data structure representing Z.

The transition from 8.25(1) to 8.25(2) in linear time requires, in case 8.5(2), going through the sequence $Y_1, \ldots, Y_p$ in order and checking for each Y_i whether or not it is directly linked to F. As F is ahead of Y_i in the order on SEGLST(e), this requires checking if any entry of the list HEAD(Y_i) lies between LOW1(F) and TAIL(F). To check this out it suffices to make one pass through HEAD(Y_i) for each Y_i. Thus, this process is again going to be linear in edges and, hence, in vertices.

We now consider the problem of 8.25(3), constructing a graph in HOMKER-NEL(A,B,F) in linear time. If BASIC CASE 8.25(1) holds, the construction is easily carried out using the data structures described above. If BASIC CASE 8.5(2) holds, then the desired linear time construction follows from LEMMA 8.16 as we now describe. We assume that the list FLIST is constructed from the reduced path that occurs in BASIC CASE 8.5(2). We refer now to FIGURE 8.17. We first go through the vertices of CYCLE(e) from TAIL(F) to TAIL(B). For each such vertex x, we go through F_xLIST in order to see if there is a segment Z with TAIL(Z) greater than TAIL(B). By LEMMA 8.14 we must find such a Z for some x with TAIL(F) $\leq$ x $<$ TAIL(B). The number of times this test is made is clearly bounded by the number of backedges f with TAIL(F) $\leq$ HEAD(f) $<$ TAIL(B). The first time such a Z is found we set that Z $= X_1$. It is easily seen that X_1 satisfies the minimality condition of LEMMA 8.16(3). We now check all vertices x in CYCLE(e) with TAIL(B) $\leq$ x $<$ TAIL(X_1). Again, for each such x we go through F_xLIST in order, checking for a Z with TAIL(Z) greater than TAIL(X_1) or with LOW1(Z) $\leq$ LOW1(F) (i.e., a retreat segment). Again by LEMMA 8.16, such a Z must be found. If no retreat segment is found, then the first such Z $= X_2$ satisfies the minimality condition of LEMMA 8.16. Again, the number of segments that must be checked for these two conditions is bounded by the number of backedges f with TAIL(B) $\leq$ HEAD(f) $<$ TAIL(X_1). This set of backedges is disjoint from the set of backedges used above to bound the tests required to locate X_1. Continuing in this way, we see that the chain of segments specified by FIGURE 8.18 can be constructed in linear time. The reduction of this chain to the FUNDAMENTAL SUBGRAPH 8.19 and from there to the COMPLETE HOMEOMORPHIC REDUCTION 8.21 can easily be seen to be carried out in linear time using the data structures previously described.

8.26 EXERCISE.

(1) Construct some nontrivial examples of nonplanar graphs and locate the Kuratowski subgraphs by the methods discussed previously.

(2) Try to construct some interesting examples of nonplanar graphs that do not contain a Kuratowski subgraph of type $K_{3,3}$.

(3) In the case of BASIC CASE 8.5(2) we have shown explicitly how to find the Kuratowski subgraph. If BASIC CASE 8.5(1) occurs, we have reduced the problem to searching for a Kuratowski subgraph in one of finitely many (up to isomorphism) nonplanar graphs. Can you be more specific about how to find a Kuratowski subgraph in the case of BASIC CASE 8.5(1)?

(4) Technically, our method for finding Kuratowski subgraphs is not a proof of Kuratowski's theorem (THEOREM 8.2) due to the fact that we have not shown explicitly that every graph HOMKERNEL(A,B,F) in BASIC CASE 8.5(1) has a Kuratowski subgraph. Kuratowski's theorem guarantees us that this is the case. If you have worked EXERCISE 8.26(3) then that result may be used, together with our discussion of BASIC CASE 8.5(2) to provide an independent proof of Kuratowski's theorem. Is there an easier way to modify our algorithm to provide an independent proof of Kuratowski's theorem?

Chapter 9

Topic III: Triconnectivity

In DEFINITION 6.95 we introduced the notion of a biconnected or "2-connected" graph. From EXERCISE 6.96(2) it is evident that a connected graph G is not biconnected if and only if it has an articulation point. The intuitive idea of an articulation point is shown in FIGURE 9.1(a). There, the graph $G = (V,E)$ has its edge set E partitioned into two subsets, F and $F^c = E - F$. For any subset $S \subseteq E$, let $V(S)$ denote the set of vertices of edges in S. For the vertex x of FIGURE 9.1(a) to be an articulation point, we must have $|F| \geq 1$, $|F^c| \geq 1$, and $|V(F) \cap V(F^c)| = 1$. If G is connected and the articulation point x together with all edges of I_x (the set of edges incident on x, see DEFINITION 6.6) are removed from the graph then G becomes disconnected. Thus an articulation point is a vertex of G whose deletion separates G into two or more components. This idea is generalized in DEFINITION 9.2.

9.1 PICTORIAL REPRESENTATION OF 1- AND 2-SEPARATION SETS.

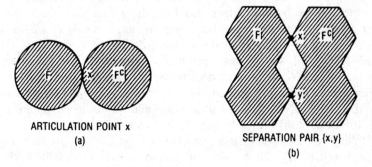

ARTICULATION POINT x

(a)

SEPARATION PAIR {x,y}

(b)

Figure 9.1

9.2 DEFINITION.

Let $G = (V,E)$ be a connected graph and let k be any positive integer. Let $\mathscr{S}_k = \{F: F \subseteq E, |F| \geq k, |F^c| \geq k, |V(F) \cap V(F^c)| = k\}$. If $\mathscr{S}_k$ is nonempty then G is called a *k-separated* graph. If F is in $\mathscr{S}_k$ then the set of vertices $V(F) \cap$

V(F^c) is called a k-separation set for G. The 1-separation sets are the *articulation points* and the 2-separation sets are called *separation pairs*.

In a certain sense, the k-separation sets provide a measure of the degree of connectedness of a graph. There are many possible variations on this idea and a general study of connectivity will not concern us here. One natural definition of connectivity is given in DEFINITION 9.3.

9.3 DEFINITION.

Let G = (V,E) be a graph. We denote by k(G) a non-negative integer called the *connectivity* of G. If G is disconnected then k(G) = 0. For connected G, if |E| = 0 then k(G) = 1, if |E| = 1 then k(G) = 2, and if G is a cycle of length 3 then k(G) = 3. For all other connected G, k(G) is the smallest integer k such that $\mathcal{S}_k$ of DEFINITION 9.2 is nonempty. We say that G is t-*connected* for any integer $0 \leq t \leq k(G)$.

We shall not use DEFINITION 9.3 except for the cases k(G) = 0,1,2,3. We want to say that the graph consisting of one vertex has connectivity 1, the graph consisting of a single edge has connectivity 2, and a cycle of length 3 has connectivity 3 for technical reasons. For these graphs $\mathcal{S}_k$ is empty for all k = 1,2,.... . sometimes these graphs are said to have "infinite connectivity" for this reason. Our graphs of the form G = (V,E) do not have loops or multiple edges (such as the edge "a" of FIGURE 6.1 or the pair of edges "e" and "f" of FIGURE 6.1). If these more general graphs are considered then the graphs consisting of a single loop, a pair of vertices joined by two edges, and a pair of vertices joined by three edges would also have "infinite connectivity." All other graphs have finite connectivity k(G). In fact, it is easy to see that k(G) is always less than or equal to the minimal degree of a vertex of G. From DEFINITION 9.3, we see that a graph is 3-connected or "triconnected" if its connectivity is 3 or more. Equivalently, we may say that *a graph G = (V,E) is triconnected if it is biconnected with at least three edges and has no separation pair* (DEFINITION 9.2). Some ideas associated with connectivity are explored in EXERCISE 9.38(1).

At this point the reader should recall the idea of a bridge graph of a cycle in a graph (DEFINITION 6.110) and related ideas (FIGURES 6.98, 6.99, DEFINITIONS 6.100, 6.101, 6.102, EXERCISE 6.109(3)). In BASIC NOTATION 8.3 we introduced some terminology for segment graphs. This terminology has obvious extensions to the slightly more general setting of bridge graphs which we now describe. Let $\mathcal{C} = (x_1,x_2,\ldots,x_k,x_1)$ be a cycle of a biconnected graph G as shown in FIGURE 9.4. Let $\mathcal{C}'$ be the corresponding broken cycle obtained by removing the edge $\{x_k,x_1\}$ from $\mathcal{C}$. We associate $\mathcal{C}'$ with a directed path $(x_1,x_2,\ldots,x_k)$ as shown in FIGURE 9.4. FIGURE 9.4 shows a bridge A relative to the cycle $\mathcal{C}$. As in BASIC NOTATION 8.3, let RANGE(A) be the vertices common to A and $\mathcal{C}$ (the "vertices of attachment" of A to $\mathscr{C}$). RANGE(A) is linearly ordered by the order of the vertices in $\mathscr{C}'$. We call the first vertex in RANGE(A) LOW1(A) and the last vertex TAIL(A). The directed path in $\mathscr{C}'$ from LOW1(A) to TAIL(A) is called SPAN(A). If $v_1 < v_2 < \ldots < v_r$ is RANGE(A) then the directed paths from v_i to v_{i+1}, $i = 1, \ldots, r-1$, are called the proper gaps of A. The directed path in $\mathscr{C}$ from v_r to v_1 is called the cospan of A. In FIGURE 9.4, SPAN(B) is contained in a proper gap of A. When this happens, we say that A *arches* B or B *is arched by* A.

9.4 BRIDGES OF A BROKEN CYCLE.

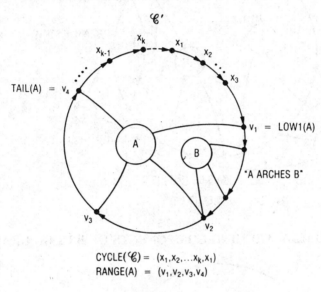

$$\text{CYCLE}(\mathscr{C}) = (x_1, x_2, \ldots x_k, x_1)$$
$$\text{RANGE(A)} = (v_1, v_2, v_3, v_4)$$

Figure 9.4

If $\mathscr{C}$ is a cycle, we denote BRGR($\mathscr{C}$) the bridge graph of $\mathscr{C}$. If $\mathscr{H}$ is a component of BRGR($\mathscr{C}$) then RANGE($\mathscr{H}$) is the union of RANGE(X) for X a vertex of $\mathscr{H}$. Let $\mathscr{C}'$ be a broken cycle of $\mathscr{C}$ with corresponding directed path $(x_1, x_2, \ldots, x_k)$. We define LOW1($\mathscr{H}$) to be the first vertex of RANGE($\mathscr{H}$) on this path and TAIL($\mathscr{H}$) to be the last vertex. As the graph G is biconnected, we always have LOW1($\mathscr{H}$) < TAIL($\mathscr{H}$) in the order on $\mathscr{C}'$. If $v_1 < v_2 < \ldots < v_r$ is RANGE($\mathscr{H}$) then the proper gaps and cospan of $\mathscr{H}$ are defined as in the previous paragraph for a single bridge. If $\mathscr{H}_1$ and $\mathscr{H}_2$ are components and RANGE($\mathscr{H}_2$) is contained in a proper gap of $\mathscr{H}_1$ then we say $\mathscr{H}_1$ arches $\mathscr{H}_2$ and we write $\mathscr{H}_1 \geqslant \mathscr{H}_2$. These ideas are illustrated in FIGURE 9.5. In FIGURE 9.5, $\mathscr{H}_1$ arches $\mathscr{H}_2$. It is possible to have components $\mathscr{H}_1$ and $\mathscr{H}_2$ such that $\mathscr{H}_1$ arches $\mathscr{H}_2$ and $\mathscr{H}_2$ arches $\mathscr{H}_1$ but $\mathscr{H}_1 \neq \mathscr{H}_2$. This can only happen if $\mathscr{H}_1$ and $\mathscr{H}_2$ have only one bridge. This situation is shown in FIGURE 9.6. Note that in FIGURE 9.6, RANGE($\mathscr{H}_1$) = RANGE ($\mathscr{H}_2$) and there are only two vertices in each set. If there are no such mutually arching bridges then the arching relation on the set of components of BRGR($\mathscr{C}$) is an order relation (define $\mathscr{H} \geq \mathscr{H}$ in this case). In EXERCISE 9.38 the reader is asked to prove THEOREM 9.7 (recall DEFINITION 1.2 of CHAPTER 1 which defines "order relation").

9.5   ARCHING RELATION ON COMPONENTS OF BRIDGE GRAPH.

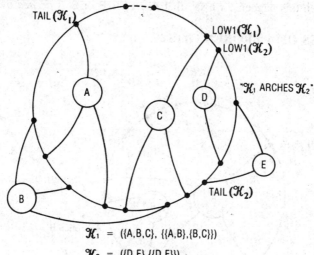

$$\mathscr{H}_1 = (\{A,B,C\}, \{\{A,B\},\{B,C\}\})$$
$$\mathscr{H}_2 = (\{D,E\},\{\{D,E\}\})$$

Figure 9.5

9.6   MUTUALLY ARCHING COMPONENTS OF BRIDGE GRAPH.

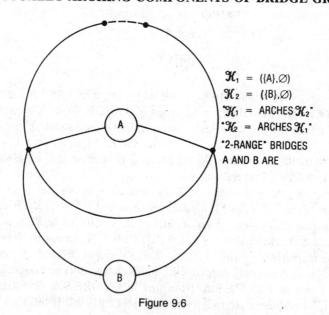

$$\mathscr{H}_1 = (\{A\},\varnothing)$$
$$\mathscr{H}_2 = (\{B\},\varnothing)$$
"$\mathscr{H}_1$ = ARCHES $\mathscr{H}_2$"
"$\mathscr{H}_2$ = ARCHES $\mathscr{H}_1$"
"2-RANGE" BRIDGES
A AND B ARE

Figure 9.6

9.7   THEOREM. (Restate to deal with mutually arching bridges!)

Let $G = (V,E)$ be a biconnected graph and let $\mathscr{C}'$ be a broken cycle of G. The arching relation on components of $BRGR(\mathscr{C})$ is an order relation.

Proof.   EXERCISE 9.38(2).

We now look more closely at the notion of a "separation pair." In DEFINITION 6.100 and EXERCISE 6.109(7) we defined the concept of a bridge relative to a subgraph. Using the definition of EXERCISE 6.109(7), for example, let $H = (\{a,b\},\phi)$ be the subgraph consisting of the two vertices a and b of G and no edges. The bridges relative to this subgraph are the equivalence classes of the equivalence relation defined in EXERCISE 6.109(7). That is, two edges e and f are equivalent if there is a path joining e to f without a or b as internal vertices. These equivalance classes are as shown in FIGURE 9.8. We call such equivalence classes *separation classes* of a,b.

9.8   SEPARATION CLASSES OF A PAIR OF VERTICES.

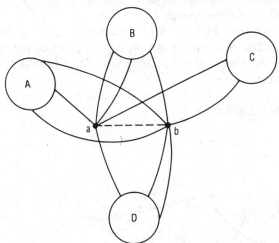

A,B,C,D ARE "SEPARATION CLASSES" OF THE PAIR {a,b}. THE
EDGE JOINING a AND b MAY BE A "TRIVIAL" SEPARATION
CLASS.

Figure 9.8

We call a separation class *nontrivial* if it has at least two edges. Thus, a pair of vertices of a biconnected graph $G = (V,E)$ is a separation pair if and only if it has at least two nontrivial separation classes.

We now develop the relationship between bridges of a cycle and separation classes of a pair of vertices {a,b}. As we have just noted, if the pair {a,b} is a

separation pair in the sense of DEFINITION 9.2 then there must exist at least
two nontrivial separation classes of {a,b}. Let $\mathscr{C}$ be a cycle containing the vertices
a and b of the separation pair {a,b}. There are three basic cases of interest to
us, shown in FIGURES 9.10, 9.11, and 9.12. The circled regions A, B, X,
etc., in these FIGURES are subgraphs, the detailed structure of which is not
shown explicitly. In FIGURE 9.10, the cycle $\mathscr{C} = (v_1, v_2, \ldots, v_8, v_1)$ lies entirely
within one separation class A. As remarked above, there must exist another
nontrivial separation class B as shown in FIGURE 9.10. Clearly, the separation
class B is also a bridge of the cycle $\mathscr{C}$. Note that the RANGE(B) = {a,b}.

9.9 DEFINITION.

Let $\mathscr{C}$ be a cycle and B a bridge of $\mathscr{C}$. If RANGE(B) has exactly two elements
then we call B a *2-range* bridge of $\mathscr{C}$. In other words, B has two vertices of
attachment to $\mathscr{C}$.

Thus, FIGURE 9.10 shows that if $\mathscr{C}$ is contained in a single separation class
then $\mathscr{C}$ must have a 2-range bridge B with RANGE(B) = {a,b}. If one considers
the bridge X in FIGURE 9.10 it is apparent that X and B are joined in BRGR($\mathscr{C}$).
Thus, in the case of FIGURE 9.10, one can have many bridges of $\mathscr{C}$ and have
BRGR($\mathscr{C}$) either connected or disconnected.

Another basic case is shown in FIGURE 9.11. In this case, the cycle has all
of its edges in separation class A except for the one edge {a,b} which is a trivial
separation class. Again, there must be a 2-range bridge B and BRGR($\mathscr{C}$) may
be connected or disconnected.

9.10 CASE I OF THEOREM 9.13.

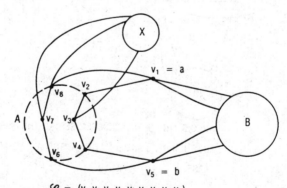

$$\mathscr{C} = (v_1, v_2, v_3, v_4, v_5, v_6, v_7, v_8, v_1)$$

A (WHICH INCLUDES X) AND B ARE SEPARATION CLASSES.

Figure 9.10

9.11   CASE II OF THEOREM 9.13.

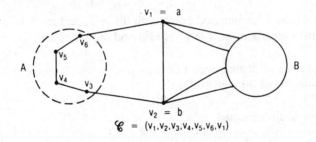

Figure 9.11

9.12   CASE III OF THEOREM 9.13.

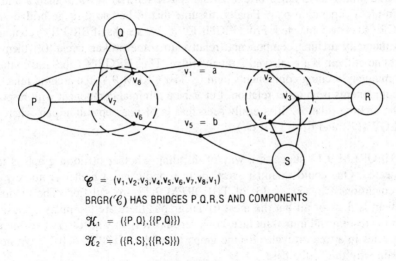

Figure 9.12

The third basic case is shown in FIGURE 9.12. In this case the cycle is contained in two separation classes. Obviously, a cycle cannot be contained in three separation classes. Case III is broken down into two subcases, where $\mathcal{C}$ has a vertex of degree 2 in G and where $\mathcal{C}$ does not have a vertex of degree 2. It is the latter case that is shown in FIGURE 9.12. Note that the fact that $\mathcal{C}$ does not have a vertex of degree 2 forces the bridge graph, BRGR($\mathcal{C}$) to have at least two components, as shown in FIGURE 9.12. One or both of these components may have only one vertex (a bridge of $\mathcal{C}$). These observations form the basis for the proof of the ''only if'' part of THEOREM 9.13.

9.13   THEOREM.

Let $G = (V,E)$ be a biconnected graph with $|E| > 3$, and let $\mathscr{C}$ be a cycle of G. $\mathscr{C}$ contains a separation pair $\{a,b\}$ of G if and only if either

(1) $\mathscr{C}$ has a vertex of degree two in G
(2) $\mathscr{C}$ has a nontrivial 2-range bridge
or
(3) BRGR($\mathscr{C}$) is disconnected

Proof.   The "only if" part follows from FIGURES 9.10, 9.11, and 9.12 and the related discussion. To prove the converse, suppose that $\mathscr{C}$ has a vertex v of degree 2 in G. If $\mathscr{C}$ has only three edges then condition (2) holds. If $\mathscr{C}$ has more than three edges then the vertices of $\mathscr{C}$ adjacent to v form a separation pair. If $\mathscr{C}$ has a nontrivial 2-range bridge B and if RANGE(B) $= \{a,b\}$ then a and b again are a separation pair. Finally, assume that $\mathscr{C}$ has no 2-range bridge and BRGR ($\mathscr{C}$) is disconnected. From FIGURE 9.6, we see that if BRGR($\mathscr{C}$) contains two mutually arching components (relative to some broken cycle $\mathscr{C}'$) then at least one of them is a nontrivial 2-range bridge. Thus BRGR($\mathscr{C}$) does not contain any mutually arching components, and by THEOREM 9.7, the arching relation on components is an order relation. Let $\mathscr{H}$ be a minimal component with respect to the arching relation. It is easily seen that $\{a,b\}$ is a separation pair where a $= \mathrm{LOW1}(\mathscr{H})$ and b $= \mathrm{TAIL}(\mathscr{H})$.

THEOREM 9.13 suggests a way of deciding whether or not a graph is triconnected. One could examine every cycle $\mathscr{C}$ and check whether or not any of the conditions (1), (2), or (3) of THEOREM 9.13 are satisfied. The obvious problem is that for all but the most trivial graphs there are too many cycles. It is an interesting and important fact, however, that it is only necessary to examine the cycles in a tree of cycles for the graph (see DEFINITION 6.107). We now explain why this is the case.

Let $G = (V,E)$ be a biconnected graph and let $\{a,b\}$ be a separation pair. If $\mathscr{C}$ is a cycle in G, then we have seen that $\mathscr{C}$ either has all edges entirely in one separation class or has edges in two classes. These two possibilities are shown in FIGURES 9.10, 9.11, and 9.12. If the cycle does not contain both a and b then the cycle cannot have edges in two different separation classes as shown in FIGURES 9.11 or 9.12 (this forces a and b to both be on $\mathscr{C}$). If $\mathscr{C}$ has all edges in one separation class it may have both a and b as vertices as in FIGURE 9.10, but it also may contain just one or neither of the vertices a and b as shown in FIGURE 9.14. In any case, we have the trivial LEMMA 9.15.

9.14   THE CYCLE IS CONTAINED IN A SEPARATION CLASS.

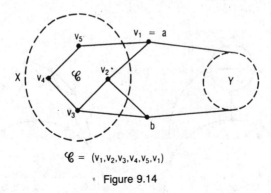

$$\mathscr{C} = (v_1, v_2, v_3, v_4, v_5, v_1)$$

Figure 9.14

9.15   LEMMA.

Let G be a biconnected graph with separation pair $\{a,b\}$. Let $\mathscr{C}$ be a cycle such that not both a and b are vertices of $\mathscr{C}$. Then the edges of $\mathscr{C}$ are all contained in one separation class of G.

A second fact we need concerns the bridges of a cycle $\mathscr{C}$ such as that of LEMMA 9.15. Again, let G be biconnected with cycle $\mathscr{C}$ and assume that $\{a,b\}$ is a separation pair with a on $\mathscr{C}$ and b not on $\mathscr{C}$. The fact that b is not on $\mathscr{C}$ implies by LEMMA 9.15 that all edges of $\mathscr{C}$ belong to the same separation class of $\{a,b\}$. FIGURE 9.16(a) shows a bridge B of $\mathscr{C}$. Note, a is not a vertex of RANGE(B), and hence, whether or not b is in B, the following is true: given any edge e of B, there is a path that does not contain a or b as interior vertices joining e to at least one edge of $\mathscr{C}$. Thus, all edges of B belong to the same separation class of $\{a,b\}$ as the edges of $\mathscr{C}$. It is also easy to see that if a is in RANGE(B) but b is not in B, then all edges of B lie in the same separation class as the edges of $\mathscr{C}$. FIGURE 9.16(b) shows the situation with a in RANGE(B) and b in B. Note in this case that the edges s,t,u,v, and w of B do not belong to the same separation class of $\{a,b\}$ as the edges of $\mathscr{C}$. These observations lead to LEMMA 9.17.

9.16   THE INTUITIVE IDEA OF LEMMA 9.17.

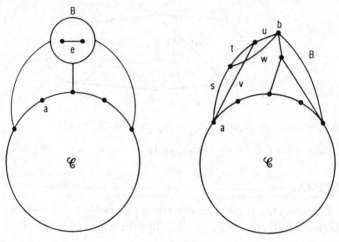

Figure 9.16

9.17   LEMMA.

Let G be a biconnected graph and let $\mathscr{C}$ be a cycle of G. Let $\{a,b\}$ be a separation pair of G with a and b not both on $\mathscr{C}$. Then a and b belong to the same bridge B of $\mathscr{C}$.

Proof.   Let X be a bridge of $\mathscr{C}$ that does not contain both a and b as vertices. As noted above, every edge of X belongs to the same separation class as the edges of $\mathscr{C}$ relative to the separation pair $\{a,b\}$. Thus, if there does not exist a bridge B with both a and b as vertices then there is only one separation class of $\{a,b\}$, contradicting the choice of a and b. Thus, the bridge B must exist.

Let G, $\mathscr{C}$, $\{a,b\}$, and B be as in LEMMA 9.17. Let $\mathscr{C}'$ be any broken cycle associated wtih $\mathscr{C}$ and let B' denote the carrier of B relative to $\mathscr{C}'$. The reader should review DEFINITION 6.102, FIGURE 6.103, and EXERCISE 6.109(3). It is shown in EXERCISE 6.109(3) that the carrier B' is just B together with the edges of the SPAN(B) in $\mathscr{C}'$. The carrier B' is a biconnected graph and, as a consequence of LEMMA 9.17, B' has both a and b as vertices (in fact, they are vertices of B). We now assert that under the hypothesis of LEMMA 9.17 the pair $\{a,b\}$ is a separation pair of B'. Using FIGURE 9.14 as an example, note that the cycle $\mathscr{C}$ is contained in a separation class X (a consequence of LEMMA 9.15). In FIGURE 9.14, for example, suppose that $\mathscr{C}'$ is $\mathscr{C} - \{v_4,v_5\}$. Then a and b are contained in the bridge $B = Y \cup \{v_3,b\} \cup \{v_2,b\}$ of $\mathscr{C}$, and B' is B together with the two edges $\{v_1,v_2\}$ and $\{v_2,v_3\}$, which are the edges of SPAN(B) relative to $\mathscr{C}'$. Generally, all separation classes of $\{a,b\}$ in G other than X belong to the bridge B. Thus these *remain* separation classes of {a,b} in the biconnected graph B' and at least one of them must be nontrivial. We must show that there is another nontrivial separation class of {a,b} in B'. In general, given any vertex c of RANGE(B) and any vertex d of B there is a path *in* B from d to c. Assume b is not on $\mathscr{C}$. Choose c ≠ a. Consider the path P in B from b to c. By interchanging the roles of a and b if necessary, we may assume that a is not on this path. The vertex c is on some edge e of $\mathscr{C}'$. Thus, the edges of P together with the edge e (totalling at least two edges) belong to a nontrivial separation class of {a,b} in B'. These edges are also in X since e is in X and hence this class is distinct from the one mentioned above. Thus {a,b} is a separation pair for B . These ideas are summarized in LEMMA 9.18.

9.18 LEMMA.

Let B be the bridge of LEMMA 9.17 that contains the separation pair {a,b} and let B' be the carrier of B relative to the broken cycle $\mathscr{C}'$. The separation pair {a,b} of G is also a separation pair of B'.

Recalling the definition of the cycle tree of a biconnected graph G (DEFINITION 6.107), we can now prove THEOREM 9.19 by induction (EXERCISE 9.38(3)).

9.19 THEOREM.

Let G be a biconnected graph and let CYCTR(G) be any cycle tree of G in the sense of DEFINITION 6.107. If {a,b} is a separation pair of G then a and b must both lie on some cycle of CYCTR(G).

Using THEOREM 9.19, we can now check the conditions of THEOREM 9.13 on a much smaller class of cycles of G.

9.20 REASONABLE TRICONNECTIVITY ALGORITHM.

Given a biconnected graph G, construct a cycle tree CYCTR(G) for G and then check each of the conditions of THEOREM 9.13 for each cycle that occurs as a vertex of CYCTR(G). Only cycles corresponding to nontrivial bridges need be checked.

The reader should "execute" ALGORITHM 9.20 on the cycle tree of FIGURE 6.108.

The reader has probably noticed that, although REASONABLE TRICONNECTIVITY ALGORITHM 9.20 reduces the number of cycles of G that one need inspect for separation pairs, at each cycle it still is necessary to consider all of the graph G. One can improve this situation by reducing the size of the graph associated with each cycle as we now describe.

FIGURE 9.22(a) shows a biconnected graph G with two bridges A and B.

The carriers of the two bridges are labeled A' and B' and are shown in FIGURE 9.22(b) and (c). The cycle $\mathscr{C}$ in this figure is (1,2,3,4,5,1) and $\mathscr{C}'$ is (1,2,3,4,5). Among the separation pairs of B' we find {5,9} {7,8}, and {2,4}. The first two pairs are separation pairs of G but the pair {2,4} is not a separation pair of G. To avoid introducing new separation pairs, such as {2,4} in this example, we introduce the idea of a *closed carrier* in DEFINITION 9.21 and *reduced carrier*, DEFINITION 9.25.

9.21 DEFINITION.

Let G be a biconnected graph with broken cycle $\mathscr{C}'$. Let X be a nontrivial bridge of $\mathscr{C}$ with SPAN(X) = $(v_1, . . ., v_p)$, $p \geq 3$. The bridge X together with the cycle $(v_1, . . ., v_p, v_1)$ will be called the *closed carrier* of X. If $p = 2$ (X has just two vertices of attachment to $\mathscr{C}$) then the *closed carrier* of X is defined to be simply the carrier of X.

The closed carriers of the bridges A and B of FIGURE 9.22 are shown in FIGURE 9.23.

9.22   THE CARRIER HAS SEPARATION PAIRS NOT IN G.

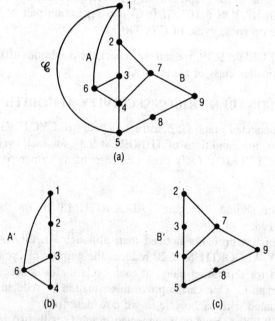

Figure 9.22

9.23 THE CLOSED CARRIERS OF BRIDGES A AND B OF FIGURE 9.22.

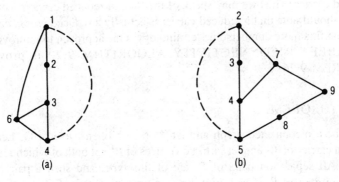

Figure 9.23

We require one more step in connection with the closed carriers of FIGURE 9.23. In both FIGURE 9.23(a) and (b) there are vertices of degree two on the span of the carrier. In FIGURE 9.23(a), for example, the vertex 2 is of degree two. Vertices of degree two can be eliminated by considering any two edges incident on a vertex of degree two as part of the same edge. Equivalently, we replace all proper gaps of the bridge by a single edge. The result for FIGURE 9.23 is shown in FIGURE 9.24. We call the resulting graphs the *reduced carriers* of $\mathscr{C}'$ as stated in DEFINITION 9.25.

9.24 THE REDUCED CARRIERS OF FIGURE 9.23.

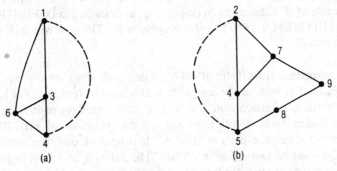

Figure 9.24

9.25 DEFINITION.

Let G be a biconnected graph and let $\mathscr{C}'$ be a broken cycle of G. Let B be a nontrivial bridge and B' its closed carrier with respect to $\mathscr{C}$. If each proper gap of B in B' is replaced by a single edge then the resulting graph will be called a *reduced carrier* of $\mathscr{C}'$. From DEFINITION 9.25 we see that for each broken cycle $\mathscr{C}'$ and each nontrivial bridge B of $\mathscr{C}'$ there is a unique (up to isomorphism) reduced carrier. Thus we may speak of the "set of reduced carriers" of $\mathscr{C}'$. The reader should note that a reduced carrier is actually a reduced *closed* carrier, but we avoid this more cumbersome terminology. One approach to improving REASONABLE TRICONNECTIVITY ALGORITHM 9.20 is provided by THEOREM 9.26.

9.26 THEOREM.

Let G be a biconnected graph and let $\mathscr{C}'$ be a broken cycle of G. Let B' be a reduced carrier of $\mathscr{C}'$ and let {a,b} be vertices of B' not both of which are vertices of $\mathscr{C}'$. All separation pairs of B' are of this type, and such a pair {a,b} is a separation pair of B' if and only if it is a separation pair of G.

Proof.   The basic idea of the proof is to consider the pair of vertices {a,b} in B' and compare the separation classes of {a,b} in B' and in G. Assume that not both a and b are vertices of $\mathscr{C}$ and $|\text{RANGE(B)}| \geq 3$. A little thought reveals that the separation classes of {a,b} in B' and in G are exactly the same except for the class associated with the edges of SPAN(B) = $(v_1,\ldots,v_p)$. In G, this class includes all edges of $\mathscr{C}$ and also all edges belonging to bridges of $\mathscr{C}$ other than the bridge B. In B', this class includes the edges obtained from $(v_1,\ldots,v_p)$ by eliminating vertices of proper gaps of B, as described in DEFINITION 9.25, and the edge $\{v_p,v_1\}$ ($|\text{RANGE(B)}| \geq 3$). By our assumptions, this class still contains at least three edges. Thus, if {a,b} is a separation pair for B' it is obviously also a separation pair for G and conversely. That all separation pairs of B' are of this type follows by noting (for $|\text{RANGE(B)}| \geq 3$) that B is a bridge of the cycle of B' obtained from $(v_1,\ldots,v_p)$ as described in DEFINITION 9.25. Apply THEOREM 9.13 to B and this cycle in B'. The case where $|\text{RANGE(B)}|$ = 2 is trivial.

It is immediate from THEOREM 9.13 that if $\mathscr{C}'$ does not contain any separation pairs of G then any bridge of $\mathscr{C}'$ is either trivial (one edge) or has at least three "vertices of attachment" to $\mathscr{C}'$ (i.e., three vertices in its range). Thus, given a broken cycle $\mathscr{C}'$ of G, we can use the conditions of THEOREM 9.13 to check for separation pairs of G on $\mathscr{C}'$. If none are found then recursively we check the reduced carriers of $\mathscr{C}'$. Thus THEOREM 9.26 seems to provide the basic recursive structure for finding a separation pair of a biconnected graph G. But there remains one small difficulty! Consider the graph of FIGURE 9.27 with cycle $\mathscr{C}$ and bridge B. Let $\mathscr{C}' = (1,2,3)$. The reduced carrier B' is shown in FIGURE 9.27(b) and is isomorphic to the graph G in this case. This is the same problem confronted by the reader in EXERCISE 6.118(3). If this case occurs then one can choose a new cycle $\mathscr{C}$ in the carrier B' that includes the edges of SPAN(B). This new cycle has at least one more edge than $\mathscr{C}$ and has the edge e, deleted in going from $\mathscr{C}$ to $\mathscr{C}'$, as a trivial bridge. Thus any closed carrier (and hence reduced carrier) of $\mathscr{C}$ has fewer edges than G and allows the recursion to proceed. The reader is asked to develop these ideas in EXERCISE 9.38(4). The new cycle and its bridges (both trivial) for the graph of FIGURE 9.27(a) are shown in FIGURE 9.27(c).

9.27 A GRAPH WITH ISOMORPHIC REDUCED CARRIER.

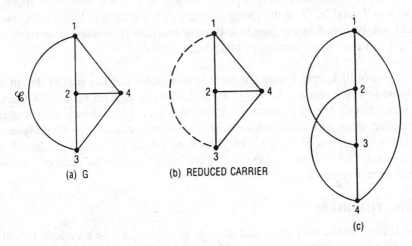

(a) G   (b) REDUCED CARRIER   (c)

Figure 9.27

We now are in a position to improve on REASONABLE TRICONNECTIV-ITY ALGORITHM 9.20. G = (V,E) is a biconnected graph with at least three edges ($|E| \geqslant 3$).

9.28 MORE REASONABLE TRICONNECTIVITY ALGORITHM.

(1) Choose a cycle $\mathscr{C}$ in G = (V,E). Let $\mathscr{C}'$ be a corresponding broken cycle.
(2) If $|E| = 3$ then STOP. G has no separation pairs. Otherwise, check the conditions of THEOREM 9.13 and see if $\mathscr{C}$ has a pair of vertices {a,b} that are a separation pair of G. If there is a separation pair STOP, otherwise go to (3).
(3) If $\mathscr{C}$ has only trivial bridges STOP, G has no separation pairs. Otherwise, if $\mathscr{C}$ has only one bridge B, replace $\mathscr{C}$ by a cycle in the carrier B', choosing the cycle such that it contains the edges of SPAN(B), and go to (2). Otherwise go to (4).
(4) Construct the reduced carriers of the nontrivial bridges of $\mathscr{C}'$ and recursively apply the algorithm to each reduced carrier.

The reader should construct some examples to illustrate the various situations that arise in ALGORITHM 9.28. The purpose of ALGORITHM 9.28 is to find a separation pair of G if one exists. We have actually characterized the set of all separation pairs in the process of proving THEOREM 9.13 and THEOREM 9.26. This result is stated in THEOREM 9.30. We need one more definition to state THEOREM 9.30.

9.29 DEFINITION.

Let G be a biconnected graph and let $\mathcal{C} = (v_1,\ldots,v_p,v_1)$ be a cycle of G with $\mathcal{C}' = (v_1,\ldots,v_p)$. Let $\{a,b\}$ be a pair of vertices of $\mathcal{C}$. Let P be the path joining a to b in $\mathcal{C}'$ and let Q be the complementary path joining a to b in $\mathcal{C}$. The pair $\{a,b\}$ will be called *bridge complete* if every bridge B (trivial and nontrivial) of $\mathcal{C}$ either has all of its vertices of attachment in P or all in Q.

A pair $\{a,b\}$ is thus bridge complete if no bridge of $\mathcal{C}$ has part of its range interior to P and part interior to Q. If a and b are not adjacent vertices of $\mathcal{C}$ and if either P or Q has all its internal vertices of degree 2 in G then $\{a,b\}$ is bridge complete. In particular, if a and b are not adjacent and are themselves the adjacent vertices to a vertex of degree 2 of G on $\mathcal{C}$ then $\{a,b\}$ is bridge complete. We now state a "cycle based" necessary and sufficient condition for a pair of vertices of G to be a separation pair.

9.30 THEOREM.

Let G be a biconnected graph and let $\mathcal{C} = (v_1,\ldots,v_p,v_1)$ be a cycle of G with $\mathcal{C}' = (v_1,\ldots,v_p)$. Then a pair $\{a,b\}$ is a separation pair of G if and only if one of the following conditions holds:

(1) The vertices a and b are on $\mathcal{C}$, are not adjacent, and the pair $\{a,b\}$ is bridge complete.
(2) The vertices a and b are on $\mathcal{C}$ and they are the vertices of attachment of a nontrivial 2-range bridge of $\mathcal{C}$.
(3) The pair $\{a,b\}$ is a separation pair for a reduced carrier of $\mathcal{C}'$.

We now indicate the tree structures analogous to the bicomponent tree (DEFINITION 6.104, FIGURE 6.105) and the tree of cycles (DEFINITION 6.107, FIGURE 6.108) that are associated with the recursion of THEOREM 9.30 and ALGORITHM 9.28. Consider the graph G of FIGURE 9.31. Relative to the broken cycle (1,2,3,4), there are two reduced carriers, shown as the sons of G in FIGURE 9.31. The bridge that produces the first carrier has the separation pair $\{1,3\}$ as vertices of attachment. The pair $\{1,3\}$ satisfies both conditions (1) and (2) of THEOREM 9.30. There are no other separation pairs on (1,2,3,4). The first son of G is triconnected as may be seen by considering the broken cycle (1,3,5,6). There are no separation pairs on this cycle and all bridges of this cycle are trivial. The second son of G in FIGURE 9.31 has two reduced carriers relative to the cycle (1,3,4,7,8). They are both "3-cycles" as shown in FIGURE 9.31.

9.31 THE REDUCED CARRIER TREE OF A GRAPH.

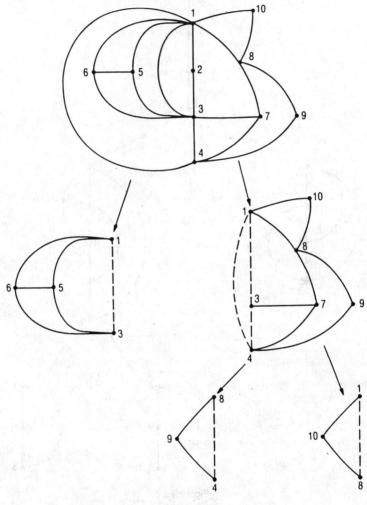

Figure 9.31

Just as in the case of FIGURE 6.105, where we observed that we had too much information labeling the vertices of the tree, we may greatly reduce the structures associated with the vertices of the reduced carrier tree (FIGURE 9.31). At each level of the recursion, we select a broken cycle and extract its reduced carriers. When the carriers are removed, all that is left is a cycle with perhaps some trivial bridges. If this process is repeated the whole graph is eventually decomposed into a tree with vertices labeled by such structures. This process is carried out for the tree of FIGURE 9.31 in FIGURE 9.32. Motivated by DEFINITION 9.33, we call trees such as that of FIGURE 9.32 *Hamiltonian structure trees.*

9.32   HAMILTONIAN STRUCTURE TREE OF FIGURE 9.31.

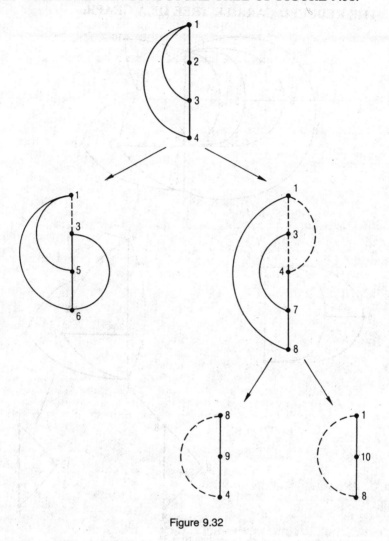

Figure 9.32

9.33   DEFINITION.

A graph G = (V,E) will be called *Hamiltonian* if there is a cycle 𝒞 that has all of V as a vertex set. The cycle 𝒞 is called a *Hamiltonian cycle for* G.

Note that all vertices of the Hamiltonian structure tree of FIGURE 9.32 are Hamiltonian graphs with Hamiltonian cycles as indicated by the vertical sequence of vertices. There are a number of interesting questions about Hamiltonian structure trees that we leave for the reader to explore in EXERCISE 9.38(5). The

Hamiltonian structure tree points out quite strikingly the importance of the test for bridge completeness, THEOREM 9.30(1). One may develop a depth first version of the search for separation pairs along the lines suggested by ALGO-RITHM 9.34.

9.34 DEPTH FIRST SEARCH FOR SEPARATION PAIRS.

(1) Given a biconnected graph G, construct a Hamiltonian structure tree such as that shown in FIGURE 9.32.
(2) Inspect the vertices of the tree constructed in step (1) in postorder, reconstructing the reduced carrier tree (see FIGURE 9.31 for an example). When a vertex of the Hamiltonian structure tree is arrived at in postorder, the carriers of its sons have been constructed and all associated separation pairs have been found. Find all separation pairs on the cycle associated with that vertex and construct the carrier associated with that vertex.

There remains two basic questions. First, how do we construct the Hamiltonian structure tree in the first place, and second, how do we perform the test for bridge completeness? Both of these procedures can be carried out using lineal spanning trees and the ideas associated with TOPICS I and II. We refer the reader to the references at the end of the chapter for details. One can construct the segment forest of the segment graph of each cycle as in TOPIC I. If the segment forest is not a tree then we know the graph is not triconnected. This approach leads to a good but not the best possible test for triconnectivity. The best test for triconnectivity of biconnected graphs G = (V,E) has worst-case complexity $0(|E|)$. It turns out that the question of the connectivity of the segment forest can be settled without constructing all of the edges of the forest. This idea leads to the linear in edges algorithm. One can, in the process of constructing the Hamiltonian structure tree of graph G, stop decomposing the reduced carriers as soon as a triconnected reduced carrier is found. One would then have a tree consisting of Hamiltonian structures and more complex triconnected graphs for some (perhaps none) of the terminal nodes. There is a natural way of splitting the Hamiltonian structures further into smaller Hamiltonian structures until the whole graph is broken up into "triconnected components." There are different approaches to the problem of decomposing a graph into triconnected components that we leave to the reader to explore in EXERCISE 9.38(6). We conclude our discussion of triconnectivity by deriving one of the most important facts about triconnected graphs, namely, that they have only one embedding (in a very natural sense) in the sphere or plane.

Two different embeddings of the same graph are shown in FIGURE 9.36. We may regard these embeddings as being in the plane or on the surface of a sphere. Intuitively, an "embedding" of a graph G = (V,E) is a representation or drawing of the graph where the vertices V are represented by distinct points on the surface and the edges E are represented by smooth arcs joining the respective vertices.

An embedding is planar if the different arcs representing edges have, at most, endpoints in common. The embeddings of FIGURE 9.36 are planar. A graph G is *planar* if it has a planar embedding. The embedding of FIGURE 9.36(a) has six *regions* or *domains* labeled $R_1, R_2, \ldots, R_6$. If we regard the embedding as being on the surface of a sphere then all domains $R_1, \ldots, R_6$ are finite. For this reason it is slightly better from an intuitive point of view to think of spherical rather than planar embeddings of graphs. Regarding the embedding of FIGURE 9.36(a) as being on the surface of a sphere, we may identify with each region its bounding cycle. With R_1 we associate the cycle $(1,2,7,1)$ where the vertices are listed in clockwise order viewed from the interior of the region. Thus with R_2 we associate the cycle $(2,3,5,6,7,2)$, etc. These bounding cycles are called the "domain boundaries" of the embedding. If the vertices and smooth arcs of a spherical embedding are allowed to drift around on the surface of the sphere without crossing over each other, we get the intuitive idea of "isotopically equivalent" embeddings. Note that the domain boundaries of two embeddings are the same if and only if the two embeddings are isotopically equivalent. We take this as intuitively obvious for our purposes. We express this fact in DEFINITION 9.35.

9.35 DEFINITION.

Two planar or spherical embeddings of a graph G are regarded as equivalent (isotopically) if they have the same domain boundaries.

Referring to FIGURE 9.36, the reader will note that the cycle $\mathscr{C} = (1,2,3,4,6,7,1)$ is a domain boundary in FIGURE 9.36(b) but not in 9.36(a). Thus these two embeddings are not equivalent. The basic result we require is that if the graph G is triconnected there can be only one embedding.

9.36   TWO DIFFERENT EMBEDDINGS OF THE SAME GRAPH.

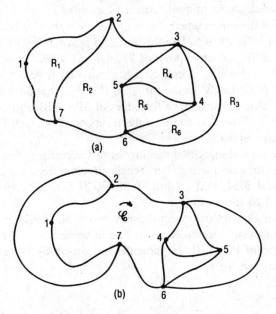

$\mathscr{C}$ is a domain boundary of (b) but not of (a).

Figure 9.36

9.37   THEOREM.

A planar triconnected graph has only one embedding in the sphere or plane up to isotopic equivalence.

Proof.   We illustrate the idea of the proof using FIGURE 9.36. Suppose there are two inequivalent embeddings. Consider the cycle $\mathscr{C} = (1,2,3,4,6,7,1)$ which is a domain boundary in FIGURE 9.36(b) but not in FIGURE 9.36(a). Because $\mathscr{C}$ is not a domain boundary in FIGURE 9.36(a) it must have at least two bridges. Because $\mathscr{C}$ is a domain boundary in FIGURE 9.36(b), these bridges can all be embedded outside of $\mathscr{C}$ and hence none of them are joined by an edge in the bridge graph of $\mathscr{C}$ (DEFINITION 6.110). Thus the bridge graph is "discrete" or without edges. Hence it is disconnected and, by THEOREM 9.13, $\mathscr{C}$ would contain a separation pair, contradicting triconnectivity of G.

9.38   EXERCISE.

(1) Characterize all graphs $G = (V,E)$ for which the set $\mathscr{S}_k$ of DEFINITION 9.2 is empty for all k. Consider also the case of more general graphs (see

DEFINITION 6.3). Prove that for all other graphs the connectivity is less than or equal to the minimal degree of a vertex.

(2) Prove that the only mutually arching components of a bridge graph are as shown in FIGURE 9.6. Use this result to prove THEOREM 9.7.

(3) Give a careful inductive proof of THEOREM 9.19.

(4) Let G = (V,E) be a biconnected graph and let B be a bridge of a broken cycle $\mathscr{C}$ of G. Let B' be the carrier of B. Prove that there always is a cycle $\mathscr{C}'$ of B' that contains all of the edges of SPAN(B). Prove that the idea of FIGURE 9.27 used to continue the recursion of ALGORITHM 9.28 (step (3)) always works.

(5) Describe a good algorithm (analogous to the planarity test of TOPIC I for example) for constructing Hamiltonian structure trees and carrying out AL-GORITHM 9.34, DEPTH-FIRST SEARCH FOR SEPARATION PAIRS. *Discuss data structures.*

(6) Define a notion of ''triconnected components'' and construct them algorithmically. Are your tricomponents unique in some sense? (See the references at the end of PART II, in particular the papers by Hopcroft and Tarjan, MacLane, and Vo.)

Chapter 10

Topic IV: Matroids

The theory of matroids or "combinatorial geometries" is becoming of increasing importance to applied mathematicians and computer scientists as a conceptual tool for unifying many seemingly unrelated ideas. The subject originated in the work of Hassler Whitney in the 1930s. The term "matroid" is intended to suggest a generalization of "matrix." As we shall see, for most purposes "matroid theory" can be viewed as a special topic within the theory of matrices. As with the other topics in this book, we wish to provide the framework for classroom or seminar discussion on the part of the readers.

There is extensive literature on the theory of matroids. Much of this literature is concerned with the technical but important attempt by mathematicians to explore all of the consequences of the axiomatic approach to the subject. Recently there has been a considerable increase of interest in the algorithmic aspects of matroid theory. Many interesting open problems can be found on this subject, especially in the area of data structures and complexity of algorithms. In this TOPIC, we shall take a tour through the theory of matroids by giving many elementary examples of the basic ideas. In order to make the theory more accessible we shall emphasize the matrix theoretic aspects of the subject. For the reader interested in the general development and other aspects of the theory of matroids, we shall give references throughout our discussion to three books that are available in most libraries: M. Aigner, *Combinatorial Theory*, Springer-Verlag, Berlin, 1979; E. Lawler, *Combinatorial Optimization, Networks and Matroids*, Holt, Rinehart and Winston, New York, 1976; and D. J. A. Welsh, *Matroid Theory*, Academic Press, New York, 1976. In these three books and in the reference list at the end of PART II as well, the reader will find many references to the research literature on the theory of matroids.

We start our discussion by giving an "abstract" definition of a matroid.

10.1 DEFINITION.

A matroid M on a finite set S is a pair $(S, \mathcal{B})$ where $\mathcal{B}$ is a collection of subsets of S satisfying

(1) All sets B in $\mathcal{B}$ have the same number of elements.
(2) If B_1 and B_2 are in $\mathcal{B}$ and x is any element of B_1 then there is some element y in B_2 such that $(B_1 - \{x\}) \cup \{y\}$ is in $\mathcal{B}$.

The elements of $\mathcal{B}$ are called *bases* of the matroid M. If all elements of $\mathcal{B}$ have cardinality k then k is called the *rank* of M. Condition (2) is called the *exchange property* for bases.

Condition (1) of DEFINITION 10.1 is straightforward but condition (2) seems a bit strange at first glance. Suppose we try to construct a matroid on $S = \underline{5} = \{1,2,3,4,5\}$. First we choose $\mathcal{B}$. For example, try $\mathcal{B} = \{\{1,2,3\}, \{1,3,4\}, \{3,4,5\}\}$. Condition (1) is satisfied so this choice for $\mathcal{B}$ is not completely ridiculous. To check (2), let $B_1 = \{1,2,3\}$ and $B_2 = \{3,4,5\}$. Choose $x = 1$ in B_1 and try to find a y in B_2 that can replace x in B_1 and have the resulting set still in the collection $\mathcal{B}$. By trying the various possibilities we see that there is no such y. Thus we have failed in our first attempt to construct a matroid. If we had chosen $\mathcal{B}$ to be the collection of *all* subsets of size 3 from $\underline{5}$ then we would clearly have obtained a matroid (called the *uniform* matroid of rank 3 on $\underline{5}$). Fortunately, there is a very simple way to generate matroids (EXAMPLE 10.2).

10.2   EXAMPLE: COLUMN AND ROW MATROID OF A MATRIX.

Consider the matrix

$$A = \begin{pmatrix} 1 & 0 & 0 & 1 & 0 \\ 0 & 1 & 0 & 1 & 1 \\ 0 & 0 & 1 & 0 & 1 \end{pmatrix}.$$

Let $S = \underline{5}$ and let $A^{(1)},\ldots,A^{(5)}$ denote the columns of A. For $Q \subseteq S$ a subset of S, let $A^{(Q)}$ denote the submatrix of A consisting of columns indexed by the elements of Q. Let $\mathcal{B}_A$ be the collection of all subsets Q of S such that $A^{(Q)}$ is a basis for the column space of the matrix A (we assume throughout this TOPIC that the reader has had a beginning level course in linear algebra). Thus for the above matrix A, $\mathcal{B}_A = \{\{1,2,3\}, \{1,2,5\}, \{1,3,4\}, \{1,3,5\}, \{1,4,5\}, \{2,3,4\}, \{2,4,5\}, \{3,4,5\}\}$. The reader is asked to show in EXERCISE 10.3 that such a collection $\mathcal{B}_A$ constructed from a matrix A is always a matroid in the sense of DEFINITION 10.1. This matroid is called the *column matroid* of A. Similarly, we could define the *row matroid* of A. We use the notation M_A to denote the column matroid of A. Note that an element $Q \in \mathcal{B}_A$ is called a *base* of the matroid M_A and the columns of $A^{(Q)}$ are a *basis* for the column space of A. In the above example, $B_1 = \{1,2,3\}$ is a base of M_A. If we take $B_2 = \{3,4,5\}$ to be another base and $x = 2$ in B_1 then we may choose $y = 4$ or $y = 5$ in B_2 to replace x in B_1 and still obtain a base. When the basis $A^{(B_1)}$ has the simple form of being the columns of the identity matrix I (as in this example) then for any $x \in B_1$, $A^{(x)} = I^{(t)}$ for some t. The element $x \in B_1$ can be replaced by any $y \in B_2$ such that $A^{(y)}$ has a nonzero entry in position t. A slight extension of this idea can be used to prove EXERCISE 10.3.

10.3   EXERCISE.

Let A be an $m \times n$ matrix with entries in a field F (this is a good point to review the definition of a field, DEFINITION 10.4). Prove that the column matroid M_A, as defined in EXAMPLE 10.2, is in fact a matroid in the sense of DEFINITION 10.1.

We shall give many examples of matroids in what follows. Virtually all of these examples will be equivalent to matroids that arise from matrices. We shall also give many examples of operations which when performed on matroids produce other matroids (deletion, contraction, truncation, extension, etc.). All of these operations transform matrix matroids into other matrix matroids. There are examples of matroids (see EXERCISE 10.21) that are not related to matrices but this class of matroids is not nearly as important to the applied mathematician as the matrix matroids. For this reason we shall, when proving results valid for all matroids, give only the proof for the matrix case when this shortens the argument. The reader interested in the more general case will find proofs in the books referred to above or in the references.

In linear algebra, given a matrix A, a basic question is that of finding a basis for the column space (or row space) of A. The standard algorithms for solving systems of linear equations focus on this problem. In the study of (matrix) matroids our attention is focused on the more general question of the nature of *all* bases for the column space of A. A number of mathematical structures that satisfy the conditions of DEFINITION 10.1 are not obviously matrices yet turn out to be bijectively equivalent to matrix matroids (in the sense of DEFINITION 10.15). The nature of these bijections is itself an interesting study. In order to develop a uniform terminology, we shall now give a short review of some important ideas from linear algebra.

Let Z denote the set of all integers (positive, negative, or zero). Note that the elements of Z together with the operation $+$ form a group (see CHAPTER 4) with identity element 0. As $a + b = b + a$ for any pair of integers, this group is commutative. We also have the operation $\times$ of multiplication which is associative: $a \times (b \times c) = (a \times b) \times c$. The integer 1 is an identity element for multiplication: $1 \times a = a \times 1 = a$ for all $a \in Z$. Furthermore, the two operations are connected by the distributive laws: $a \times (b + c) = (a \times b) + (a \times c)$ and $(b + c) \times a = (b \times a) + (c \times a)$ for all a, b, and c. Any set S together with a pair of binary operations $+$ and $\times$ satisfying these conditions is called a *ring*. If $a \times b = b \times a$ for all a and b then the ring is said to be *commutative* (the operation $+$ is commutative in any ring). Thus, Z is a commutative ring. The polynomials Z[t] in the variable t with coefficients in Z is another commutative ring. The 2×2 matrices with entries in Z is a noncommutative ring. An important special class of rings is given by DEFINITION 10.4. Recall that an element a of a ring has an *inverse* with respect to the operation $\times$ if there is an element b of the ring such that $a \times b = b \times a = 1$ (the element b is denoted by a^{-1}).

10.4 DEFINITION.

A commutative ring S is called a *field* if every nonzero element a has an inverse a^{-1} with respect to multiplication.

10.5 EXAMPLES OF FIELDS.

The rational numbers Q, the real numbers R, and the complex numbers C are the most familiar examples of fields. If t is a variable then the rational functions Q(t) with coefficients in Q form a field. The elements of Q(t) are ratios of polynomials in t with coefficients in Q. For example, $(3.5t^5 + 4)/(t^3 + t + 1)$ is an element of Q(t). Its inverse is $(t^3 + t + 1)/(3.5t^5 + 4)$. Similarly, we have the rational function fields R(t) and C(t). Many variations are possible. One might consider rational functions in several variables. One example that we shall consider below is the case where $(z_{i,j})$ is a matrix of variables. The field $Q(z_{i,j})$ is the field of rational functions in these variables with coefficients in Q. For example, $(2z_{1,1}^6 + 3z_{1,2}z_{2,3}^8)/(4z_{1,3} + 5z_{2,2}^7)$ is such a function.

10.6 EXAMPLES OF FINITE FIELDS.

If n is an integer then the integers modulo n under addition and multiplication form a commutative ring. If n = 6, for example, then the element 5 is its own inverse as $5 \times 5 = 25 \equiv 1$ (mod 6). The elements 2, 3, and 4, however, have no inverse. If n = p is a prime then Z_p, the integers mod p, form a field (check this!). Such fields are called *finite fields* because they have finitely many elements. If a field has the property that by adding 1 to itself, $1 + 1 + \ldots + 1$, a certain number of times one gets 0 then the field is said to be of *characteristic* p where p is the smallest number of such summands that gives 0 (this number is always a prime). Thus each finite field Z_p is of characteristic p. The rational function fields $Z_p(t)$ in a variable t are of characteristic p but have infinitely many elements (the degrees of the polynomials may be arbitrarily large). It is an interesting fact that for every prime p and positive integer k there is a finite field with p^k elements. This field is called the *Galois field* GF(p^k) and has characteristic p. All finite fields are of this type. These fields, for k > 1, are awkward to work with although easy to construct in principle. The idea can be illustrated for p = 2, k = 2. Consider the polynomials $Z_2[t]$ (polynomials in the variable t with coefficients in Z_2). First form the polynomial $t^{p^k} - t$ (this is done in the general case) which is the same as $t^4 - t = t^4 + t$ in the case p = 2, k = 2. The polynomial $t^4 + t$ factors into $t(t + 1)(t^2 + t + 1)$ as is easily checked by direct computation. Thus, 0 and 1 are roots of $t^4 + t$. The polynomial $t^2 + t + 1$ is "irreducible over Z_2" in that neither of the two elements 0 or 1 of Z_2 are roots of this polynomial. This is reminiscent of the irreducible polynomial $t^2 + 1$ over the real field R. The complex number i is a "symbolic" root of this polynomial and is used together with R to construct the complex numbers. All this means is that we treat i as if it were a variable in multiplication and addition and then use the relation $i^2 = -1$ to simplify the answer as much as possible. Thus we may do the same thing with $t^2 + t + 1$. Let r be the symbolic root (i.e., $r^2 + r + 1 = 0$). It is easy to check that r + 1 is also a root (in the complex number case $-i$ is the other root). The elements 0, 1, r, and r + 1 are the elements of GF(4). Addition is done in the obvious way $(r + (r + 1) = 2r + 1 = 1$, etc.). Multiplication is done by thinking of r as a variable and then using the relation $r^2 + r + 1 = 0$ to simplify the answer $(r(r + 1) = r^2 + r = 1$, $r^2 = r + 1$, $(r + 1)^2 = r^2 + 2r + 1 = (r + 1)$ $+ 1 = r$, etc.). The reader should make up a table of rules for addition and multiplication in GF(4). In principle, $GF(p^k)$ can be constructed in exactly the same way by adjoining all roots of $t^{p^k} - t$ (these roots can easily be shown to be distinct). Of course, rational function fields in one or more variables can be formed over any of these "Galois fields."

We now take a look at some ideas in elementary matrix theory that are very useful in discussing matroids. Consider the matrix A shown in FIGURE 10.7(a). This matrix is in "row echelon form." The word "echelon" is a military term standing for a certain steplike formation of troops suggested by the pattern of nonzero elements in this matrix canonical form. Note that the first nonzero entry in row 1 of A (FIGURE 10.7(a)) is in column 2. The first nonzero entry in row 2 of A is in column 4. The first nonzero entry of row 3 is in column 7. We call these columns (2, 4, and 7 in this case) the *principal columns* of A. All of the rest of the rows of A are zero. Note also in the case of FIGURE 10.7(b) that the columns $A^{(2)}$, $A^{(4)}$, and $A^{(7)}$ are *unit* column vectors (one entry 1 and the rest 0). In this case, A is said to be in *unit row echelon form*. These ideas extend in the obvious way to matrices of any size over any field so we may say whether or not an m × n matrix over a field F is in row echelon form or unit row echelon form. These ideas may be found in most linear algebra books. In general, the sequence of principal columns will be of the form $A^{(i_1)},. . .,A^{(i_p)}$ where $i_1 < i_2 < ... < i_p$ and the first nonzero entry of row t will be in column i_t.

10.7 UNIT ROW ECHELON FORM (Principal columns indicated ↓).

$$
A = \begin{pmatrix}
0 & 1 & -2 & 0 & 1 & 1 & 0 & 1 & 2 \\
0 & 0 & 0 & 1 & -2 & 3 & 0 & 1 & 2 \\
0 & 0 & 0 & 0 & 0 & 0 & 1 & 2 & 1 \\
0 & 0 & 0 & 0 & 0 & 0 & 0 & 0 & 0 \\
0 & 0 & 0 & 0 & 0 & 0 & 0 & 0 & 0
\end{pmatrix}
$$
(a)

$$
A = \begin{pmatrix}
0 & 1 & -2 & 0 & 1 & 1 & 0 & 1 & 2 \\
0 & 0 & 0 & 1 & -2 & 3 & 0 & 1 & 2 \\
0 & 0 & 0 & 0 & 0 & 0 & 1 & 2 & 1
\end{pmatrix}.
$$
(b)

The reader will recall that the row canonical form or unit row canonical form is used in solving the equation $Bx = y$ where B is an m × n matrix and x and y are $n \times 1$ and $m \times 1$ column vectors, respectively ("Gaussian elimination"). The idea is that by using elementary row operations a nonsingular matrix P can be constructed such that $PB = A$ is in unit row canonical form. One then solves $Ax = Py$ quite easily. It is worthwhile taking a closer look at this latter process in the case $y = 0$ (the $m \times 1$ zero vector). Consider the equation $Ax = 0$ with A as in FIGURE 10.7(b) (in this case 0 stands for the 3×1 column vector of zeroes). It is useful to introduce some additional notation.

10.8 NOTATION.

If B is an $m \times n$ matrix and $1 \leq i_1 < i_2 < \ldots < i_p \leq m$ and $1 \leq j_1 < j_2 < \ldots < j_q \leq n$ are sequences of integers then let $B[i_1, \ldots, i_p | j_1, \ldots, j_q]$ denote the $p \times q$ matrix obtained from B by keeping the entries of B in the intersection of rows $i_1, \ldots, i_p$ with columns $j_1, \ldots, j_q$. Referring to FIGURE 10.7(b), $A[1,2|6,9]$ $= \begin{pmatrix} 1 & 2 \\ 3 & 2 \end{pmatrix}$. Similarly, let $B(i_1, \ldots, i_p | j_1, \ldots, j_q)$ be the $(m - p) \times (n - q)$ matrix formed by keeping the entries in the intersection of all rows other than $i_1, \ldots, i_p$ with all columns other than $j_1, \ldots, j_q$. We also define the mixed notations $B(i_1, \ldots, i_p | j_1, \ldots, j_q]$ and $B[i_1, \ldots, i_p | j_1, \ldots, j_q)$ with the obvious meanings. $B(\phi | j_1, \ldots, j_q]$ means delete no rows and keep columns $j_1, \ldots, j_q$. Thus $B(\phi | j_1, \ldots, j_q] = B[1, \ldots, m | j_1, \ldots, j_q] = B^{(Q)}$, $Q = \{j_1, \ldots, j_q\}$.

Using NOTATION 10.8 and referring to the 3×9 matrix A of FIGURE 10.7(b), we may easily write down a 9×6 matrix N such that $AN = \theta$ (the 3×6 zero matrix) and such that the columns of N are a basis for the null space of A (the space of all 9×1 column vectors x such that $Ax = 0$). Note again that *columns* 2, 4, and 7 are the principal columns of A (as defined above). FIGURE 10.9(a) shows a 9×6 array in which *rows* 2, 4, and 7 (corresponding to the principal column's indices) have been left blank and the array that is left has been filled with the negative of the 6×6 identity matrix. The array consisting of rows 2, 4, and 7 is a 3×6 array. In FIGURE 10.9(b) this array has been filled with the 3×6 array obtained from A by crossing off the principal columns (2, 4, and 7). The resulting matrix is N. The general situation is stated in THEOREM 10.10.

10.9 AN EXAMPLE OF THEOREM 10.10.

	1	2	3	4	5	6
1	-1	0	0	0	0	0
2						
3	0	-1	0	0	0	0
4						
5	0	0	-1	0	0	0
6	0	0	0	-1	0	0
7						
8	0	0	0	0	-1	0
9	0	0	0	0	0	-1

(a) FILLING IN THE IDENTITY

	1	2	3	4	5	6
1	-1	0	0	0	0	0
2	0	-2	1	1	1	2
3	0	-1	0	0	0	0
4	0	0	-2	3	1	2
5	0	0	-1	0	0	0
6	0	0	0	-1	0	0
7	0	0	0	0	2	1
8	0	0	0	0	-1	0
9	0	0	0	0	0	-1

(b) THE MATRIX N.

Figure 10.9

10.10 THEOREM.

Let A be a p $\times$ n matrix with entries in a field F. Suppose that $A(\phi|i_1,\ldots,i_p]$ is the p $\times$ p identity matrix I. Then the n $\times$ (n$-$p) matrix N defined by $N(i_1,\ldots,i_p|\phi) = -I$ and $N[i_1,\ldots,i_p|\phi) = A(\phi|i_1,\ldots,i_p)$ satisfies $AN = \theta$ (the p $\times$ (n$-$p) zero matrix) and the columns $N^{(1)},\ldots,N^{(n-p)}$ of N are a basis for the null space of A.

Proof. The fact that $AN = \theta$ follows directly by the rule for multiplying matrices. From elementary linear algebra, we know that the null space of A must have dimension n$-$p. This is obviously the rank of N so the columns of N are a basis for the null space of A.

Note that in THEOREM 10.10 we did not have to assume that A was in unit row canonical form. If A is in unit row canonical form then the submatrix equal to I obviously exists (consider the principal columns). In a course in linear algebra, we learn that any matrix B can be reduced to unit row canonical form by a sequence of "elementary row operations." This is equivalent to saying that there always exists a nonsingular matrix P such that PB = A is in unit row canonical form.

10.11 LEMMA.

Let A be an m $\times$ n matrix with entries in a field F and let B = PA where P is nonsingular. Then for c_i, $i = 1, \ldots, n$, in F, $\sum_{i=1}^{n} c_i A^{(i)} = 0$ if and only if $\sum_{i=1}^{n} c_i B^{(i)} = 0$. In other words, the columns of A and B satisfy exactly the same linear relations.

Proof. Note that $\sum c_i B^{(i)} = 0$ if and only if $\sum c_i (PA)^{(i)} = 0$ if and only if $\sum c_i P(A^{(i)}) = 0$ if and only if $P \sum c_i A^{(i)} = 0$ if and only if $\sum c_i A^{(i)} = 0$ (using the fact that P is nonsingular). The expression $P(A^{(i)})$ denotes the product of the $m \times m$ matrix P and the $m \times 1$ column vector $A^{(i)}$.

An important consequence of LEMMA 10.11 is the fact that the unit row canonical form is unique.

10.12 EXERCISE.

Let A be an $m \times n$ matrix and P and Q nonsingular matrices such that PA and QA are both in unit row canonical form. Prove that $PA = QA$. Give an example to show that $P \neq Q$ is possible. This result says that the unit row canonical form of a matrix A is unique. *Hint.* Show that the location of the principal columns is the same in PA and QA and then use LEMMA 10.11.

This ends our brief review of linear algebra. We now define the important concept of isomorphism of matroids.

10.13 DEFINITION.

Let $M = (S, \mathcal{B})$ and $M' = (S', \mathcal{B}')$ be two matroids. We say that M is isomorphic to M' with isomorphism φ if (1) $\varphi: S \to S'$ is a bijection and (2) $\varphi(B) \in \mathcal{B}'$ if and only if $B \in \mathcal{B}$. Note: $\varphi(B) = \{\varphi(x): x \in B\}$.

In other words, a bijection from S to S' that induces a bijection between bases defines an isomorphism between matroids.

Let A be a matrix with entries in a field F. If A is $m \times n$, then A is specified by the ordered sequence of column vectors $(A^{(1)}, \ldots, A^{(n)})$. For future reference, we state formally the definition of column matroid of a matrix A.

10.14 DEFINITION.

Let $A = (A^{(1)}, \ldots, A^{(n)})$ be an $m \times n$ matrix. Let $S = \underline{n}$ and let $\mathcal{B}_A$ be the collection of all subsets $Q \subseteq \underline{n}$ with the property that the columns of $A^{(Q)}$ form a basis for the column space of A. Then $M_A = (S, \mathcal{B}_A)$ is a matroid called the *column matroid* of the matrix A (see EXAMPLE 10.2).

The following definition (DEFINITION 10.15) is central to our discussion of matroids.

10.15   DEFINITION.

Let $M = (S, \mathscr{B})$ be a matroid and let $(s_1, s_2, \ldots, s_n)$ be a linear ordering of S. An $m \times n$ matrix $A = (A^{(1)}, \ldots, A^{(n)})$ with entries in a field F will be called a *matrix representation* of N with respect to $(s_1, \ldots, s_n)$ if the map $\varphi(s_i) = i$ is an isomorphism between M and the column matroid M_A. If M has a matrix representation for some F, then M is said to be a *representable* matroid.

10.16   REMARK.

It is important to be aware that an $m \times n$ matrix A is an *ordered sequence* $(A^{(1)}, \ldots, A^{(n)})$ of vectors and not just a *set* of vectors. The matrix representation of DEFINITION 10.15 defines a map $\varphi(s_i) = i$ associated with the matrix A and the linear ordering of S, $(s_1, \ldots, s_n)$. If we change the ordering to $(s_{\sigma(1)}, \ldots, s_{\sigma(n)})$ where σ is some permutation of $\underline{n}$ and change the matrix to $B = (A^{\sigma(1)}, \ldots, A^{\sigma(n)})$ then B is a different matrix representation of the same matroid. This representation is with respect to the linear ordering $s_{\sigma(1)}, \ldots, s_{\sigma(n)}$. In general, we shall want to choose the linear ordering $(s_1, \ldots, s_n)$ such that the matrix representation A has a nice form. A natural choice is to pick $s_1, \ldots, s_k$ to be a base if M has rank k. For a fixed linear order $(s_1, \ldots, s_n)$ we still have quite a bit of freedom in choosing A. From LEMMA 10.11, we see that if A is a matrix representation of M with respect to $(s_1, \ldots, s_n)$ then so is PA where P is any nonsingular $m \times m$ matrix. Thus we may assume that A is in unit row canonical form. Also, if $A = (A^{(1)}, \ldots, A^{(n)})$ is a matrix representation of M with respect to $(s_1, \ldots, s_n)$ then so is $B = (t_1 A^{(1)}, \ldots, t_n A^{(n)})$ where the t_i are nonzero elements of the field F. Putting these various facts together, if we choose $s_1, \ldots, s_k$ to be a base of M and assume A is in unit row canonical form then the first k columns of A are the principal columns and rows $k+1, \ldots, m$ of A are all zero. We may discard these rows. Thus A may be taken to be a $k \times n$ matrix of rank k such that $A(\phi|1, \ldots, k)$ is the $k \times k$ identity. By choosing the t_i properly we may assume each nonzero column $A^{(i)}$ with $i > k$ has at least one entry equal to 1. We shall now see a number of examples of the use of these ideas.

10.17   UNIFORM MATROIDS.

The "uniform matroids" are an example of a class of representable matroids. The matroid $\mathscr{U}_{k,S} = (S, \mathscr{P}_k(S))$ where $\mathscr{P}_k(S)$ is the set of all subsets of size k of S is called the *uniform matroid of rank k on* S. If $|S| = n$ then $\mathscr{U}_{n,S}$ is called the *free* matroid on S. The $n \times n$ identity matrix is a matrix representation of the free matroid over any field F. For notational convenience, let $\mathscr{U}_{k,n} \equiv \mathscr{U}_{k,\underline{n}}$ denote the uniform matroid of rank k over $S = \underline{n} = \{1, 2, \ldots, n\}$.

By REMARK 10.16, if A is a matrix representation of $\mathscr{U}_{2,4}$ then we may assume that $A = \begin{pmatrix} 1 & 0 & 1 & 1 \\ 0 & 1 & x & y \end{pmatrix}$ where x and y are nonzero and $x \neq y$. Thus we see that $\mathcal{U}_{2,4}$ is representable over any field except GF(2), the field of two elements (in that field we would be forced to have x = y). The situation for $\mathcal{U}_{k,n}$ is more complicated with regard to its representability over specific fields. There is one field F for which the representability of $\mathcal{U}_{k,n}$ is trivial, however. Let Z = $(z_{i,j})$ be a k × n matrix with entries variables $z_{i,j}$. Regard these variables as elements of the rational function field $Q(z_{i,j})$ (see EXAMPLE 10.6). Note that the determinants of any k × k submatrix of Z is a nonzero polynomial in the variables $z_{i,j}$ and hence is a nonzero element of the field $Q(z_{i,j})$. Thus any k columns of the matrix Z are linearly independent and hence the column matroid of Z is $\mathcal{U}_{k,n}$. Thus every uniform matroid is representable over some field.

10.18   EUCLIDEAN REPRESENTATIONS AND FANO⁻, FANO.

FIGURE 10.19(a) shows a planar configuration of points and lines. We can use such a diagram to define a collection $\mathcal{B}$ of subsets of $\underline{7}$ (the set of vertex labels of the diagram) as follows: let $\mathcal{B}$ be all subsets of size 3 of $\underline{7}$ that *do not* lie on the same line segment. We claim that $(\underline{7}, \mathcal{B})$ is a matroid of rank 3. Note that each pair of lines meets in exactly one point. Let $B_1 = \{q,r,s\}$ and $B_2 = \{t,u,v\}$ be two sets in $\mathcal{B}$. The case $|B_1 \cap B_2| = 2$ is trivial, so suppose $|B_1 \cap B_2| < 2$. Without loss of generality, it suffices to show that one of the sets $\{t,r,s\}$, $\{u,r,s\}$ or $\{v,r,s\}$ is in $\mathcal{B}$ (i.e., the exchange property for bases holds). Clearly, there are at least two distinct sets in this collection. If neither of these sets is in $\mathcal{B}$ then we would have two distinct lines with two points in common. Thus one of these two sets is in $\mathcal{B}$ and the exchange property for bases holds. This type of diagrammatic representation of matroids is called a *Euclidean representation of the matroid* (see Welsh, p. 30). FIGURE 10.19(b) is a little more interesting. One additional line, the curved line joining 3, 2, and 5, has been added. It is still the case that two distinct lines meet in only one point so the same argument works for FIGURE 10.19(b) as for FIGURE 10.19(a) to define a matroid. The matroid of FIGURE 10.19(b) is called the *Fano matroid* (Aigner, p. 259; Welsh, p. 32) and that of FIGURE 10.19(a) the *Fano⁻ matroid* (it is missing a line!). The configuration of points and lines of FIGURE 10.19(b) is an example of a mathematical structure called a *projective plane*. There is a close connection between the study of projective spaces and matroids (Aigner, p. 55; Welsh, p. 193).

10.19 THE MATROIDS FANO⁻ AND FANO.

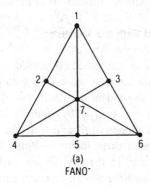
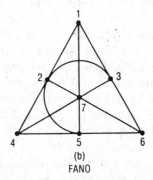

Figure 10.19

10.20 MATRIX REPRESENTATIONS OF FANO⁻ AND FANO.

Consider again FIGURE 10.19. Imagine the diagram of FIGURE 10.19(a) embedded in a plane in ordinary 3-space, R^3, and assume that the plane does not contain the origin (the plane $z = 1$, for example, if (x,y,z) denotes points of R^3). Each of the points $1,2,\ldots,7$ of the diagram of FANO⁻ then corresponds to a 3-tuple in R^3. If A is a matrix with these three tuples as column vectors then A is obviously a matrix representation of FANO⁻. Thus FANO⁻ is representable over the real field and obviously also over the rationals. To gain a deeper insight, we use the ideas discussed in REMARK 10.16. We claim that if A is a 3×7 matrix representation of either FANO⁻ or FANO over a field F then we may assume that A has the following form:

$$\underline{1} \quad \underline{2} \quad \underline{3} \quad \underline{4} \quad \underline{5} \quad \underline{6} \quad \underline{7} \text{ (COLUMNS)}$$

$$A = \begin{pmatrix} 1 & 0 & 0 & 1 & x & 1 & 1 \\ 0 & 1 & 0 & a & 1 & 0 & d \\ 0 & 0 & 1 & 0 & c & b & e \end{pmatrix}.$$

In the matrix A, the field elements a, b, c, d, and e are all nonzero. We shall show that if A represents FANO⁻, then x is nonzero, and if A represents FANO, then x is zero. The fact that A can be assumed to be of this form follows in an elementary way from the definition of FANO⁻ and FANO as given in FIGURE 10.19. We indicate the reasoning and let the reader fill in the details. $A(\phi|1,2,3]$ is the 3×3 identity as $\{1,2,3\}$ is a base in both matroids (we assume A is in unit row canonical form). In either matroid, we have that $\{1,2,3\}$ is a base but $\{1,2,4\}$ is not a base. Thus, no matter what the field of entries of A we must have that $A^{(4)}$ is a nontrivial linear combination of $A^{(1)}$ and $A^{(2)}$. For this reason, $A^{(4)}$ is shown as having exactly two nonzero entries as one would get from taking a nontrivial linear combination of $A^{(1)}$ and $A^{(2)}$. By REMARK 10.16, we may assume one of the entries of $A^{(4)}$ is 1 (which we take to be the first entry in this case). The rest of the structure of A follows in a similar manner from FIGURE 10.19 ($A^{(6)}$ is a nontrivial linear combination of $A^{(1)}$ and $A^{(3)}$, $A^{(5)}$ is a combination of $A^{(4)}$ and $A^{(6)}$, etc.). We now must deal with the fact that $\{2,3,5\}$ is a base in FANO$^-$ but not in FANO. Clearly, columns $A^{(2)}$, $A^{(3)}$, and $A^{(5)}$ are linearly independent if and only if $x \neq 0$. Note also that various other identities on the entries of A follow from the linear dependence relations on the columns of A by taking determinants: columns 1, 7, and 5 dependent implies that $e - dc = 0$; columns 2, 7, and 6 dependent implies that $e - b = 0$; columns 3, 7, and 4 dependent implies that $a - d = 0$; and columns 4, 5, and 6 dependent implies that $b - xab + ac = 0$. The first three of these identities imply that $b - ac = 0$ in either the FANO$^-$ or FANO case. In the FANO case, when $x = 0$, the identity $b - xab + ac = 0$ becomes $b + ac = 0$. Hence we must have $2b = 0$ in the FANO case. But $\{1,2,6\}$ independent implies that $b \neq 0$. Thus in the FANO case we must have $2 = 0$ (i.e., the field must have characteristic 2). In fact, we can easily check that $x = 0$, $a = b = c = d = e = 1$ gives a representation A of FANO over any field of characteristic 2. If $x \neq 0$ then the two identities $b - ac = 0$ and $b - xab + ac = 0$ imply that $2b - xab = 0$. Thus the fact that x, a, and b are nonzero forces $2 \neq 0$. From this we easily conclude that FANO$^-$ is representable over F if and only if F does not have characteristic 2. This field incompatibility of FANO$^-$ and FANO can be used to construct a matroid not representable over any field (EXERCISE 10.21(1)).

10.21 EXERCISE.

(1) Let $M_1 = (S_1, \mathcal{B}_1)$ and $M_2 = (S_2, \mathcal{B}_2)$ be two matroids with $S_1 \cap S_2 = \phi$. Define the direct sum, $M_1 + M_2$, of M_1 and M_2 to be the matroid $(S_1 \cup S_2, \mathcal{B})$ where $\mathcal{B} = \{B_1 \cup B_2 : B_1 \in \mathcal{B}_1, B_2 \in \mathcal{B}_2\}$. Prove that $M_1 + M_2$ satisfies DEFINITION 10.1 and hence is a matroid. Show that FANO$^-$ + FANO is not representable over any field. *Hint:* If A_1 and A_2 are matrix representations of M_1 and M_2 over a field F then the direct sum

$$A_1 \oplus A_2 = \begin{array}{|c|c|} \hline A_1 & 0 \\ \hline 0 & A_2 \\ \hline \end{array}$$

is a representation of $M_1 + M_2$ over F.

(2) This exercise is concerned with another nonrepresentable matroid called the VAMOS matroid (Welsh, pp. 140, 188, in a slightly different form). Let VAMOS = $(S, \mathcal{B})$ where S is a set of eight elements which, for conceptual convenience, we label $\{a_1, b_1, a_2, b_2, a_3, b_3, a_4, b_4\}$ and $\mathcal{B}$ is the set of *all* subsets of S of four elements *except* $\{a_1, b_1, a_3, b_3\}$, $\{a_1, b_1, a_4, b_4\}$, $\{a_2, b_2, a_3, b_3\}$, $\{a_2, b_2, a_4, b_4\}$, $\{a_3, b_3, a_4, b_4\}$. In other words, for all pairs $1 \leq i < j \leq 4$ the set $\{a_i, b_i, a_j, b_j\}$ is a base *only* when $i = 1$ and $j = 2$.

(a) Show that VAMOS satisfies the conditions of DEFINITION 10.1 and hence is a matroid.

(b) Without using the fact that $\{a_3,b_3,a_4,b_4\}$ is or is not a base, show that if VAMOS is representable over a field F then it must have a matrix representation A of the following form (a, b, c, d, e, f, g, s, and t are nonzero, $s \neq 1$, $t \neq 1$)

$$
A = \begin{array}{c} \begin{array}{cccccccc} a_1 & b_1 & a_2 & b_2 & a_3 & b_3 & a_4 & b_4 \end{array} \quad \text{COLUMNS} \\ \begin{pmatrix} 1 & 0 & 0 & 0 & 1 & 1 & 1 & 1 \\ 0 & 1 & 0 & 0 & a & a & e & e \\ 0 & 0 & 1 & 0 & c & tc & f & sf \\ 0 & 0 & 0 & 1 & d & td & g & sg \end{pmatrix} \end{array}
$$

Hint. Consider the 2×2 submatrix $A[1,2|5,6]$, for example. A priori, it could be any 2×2 matrix $\begin{pmatrix} w & x \\ y & z \end{pmatrix}$. But the fact that $\{a_2,b_2,a_3,b_3\}$ is not a base means that the 4×4 matrix $A(\phi|3,4,5,6]$ is singular and thus the determinant of $\begin{pmatrix} w & x \\ y & z \end{pmatrix}$ is zero. Hence $\begin{pmatrix} w \\ y \end{pmatrix} = p\begin{pmatrix} x \\ z \end{pmatrix}$ for some field element p. Using the ideas of REMARK 10.16, we have chosen to make the first nonzero entry in each nonprincipal column of A a one. If $x = 0$ then columns 2, 3, 4, and 6 of A would be linearly dependent as $A(\phi|2,3,4,6]$ would have first row all 0's. This contradicts the fact that $\{2,3,4,6\}$ is a base. Thus $x \neq 0$ and similarly $y \neq 0$. Normalizing to make the first entries of columns 5 and 6 of A equal to 1 we see that we can assume that $A[1,2|5,6] = \begin{pmatrix} 1 & 1 \\ a & a \end{pmatrix}$ for some nonzero a (as shown above). By repeating this type of argument, the rest of the matrix A is determined.

(c) Show that the determinant of the 4×4 submatrix $A(\phi|5,6,7,8]$ is $(t - 1)(s - 1)(fd - cg)(e - a)$ and this expression is nonzero. This forces $\{a_3,b_3,a_4,b_4\}$ to be a base in any matroid represented by A. Hence VAMOS is not representable for any F.

(3) Let S be a set and let $\mathcal{F}$ (the "forbidden sets") be a collection of subsets of S, each subset of size k. In other words, if $\mathcal{P}_k(S)$ denotes all subsets of S of size k then $\mathcal{F} \subseteq \mathcal{P}_k(S)$. Let $\mathcal{B} = \mathcal{P}_k(S) - \mathcal{F}$. Show that if for every pair of distinct elements F_1 and F_2 of $\mathcal{F}$, $|F_1 \cap F_2| \leq k-2$, then $M = (S,\mathcal{B})$ is a matroid. *Hint.* Let B_1 and B_2 be in $\mathcal{B}$. Given $x \in B_1$ choose any two elements y_1 and y_2 in B_2. Could both $(B_1 - \{x\}) \cup \{y_1\}$ and $(B_1 - \{x\}) \cup \{y_2\}$ be in $\mathcal{F}$? Are the matroids $FANO^-$, $FANO$, and VAMOS of this type?

Although the nonrepresentable matroids of EXERCISE 10.21 are interesting and can be pursued further (see the references at the end of PART II) our goal in this TOPIC is to focus on representable matroids. The general structure of the rest of this TOPIC is as follows:

(1) give many examples of matroids (all of which will turn out to be representable)
(2) describe operations on matroids that produce new matroids (these operations will preserve representability)
(3) analyze, in the spirit of the previous TOPICS, the recursive structure of matroids

We begin by describing other possible axiom systems for matroids besides DEFINITION 10.1 and explaining their meaning in matrix terms. *The set S is always assumed to be finite.*

10.22   DEFINITION.

Let $M = (S,\mathcal{B})$ be a matroid. The collection $\mathcal{I} = \{X$: there exist $B \in \mathcal{B}$ such that $X \subseteq B\}$ is called the collection of *independent sets* of the matroid M.

If the matrix M is the column matroid of an m $\times$ n matrix A then a subset $X \subseteq \underline{n}$ is an independent set if and only if the set of columns $A^{(X)}$ is linearly independent. The definition of matroids in terms of independent sets is given in DEFINITION 10.23 (Welsh, p. 7).

10.23   DEFINITION.

(Independent set axioms).   A set S together with a collection $\mathcal{I}$ of subsets of S (called independent sets) satisfying

(I1) $\phi \in \mathcal{I}$.
(I2) If $Y \in \mathcal{I}$ and $X \subseteq Y$ then $X \in \mathcal{I}$ ("hereditary" property).
(I3) If X and Y are in $\mathcal{I}$ with $|Y| = |X| + 1$ then there is some $y \in Y - X$ such that $X \cup \{y\} \in \mathcal{I}$.

defines a matroid on S.

The more serious student will want to show the equivalence of DEFINITION 10.1 and DEFINITION 10.23 as axiom systems for a matroid. If one starts with DEFINITION 10.23, $\mathcal{B}$ is the set of elements of $\mathcal{I}$ of maximal size. If A is an m $\times$ n representation matrix of M over a field F and $X = \{x_1, \ldots, x_k\}$ and Y independent sets of M with $|X| = k$, $|Y| = k+1$, then we may assume (REMARK 10.16) that the first k columns of A correspond to the elements of X and that A has the form

$$A = \begin{array}{c} \begin{array}{ccccccc} x_1 & x_2 & \cdots & x_k & y \in Y & & \end{array} \\ \left(\begin{array}{ccccccc} 1 & 0 & \cdots & 0 & y_1 & & \\ 0 & 1 & \cdots & 0 & y_2 & & \\ \vdots & \vdots & & \vdots & \vdots & * & * \\ 0 & 0 & \cdots & 1 & y_k & & \\ \hline 0 & 0 & \cdots & 0 & y_{k+1} & & \\ \vdots & \vdots & & \vdots & * & \vdots & * \\ 0 & 0 & \cdots & 0 & y_m & & \end{array} \right) \end{array} \quad \text{and} \quad \begin{pmatrix} y_{k+1} \\ \vdots \\ y_m \end{pmatrix} \neq \begin{pmatrix} 0 \\ \vdots \\ 0 \end{pmatrix}.$$

Referring to I3, it is evident from elementary matrix theory that some $y \in Y$ must correspond to a column of A that has a nonzero entry in one of rows $k + 1$ to m of A. This is a y that can be added to X as asserted in I3.

Another set of axioms for a matroid is in terms of "rank functions" (Welsh, p. 8).

10.24 DEFINITION.

(Rank axioms).   Let $\mathcal{P}(S)$ denote the set of all subsets of S. A function $\rho: \mathcal{P}(S) \rightarrow \{0,1,2,3,\ldots\}$ is called a *rank function* for S if

(R1) $\rho(\phi) = 0$.
(R2) For all $X \in \mathcal{P}(S)$ and $y \in S$, $\rho(X) \le \rho(X \cup \{y\}) \le \rho(X) + 1$.
(R3) If $\rho(X \cup \{y\}) = \rho(X \cup \{z\}) = \rho(X)$ then $\rho(X \cup \{y\} \cup \{z\}) = \rho(X)$.

A set S together with a rank function defines a matroid.

To relate DEFINITION 10.24 to DEFINITION 10.1, a set B is a base for the matroid defined in terms of a rank function if $\rho(B \cup \{x\}) = \rho(B)$ for all $x \in S$ and B is minimal with respect to this property. For representable matroids, the rank function $\rho(X)$ is just the rank of the submatrix of the columns in the matrix representation that correspond to X. Conditions R1, R2, and R3 follow from elementary linear algebra in the representable case.

The following is an equivalent definition of matroids in terms of rank.

10.25 DEFINITION (More rank axioms).

If a function $\rho: \mathcal{P}(S) \rightarrow \{0,1,2,3,\ldots\}$ satisfies

(MR1) $0 \le \rho(X) \le |X|$ for all $X \in \mathcal{P}(S)$.
(MR2) $X \subseteq Y$ implies $\rho(X) \le \rho(Y)$ for all $X,Y \in \mathcal{P}(S)$.
(MR3) $\rho(X \cup Y) + \rho(X \cap Y) \le \rho(X) + \rho(Y)$ for all X,Y in $\mathcal{P}(S)$.

then S together with ρ defines a matroid.

Again, if M is a representable matroid the rank $\rho(X)$ is just the dimension of the space spanned by the columns corresponding to X in the representation matrix. The reader should prove MR3 for the representable case. In general, for both DEFINITIONS 10.24 and 10.25 one should show that the rank axioms imply DEFINITION 10.1 and conversely. We shall not do that here. If one starts with DEFINITION 10.1 then $\rho(X)$ is defined to be the size of a maximal independent subset of X (independent subsets being simply subsets of bases as in DEFINITION 10.22). In starting with a rank function one defines the bases B as above (just following DEFINITION 10.24). For example, in the matrix A of EXAMPLE 10.20 $\rho\{1,2,4\} = 2$.

Another set of axioms for a matroid can be based on the linear algebraic idea of "closure."

10.26 DEFINITION.

Let S be a set and let c: $\mathscr{P}(S) \to \mathscr{P}(S)$ be a function on subsets of S satisfying

(CL1) $X \subseteq c(X)$ for all $X \in \mathscr{P}(S)$.
(CL2) For all $X,Y \in \mathscr{P}(S)$, if $X \subseteq Y$ then $c(X) \subseteq c(Y)$.
(CL3) For all $X \in \mathscr{P}(S)$, $c(X) = c(c(X))$.
(CL4) For all $x,y \in S$ and $X \in \mathscr{P}(S)$, if $y \notin c(X)$ but $y \in c(X \cup \{x\})$ then $x \in c(X \cup \{y\})$.

Then S together with c defines a matroid. The function c is called the *closure operator* of a matroid. A set X is *closed* if $c(X) = X$, *spanning* if $c(X) = S$. The closed sets are also called *flats* or *subspaces*.

Let M be a representable matroid on S with matrix A. For $X \subseteq S$ the closure of X, $c(X)$, is the largest Q such that the columns of $A^{(Q)}$ are linearly dependent on the columns associated with X. For example, in the matrix associated with EXAMPLE 10.20 $c(\{1,4\}) = \{1,2,4\}$. If one starts with DEFINITION 10.26 then one defines the set $X \subseteq S$ to be an independent set if for all $x \in X$, $c(X - \{x\})$ does not contain x. These independent sets can then be shown to satisfy DEFINITION 10.23. If one starts with the rank function definition, DEFINITION 10.24, then one defines the closure operator c by $c(X) = \{y: \rho(X \cup \{y\}) = \rho(X)\}$. The function c can also be defined in terms of the independent sets (DEFINITION 10.23) as $\rho(X)$ can be defined as the maximal size of an independent set contained in X.

Another standard definition of a matroid can be based on the idea of a "hyperplane." In linear algebra, if V is a vector space of dimension n then a subspace H of dimension $n-1$ is called a "hyperplane." Clearly, if x is in V but not in H then the linear closure (or "span") of $H \cup \{x\}$ is V. In a general matroid on S, a hyperplane H is best defined in terms of the closure operator c as a closed set (or flat or subspace, DEFINITION 10.26) $H \neq S$ such that for all $x \notin H$,

$c(H \cup \{x\}) = S$. In the representable case, if A is an m × n matrix of rank $r + 1$ and the first p columns of A correspond to a hyperplane H then the matrix of A can be assumed to have the unit row canonical form shown in FIGURE 10.27.

10.27 HYPERPLANE H IN UNIT ROW CANONICAL FORM.

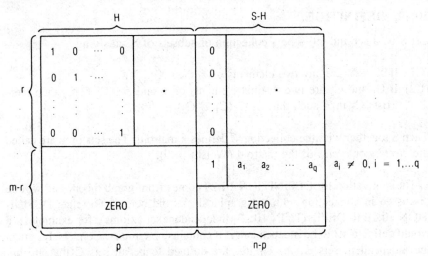

REPRESENTATION OF MATROID ON S IN UNIT ROW CANONICAL FORM WITH HYPERPLANE H

Figure 10.27

A matroid can be defined in terms of the notion of a hyperplane. One way of doing this is given in DEFINITION 10.28 (Welsh, p. 39).

10.28 DEFINITION.

Let S be a set and let $\mathcal{H}$ be a collection of proper subsets of S satisfying

(H1) If H_1 and H_2 are in $\mathcal{H}$ with $H_1 \neq H_2$ then $H_1 \not\subseteq H_2$.

(H2) If $H_1, H_2 \in \mathcal{H}$ with $H_1 \neq H_2$ and $x \notin H_1 \cup H_2$ there exists $H_3 \in \mathcal{H}$ such that

$$H_3 \supseteq (H_1 \cap H_2) \cup \{x\}.$$

The set S together with $\mathcal{H}$ defines a matroid.

Intuitively, the best way to think of the conditions of DEFINITION 10.28 is to regard H_1, H_2, and H_3 as planes through the origin in 3-space. The reader should think of how the hyperplane definition relates to at least one of our other definitions of a matroid. For example, the closed sets of DEFINITION 10.26 can be defined as the sets obtained by taking S together with all hyperplanes and all possible intersections of hyperplanes. Our final definition of a matroid is in terms of structures closely related to hyperplanes called "circuits." Hyperplanes and circuits are "dual" concepts in a sense, explained in 10.70 and the related discussions.

10.29 DEFINITION.

Let S be a set and let $\mathscr{C}$ be a collection of subsets of S satisfying

(C1) If $X \neq Y$ are any two elements of $\mathscr{C}$ then $X \not\subset Y$.
(C2) If C_1 and C_2 are two distinct elements of $\mathscr{C}$ and $z \in C_1 \cap C_2$ then there exists C_3 in $\mathscr{C}$ such that $C_3 \subset (C_1 \cup C_2) - \{z\}$.

Then S together with the collection $\mathscr{C}$ defines a matroid. The sets of $\mathscr{C}$ are called the *circuits* or *cycles* of the matroid (Welsh, p. 9).

The motivation for DEFINITION 10.29 comes from graph theory and will be discussed in connection with the graphical matroid below. To relate DEFINITION 10.29 to DEFINITION 10.23 (independent set axioms), for example, we would define a set to be independent if it contains no circuits. Conversely, given the independent sets $\mathscr{I}$, the circuits are defined to be all sets C that are not independent but become independent upon the removal of any element (the "minimal dependent sets"). The circuits of a representable matroid have a very nice description in terms of the unit row canonical form. Suppose that M is representable and has representation matrix A. Assume that $C = \{x_1, x_2, . . ., x_p\}$ is a circuit and x_i corresponds to the ith column of the matrix A. If A is in unit row canonical form we have FIGURE 10.30.

10.30 A CYCLE IN UNIT ROW CANONICAL FORM.

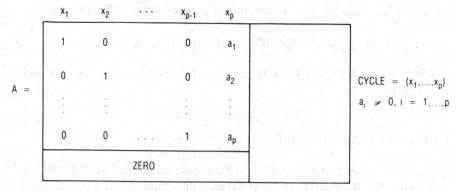

Figure 10.30

To summarize, in DEFINITIONS 10.23, 10.24, 10.25, 10.26, 10.28, and 10.29 we have given alternative descriptions of a matroid. This means that we could have taken any one of these definitions as *the* definition of a matroid and the others would be theorems derivable from this definition. In particular, for representable matroids these statements are all theorems about matrices and none of them are very difficult to prove. In a rigorous course about general matroids the equivalence of all of these definitions would be demonstrated (see Welsh, 1976; and Aigner, 1979).

10.31 EXERCISE.

(1) In the case of representable matroids, give examples of all of the terms (bases, independent sets, rank functions, closure, flats, hyperplanes, and circuits) and conditions (I3, R2, R3, MR2, MR3, CL3, CL4, H1, H2, C2) that occur in connection with 10.23–10.29.

(2) Justify the canonical forms of FIGURES 10.27 and 10.30. Let M be a representable matroid, B a base of M, and y an element of M, $y \notin B$. Show that there is a unique circuit of M containing y and having all other elements in B. Show $(B - \{x\}) \cup \{y\}$ is a base if and only if x is in this circuit.

(3) Pick two definitions from DEFINITIONS 10.23, 10.24, 10.25, 10.26, 10.28, and 10.29 and show carefully that they are equivalent to DEFINITION 10.1.

(4) Suppose that condition (2) of DEFINITION 10.1 is replaced by (2′) "If B_1 and B_2 are in $\mathcal{B}$ and $x \in B_1$ then there exists y in B_2 such that $(B_1 - \{x\}) \cup \{y\}$ and $(B_2 - \{y\}) \cup \{x\}$ are in $\mathcal{B}$." Note that this condition is stronger than condition (2) of DEFINITION 10.1, as not only does y replace x, but the *same* y can be replaced by x. It is the case, however, that DEFINITION 10.1 with conditions (1) and (2′) is another equivalent definition of a matroid. One must show that conditions (1) and (2) imply conditions (1) and (2′), as the reverse implication is trivial. Prove this for the case of representable matroids and then try to give a proof for the general case. *Hint.* Let A be an $r \times n$ representation matrix of a matroid M of rank r. Let B_1 and B_2 be bases with corresponding columns $A^{(B_1)}$ and $A^{(B_2)}$. By using elementary row operation, if necessary, we may assume that the submatrix $A^{(B_2)}$ is the identity I_r. Note that $A^{(B_1)}$ is nonsingular $r \times r$. Thus the problem becomes, given an $r \times r$ nonsingular matrix $N = (N^{(1)}, N^{(2)}, \ldots, N^{(r)})$ and an integer $1 \le t \le r$, find an integer $1 \le j \le r$ such that both matrices $(N^{(1)}, \ldots, N^{(t-1)}, I_r^{(j)}, N^{(t+1)}, \ldots, N^{(r)})$ and $(I^{(1)}, \ldots, I_r^{(j-1)}, N^{(t)}, I_r^{(j+1)}, \ldots, I_r^{(r)})$ are nonsingular. For the general case feel free to choose any one of the equivalent definitions of a matroid given above!

(5) A stronger version of problem (4) is true. Let M be a matroid and B_1 and B_2 bases. For any subset $X \subseteq B_1$ there is a subset $Y \subseteq B_2$ such that $(B_1 - X) \cup Y$ and $(B_2 - Y) \cup X$ are bases. Prove this for the representable case. *Hint.* A beautiful proof is given in the introduction to the paper by Greene and Magnanti, (1975). A proof of the general case is given by Greene and

Magnanti (1975) and also by Woodall (1974) in "An exchange theorem for bases of matroids" J. Comb. Theory (B), vol. 16 (1974), 227–229. The latter proof uses some ideas that we shall not prove until later (THEOREM 10.148).

We now develop the very important notion of duality for matroids. The reader should recall NOTATION 10.8, EXAMPLE 10.9, THEOREM 10.10 and LEMMA 10.11.

10.32   NOTATION.

Let M be a matroid on S and let A be a matrix representation of S with respect to the ordering $s_1, s_2, \ldots, s_n$. If $X \subseteq S$, $X = \{s_{i_1}, \ldots, s_{i_t}\}$ with $i_1 < \ldots < i_t$ then $A^{(X)} = (A^{(i_1)}, \ldots, A^{(i_t)}) = A(\phi | i_1, \ldots, i_t]$ will be called the *submatrix of* A *corresponding to* X. We use the notation A^+ to denote the standard transpose of A. Thus, if $A(i,j)$ denotes the entry of A in the ith row and j^{th} column, $A(i,j) = A^+(j,i)$ for all i and j. Don't confuse $A(i,j)$ with $A(i|j)$, the latter being the submatrix of A obtained by deleting row i and column j. In terms of NOTATION 10.8, $A(i,j) = A[i|j]$.

10.33   DEFINITION.

Let $M = (S, \mathcal{B})$ be a matroid. Let $\mathcal{B}^* = \{S - B : B \in \mathcal{B}\}$. Then $M^* = (S, \mathcal{B}^*)$ is a matroid called the *dual of* M.

The fact that M* is a matroid follows directly from DEFINITION 10.1 using the fact that the conditions of DEFINITION 10.1 hold for M (EXERCISE 10.46(4)). The next theorem shows that M* is representable if M is representable.

10.34   THEOREM.

Suppose that the m × n matrix A of rank r is a representation of the matroid $M = (S, \mathcal{B})$ with respect to the ordering $s_1, s_2, \ldots, s_n$ of S. Let N be an n × q matrix of rank $n - r$ such that $AN = \theta$ (the m × q zero matrix). Then N^+ is a representation of M* with respect to $s_1, s_2, \ldots, s_n$.

Proof.   By using elementary row operations we can convert A to a matrix with first r rows linearly independent and remaining $m - r$ rows zero (unit row canonical form will do this). The new matrix is still a representation of M (REMARK 10.16). Thus we may assume that $m = r$ and similarly that $q = n - r$. Given a base $B = \{s_{i_1}, \ldots, s_{i_r}\}$ of M, the submatrix $A^{(B)} = A(\phi | i_1, \ldots, i_r]$ of A·is a basis for the column space of A. We must show that $N(i_1, \ldots, i_r | \phi)$, the submatrix of N consisting of *rows* corresponding to $S - B$, is a basis for the row space of N (hence of the column space of N^+). Let P be an r × r nonsingular matrix such that $\tilde{A} = PA$ has $\tilde{A}(\phi | i_1, \ldots, i_r] = I_r$, the r × r identity matrix (one can use elementary row operations to construct P). By THEOREM 10.10, choose $\tilde{N}$ such that $\tilde{N}(i_1,\ldots,i_r|\phi) = I_{n-r}$ and $\tilde{A}\tilde{N} = \theta$. Thus the columns of $\tilde{N}$ are a basis for the null space of $\tilde{A}$ and hence of A. By representing the columns of N in terms of the columns of $\tilde{N}$ we can find a nonsingular $(n-r) \times (n-r)$ matrix Q such that $\tilde{N}Q = N$. The row matroid of N is thus the same as that of $\tilde{N}$ and, hence, $N(i_1,\ldots,i_r|\phi)$ is a basis for the row space of N.

THEOREM 10.34 provides an interesting joint matrix representation of a representable matroid and its dual. Let $M = (S,\mathscr{B})$ be a representable matroid, $S = \{s_1,\ldots,s_n\}$, where $B = \{s_1,s_2,\ldots,s_r\}$ is a base. We may choose an $r \times n$ representation matrix A of M in canonical form with respect to the ordering $s_1,s_2,\ldots,s_n$. Thus $A = (I_r,\hat{A})$ has its first r columns equal to those of the $r \times r$ identity matrix. By THEOREMS 10.10 and 10.34 the matrix $N = \begin{pmatrix} \hat{A} \\ -I_{n-r} \end{pmatrix}$ is a row representation of M*. By REMARK 10.16, we may multiply the last $n-r$ rows of N by -1 and still have a row representation B of M*. Thus we may jointly represent M and M* in the following tabular form.

10.35 JOINT REPRESENTATION OF M AND M*.

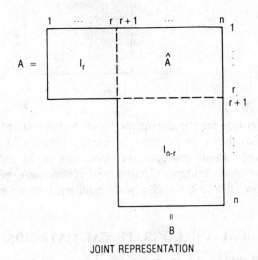

JOINT REPRESENTATION

Figure 10.35

10.36 EXAMPLE OF JOINT REPRESENTATION.

If the matrix

$$A = \begin{pmatrix} 1 & 0 & 0 & | & 1 & 3 & 2 & 0 \\ 0 & 1 & 0 & | & 1 & 2 & 0 & 1 \\ 0 & 0 & 1 & | & 0 & 0 & 1 & 1 \end{pmatrix}$$

represents the matroid M with respect to the ordering $s_1, \ldots, s_7$ then

$$
B = \begin{pmatrix}
1 & 3 & 2 & 0 \\
1 & 2 & 0 & 1 \\
0 & 0 & 1 & 1 \\
\hline
1 & 0 & 0 & 0 \\
0 & 1 & 0 & 0 \\
0 & 0 & 1 & 0 \\
0 & 0 & 0 & 1
\end{pmatrix}
$$

is a *row* representation of M^* with respect to $s_1, \ldots, s_n$. The joint representation is

	1	2	3	4	5	6	7	
A =	1	0	0	1	3	2	0	1
	0	1	0	1	2	0	1	2
	0	0	1	0	0	1	1	3
				1	0	0	0	4
				0	1	0	0	5
				0	0	1	0	6
				0	0	0	1	7

$$\underset{B}{\parallel}$$

The principal reason for introducing the "joint representation" is conceptual. The representation shows the complete symmetry between M and M^* and is useful in studying various concepts and operations on M and M^* (circuits, cocircuits, components, bridges, deletion, and contraction). We shall discuss these ideas below, but first we give some additional important examples of matroids.

10.37   GRAPHICAL AND COGRAPHICAL MATROIDS.

In the study of matroids, it is more natural to work with the general definition of a graph (DEFINITION 6.3). Consider the graph G shown in FIGURE 10.38. Note that every triple of edges $\{x,y,z\}$ defines a spanning tree except for $F_1 = \{a,b,c\}$ and $F_2 = \{c,d,e\}$. It is easily seen that $M_G = (E, \mathscr{B})$ is a matroid where the set of bases $\mathscr{B}$ is the set of all triples of edges that form a spanning tree of G. In this case, one can use the argument of EXERCISE 10.21(3). It is not difficult to show that for any connected graph $G = (V,E,\varphi)$ the pair $M_G = (E,\mathscr{B})$, where $\mathscr{B}$ is the set of all collections of edges that form a spanning tree of G, is a matroid (sometimes called the "cycle matroid" of G, EXERCISE 10.46(1)). For a disconnected graph G, we take M_G to be the direct sum (EXERCISE 10.21(1)) of the matroids associated with each connected component. Any matroid M that is isomorphic to a matroid M_G for some graph G will be called a *graphical matroid*. If M is graphical, then M* (which is isomorphic to M_G^* for some G) is called *cographical*. The bases of M_G^* are the complements of *spanning* trees (assume G is connected). These bases are called *cotrees* of G.

10.38 GRAPH, TREE, AND COTREE.

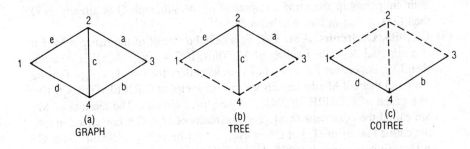

Figure 10.38

Note that in FIGURE 10.38(b) the "tree" is in fact a spanning tree. A "cotree" in the sense we are using it here is the complement of a *spanning* tree. For general matroids, one uses the term *base* for spanning tree and *cobase* for cotree. The independent sets in the cographical matroid are all subsets of cotrees. Thus a set is independent in M_G^* if it is a subset of the set of chords (DEFINITION 6.47) of some spanning tree for G (assume G is connected). A set is a base in M_G^* if it is the set of chords of some spanning tree. In DEFINITIONS 10.28 and 10.29 we gave characterizations of hyperplanes and circuits in a matroid M. We discussed the meanings of these ideas for representable matroids (FIGURES 10.27, 10.30). We now review some of this terminology and give examples for graphical matroids M_G, G a connected graph.

10.39 TERMINOLOGY REVIEW.

$M = (S, \mathcal{B})$ defined in terms of bases.

(1) **Independent Sets.** Any subset of a base of M is an *independent* set. In the case of a graphical matroid M_G, the independent sets are the subforests of G (DEFINITION 6.47). A set not contained in any base of M is called *dependent*.

(2) **Rank Function.** If $Q \subseteq S$ then $\rho(Q)$, the *rank* of Q, is the size of the largest independent set of M contained in Q. In the graphical case, Q is a set of

edges and hence defines a subgraph of G. The rank of Q is the size of any spanning forest for Q (DEFINITIONS 6.47, 6.90 and EXERCISE 6.94(1)). Recall that, by our definition, the components of a spanning forest for Q are spanning trees for the components of Q.

(3) **Closure** or **Span**. If $Q \subseteq S$ then $c(Q)$, the *closure* or *span* of Q, is $\{x: \rho(\{x\} \cup Q) = \rho(Q)\}$. In the graphical case, $c(Q)$ is Q together with all edges of G both of whose endpoints lie in the same component of Q. In FIGURE 10.38(a), the closure of $Q = \{a,b\}$ is $\{a,b,c\}$.

(4) **Closed Sets, Flats, Subspaces**. If $Q \subseteq S$ and $c(Q) = Q$ then Q is a *closed set* or *flat* or *subspace* of M. In the graphical case, if every edge in G with both endpoints in the same component of the subgraph Q is already in Q then Q is closed (a flat, a subspace).

(5) **Circuits, Cocircuits**. A set $C \subseteq S$ is called a circuit of the matroid M if it is a minimal dependent subset of M. Thus, if $C = \{x_1, . . .,x_p\}$ is a circuit then C is dependent but $C - \{x_i\}$ is independent for $i = 1, . . .,p$. For the graphical matroid M_G the circuits are just the cycles of G (DEFINITION 6.10). The graph of FIGURE 10.38(a) has just three circuits. The circuits of M* are called the *cocircuits* of M. The cocircuits of M_G, G a connected graph, are called *cutsets* of G. Let $C^* = \{y_1, . . .,y_q\}$ be such a cocircuit. Then C* is by definition a circuit in M_G^*. This means that $\{y_1, . . .,y_{q-1}\}$ is independent in M_G^* and hence is a subset of a set of chords of a spanning tree T for G. But C* is dependent in M_G^* and thus y_q must be an edge of T. Note that H $= G - C^*$ must be disconnected, for otherwise we could find a spanning tree T for G for which C* would be a set of chords. We have just observed that $H' = G - \{y_1, . . .,y_{q-1}\}$ is connected. Thus when y_q is removed from H' we disconnect H' but only into two components (the removal of a single edge from a connected graph can at most create one extra component). We may thus think of a cocircuit (or cutset) of a connected graph G as being a set of edges whose removal creates one extra component but if any proper subset of these edges is removed the graph remains connected. One way to construct such sets is to construct first a spanning tree T for G and pick an edge y_q in T. Let $\{y_1, . . .,y_{q-1}\}$ be all chords of T with vertices in different components of $T - \{y_q\}$. The set $C^* = \{y_1, . . .,y_q\}$ is a cocircuit. As an example, we consider the graph of FIGURE 10.38(a). Let T be the spanning tree defined by the edge set $\{a,e,d\}$. Take $q = 3$ and define $y_q = \{e\}$. Thus $C^* = \{b,c,e\}$ is a cocircuit. All cocircuits can be constructed in this way.

(6) **Hyperplanes**. If $M = (S,\mathcal{B})$ has rank r and $H \subseteq S$ is a closed set of rank $r-1$ then H is called a *hyperplane*. If H is a hyperplane and $x \notin H$ then $c(H \cup \{x\}) = S$. In FIGURE 10.38(a), the set $\{a,b,c\}$ is a hyperplane.

We now show that the graphical matroids are representable. They are in fact representable over *every* field. Such matroids are called *regular* as given in DEFINITION 10.40. Many matroids of combinatorial interest are *not* regular (or binary in the sense of DEFINITION 10.40) as we shall see below.

10.40 DEFINITION.

Let M be a matroid. If for every field F there exists a matrix representation A of M with entries in F then M is called a *regular* matroid. A matroid representable over GF(2) is called *binary*.

It turns out that a matroid M is regular if it is representable both over GF(2) and over some other field not of characteristic 2 (see Aigner, 1979, Theorem 7.35, p. 344). We shall now show that for any graph G the matroid M_G is regular. We do this directly by giving a representation valid for all fields F. First we introduce some notation.

10.41 NOTATION.

Let $G = (V;E,\varphi)$ be a graph and let M_G be its associated matroid. Let A be a matrix representation of M_G with respect to the ordering $e_1,\ldots,e_n$ of the edges E of G. For any $e \in E$ we use the notation $A^{(e)}$ to denote the column of A corresponding to e (thus $A^{(e_i)} = A^{(i)}$ is the ith column of A). For any column vector Z, we denote the tth entry of Z by Z(t). Assume that the vertices V of G are linearly ordered and let $\varphi(e_i) = \{u_i,v_i\}$ where $u_i < v_i$. The matrix A with columns and rows indexed by the linearly ordered sets E and V respectively and defined by $A^{(e_i)}(u_i) = -1$, $A^{(e_i)}(v_i) = +1$, and $A^{(e_i)}(t) = 0$ for all other values of t will be called the *natural representation* of M_G with respect to these linear orders on E and V. We now prove that this "natural representation" is in fact a representation (THEOREM 10.42). See also EXAMPLE 10.43.

10.42 THEOREM.

Let G be a graph and let F be a field. The matroid M_G is representable over F.

Proof. We show that the natural representation defined in NOTATION 10.41 is in fact a representation of M_G. We do this by showing that a subset $X \subseteq E$ is independent in M_G if and only if the corresponding set of columns $A^{(X)}$ is linearly independent over F. First, suppose that X is independent in M_G. Thus, the edges of X define a subforest of G. Consider $Z = \sum_{e \in X} a_e A^{(e)}$, $a_e \in F$, and let $X' = \{e: a_e \neq 0\}$. The set of edges X' defines a subforest of G. Let $f = \{u,v\}$ be a pendant edge of X' and let v be its vertex of degree 1. Clearly, $Z(v) = \pm a_f \neq 0$ and thus the vector Z is zero only when X' is empty. This shows that $A^{(X)}$ is linearly independent. Conversely, suppose that X is a dependent subset of M_G and let C be a cycle in X. Obviously $\sum_{e \in C} a_e A^{(e)}$ is the zero vector for some choice of $a_e = \pm 1$. Thus $A^{(X)}$ is a linearly dependent set of columns.

10.43   EXAMPLES OF THE NATURAL REPRESENTATION.

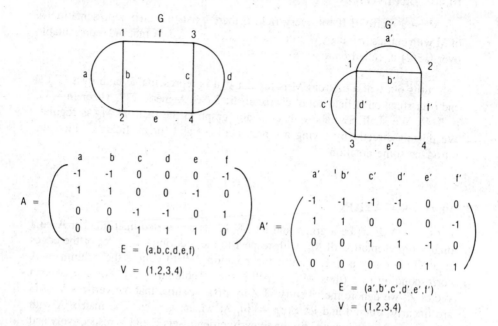

$$A = \begin{pmatrix} a & b & c & d & e & f \\ -1 & -1 & 0 & 0 & 0 & -1 \\ 1 & 1 & 0 & 0 & -1 & 0 \\ 0 & 0 & -1 & -1 & 0 & 1 \\ 0 & 0 & 1 & 1 & 1 & 0 \end{pmatrix}$$

$$E = (a,b,c,d,e,f)$$
$$V = (1,2,3,4)$$

$$A' = \begin{pmatrix} a' & b' & c' & d' & e' & f' \\ -1 & -1 & -1 & -1 & 0 & 0 \\ 1 & 1 & 0 & 0 & 0 & -1 \\ 0 & 0 & 1 & 1 & -1 & 0 \\ 0 & 0 & 0 & 0 & 1 & 1 \end{pmatrix}$$

$$E = (a',b',c',d',e',f')$$
$$V = (1,2,3,4)$$

THEOREM 10.42 tells us that the graphical matroids are a special subclass of representable matroids and provides a strong link between linear algebra and graph theory. In passing from G to M_G, however, certain basic geometric information is lost. For example, if G = (V,E) is any tree then M_G is the free matroid (E,{E}). The map G → M_G is "tree blind." If G is biconnected (DEFINITION 6.95) a little more can be said about reconstructing G from M_G. Consider the two biconnected graphs G and G' of EXAMPLE 10.43. They obviously have the same set of cycles up to the isomorphism x → x' and thus the matroids M_G and M_G' are isomorphic. In the case of biconnected graphs such as these, Whitney (1933, pp. 245–254) defined an operation based on separation pairs (DEFINITION 9.2) called "twisting" and showed that any two biconnected graphs with the same associated matroid can be transformed from one to the other by a succession of "twistings." Moreover, if G is triconnected (DEFINITION 9.3 and following paragraph) then G is essentially determined by its associate matroid. Since M_G for an arbitrary graph G is a direct sum of the matroids associated wtih the biconnected components of G *independent of how these components are pieced together in* G, these results are of little help in reconstructing G from M_G as the example of trees shows. For a discussion of these topics and for references the reader is referred to Welsh (Chapter 6).

Given a graph G and its associated matroid M_G, we can also look at the dual matroid M_G^*. Historically, there are two other notions of duality for graphs, the "geometric dual" and the "abstract dual." We briefly discuss these ideas here and refer the reader to Aigner (Chapter VI) and Welsh (Chapter 6) for more complete discussions. First we consider the "geometric dual." Consider FIGURE 10.44. The solid lines represent an embedding of a planar graph G (paragraph preceding DEFINITION 6.110). To construct the geometric dual of G given this embedding, put a dot inside each region including the exterior or unbounded region (if we imagine the embedding on the surface of a sphere then all regions are bounded). An edge such as edge e of FIGURE 10.44 is called an *isthmus* (any pendant edge is also an isthmus). Removing e disconnects G. Any edge x that is not an isthmus bounds two regions. For each such edge x construct a dashed line x' crossing x and joining the dots in the two regions bounded by x. For the isthmus e construct a dashed line e' that forms a loop as shown in FIGURE 10.44. The resulting graph represented by the dots and dashed edges defines another planar graph G* called the *geometric dual* of G with respect to the given embedding. Note first of all that the geometric dual is defined only for planar graphs and depends on an embedding of that graph. For each edge x of G there is a corresponding edge x' of the dual G*. Thus the number of edges of G and G* is the same. The reader should check that under this correspondence the circuits of G in FIGURE 10.44 become the cutsets or co-circuits of the graph G* and a loop becomes an isthmus. Trees in G become cotrees in G* under the map $x \rightarrow x'$. Note that $G = (G*)*$ with the embeddings shown. In general, for any planar graph G, M_G^* is isomorphic to M_G*. Thus, up to isomorphism, M_G* does not depend on the embedding of G used to construct G*. On the other hand, if G_1^* and G_2^* are two geometric duals of G constructed from two different embeddings then it is possible that G_1^* and G_2^* are nonisomorphic graphs. FIGURE 10.45 shows two embeddings of the same graph that give rise to nonisomorphic geometric duals (isomorphic to the graphs of FIGURE 10.43).

10.44 A GRAPH AND ITS GEOMETRIC DUAL FROM AN EMBEDDING.

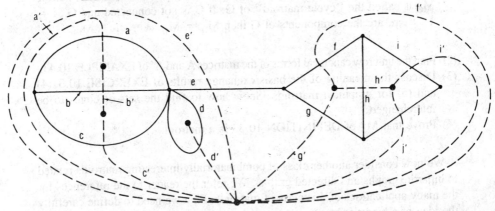

Figure 10.44

10.45 NONISOMORPHIC GEÓMETRIC DUALS OF THE SAME GRAPH.

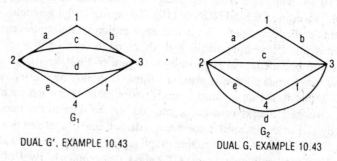

DUAL G', EXAMPLE 10.43   DUAL G, EXAMPLE 10.43

Figure 10.45

As we have remarked, the concept of a geometric dual is restricted to planar graphs. Suppose that starting with a nonplanar graph G we form M_G and then M_G^*. It might happen that there is some graph H such that M_G^* is isomorphic to M_H. Such an H would be called an *abstract dual* of G. It turns out that this can never happen. M_G^* is never a graphical matroid if G is nonplanar. If G is planar there can exist abstract duals H that are not geometric duals but only if G is not biconnected. For biconnected graphs the abstract and geometric duals are the same.

10.46 EXERCISE.

(1) Let $G = (V,E,\varphi)$ be a connected graph and let $M_G = (E,\mathscr{B})$ where $\mathscr{B}$ is the set of all spanning trees for G. Prove that M_G is a matroid. The matroid M_G is called the "cycle matroid" of G. If G is not connected and G_i, $i = 1,\ldots,p$, are the components of G then $M_G = M_{G_1} + \ldots + M_{G_p}$.

(2) Find the unit row canonical forms of the matrices A and A' of EXAMPLE 10.43.

(3) Discuss the meaning of the basis exchange results of EXERCISE 10.31(4) and (5) for graphical matroids. Show how to find the sets of edges to be interchanged.

(4) Prove that M* of DEFINITION 10.33 is a matroid.

We now consider another class of combinatorially interesting matroids related to bipartite graphs and directed graphs. We refer the reader to the references for the many applications of this class of matroids. First we need to define carefully the idea of a bipartite graph.

10.47   DEFINITION.

A graph $G = (V,E,\varphi)$ is *bipartite* if there exists a partition of V into two nonempty subsets V_1 and V_2 such that for all $e \in E$, $|\varphi(e) \cap V_1| = |\varphi(e) \cap V_2| = 1$. In words, each e has one vertex in V_1 and the other vertex in V_2. For a given G, the choice of V_1 and V_2 may not be unique so we introduce the notation $G = (V_1,V_2,E,\varphi)$ when we wish to be specific about the underlying partition. In this case, we call V_1 the *first block* and V_2 the *second block* of the bipartite graph G.

A diagrammatic representation of the bipartite graph is shown in FIGURE 10.48. The set $V_1 = \underline{6}$, and the set $V_2 = \underline{6}'$. Each edge is represented as directed from V_1 to V_2. Strictly speaking, the bipartite graph is not a directed graph but it is often convenient to represent the graph with the edges directed from the first to the second block (in cases where the blocks have been ordered).

10.48   A BIPARTITE GRAPH.

$G = (\underline{6},\underline{6}',E,\varphi)$

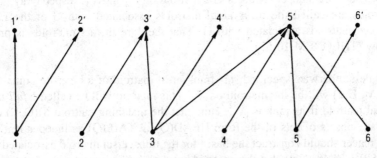

Figure 10.48

We now define the concept of a *matching* in a graph (not necessarily bipartite).

10.49   DEFINITION.

Let $G = (V,E,\varphi)$ be a graph (DEFINITION 6.3). A subset $Q \subseteq E$ with the property that $e,f \in Q$, $e \neq f$, implies that $\varphi(e) \cap \varphi(f) = \phi$ is called a *matching* in G. Thus a matching is simply a collection of edges of G whose vertex sets are disjoint. If Q is a matching and $\{\varphi(e): e \in Q\}$ is a partition of V (i.e., contains all vertices of V) then Q is called a *complete* matching. If $G = (V_1,V_2,E,\varphi)$ is a bipartite graph with blocks V_1 and V_2 and Q is a matching in G then we define $TAIL(Q) = \{x: x \in \varphi(e) \cap V_1$ for some $e \in Q\}$ and $HEAD(Q) = \{x: x \in \varphi(e) \cap V_2$ for some $e \in Q\}$.

In the graph of FIGURE 10.44, $Q = \{a,f,j\}$ is a matching (in fact a complete matching). Associated with any graph are matroids called "matching matroids" of the graph.

10.50   DEFINITION (MATCHING MATROIDS).

Let $G = (V,E,\varphi)$ be a graph (DEFINITION 6.3). Let $\mathcal{M}$ denote the set of all matchings of G. For any matching Q, let $\varphi(Q) = \bigcup_{e \in Q} \varphi(e)$. If we let $\mathcal{I} = \{X: X \subseteq \varphi(Q), Q \in \mathcal{M}\}$ then $\mathcal{I}$ is the collection of independent sets of a matroid on V. For any subset $S \subseteq V$, the matroid $M(G,S) = (S,\mathcal{I}_S)$ where $\mathcal{I}_S$ is the set of all elements of $\mathcal{I}$ contained in S is called a *matching matroid*.

It is not difficult to verify that the "matching matroids" of DEFINITION 10.23 are in fact matroids (EXERCISE 10.56(1)). The matching matroids turn out to be a special case of an important class of matroids related to bipartite graphs, which we now discuss.

10.51   DEFINITION (TRANSVERSAL OR SIMPLE BIPARTITE INDUCED MATROIDS).

Let $G = (V_1,V_2,E,\varphi)$ be a bipartite graph. Then, referring to DEFINITION 10.49, {HEAD(Q): $Q \in \mathcal{M}$} and {TAIL(Q): $Q \in \mathcal{M}$} where Q ranges over all matchings $\mathcal{M}$ of G are the independent sets of a matroid on V_2 and V_1, respectively. These matroids are called the *transversal* matroids associated with G or the *simple induced* matroids associated with G. That they are in fact matroids is proved below (THEOREM 10.53).

Unless otherwise specified, *the* transversal matroid of a bipartite graph $G = (V_1,V_2,E,\varphi)$ will be the matroid on V_2. This matroid will be called a *full* transversal matroid if its rank is $|V_1|$. Note that the matching matroid $M(G,V)$ on G has all subsets of sets of the form HEAD(Q) $\cup$ TAIL(Q) as independent sets. The reader should construct the bases for the transversal matroid associated with FIGURE 10.48. Note that this matroid has rank 5 (the largest size of a matching for this bipartite graph). It is a remarkable fact that the transversal matroids and the matching matroids are the same up to isomorphism (Welsh, Chapter 14). We shall prove below that the transversal matroids (and hence the matching) matroids are representable. In contrast to the graphical matroids, the transversal matroids (as a class) are neither binary nor regular in the sense of DEFINITION 10.40. Transversal matroids have an important generalization which we now define.

10.52   DEFINITION (BIPARTITE INDUCED MATROIDS).

Let $G = (V_1,V_2,E,\varphi)$ be a bipartite graph. Let $M_1 = (V_1,\mathcal{I}_1)$ be a matroid on V_1 with independent sets $\mathcal{I}_1$. Then the set {HEAD(Q): $Q \in \mathcal{M}$ and TAIL(Q) $\in \mathcal{I}_1$} is the set of independent sets of a matroid on V_2. This matroid is called the *induced matroid on* V_2 from M_1. The proof that it is in fact a matroid is given below for the representable case (THEOREM 10.55).

As a simple example of a bipartite induced matroid, consider the bipartite graph $G = (\underline{6},\underline{6}',E,\varphi)$ of FIGURE 10.48. Let M_1 be the uniform matroid of rank 2 on $V_1 = \underline{6}$. Then the induced matroid on $\underline{6}'$ is of rank 2 but not uniform on $\underline{6}'$ as $\{1',2'\}$ is not a base. By symmetry, one could obviously have started with a matroid M_2 on V_2 in DEFINITION 10.52 and induced a matroid on V_1. Note that the transversal or simple bipartite induced matroid of DEFINITION 10.52 can be regarded as the matroid induced on V_2 by the free matroid on V_1.

We shall now show that if the matroid M_1 is representable then the associated bipartite matroid is also representable. We shall show this by explicitly constructing a representation matrix. To understand the idea, it is best to consider the case of transversal or simple induced matroids first. The reader should recall the rational function field $F(z_{i,j})$ of EXAMPLE 10.5 and the notational conventions of NOTATION 10.32.

10.53 THEOREM.

Let $G = (V_1,V_2,E,\varphi)$ be a bipartite graph with $V_1 = (a_1,. . .,a_m)$ and $V_2 = (b_1,. . .,b_n)$. Let $z_{i,j}$ be variables and $F(z_{i,j})$ the corresponding rational function field over a field F (EXAMPLE 10.5). Define an $m \times n$ matrix Z with entries in $F(z_{i,j})$ by $Z(i,j) = z_{i,j}$ if $\{a_i,b_j\}$ is an edge of G and $Z(i,j) = 0$ otherwise. For any subset $X \subseteq V_2$, the corresponding columns $Z^{(X)}$ of Z are linearly independent if and only if $X = \text{HEAD}(Q)$ for some matching Q of G. Thus, the transversal matroid of DEFINITION 10.51 is in fact a matroid and Z is a matrix representation of this matroid with respect to the ordering $(b_1,. . .,b_n)$ of V_2.

Proof. Note that the definition of Z depends only on G (and no assumptions about the transversal matroid). Thus, verifying the assertions of the theorem shows simultaneously that the "transversal matroid" of DEFINITION 10.51 is in fact a matroid and is representable. First, we observe that given $X \subseteq V_2$, $X = (x_1,. . .,x_k)$, there exists a matching Q of G such that $\text{HEAD}(Q) = X$ if and only if there is a $Y = (y_1,. . .,y_k)$ in V_1 and a permutation $\tau \in S_k$ such that $\prod_{t=1}^{k} Z(y_t,x_{\tau(t)}) \neq 0$ where $Z(y_t,x_{\tau(t)}) = Z_{t,\tau(t)}$. Let $Z[Y|X]$ denote the $k \times k$ square submatrix of Z obtained by keeping the rows corresponding to Y and the columns corresponding to X (NOTATION 10.8). Since the $z_{i,j}$ are independent variables, we have $\det Z[Y|X] = \sum_{\sigma \in S_k} \text{sgn}\,(\sigma) \prod_{t=1}^{k} Z(y_t,x_{\sigma(t)}) \neq 0$ if and only if there is a $\tau \in S_k$ such that $\prod_{t=1}^{k} Z(y_t,x_{\tau(t)}) \neq 0$. Putting these facts together, we see that there is a matching Q of G such that $\text{HEAD}(Q) = X$ if and only if there is a subset Y of V_1 such that $\det Z[Y|X] \neq 0$. The latter condition holds if and only if the columns of Z corresponding to X are linearly independent.

We now consider an example of the ideas in THEOREM 10.53. A bipartite
graph $G = (\underline{4}, \underline{6'}, E, \varphi)$ and the associated matrix Z are shown in FIGURE 10.54.

10.54   AN EXAMPLE OF THEOREM 10.53.

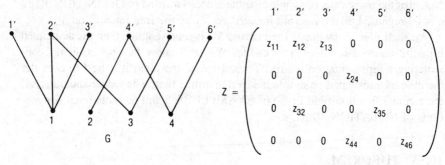

REPRESENTATION Z

Figure 10.54

Referring to the proof of THEOREM 10.53 and using the matrix Z of
FIGURE 10.54, let $X = (2',3',4',6') = (x_1,x_2,x_3,x_4)$ and $Y = (1,2,3,4) =$
(y_1,y_2,y_3,y_4). With $\tau = \begin{pmatrix} 1\,2\,3\,4 \\ 2\,3\,1\,4 \end{pmatrix}$ we obtain $\prod_{t=1}^{4} Z(y_t,x_{\tau(t)}) = z_{13}\,z_{24}\,z_{32}\,z_{46} \neq$
0. Thus $Q = \{\{y_t,x_{\tau(t)}\}: t = 1,\ldots,4\} = \{\{1,3'\},\{2,4'\},\{3,2'\},\{4,6'\}\}$ is a match-
ing.

Note that if we multiply the second row of z (FIGURE 10.54) by $z_{44}\,z_{24}^{-1}$ and
subtract the result from the 4th row of z we obtain

$$\begin{array}{c} 1'\ \ 2'\ \ 3'\ \ 4'\ \ 5'\ \ 6' \\ \begin{pmatrix} z_{11} & z_{12} & z_{13} & 0 & 0 & 0 \\ 0 & 0 & 0 & z_{24} & 0 & 0 \\ 0 & z_{32} & 0 & 0 & z_{35} & 0 \\ 0 & 0 & 0 & 0 & 0 & z_{46} \end{pmatrix} \end{array}.$$

Using REMARK 10.16, we can make the first nonzero entry in each column a
1 to obtain

$$W = \begin{array}{c} 1'\quad 2'\quad 3'\ 4'\ 5'\ 6' \\ \begin{pmatrix} 1 & 1 & 1 & 0 & 0 & 0 \\ 0 & 0 & 0 & 1 & 0 & 0 \\ 0 & z_{32}z_{12}^{-1} & 0 & 0 & 1 & 0 \\ 0 & 0 & 0 & 0 & 0 & 1 \end{pmatrix} \end{array}$$

It is evident that the only circuits in the matroid represented by W (which is the
same as the matroid represented by Z) are $\{1',3'\}$, $\{2',3',5'\}$, and $\{1',2',5'\}$. If

we set $z_{32} = z_{12} = 1$ in W we obtain the same set of circuits and thus the transversal matroid of FIGURE 10.54 is also represented by

$$Z' = \begin{array}{c} \begin{array}{cccccc} 1' & 2' & 3' & 4' & 5' & 6' \end{array} \\ \begin{pmatrix} 1 & 1 & 1 & 0 & 0 & 0 \\ 0 & 0 & 0 & 1 & 0 & 0 \\ 0 & 1 & 0 & 0 & 1 & 0 \\ 0 & 0 & 0 & 0 & 0 & 1 \end{pmatrix} \end{array}$$

The transversal matroid of FIGURE 10.54 is thus representable over every field. This is not the case for all transversal matroids as we remarked above. The uniform matroid $\mathcal{U}_{2,4}$ is obviously isomorphic to a transversal matroid but is easily seen not to be representable over GF(2) (EXERCISE 10.56(3)). The process of going from Z to Z' is of interest in general. Given the representation Z over the field $F(z_{ij})$ we would like to find a representation Z' over a less exotic field, such as the rational numbers. Some aspects of this question are considered in EXERCISE 10.56(4).

We now consider the slightly more complicated case of the bipartite induced matroids of DEFINITION 10.52. We restrict our attention to the case where M_1 is representable (the general case may be found in Welsh, Chapter 8). In this case the fact that the bipartite induced matroid is in fact a matroid and is representable over $F(z_{i,j})$ follows easily from a standard result in linear algebra called the Cauchy-Binet theorem (the reader may wish to consult a textbook on linear algebra to review this theorem). To illustrate how the representation matrix for a bipartite induced matroid is constructed, consider again the bipartite graph G of FIGURE 10.54. Let the field F be the rational numbers and let Z be as in FIGURE 10.54. Take M_1 to be the uniform matroid of rank 2 on $\underline{4} = V_1$. One possible representation matrix of M_1 is

$$A = \begin{array}{c} \begin{array}{cccc} 1 & 2 & 3 & 4 \end{array} \\ \begin{pmatrix} 1 & 0 & 1 & 1 \\ 0 & 1 & 1 & 2 \end{pmatrix} \end{array}$$

Our next theorem, THEOREM 10.55, asserts that $B = AZ$ is a representation of the bipartite induced matroid. In this case,

$$B = \begin{pmatrix} z_{11} & z_{12} + z_{32} & z_{13} & z_{44} & z_{35} & z_{46} \\ 0 & z_{32} & 0 & z_{24} + 2z_{44} & z_{35} & 2z_{46} \end{pmatrix}$$

10.55 THEOREM.

Let $G = (V_1, V_2, E, \varphi)$ be as in THEOREM 10.53 and let $M_1 = (V_1, \mathcal{I}_1)$ be a matroid on V_1. Assume that M_1 has an $r \times m$ representation matrix A with entries in a field F. Let Z be the $m \times n$ matrix of THEOREM 10.53 and let $B = AZ$. For any $X \subseteq V_2$ the corresponding columns $B^{(X)}$ are linearly independent if and only if $X = HEAD(Q)$ for some matching Q of G with $TAIL(Q) \in \mathcal{I}_1$.

Thus the bipartite induced matroids of DEFINITION 10.52 are in fact matroids with $B = AZ$ as representation matrices.

Proof. "Bipartite induced matroids" of DEFINITION 10.52 are matroids even if M_1 is not representable (Welsh, Chapter 8). We assume representability of M_1. For notational convenience, assume $V_1 = \underline{m}$ and $V_2 = \underline{n}$. We again use NOTATION 10.8. Let $X \subseteq \underline{n}$ with $|X| = k$. The columns $B^{(X)}$ are linearly independent if and only if there is a $Y \subseteq \underline{r}$, $|Y| = k$, such that $\det B[Y|X] \neq 0$. The Cauchy-Binet theorem states that $\det B[Y|X] = \sum_T \det A[Y|T] \det Z[T|X]$ where the sum is over all subsets $T \subseteq \underline{m}$ with $|T| = k$. But this latter sum (over T) is nonzero if and only if there exists $T_0 \subseteq \underline{m}$, $|T_0| = k$, such that $\det A[Y|T_0] \neq 0$ and $\det Z[T_0|X] \neq 0$. The "only if" part of this assertion is trivial. For the "if" part we again use the independence of the variables $z_{i,j}$. But $\det A[Y|T_0] \neq 0$ for some Y if and only if $A^{(T_0)}$ is linearly independent and, thus, $T_0 \in \mathcal{I}_1$. Also, $\det Z[T_0|X] \neq 0$ for some T_0 if and only if $Z^{(X)}$ is linearly independent in the transversal matroid of G by THEOREM 10.53. The result follows.

10.56 EXERCISE.

(1) Prove that the "matching matroids" of DEFINITION 10.50 are in fact matroids (see Lawler, Chapter 7, or Welsh, Chapter 14).

(2) Let $\mathcal{A} = \{A_i : i \in I\}$ be a family of subsets of a set S. If $I' \subseteq I$ is a subset of I and $T = \{a_i : i \in I'\}$ is a collection of $|I'|$ elements of S such that $a_i \in A_i$ for all $i \in I'$, then T is called a *partial transversal* for $\mathcal{A}$. If $I' = I$ then T is called a *full transversal* for the family $\mathcal{A}$ or a *system of distinct representatives* for $\mathcal{A}$. The fact that the collection of all transversals for $\mathcal{A}$ form the independent sets of a representable matroid on S follows from THEOREM 10.53. Explain. Give an example and show how to construct the representing matrix. The famous Phillip Hall condition for the existence of a system of distinct representatives (see CHAPTER 5, Section D) has an extension to matroids, called "Rado's Theorem." Learn the statement and proof of this theorem and give some examples. *Hint.* Discussions and references may be found in Welsh (Chapter 7) and Aigner (Chapter VIII).

(3) Show that the uniform matroid $\mathcal{U}_{2,4}$ is isomorphic to a transversal matroid. Show that $\mathcal{U}_{2,4}$ is not representable over GF(2).

(4) Given the matrix Z of THEOREM 10.53 with variable entries and given a field F we wish to substitute values in F for the variables to obtain a matrix Z' which is still a representation of the same transversal matroid. What is a good way of doing this in general (it may not always be possible, depending on G and F)? Such a Z' was constructed in the discussion following EXAMPLE 10.54. Another way to look at this problem is to consider the polynomial $p(z_{i,j})$, which is the product of all nonzero $r \times r$ subdeterminants of Z where r is the rank of Z. Finding Z' amounts to finding a set $z'_{i,j}$ of

values of the $z_{i,j}$ on which p does not vanish. From a probabilistic point of view almost all values of the $z_{i,j}$ are not roots of p if F is an infinite field such as the rational numbers or real numbers. Thus, this problem should be easy to solve for such fields! What about the more general case of the bipartite induced matroids? In the discussion following EXAMPLE 10.54, the Z' found for the transversal matroid was such that AZ' is a representation for the induced matroid. Is this just a coincidence or is it true in general?

(5) Let S be a set and let $\Pi = \{B_1,. . .,B_m\}$ be a partition of S into m blocks (CHAPTER 1, DEFINITION 1.3). Let d_i, $i = 1,. . .,m$ be non-negative integers. Show that $\mathcal{I} = \{I: I \subseteq S$ and $|I \cap B_i| \leq d_i$ for $i = 1,. . .,m\}$ is the collection of independent sets for a representable matroid on S. This matroid is called a *partition matroid* (see Lawler, Chapter 7). *Hint.* This is an easy corollary of THEOREM 10.53. Give an example and show how to construct representing matrices.

(6) Let $M_1 = (S_1,\mathcal{I}_1)$ be a representable matroid with independent sets $\mathcal{I}_1$ and let f: $S_1 \to S_2$ be a function with domain S_1 and range S_2. Prove that $M_2 = (S_2,\mathcal{I}_2)$ where $\mathcal{I}_2 = \{f(X), X \in \mathcal{I}_1\}$ is a representable matroid with independent sets $\mathcal{I}_2$. Discuss the problem of finding representing matrices. The matroid M_2 is denoted by $f(M_1)$. *Hint.* Construct a bipartite graph of the form $G = (S_1,S_2,E,\varphi)$ and apply THEOREM 10.55. Even if M_1 is not representable, $f(M_1)$ is a matroid (see Welsh, Chapter 8).

(7) Let $M_1,. . .,M_k$ be matroids on a fixed set S with independent sets $\mathcal{I}_1,. . .,\mathcal{I}_k$. Define a new matroid M, called the *union* of the M_i and denoted by $\bigvee_{i=1}^{k} M_i$ to be the matroid on S with independent sets $\{X: X = X_1 \cup X_2 . . . \cup X_k, X_i \in \mathcal{I}_i, i = 1,. . .,k\}$. Show that if the M_i are representable then M is a representable matroid and discuss the problem of finding representing matrices. *Hint.* Make an isomorphic copy M_i' of each M_i on disjoint sets S_i'. Let $M' = M_1' + . . . + M_k'$ be the direct sum of these copies (EXERCISE 10.21(1)). Define f: $M' \to M$ such that f: $M_i' \to M_i$ is an isomorphism for each i and apply 10.56(6) above. The union of matroids is a matroid even if the M_i are not representable (Welsh, Chapter 8, Section 3; and Welsh, Chapter 9, Section 6).

We now discuss an important class of matroids that are dual to transversal and bipartite induced matroids. These matroids arise from directed graphs (DEFINITION 6.3).

10.57 DEFINITION.

Let $G = (V,E,\varphi)$ be a directed graph and let $Y \subseteq V$. We say that a subset X $\subseteq$ V is *linked* into Y if there exists $|X|$ vertex disjoint directed paths in G, each path starting at a vertex of X and ending at a vertex of Y. If $|X| = |Y|$ we say that X is *linked onto* Y. A single vertex is regarded as a path, so Y is always linked onto Y.

As an example, consider the graph of FIGURE 10.58(a). Let $Y = \{6,7\}$. Then $X = \{1,2\}$ is linked onto Y by the pair of paths $(1,3,5,7)$ and $(2,4,6)$. Also $X = \{2,3\}$ is linked onto Y by the pair of paths $(2,4,6)$ and $(3,5,7)$. As single vertices are regarded as trivial paths, $X = \{4,7\}$ is linked onto Y by the pair of paths $(4,6)$ and (7). Also, Y is linked onto Y by the pair of paths (6), (7). It turns out that the set of all such X that are linked onto a fixed set Y is the set of bases for a matroid on $S = \underline{7}$. This is a special case of a more general construction.

10.58   TRANSFORMING A DIGRAPH INTO BIPARTITE GRAPH.

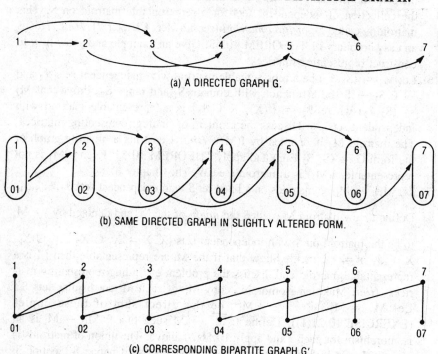

(a) A DIRECTED GRAPH G.

(b) SAME DIRECTED GRAPH IN SLIGHTLY ALTERED FORM.

(c) CORRESPONDING BIPARTITE GRAPH G'.

Figure 10.58

10.59   DEFINITION.

Let $G = (V,E,\varphi)$ be a directed graph or "digraph" for short. Let M_0 be a matroid on V and let $L(G,M_0)$ be the collection of all subsets of V that can be linked onto an independent set of M_0. We show in THEOREM 10.62 that $L(G,M_0)$ is the collection of independent sets of a matroid on V. We call this matroid the *digraph induced matroid of* M_0 *in G*.

The key to understanding digraph induced matroids is the transformation shown in FIGURE 10.58 which maps a digraph G to a bipartite graph G'.

FIGURE 10.58(a) shows a digraph G. In FIGURE 10.58(b) we see the same digraph but each vertex v has been relabeled with a pair of symbols v and Ov. The edges are drawn so that their tails are close to the symbols Ov and their heads close to the symbols v. In FIGURE 10.58(c) we see a directed graph G' = (OV,V,E',φ') where V = $\underline{7}$ and OV = {Oi: i $\in$ $\underline{7}$}. Each pair {Ov,v} is an edge in G' and all other edges of the form {Ov,w} correspond to directed edges (v,w) of G. Given G' we can obviously reconstruct G so this transformation is invertible. The transformation from G to G' extends in the obvious manner to any digraph G.

10.60 NOTATION.

Let G = (V,E,φ) be a digraph and let G' = (OV,V,E',φ') be the corresponding bipartite graph (see FIGURE 10.58). Let Q be a matching in G' with TAIL(Q) and HEAD(Q) as defined in DEFINITION 10.49. Let ZIG(Q) = {v: v $\in$ V, v $\notin$ HEAD(Q) but Ov $\in$ TAIL(Q)} and let ZAG(Q) = {Ov: Ov $\notin$ TAIL(Q) but v $\in$ HEAD(Q) }. For example, consider the graph G' of FIGURE 10.58(c) with Q = {{01,1}, {02,4}, {04,6}, {03,5}, {05,7}}. Then ZIG(Q) = {2,3} and ZAG(Q) = {06,07}. The trivial bijection Ov $\rightarrow$ v takes OV to V. We denote by CTAIL(Q) and CHEAD(Q) the complements of the sets TAIL(Q) and HEAD(Q).

10.61 LEMMA.

Let G = (V,E,φ) be a digraph and let G' = (OV,V,E',φ') be its corresponding bipartite graph (FIGURE 10.58). For subsets X and Y of V, X is linked onto Y in G if and only if there is a matching Q in G' with X = CHEAD(Q) and OY = CTAIL(Q).

Proof. An example gives the idea. Let G be the graph of FIGURE 10.58(a) and let X = {1,2} and Y = {6,7}. The paths (1,3,5,7) and (2,4,6) link X onto Y. From the path (1,3,5,7) we construct the set of edges {{01,3}, {03,5}, {05,7}} and from the path (2,4,6) we construct the set of edges {{02,4}, {04,6}}. The union of these two sets is the desired matching Q. Note that HEAD(Q) = {3,4,5,6,7} and TAIL(Q) = {01,02,03,04,05}. Thus, X = CHEAD(Q) and OY = CTAIL(Q). The same idea works in general.

Let X be linked onto Y by |X| vertex disjoint directed paths. Divide the vertices of V-X into two classes, those vertices that lie on some linking path and those that do not. If v is in the former class and (u,v) is the corresponding edge of a linking path then add the edge {Ou,v} to Q. If v is in the latter class, add {Ov,v} to Q. By construction, HEAD(Q) = V − X or, equivalently, X = CHEAD(Q). It is easily verified that OY = CTAIL(Q). Note also that OY − OX = ZAG(Q) and X − Y = ZIG(Q). From these latter observations it is easily seen how, starting with Q, one can reconstruct the linking paths and thus prove the converse.

The next result, THEOREM 10.62, follows easily from LEMMA 10.61.

10.62   THEOREM.

Let $G = (V,E,\varphi)$ be a digraph and let $G' = (OV,V,E',\varphi')$ be its corresponding bipartite graph (as in FIGURE 10.58). Let M_0 be a matroid on V, let M_0^* be its dual, and let OM_0^* be the isomorphic copy of M_0^* under the trivial bijection $v \to Ov$. Then the digraph induced matroid of M_0 in G is the dual of the bipartite induced matroid of OM_0^* in G'. In particular, if M_0 is representable then the digraph induced matroid of M_0 in G is representable.

Proof.   The fact that the digraph induced matroid of M_0 in G is the dual of the bipartite induced matroid of OM_0^* in G' is a direct consequence of LEMMA 10.61 and the relevant definitions (DEFINITION 10.52 and 10.59). If M_0 is representable then so is M_0^* by THEOREM 10.14. By THEOREM 10.55, the bipartite induced matroid of OM_0^* is thus representable. Again applying THEOREM 10.14 we see that the digraph induced matroid of M_0 in G is representable.

10.63   EXERCISE.

(1) Construct a good example to illustrate THEOREM 10.62. By looking carefully at the results quoted in the proof of THEOREM 10.62, show how to construct a representation matrix for digraph induced matroids when M_0 is representable.

(2) Consider THEOREM 10.62 in the case where M_0 is the trivial matroid $(V,\{Y\})$ where Y is a subset of V (in other words, M_0 has only one base, the set Y). In this case, the diagraph induced matroid of M_0 is called a *strict gammoid* and we denote it by $M(G,Y)$. Show how to construct representation matrices for strict gammoids.

(3) A classical result (Welsh, Chapter 13, Section 2) states that a matroid is a strict gammoid if and only if its dual is a full transversal matroid. Prove this result. *Hint.* A full transversal matroid is defined by DEFINITION 10.51 and the following remarks. An alternative point of view is found in EXERCISE 10.56(2). Look carefully at LEMMA 10.61 for the idea of the proof.

(4) Let $M(G,Y)$ be a strict gammoid and let $S \subseteq V$, where $G = (V,E,\varphi)$. Let $\mathscr{I}_S$ be the set of all independent sets of $M(G,Y)$ contained in S. Then $\mathscr{I}_S$ is the set of independent sets of a matroid $M(G,Y,S)$ on S. These matroids are called *gammoids*. How would you construct representation matrices for gammoids?

(5) The study of induced matroids has been generalized to mathematical systems called "linking systems" (see Schrijver, 1978). Formally, a *linking system* is a triple $(X,Y,\wedge)$ where X and Y are finite sets and $\wedge$ is a collection of pairs (P,Q) of subsets, $P \subseteq X$ and $Q \subseteq Y$. The collection $\wedge$ must satisfy the following conditions:

   (i)   If $(P,Q) \in \wedge$ and $x \in P$ then there is some $y \in Q$ such that
         $(P - \{x\},Q - \{y\}) \in \wedge$.

(ii) If $(P,Q) \in \wedge$ and $y \in Q$ then there is some $x \in P$ such that
$(P - \{x\}, Q - \{y\}) \in \wedge$.
(iii) If (P_1,Q_1) and (P_2,Q_2) are in $\wedge$ then there exists (P,Q) in $\wedge$ with
$P_1 \subseteq P \subseteq P_1 \cup P_2$ and $Q_2 \subseteq Q \subseteq Q_1 \cup Q_2$.

Axiom (iii) seems a bit strange at first glance. It is sometimes called "the Mendelsohn-Dulmage condition." It corresponds to a fundamental property of matrices. Observe that if $(X,Y,\wedge)$ is a linking system and $(P,Q) \in \wedge$ then $|P| = |Q|$. Let A be a matrix over a field F and let X be the row and Y the column indices of A. Let $\wedge$ be the collection of all (P,Q) such that the submatrix $A[P|Q]$ is nonsingular. Prove that $(X,Y,\wedge)$ is a linking system. *Hint:* To prove condition (iii), assume without loss of generality that $X = P_1 \cup P_2$ and $Y = Q_1 \cup Q_2$. Extend P_1 to a basis P for the row space of A and extend Q_2 to a basis Q for the column space of A. Show that $A[P|Q]$ is nonsingular (this depends only on the fact that P and Q are bases) and hence $(P,Q) \in \wedge$ is the required pair. Isomorphism of linking systems and hence representability of linking systems can now be defined in a way analogous to DEFINITIONS 10.13 and 10.15. What is the combinatorial interpretation of the linking system of the matrix Z of THEOREM 10.53?

We now consider some important transformations on matroids. These transformations are called *restriction, contraction, truncation, elongation, series extension,* and *parallel extension.* All of these operations transform representable matroids into representable matroids. The first two, restriction and contraction, are by far the most important from our point of view and will be the basis for our recursive analysis of the structure of matroids. In all cases, we shall emphasize the matrix theoretic aspects of these operations.

10.64 DEFINITION.

Let $M = (S,\mathscr{B})$ be a matroid with $\mathscr{B}$ the set of bases. Let $P \subseteq S$ be any nonempty subset. Let $\mathscr{I}$ denote the set of independent sets of M and let $\mathscr{I}_P$ denote those elements of $\mathscr{I}$ that are contained in P. Then $(P,\mathscr{I}_P)$ is a matroid called the *restriction of M to P.* We denote this matroid by MrtoP. If $Q = S - P$ then we say the MrtoP is the matroid obtained by *deleting* Q. We shall also write D_QM for MrtoP.

It is trivial to show that MrtoP is a matroid. Note that the bases of MrtoP are the maximal independent sets of M contained in P.

10.65 DEFINITION.

Let $M = (S,\mathscr{B})$ be a matroid as in DEFINITION 10.64. Let Q be a subset of S and let $P = S - Q$. Then the set of all subsets of Q of the form B-X where B is a base of M and X is a base of MrtoP is the set of bases of a matroid on

Q. This matroid is called the *contraction of* M *to* Q. We denote this matroid by M<u>cto</u>Q. We say that M<u>cto</u>Q is the matroid obtained by *contracting the set* P *from* M. When emphasis is to be placed on the contracted set P rather than the set Q, we write C_PM for the matroid M<u>cto</u>Q.

   The proof that M<u>cto</u>Q is a matroid in the general case is left to the reader (EXERCISE 10.71(1)). There seems to be some disagreement in the literature as to the notation for "restriction to" and "contraction to." Our notation is nonstandard but also unforgettable! The reader should note the meaning of DEFINITION 10.65 in the case where P = {x} consists of only one element. In that case, the bases of M<u>cto</u>Q = C_xM are all bases of M that contain x with ·x removed. If x is not contained in any base then C_xM = D_xM.

   We now consider the case where M is a representable matroid with representation matrix A. In this case both M<u>rto</u>P and M<u>cto</u>Q are representable and their representation matrices are easily obtainable from A.

10.66 THEOREM.

Let M = (S,$\mathscr{B}$) be a representable matroid of rank r and let A be an r × n representation matrix of M with respect to the linear order $s_1,\ldots,s_n$. Let P and Q = S − P be nonempty subsets of S and assume that P = $\{s_1,\ldots,s_p\}$. Suppose that A has the following block upper triangular form:

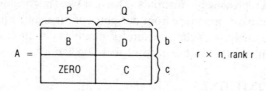

We assume (using NOTATION 10.8) that B = A[1,. . .,b|P] has rank b and C = A[b+1,. . .,r|Q] has rank c where b + c = r. Then B is a matrix representation of M<u>rto</u>P and C is a matrix representation of M<u>cto</u>Q. Such a representation matrix A always exists (row echelon form) and hence M<u>rto</u>P and M<u>cto</u>Q are representable.

Proof. It is trivial that B is a representation of M<u>rto</u>P. In fact, no matter what the form of the matrix A, the matrix $A^{(P)}$ formed from the columns corresponding to P is a representation of M<u>rto</u>P. Thus, suppose that X ⊆ P and the columns $B^{(X)}$ span the column space of B (in other words, X is a base of M<u>rto</u>P). Choose Y ⊆ Q such that the columns corresponding to X ∪ Y are a basis for the column space of A. We must show that $C^{(Y)}$ is a basis for the column space of C. But the fact that the $r \times r$ matrix $A(\phi|X \cup Y]$ has nonzero determinant implies that det $C(\phi|Y]$ is nonzero. (Note that by the assumption $A(\phi|X \cup Y]$ is in block upper triangular form with diagonal blocks the $b \times b$ and $c \times c$ matrices $B(\phi|X]$ and $C(\phi|Y]$.) Hence the columns $C^{(Y)}$ form a $c \times c$ nonsingular submatrix of C and so span the column space of C.

10.67 REMARK.

Let $M = (S,\mathscr{B})$ be a representable matroid of rank r and let A be a representation of M, not necessarily of the form shown in THEOREM 10.66. Let $Q \subseteq S$ and $X \subseteq \underline{r}$ and suppose that $A[X|Q]$ is the zero matrix and $A(X|Q]$ has rank $r - |X|$. Then $A[X|Q]$ is a representation of the matroid MctoQ. This follows since by permuting rows and columns of A (corresponding to a different ordering on S) this situation can be reduced to that of THEOREM 10.66.

The conceptual device of the "joint representation" of FIGURES 10.35 and 10.36 is very useful for understanding THEOREM 10.66 and REMARK 10.67. The general situation is shown in FIGURE 10.68. In FIGURE 10.68, $P = P_1 \cup P_2$ is an arbitrary proper subset of the elements S of M and $Q = Q_1 \cup Q_2$ is its complement. P_1 is a base for MrtoP and Q_1 is an extension of P_1 to a base for M. The reader should explain why the matrix A of FIGURE 10.68 can be assumed to have the form shown. Comparing the matrix of FIGURE 10.68 with that of FIGURE 10.35, we have $I_r = I_a \oplus I_b$ (matrix direct sum) and $I_{n-r} = I_c \oplus I_d$. Also we have $\hat{A} = \begin{pmatrix} A_1 & A_2 \\ ZERO & A_3 \end{pmatrix}$. Denote by A the $r \times n$ matrix in FIGURE 10.68 that represents M and by B the $nx(n-r)$ matrix that is a row representation of M*. Note that the submatrix $A[Q_1|P_2]$ is the zero matrix (we use the association between the rows of B and S to index rows of A as shown in FIGURE 10.68). Thus, by REMARK 10.67, the matrix $A[Q_1|Q] = (I_b,A_3)$ is a representation of MctoQ in unit row canonical form. The matrix $A[P_1|P] = (I_a,A_1)$ is a representation of MrtoP in unit row canonical form. The subarrays (see FIGURE 10.68)

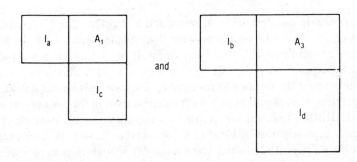

$$I_a \quad A_1 \qquad\qquad I_b \quad A_3$$

and

$$I_c \qquad\qquad\qquad I_d$$

are respectively the joint representations of M$\underline{\text{rto}}$P with (M$\underline{\text{rto}}$P)* and M$\underline{\text{cto}}$Q with (M$\underline{\text{cto}}$Q)*

10.68 RESTRICTION, CONTRACTION, AND THE JOINT REPRESENTATION.

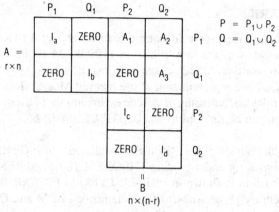

Figure 10.68

The following theorem, THEOREM 10.69, is suggested by FIGURE 10.68.

10.69 THEOREM.

Let $M = (S,\mathcal{B})$ be a matroid and let P and Q be subsets of S. Then (M$\underline{\text{rto}}$P)* $= M*\underline{\text{cto}}P$ and (M$\underline{\text{cto}}$Q)* $= M*\underline{\text{rto}}Q$.

Proof. We consider the joint representation of FIGURE 10.68. As noted above, the subarray consisting of I_a, A_1, and I_c is the joint representation of M$\underline{\text{rto}}$P and (M$\underline{\text{rto}}$P)*. It follows from REMARK 10.67 applied to the row representation B of M* shown in FIGURE 10.68 that the submatrix of B consisting of A_1 and I_c is a row representation of M*$\underline{\text{cto}}$P. Thus (M$\underline{\text{rto}}$P)* $= M*\underline{\text{cto}}P$. The other result follows in the same manner by considering the subarray consisting of I_b, A_3, and I_d, which is the joint representation of M$\underline{\text{cto}}$Q and (M$\underline{\text{cto}}$Q)*.

We conclude our discussion of restriction and contraction by reminding the reader of the dual relationship between hyperplanes and cycles alluded to in connection with FIGURES 10.27 and 10.30. If $M = (S,\mathcal{B})$ is a matroid and H $\subseteq$ S a hyperplane, then S $-$ H $=$ C is a cycle in M*. This is not difficult to prove in general. The situation for the representable case is shown in FIGURE 10.70. A hyperplane H is shown in unit row canonical form in the joint representation. As in FIGURE 10.68, the r $\times$ n matrix A is a column representation of M and B is a row representation of M*. Let $A_{(i)}$ denote the ith row of A and let supp($A_{(i)}$) denote the *support* of $A_{(i)}$, which is the set $\{j: A(i,j) \neq 0\}$. Note in FIGURE 10.70

that $C = S - H = \text{supp}(A_{(r)})$ and that the matrix $B[C|\phi)$ represents a cycle in the row representation matrix B. This is the idea behind the statement that "S − H is a cycle in M*" in the representable case. The reader is asked to explore these ideas further in EXERCISE 10.71(2).

10.70 THE RELATIONSHIP BETWEEN HYPERPLANES IN M AND CYCLES IN M*.

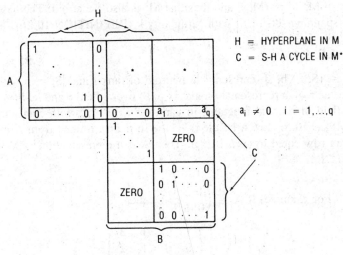

Figure 10.70

10.71 EXERCISE.

(1) Let $M = (S,\mathcal{B})$ be a matroid and let $Q \subseteq S$. Prove that $M\text{ctoQ}$ (DEFINITION 10.65) is a matroid.

(2) Let $M = (S,\mathcal{B})$ be a representable matroid with joint representation, as shown in FIGURE 10.68. Let P and Q be as shown in FIGURE 10.68. Discuss the relationships between hyperplanes and cycles in M and hyperplanes and cycles in $M\text{rtoP}$ and $M\text{ctoQ}$ (see Welsh, Chapter 4, for the general case). What happens to these relationships under duality?

We now define two additional operations on a matroid called *truncation* and *elongation*. As with restriction and contraction, these operations preserve representability.

10.72 DEFINITION.

Let $M = (S,\mathcal{B})$ be a matroid of rank r. Let $1 \leq j < r$ and $r < k \leq n$ where $n = |S|$. Let $B_j = \{B - X: X \subseteq B, |X| = r - j \text{ and } B \in \mathcal{B}\}$. Let $\mathcal{B}^k = \{B \cup X: X \subseteq S - B, |X| = k - r \text{ and } B \in \mathcal{B}\}$. Then $M_j = (S,\mathcal{B}_j)$ and M^k

$= (S,\mathscr{B}^k)$ are matroids on S of rank j and k, respectively. M_j is called the *truncation of M to j* and M^k is called the *elongation of M to k*.

10.73   REMARK.

The independent sets of M_j are just the independent sets of M that have cardinality less than or equal to j. Using the independent set characterization of a matroid (DEFINITION 10.23) the fact that M_j is a matroid follows easily. It is easy to check that $M^*_{n-k} = (M^k)^*$ and thus that M^k is also a matroid. The bases of M^k are the spanning sets of M with cardinality k (DEFINITION 10.26).

10.74   LEMMA.

Let $M = (S,\mathscr{B})$ be a representable matroid of rank r and $|S| = n$ with $r < n$. Let A be an $r \times n$ representation matrix of M over a field F and let $F(x_1,\ldots,x_n)$ be the field of rational functions in variables $x_1,\ldots,x_n$ with coefficients in F (EXAMPLE 10.5). Let $\hat{A}$ be the $(r+1) \times n$ matrix formed from A by adding one extra row equal to $(x_1,\ldots,x_n)$. Then $\hat{A}$ is a representation of $M^{(r+1)}$ over $F(x_1,\ldots,x_n)$.

Proof.   For example, if $A = \begin{pmatrix} 1 & 2 & 1 & 3 \\ 0 & 1 & 1 & 2 \end{pmatrix}$ then

$$\hat{A} = \begin{pmatrix} 1 & 2 & 1 & 3 \\ 0 & 1 & 1 & 2 \\ x_1 & x_2 & x_3 & x_4 \end{pmatrix}.$$

Let $Q \subseteq S$ be such that $|Q| = r + 1$. Consider the $(r+1) \times (r+1)$ square submatrix $\hat{A}(\phi|Q)$ gotten by keeping all rows of $\hat{A}$ and all columns corresponding to Q. By expanding along the last row of $\hat{A}$, note that $\det \hat{A}(\phi|Q) = \sum_{t \in Q} a_t x_t$ where a_t is equal, except possibly for sign, to the determinant of an $r \times r$ square submatrix of A. Thus $\det \hat{A}(\phi|Q) \neq 0$ if and only if $Q = B \cup \{y\}$ where B is a base of M (i.e., $\det A(\phi|B) \neq 0$) and $y \in S - B$. Thus, $\hat{A}$ is a representation of the elongation $M^{(r+1)}$ as was to be shown.

10.75   THEOREM.

If M is a representable matroid then any truncation M_j or elongation M^k is representable.

Proof.   The elongation M^k can be obtained by a succession of one step elongations as in LEMMA 10.74. Thus M^k is representable over the resulting field of rational functions. Using the relationship $M^*_{n-j} = (M^j)^*$ of REMARK 10.73, the representability of M_j follows from THEOREM 10.34.

The reader is asked to explore some additional aspects of truncations and elongations in EXERCISE 10.79. We now discuss our two final transformations—*series extension* and *parallel extension*.

10.76 DEFINITION.

Let $M = (S, \mathscr{B})$ be a matroid with $e \in S$. Let $S(f) = S \cup \{f\}$ where f is not in S. Define $s\mathscr{B}(e,f) = \{B \cup \{f\}: B \in \mathscr{B}\} \cup \{B \cup \{e\}: B \in \mathscr{B}, e \notin B\}$. Define $p\mathscr{B}(e,f) = \mathscr{B} \cup \{(B-\{e\}) \cup \{f\}: B \in \mathscr{B} \text{ with } e \in B\}$. Then both $s\mathscr{B}(e,f)$ and $p\mathscr{B}(e,f)$ are sets of bases for a matroid on $S(f)$. The matroid $sM(e,f) = (S(f), s\mathscr{B}(e,f))$ is called the *series extension of* M *by* f *at* e and the matroid $pM(e,f) = (S(f), p\mathscr{B}(e,f))$ *is called the parallel extension of* M *by* f *at* e.

The verification that series and parallel extensions are in fact matroids and the proof that $(sM(e,f))^* = pM^*(e,f)$ are left to the reader (EXERCISE 10.79(3)). The intuitive idea behind series and parallel extensions comes from graph theory and electrical network theory. The interested reader should look at the paper by Minty (1966). A graph G with an edge e and a series and parallel extension of G by f at e are shown in FIGURE 10.78. If M is representable then it is trivial to show that $sM(e,f)$ and $pM(e,f)$ are also representable. Suppose, for example, that M has representation matrix A, where A is $r \times n$, has rank r, and has entries in a field F. Let the columns of A correspond to the ordering $s_1, \ldots, s_n$ on S and take $e = s_i$. Then the matrix $\hat{A} = (A, A^{(i)})$ formed from A by adding another copy of the ith column of A to the end of A is obviously a representation of $pM(e,f)$ with respect to the ordering $s_1, \ldots, s_n, f$. The representability of $sM(e,f)$ follows by duality. We state these results in THEOREM 10.77.

10.77 THEOREM.

Let $M = (S, \mathscr{B})$ be a representable matroid over a field F. Then any series or parallel extension of M is a representable matroid over the same field.

Proof. The proof is as described above. If A represents M with respect to the ordering $s_1, \ldots, s_n$ and $e = s_i$, then the augmented matrix $\hat{A} = (A, A^{(i)})$ represents $pM(e,f)$ with respect to the ordering $s_1, \ldots, s_n, f$. The fact that $(sM(e,f))^* = pM^*(e,f)$ (EXERCISE 10.79(3)), together with the fact that M^* is representable if M is, gives the representability of $sM(e,f)$. .

10.78 SERIES AND PARALLEL EXTENSIONS OF A GRAPH.

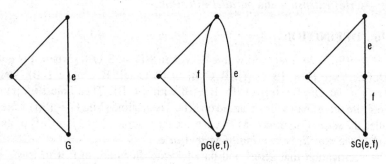

Figure 10.78

10.79 EXERCISE.

(1) Let $M = (S,\mathcal{B})$ be a matroid of rank r with r × n representation matrix A. Show how to construct the representation of the truncation $M_{(r-1)}$.

(2) Prove that $M^*_{n-k} = (M^k)^*$ where M is a matroid of rank r. If M is representable, interpret the case $k = r + 1$ in terms of the joint representation (such as was done for restriction and contraction in FIGURE 10.68).

(3) Let $M = (S,\mathcal{B})$ be a matroid. Prove that the series and parallel extensions sM(e,f) and pM(e,f) are matroids and that $(sM(e,f))^* = pM^*(e,f)$. Interpret this latter identity in terms of the joint representation in the case where M is representable.

(4) Let M be a representable matroid with representation matrix A. Show how to construct the representation matrix of sM(e,f).

We now discuss the important concept of *connectivity* of matroids. In order to obtain an intuitive feeling for matroid connectivity, we consider first an example.

10.80 A DISCONNECTED MATROID.

Consider the representable matroid $M = (\underline{8},\mathcal{B})$ with representation matrix

$$
\begin{array}{cccccccc}
1 & 2 & 3 & 4 & 5 & 6 & 7 & 8 \quad \text{COLUMNS}
\end{array}
$$

$$
A = \begin{pmatrix}
0 & 0 & -1 & 2 & 0 & 0 & 1 & 0 \\
0 & 0 & 0 & 0 & 2 & 1 & 0 & 1 \\
1 & 0 & 1 & 2 & 0 & 0 & 0 & 0 \\
0 & 1 & 0 & 0 & 1 & 0 & 0 & 0
\end{pmatrix}.
$$

Note that A is a 4 × 8 matrix of rank 4 and that the submatrix $A^{(Q)} = A(\phi|Q]$, where $Q = \{1,2,7,8\}$, is a permutation of the columns of the 4 × 4 identity matrix. We call a matrix A that has such a submatrix *standard with respect to* Q (DEFINITION 10.83) or simply *standard*. Note also that it is possible to permute the columns and the rows of A such that the following matrix A is obtained:

$$
\begin{array}{ccccccccc}
 & 7 & 1 & 3 & 4 & 8 & 2 & 5 & 6 & \text{COLUMNS}
\end{array}
$$

$$
\hat{A} = \left(\begin{array}{cccc|cccc}
1 & 0 & -1 & 2 & 0 & 0 & 0 & 0 \\
0 & 1 & 1 & 2 & 0 & 0 & 0 & 0 \\
\hline
0 & 0 & 0 & 0 & 1 & 0 & 2 & 1 \\
0 & 0 & 0 & 0 & 0 & 1 & 1 & 0
\end{array}\right) = B \oplus C .
$$

The matrix $\hat{A}$ is also a representation of the matroid M but with respect to the new ordering 7,1,3,4,8,2,5,6. Observe that A is a direct sum of two 2×4 standard matrices B and C. Whenever one can so rearrange a standard representation matrix of M in such a way that it decomposes into a direct sum of smaller standard matrices then the matroid M is said to be *disconnected*. The elements of M corresponding to the direct summands B and C in $\hat{A}$ for this example are {7,1,3,4} for the first summand and {8,2,5,6} for the second summand. Since neither of these summands can be further decomposed by row and column permutations, they represent *connected* matroids which are called the *connected components* of M (DEFINITION 10.85). As we shall see in EXAMPLE 10.81, connected components in a graphical matroid M_G correspond to *biconnected* components in G (DEFINITION 6.95). In EXAMPLE 10.82 we show that finding connected components in a representable matroid is equivalent to finding the *ordinary graphical connected components* in a certain associated graph. In general, for a graphical matroid M_G, this graph will not be G. We have constructed the connected components of M from a standard representation A. As matroids, these connected components do not depend on the choice of A (THEOREM 10.86).

10.81   CONNECTIVITY IN GRAPHICAL MATROIDS.

Consider the graph $G = (5,\{a,b,c,d,e,f\},\varphi)$ defined by the following diagram:

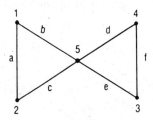

Figure 10.81

The natural representation over GF(2) (NOTATION 10.41) of the matroid M_G of this graph is, using the usual order on $\underline{5}$,

$$
\begin{array}{cccccc}
a & b & c & d & e & f \quad \text{COLUMNS}
\end{array}
$$

$$
A = \begin{pmatrix}
1 & 1 & 0 & 0 & 0 & 0 \\
1 & 0 & 1 & 0 & 0 & 0 \\
0 & 0 & 0 & 0 & 1 & 1 \\
0 & 0 & 0 & 1 & 0 & 1 \\
0 & 1 & 1 & 1 & 1 & 0
\end{pmatrix}.
$$

This matrix is not standard, but by elementary row operations it is equivalent to (a last row of zeroes in $\hat{A}$ is omitted):

$$
\begin{array}{cccccc}
a & b & c & d & e & f \quad \text{COLUMNS}
\end{array}
$$

$$
A = \left(\begin{array}{ccc:ccc}
1 & 0 & 1 & 0 & 0 & 0 \\
0 & 1 & 1 & 0 & 0 & 0 \\
\hdashline
0 & 0 & 0 & 1 & 0 & 1 \\
0 & 0 & 0 & 0 & 1 & 1
\end{array}\right) = B \oplus C.
$$

The matrix $\hat{A}$ is a direct sum of two standard 2×3 matrices B and C. B and C cannot, by row and column permutations alone, be further decomposed as direct sums and hence the matroid on $\{a,b,c\}$ represented by B and the matroid on $\{d,e,f\}$ represented by C are the *components* of M_G. These sets of edges correspond to the bicomponents of G. We shall see below that this is true for any graph G (COROLLARY 10.89).

10.82   CONNECTED COMPONENTS AND THE COLUMN INCIDENCE GRAPH.

Consider once again the matrix A of EXAMPLE 10.80. For any column $A^{(j)}$, the *support* of $A^{(j)}$ or supp $(A^{(j)})$ is the set of all row indices i such that $A(i,j)$ is nonzero (DEFINITION 10.84). Thus, in our example, supp $(A^{(4)}) = \{1,3\}$ and supp $(A^{(5)}) = \{2,4\}$. We define a graph on the set $S = \underline{8}$ by specifying $\{p,q\}$ to be an edge if supp $(A^{(p)}) \cap$ supp$(A^{(q)})$ is nonempty. We call this graph the *column incidence graph* of A and denote it by CIG(A) (DEFINITION 10.84). For our example, CIG(A) is represented by the following diagram:

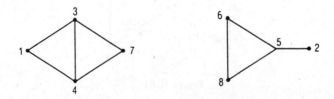

Note that the connected components of CIG(A) have as vertex sets the elements of the connected components of the matroid M represented by A. This is true in general (THEOREM 10.86). A must be standard (DEFINITION 10.83).

We now develop these ideas more formally.

10.83 DEFINITION.

An r × r matrix P whose columns are a rearrangement of the columns of the identity matrix is called a *permutation matrix*. If A is an r × n matrix and Q a set of column indices such that the submatrix $A^{(Q)}$ is a permutation matrix then we say that A is in *standard form with respect to* Q. If such a matrix A is a representation matrix of a matroid M = (S,$\mathcal{B}$) and the set S, in some order, is used to index the columns of A then Q may be taken to be a subset of S. In this case Q is a base of M. A representation matrix A will be called a *standard representation* of M if it is in standard form with respect to some Q. These definitions extend in the obvious way to row representation matrices.

10.84 DEFINITION.

Let A be an r × n matrix and $A^{(j)}$ a column of A. The *support* of $A^{(j)}$ is the set of row indices i such that $A(i,j) \neq 0$. Similarly, we define the support of a row $A_{(i)}$ to be the set of column indices j such that $A(i,j) \neq 0$. We denote the support of $A^{(i)}$ by supp $(A^{(i)})$. If A is a representation matrix of a matroid M = (S,$\mathcal{B}$) then we define a graph, called the *column incidence graph* and denoted by CIG(A), on S with edge set the set of distinct pairs of column indices {p,q} such that supp $(A^{(p)}) \cap$ supp $(A^{(q)})$ is nonempty. In an analogous way we define the *row incidence graph* RIG(A).

The matrix A of EXAMPLE 10.80 is in standard form with respect to Q = {1,2,7,8}. The graph CIG(A) for this example is shown in EXAMPLE 10.82. We now define the important concept of connectivity for matroids.

10.85 DEFINITION.

Let M = (S,$\mathcal{B}$) be a matroid and let the r × n matrix A be a standard representation of M. We say that M is *connected* if the graph CIG(A) is connected. Otherwise, M is *disconnected*. If M is disconnected, and $L_i = (S_i, E_i)$, i = 1,...,t are the connected components of CIG(A), then $M_i = M \underline{to} S_i$, i = 1,...,t are the *connected components* of M. If $|S_i| = 1$ then M_i is called a *trivial* component.

The matroid M of EXAMPLE 10.80 is disconnected and the two connected components are represented by the matrices B and C as shown. If A has a zero column then CIG(A) is disconnected. It would seem from DEFINITION 10.85 that the connectivity of a matroid M depends on the choice of the standard matrix representation A. This is not the case as we now show.

10.86 THEOREM.

Let $M = (S,\mathscr{B})$ be a matroid and let the $r \times n$ matrix A be a standard representation of M with respect to $Q \subseteq S$. Two distinct elements x and y in S lie on a common cycle C of M if and only if x and y belong to the same component of the column incidence graph CIG(A).

Proof. Suppose first that x and y do not belong to the same component of CIG(A). If either $A^{(x)}$ or $A^{(y)}$ is zero they obviously do not lie on a common cycle. Thus assume $A^{(x)}$ and $A^{(y)}$ are nonzero. Just as in EXAMPLE 10.80, we can permute rows and columns of A to obtain a matrix $\hat{A} = B \oplus C \oplus \ldots$ where the direct summands B,C,... are standard representations for the nontrivial components of M. (See EXERCISE 10.96(1).) The columns in the representation A corresponding to x and y have their supports in different blocks of the direct sum decomposition $B \oplus C \oplus \ldots$ of $\hat{A}$. For this reason it is apparent that x and y cannot both belong to any minimal dependent subset of columns of $\hat{A}$. Thus x and y are not contained in any common cycle.

For the converse, we assume that x and y lie in the same component of CIG(A). Let $x = e_1,\ldots,e_p = y$ be a path *of minimal length* in CIG(A) joining x to y. To simplify the notation we assume that the columns of A corresponding to $e_1,\ldots,e_p$ are the first p columns of A. By rearranging the rows when necessary, we may assume that A has the following form where a_1, a_1', ..., a_2, a_2', ..., a_{p-1}, a_{p-1}' are all nonzero:

$$A = \begin{array}{c|cccccccc|c}
 & x = e_1 & e_2 & e_3 & e_4 & \ldots & e_{p-2} & e_{p-1} & e_p = y & \\
\hline
 & a_1 & a_1' & 0 & 0 & \ldots & 0 & 0 & 0 & \\
 & 0 & a_2 & a_2' & 0 & \ldots & 0 & 0 & 0 & \\
 & 0 & 0 & a_3 & a_3' & \ldots & 0 & 0 & 0 & * \\
 & \vdots & \vdots & \vdots & \vdots & & \vdots & \vdots & \vdots & \\
 & 0 & 0 & 0 & 0 & \ldots & a_{p-2} & a_{p-2}' & 0 & \\
 & 0 & 0 & 0 & 0 & \ldots & 0 & a_{p-1} & a_{p-1}' & \\
\hline
 & & & & * & & & & & \\
\end{array}$$

The fact that A has such a form is a consequence of the minimality of the path joining x to y (EXERCISE 10.96(2)). We now apply a sequence of elementary row operations, using first row $p-1$ of A, then row $p-2$ of A, etc. In the first sequence of row operations we use row $p-1$ with the entry a_{p-1} as the pivot to eliminate all entries in column e_{p-1} except for a_{p-1}. In doing this, we introduce a nonzero entry in the position $p-2$ of column e_p. We now use row $p-2$ with a_{p-2} as the pivot to eliminate all other entries in columns e_{p-2}. In doing this, we introduce a nonzero entry in the position $p-3$ of column e_p. Continuing in this manner until we finally use a_1 as a pivot in row 1 to eliminate all other entries in column e_1, we obtain (after multiplying column 1 by a_1^{-1}, column 2 by a_2^{-1}, etc.) the following equivalent representation $\bar{A}$, where $k_i \neq 0$, $i = 1,\ldots,p-1$:

$$
\tilde{A} =
\begin{array}{c}
 \\
\end{array}
$$

	e_1	e_2	e_3	e_4	...	e_{p-2}	e_{p-1}	e_p	
	1	0	0	0	...	0	0	k_1	
	0	1	0	0	...	0	0	k_2	
	0	0	1	0	...	0	0	k_3	
$\tilde{A} =$	0	0	0	0	...	1	0		*
	0	0	0	0	...	0	1	k_{p-1}	
	0	0	0	0			0	k_p	
	0	0	0	0			0	k_r	

Note that in $\tilde{A}$, $k_1,. . .,k_{p-1}$ are nonzero and thus $\underline{p-1} \subset \mathrm{supp}\,(A^{(e_p)})$. Observe also that $\tilde{A}$ is in standard form with respect to $\tilde{Q}$ where $\tilde{Q}$ is $\{e_1,. . .,e_{p-1}\}$ together with all elements $q \in Q$ such that $A^{(q)}$ is a column of the identity matrix with its 1 in row p or greater (these columns are not changed by the sequence of row operations used in converting A to $\tilde{A}$). If the reader will now recall the canonical form for cycles (FIGURE 10.30), then it will be obvious that the columns of $\tilde{A}$ consisting of $A^{(e_p)}$ together with all $A^{(q)}$ with $q \in \tilde{Q}$ and supp $(A^{(q)}) \subseteq \mathrm{supp}\,(A^{(e_p)})$ represents a cycle that contains $x = e_1,. . .,e_p = y$. Thus we have constructed a cycle containing both x and y (in fact it contains all elements on a minimal path in CIG(A) joining x to y). This completes the proof of THEOREM 10.86.

10.87 COROLLARY.

The vertex sets of the components of the graph CIG(A) do not depend on the choice of the standard representation A of $M = (S,\mathcal{B})$.

Proof.   Let x and y be in S. By THEOREM 10.86, x and y belong to the same component of CIG(A) if and only if x and y are on a common cycle of M. The latter condition depends only on M and not on A.

10.88 REMARK.

The components of CIG(A) define a partition of the set S. Thus the relation "x ~ y if x = y or if x and y lie on a common cycle" is an equivalence relation. This is the standard way of defining the connected components of a matroid M in the general case. One defines a matroid M (not necessarily representable) to be connected if given any two x and y in S, either $x = y$ or x and y lie on a common cycle (see Welsh, Chapter 5). For an approach to the general case along the lines we have taken, see the paper by Krogdahl, referenced at the end of PART II (Math., Rev. 58 #27568).

10.89 COROLLARY.

Let G be a graph and let M_G be its cycle matroid. M_G is connected if and only if G is biconnected.

Proof.   G is biconnected if and only if any two edges x and y of G lie on a common cycle.

10.90   REMARK.

From THEOREM 10.86, it is evident (see EXERCISE 10.96(1)) that a representable matroid $M = (S,\mathscr{B})$ of rank r always has a representation of the form:

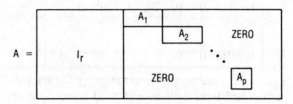

$$A = \begin{array}{ccc} & A_1 & \\ & A_2 & \text{ZERO} \\ I_r & & \ddots \\ & \text{ZERO} & A_p \end{array}$$

A_i NONZERO, CIG(I_{r_i},A_i) CONNECTED i,...,p.

Figure 10.90

If each A_i is an $r_i \times n_i$ matrix then the matrix (I_{r_i},A_i) is a representation of the ith nontrivial component of M. This canonical form is useful in connection with the joint representation of $M = (S,\mathscr{B})$ and M*, which now has the form (take $S = \underline{n}$) shown in FIGURE 10.91.

10.91   JOINT REPRESENTATION OF COMPONENTS OF M AND M*.

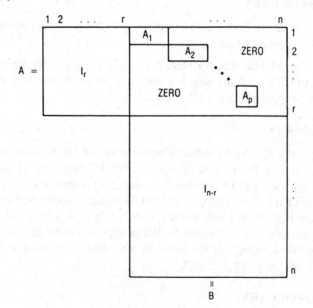

Figure 10.91

From the symmetry of the joint representation of FIGURE 10.91 it is evident that the following corollary is valid.

10.92 COROLLARY.

Let $M = (S, \mathcal{B})$ be a matroid and $M^* = (S, \mathcal{B}^*)$ be its dual. Then x and y in S belong to the same connected component of M if and only if they belong to the same connected component of M^*. In other words, x and y are on a common cycle of M if and only if they are on a common cycle of M^*. Trivial components are the same in M and M^* with (using the terminology of EXERCISE 10.96(1)) loops becoming coloops and conversely.

We conclude our discussion of connectivity of matroids with the important concept of the bridges of a subset of a matroid. The reader should recall FIGURES 6.98 and 6.99 and DEFINITIONS 6.100 and 6.101. These ideas are extended to matroids by DEFINITION 10.93 (recall DEFINITIONS 10.64 and 10.65 and associated discussion).

10.93 DEFINITION.

Let $M = (S, \mathcal{B})$ be a matroid and let $T \subseteq S$ be a subset. The connected components of $C_T M = M\underline{cto}(S - T)$ are called the *bridges* of T in M.

Again, the joint representation of M and M^* gives a very clear intuitive picture of the bridges of a representable matroid. Consider FIGURE 10.94.

10.94   JOINT REPRESENTATION OF BRIDGES.

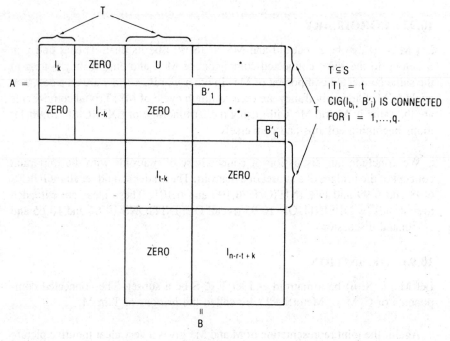

Figure 10.94

To understand FIGURE 10.94, the reader should recall FIGURE 10.68 and the related discussion. Note that in FIGURE 10.94, the submatrix (I_k, U) represents $M\underline{\text{rto}}T$ and the submatrix $(I_{r-k}; B'_1 \oplus B'_2 \oplus \ldots \oplus B'_q)$ represents $M\underline{\text{cto}}$ $(S - T) = C_T M$. We have assumed that $CIG(I_{b_i}, B'_i)$, $b_i = |B'_i|$, is connected for all i and hence that this latter matrix is the canonical form of REMARK 10.90 for the connected components of $C_T M$ and hence for the bridges of T in M. For simplicity we assume $C_T M$ does not have loops or coloops (EXERCISE 10.96(1)).

From the ideas associated with FIGURE 10.68 it is clear that the submatrix

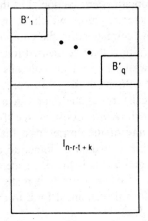

is a representation of M*<u>rto</u> (S − T). We thus have the following basic result.

10.95 COROLLARY.

Let M = (S,$\mathscr{B}$) be a matroid and let T ⊆ S. The partition of S − T induced by the connected components of $C_T M$ is the same as the partition of S − T induced by the connected components of $D_T M^*$. In other words, the bridges of T in M correspond to the connected components of S − T in $D_T M^*$.

COROLLARY 10.95 is true for general matroids. The notion of a bridge plays an important role in the classical work by W. T. Tutte, *Introduction to the Theory of Matroids*, American Elsevier, New York, 1970 (Chapter 4, in particular).

10.96 EXERCISE.

(1) This exercise is directed towards understanding the canonical form of RE-MARK 10.90. Let M = (S,$\mathscr{B}$) be a matroid where, for notational simplicity, we take S = $\underline{n}$.

(a) An element x ∈ S is a *loop* of M if it does not belong to any base and a *coloop* if it belongs to every base. Show that x is a loop (coloop) of M if and only if it is a coloop (loop) of M*. If M is representable and A is an r × n representation matrix of M, show that x is a loop of M if and only if the corresponding column $A^{(x)}$ is zero. If A is in standard form, A = $(I_r, \tilde{A})$ where I_r is the r × r identity and $\tilde{A}$ is rx(n − r), show that x is a coloop if and only if 1 ≤ x ≤ r and the row $\tilde{A}_{(x)}$ is zero. Thus for A = $(I_r, \tilde{A})$, x is a loop if and only if x > r and the column $\tilde{A}^{(x)}$ is zero and x is a coloop if and only if x ≤ r and the row $\tilde{A}_{(x)}$ is zero. For loops and coloops in the graphical case see FIGURE 10.44 and the related discussion.

(b) Prove that if M is representable then it has a representation of the form shown in REMARK 10.90. *Hint*. Let $1,\ldots,r$ be a base of M which by definition must contain every coloop. Let there be i coloops, $r-i+1,$ $\ldots,r$. Suppose there are j loops which we list last, $n-j+1,\ldots,n$. The blocks A_i will now correspond to the components of CIG(A) restricted to $r+1,\ldots,n-j$. Show that the desired form can be achieved by some permutation of rows $1,\ldots,r-i$ and columns $r+1,\ldots,n-j$. What happens to loops and coloops in the joint representation?

(2) Show that the canonical form of the matrix A of the proof of THEOREM 10.86 can be obtained. *Hint*. Look at the first row of A, which is $(a_1,a_1',0,0,\ldots,0)$. If any of the entries past the second entry, say the tth entry, were nonzero then e_1 would be joined to e_t in CIG(A) contradicting the minimality of the path. This is the basic idea. What can you say about the structure of $A[p,\ldots,r|1,\ldots,p]$? Is it really necessary for the path to have minimal length for this canonical form to exist?

10.97   REMARKS CONCERNING RECURSION.

A fundamental technique in this book has been the global or geometric analysis of recursions. This was our approach to the Towers of Hanoi problem of FIGURES 6.35 and 6.36 and the associated discussion. Other examples were studied in EXERCISE 6.40 including set partitions, bit configurations, permutations, and Gray codes. The bicomponent tree of DEFINITION 6.104 and the tree of cycles of DEFINITION 6.107 are again examples of this technique. The planarity test of *procedure* 6.113 is based on these concepts. Tree structures associated with recursion were central to the algorithms developed in Chapters 7, 8, and 9. We now take this approach to matroids by developing the trees and graphs most naturally associated with the restriction and contraction operations of DEFINITIONS 10.64 and 10.65.

10.98   DELETION AND CONTRACTION IN GRAPHICAL MATROIDS.

Perhaps the most natural framework for studying restrictions and contractions is in connection with graphs. If $G(V,E,\varphi)$ is a graph and M_G is its associated cycle matroid then we let $D_a M_G$ denote the matroid obtained from M_G by deleting the edge a and let $C_a M_G$ be the matroid obtained by contracting a. Both of these matroids are again cycle matroids of graphs. Let $\varphi(a) = \{p,q\}$. $D_a M_G$ is the cycle matroid of the graph $(V,E-\{a\},\varphi)$ which we denote by $D_a G$ and $C_a M_G$ is the cycle matroid of the graph $C_a G = (\kappa V, E-\{a\},\kappa\varphi)$ where the function $\kappa: V \to V$ is defined by $\kappa(v) = v$ for $v \neq q$ and $\kappa(q) = p$. Geometrically, the graph $D_a G$ is obtained from G by simply removing the edge a and $C_a G$ is obtained by shrinking the edge a until its two endpoints join. In this shrinking process, a disappears and the vertices of other edges attached to vertices of a coalesce. The reader should recall the concept of loops and coloops in graphs (FIGURE 10.44 and related discussion) and in matroids (EXERCISE 10.96(1)). If b is an edge in G with the same endpoints as a then b will become a loop in C_aG. Similarly, the operation D_a can create coloops. If a is a loop or coloop C_aG and D_aG have isomorphic matroids (see FIGURE 10.99). If the edges of G are ordered a,b,. . . and successive deletions and contractions are done on these edges then a tree structure is created as in FIGURE 10.99.

10.99   DELETE-CONTRACT TREE T(G) FOR A GRAPH G.

(edge ordering a,b,c,d).

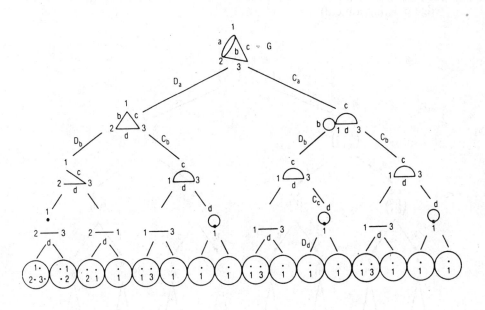

Figure 10.99

If $M = (S,\mathscr{B})$ is a matroid and an ordering on the elements of S is specified then we may also construct a delete-contract tree for M. We shall be concerned primarily with the case of representable matroids. The matroid M_G of the graph of FIGURE 10.99 is represented by the GF(2) matrix

$$A = \begin{pmatrix} 1 & 1 & 1 & 0 \\ 1 & 1 & 0 & 1 \\ 0 & 0 & 1 & 1 \end{pmatrix}.$$

with columns labeled $\begin{matrix} a & b & c & d \end{matrix}$

In unit row canonical form, the matrix A becomes

$$A' = \begin{pmatrix} \overset{a}{1} & \overset{b}{1} & \overset{c}{0} & \overset{d}{1} \\ 0 & 0 & 1 & 1 \end{pmatrix}.$$

Starting with A' and the ordering a,b,c,d specified by the ordering of the columns of A', we show a delete-contract tree of the matroid M_G in FIGURE 10.100.

10.100   DELETE-CONTRACT TREE T(M) OF A MATROID M.

(edge ordering a,b,c,d).

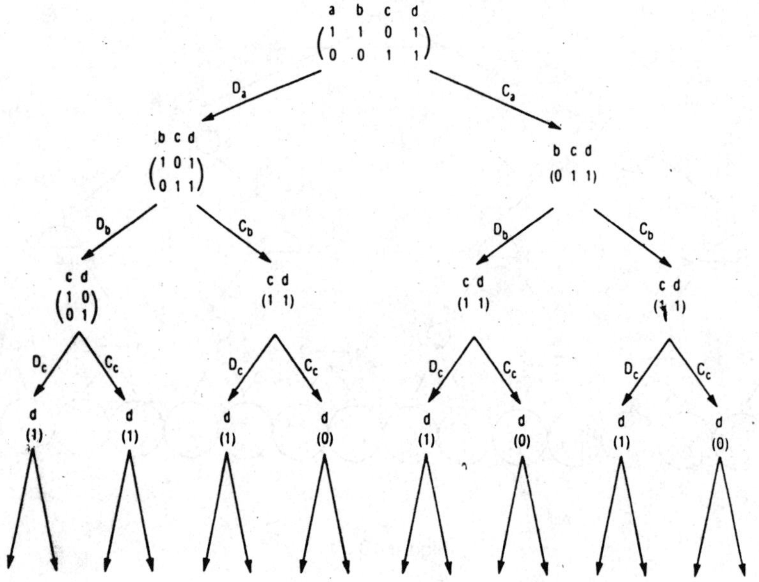

Figure 10.100

Observe that the labeled, ordered, rooted, binary trees of FIGURES 10.99 and 10.100 have the same structure although they are formally different since their vertex labels are different. The information represented in the terminal vertices of the tree T(G) by sets of isolated vertices does not make sense (in that form) for matroids. In constructing the tree T(M) of FIGURE 10.100, the basic operation required is deletion or contraction of the first column $U^{(1)}$ of a matrix

U in unit row canonical form. If this column is zero (i.e., corresponds to a loop of the matroid represented by U) then the matrix $U(\phi|1)$ obtained by its removal is a representation of both the deletion and contraction matroids with respect to the entry of the matroid associated with this column. This matrix is put into unit row canonical form and becomes both the left and right son of U. If $U(1,1)$ is the only nonzero entry in the first row of U then $U^{(1)}$ corresponds to a coloop. In this case, the submatrix $U(1|1)$ obtained by deleting row 1 and column 1 represents both the deletion and contraction matrices. This matrix is already in unit row canonical form. In all other cases, $U(\phi|1)$, after being put into unit row canonical form, represents the left son of U in FIGURE 10.100 and $U(1|1)$, already in unit row canonical form, represents the right son. For example, in

FIGURE 10.100, $U = \begin{pmatrix} \overset{b}{1} & \overset{c}{0} & \overset{d}{1} \\ 0 & 1 & 1 \end{pmatrix}$ is transformed by deletion of b into $\begin{pmatrix} \overset{c}{0} & \overset{d}{1} \\ 1 & 1 \end{pmatrix}$ which

is then put into unit row canonical form to become $\begin{pmatrix} \overset{c}{1} & \overset{d}{0} \\ 0 & 1 \end{pmatrix}$, which is the

left son in this case. If U is a $1 \times t$ matrix then every zero entry corresponds to a loop of the matroid represented by U. If $U(1,1)$ is nonzero then the left son is the matrix $U(\phi|1)$ as above but the right son (the contraction) is the $1 \times (t-1)$ zero matrix. If $U(1,1)$ is zero, both the left and right sons of U are the deletion $U(\phi|1)$ as above. We shall use these ideas in the following material, so the reader should study FIGURE 10.100 carefully.

The reader should note that there is much symmetry in the delete-contract trees of most graphs due to the fact that the subtrees of a loop or coloop are identical. These and other symmetries that appear allow one to represent a delete-contract tree as a directed graph or "reduced tree" in the same way that was done in PART I (see for example, FIGURES 1.41 to 1.44 and FIGURE 3.6 of PART I). The reduced tree for FIGURES 10.99 and 10.100 is shown in FIGURE 10.101. As one would expect, the most dramatic such symmetries arise in the case of the complete graphs. The case of K_5 is given by the intriguing directed graph of FIGURE 10.102. We shall say more about this directed graph later in connection with computing certain polynomials associated with the complete graph. The basic idea in both FIGURE 10.101 and FIGURE 10.102 is that there is a natural correspondence (bijection) between directed paths of maximal length in these graphs and paths from the root to a leaf in the corresponding delete-contract trees.

10.101 REDUCED DELETE-CONTRACT TREE FOR FIGURE 10.99.

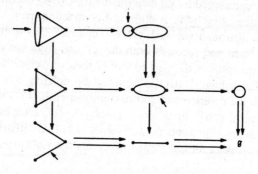

Right means contract, down means delete edge marked by small arrow.

Figure 10.101

10.102 REDUCED DELETE-CONTRACT TREE FOR THE COMPLETE GRAPH K_5.

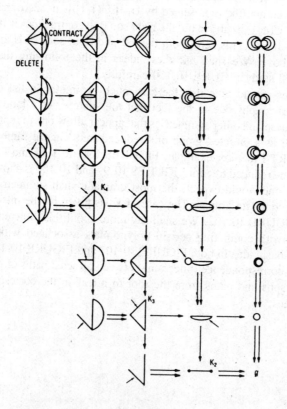

Figure 10.102

In a certain sense, the tree T(G) or T(M) contains too much information for working with numerical functions and polynomials associated with graphs and matroids. Each vertex of T(G) or T(M) is labeled by an edge of G or an element of M together with another graph G' or matroid M'. Each such G' or M' is derived by a sequence of deletions or contractions of elements of G or M.

10.103 DEFINITION.

Let M = (S,$\mathcal{B}$) be a matroid. A matroid M' obtained from M by a sequence of deletions and/or contractions of elements of S is called a *minor* of M. For a graph G, a graph G' obtained by a sequence of deletions and/or contractions of edges of G will be called a *graphical minor*. If M' is obtained by deletions only it will be called a *submatroid* of M.

10.104 REMARK.

If M = (S,$\mathcal{B}$) is a matroid and a,b $\in$ S are any two elements, then one has the following commutative rules: $D_aD_bM = D_bD_aM$, $D_aC_bM = C_bD_aM$, and $C_aC_bM = C_bC_aM$. These rules are easily verified for the representable case where one may assume that a and b correspond to the first two columns of a representation matrix A in unit row canonical form. The general case is a routine exercise. These rules mean that, as a matroid, a minor depends only on the deletions and contractions involved and not on their order. This rule is also valid for graphical minors (up to isomorphism of graphs).

We now define the basic combinatorial object required for our discussion of the delete-contract recursion, the *CNL tree*, DEFINITION 10.105. Associated with each internal vertex of a tree T(M) (or T(G)) is an element of M (or edge of G) together with a minor X. We denote this pair by (e,X). We have not formally defined T(G) or T(M) but have given examples in FIGURE 10.99 and FIGURE 10.100. Formally, if M = (S,$\mathcal{B}$) is a matroid and the elements of S are linearly ordered, say a,b,c,. . ., then T(M) would be defined recursively with respect to this order. T(M) is a binary ordered rooted tree with vertices labeled by pairs (e,X) where e $\in$ X and X is a minor of M. The root of T(M) is labeled (a,M). If a vertex is labeled (e,X) then its left son is labeled (f,D_eX) and its right son is labeled (f,C_eX) where f is the successor to e in the linear order on S. In FIGURES 10.99 and 10.100 we labeled the vertices with X rather than formally writing down (e,X) as the e for each X is obvious from the notation used. If it is necessary to be explicit about the linear order $\leq$, we write T(G,$\leq$) or T(M,$\leq$) instead of T(G) or T(M). In the case where M is representable, we shall adopt the convention of FIGURE 10.100 for specifying the pair (e,M) unless otherwise stated.

10.105 DEFINITION.

Let M be a matroid and let T(M,$\leq$) be its delete-contract tree with respect to a linear order $\leq$ on S as defined above. If each vertex label (e,X) of T(M,$\leq$) is replaced by a C if e is a coloop of X, an L if e is a loop, and an N if e is neither, then the resulting tree will be called the *CNL-tree of* M *with respect to the linear order* $\leq$ and will be denoted by CNL(M,$\leq$) or simply CNL(M). Similarly, if G is a graph we define the CNL-tree, CNL(G,$\leq$), of G to be the tree CNL(M_G,$\leq$).

The CNL-tree corresponding to FIGURES 10.99 and 10.100 is shown in FIGURE 10.106.

10.106   THE CNL-TREE OF FIGURES 10.99 AND 10.100.

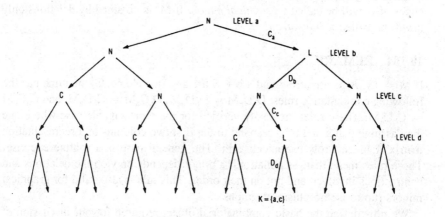

Figure 10.106

10.107   REMARK.

We emphasize that the CNL-tree is *with respect to a linear order* $\leq$ on the elements of M. If the linear order is a,b,. . .,e,f,. . .,h then we refer to the vertices of the CNL-tree at "level e" with the obvious meaning. The root of the CNL-tree is at level a. If M = (S,$\mathcal{B}$) then the leaves of CNL(M,$\leq$) will be assigned level $|S| + 1$ as the vertices at the next to last level correspond to the last element of S. We adopt our usual convention for rooted trees and direct each edge of the CNL-tree away from the root (see FIGURE 10.106). If the tail of such an edge is at level e, we say that that edge is "from level e" or "at level e."

We now define a bijection between paths in a CNL-tree of a matroid M and submatroids of M. Such submatroids are of the form M$\underline{\text{rto}}$K, K $\subseteq$ S, and thus correspond to subsets of S.

10.108 DEFINITION.

Let M = (S,$\mathcal{B}$) be a matroid and let CNL(M,$\leq$) be its CNL-tree relative to a fixed linear order $\leq$ on S. If K is a subset of S we define a path PATH(K,$\leq$) in CNL(M,$\leq$). If e is in K then the edge in PATH(K,$\leq$) from level e goes to the right; otherwise, to the left. We specify PATH(K,$\leq$) by a sequence XY . . . Z of deletions D_e or contractions C_e where D_e means the corresponding edge of PATH(K,$\leq$) goes left from e and C_e means it goes right from e. Similarly, if G is a graph and K a subset of edges of G, we define PATH(K,$\leq$).

The path $C_aD_bC_cD_d$ corresponding to K = {a,c} is shown in FIGURE 10.106. If M = (S,$\mathcal{B}$) is a matroid and M* its dual then CNL(M,$\leq$) and CNL(M*,$\leq$) are related in a very simple way as specified by THEOREM 10.109. We write CNL(M) and CNL(M*) for these trees as the order $\leq$ is the same in both cases.

10.109 THEOREM.

Let M be a matroid and let $(CNL(M))^+$ be the ordered rooted tree obtained from CNL(M) by reflecting CNL(M) through a vertical axis through its root and changing every C to an L and every L to C. If M* is the dual of M then CNL(M*) = $(CNL(M))^+$.

Proof. This result is a direct consequence of THEOREM 10.69 and EXERCISE 10.96(1). EXERCISE 10.96(1) states that e is a loop (coloop) of M if and only if e is a coloop (loop) of M*. From THEOREM 10.69 we have that $(D_e(M))^* = C_e(M^*)$ and $(C_e(M))^* = D_e(M^*)$. These facts together imply the result.

The reader should verify THEOREM 10.109 directly by computing the geometric dual G* of the graph of FIGURE 10.99 (as in FIGURE 10.44) and then computing its CNL-tree. We call $(CNL(M))^+$ the *conjugate mirror image* of CNL(M).

We now use a CNL-tree of a matroid as a geometric device to describe and relate various important numerical functions and polynomials associated with matroids.

10.110 NOTATION.

Let M = (S,$\mathcal{B}$) be a matroid. Let e(M) = |S| be the number of elements of M and r(M) be the rank of M. The corank of M (i.e., the rank of M*) will be denoted by c(M). Clearly, c(M) + r(M) = e(M). If K is a submatroid of M, we define the *brokenness* b(K) to be r(M) − r(K). For a graph G, e(G) = $e(M_G)$, r(G) = $r(M_G)$, and c(G) = $c(M_G)$ denote the number of edges, rank, and corank (or "nullity") of G. We have already encountered these ideas for graphs in DEFINITION 6.90 and EXERCISE 6.94. In particular for graphs, we let v(G) be the number of vertices of G and let p(G) be the number of connected components of $\overset{.}{G}$. Note that $v(G) = p(G) + r(G)$. If K is a spanning subgraph of G (DEFINITION 6.87), then $b(K) = p(K) - p(G)$.

We next define the important ideas of internal and external activity of elements of a matroid relative to a subset K of the matroid.

10.111 DEFINITION.

Let $M = (S,\mathcal{B})$ be a matroid and let $\leq$ be a linear order on S. Let $K \subseteq S$ be a collection of elements of M. We say that an element x of M, $x \notin K$, is *externally active* relative to K and $\leq$ if for some subset $J \subseteq K$, $J \cup \{x\}$ is a circuit of M and $x > y$ for all $y \in J$. We say that an element $x \in K$ is *internally active* relative to K and $\leq$ if x is externally active relative to $S - K$ and $\leq$ in M^*. The number of externally active elements of K in M relative to $\leq$ will be denoted by $ex(K,M,\leq)$. Similarly, $in(K,M,\leq)$ denotes the number of internally active elements. These numbers are called the *external* and *internal activity* of K in M relative to $\leq$.

The reader should think about the geometric meaning in graphs of internal and external activity. Related ideas are to be found in DEFINITION 6.90, *procedures* 6.91 and 6.92, EXAMPLE 6.93, and EXERCISE 6.94. Note that if x is a loop of M and $x \notin K$ then x is trivially externally active relative to K.

10.112 EXAMPLE.

We now consider the computation of the external activity of a set K in the case of a representable matroid $M = (S,\mathcal{B})$. Take $S = \{a,...,h\}$ in that order and let M be the column matroid of the following matrix

$$
\begin{array}{c}
\quad\; a \quad b \quad c \quad d \quad e \quad f \quad g \quad h \\
A = \begin{pmatrix}
1 & 1 & 0 & 2 & 0 & 1 & 1 & 1 \\
0 & 2 & 1 & 1 & 0 & 2 & 0 & 0 \\
0 & 1 & 0 & 0 & 1 & 1 & 2 & 0 \\
0 & 1 & 0 & 0 & 0 & 0 & 0 & 1
\end{pmatrix}
\end{array}
$$

Let $K = \{a,c,e,f\}$. We assume that A is chosen such that the submatrix $A^{(K)}$ consisting of the columns corresponding to K is in unit row canonical form as indicated in the above matrix A. Then $PATH(K,\leq) = PATH(K)$ is $C_aD_bC_c$-$D_dC_eC_fD_gD_h$. We now compute representation matrices for the successive minors C_aM, $D_bC_aM,...$ corresponding to the vertices of T(M) along this path. It is convenient here to modify slightly the conventions of FIGURE 10.100 for representing these minors. We obtain the following sequence:

$$A \xrightarrow{C_a} \begin{pmatrix} 2 & 1 & 1 & 0 & 2 & 0 & 0 \\ 1 & 0 & 0 & 1 & 1 & 2 & 0 \\ 1 & 0 & 0 & 0 & 0 & 0 & 1 \end{pmatrix} \xrightarrow{D_b} \begin{pmatrix} 1 & 1 & 0 & 2 & 0 & 0 \\ 0 & 0 & 1 & 1 & 2 & 0 \\ 0 & 0 & 0 & 0 & 0 & 1 \end{pmatrix} \xrightarrow{C_c}$$

$$\begin{array}{ccccc} d & e & f & g & h \end{array}$$
$$\begin{pmatrix} 0 & 1 & 1 & 2 & 0 \\ 0 & 0 & 0 & 0 & 1 \end{pmatrix} \xrightarrow{D_d} \begin{pmatrix} e & f & g & h \\ 1 & 1 & 2 & 0 \\ 0 & 0 & 0 & 1 \end{pmatrix} \xrightarrow{C_e}$$

$$\begin{array}{ccc} f & g & h \end{array}$$
$$(0 \quad 0 \quad 1) \xrightarrow{C_f} (0 \quad 1) \xrightarrow{D_g} \phi$$

The corresponding path in CNL(M,$\leq$), with vertex labels shown, is

$$\begin{array}{cccccccc} & C_a & D_b & C_c & D_d & C_e & C_f & D_g & D_h \\ N & \to & N \to & N \to & L \to & N \to & L \to & L \to & C \to \end{array}$$

With the matrix A in the form shown above it is easy to find the elements of M that are externally active relative to K. Consider d and the corresponding column $A^{(d)}$. Note that this column is a linear combination of columns $A^{(a)}$ and $A^{(c)}$, which are the principal columns of $A^{(K)}$ that come before $A^{(d)}$. Similarly, $A^{(g)}$ is a linear combination of the principal columns of $A^{(K)}$ that come before it. These are the only two columns of $S - K$ with this property and they are precisely the columns corresponding to elements that are externally active relative to K. The column $A^{(b)}$ has only one principal column of $A^{(K)}$ before it and does not have this property. The reader should check that in general the externally active elements relative to a set K are those whose columns are spanned by the principal columns of $A^{(K)}$ that come before it. Note that an element x not in K is spanned by the principal columns of $A^{(K)}$ that come before it if and only if the corresponding edge of PATH(K) at level x is of the form $L \xrightarrow{D_x}$. Check in the above example that the edges corresponding to y = d and x = g are of this form. This idea leads to LEMMA 10.113.

10.113 LEMMA.

Let M $=$ (S,$\mathcal{B}$) be a matroid with S linearly ordered by $\leq$ and K $\subseteq$ S. Let x be an element of M but x $\notin$ K. Then x is externally active relative to K and $\leq$ if and only if the vertex of PATH(K,$\leq$) at level x in CNL(M,$\leq$) is labeled L.

Proof. If x is a loop in M then the result is trivial. Assume x is not a loop. First suppose that x is externally active relative to K and $\leq$. Divide the vertices of PATH(K,$\leq$) that are at levels less than x into two classes P and Q. If the edge of PATH(K,$\leq$) at the element y $<$ x goes left (corresponding to D_y) add y to P, otherwise add y to Q (corresponding to C_y). Note that by definition of

PATH$(K,\leq)$, $Q \subseteq K$. We must show that x is a loop in the minor D_PC_QM and thus is labeled L. The fact that x is externally active implies that there exists a subset $J \subseteq Q$ such that $J \cup \{x\}$ is a circuit of M. Let A be a representation matrix of M and denote by C_JA the corresponding matrix for C_JM (obtained as in EXAMPLE 10.112, for example). As the column $A^{(x)}$ is linearly dependent on the set of columns $A^{(J)}$ it is evident from the way contractions are performed on matrices that the column $(C_JA)^{(x)}$ is zero. Thus the column corresponding to x is still zero in the matrix D_PC_QA which represents D_PC_QM. Thus x is a loop, as was to be shown.

Suppose now that the vertex of PATH$(K,\leq)$ at level x in CNL$(M,\leq)$ is labeled L. This means that x is a loop in the minor D_PC_QM where P and Q are as in the previous paragraph. Thus the column $(D_PC_QA)^{(x)}$ must be zero. This implies that the column $(C_QA)^{(x)}$ must be zero as deletions cannot change a column from nonzero to zero. Thus x is a loop in C_QM. From the way contractions are performed on matrices it is evident that $A^{(x)}$ is linearly dependent on the columns $A^{(Q)}$ and, by letting $J \subseteq Q$ be a minimal subset of Q such that $A^{(x)}$ depends on $A^{(J)}$ we obtain the required circuit $J \cup \{x\}$ with the elements of J less than x relative to $\leq$. Thus x is externally active relative to K and $\leq$ as was to be shown.

Using duality in the form of THEOREM 10.109, we have LEMMA 10.114.

10.114   LEMMA.

Let M and K be as in LEMMA 10.113. An element $x \in K$ is internally active relative to K if and only if the vertex of PATH$(K,\leq)$ at level x in CNL$(M,\leq)$ is labeled C.

We now come to the basic theorem, THEOREM 10.115, which gives the geometric interpretation of the numerical parameters associated with a matroid M (NOTATION 10.110 and DEFINITION 10.111) in terms of the CNL-tree. Note that if $M = (S,\mathscr{B})$ is a matroid and $K \subseteq S$ is a subset of S then K determines the submatroid MrtoK. Thus we may use the terms "subset" and "submatroid" interchangeably. In the case of a graphical matroid M_G, K is a subset of edges. When we speak of K as a subgraph of G we mean the associated spanning subgraph (DEFINITION 6.89). This means that the vertex set of K is taken to be the vertex set of G so $v(K) = v(G)$.

10.115   THEOREM.

Let $M = (S,\leq)$ be a matroid and $K \subseteq S$ a subset which we identify as above with the submatroid M:toK obtained by restricting M to K. Let S be linearly ordered by $\leq$. For PATH$(K,\leq)$ in CNL$(M,\leq)$ we have the following geometric interpretations of the parameters of NOTATION 10.110 and DEFINITION 10.111:

10.116 Remark

(1) The number of elements of K, e(K), is the number of right edges in PATH(K,≤).
(2) The rank of K, r(K), is the number of right edges in PATH(K,≤) with C or N tails.
(3) The corank of K, c(K) = |K| − r(K), is the number of right edges in PATH(K,≤) with L tails.
(4) The external activity of K, ex(K,M,≤), is the number of left edges in PATH(K,≤) with L tails.
(5) The internal activity of K, in(K,M,≤), is the number of right edges in PATH(K,≤) with C tails.
(6) The brokenness of K, b(K) = r(M) − r(K), is the number of left edges in PATH(K,≤) with C tails.
(7) If M = G is a graph and K is a spanning subgraph of G, then v(K) = p(G) plus the number of right edges of PATH(K,≤) with N tails plus the number of C vertices of PATH(K,≤).

Proof. The reader should interpret each of the above statements in terms of FIGURES 10.99, 10.100, 10.106, and, most importantly, in terms of EXAMPLE 10.112. We shall, as usual, use representability in the proof although the result is true in general.

Statement (1) follows immediately from the definition of PATH(K,≤), DEFINITION 10.108. Since r(K) + c(K) = e(K), from (1) it suffices to show either (2) or (3). The validity of (3) is easily seen for the representable case using the ideas of EXAMPLE 10.112. An edge of PATH(K,≤) has an L tail and goes right at level x if and only if the column $A^{(x)}$ is linearly dependent on the principal columns of the submatrix $A^{(K)}$ that are to the left of it. The number of such columns $A^{(x)}$, is clearly the nullity of the matrix $A^{(K)}$ as this matrix is in unit row canonical form. Since the nullity of $A^{(K)}$ is the corank, c(K), statement (3) and hence statement (2) is valid. Statement (4) is a restatement of LEMMA 10.113. The fact that the edge is a "left edge" in statement (4) is equivalent to x ∉ K. In the same manner, statement (5) follows from LEMMA 10.114. To prove statement (6), look at PATH(S-K,≤) in CNL(M*,≤) using THEOREM 10.109 and then apply (3). It is easy to verify directly that the corank, C*(S-K) of S-K in M* is r(M) − r(K) = b(K). Statement (7) follows from (2) and (6), noting that r(K) + p(K) = v(K).

10.116 REMARK.

In the case of a graphical matroid, M_G, $r(M_G) = r(G)$ in the sense of DEFINITION 6.90. But r(G) = v(G) − p(G) where v denotes vertices and p denotes components. Thus, for graphs, brokenness becomes b(K) = (v(G) − ₁(G)) − (v(K) − p(K)) = p(K) − p(G), using our assumption that K is a spanning subgraph and hence v(K) = v(G). Thus b(K) measures the increase in disconnectedness of K over G and hence the name "brokenness." It is worthwhile to interpret statement (6) of THEOREM 10.115 directly in terms of matrices. Clearly, b(K) does not depend on the linear order on S, so choose ≤ such that the elements of K come first. Let $r(K) = i$ and $r(M) - r(K) = j$. Choose an $r(M) \times n$ representation matrix A for M that is in standard form with respect to $Q = \{1,\ldots,i\} \cup \{n-j+1,\ldots,n\}$ in the sense of DEFINITION 10.86. Thus A may be assumed to be as follows:

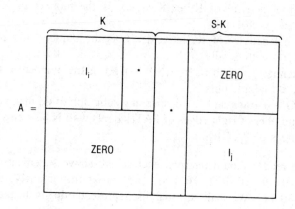

With this ordering, the contractions or right edges of PATH$(K,\leqslant)$ are all first, followed by all deletions or left edges. Obviously, from this form for A, the only deleted coloops correspond to the last j columns of A. These are the $j = r(M) - r(K)$ left edges of PATH$(K,\leqslant)$ with C tails as asserted in statement (6) of THEOREM 10.115.

There is a natural intuitive way to think about the statements of THEOREM 10.115. Imagine starting at the root of the CNL-tree and descending the tree to a leaf. At each vertex, choose whether or not to go right or left at random. At the end, a path PATH$(K,\leqslant)$ has been created. The set K corresponds to the vertices x of CNL$(M,\leqslant)$ at which a right edge was chosen. Starting at the root, one knows nothing about K. As each edge of PATH$(K,\leqslant)$ is added, one learns more information. THEOREM 10.115 tells us what new information we gain about the basic numerical parameters of K as each new edge is added to the path. These parameters are initialized at the root to be $(v,e,r,c,ex,in,b) = (p(G),0,0,0,0,0,0)$. FIGURE 10.117 summarizes the way our information about these parameters changes as edges are added to PATH$(K,\leqslant)$. Thus, if a left edge with C tail is added we may increase b and v by one, if a right edge with C tail is added we may increase v,e,r,in, by one, etc. In the end, we will have the correct parameters for K.

One can easily characterize when K is independent in terms of PATH$(K,\leqslant)$. A subset $K \subseteq S$ is independent if and only if PATH$(K,\leqslant)$ has no right edges with L tails. If in addition, PATH$(K,\leqslant)$ has no left edges with C tails then K is a base (and conversely, see EXERCISE 10.137(2)).

10.117 SUMMARY OF THEOREM 10.115.

(Labels on an edge indicate that these parameters increase by one when an edge of this type is added to PATH(K,≤).

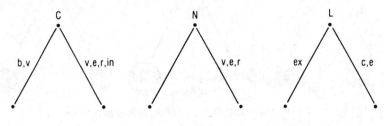

Figure 10.117

In Theorem 10.115 and FIGURE 10.117 we are dealing with parameters of submatroids associated with paths, PATH(K,≤). We might just as well look at these parameters associated with the minors of the delete-contract tree T(M). FIGURES 10.118(a) and 10.118(b) show what happens in this case. FIGURE 10.118(a) shows the general situation for matroids. The parameters v,p which represent the number of vertices and components in a graphical minor are defined only in the graphical case. The meaning of FIGURE 10.118(a) is analogous to that of FIGURE 10.117. A minor obtained by deleting a coloop of a minor X corresponds to a left edge with a C tail in FIGURE 10.118(a). This minor will have parameters p,e, and r decreased by one from X. Contracting a coloop of X results in a decrease by one in v,e, and r as indicated, etc. The parameters "in" and "ex" are only defined for submatroids. The proof that FIGURE 10.118(a) is correct is left as an exercise (EXERCISE 10.137(4)). It is very easy to see why FIGURE 10.118(a) is correct in the graphical case. This idea is shown in FIGURE 10.118(b).

10.118 ANALOG OF FIGURE 10.117 FOR MINORS.

(Labels indicate which parameters decrease)

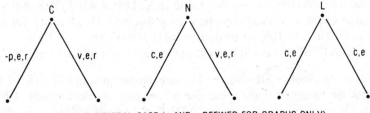

(a) THE GENERAL CASE (p AND v DEFINED FOR GRAPHS ONLY).

Figure 10.118a

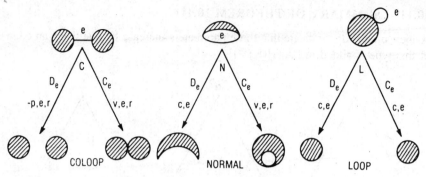

(b) THE GRAPHICAL CASE (PICTORIAL REPRESENTATION).

Figure 10.118b

The CNL-tree provides a convenient geometric framework for discussing certain classical polynomials associated with matroids. We begin with the Whitney polynomial.

10.119 DEFINITION.

Let $M = (S, \leqslant)$ be a matroid. For each $K \subseteq S$ let $b(K) = r(M) - r(K)$ be the brokenness of K as above (NOTATION 10.110). The polynomial in variables x and y

$$W_M(x,y) = \sum_{K \subseteq S} x^{b(K)} y^{c(K)}$$

where c is the corank and the sum is over all subsets K of S is called the *Whitney polynomial of* M.

To interpret the Whitney polynomial in terms of CNL-trees, compare FIGURE 10.121 with FIGURES 10.117 and 10.106. Imagine that the edges of the CNL-tree, CNL($M, \leqslant$) have been labeled as in FIGURE 10.120 where every left edge with a C tail is given a label or "weight" x and every right edge with an L tail is given weight y. The reader should label FIGURE 10.106 accordingly. Imagine traversing the CNL-tree, with edges so labeled, from the root to a leaf along the path PATH($K, \leqslant$) corresponding to K. Define w(PATH($K, \leqslant$)) to be the product of the weights of the edges along this path. For example, for K = $\{a,c,d\}$ in FIGURE 10.106, the product would be $(1)(1)(1)(y) = y$. Then $W_M(x,y) = \sum\limits_{K \subseteq S} w(PATH(K, \leqslant))$ is the sum of such weights over all such paths. To see why this is true, look at FIGURE 10.117 and compare it with FIGURE 10.120. Note that the values of b and c increase by one exactly when an edge labeled with an x or a y is traversed. Thus w(PATH($K, \leqslant$)) = $x^{b(K)} y^{c(K)}$ is summed over all K and $W_M(x,y)$ is the result. As an example, the reader should compute the Whitney polynomial associated with the CNL-tree of FIGURE 10.106.

10.120   CNL WEIGHTS FOR THE WHITNEY POLYNOMIAL AS A SUM OVER SUBMATROIDS.

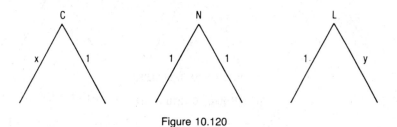

Figure 10.120

From a geometric point of view, FIGURE 10.120 together with FIGURE 10.117 can be regarded as the definition of the Whitney polynomial. We are now in a position to exploit our knowledge of the CNL-tree to give alternative representations of the Whitney polynomial. For example, both FIGURES 10.121(a) and (b) represent the Whitney polynomial. In FIGURE 10.121(a) the weight y that was on every right edge with L tail has been made 0 and the weight of every left edge with L tail has been made $1 + y$. Recall, however, that the subtrees of an L or C vertex are identical. Thus the sum of $w'(\text{PATH}(K, \leqslant))$ for these new weights over all K is still $W_M(x,y)$. Using the same idea, we may modify the weights of the edges with C tail as shown in FIGURE 10.121(b) and still obtain $W_M(x,y)$. As previously covered (see also EXERCISE 10.138(2)), a subset $K \subseteq S$ is independent in M if and only if $\text{PATH}(K, \leqslant)$ contains no right edges with L tails and is a basis if and only if $\text{PATH}(K, \leqslant)$ contains no right edges with L tails *and* no left edges with C tails. The zero weights of FIGURES 10.121(a) and (b) force the sum of weights to be over these two classes of sets respectively, so we obtain COROLLARY 10.122.

10.121   WHITNEY POLYNOMIAL AS SUM OVER INDEPENDENT SETS AND BASES.

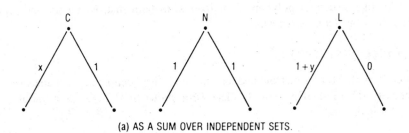

(a) AS A SUM OVER INDEPENDENT SETS.

Figure 10.121a

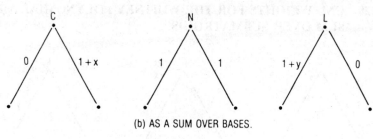

(b) AS A SUM OVER BASES.

Figure 10.121b

10.122 COROLLARY.

Let $M = (S,\mathscr{B})$ be a matroid with bases $\mathscr{B}$ and independent sets $\mathscr{I}$. Let "b" be the brokenness, "in" the internal activity and "ex" the external activity as defined in NOTATION 10.110 and DEFINITION 10.111. Then

$$W_M(x,y) = \sum_{I \in \mathscr{I}} x^{b(I)}(1+y)^{ex(I)}$$

$$W_M(x,y) = \sum_{B \in \mathscr{B}} (1+x)^{in(B)}(1+y)^{ex(B)}.$$

Proof. We have noted above that the weights of FIGURES 10.121(a) and (b) give the Whitney polynomial. By comparing these figures with FIGURE 10.117 we see that the weights $1+x$ and $1+y$ correspond to edges that count changes in internal and external activity, respectively.

10.123 REMARK.

A basic recursion for the Whitney polynomial follows from FIGURE 10.121(b). Let $H = D_e(M)$ and let $K = C_e(M)$. Then

$$W_M(x,y) = \begin{cases} (1+y)W_H(x,y), & e \text{ a loop} \\ (1+x)W_K(x,y), & e \text{ a coloop} \\ W_H(x,y) + W_K(x,y), & e \text{ neither} \end{cases}$$

where $W_Z(x,y) = 1$ if Z is empty.

Another structural polynomial of interest in both matroid theory and graph theory is the *Tutte polynomial*.

10.124 DEFINITION.

Let $M = (S,\mathscr{B})$ be a matroid and let "in" and "ex" denote internal and external activity (DEFINITION 10.111). The *Tutte polynomial* $T_M(x,y)$ in variables x and y is defined by

$$T_M(x,y) = \sum_{B \in \mathscr{B}} x^{in(B)} y^{ex(B)}.$$

Because the parameters "in" and "ex" depend on the linear order on S, it might seem, a priori, that the Tutte polynomial T_M might depend on the linear order also. However, using COROLLARY 10.122, we see immediately that

$$T_M(x,y) = W_M(x-1,y-1).$$

Since W_M obviously is not order dependent, neither is T_M.

Note that the Tutte polynomial can also be written in the following form:

$$T_M(x,y) = \sum_{i,j} t_{ij}(M)x^i y^j$$

where $t_{ij}(M)$ denotes the number of bases B with $in(B) = i$ and $ex(B) = j$. If M^* is the dual of M note that $t_{ij}(M) = t_{ji}(M^*)$.

The weights for the CNL-tree that give the Tutte polynomial $T_M(x,y)$ are shown in FIGURE 10.125.

10.125 CNL WEIGHTS FOR THE TUTTE POLYNOMIAL.

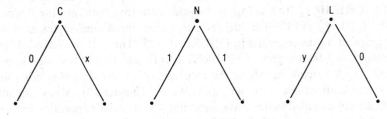

Figure 10.125

For the Tutte-Grothendieck invariants (REMARK 10.126 below) $x = \dfrac{\lambda(C)+\mu(C)}{\mu(N)}$, $y = \dfrac{\lambda(L)+\mu(L)}{\lambda(N)}$.

10.126 REMARK.

The fact that the Tutte and Whitney polynomials are related by a simple change of variable is a special case of a more general idea involving functions defined recursively on matroids using the delete-contract recursion. Suppose f(M) is a function on matroids such that for an element e of M

$$f(M) = \lambda(e,M)f(D_e(M)) + \mu(e,M)f(C_e(M)),$$

where λ and μ depend only on whether e is a loop, coloop, or neither of M, say $\lambda(L)$, $\lambda(C)$, $\lambda(N)$, $\mu(L)$, $\mu(C)$, $\mu(N)$. Also suppose $f(Z) = k$ for Z empty. Then

$$f(M) = k\lambda(N)^{c(M)} \mu(N)^{r(M)} T_M(x,y)$$

where

$$x = \frac{\lambda(C) + \mu(C)}{\mu(N)}, \quad y = \frac{\lambda(L) + \mu(L)}{\lambda(N)} \quad \text{(see FIGURE 10.125)}.$$

The CNL weights for f are shown in FIGURE 10.127(a). Let $s = 1/\mu(N)$ and $t = 1/\lambda(N)$. Multiply all edges of FIGURE 10.127(a) that have a C tail by s and multiply all right edges with N tails by s. Multiply all other edges of FIGURE 10.127(a) by t. The resulting weights, shown in FIGURE 10.127(b), compute $s^{r(M)}t^{c(M)}f(M)$. To understand the reason for this transformation, look at FIGURE 10.118(a). Notice that the edges that we have multiplied by an s correspond exactly to edges where there is a decrease in rank in going to the associated minor. Those edges we have multiplied by t correspond to a decrease in corank. In computing f(M) we sum the product of the weights over all paths from the root to a leaf of the tree weighted as in FIGURE 10.127(a). In terms of the tree T(M) of FIGURE 10.118(a), the total decrease in rank r along any such path is r(M) as the leaves of T(M) have rank zero. This gives the factor $s^{r(M)}t^{c(M)}$ that relates the functions associated with weights of FIGURES 10.127(a) and 10.127(b). The weights of FIGURE 10.127(c) are clearly equivalent to those of FIGURE 10.127(b) using the same idea involved in transforming FIGURE 10.120 to FIGURE 10.121. This proves the desired representation of f in terms of T_M as indicated in FIGURE 10.125. The trick we have just used of interrelating the weights of FIGURES 10.117 and 10.118 is a useful one to remember. A function satisfying the recursion of f is sometimes referred to as a "Tutte-Grothendieck invariant" (see Welsh, Chapter 15). Many important functions are included in this class, including a wide class of partition functions in statistical mechanics (EXERCISE 10.137(9)).

10.127   WEIGHTS FOR A GENERAL TUTTE-GROTHENDIECK INVARIANT (REMARK 10.126).

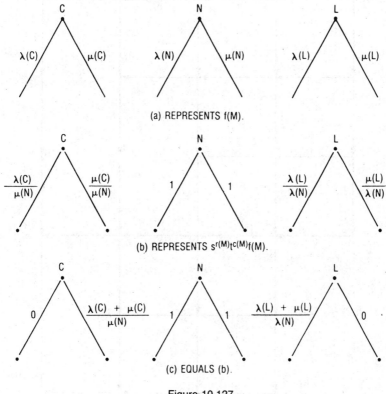

Figure 10.127

It is beyond the scope of this book to go into the interesting relationship between reduced delete-contract trees such as that shown for K_5 in FIGURE 10.102 and polynomials such as T_M and W_M. If the weights of FIGURE 10.125 are applied to FIGURE 10.102, we obtain the interesting directed graph of FIGURE 10.128. The sum of the weighted paths of this graph is the Tutte polynomial for K_5 (EXERCISE 10.137(7)).

10.128   THE TUTTE POLYNOMIAL OF K_5.

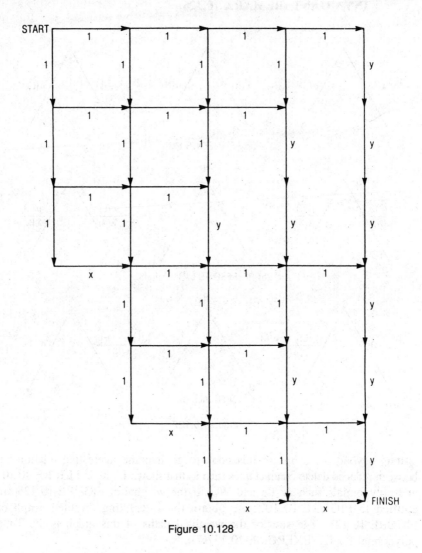

Figure 10.128

(For each directed path from START to FINISH take the product of the weights of its edges. Sum over all such paths.)

Another important polynomial associated with a matroid M is the *chromatic polynomial* P(M,x). The chromatic polynomials were originally defined for graphs. Suppose we are given a graph $G = (V,E,\varphi)$. Let X^V denote the set of all functions from V to a finite set X. Intuitively, we imagine that X is a collection of colors with which we are going to color the vertices of G. Each coloring corresponds to a function $f \in X^V$. A function or "coloring" f is *proper* for G if for any edge e in G, the pair of vertices $\varphi(e) = \{u,v\}$ incident on e have different colors (i.e., $f(u) \neq f(v)$). We make the convention that if G has a loop then it has no proper functions. A graph G is x-*colorable* if there is a proper function in $\underline{x}^V$ ($\underline{x} = \{1,2,\ldots,x\}$). A difficult theorem in graph theory states that every planar graph is 4-colorable. The *chromatic number* of a graph G is the minimum x such that $\underline{x}^V$ has a proper function for G.

10.129 DEFINITION.

Let G be a graph and let $C(x,G)$ denote the number of proper functions for G in $\underline{x}^V$ (as just described). The function $C(x,G)$ is easily seen to be a polynomial in x (REMARK 10.130) and is called the *chromatic polynomial of* G.

We shall use the CNL-tree of a matroid M to define the chromatic polynomial $P(M,x)$ of M (FIGURE 10.131, DEFINITION 10.132). It will turn out that for a graph G, $P(M_G,x) = x^{-p(G)}C(x,G)$ where $p(G)$ is the number of components of G and M_G is the cycle matroid of G. This is a little bit awkward but is standard terminology.

10.130 REMARK.

If T_n is the graph with n vertices and no edges, then $C(x,T_n) = x^n$. In general, it is easily shown that $C(x,G) = C(x,D_eG) - C(x,C_eG)$ for any edge e of G. It follows from these facts that $C(x,G)$ is a polynomial in x (use induction).

Referring again to FIGURE 10.99, notice that the leaves of the tree $T(G)$ shown there are all graphs of the form T_n (no edges, n vertices for some n). To each corresponding leaf in FIGURE 10.106, assign weight x^n where n is the number of vertices in that leaf in FIGURE 10.99. To each edge of the CNL-tree shown in FIGURE 10.106, assign weight $+1$ if it is a left edge and -1 if it is a right edge. For each path from the root to a leaf in FIGURE 10.106, take the product of the edge weights and the weight of the terminal vertex (the leaf). Adding these terms over all paths gives the chromatic polynomial of the given graph G. In this case $C(x,G) = x(x-1)(x-2) = x^3 - 3x^2 + 2x$. The reader should carry out this computation. This computation works because it is the obvious implementation of the recursion of REMARK 10.131. But now look at FIGURE 10.118 and notice the parameter $-p$ on the left edge with C tail. If we label each left edge with C tail in FIGURE 10.106 with an x and replace all labels on leaves by $+1$ then again summing weighted paths we get essentially the same polynomial as before. Each path with weight $\pm x^n$ before now gets weight $\pm x^{n-p(G)}$. The reader should again carry out the computation on FIGURE 10.106 to get $x^2 - 3x + 2$. Thus if $K_G(x)$ represents this new polynomial we have $C(x,G) = x^{p(G)}K_G(x)$. The weights used to compute $K_G(x)$ are those that we shall use to define the chromatic polynomial of a matroid. See FIGURE 10.131 and DEFINITION 10.132.

10.131   CNL WEIGHTS FOR THE CHROMATIC POLYNOMIAL OF A MATROID.

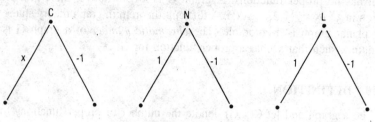

Figure 10.131

10.132   DEFINITION.

Let $M = (S, \mathscr{B})$ be a matroid and let CNL(M) be a CNL-tree for M (DEFINITION 10.105). Assign weights to the edges of CNL(M) as shown in FIGURE 10.131. For each path from the root to a leaf of CNL(M) take the product of the weights of the edges along that path. Sum these expressions over all paths. The resulting polynomial P(M,x) will be called the *chromatic polynomial of* M.

10.133   REMARK.

As we have noticed above, if G is a graph and M_G is its cycle matroid then $P(M_G,x) = x^{-p(G)}C(x,G)$ where $p(G)$ is the number of components of G and $C(x,G)$ is the usual graphical chromatic polynomial of G (DEFINITION 10.129). By comparing FIGURE 10.131 and FIGURE 10.117 we can represent P(M,x) as a sum over all subsets (or equivalently, submatroids) $H \subseteq S$ as

$$P(M,x) = \sum_{H \subseteq S} (-1)^{e(H)} x^{b(H)}.$$

In this expression $b(H) = r(M) - r(H)$ is the "brokenness" of H (NOTATION 10.110) and $e(H)$ is the number of elements of H. This expression for P(M,x) follows in the usual manner by observing that x occurs as a weight on left edges with a C tail and these edges are precisely where the parameter b changes value according to FIGURE 10.117. Similarly, the weight -1 occurs where e changes value. From this expression for P(M,x) it is obvious that it does not depend on the choice of CNL-trees.

10.134 ALTERNATIVE CNL WEIGHTS FOR THE CHROMATIC POLYNOMIAL.

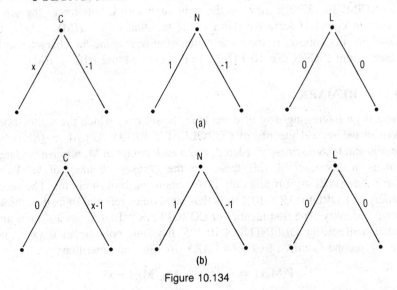

Figure 10.134

In FIGURE 10.134 we see some alternative choices of weights for P(M,x). As we observed before, the two subtrees of a vertex labeled L or C in the CNL-tree are identical. We may thus alter the weights on the edges connecting a C or L vertex to the sons of that vertex in any way that preserves their sum. This alteration will not change the function being defined by these weights (in this case P(M,x)). As the sum of the weights associated with the L vertex in FIGURE 10.131 is zero, we may replace these weights with zero as in FIGURE 10.134(a). Similarly, the weights associated with the C vertex are altered in FIGURE 10.134(b). COROLLARY 10.135 follows easily from the transformations of FIGURE 10.134.

10.135 COROLLARY.

Let M be a matroid and P(M,x) its chromatic polynomial. Using the notation X(*statement*) = 0 if *statement* is false and 1 if *statement* is true, we have (using again NOTATION 10.110)

$$P(M,x) = (-1)^{r(M)} \sum_{I} (-x)^{b(I)} \, X \text{ (I independent, ex(I)} = 0)$$

and

$$P(M,x) = (-1)^{r(M)} \sum_{B} (1-x)^{in(B)} \, X \text{ (B a base, ex(B)} = 0).$$

Proof. The proof follows in the standard manner from FIGURE 10.117. In the case of the first identity, we use the weights of FIGURE 10.134(a). The 0 on the left edge with L tail forces the external activity to be zero. As a path corresponds to an independent set if and only if it has no right edge with L tail (EXERCISE 10.137(2)), the 0 on the right edge with L tails forces the sum to be over independent sets. We use also the fact that $r(I) = r(M) - b(I)$. The second identity follows in the same manner but now using the characterization of bases from EXERCISE 10.137(2). In this case we use $r(B) = r(M)$.

10.136   REMARK.

There is an interesting way of describing the set over which the summation is taken in the second identity of COROLLARY 10.135. Let $M = (S,\mathcal{B})$ be a matroid and let S be linearly ordered. From each circuit in M, remove the largest element in this ordering. Call these sets the "broken circuits" of M. Then a base B has $ex(B) = 0$ if and only if it contains no broken circuit. The second identity of COROLLARY 10.136 is thus sometimes referred to as the "broken circuit" identity. The first identity of COROLLARY 10.136 has a similar interpretation. Recalling DEFINITION 10.125, the Tutte polynomial $T_M(x,y)$, note that the second identity of COROLLARY 10.136 can be written

$$P(M,x) = (-1)^{r(M)} \sum_i t_{io}(M)(1-x)^i$$

where $t_{ij}(M)$ is the coefficient of $x^i y^j$ in $T_M(x,y)$. If $P(M,x)$ is written in the form

$$P(M,x) = (-1)^r \sum_{k \geq 0} (-1)^k a_k x^k$$

then the a_k are called the *Whitney numbers of the first kind*.

10.137   EXERCISE.

(1) Extend FIGURE 10.102 to K_6.
(2) Let $M = (S,\mathcal{B})$ be a representable matroid and let CNL(M,$\leq$) be a CNL-tree for M. Prove that $K \subseteq S$ is an independent set if and only if PATH(K,$\leq$) has no right edges with L tails. Prove that an independent set K is a base of M if and only if PATH(K,$\leq$) has no left edges with C tails. *Hint:* The idea for the proof can be found in EXAMPLE 10.112. The result is true for general matroids.
(3) Let M be a matroid with CNL-tree CNL(M,$\leq$). Suppose that the edges of CNL(M,$\leq$) are weighted with elements from a field or commutative ring and we are considering $W(M) = \sum_{K \subseteq S} w(PATH(K,\leq))$ where $w(PATH(K,\leq))$ is the product of the weights of the edges in PATH(K,$\leq$). Suppose that the two edges directed downward from each C vertex have weights α and β and that these weights are changed to α' and β' where $\alpha' + \beta' = \alpha + \beta$. Show that W(M) is unchanged. Show the same for an L vertex.
(4) Prove that Figure 10.118(a) is correct for representable matroids.

(5) Let M be a matroid and M* its dual. Show that the Tutte polynomials are related by $T_M(x,y) = T_M*(y,x)$ or, in terms of coefficients, $t_{ij}(M) = t_{ji}(M*)$. In addition, show that $t_{10}(M) = t_{01}(M)$ if M has no loops or coloops. In other words, the coefficients of x and y are the same in $T_M(x,y)$ for such M. *Hint:* The fact that $t_{ij}(M) = t_{ji}(M*)$ follows easily from the definitions and can be interpreted in terms of paths in CNL(M) and CNL(M*) using THEOREM 10.109. The equality of $t_{10}(M)$ and $t_{01}(M)$ can also be interpreted in terms of paths in CNL(M).

(6) Extend FIGURE 10.128 to include K_7. What is the general rule? Give a formula for computing the Tutte polynomial of K_n and see if you can compute the Tutte polynomial of K_8.

(7) Let M be a representable matroid and let CNL(M) be a CNL-tree with respect to the ordering a,..,f of the elements of M. All vertices at level f in CNL(M) are labeled with either a C or an L. Prove that M is connected if and only if f is the only level of CNL(M) with this property. The result is true in general.

(8) Show that given CNL(M,$\leq$) in the form of FIGURE 10.106 (i.e., the ordered rooted binary tree with labels C, N, and L and the ordered list of levels a,b,. . .) one can reconstruct the bases of M and hence M = (S,$\mathcal{B}$).

(9) In theoretical statistical mechanics graph theoretic models are used to study physical systems. From these models, functions called "partition function" are calculated. These functions are used to compute physical quantities such as energy and specific heat. The latter quantity, which exhibits singular behavior in the limit, is of particular interest in these calculations. A famous classical example is the two-dimensional Ising model for ferromagnetism (as well as gas condensation and order-disorder transition in alloys). In this model, the vertices of a two-dimensional rectangular grid or graph G = (V,E) are imagined to be an orderly array of particles, each particle i having a variable or "spin" $\sigma(i)$ associated with it.

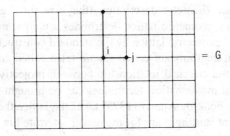

The spin $\sigma(i)$ can be $+1$ or -1. The partition function Z_G for the two-dimensional Ising model has the form

$$Z_G = \sum_\sigma \exp\left[\sum_{\{i,j\}} K_{ij}(\sigma(i)\sigma(j) - 1)\right]$$

where σ ranges over all functions $\{-1, +1\}^V$ and $\{i,j\}$ ranges over all edges of G. The K_{ij} are functions of the absolute temperature of the system. In the case where the K_{ij} are independent of i and j (say $K_{ij} = K$) the partition function Z_G can be written in the form of a subgraph expansion of the type we have been studying:

$$Z_G = \sum_{H \subseteq E} \gamma^{e(H)} \delta^{e(G) - e(H)} 2^{p(H)}$$

Here e and p are as defined in NOTATION 10.110 and the subgraph defined by H is its spanning subgraph (i.e., $v(H) = v(G)$). In terms of K, $\gamma = 1 - e^{-2K}$, $\delta = e^{-2K}$. Express Z_G in this form in terms of the Tutte polynomial and the Whitney polynomial. Try to compute Z_G for some small rectangular graphs. The reader interested in studying these matters further should read the article by J. Essam, "Graph Theory and Statistical Physics," Discrete Math., v. 1, no. 1 (1971), 83-112. The above subgraph expansion appears on page 91 of this article. Another source for this type of problem is the book by N. L. Biggs, "Interaction Models," London Math. Soc. Lecture Note Series 30, Cambridge University Press, 1971.

10.138   REMARK.

At this point, by frequently resorting to the assumption of representability, we have covered most of the basic theoretical ideas of matroid theory. The representable case is particularly important for the applied mathematician or computer scientist as the assumption of representability is a great help in algorithm design. A more general point of view, that of lattice theory, has been omitted from our discussion. A set together with an order relation (DEFINITION 1.2, PART I) is called a *poset*. A poset in which every pair of elements has a unique least upper bound and greatest lower bound is called a *lattice*. With any matroid M one can associate a lattice called the *lattice of flats* of the matroid. The order relation is set inclusion. The class of lattices that arise from matroids has a very nice purely lattice theoretic description (they are the "geometric lattices"). Conversely, every geometric lattice determines a unique matroid. The matroid that arises from a geometric lattice by the standard construction is without loops or coloops. Such matroids are called *simple* (also called *combinatorial geometries*). Through the classical relationship between projective spaces and lattice theory, additional mathematical techniques can be brought to bear on the study of matroids. The book by Aigner (1979) takes the lattice theoretic point of view and is an excellent starting point for the reader interested in learning more about these ideas.

An area with perhaps even more interest to the reader at this point is the study of matroid algorithms. The book by Lawler (1976) is a good place to start a study of this subject. There are many interesting unsolved research problems in regard to data structures and complexity of matroid algorithms. We list a number of references to the current literature in this field at the end of this chapter. We now close our discussion of matroids with a brief discussion of some important ideas associated with matroid algorithms.

10.139 THE GREEDY ALGORITHM.

As we have seen on a number of occasions, Gaussian elimination or "row canonical form" (see FIGURE 10.7 and the related discussion) is very important in understanding the structure of representable matroids. The extension of the row canonical form algorithm to general matroids is called the "greedy algorithm." Suppose we are given a matroid $M = (S, \mathcal{I})$ with an ordering $s_1, s_2, \ldots, s_n$ on the elements of S, and $\mathcal{I}$ the collection of independent sets. Let $1 \leq t \leq r$, where r is the rank of M. The following procedure, GREEDY(M,t) selects an independent set of size t which we call the *principal independent set* of M with respect to the order $s_1, s_2, \ldots, s_n$.

procedure GREEDY(M,t) [produces the principal independent set $(s_{i_1}, \ldots, s_{i_t})$].
begin
    $s_{i_1} := $ the first nonloop of S with respect to the order $s_1, \ldots, s_n$;
    for $k = 2$ to t *do* let s_{i_k} be the first element of S that is independent of
        $(s_{i_1}, \ldots, s_{i_{k-1}})$;
end

If M is a representable matroid with representation matrix A in row canonical form (or unit row canonical form) then the principal columns of A, as discussed in connection with FIGURE 10.7, correspond to the principal independent set, or base in this case, $(s_{i_1}, \ldots, s_{i_r})$. Thus, in the representable case the row canonical form algorithm is a way of implementing the GREEDY ALGORITHM (see also EXERCISE 10.151(1)). The GREEDY ALGORITHM gets its name because it always grabs the first available element to add to the independent set being constructed. Greedy algorithms for graphs were the subject of EXERCISE 6.94(4). LEMMA 10.140 states the main property of the principal independent set.

10.140 LEMMA.

Let $(s_{i_1}, \ldots, s_{i_t})$ be the elements of the principal independent set in the order they are produced by GREEDY(M,t). Let $(s_{j_1}, \ldots, s_{j_t})$ be any other independent set of cardinality t in order $(j_1 < \ldots < j_t)$. Then $i_1 \leq j_1, \ldots, i_t \leq j_t$. (We say that $(s_{i_1}, \ldots, s_{i_t})$ is *pointwise minimal* among all independent sets of size t when this condition holds.)

Proof. The reader may wish to read TERMINOLOGY REVIEW 10.19. Let $I_2 = \text{span}\{s_{i_1}, \ldots, s_{i_2 - 1}\}, \ldots, I_t = \text{span}\{s_{i_1}, \ldots, s_{i_t - 1}\}$. Then $I_2 \subseteq I_3 \subseteq \ldots \subseteq I_t$ and rank $(I_j) = j - 1$ for $j = 2, \ldots, t$. Thus if $(s_{j_1}, \ldots, s_{j_t}) = Q$ is independent then $|I_j \cap Q| \leq j - 1$ for $j = 2, \ldots, t$. Thus $i_1 \leq j_1, i_2 \leq j_2, \ldots, i_t \leq j_t$ as was to be shown.

10.141 WEIGHTS FOR THE GREEDY ALGORITHM.

Let $M = (S, \mathcal{I})$ be a matroid with independent sets $\mathcal{I}$. Let $W: \mathcal{I} \to L$ where L is a linearly ordered set. Asssume that S is linearly ordered $s_1, s_2, \ldots, s_n$ as above. For X and Y in $\mathcal{I}$, we say that X *is pointwise less than* Y *relative to the order* $s_1, \ldots, s_n$ *on* S if when X and Y are ordered $x_1, \ldots, x_t$ and $y_1, \ldots, y_t$ relative to the order on S we have $x_i \leqslant y_i$ for i = 1, \ldots, t. Note that we require that X and Y have the same cardinality. If $W(X) \leqslant W(Y)$ whenever X is pointwise less than Y then we say that W is a *greedy weight*. If w: $S \to R$, R the real numbers, $W(s_1) \leqslant \ldots \leqslant W(s_n)$, then $W(X) = \overset{t}{\underset{i=1}{\Sigma}} w(x_i)$ is obviously a greedy weight. If $\bar{W}(X) = \min \{w(x): x \in X\}$ then $\bar{W}$ is a greedy weight. Clearly, if $|Q| = t$, is the principal independent set, selected by the greedy algorithm, then W(Q) is minimal over W applied to independent sets of size t whenever W is a greedy weight. Thus, if one is given the function w and wants to minimize W or $\bar{W}$ (defined from w as above) then one chooses the order on S such that $w(s_1) \leqslant w(s_2) \leqslant \ldots \leqslant w(s_n)$. Applying the greedy algorithm produces a minimal independent set of the desired size. If one wants to maximize W then one chooses the linear order on S such that $w(s_1) \geqslant w(s_2) \geqslant \ldots \geqslant w(s_n)$.

In a certain sense, the fact that the greedy algorithm works to produce a pointwise minimal independent set characterizes matroids.

10.142 DEFINITION.

A pair $(S, \mathcal{I})$ where S is a set and $\mathcal{I}$ a nonempty collection of subsets is called a *hereditary set system*, HSS, if whenever Y is in $\mathcal{I}$ and $X \subset Y$ then X is in $\mathcal{I}$. The pair $(S, \mathcal{I})$ satisfies the exchange property, EXP, if whenever X and Y are in $\mathcal{I}$ with $X \subset Y$ then there exists $y \in Y-X$ such that $X \cup \{y\}$ is in $\mathcal{I}$. (If $(S, \mathcal{I})$ satisfies both HSS and EXP then it is a matroid.)

If $(S, \mathcal{I})$ is a hereditary system one can define the obvious analog of the greedy algorithm, GREEDY$((S, \mathcal{I}), t)$, where t is less than or equal to the size of the largest set in $\mathcal{I}$. To do so, first order the elements of S, $s_1, s_2, \ldots, s_n$. Let s_{i_1} be the first element that belongs to some set in the collection $\mathcal{I}$. In general, let s_{i_k} be the first element of S greater than $s_{i_{k-1}}$ such that $\{s_{i_1}, \ldots, s_{i_{k-1}}, s_{i_k}\}$ is in $\mathcal{I}$. THEOREM 10.144 states that if the greedy algorithm applied to a hereditary set system always produces a pointwise minimal element of $\mathcal{I}$ then the hereditary set system is in fact a matroid.

10.143 THEOREM.

Let $(S, \mathcal{I})$ be a hereditary set system. If for any order $s_1, \ldots, s_n$, GREEDY$((S, \mathcal{I}), t)$ always produces a pointwise minimal set of size t then $(S, \mathcal{I})$ satisfies the exchange property, EXP. Thus, $(S, \mathcal{I})$ is a matroid.

Proof. Let X and Y be in $\mathscr{I}$, $|X| < |Y|$. Order the elements of S such that X comes first, then Y-X, and then S-X-Y. By assumption Y-X is nonempty. If there is no y in Y-X such that $X \cup \{y\}$ is in $\mathscr{I}$ then GREEDY$((S,\mathscr{I}),t)$, $t = |Y|$, would select all of X followed by some elements of S-X-Y. This set is clearly not pointwise minimal when compared to Y.

There is an extension of the idea of a matroid that relates to our discussion of the greedy algorithms. These structures are called "greedoids" and may be viewed as a generalization of matroids or a specialization of the general problem of efficient backtracking algorithms (see FIGURE 31 of CHAPTER 1 for the basic idea of backtracking). Let $M = (S,\mathscr{I})$ be a matroid of rank r and suppose that $S_1 \subset S_2 \subset \ldots \subset S_r$ are closed subsets of M, rank$(S_i) = i$. Thus $S_r = S$. Let $A_i = S_i - S_{i-1}$ for $i = 2,\ldots,r$, $A_1 = S_1$. Let $\mathscr{A}_t = A_1 \times \ldots \times A_t$ for $t = 1,\ldots,r$ and let $\mathscr{L} = \bigcup_{t=1}^{r} \mathscr{A}_t$. Then $\mathscr{L}$ is a collection of vectors over S. The entries in these vectors are all distinct. Furthermore, if $v = (x_1,\ldots,x_t) \in \mathscr{L}$ and $j < t$ then $(x_1,\ldots,x_j) \in \mathscr{L}$. We call such a vector system a *hereditary vector system*, or *hereditary language* if it satisfies this latter condition. Thus the $\mathscr{L}$ just defined is an example of a hereditary language.

10.144 DEFINITION.

Let S be a set and let $\mathscr{L}$ be a nonempty collection of vectors with entries in S. If for any $(x_1,\ldots,x_t) \in \mathscr{L}$ and any $j < t$, $(x_1,\ldots,x_j)$ is in $\mathscr{L}$ then $\mathscr{L}$ will be called a *hereditary vector system* or *hereditary language* over S. If $\mathscr{L}$ is a hereditary language over S such that for any $(x_1,\ldots,x_j) \in \mathscr{L}$ and $(y_1,\ldots,y_t) \in \mathscr{L}$ with $j < t$ there exists k, $1 \leq k \leq t$, such that $(x_1,\ldots,x_j,y_k) \in \mathscr{L}$ then $\mathscr{L}$ will be called a *greedoid*.

In the above example, order S such that all nonloops of A_1 are first, all nonloops of A_2 second, etc. Put all loops last. Then, GREEDY(M,t) produces the lexicographically minimal element of $\mathscr{A}_t$. In terms of the hereditary language $\mathscr{L}$, this corresponds first, choosing a minimal vector of length 1, then extending this to a minimal vector of length 2, etc., until a minimal vector of length t is obtained. Minimal in all cases means lexicographically. By putting weight functions on vectors of $\mathscr{L}$ where $\mathscr{L}$ is any hereditary language and successively maximizing or minimizing extensions of vectors one can generalize the greedy algorithm. Another natural hereditary language associated with a matroid $M = (S,\mathscr{I})$ is to take $\mathscr{L}$ to be the set of all orderings of sets of $\mathscr{I}$. An interesting greedoid associated with rooted graphs is defined in EXERCISE 10.151(2). References are listed at the end of the chapter for the reader interested in studying greedoids.

We conclude our discussion of matroids with a brief look at two closely related problems that are the starting point for a number of interesting algorithms.

10.145   THE MATROID PARTITIONING PROBLEM.

We are given a set S and p matroids on this set: $M_1 = (S, \mathscr{B}_1), \ldots, M_p = (S, \mathscr{B}_p)$. The problem is to determine whether or not S can be written as a disjoint union $E_1 \cup E_2 \cup \ldots \cup E_p$ of sets where each E_i is an independent set in the matroid M_i. This is equivalent to finding a collection of bases $B_1, B_2, \ldots, B_p$ whose union is S, each B_i a base of M_i. The B_i need not be disjoint. If such a collection of B_i has been found then one can take $E_1 = B_1$, $E_2 = B_2 - B_1$, etc., to obtain a disjoint collection of independent sets whose union is S. Conversely, if the E_i has been found then each E_i may be extended to a base to obtain the B_i. Suppose that $X \subseteq S$ is some subset of S. If the partitioning E_i exists, then each $X \cap E_i$ is an independent set, so obviously, the rank of X in the matroid M_i, denoted by $\rho_i(X)$, is greater than or equal to $|X \cap E_i|$. Thus $|X| \leq \rho_1(X) + \ldots + \rho_p(X)$. We show that this condition is also sufficient to guarantee the existence of an independent set partition (see THEOREM 10.149).

10.146   THE MATROID INTERSECTION PROBLEM.

We are again given a fixed set S and matroids $M_1, \ldots, M_p$ on S. In addition, we are given an integer k. We wish to determine whether or not there is a subset $E \subseteq S$ that has cardinality k and is independent in all of the M_i. For $p > 2$ no reasonable methods are known for resolving this question. For $p = 2$ a variety of good algorithms are known. In this special case, $p = 2$, the matroid intersection problem is equivalent to the matroid partitioning problem for $p = 2$. Although not the best from the point of view of algorithms, there is an easy way to see the connection between the two problems using truncations of matroids (DEFINITION 10.72). Let M and N be two matroids on S and let k be less than or equal to the minimal rank of these two matroids. Let M_k and N_k be the truncation of these matroids to k. All independent sets of size k have now become bases. Clearly, M and N have a common independent set of size k if and only if M_k and N_k have a common base of size k. But this latter condition happens if and only if M_k and N_k^* have disjoint bases. The rank of the dual N_k^* is $n - k$, $n = |S|$, so M_k and N_k^* have disjoint bases if and only if they partition S in the sense of the matroid partitioning problem. Assuming the result of THEOREM 10.149 we have the following THEOREM 10.147.

10.147   THEOREM (Edmonds' intersection theorem).

Let M_1 and M_2 be two matroids on a set S with rank functions ρ_1 and ρ_2. M_1 and M_2 have a common independent set of cardinality k if and only if either one of the following two conditions holds:

(1) For all $X \subseteq S$, $|X| \leq \bar{\rho}_1(X) + \bar{\rho}_2^*(X)$, $\bar{\rho}_1$ the rank function of the truncation $(M_1)_k$ and $\bar{\rho}_2^*$ the rank function of the dual $(M_2)_k^*$ or

(2) For all $X \subseteq S$, $k \leq \rho_1(X) + \rho_2(S-X)$.

Proof. Condition (1) is immediate from the discussion of THE MATROID INTERSECTION PROBLEM 10.146 above together with THEOREM 10.149. To see the equivalence of conditions (1) and (2) we need the following fact relating the rank functions ρ and ρ^* of a matroid M of rank k on S and its dual M^*: For any $X \subseteq S$, $|X| - \rho^*(X) + \rho(S-X) = k$. The validity of this result in the representable case is very easy to see in terms of the joint representation (FIGURE 10.148). In the general case, the proof is also very easy (see Welsh, Chapter 2, Theorem 2). Given this fact we note that ρ_2, interpreted in terms of the discussion of THE MATROID INTERSECTION PROBLEM 10.146 is the rank function of the truncation $(M_2)_k$ which has rank k. Thus, the above identity becomes $|X| - \bar{\rho}_2^*(X) + \bar{\rho}_2(S-X) = k$, which, upon substitution into (1) gives $k \leqslant \bar{\rho}_1(X) + \bar{\rho}_2(S-X)$. This is not quite (2) but note that (2) is equivalent to $k \leqslant \min (k,\rho_1(X)) + \min (k,\rho_2(S-X))$. This gives the result as $\bar{\rho}_1(X) = \min (k,\rho_1(X))$ and $\bar{\rho}_2(X) = \min (k,\rho_2(S-X))$.

Condition (2) of THEOREM 10.147 is the one usually associated with this result under the name "Edmond's Intersection Theorem."

10.148 JOINT REPRESENTATION FOR RELATING RANKS IN M AND M*.

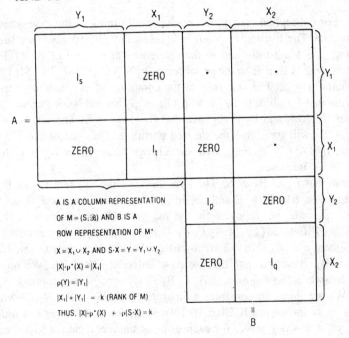

Figure 10.148

A is a column representation of $M = (S,\mathscr{B})$ and B is a row representation of M^*. Note the following:

$$X = X_1 \cup X_2 \text{ and } S - X = Y = Y_1 \cup Y_2.$$

$$|X| - \rho^*(X) = |X_1|$$

$$\rho(Y) = |Y_1|$$

$$|X_1| + |Y_1| = k \text{ (rank of M)}$$

Thus,

$$|X| - \rho^*(X) + \rho(S - X) = k.$$

It remains for us to establish the assertions of THE MATROID PARTITION-ING PROBLEM, 10.145. See FIGURE 10.150 in connection with the proof of THEOREM 10.149.

10.149 THEOREM.

Let $M_i = (S, \mathcal{B}_i)$, $i = 1, \ldots, p$ be matroids on a set S with rank functions ρ_i, $i = 1, \ldots, p$. The set S can be written as a disjoint union $E_1 \cup E_2 \cup \ldots \cup E_p$ of sets E_i where each E_i is independent in M_i if and only if for all subsets $X \subseteq S$, $|X| \leq \rho_1(X) + \rho_2(X) + \ldots + \rho_p(X)$.

Proof. For conceptual clarity, the reader should think of the case where M is representable. The method of proof is valid in the general case (see the paper by Greene and Magnanti cited in the references at the end of PART II). The proof for $p > 2$ is similar to the proof for $p = 2$ (EXERCISE 10.151(4)) so we shall assume $p = 2$. The necessity of the condition of the theorem is trivial so we assume that for all $X \subseteq S$, $|X| \leq \rho_1(X) + \rho_2(X)$ and show that we can find two bases $B_1 \in \mathcal{B}_1$ and $B_2 \in \mathcal{B}_2$ such that $B_1 \cup B_2 = S$. The sets $E_1 = B_1 - B_2$, $E_2 = B_2$ will then give the desired partition. The idea of the proof is to show that if $B_1 \cup B_2 \neq S$ then we can change either B_1 or B_2 in such a way that $|B_1 \cup B_2|$ increases.

Suppose that $B_1 \cup B_2 \neq S$. The hypothesis of the theorem forces $B_1 \cap B_2 \neq \phi$ (otherwise take $X = S$ and obtain a contradiction). Let $z \notin B_1 \cup B_2$ and let $A_z \cup \{z\} = C_z$ be the cycle (in the matroid M_1) containing z in $\{z\} \cup B_1$ (see EXERCISE 10.31(2)). If $A_z \cap B_1 \cap B_2$ is nonempty then exchange z for some element $u \in A_z \cap B_1 \cap B_2$ to change B_1 to $(B_1 - \{u\}) \cup \{z\}$. Call this new basis B_1 again and note that we have enlarged $|B_1 \cup B_2|$. We now show how to enlarge $|B_1 \cup B_2|$ even if $A_z \cap B_1 \cap B_2 = \phi$. Thus, suppose $A_z \subseteq B_1 - B_2$. We are going to construct a bipartite graph $G = (V_1, V_2, E)$ where $V_1 = V_2 = S$ as shown in FIGURE 10.150. First, for each $x \in A_z$ add a directed edge (x,y), $x \in V_1$, $y \in V_2$, for each y in the unique cycle (in M_2) formed by x with elements of B_2. Now look at each y that is the head of one of these edges (x,y). Add an edge (y,t), $y \in V_2$, $t \in V_1$ for each t on the cycle (in M_1) formed by y and elements of B_1. Repeat this process (going back and forth between $B_1 \subseteq V_1$ and $_2 \subseteq V_2$ until the *first time* a new edge added to G contains a vertex w of $B_1 \cap B_2$ (in either V_1 or V_2, see FIGURE 10.150(a)). We discuss why we must eventually produce such a vertex w of $B_1 \cap B_2$ below, so assume this for the moment. Call the resulting graph $G = (V_1, V_2, E)$. We thus have a directed path $x = a_1, b_1, b_2, \ldots, a_{q-1}, b_{q-1}, a_q = w$ joining $x \in A_z \subseteq V_1$ to $w \in B_1 \cap B_2$. We assume without loss of generality that $w \in V_1$. This path is of minimal length among all such paths joining x to w in G. We think of this path as describing a sequence of replacements to be made on the bases B_1 and B_2. First replace x in B_1 by z, then replace b_1 in B_2 by $x = a_1$. *The bases are now changed, but call them B_1 and B_2 again.* Now replace a_2 in B_1 by b_2 and b_2 in B_2 by a_2, etc., until finally w in b_1 is replaced by b_{q-1}. We leave it to the reader to verify that these substitutions can all be made (it is an immediate consequence of the minimality of the path from x to w). The net result is the following replacement:

$$B_1: = \left(B_1 - \bigcup_{i=1}^{q} \{a_i\} \right) \cup \{z\} \cup \bigcup_{i=1}^{q-1} \{b_i\}$$

$$B_2: = \left(B_2 - \bigcup_{i=1}^{q-1} \{b_i\} \right) \cup \bigcup_{i=1}^{q-1} \{a_i\}.$$

Hence $|B_1 \cup B_2|$ has been increased by one. Repeating this procedure eventually results in $B_1 \cup B_2 = S$.

It remains to be shown that the path $x = a_1, b_1, a_2, b_2, \ldots, w$ with $w \in B_1 \cap B_2$ exists. If it did not, the inductive procedure described above for constructing $G = (V_1, V_2, E)$ would reach a point where no new vertices can be added, at which point we stop and call the resulting graph $G = (V_1, V_2, E)$. Let $Y \subseteq B_1 - B_2 \subseteq V_1$ be the vertices of edges in E that belong to V_1 and let $Z \subseteq B_2 - B_1$ be the vertices of edges in E that belong to V_2. (See FIGURE 10.150(b).) Take $X = \{z\} \cup Y \cup Z$ and note that by construction $\{z\} \cup Y$ is in the span of Z (in M_2) and Z is in the span of Y (in M_1). Our hypothesis would then require that

$$1 + |Y| + |Z| = |X| \leq |Y| + |Z|,$$

a contradiction. Thus, prior to the point in our construction where no new vertices are added, we must encounter a vertex in $B_1 \cap B_2$ in either V_1 or V_2. This completes the proof.

10.150   IDEA OF THE MATROID PARTITIONING ALGORITHM, THEOREM 10.150.

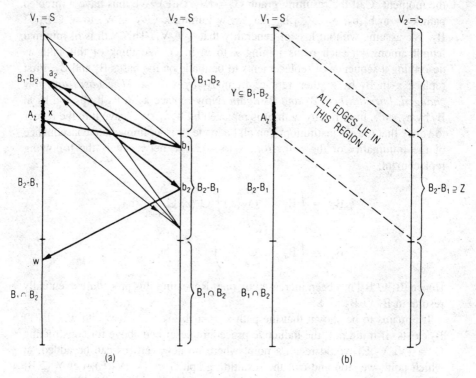

Figure 10.150

10.151   EXERCISE.

(1) Consider the following approach to the greedy algorithm: A is a representation matrix of a matroid $M = (S, \mathcal{B})$ with respect to the ordering $s_1, s_2, \ldots, s_n$ of S.

STEP 0   Set $k = 1$.

STEP 1   If column k of A is zero go to STEP 2. Otherwise, choose any nonzero entry in column k, say a_{ij} and, by using elementary *column* operations eliminate all other entries in row i.

STEP 2   If $k < n$ then let $k := k + 1$ and go to STEP 1. Else, STOP.

Prove that the nonzero columns of the resulting matrix, say $i_1, \ldots, i_r$, correspond to the principal independent set (in this case base) $\{s_{i_1}, \ldots, s_{i_r}\}$. In other words, if the matrix A were put into row canonical form then the principal columns would be columns $i_1, \ldots, i_r$. This algorithm, in contrast to the row canonical form algorithm, produces a matrix that no longer represents M.

(2) Let G = (V,E) be a connected graph rooted at v. Define $\mathcal{L}$ to be all sequences of edges $(e_1, e_2, \ldots, e_k)$, $1 \leq k \leq |V|$, with the property that for any t, $1 \leq t \leq k$, the set of edges $\{e_1, e_2, \ldots, e_t\}$ defines a subtree of G rooted at v. Prove that $\mathcal{L}$ is a greedoid. $\mathcal{L}$ is called the "branching greedoid" or "search greedoid" of the rooted graph G.

(3) What is the analog of "depth first search" for representable matroids? In particular what should correspond to the depth first sequence of edges for a graph, DFE(T), of DEFINITION 6.30? What should be the analog of the "lineal spanning tree" and "backedge graph" of *Procedure* 7.3 for representable matroids?

(4) Extend the proof of THEOREM 10.149 to p > 2. Describe an algorithm for partitioning M based on your proof in the case where M is representable.

REFERENCES

GRAPHS, TREES, AND RECURSION

The literature on graph theory, graph algorithms, and matroids is extensive. We shall begin by listing some books that will help the reader get an overall feeling for the subject. We then give references for each of the TOPICS. More important than any fixed listing of references is the knowledge of how to use the various data bases that summarize the state of knowledge in graph theory and matroid theory. We use the references for TOPIC IV: MATROIDS, to give an explanation of how these data bases are organized. We use the format of MATHEMATICAL REVIEWS and COMPUTER SCIENCE REVIEWS to instruct the reader in the use of these important sources of information.

The following books most closely fit our approach to graph theory:

Aho, A.O., Hopcroft, J.E., and Ullman, J.D., *The Design and Analysis of Computer Algorithms*, Addison-Wesley, Reading, Mass., 1974.

Baase, S., *Computer Algorithms: Introduction to Design and Analysis*, Addison-Wesley, Reading, Mass., 1978.

Even, S., *Graph Algorithms*, Computer Science Press, Rockville, Md., 1979.

Reingold, E., Nievergelt, J., and Deo, N., *Combinatorial Algorithms: Theory and Practice*, Prentice-Hall, Englewood Cliffs, N.J., 1977.

For general background in graph theory, the reader can consult the following:

Liu, C.L., *Introduction to Combinatorial Mathematics*, McGraw-Hill, New York, 1968.

Tucker, A., *Applied Combinatorics*, John Wiley, New York, 1980.

For a good selection of classical topics in graph theory and an extensive bibliography, see:

Behzad, M., Chartand, G., and Lesniak-Foster, L., *Graphs and Digraphs*, Wadsworth International Group, Belmont, Calif., 1979.

In addition to the books just listed, there are numerous other interesting books on various aspects of graph theory and matroid theory. The following is a sampling:

Behzad, M., and Chartrand, G., *Introduction to the Theory of Graphs*, Allyn and Bacon, Boston, 1971.

Bellman, R., Cooke, K., and Lockett, J., *Algorithms, Graphs and Computers*, Academic Press, New York, 1970.

Berge, C., *The Theory of Graphs and Its Applications*, John Wiley, New York, 1962.

Berge, C., and Ghouila-Hourie, A., *Programming, Games, and Transportation Networks*, John Wiley, New York, 1965.

Berge, C., *Graphs and Hypergraphs,* North-Holland, Amsterdam, 1973.

Berztiss, A., *Data Structures: Theory and Practice,* Academic Press, New York, 1971.

Biggs, N., *Algebraic Graph Theory*, Cambridge Univ. Press, New York, 1974.

Biggs, N., *Interaction Models*, London Math. Soc. Lecture Notes 30, Cambridge U. Press, 1976.

Biggs, N., Lloyd, E., and Wilson, R., *Graph Theory 1736–1936*, Clarendon Press, Oxford, 1976.

Bollabas, B., *Graph Theory: An Introductory Course*, Springer-Verlag, Berlin, 1971.

Bollabas, B., *Extremal Graph Theory*, Academic Press, New York, 1978.

Bondy, J., and Murty, U., *Graph Theory With Applications*, American Elsevier, New York, 1976.

Busacker, R., and Saaty, T., *Finite Graphs and Networks*, McGraw-Hill, New York, 1965.

Carre, B., *Graphs and Networks*, Clarendon Press, New York, 1979.

Chartrand, G., *Graphs as Mathematical Models*, Prindle, Weber, Schmidt, Boston, 1977.

Chen, W., *Applied Graph Theory: Graphs and Electrical Networks*, American Elsevier, New York, 1976.

Coppobianco, M., and Mulluzzo, J., *Examples and Counterexamples in Graph Theory*, North-Holland, Amsterdam, 1978.

Deo, N., *Graph Theory With Applications to Engineering and Computer Science*, Prentice-Hall, Englewood Cliffs, N.J., 1963.

Ford, L.R., Jr., and Fulkerson, D.R., *Flows in Networks*, Princeton Univ. Press, Princeton, 1962.

Fujii, J.N., *Puzzles and Graphs*, Washington National Conference of Teachers of Mathematics, Washington, D.C., 1966.

Garey, M.R., and Johnson, D.S., *Computers and Intractability, A Guide to the Theory of NP-Completeness*, Freeman, San Francisco, 1979.

Golumbic, M.C., *Algorithmic Graph Theory and Perfect Graphs*, Academic Press, New York, 1980.

Graver, J.E., and Watkins, M.E., *Combinatorics With Emphasis on the Theory of Graphs*, Springer-Verlag, Berlin, 1977.

Harary, F., *Graph Theory*, Addison-Wesley, Reading, Mass., 1969.

Harary, F., and Palmer, E., *Graphical Enumeration*, Academic Press, New York, 1973.

Lawler, E.L., *Combinatorial Optimization: Networks and Matroids*, Holt, Rinehart, and Winston, New York, 1976.

Maeda, W., *Graph Theory*, Wiley-Interscience, New York, 1972.

Marshall, C.W., *Applied Graph Theory*, Wiley-Interscience, New York, 1971.

Maxwell, L.M., and Reed, M.B., *The Theory of Graphs: A Basis for Network Theory*, Pergamon Press, New York, 1971.

Minieka, E., *Optimization Algorithms for Networks and Graphs*, Marcel Dekker, New York 1978.

Moon, J.W., *Topics on Tournaments*, Holt, Rinehart and Winston, New York, 1968.

Read, R.C., ed., *Graph Theory and Computing*, Academic Press, New York, 1972.

Ore, O., *Theory of Graphs*, American Mathematical Society, Providence, RI, 1962.

Ore, O., *Graphs and Their Uses*, Random House, New York, 1963.

Seshu, S., and Reed, M.B., *Linear Graphs and Electrical Networks*, Addison-Wesley, Reading, Mass., 1961.

Tutte, W.T., *Introduction to the Theory of Matroids*, American Elsevier, New York, 1971.

Welsh, D.J.A., *Matroid Theory*, Academic Press, New York, 1976.

Wilson, R., *Introduction to Graph Theory*, Academic Press, New York, 1972.

OPEN LITERATURE ARTICLES

Most of the topics covered in the BASIC CONCEPTS section are covered in more depth in the individual TOPICS sections to which references are given below. One exception is the material on inversion in trees. The following references relate to this subject:

André, D., *Sur les permutations alternées*, J. Math. Pures Appl. *7* (1881), 167–184.

Beissinger, J.S., *On external activity and inversions in trees*, J. Comb. Theory, Series B, *33* (1982), 87–92.

Gessel, I., and Wang, D.-L., Depth first search as a combinatorial correspondence, J. Combin. Theory, Series A, *26* (1979), 308–313.

Kreweras, G., *Une famille de polynomes ayant plusieurs propriétés énumératives*, Period. Math. Hungar. *11* (1980), 38–45.

Mallows, C.W., and Riordan, J., *The inversion enumerator for labelled trees*, Bull. Amer. Math. Soc., *74* (1968), 92–94.

Pansiot, J.-J., *Nombres d'Euler et inversions dans les arbres*, Europ. J. Combinatorics, *3* (1982), 259–262.

Tutte, W.T., *A contribution to the theory of chromatic polynomials* Canad. J. Math. *6* (1953), 80–91.

Viennot, G., *Quelques algorithmes de permutations*, Astérisque *38–39* (1976), (Soc. Math. de France), 275–293.

Viennot, G., *Une interprétation combinatoire des développements en série entiére des fonctions elliptiques de Jacobi,''* J. Combin. Theory, Series A, *29* (1980), 121–133.

TOPIC I: DEPTH FIRST SEARCH AND PLANARITY

The following references relate to the algorithmic aspects of planarity and obstructions to planarity:

Auslander, L., and Parter, S.V., *On imbedding graphs in the plane*, J. Math. Mech. *10* (1961), 517–523.

Chung, S.H., and Roe, P.H., *Algorithms for testing the planarity of a graph* in the Proceedings of the Thirteenth Midwest Symposium on Circuit Theory, University of Minnesota (Minneapolis, Minnesota, May 1970), VII.4.1–VII.4.12.

Cori, R., *Un code pour les graphes planaires*, Astérisque, 1975 (Soc. Math. de France) 169 pp.

Demoucron, G., Malgrange, Y., and Pertuiset, R., *Graphes planaires: reconnaissance et construction des représentations planaires topologiques*, Rev. Francaise Recherche Opérationelle *8* (1965), 34–47.

Deo, N., *Note on Hopcroft and Tarjan's planarity algorithm*, J. Assoc. Comp. Mach. *23* (1976), 74–75.

Goldstein, A.J., *An efficient and constructive algorithm for testing whether a graph can be embedded in a plane*, Graph and Combinatorics Conference, Contract no. NONR 1858–(21), Office of Naval Research Logistics Proj., Dept. of Math. (Princeton Univ., May 16–18, 1963). 2 pp.

Hopcroft, J., and Tarjan, R., *Efficient planarity testing*, J. Assoc. Comp. Mach., *21* (1974), 549–568.

Hopcroft, J., and Tarjan, R., "Isomorphism of planar graphs," in *Complexity of Computer Computations* (R.E. Miller and J.W. Thatcher, Editors) Plenum Press, New York, (1972).

Kuratowski, C., *Sur le probléme des corbes gauches en topologie*, Fund. Math. *15* (1930), 271–283.

LaPaugh, A.S., and Rivest, R.L., *The subgraph homeomorphism problem*, in Tenth Annual ACM Symposium on Theory of Computing (San Diego, May 1978) (ACM, 1978), pp. 40–50.

Lempel, A., Even, S., and Cederbaum, I., *An algorithm for planarity testing of graphs*, in International Symposium Theory of Graphs (P. Rosensteiehl, ed.) (Rome, July 1966) Gordon and Breach, New York, (1967), 215–232.

Mei, P., and Gibbs, N., *A planarity algorithm based on the Kuratowski theorem*, in Proc. AFIPS, 1970, SJCC, Vol. 36 (AFIPS Press, Montvale, New Jersey), 91–95.

Penaud, J.G., *Algorithmes de planarité*, Journées de Combinatoire et d'Informatique de Bordeaux, (Juin 1975), 279–304.

Riengold, E.M., Nievergelt, J., and Deo, N., *Combinatorial Algorithms*, Prentice-Hall, Englewood Cliffs, New Jersey, 1977, (Sect. 8.6. p. 364, and p. 399, Problem 51).

Rubin, F., *An improved algorithm for testing the planarity of a graph*, IEEE Trans. Comp., *C-24* (1975), 113–121.

Tarjan, R., *An efficient planarity algorithm*, STAN-CS-244-71, Comp. Sci. Dept., Stanford University, November 1971.

Tarjan, R., *Depth-first search and linear graph algorithms*, SIAM J. Comp. *1* (1972), 146–159.

Tarjan, R., *Complexity of combinatorial algorithms*, SIAM Rev. *20* (1978), 457–492.

Williamson, S.G., *Embedding graphs in the plane—Algorithmic aspects*, Annals of Discrete Math. *6* (1980), 349–384.

Williamson, S.G., *Finding a Kuratowski subgraph in linear time*, IRMA, Strasbourg, (Dept. de Math., University Louis Pasteur, 7 rue R. Descartes, 67084, Strasbourg), 89/P-47 (March 1980).

TOPIC III: TRICONNECTIVITY

The following references relate to our discussion of connectivity and, in particular, triconnectivity:

Even, S., and Tarjan, R., *Network flow and testing graph connectivity*, SIAM J. Comp. *4* (1975), 507–518.

Even, S., and Tarjan, R., *Algorithm for determining whether the connectivity of a graph is at least k*, SIAM J. Comp. *4* (1977), 393–396.

Fontet, M., *Test d'isomorphie de deux graphes planaires*, Journées de Combinatoire et d'Infórmatique de Bordeaux, (Juin 1975), 125–138.

Hopcroft, J., and Tarjan, R., *Isomorphism of planar graphs*, in Complexity of Computer Computations (R. Miller and J. Thatcher, eds.), Plenum Press, New York, 1972.

Hopcroft, J., and Tarjan, R., *Dividing a graph into triconnected components*, SIAM J. Comp. *2* (1973), 135–158.

MacLane, S., *A structural characterization of planar combinatorial graphs*, Duke Math. J. *3* (1937), 460–472.

Tarjan, R., *Depth-first search and linear graph algorithms*, SIAM J. Comp. *1* (1972), 146–159.

Tutte, W., *Connectivity in Graphs*, University of Toronto Press, 1966.

Vo, K.P., *Segment graphs, Depth-first cycle bases, 3-connectivity and planarity of graphs*, Linear and Multilinear Alg. *13* (1983), 119–141.

Vo, K.P., *Finding triconnected components of graphs*, Linear and Multilinear Alg. *13* (1983), 143–165.

TOPIC IV: MATROIDS

The general references for this TOPIC are the following three books mentioned at the beginning of our discussion of matroids:

Aigner, M., *Combinatorial Theory*, Springer-Verlag, Berlin, 1979.

Lawler, E., *Combinatorial Optimization, Networks and Matroids*, Holt, Rinehart and Winston, New York, 1976.

Welsh, D.J.A., *Matroid Theory*, Academic Press, New York, 1976.

The following are mentioned in the text and are directly related to our discussion:

Essam, J., *Graph Theory and Statistical Physics*, Discrete Math., *1* (1971), 83–112.

Greene, C., and Magnanti, T.L., *Some Abstract Pivot Algorithms*, SIAM J. Applied Math. *29*, no. 3 (1975), 530–539.

Minty, G., *On the axiomatic foundations of the theories of directed linear graphs, electrical networks and network programming*, Jour. Math. Mech., *15*, (1966), 485–520.

Shrijver, A., *Matroids and Linking Systems*, Math. Centrum, Amsterdam, 1978.

Tutte, W.T., *Introduction to the Theory of Matroids*, American Elsevier, New York, 1970.

Whitney, H., *2-isomorphic graphs*, Am. J. Math. *55* (1933), 245–254.

Woodall, D.R., *An exchange theorem for bases of matroids*, J. Comb. Theory (B), *16* (1974), 227–220.

On the topic of greedoids, we recommend the following:

Bjorner, A., "On matroids, groups and exchange languages," Matematiska Institutionen, Stockholms Universitet, Box 6701, 113 85 Stockholm, Sweden, 1983, No. 6.

Korte, B., and Lovasz, L., *Greedoids—a structural framework for the greedy algorithm*, (Proc. of the Silver Jubilee Conf. on Combinatorics, 1982), Academic Press, New York.

We now cover the additional references for matroids by acquainting the reader with the use of two on-line interactive databases—MATHFILE and INSPEC.

The reader will find that these databases are much more useful than any standard bibliography both for learning what has gone on in the past, and for keeping up with new developments.

The first thing the reader should do is to go to the library and become acquainted with *Mathematical Reviews, Electrical and Electronics Abstracts,* and *Computer and Control Abstracts.* The first is published by the American Mathematical Society (AMS) and the latter two are published by the Institution of Electrical Engineers (IEEE). Browse through these reviews. (Your reference librarian might help you to understand them. The reader will then appreciate the complexity of extracting selective information from such a massive amount of data. It is the purpose of MATHFILE and INSPEC to assist in this task).

MATHFILE is the computerized bibliographic database of the AMS corresponding to *Mathematical Reviews.* Your librarian can explain to you how one gains access to this database. The great advantage of such a computerized database is that it is "interactive." The user's interests are specified by a Boolean combination of searchable parameters (authors to be included or exluded, keywords of phrases to be included or excluded, etc.). The retrieval software then extracts from MATHFILE the number of entries that satisfy these conditions. The user decides if these items (citations of reviews in *Mathematical Reviews*) should be printed. If there are too many or too few such entries, the searchable parameters might first be changed to contract or enlarge the list. The ability to query MATHFILE in this interactive fashion greatly enhances the useability of *Mathematical Reviews.*

Another important use of MATHFILE is as an "alerting service" or "SDI (selective dissemination of information) service." To use MATHFILE in this manner, the user again constructs a profile of his or her interests using a Boolean combination of searchable parameters. This profile is then kept on record in the accessing software together with a notification interval specified by the user. The user is then notified on an ongoing basis of the appearance in *Mathematical Reviews* of items satisfying the specified conditions. At the present time, MATHFILE contains all the bibliographic information contained in all of the headings of entries in *Mathematical Reviews* since 1973. The reviews themselves are contained in the file after January 1980.

The organization and use of the database INSPEC is similar to that of MATHFILE. In the case of INSPEC, references correspond to *Physics Abstracts, Electrical and Electronics Abstracts,* and *Computer and Control Abstracts.*

We now give some selected references from *Mathematical Reviews, Electrical and Electronics Abstracts,* and *Computer and Control Abstracts.* The first collection of references is from *Mathematical Reviews.* Each citation has an identifying number. Prior to 1980 these numbers are of the form "58 #27507" and after 1979 they look like "82k:05002." The identifier "58 #27507" refers to the volume number 58 and review number 27507. The identifier "82k:05002" refers to volume 82k and review number 05002. In this latter numbering scheme, 82 gives the year of the volume in which the review appeared and 05 is a subject code (these are listed in each volume of the reviews).

The second collection of references has citations from either *Electrical and Electronics Abstracts* or *Computer and Control Abstracts*, or perhaps both. Identifying numbers are of the form "1008361 B8301164, C83005066." The first number is an INSPEC identifier. It is convenient to keep these numbers since more than one source of reviews is involved. The identifier B8301164 specifies that the review is from *Electrical and Electronics Abstracts* (this is specified by the "B"), dated 1983, with the specified review number. The second identifier has the same format but refers to the review from *Computer and Control Abstracts*.

SELECTED REFERENCES ON MATROIDS CLASSIFIED BY ISSUE
(*Mathematical Reviews*)

Issue No. 83f (June 1983)

Cunningham, William H.   83f:05015
  On matroid connectivity.
  J. Combin. Theory Ser. B 30 (1981), no. 1, 94–99.

Seymour, P.D.; Walton, P.N.   83f:05017
  Detecting matroid minors.
  J. London Math. Soc. (2) 23(1981), no. 2, 193–203.

Issue No. 83c (Mar 1983)

Recksi, A.   83c:05039
  An algorithm to determine whether the sum of some graphic matroids is graphic.
  Algebraic Methods in Graph Theory, Vol. 1, II (Szeged, 1978), pp. 647–656, Colloq. Math. Soc. Janos Bolyai, 25, North-Holland, Amsterdam, 1981.

Issue No. 83b (Feb 1983)

Jensen, P.M.   83b:05050
  Binary fundamental matroids.
  Algebraic Methods in Graph Theory, Vol. I, II (Szeged, 1978), pp. 281–296. Colloq. Math. Soc. Janos Bolyai, 25, North-Holland, Amsterdam, 1981.

Syslo, M.M.   83b:05085
  On some problems related to fundamental cycle sets of a graph.
  The Theory and Applications of Graphs (Kalamazoo, Mich., 1980), pp. 577–588, Wiley, New York, 1981.

Issue No. 82k (Nov 1982)

Algebraic methods in graph theory. Vol I, II   82k:05002

Papers from the Conference held in Szeged, August 24–31, 1978.
Edited by L. Lovasz and Vera T. Sos.
Colloquia Mathematica Societatis Janos Bolyai, 25.
North-Holland Publishing Co., Amsterdam-New York, 1981. 847 pp.

Perfect, Hazel   82k:05041
Independence theory and matroids.
Math. Gaz. 65 (1981), no. 432 103–111.

Vol. 82 Nos. e–f (May–June 1982)

Hausmann, D.; Korte, B.   82f:05025
Algorithmic versus axiomatic definitions of matroids.
Mathematical Programming at Oberwolfach (Proc. Conf., Math. Forschunginstitut,
Oberwolfach, 1979).
Math. Programming Stud. No. 14 (1981), 98–111.

Oxley, James
On connectivity in matroids and graphs.
Trans. Amer. Math. Soc. 265 (1981), no. 1, 47–58.

Vol. 82 Nos. a–b (Jan–Feb 1982)

Gabow, Harold N.; Tarjan, Robert E.   82b: 68056
Efficient algorithms for simple matroid intersection problems.
20th Annual Symposium on Foundations of Computer Science (San Juan, Puerto
Rico, 1970) pp. 196–204, IEEE, New York, 1979.

Lawrence, Jim; Weinberg, Louis   82a:05040
Unions of oriented matroids.
Combinatorics 79 (Proc. Colloq., Univ. Montréal, Montreal, Que., 1979), Part I.
Ann. Discrete Math. 8 (1980), 29–34.

Seymour, P.D.   82a:05041
On Tutte's characterization of graphic matroids.
Combinatorics 79 (Proc. Colloq., Univ. Montréal, Montreal, Que., 1979), Part I.
Ann. Discrete Math. 8 (1980), 83–90.

Vol. 81 Nos. k–m (Nov–Dec 1981)

Inukai, Thomas; Weinberg, Louis   81m:05056
Second International Conference on Combinatorial Mathematics (New York, 1978)
pp. 289–305, Ann. New York Acad. Sci., 319, New York Acad. Sci., New York,
1979.

Vol. 81 Nos. g–h (July–Aug 1981)

Dawson, Jeremy E.   81g:05041
A note on some algorithms for matroids.
J. Math. Anal. Appl. 75 (1980), no. 2, 611–615.

Vol. 81 Nos. e–f (May–June 1981)

Kelmans, A.K.   81f:05056
Concept of a vertex in a matroid and 3-connected graphs.
J. Graph Theory 4 (1980), no. 1, 13–19.

Bixby, Robert E.; Cunningham, William H.   81e:05053
Matroids, graphs, and 3-connectivity.
Graph Theory and Related Topics (Proc. Conf., Univ. Waterloo, Waterloo, Ont., 1977), pp. 91–103, Academic Press, New York, 1979.

Vol. 81 Nos. a–b (Jan–Feb 1981)

Matthews, Laurence   81a:05030
Properties of bicircular matroids (French summary).
Problèmes Combinatoires et Theorie Des Graphes (Colloq. Internat. CNRS, Univ. Orsay, Orsay, 1976), pp. 289–190, Colloques Internat. CNRS, 260, CNRS, Paris, 1978.

Földes, S.; Hammer, P.L.   80c:05110
On a class of matroid-producing graphs.
Combinatorics (Proc. Fifth Hungarian Colloq., Keszthely, 1976), Vol. I, pp. 331–352, Colloq. Math. Soc. Jànos Bolyai, 18, North-Holland, Amsterdam, 1978.

Recski, A.   80c:94018
Contributions to the n-port interconnection problem by means of matroids.
Combinatorics (Proc. Fifth Hungarian Colloq., Keszthely, 1976), Vol. II, pp. 877–892, Colloq. Math. Soc. Jànos Bolyai, 18, North-Holland, Amsterdam, 1978.

Gyori, E.; Milne, E.C.   80b:05019
A theorem of the transversal theory for matroids of finite character.
Discrete Math. 23 (1978), no. 3, 235–240.

Ingleton, A.W.   80b:05020
Transversal matroids and related structures.
Higher Combinatorics (Proc. NATO Advanced Study Inst., Berlin, 1976), pp. 117–131, NATO Adv. Study Inst. Ser., Ser. C: Math. and Phys. Sci., 31, Reidel, Dordrecht, 1977.

Recski, A.   80b:94051
Matroidal structure of n-ports.
Combinatorics (Proc. Fifth Hungarian Colloq., Keszthely, 1976), Vol. II, pp. 893–909, Colloq. Math. Soc. Jànos Bolyai, 18, North-Holland, Amsterdam, 1978.

Matthews, Laurence   80a:05103
Matroids on the edge sets of directed graphs.

Optimization and Operations Research (Proc. Workshop, Univ. Bonn, Bonn, 1977), pp. 193–199, Lecture Notes in Econom. and Math. Systems, 157, Springer, Berlin, 1978.

Andreae, Thomas   80a:05160
Matroidal families of finite connected nonhomeomorphic graphs exist.
J. Graph Theory 2 (1978), no. 2, 149–153.

Vol. 58 Part 6 (Dec 1979)

Higher Combinatorics   58 #27507
Proceedings of the NATO Advanced Study Institute Held in Berlin, September 1–10, 1976.
Edited by Martin Aigner.
NATO Advanced Study Institute Series. Ser. C: Mathematical and Physical Sciences, 31.
D. Reidel Publishing Co., Dordrecht-Boston, Mass. 1977. xiii + 256 pp. $24.00.
ISBN 90-277-0795-2.

Contains a chapter on matroids.

Brylawski, Tom   58 #27566
Connected matroids with the smallest Whitney numbers.
Discrete Math. 18 (1977), no. 3, 243–252.

Krogdahl, Stein   58 #27568
The dependence graph for bases in matroids.
Discrete Math. 19 (1977), no. 1, 47–59.

Vol. 58 Part 5 (Nov 1979)

Bixby, Robert E.   58 #21721
A simple proof that every matroid is an intersection of fundamental transversal matroids.
Discrete Math. 18 (1977), no. 3, 311–312.

Bixby, Robert E.   58#21722
Kuratowski's and Wagner's theorems for matroids.
J. Combinatorial Theory Ser. B 22 (1977), no. 1, 31–53.

Bruter, C.   58 #21723
Sur différents problèmes posés en theorie des matrolïdes.
Publ. Inst. Statist. Univ. Paris 18 (1969), no. 3, Exp. no. 1, 1–96.

Matthews, Laurence R.   58 #21732
Bicircular matroids.
Quart. J. Math. Oxford Ser. (2) 28 (1977), no. 110, 213–227.

Vol. 58 Part 4 (Oct 1979)

Matthews, Laurence R.; Oxley, James G.   58 #16348
Infinite graphs and bicircular matroids.
Discrete Math. 19 (1977), no. 1, 61–65.

Vol. 58 Part 2 (Aug 1979)

Cunningham, W.H.   58 #5295
Chords and disjoint paths in matroids.
Discrete Math. 19 (1977), no. 1, 7–15.

Vol. 58 Part 1 (July 1979)

Minieka, Edward   58 #311
Finding the circuits of a matroid.
J. Res. Nat. Bur. Standards Sect. B 80B (1976), no. 3, 337–342.

Donald, J.D.,; Holzmann, C.A.; Tobey, M.D.   58 #377
A characterization of complete matroid base graphs.
J. Combinatorial Theory Ser. B 22 (1977), no. 2, 139–158.

Vol. 57 Part 1 (Jan–Mar 1979)

Seymour, P.D.   57 #2960
The matroids with the max-flow min-cut property.
J. Combinatorial Theory Ser. B 23 (1977), no. 2–3, 189–222.

Aigner, Martin   57 #123
Kombinatorik. II.
Matroide und Transverltheorie.
Hochschultext.
Springer-Verlag, Berlin-New York, 1976. xviii + 32 pp. DM 34.00; $14.00.

Vol. 56 Part 1 (July–Sept 1978)

Tomizawa, Nobuaki   56 #5337
Strongly irreducible matroids and principal partition of a matroid in strongly irred-
ucible minors.
Electron. Commun. Japan 59 (1976), no. 2, 1–10.

Las Vergnas, M.   56 #5365
Degree-constrained subgraphs and matroid theory.
Infinite and finite sets (Colloq., Keszthely, 1973; Dedicated to P. Erdős on his 60th
birthday), Vol. III, pp. 1473–1502. Colloq. Math. Soc. János Bolyai, Vol. 10,
North-Holland, Amsterdam, 1975.

Murty, U.S.R.   56 #2851
Extremal matroids with forbidden restrictions and minors (Synopsis).
Proceedings of the Seventh Southeastern Conference on Combinatorics, Graph Theory,
and Computing (Louisiana State Univ., Baton Rouge, La., 1976), pp. 463–468.
Congressus Numerantium, no. XVII, Utilitas Math., Winnipeg, Man., 1976.

Szamkolowicz, Lucjan   56 #166
    On problems of the elementary theory of graphical matroids.
    Recent Advances in Graph Theory (Proc. Second Czechoslovak Sympos., Prague,
    1974), pp. 501–505. Academia, Prague, 1975.

Vol. 55 Part 2 (Apr–June 1978)

Seymour, P.D.   55 #12549
    A note on the production of matroid minors.
    J. Combinatorial Theory Ser. B 22 (1977), no. 3, 289–295.

Mauer, Stephen B.   55 #10296
    Intervals in matroid basis graphs.

    The basis graph of a matroid M is a graph whose vertices are the bases of M, with
    two vertices connected by an edge if each can be obtained fom the other by exchanging
    a single element.

Yamamoto, Yoshitsugu   55 #10298
    An algorithm for finding a common basis of two matroids.
    Keio Engrg. Rep. 29 (1976), no. 4, 41–51.
    An algorithm is presented for finding a common basis for two matroids, when such
    a basis exists. The algorithm presented is a modification of Edmond's intersection
    algorithm, which solves a more general class of problems.

Vol. 55 Part 1 (Jan–Mar 1978)

Wilde, P.J.   55 #5470
    Matroids with given restrictions and contractions.
    J. Combinatorial Theory Ser. B 22 (1977), no. 2, 122–130.

Seymour, P.D.   55 #2622
    A forbidden minor characterization of matroid ports.
    Quart. J. Math. Oxford Ser. (2) 27 (1976), no. 108, 407–413.

Vol. 54 Part 2 (Oct–Dec 1977)

Murty, U.S.R.   54 #10053
    On the number of bases of a matroid.
    Proc. Second Louisiana Conf. on Combinatorics, Graph Theory, and Computing
    (Louisiana State Univ., Baton Rouge, La., 1971), pp. 387–410. Louisiana State
    Univ., Baton Rouge, La., 1971.

Milnor, E.C.   54 #7270
    Transversal theory.

Proceedings of the International Congress of Mathematicians (Vancouver, B.C., 1974), Vol. 1, pp. 155–169. Canad. Math. Congress, Montreal, Que., 1975.

In this expository paper the author describes the most important results in the field now known as transversal theory. In addition to the standard results relating to Hall's marriage theorem and its consequences, he includes a discussion on various infinite extensions of Hall's theorem, and on the use of pre-independence structures (matroids). This article concludes with an extensive bibliography.

Richardson, W.R.H.   54 #7296
Decomposition of chain-groups and binary matroids.
Proceedings of the Fourth Southeastern Conference on Combinatorics, Graph Theory, and Computing (Florida Atlantic Univ., Boca Raton, Fla., 1973), pp. 463–476. Utilitas Math., Winnipeg, Man., 1973.

Las Vergnas, Michel   54 #7295
Extensions normales d'une matroïde, polynôme de Tutte d'un morphisme. (English summary).
C.R. Acad. Sci. Paris Ser. A-B 280 (1975), no. 22, Ai, A1479–A1482.

Author's summary: "This note is concerned with the study of extensions of matroids, the normal extension. A normal extension is characterized within a given matroid by a bundle of flats. An expression of the rank function is obtained in a particular case. Tutte polynomials are considered for morphisms."

Simões-Pereira, J.M.S.   54 #7298
On matroids on edge sets of graphs with connected subgraphs as circuits. II.
Discrete Math. 12 (1975), 55–78.
(Part I has been reviewed [Proc. Amer. Math. Soc. 38 (1973), 503–506; MR 47 #3214]).

Todd, Micheal J.   54 #7299
Characterizing binary simplicial matroids.
Discrete Math. 16 (1976), no. 1, 61–70.

A binary simplicial matroid is a matroid whose circuits are combinatorial generalizations of simple polytopes. The author gives necessary and sufficient conditions for a matroid to be isomorphic to such a binary simplicial matroid.

Vol. 54 Part 1 (July-Sept 1977)

Las Vergnas, Michel   54 #5018
On certain constructions for matroids.
Proceedings of the Fifth British Combinatorial Conference (Univ. Aberdeen, Aberdeen, 1975), pp. 395–404. Congressus Numerantium, No. XV, Utilitas Math., Winnipeg, Man., 1976.

Constructions are with respect to geometric lattices.

Brualdi, R.A.   54 #115
Matroids induced by directed graphs, a survey.
Recent Advances in Graph Theory (Proc. Second Czechoslovak Sympos. Prague, 1974), pp. 115–134. Academia, Prague, 1975.

Vol. 53 Part 2 (Apr-June 1977)

Bruter, C.P.   53 #13002
Les matroïdes. Nouvel outil mathématique.
Initiation aux Nouveautés de la Science, 21. Dunod. Paris 1970. xii + 192 pp.

Recski, András   53 #13004
On the sum of matroids. II.
Proceedings of the Fifth British Combinatorial Conference (Univ. Aberdeen, Aberdeen, 1975), pp. 515–520. Congressus Numerantium, No. XV, Utilitas Math., Winnipeg, Man., 1976.
Part I [Acta. Math. Acad. Sci. Hungar. 24 (1973), 329–333; MR 48 #3772].

Brualdi, Richard A.   53 #10589
Transversal theory and graphs.
Studies in graph theory, Part I, pp. 23–88. Studies in Math, Vol. 11, Math. Assoc. Amer., Washington D.C., 1975.

Bixby, Robert E.   53 #10622
A strengthened form of Tutte's characterization of regular matroids.
J. Combinatorial Theory Ser. B 20 (1976), no. 3, 216–221.

Vol. 52 Part 3 (Nov–Dec 1976)

Ingleton, A.W.   52 #13442
Non-base-orderable matroids.
Proceedings of the Fifth British Combinatorial Conference (Univ. Aberdeen, Aberdeen, 1975), pp. 355–359. Congressus Numerantium, no. XV, Utilitas Math., Winnipeg, Man., 1976.

Dinolt, George W.   52 #10457
An extremal problem for non-separable matroids.
Théorie des matroïdes (Recontre Franco-Britannique, Brest, 1970), pp. 31–49. Lecture Notes in Math., Vol. 211, Springer, Berlin, 1971.

Holzmann, C.A.; Norton, P.G.; Tobey, M.D.   52 #10458
A graphical representation of matroids.
SIAM J. Appl. Math. 25 (1973), 618–627.

Hull, Bradley   52 #10459
Two algorithms for matroids.
Discrete Math. 13 (1975), no. 2, 121–128.
Closure and cocircuits.

von Randow, Rabe   52 #10460
Introduction to the theory matroids.
Lecture Notes in Economics and Mathematical Systems, Vol. 109.
Springer-Verlag, Berlin-New York, 1975. ix + 102 pp. DM 18.00; $7.80.

Woodall, D.R.   52 #10462
An exchange theorem for bases of matroids.
J. Combinatorial Theory Ser. B 16 (1974), 227–228.

SELECTED REFERENCES ON MATROIDS
(*Electrical and Electronics Abstracts* (B)
and Computer and Control Abstracts (C))

1069603   C83022907
On decomposition theory: Duality
Naylor, A.W.
Industrial Tech. Inst., Ann Arbor, MI, USA
IEEE Trans. Syst. Man and Cybern. (USA) Vol. SMC-13, no. 2, 215–21, March–April 1983. Coden: ISYMAW. ISSN: 0018-9472
U.S. Copyright Clearance Center Code: 0018-9472/83/0300-02—15$01.00

1057085   B83029075, C83019769
The lattice of convex sets of an oriented matroid
Edelman, P.H.
Dept. of Math., Univ. of Pennsylvania, Philadelphia, PA, USA
J. Comb. Theory, Ser. B (USA), Vol. 33, no. 3, 239–44, Dec. 1982. Coden: JCTHAR. ISSN: 0095-8956
U.S. Copyright Clearance Center Code: 0095-8956/82/060239—06$02.00/0

1055423   C83020815
Connectivity and edge-disjoint spanning trees
Gusfield, D.
Dept. of Computer Sci., Yale Univ., New Haven, CT, USA
Inf. Process. Lett. (Netherlands), Vol. 16, no. 2, 87–9, 26 Feb 1983. Coden: IFPLAT. ISSN: 0020-0190
U.S. Copyright Clearance Center Code: 0020-0190/83/0000-00-00/$03.00

1040804   B83022868
Integral decomposition in polyhedra
McDiarmid, C.
Wolfson Coll., Oxford, England
Math. Program (Netherlands), Vol. 25, no. 2, 1883–98, Feb. 1983. Coden: MHPGA4. ISSN: 0025-5610

1008361   B83011647, C83007588
Determining minimal cuts with a minimal number of arcs
Hamacher, H.
Univ. of Florida, Gainesville, FL, USA
Networks (USA), Vol. 12, no. 4, 493–504, Winter 1982. Coden: NTWKAA. ISSN: 0028-3045
U.S. Copyright Clearance Center Code: 0028-3045/82/040493—12$02.20

992527   B83006240, C83005066
Decomposition of group flows in regular matroids
Hamacher, H.
Dept. of Math., Univ. of Koln, Koln, Germany
Computing (Austria), Vol. 29, no. 2, 113–33, 1982. Coden: CMPTA2. ISSN: 0010-485X
U.S. Copyright Clearance Center Code: 0010-485X/82/0029/01-13/$04.20

992453   B83006165, C83003739
Packing subgraphs in a graph
Cornuejols, G.; Hartvigsen, D.; Pulleyblank, W.
Core. Louvain-La-Neuve, Belgium Oper. Res. Lett. (Netherlands), Vol. 1, no. 4, 139–
43, Sept. 1982. Coden: ORLED5. ISSN: 0167-6377
U.S. Copyright Clearance Center Code: 0167-6377/82/0000-00-00/$02.75

939461   B82050686, C82036727
Closure in independence systems
Matthews, L.
British Railways Board, London, England
Math. Oper. Res. (USA), Vol. 7, no. 2, 159–71, May 1982. Coden:
MOREDQ

939428   B82050653, C82036692
*A sufficient condition for any two matroidally isomorphic graphs with the same edge
set to have a common tree*
Shinoda, S.; Wai-Kai Chen; Kuwahara, T.
Dept. of Electrical Engng., Chuo Univ., Tokyo, Japan
Sponsor: IEEE
1982 International Symposium on Circuits and Systems, 601-4, Vol. 2, 1982, 10–12
May 1982, Rome, Italy
Publ.: IEEE, New York, USA
3 vol. 1258 pp.

922099   B82045114, C82032760
Admissible transformations and their application to matching problems
Burkhard, R.E.; Derigs, U.
Math. Inst., Univ. Zu Koln, Koln, Germany
Hansen, P. (Editors)
Studies on Graphs and Discrete Programming, 23–38, 1981
Publ.: North-Holland, Amsterdam, Netherlands. ISBN 0 444 86216 1

922069   B82045084   C82032727
Principal partition in 2-parity problems
Kajitani, Y.; Ueno, S.
Dept. of Electrical and Electronic Engng., Tokyo Inst. of Technol., Ookayama, Me-
guro-Ku, Tokyo, Japan
Sponsor: IEEE
1982 International Symposium on Circuits and Systems, 150-3, Vol. 1, 1982, 10–12
May 1982, Rome, Italy
Publ.: IEEE, New York, USA
3 vol., 1258 pp.

922064   B82045079   C82032722
Combinatorial optimization: algorithms and complexity
Papadimitriou, C.H.; Steiglitz, K.
1982
Publ.: Prentice-Hall, Englewood Cliffs, NJ, USA
XVI + 496 pp. ISBN 0 13 152462 3

921992   B82045007   C82032637
A weighted matroid intersection algorithm
Frank, A.
Res. Inst. for Telecommunication, Budapest, Hungary
J. Algorithms (USA), Vol. 2, no. 4, 328–36, Dec. 1981. Coden: JOALDV

905832   B82039870   C82028982
Leontief substitution systems and matroid complexes
Provan, J.S.; Billera, L.J.
State Univ. of New York, Stony Brook, NY, USA
Math. Oper. Res. (USA), Vol. 7, no. 1, 81–7, Feb. 1981. Coden: MOREDQ

905816   B82039854   C82028966
Alpha-balanced graphs and matrices and GF(3)-representability of matroids
Truemper, K.
Univ. of Texas, Dallas, TX, USA
J. Comb. Theory, Ser. B (USA), Vol. 32, no. 2, 112–39, April 1982. Coden: JCTHAR

905799   B82039836   C82028949
The independent sets of rank K of a matroid
Purdy, G.
Math. Dept., Texas A and M Univ., College Station, TX, USA
Discrete Math. (Netherlands), Vol. 38, no. 1, 87–91, Jan. 1982. Coden: DSMHA4

891122   B82038760
Power system topological observability using a direct graph-theoretic approach
Quintana, V.H.; Simoes-Costa, A.; Mandel, A.
Dept. of Electrical Engng., Univ. of Waterloo, Waterloo, Ontario, Canada
IEEE Trans. Power Appar. and Syst. (USA), Vol. Pas-101, no. 3, 617–26.

873131   B82028794   C82020558
Probabilistic analysis of the performance of greedy strategies over different classes of combinatorial problems
Ausiello, G.; Protasi, M.
Instituto di Automatica, Univc. di Roma, Italy
Gecseg, F. (Editors)
Fundamentals of Computation Theory, Proceedings of the 1981 International FCT-Conference, 24–33, 1981
24–28 Aug. 1981, Szeged, Hungary
Publ.: Springer-Verlag, Berlin, Germany
X + 471 pp. ISBN 3 540 108544 8

873038   B82028700   C82020446
Signed graphs
Zaslavsky, T.
Ohio State Univ., Columbus, OH, USA
Discrete Appl. Math. (Netherlands), Vol. 4, no. 1, 47–74, Jan. 1982. Coden: DAMADU

856966   B82024172   C82017226
On characterizations of binary and graphic matroids

Doignon, J.-P.
Univ. Libre de Bruxelles, Bruxelles, Belgium
Discrete Math. (Netherlands), Vol. 37, no. 21-3, 299–301, Dec. 1981. Coden: DSMHA4

856954   B82024160   C82017214
Matroids and multicommodity flows
Seymour, P.D.
Merton Coll., Univ. of Oxford, Oxford, England
Eur. J. Comb. (GB), Vol. 2, no. 3, 257–90, Sept. 1981. Coden: EJOCDI

856944   B82024150   C82017204
A necessary and sufficient condition of embeddability for semimodular lattices
Percsy, N.
Dept. de Math., Univ. de L'Etat a mons, Mons, Belgium
Eur. J. Comb. (GB), Vol. 2, no. 2, 173–7, June 1981. Coden: EJOCDI

856940   B82024146   C82017200
A constructive approach to the critical problem for matroids
Jaeger, F.
Lab. Imag. Grenoble, France
Eur. J. Comb. (GB), Vol. 2, no. 2, 137–44, June 1981. Coden: EJOCDI

841947   B82019198   C82013612
Hamiltonicity and combinatorial polyhedra
Naddef, D.; Pulleyblank, W.R.
Lab. d'Informatique et de Math. Appl. de Grenoble, Grenoble, France
J. Comb. Theory, Ser. B (USA), Vol. 31, no. 3, 297–312, Dec. 1981. Coden: JCTHAR

841921   B82019172   C82013571
The ellipsoid method and its consequences in combinatorial optimization
Grotschel, M.; Lovasz, L.; Schrijver, A.
Inst. für Okonometrie und Operations Res., Univ. Bonn, Bonn, Germany
Combinatorica (Netherlands), Vol. 1, no. 2, 169–97, 1981. Coden: COMBDI

841911   B82019162   C82013561
On matroids and Sperner's lemma
Lindstrom, B.
Dept. of Math., Univ. of Stockholm, Stockholm, Sweden
Eur. J. Comb. (GB), Vol. 2, no. 1, 65–6, March 1981. Coden: EJOCDI

841910   B82019161   C82013560
Matroids on the bases of simple matroids
Lindstrom, B.
Dept. of Math., Univ. of Stockholm, Stockholm, Sweden
Eur. J. Comb. (GB), Vol. 2, no. 1, 61–3, March 1981. Coden: EJOCDI

810603   B82008594   C82005736
On products of matroids
Las Vergnas, M.
Univ. of Pierre et Marie Curie, Paris, France
Discrete Math. (Netherlands), Vol. 36, no. 1, 49–55, Aug. 1981. Coden: DSMHA4

810598   B82008589   C82005721
Incidence matrices of subsets—a rank formula
Linial, N.; Rothschild, B.L.
Dept. of Math., Univ. of California, Los Angeles, CA, USA
SIAM J. Algebraic and Discrete Methods (USA), Vol. 2, no. 3, 333–40, Sept. 1981.
Coden: SJAMOU

798067   B82004838   C82003046
Whitney connectivity of matroids
Inukai, T.; Weinberg, L.
Comsat Labs., Clarksburg, MD, USA
SIAM J. Algebraic and Discrete Methods (USA), Vol. 2, no. 2, 108–20, June 1981.
Coden: SJAMOU

786187   B82000331   C82000226
A characterization of binary geometries by a double elimination axiom
Fournier, J.-C
Univ. de Paris VI, Montgeron, France
J. Comb. Theory, Ser. B (USA), Vol. 31, no. 2, 249–50, Oct. 1981. Coden: JCTHAR

773756   B81050207   C81034345
On Tutte's extension of the four-colour problem
Seymour, P.D.
Merton Coll., Oxford, England
J. Comb. Theory, Ser. B (USA), Vol. 31, no. 1, 82–94, Aug. 1981. Coden: JCTHAR

773589   B81050076   C81034177
Amalgamation of matroids and its applications
Nesetril, J.; Poljak, S.; Turzik, D.
Kzaa Mff Ku, Charles Univ., Praha, Czechoslovakia
J. Comb. Theory, Ser. B (USA), Vol. 31, no. 1, 9–22, Aug. 1981. Coden: JCTHAR

761581   C81031458
Vth Symposium on Operations Research
Methods Oper. Res. (Germany), Vol. 40, 1981. Coden: MEORDE
Vth Symposium on Operations Research, 25–27 Aug. 1980, Cologne, Germany

761275   B81044923   C81031146
A class of matroids derived from saturated chain partitions of partially ordered sets
Denig, W.A.
Dept. of Math., The Citadel, Charleston, SC, USA
J. Comb. Theory, Ser. B (USA), Vol. 30, no. 3, 302–17, June 1981. Coden: JCTHAR

761254   C81031125
Hyperplane reconstruction of the Tutte polynomial of a geometric lattice
Brylawski, T.H.
Dept. of Math., Univ. of North Carolina, Chapel Hill, NC, USA
Discrete Math. (Netherlands), Vol. 35, 25–38, July 1981. Coden: DSMHA4

761234   C81031100
On a classification of independence systems
Euler, R.

Math. Inst., Univ. Koln, Koln, Germany
Methods Oper. Res. (Germany), Vol. 40, 299–302, 1981. Coden: MEORDE
Vth Symposium on Operations Research, 25–27 August, 1980, Cologne, Germany

757395 B81044998 C81027957
Mathematische Optimierung (Mathematical Optimization)
Math. Program. Stud. (Netherlands), no. 14, Jan. 1981. Coden: MPSTDF
Mathematische Optimierung (Mathematics Optimization), 6–12, May 1979, Ober-
wolfach, Germany

745226 A81079926 B81039603 C81027936
An elementary approach to the principal partition of a matroid
Narayanan, H.; Vartak, M.N.
Dept. of Electrical Engng., Indian Inst. of Technol., Bombay, India
Trans. Inst. Electron. and Commun. Eng., Jpn., Sect. E (Japan), Vol. E64, no. 4,
227–34, April 1981. Coden: TIEEDU

745193 C81027903
A quantifier for matroid duality
McKee, T.A.
Dept. of Math., Wright State Univ., Dayton, OH USA
Discrete Math. (Netherlands), Vol. 34, no. 3, 315–18, June 1981. Coden: DSMHA4

738455 B81039574 C81024783
Recognizing graphic matroids
Seymour, P.D.
Merton Coll., Oxford, England
Combinatorica (Netherlands), Vol. 1, no. 1, 75–8, 1981.

738451 B81039570 C81024779
On matroid intersections
Groflin, H.; Hoffman, A.J.
IBM T.J. Watson Res. Center, Yorktown Heights, NY, USA
Combinatorica (Netherlands), Vol. 1, no. 1, 43–7, 1981.

731951 C81025206
Minimal cost flows in regular matroids
Burkhard, R.E.; Hamacher, H.
Univ. of Cologne, Cologne, Germany
Math. Program. Stud. (Netherlands), No. 14, 32–47, Jan. 1981. Coden: MPSTDF
Mathematische Optimierung (Mathematical Optimization), 6–12 May 1979, Ober-
wolfach, Germany

731642 B81035821 C81024847
Directed trees and bases
Shinoda, S.; Kajitani, Y.; Wai-Kai Chen
Faculty of Sci. and Engng., Chuo Univ., Tokyo, Japan
Sponsor: Naval Postgraduate School; Univ. Santa Clara; IEEE Conference Record of
the Fourteenth Asilomar Conference on Circuits, Systems and Computers, 173–7,
1980, 17–19 Nov. 1980, Pacific Grove, CA, USA
Publ.: IEEE, New York, USA
VIII + 520 pp.

731619   C81024822
Intersection theory for graphs
Brylawski, T.
Dept. of Math., Univ. of North Carolina, Chapel Hill, NC, USA
J. Comb. Theory, Ser. B (USA), Vol. 30, no. 2, 233–46, April 1981. Coden: JCTHAR

706113   B81027012   C81018762
Some properties of perfect matroid designs
Deza, M.; Singhi, N.M.
CNRS, Paris, France
Srivastava, J. (editor)
Sponsor: US Air Force Office of Sci. Res.; Office Naval Res.
Combinatorial Mathematics, Optimal Designs and Their Applications, A Symposium,
57–76, 1980, 5–9 June 1978, Fort Collins, CO, USA
Publ.: North-Holland, Amsterdam, Netherlands
VIII + 391 pp.   ISBN 0 444 86048 7

706077   C81018726
On a generalization of linear independence in finite-dimensional vector spaces
Feinberg, M.
Dept. of Chem. Engng., Univ. of Rochester, Rochester, NY, USA
J. Comb. Theory, Ser. B (USA), Vol. 30, no. 1, 61–9, Feb. 1981. Coden: JCTHAR

706057   C81018706
On a classification of independence systems
Euler, R.
Math. Inst., Univ. Zu Koln, Koln, Germany
Discrete Appl. Math. (Netherlands), Vol. 2, no. 4, 357–90, Dec. 1980. Coden: DA-MADU

706033   C81018682
Local complementation and interlacement graphs
de Fraysseix, H.
Lab. de Phys. Math., Coll. de France, Paris, France
Discrete Math., (Netherlands), Vol. 33, no. 1, 29–35, Jan. 1981. Coden: DSMHA4

692574   C81016068
Combinatorics 79. Proceedings of the Joint Canada-France Combinatorial Colloquium
Deza, M.; Rosenberg, I.G. (Editors)
Combinatorics 79. Proceedings of the Joint Canada-France, Combinatorial Colloquium,
1980
Combinatorics 79. Proceedings of the Joint Canada-France Combinatorial Colloquium,
11–16 June 1979, Montreal, Que., Canada
Publ.: North-Holland, Amsterdam, Netherlands
2 vols. (XXII + 309 + VII + 309), pp.   ISBN 0 444 86112 2

692520   C81016013
An algorithmic approach to algebraic flows in regular matroids
Hamacher, H.
Univ. of Koln, Koln, Germany
Methods Oper. Res. (Germany), no. 37, 277–80, 1980. Coden: MEORDE
IV Symposium on Operations Research, 10–12 Sept., 1979, Saarbrucken, Germany

678979 B81018733 C81013294
Use of matroid theory in operations research, circuits and systems theory
Iri, M.; Fujishige, S.
Faculty of Engng., Univ. of Tokyo, Bunkyo-Ku, Tokyo, Japan
Int. J. Syst. Sci. (GB), Vol. 12, no. 1, 27–54, Jan. 1981. Coden: IJSYA9

678974 C81013289
Factor group of the automorphism group of a matroid basis graph with respect to the automorphism group of the matroid
Astie-Vidal, A.
Univ. Paul Sabatier, Toulouse, France
Discrete Math. (Netherlands), Vol. 32, no. 3, 217–24, Dec. 1980. Coden: DSMHA4

651062 C81006607
Finding K edge-disjoint spanning trees of minimum total weight in a network: an application of matroid theory
Clausen, J.; Hansen, L.A.
Univ. of Copenhagen, Copenhagen, Denmark
Math. Program. Stud. (Netherlands), no. 13, 88–101, Aug. 1980. Coden: MPSTDF

650853 B81009931 C81006398
Rank-axiomatic characterizations of independent systems
Euler, R.
Math. Inst., Univ. Koln, Koln, Germany
Discrete Math. (Netherlands), Vol. 32, no. 1, 9–17, Oct. 1980. Coden: DSMHA4

622633 C81000474
Converting linear programs to network problems
Bixby, R.E.; Cunningham, W.H.
Northwestern Univ., Evanston, IL, USA
Math. Oper. Res. (USA), Vol. 5, no. 3, 321–57, Aug. 1980. Coden:
MOREDQ

611926 C80034237
Convexity in oriented matroids
Las Vergnas, M.
CNRS, Univ. Pierre et Marie Curie, Paris, France
J. Comb. Theory, Ser. B (USA), Vol. 29, no. 2, 231–43, Oct. 1980. Coden: JCTHAR

599240 C80031125
A technique for determining blocking and anti-blocking polyhedral descriptions
Huang, H.-C.; Trotter, L.E., Jr.
Nanyang Univ., Singapore
Math. Program. Stud. (Netherlands), no. 12, 197–205, April 1980. Coden: NPSTDF

586711 C80027891
Decomposition of regular matroids
Seymour, P.D.

Merton Coll., Oxford Univ., Oxford, England
J. Comb. Theory, Ser. B (USA), Vol. 28, no. 3, 305–59, Jan. 1980. Coden: JCTHAR

513698   C80015671
The complexity of restricted minimum spanning tree problems
Papadimitriou, C.H.; Yannakakis, M.
Lab. for Computer Sci., MIT, Cambridge, MA USA
Maurer, H.A. (Editor)
Automata, Languages and Programming, 460–70, 1979, 16–20 July 1979, Graz, Austria
Publ.: Springer-Verlag, Berlin, Germany
IX + 684 pp.   ISBN 3 540 09510 1

INDEX